W9-AXH-872

HISTORY OF RUSSIAN LITERATURE

SLAVISTISCHE DRUKKEN EN HERDRUKKEN

*

SLAVISTIC PRINTINGS AND REPRINTINGS

uitgegeven door | edited by

C. H. VAN SCHOONEVELD

XII

MOUTON & CO · 1971 · 'S-GRAVENHAGE

HISTORY OF
RUSSIAN LITERATURE

FROM THE ELEVENTH CENTURY TO
THE END OF THE BAROQUE

by

DMITRIJ ČIŽEVSKIJ

WITH 34 PLATES

THIRD PRINTING

MOUTON & CO · 1971 · 'S-GRAVENHAGE

FIRST PRINTING 1960
SECOND PRINTING 1962

PRINTED IN THE NETHERLANDS BY
MOUTON & CO., PRINTERS, THE HAGUE

PREFACE

This work is an attempt to present a history of Early Russian Literature in text-book form. It is designed for those commencing Slavonic studies but can of course be of use to non-Slavists too. Its task is to provide the most important material in a way which corresponds to modern scholarly interpretation. The available text-books in foreign languages and popular accounts cannot perform this task, since they depict Russian literature up to the 19th century only in broad outline. That is to say, in terms so broad that hardly anything but a few names remains in the reader's memory. Moreover, many of them base their accounts on entirely anti-quated Russian works. Those who have a command of the Russian lan-guage resort therefore to modern Russian text-books. One of these, the excellent text-book of N. K. Gudzij, is available also in English trans-lation, but the edition which served as the basis for the English version has already been essentially modified by the author himself. The new editions of Gudzij's text-book and the almost inaccessible collective history of literature published by the Academy of Sciences of the USSR can hardly satisfy the needs of the foreign reader. The official policy and requirements of the Soviet Russian authorities exert considerable pressure on the presentation of the material. It lacks an adequate portrayal of religious literature, so important in this period of Russian literature. It lacks, too, a solid formal analysis of works, for such would bring the accusation of "formalism" on the authors. And last, but not least, it represents in one way or another some tendencies which, if they do not entirely undermine the possibility of an objective presentation, to some extent strongly hamper such a method. The significance given to the religious life of the past is reduced to a minimum. The role of foreign influences is conveniently passed over in silence, so that now even the important translated works disappear entirely from the text-books. Fre-quently, works are condemned or praised according to their political significance, and even from the present point of view; thus the polemical works of the 16th century are judged according to their significance for the ideology of the Great Russian Empire and not according to their literary or intellectual-historical value. Attempts are made to represent all the periods of Russian literary history as "brilliant" or "flourishing", and in order to fill the "gaps" monuments are introduced into the picture which in no case merit inclusion. In addition, other extra-literary criteria are becoming increasingly prominent in the accounts. Consequently, the use of these books, although useful in many respects, produces no small confusion in the minds of those readers who cannot or do not want to read the texts of the original works.

I am attempting here, on the basis of my teaching experience (eighteen years in Germany and five years in the United States), to provide such a selection and presentation of material as will bring Old Russian literature closer to the foreign student. Of this selection and this presentation I should now like to say a few words.

My selection is motivated by the wish to present a history of *literature* and not a complete history of *letters*. Hence I treat many monuments perhaps in a rather step-motherly fashion, but, I hope, justly from the literary historian's point of view; to these belongs first of all the translated literature, mainly works in which the purely literary qualities have no significance. Besides, I want to give primarily a history of *original* literature. Therefore the translated monuments are somewhat pushed into the background. Nevertheless, to those which exercised a significant influence on original works I have devoted as much attention as space has permitted.

The literary-historical presentation required analyses of style, which of course, due to lack of space, are often somewhat cursory. In some sections I had to begin further back and treat in a somewhat specialised manner some general questions (the development of the literary language, prosody, etc.). Some problems equally important, such as the question of literary genre influences, I could only touch in passing. I also did not want to neglect entirely the intellectual-historical bases of the development of literature, and so, in certain passages, some further digressions proved necessary. However, as I am hoping to publish in the very near future an intellectual history of Russia, I imposed upon myself further restraint in the treatment of these questions.

I also hold a view which is nowadays shared by most scholars, but still is not noticeably prominent in the accounts of Russian literature. This is the conception that the so-called "Old Russian literature" had in no sense a uniform character and was in no way static. During the eight centuries with which my book is concerned, there were literary revolutions and changes; in every single period there were literary trends, currents and "schools". It may be doubted whether the limits of the literary eras drawn by me (particularly between the 15th and the 16th centuries) are convincing and in the right places. To be sure I have attempted to support my plan of development by the characterization of every period. That I am fully aware of the difficulties of any division into periods, the reader may gather from my *Outline of Comparative Slavic Literature* (Boston, 1952).

The distribution of material in each of the larger sections has been made according to genres. Therefore the reader will sometimes find himself led to refer to other pages. To this end, I hope, he will be helped by the indices, to the compilation of which I have attached much importance. The indices will also help the reader to find the necessary material in those parts which are set in small type, and which are suited and intended more for reference than for study.

References to scholars are lacking in the text. I have also avoided polemics as far as possible. I have mentioned differing views of other authors only in cases where silence was impossible, as in cases where entirely baseless judgements have been made by contemporary Soviet scholars, for instance, that the political writings of the 16th century surpass the contemporary West European works, or that Zinovij Otenskij is to be reckoned as equal to St. Thomas Aquinas, and so on, or where groundless parallels with foreign literatures are introduced (for example: Castiglione and Boccaccio to *Domostroj*). I had also to take a stand, though briefly, on the question which has virtually become a curse on the history of literature, the entirely unfounded hypothesis of the falsification of The Tale of Igof's Campaign. As I often had to content myself here with merely an outline, I shall express myself in detail on a number of questions in specialised studies, some of which will soon appear or will have already been published upon the appearance of this book.

The texts and quotations, when quoted in Cyrillic, are always accompanied by a translation. The orthography until the 16th century is that of the original edition; for the 17th and 18th centuries, however, I have used (with few exceptions) the modern spelling.

It was impossible to treat in detail in all instances the events of Russian history and the notions of poetics and literary theory. The reader will sometimes have to turn to reference works or to the relevant literature; one would like to assume in every reader of a scholarly work the habit of using at least an encyclopaedia. The literary references which – where ever possible – are given in every chapter, lay no claim to completeness; I give mainly references to publications of texts and only to the most essential literature; on many occasions I have confined myself to naming the works in which further literary references can be found. In some cases I have added to a literary reference a short explanatory note, mostly in those instances when an older work is dealt with, which, however, is still worthy of being read, or when a work is tendentious in one or another sense and thus is to be used with caution.

As usual, I have read all the texts mentioned in this work, as far as they are published. On the other hand, I could not examine some works; oddly enough, these are mostly works of recent times (for example, the publications of some Soviet Universities). As to the MSS, I was able to use only numerous later MSS of the Old Believers, which are almost without importance for this book.

The period between the 11th and 13th centuries, which, in my opinion, influenced only in some points the later development of Russian (Great Russian) literature in its proper sense, and the very content of which was about to be subjected to a re-interpretation, I have treated in a separate work (*Geschichte der altrussischen Literatur im 11., 12. und 13. Jahrhundert: Kiever Epoche*, Frankfurt a.M., 1948). This latter book is written on a different scale and with a somewhat different intention. Here I give a different account of that period; I needed to revise the opinions previously expressed in only a few points. Among the reviewers of the book I am indebted especially to Max Vasmer, even if I cannot accept all his objections.

I am indebted to those of my friends, pupils and colleagues with whom I was able to discuss some questions treated in this work.

Whether I have been successful in this book in giving *non multa, sed multum*, which was my intention, this the readers and the critics will be better able to judge than I myself am.

DMITRIJ ČIŽEVSKIJ

CONTENTS

I

THE PREHISTORIC PERIOD

1. The oldest dated monument of East Slavonic literature is the Gospel, transcribed for the Novgorod *posadnik* (alderman) Ostromir in 1056–7. There is a later copy of the manuscript of the Books of the Prophets, dated 1073. It may be presumed that individual monuments extant in later transcriptions had already appeared by the end of the 10th century (see III, 4, 2). The 10th-century treaties between Rus' and the Greeks are entered in the Chronicle, but it is not known when their Slavonic text appeared. In any case, systematic literary activity only began after the acceptance of Christianity in 988.

2. There is no doubt that even before the appearance of written records, the Eastern Slavs had a folk-lore, but no monuments of it have come down to us. In the middle of the 19th century the romantics considered the contemporary folk-lore of the Eastern Slavs as extremely close to or even identical with that of the pre-Christian era. Such belief is now completely undermined: on the one hand, by comparison between the language of the old East Slavonic monuments and contemporary folk-lore, and on the other, by knowledge of the general trends of folk-lore evolution. The language of contemporary folk-lore represents on the whole an entirely different stage of development of the East Slavonic languages. The folk-lore of all nations has a tendency to modification and "modernisation". It is absolutely impossible to attribute the characteristics of modern folk-lore to that of ten centuries ago. All attempts, therefore, to begin a history of literature with a characterisation of "folk literature" must be considered as unscientific.

3. The only way to get to know the folk-lore of the Eastern Slavs in the pre-Christian and early Christian eras is to establish traces of folk-lore tradition or at least references to folk-lore in the old written monuments. Unfortunately, such traces and references are very few.

References to songs and music in the old monuments of literature are merely fortuitous. In most cases they are references to "devilish" or "laic" songs condemned by Christian writers. Musical instruments (psaltery, pipes, tambourines, horns) are also mentioned, but we do not know whether they were popular at that time nor when they became so. Certain similarities between a very few written monuments and contemporary folk-lore also testify to the fact that modern folk-lore (as may be proved for various nations) has borrowed several motifs and formal elements from written literature.

Beginning with the 12th century, it is true that ritual songs, *koljadki*, as well as popular ritual feasts, *rusalii* and *kupalii*, are mentioned; but no word is said about secular songs in this connection. One may merely deduce that some kind of songs had existed, but no definite conclusion can be drawn about their form or content. Copies of East Slavonic songs are extant only from the 16th century.

4. Only two aspects of folk-lore – "laments" and proverbs – are attested more concretely.

Laments are mentioned frequently enough, and references to them can also be found in the translated literature, and even in the Bible, as laments for the dead were and are found among many peoples of the ancient and modern worlds. The frequent references in the Chronicle to laments for dead princes are not convincing, as we are told that foreigners – Jews, Germans, and even Turks – also "lamented". Moreover, the Chronicle speaks about men's laments, whereas these were and are usually performed by women in the societies with whose laments we are familiar. *Plakat'sja* (to lament) undoubtedly was simply a synonym of the word *pečalit'sja* (to grieve). More convincing are those imitations of laments which we find frequently enough in literary works from the 11th century onwards. There are here some similarities in content with the modern dirges of the Eastern Slavs: memories of the deceased person (who is compared for instance to "the sun"), an exaggeratedly gloomy representation of the unhappy state of the living, a regret that the mourner did not die together with the deceased. Laments are now performed not only for the dead, but also when other misfortunes occur: fires and the conscription of relatives into the army. Under the year 988, we read in the Chronicle, next to an announcement about the foundation of schools in Kiev Rus', and the compulsory recruitment of pupils into them: "The mothers of these children lamented for them as for the dead" – interesting evidence of the broadened function of laments. There remains, however, the possibility that the form of lament had been taken from the higher strata of society or had changed under their influence; laments might have come to them from Byzantium, where they did exist.

5. Proverbs and sayings have come down to us through various monuments, especially the Chronicle. For instance: "If the wolf gets accustomed to walk into the fold, he will steal all the flock", "Death is the same for everybody", "The dead know no shame", "Without killing the bees, there is no honey". There occurs also a kind of adage which is widespread even to this day, namely poking fun at a particular tribe, country or town. There are similarities in form between proverbs from the old monuments and modern ones. The proverb *Rusi jest' veselije piti, ne možem bez togo byti* ("Rus' rejoices in drinking, we cannot live without it"), which occurs in the Chronicle, includes the basic elements of the proverbial style: two approximately equal parts (propositions), parallel or antithetic in meaning, or one conditioning the other; these two parts either rhyme (as here *piti:byti*) or are linked by alliteration, as in some proverbs from the old texts. But it is impossible simply to consider all or even the majority of contemporary proverbs as old and expressing popular wisdom, for the reason that a considerable part of modern East Slav proverbs are translations from Greek (as in Western Europe they are translations from Latin). To this type belong for instance: "I'd be glad to go to heaven, but sins prevent me"; "Don't spit into the well, you may yet have to drink water from it"; "What is written by pen, an axe will not hew"; "One old friend is better than two new ones", etc.; which exist in the tradition of various Eastern Slav nations and occur also among other Slavs. When translated, the verbal form adapted itself to the peculiarities of the Slavonic languages.

6. Another type of folk-lore, the heroic epos, may with some certainty be said to have existed among the ancient Eastern Slavs (see III, 9; IV, 6). A whole series of archaic expressions in modern folk-lore and several invariable formulas in old monuments and contemporary folk literature may also derive from fragments of East Slavonic folk-lore which is not necessarily always pre-Christian or early Christian; some of the expressions may have originated in the 14th, 15th and 16th centuries.

A series of legends included in the Chronicle and referring to events of the 9th–10th centuries may also be added to the remains of the prehistoric period. To these belong, the legend of the summoning of the Varangian princes; the legend of the foundation of the city of Kiev by three brothers;

and many others. As a great many parallels to some of these legends can be found in the folk-lore of other nations – parallels, moreover, which have been preserved in ancient writings – opinions have been frequently expressed and corroborated that the Slavs borrowed these legends from other nations, mainly from the Varangians (Scandinavians). Let us consider two especially striking instances.

The Chronicle recounts the death of Prince Oleg (under the year 912; this legend had been recorded no earlier than the seventies of the 11th century). Oleg had been told by soothsayers that he would meet death from his favourite horse. He ceased to ride this horse, but ordered it to be fed and cared for. After some time he learned that the horse had already died. Oleg laughed at the prophecy of the soothsayers, and expressed a wish to see the carcass of the horse. When he drew near to it, a serpent crawled from the skull and stung him. Thus the prophecy came true. – This legend, as told by the chronicler, is one of two variants of the tales about Oleg's death; according to the second tale Oleg died in Scandinavia, probably a natural death. The tale, in its turn, is one of the variants of the popular legend about a hero's death from a dead creature or an inanimate object, as foretold to him. Thus the hero is killed by the tooth of a dead boar; by a felled tree a splinter of which pricks him; by a stone statue of a lion in whose mouth a scorpion is hidden who stings the hero; and so forth. A tale similar in its general features to that of Oleg's death is still current among Icelandic sagas: there the hero Odd, to whom a witch predicts death from his horse (it is simply stated that a serpent will crawl out of the horse's skull) – kills the horse and buries it deep under the sands. Odd sets out on his wanderings and returns after 300 years; during that time the winds have swept the sand from the horse's skeleton, and the prophecy is fulfilled. – It must be admitted that the tale from the Chronicle bears all the marks of greater originality; the fantastic elements are absent from it (Odd wanders 300 years); it is recounted more absorbingly; the reader learns about the cause of death only in the last sentence of the tale, whereas in the saga of Odd the serpent has already been mentioned in the prophecy, and the element of surprise in the fulfilment of the prophecy narrows down to the fact that the skeleton of the buried horse came to the surface. This greater simplicity and archaism of the legend of Oleg makes any borrowing from the Icelandic tradition (through the Varangians) doubtful.

Another interesting tale concerns Ol'ga's vengeance on the Drevljane who had killed her husband. Unable to take their capital by arms, Ol'ga demands from them only "a small tribute", promising to retreat from the

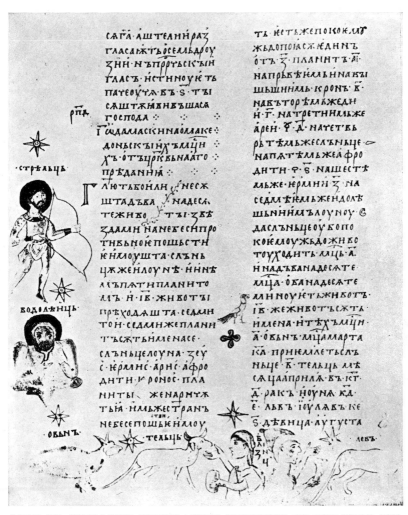

LEAF 251 FROM THE COMPILATION (*IZBORNIK*) OF THE YEAR 1073
Calender notations with in the margins representations of the signs of the Zodiac.

II

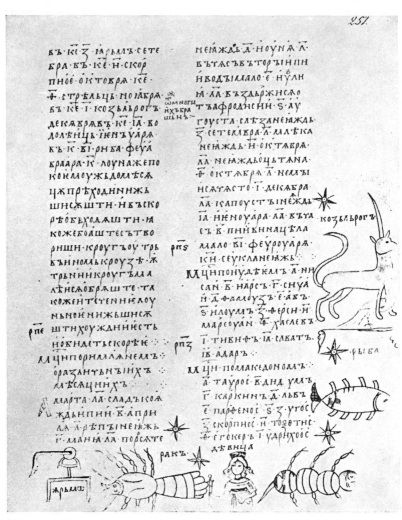

LEAF 252 FROM THE COMPILATION (*IZBORNIK*) OF THE YEAR 1073
Calender notations with in the margins representations of the signs of the Zodiac.
(in place of Libra, "Yoke", see lower left).

town. The tribute consists of three sparrows and pigeons from every house. Burning brimstone is tied to the birds and they are set free: they return to their nests and set fire to every dwelling. This tale, too, is a variant of the migratory legend about animals to whom burning objects are attached in order to cause fire in the enemy camp: thus the biblical Samson drove foxes with firebrands tied to their tails into the fields of the Philistines, while Hannibal is said to have turned bulls with burning torches, against the Romans. But there are also tales about birds which bring fire: Czech tales of much later date (one of them recounts that the Tartars captured Kiev in this manner in 1240). There are also Scandinavian legends, but in this case too the tale in the Chronicle seems to be earlier. In the Scandinavian tales the warriors catch the birds in the woods, while Ol'ga receives them from the population of the besieged town, and thus the reason why the birds fly to the town and not to the woods is explained; moreover, the inhabitants themselves contribute to the destruction of their own city. There is no particular necessity to presume any influence, in this instance, either, the more so as the oldest Scandinavian records of this legend are a hundred years later than the ones in the Chronicle.

Similarly, one cannot speak with certainty about other legends being borrowed. In any case, these legends existed before their inclusion in the Chronicle, probably still in pre-Christian times.

7. Traces of pre-literary Varangian influence may be seen also in several other passages and characteristics of the Chronicle. They may be found primarily in the few instances where a somewhat scornful attitude to the Slavs is apparent in one form or another. Thus, in the tale of the march on Constantinople, the Slavs lay hands on fine silks in the sharing of the loot. They make sails out of it; the sails get torn by the wind, and the Slavs decide to return to their linen sails. The Varangians, on the other hand, made sails out of heavy silk (*pavoloki*) and these proved fit for use. In the tale about the internecine war of 1015, the Kiev warriors make fun of the Novgorodians: "You, carpenters..." These words too are most appropriate coming from the Varangians. – There are tales about the vengeance of Prince Jaroslav on the inhabitants of Novgorod who had decimated his Varangian bodyguard; and about Ol'ga's vengeance on the Drevljane. In both cases the avengers first pronounce the enigmatic phrase: "It is no more in my power to resurrect them (or: my husband)." In all probability this phrase signified the declaration of a bloody vengeance which abolished all moral standards, including the laws of hopitality (in both tales the princes killed their guests.) It is evident that in both cases the Slavs did not understand the Varangian formula of declaration of a bloody vengeance. Such tales, however, could have naturally originated among the Varangians.

8. There are some characteristics of style common to the annalistic legends and the Scandinavian sagas. Such, for instance, are the verbal riddles. These riddles are also to be found in the tale of Ol'ga's vengeance on the Drevljane. Ol'ga suggests to the envoys sent to her by the Drevljane, that they demand to be carried from the Dniepr by boat to Kiev: the Scandinavians used to bury their dead in boats. The Slav envoys did not understand this riddle, and they were thrown together with the boats into a pit and buried alive. The third vengeance consisted in Ol'ga offering the Drevljane to "brew some mead" in order to keep the wake (*trizny*) on the grave of her husband buried in the land of the Drevljane: "to brew mead" (or "beer" etc.) and to feast was a symbol of war even much later (cf. "The Tale of Igof's Campaign" and "The Tale of Rjazan''s Ruin"). The Drevljane did not understand this riddle either; moreover, during the wake Ol'ga's warriors killed the Drevljane who took part in it. – In exactly the same way, during the 1015 war (see above) Prince Jaroslav the Wise with but a small army at the gates of Kiev, sends a messenger to the town to ask some friend what he is to do: "Little mead has been brewed, and there are many body-guards?" He answers: "If little mead has been brewed and there are many body-guards, then drinks must be given in the evening." "And Jaroslav understood", the Chronicle adds, "that the battle ought to take place at night." As we have said, verbal riddles are typical of Scandinavian and Icelandic sagas. They are found in the Chronicle at a much later date, too.

A second characteristic is the presence of the vague, undeveloped metaphors akin to riddles (Scandinavian *kenningar*) in which a simple noun is changed into a twoterm formula: e.g. ship – "sea-horse", blood – "the sword's dew", etc. However, single-term metaphors of the same type also occur; parallel phenomena are to be found among other Indo-European peoples, such as the Greeks, Indians and Celts. Undeveloped metaphors of a similar type which, however, frequently replace a verb instead of a noun, may be found in "The Tale of Igof's Campaign": "the new moon" – son of the prince; "the green mantle" – grass; "feast" – battle. In "The Tale of Igof's Campaign" we find: "There was not enough of the red wine here. Here, the feast put an end to the lives of brave Russian sons"; or, in "The Tale of Rjazan''s Ruin" battles are indicated by the words "to pour a cup" for somebody… or, in order to denote a victorious march up to

any river, it is said that the leader of the march drank water out of this
river with his helmet: "at that time Vladimir Monomach drank water out
of the Don with a golden helmet" (the Hypatius Chronicle, also in "The
Tale of Igoŕ's Campaign"). This artifice, however, is only very seldom
found in the Chronicle; it is more frequent in epic works such as "The
Tale of Igoŕ's Campaign" and "The Tale of Rjazan"s Ruin" (cf. IV, 7, 3).

The third stylistic trait (common to the Chronicle legends and the
Scandinavian sagas) is the decomposition of the description of the action
into dialogues between heroes. We shall deal with this when analysing
the Chronicle.

The fourth characteristic in which the influence of the Scandinavian
sagas can also be seen, is the great number of alliterations, especially in
the legendary parts of the Chronicle. In other parts and in the religious
literature of that time there is no alliteration. Alliterations, however, are
so widespread in the literatures of the Indo-European peoples (not only in
poetry) that the possibility of an independent rise of this peculiarity of
style among the Slavs is conceivable (in Byzantine literature alliteration
did not play any conspicuous role). Here are examples from tales which
we have already mentioned. In the tale of Oleg we meet the following
alliterations:

И приспѣ осень,	и-п-о
и помяну Олегъ конь свой,	и-п-о-к
иже бѣ поставил кормити	и-п-к
и не всѣдати на нь,	и-н-в-н
бѣ бо въпрашалъ волъхвовъ и кудесникъ	б-б-в-в-к
„отъ чего ми есть умрети?"	

. . . .

И повелѣ осѣдлати коня:	и-п-к
„а то вижю кости его"	к -е
И прииде на мѣсто,	и -п
идеже бѣша лежаще кости его голы	и-л-к-е-г
и лобъ голъ	и-л-г
и ссѣде с коня,	и-с-с-к
и посмѣяся рече:	и
„Отъ сего ли лба	с-с-л
смерть было взяти мнѣ?"	с-л-л
и вступи ногою на лобъ	и-в-н-н-л
и выникнувши змиа изо лба	и-в-и-л

("And autumn came and Oleg thought of his horse whom he had ordered to be fed; but he did not saddle him, as he had asked the magicians and sorcerers: "What is my death to be?"... And he ordered a horse to be saddled: "I shall go to see its bones." And he arrived at the place where its bones lay uncovered and its skull, and he unsaddled his horse and laughed, saying: "Am I to receive death from this skull?" And he trod with his foot upon the skull, and a snake crawled out of the skull.")

Here is an excerpt from the tale about the 1015 war:

„Что ты тому велиши творити?	т-т-в-т
меду мало варено,	м-м-в
а дружины много"	м

. . . .

„Даче меду мало,	д-м-м
а дружины много,	д-м
да къ вечеру вдати"	д-в-в

("What do you advise us to do? Little mead has been brewed, and the body-guard (army) is numerous"... "If there is little mead and many warriors, then (mead) must be given in the evening.")

Such passages are not infrequent, but they are rarer in the parts of the Chronicle devoted to the 11th and 12th centuries than in the legends about the events of the 10th and the beginning of the 11th century copied by the chronicler.

As has been said already, alliteration is so widespread in the literatures of the Indo-European peoples that it is not necessary to infer that it was an influence of the Scandinavian sagas. In any case, the use of alliteration is characteristic of the Slavonic legends which had existed before their inclusion in the Chronicle.

9. We frequently come across tales, legends and stories among various nations, especially Indo-European, very similar to the tales, legends and stories of the Eastern Slavs (we may cite the tales about the fight between a son and a father whom the son does not know. Such stories are to be found among the Greeks, Germans, Celts, Persians and Slavs). It has been concluded from this that such tales were inherited by all these nations from the "pre-Indo-European" era, when the forefathers of these nations belonged to one ethnic and linguistic entity. Unfortunately, to this day there are no authoritative criteria which would confirm the existence of such a primary community, or prove either that such tales did not pass from one nation to another by way of borrowing; or that they did not originate independently of each other among various nations. Various ideas as to the "Indo-European inheritance", which should have remained in popular tradition in the contemporary Slavonic folk-lore from prehistoric times can sometimes be found in popular literature and even in text-books. Almost all of them without exception belong to the field of insufficiently founded conjectures.

Remains of Indo-European and pre-Slav antiquity can be traced with complete certainty in the field of language – phonetics, morphology, syntax and vocabulary: this has some significance for the history of literature. The determination of the basis of pre-Slav and ancient East Slav metrics, i.e. of the laws of rhythm of the language, is of even greater significance. There is hope that in this field science will come to some conclusions about the laws of metrics and, consequently, about the verse of ancient Rus'.

TRANSLATED AND BORROWED LITERATURE

1. The beginnings of literature among the Eastern Slavs are linked with the adoption of Christianity. There had probably been some Christians in Rus' before the conversion of the whole country in 988. We know with certainty about the adoption of Christianity by Princess Ol'ga in the second half of the 10th century. We know about the existence of Varangian Christians in Kiev. Already then it was possible to get literary works in Church Slavonic, on the whole well understood by the Eastern Slavs too. These works came originally from the Slav countries which had already adopted Christianity in the 9th century – from Czechs and Bulgarians who, shortly after the creation of the Slavonic alphabet (around 862) and after the first translations of prayer books, created a literature well varied in content and surpassing in volume all the literatures in national languages which then existed in embryo in Europe. Probably soon after the conversion the copying of borrowed literature started among the Eastern Slavs, mainly in Kiev and Novgorod. According to the Chronicle, copying and translation was being organised in Kiev during the reign of Jaroslav the Wise (1019–54). Later, translating activity continued, either in Byzantium – especially for the Eastern Slavs, or in the monasteries on Mount Athos.

We shall deal first with the translated and borrowed literature of the oldest period (11th–13th centuries). This literature showed quite a considerable influence on the original literature, by forming the taste of readers and writers and by providing a model for imitation, or for learning literary craft.

2. The first group of works which reached the Eastern Slavs were books needed for Christian worship.

They were translations of passages from the Holy Scriptures which were read during service. These translations had been made by the missionaries of the Slavs – Cyril and Methodios. The Gospel existed in two forms: as a text of those passages which were read in church throughout the year – *Evangelije-aprakos* (such was the Ostromir Gospel of 1056–7 preserved in the oldest dated East Slavonic manuscript); and the full text of the Gospel – *Četveroevangelije* (Tetraevangelion). In addition, there existed in two analogous forms "The Apostle", i.e. The Acts of the Apostles and the Epistles. The Book of Psalms played the most important role among the books of the Old Testament (explanations of difficult passages were sometimes provided). Not all of the remaining books were as yet translated; it seems that the historical ones were those missing. The others were mostly known in the form of the *Paremejnik* (quotations from Bible). The books of the Holy Scriptures were read not only in church but also by individual readers. The literary historian, of course, must not forget the highly poetic qualities of the biblical books, which provide examples of various styles (narrative, religious poetry, parables). The translations were accompanied by comments explaining difficult passages, mainly in the Psalter and the Books of the Prophets.

The liturgical books containing prayers and chants already belong to the field of purely religious poetry. The Chronicle tells us about the aesthetic impression of worship. Instruction for the religious service and texts were provided by the *Služebnik* (Liturgicon) and the *Trebnik* (Sacramentarion). The chants were collected in two books of *Triod'* (Triodion) and *Oktoich* (Oktoechos) in which church songs for the whole year were assembled. *Služebnye Minei* (Menaea) were books of songs in honour of the saints.

3. Side by side with the liturgical books, a different religious literature consisting mainly of hagiographic works and sermons, was also translated.

Hagiographic literature existed in two forms: as separate "Lives" and as a collection of "Lives". The "Lives" were collections of saints' biographies. They varied greatly in type, ranging from dry schematic outlines to bulky religious novels with episodes developed in detail and with religious and moralising asides. Among them adaptations of migratory legends, connected with the name of one saint or another, are also to be found. Thus we find among them a legend similar to the subject of *Faust* (the life of Filaret Milostivyj), a tale about demons obeying a saint (the life of Conon of Isauria), etc. To the more important and sometimes quite bulky Lives belonged, for instance, in the oldest period, the Life of Anthony the Great, the founder of monasticism; the Life of Sabas of Palestine, an ascetic whose ideology influenced the Kiev-Pečerskij monastery; the Life of St. Nicholas; the Life of Andreas Salos; the Life of Alexis who left his wife on the day of the wedding, wandered among strangers and died in the house of his parents as a vagabond unrecognised by anybody. The Lives of the Slav missionaries Cyril and Methodios and the Lives of Czech saints, two Lives of St. Václav (Wenceslas) and a Life of St. Ljudmila, also found their way to the Eastern Slavs.

Short Lives were collected into a miscellany. *Prolog* (Synaxarion or Menologion) was a collection of short Lives arranged according to the days of the year. Their translation was made by the Eastern Slavs probably in the 12th century. The *Prolog* was enriched on East Slav soil by other translated and original material: it soon became three times larger than the Greek original. Here we also find individual moralising tales, for instance about the beggar whose prayer was "more gratifying to the Lord" than the prayer of the bishop; about how Christ in the guise of a pauper visited the abbot, etc. Here we find also striking aphorisms and maxims.

To a second type of hagiographic collections belong the "Paterikons" – collections of short stories about individual episodes from the lives of the saints, and sometimes of the sinners. Already Methodios had translated a paterikon (probably "Verba Patrum"), which also reached the Eastern Slavs. Well known were the paterikons named after the place where the action of their narrative took place: "Paterikon of Sinai" (Palladius, 4th century), "Paterikon of Skete" (tales from Egypt, Moschos, 7th century), *Limonar'* (Leimonarion, "The Spiritual Meadow"), "Paterikon of Rome" (Pope Gregory's, 7th century, translated from Latin). Later, on the basis of translated paterikons compilations were made. They also served as models for original works (the 11th century tale about Isaakij, see III, 3, 4). We find in the paterikons short tales, for instance about the monk Gerasim who befriended a lion in the desert (the theme of Bernard Shaw's *Androclus and the Lion*); about the hermit who in his isolation did not know whether the world still existed. We also find individual aphorisms ("Pride is the mother of all evil") or short witty dialogues, e.g. one hermit meets the devil who confides to him: "Everything that you do, I do, too: you fast – I don't eat at all; you sleep little – I don't sleep at all; ... But you surpass me in humility."

It is not surprising that hagiographic literature was used by writers for a long time, not only by authors of the Lives, but also by later poets and novelists: in the 19th and 20th centuries by Puškin, Gogol', Herzen, Dostoevskij, Leskov, Remizov.

4. The sermon-literature, to which the best models of Greek Church pulpit oratory belonged, was as widely translated. This literature has not been studied sufficiently yet. In any case, among the translated sermons we find the works of John Chrysostomos (Zlatoustyj), Basil the Great, Gregory of Nazianzus, and a whole series of other classics of homiletic art. The sermons were designed to be read. They were sometimes collected in miscellanies. From the 11th century the manuscript of thirteen sermons by Gregory of Nazianzus (among them quotations from Plato and Homer) has been preserved; from the 12th century – the manuscript of the collection of sermons by Zlatoustyj, "Zlatostruj", translated in the 10th century in Bulgaria but linguistically revised and somewhat abbreviated in Kiev. Original sermons of the 10th century Bulgarian preachers also penetrated to the Eastern Slavs, namely those of the pupil of Cyril and Methodios, Kliment of Velica, and of Kozma the Presbyter who polemised against heretics.

The sermons provided models of different styles: they ranged from a dry enumeration of sins or virtues to a sharp unmasking of social injustices, or descriptions of scenes of nature. Such, for instance, is one sermon from "Zlatostruj": Chrysostomos compares the soul of a meek man to a picture of nature at peace: "On the top of the mountain where a pure wind blows, where the sun shines, where the springs are pellucid and the various flowers are fragrant and beautiful, and where the gardens are marvellous... And his voice is sweet to those who listen to it, as if at the top of the oak trees singing birds were perched, nightingales, swallows and bullfinches having joined their voices into one sound; or as if the wind blew lightly from the East, shook the quivering leaves and talked in the groves, as if the top of the mountain were covered with flowers – purple, red and white ones... and a light breeze blew over them and rippled them into waves... And from the mountain a stream flows, which murmurs gently beating against the stones... When you see such a scene, you understand how pleasing is a patient and gentle man." Chrysostomos compares the soul of an irritable man to a noisy city, described just as colourfully.

5. The series of translated works bears a theological character, giving an exposition of Christian religious teaching. Also known in translation were some commentaries on the Holy Scriptures (on the Gospel by the Bulgarian writer of the 10th century, Constantine the Presbyter, and on the Apocalypse). Theological treatises are "Climax" by John Klimakos, a collection of reflections on the degrees of Christian ideals, and "Theology" by John Damascenus, a system of theology in which some philosophical questions are also expounded. These treatises provided inter alia the basis for the theological, philosophical and psychological Slavonic terminology.

6. The so-called "Apocrypha" – religious works not recognised by the Church – constitute a very large group. They are mostly tales about those figures and events of sacred history about which very little is said in the Holy Scriptures. Such tales employed both ecclesiastical and migratory legends. In some cases the apocrypha were used by heretics for expounding their ideas. Apocrypha which contradicted Christian teaching were strictly forbidden by the Church, but other apocrypha were tolerated.

From the events of the Old Testament the apocrypha recount the lives of Adam and Eve, Noah, Abraham, Moses, David and Solomon. There are sermons ("The Commandments of the Twelve Patriarchs") and prophecies, especially about the end of the world. The Old Testament apocrypha originated partly in Hebrew literature, but reached the Slavs through the Greeks.

Events of the New Testament are told by apocrypha which had already originated on Christian soil: they narrate Christ's childhood ("The Gospel of Thomas"); the life of the Virgin Mary ("The Gospel of Jacob"); details of Jesus' life, the judgment on Him. "The Gospel of Nicodemus" existed in two Slavonic translations, one of which was made from the Latin.

There are also apocryphal Lives of the saints, which tell of fabulous miracles or contain non-Evangelical prophecies about the end of the world. There are also apocryphal sermons and prayers.

The apocrypha reached the Slavs gradually: some of them already in the earliest period, others later, probably before the 16th century. In manuscripts of the 11th–13th centuries there are extant. "The Virgin's Travel through the Pains", a tale about the torments of the sinners in hell; "The Word of Aphroditian", a tale of how the idols fell in Persia at the moment of Christ's birth. A number of apocrypha are used in ancient monuments; thus, in the Chronicle, in the sermon which the Greek missionary preached to Prince Vladimir, the apocrypha are mentioned. A series of apocryphal motifs are found in "The Pilgrimage of Abbot Daniil", and others. Still more apocryphal themes can be seen on the ancient icons; this, however, does not always prove the existence of the given apocrypha in Rus': the icons could have used Greek models directly. Among the apocrypha already known to the Eastern Slavs in the 11th–13th centuries, mention must be made of tales about the creation of the world, in which a certain role is ascribed to the devil (these apocrypha are the work of the Bulgarian dualistic sect, the Bogomils of the 10th–11th centuries), and tales about Adam and Eve. Among the apocrypha from the New Testament we must mention: "The Tree of the Cross", the tree from which was made the cross on which Christ was crucified was said to have grown on Adam's tomb and in this way Adam's skull was entwined in the tree's roots, found its way to Golgotha, and Jesus's blood was dripping on it "washing away Adam's sins" – a naive tale based on the metaphor "washing away of sins". Finally, there were apocrypha recounting the secrets of heaven ("Enoch's Book") and the end of the world (the apocalypses of Baruch and Isaiah, "The Revelations of Methodios of Patara").

The apocrypha had an enormous influence on world literature: their echoes are found in the literature of the Middle Ages, in Dante, Milton, Klopstock, Ševčenko ("Marija"), Dostoevskij, Rilke ("Marienlieder"), Remizov, and others. The apocrypha were not regarded with as much respect as the Books of the Holy Scriptures and, therefore, considerable changes were made when they were copied, in style as well as in content. The apocrypha also had a certain influence on the old writers' art of narration. But on the whole the influence of secular literature was greater.

7. Secular literature consisted primarily of scientific literature, that is "scientific" in the context of that time. It was a literature which provided the reader with the facts of "secular science" or, rather, with what the authors considered facts.

The first group of scientific works was historical. The chronicle of John Malalas, an author of the 6th century, had already been translated in Bulgaria: it gave an account of ancient and Byzantine history up to Justin. It is written in a lively and picturesque style. Among other things in the first volumes, the history of the ancient world and Greek mythology is expounded. Later these accounts became part of "chronographs" (cf. III, 10, 4). This is how readers acquired their knowledge of antiquity. – More detailed but dry is the chronicle of George Hamartolos of the 9th century, which provides mainly a history of Byzantium and was translated in all probability at Kiev in the 11th century. Although Hamartolos gives quite a lot of cultural, historical and even philosophical material, these passages were not always successfully rendered in translation. Hamartolos was later also included in the "chronographs". – Also translated at Kiev in the 11th century, and of the greatest importance, was the "History of the Judean Wars" (i.e. of the last decades of the existence of the independent Jewish State and the destruction of Jerusalem), by Josephus Flavius. The translation often gives a very picturesque version of the Greek text. The additions about Christ and John the Baptist are of rather vague origin. Josephus' book is a beautiful model of a martial tale. The great influence of Josephus on the original historical literature of old Rus' is undoubted. A series of turns of phrases which are constantly repeated are taken from him: "The arrows darkened the sun", "The arrows showered like rain", the dead "fell like sheaves", and so forth. Also from Josephus is taken a complete short description of battle: "And one could hear the tilting of the spears and the clatter of the swords, and see the splinters of the shields, and the earth soaked with blood"; or: "While the archers were shooting their arrows, and the spearmen were fighting with their spears, and the ballista hurled stones, people did not dare to stand on the walls"; or again the characterisation of the Roman warriors: "Their order is such that they pass by quickly, and their ears listen attentively while their eyes look for the signal, and their hands are ready for battle. That is why they can do at once what they desire." The long tales are in a similar style.

Šestodnev and *Fiziolog* are works of natural history. The first of these, "Hexaemeron", gives general information about nature in the form of a commentary on the history of the six days of the Creation. One can also find here philosophical discussions and information about astronomy and natural history, and sometimes more striking scenes and praise of God for His work. There existed in translation the "Hexaemeron" of Basil the Great and its adaptation by the Bulgarian writer John the Exarch (9th–10th centuries) who completed Basil's material from other Greek sources. – A popular work was the "Physiologus", a collection of short tales about real and fabulous animals (phoenix), with symbolic comment on these tales. – The geographic and cosmographic outline of Cosmas Indikopleustes provided a description of the earth according to the popular conception of that time (the earth is a rectangular plane) and some information about exotic animals. The manuscripts were often embellished with drawings.

Of lesser historical interest are the translations in various editions of the ecclesiastical and juridical monument *Kormčaja* (Nomokanon). The first translation had already been made by Methodios.

8. The popular scientific branch of literature was represented by miscellanies. First of all there was the *Izbornik* of 1073, copied from the Bulgarian original for Prince Svjatoslav of Kiev. This miscellany contains theological as well as historical essays (the history of oecumenical councils, chronology) and, among other things, a treatise on poetics by George Choiroboskos containing a short outline of "tropes and figures of speech" with examples. Hyperbole is illustrated by the example: "The man rushes along like the wind"; metaphor by: "The Tsar – shepherd of the people", "Coal – the fire's kinsman"; various aspects of irony are explained by examples. All the tropes and figures mentioned amount to twenty-seven (with subdivisions). This manual of poetics is found in copies up to the 15th century.

A second type of miscellanies, of importance to the history of literature, are the florilegia – collections of quotations and adages. The most popular of these was *Pčela* ("The Bee" = "Melissa"), translated probably in Kiev in the 12th century, composed in the 7th century by Maximus the Confessor. *Pčela* contains texts from the Holy Scriptures, systematically arranged and followed in each chapter by quotations from the Church Fathers and then by quotations from secular literature, including ancient literature (there are many quotations from the philosophers, Greek tragedians, etc.). Some of the aphorisms are enlarged to the extent of stories. Here are a few examples of aphorisms: to Aristotle is ascribed i.a. the saying: "He is stronger who triumphs over passion than he who conquers warriors"; to Plato: "He who accepts great power must have great sagacity"; "The beginning of knowledge is to understand one's lack of knowledge." Many aphorisms are of secular character: Alexander the Great is alleged to have replied to the warriors who wanted to attack the enemy at night: "This would not be a princely victory" (the code of chivalry). Both the aphorisms and anecdotes from *Pčela* and several similar miscellanies (one of them enters into the composition of the *Izbornik of* 1076) later served as the basis of popular anecdotes, tales and proverbs.

Scientific literature did not succeed in laying the foundations of independent scientific works, but traces of the beginning of such works have been preserved (about Klim Smoljatič and Kirik see IV, 12). This literature supported certain fundamental traits of the medieval conception of the world: first of all a conviction of the symbolic significance of universal existence, then faith in the religious significance of historical events.

9. A considerable part of the translations consisted of novels of various types. First of all there are the heroic historical romances.

The first of these is *Aleksandrija* ("Alexandreis") the story of Alexander the Great, a favourite theme of medieval literature. The text translated was that ascribed to the nephew of Aristotle, Kallisthenes, but in reality it originated in the 2nd–3rd centuries A.D., and incorporated into the original story of Alexander many fantastic motifs: he is the son of the Egyptian king-priest Nektaneb; his march to the East brings him into fantastic countries where there are men-monsters with dog-heads, six arms, and so forth. Christian motifs are also interwoven into the tale. The Bulgarian translation reached the Eastern Slavs probably as early as the 12th century, and perhaps even in the 11th century. "Aleksandrija" left some traces in historical literature, as well as in the remains of the epos. Later it entered into the chronographs.

The *Trojanskoe dejanie*, "The Deeds of Troy", in a different version from that of Homer's (it was ascribed to Dyktis who had "heard it from Odysseus"), came to the Eastern Slavs as part of the Chronicle of Malalas. On the whole, a vast complex of Greek legends finds its way into the narrative. The story did not have a great influence on the literature of the 11th–13th centuries, but did enter into the composition of the chronographs.

The most interesting work (it has been preserved in four copies, three of which are defective; the fourth was burned, only small extracts of it are extant) is *Devgenievo dejanie* ("The Deeds of Digenis"), a story about a Byzantine semi-mythical hero, Digenis Akritas. The old Greek text is not extant, only later Greek epic songs are known. The subject of this novel is as follows: the Arabian king Amir abducted a Greek girl; persecuted by her brothers, he decided to embrace Christianity. From this union Digenis was born (in Greek "born of two races"). From his childhood he already reveals the character of a real hero: while hunting he kills an elk, a bear and a lion; he also kills a hydra-headed dragon which attacked him. Then his military feats commence: king Filipat and his daughter Maksimiana invite him to their palace in a polite letter but, when he arrives, he is attacked by their army which he conquers. From Filipat and Maksimiana, Digenis learns that there is a still stronger enemy, Stratig, whose daughter, Stratigovna, is even prettier than Maksimiana. Digenis betakes himself there, shows himself a gallant cavalier, plays serenades under the windows of Stratigovna and makes her fall in love with him. She flees with him and Digenis achieves victory over Stratig's army, which has set off after him. After this Digenis also defeats king Vasilij (Basil). According to a prophecy, Digenis has only twelve years of life left, but in the Greek songs he still lives through various adventures. The Slavonic manuscripts, however, end here. The Kiev translation dates from no later than the 12th century. The conjecture (H. Grégoire) that there had been two different translations is very plausible. The romance is recounted in an extremely picturesque language; the descriptions of Digenis's appearance and of his clothes are also very colourful: Digenis is "beautiful, his face is (white) like snow and red like a poppy, his hair is like gold, his eyes as big as saucers"; he wears "black clothes interwoven with gold, and his oversleeves are set with expensive pearls, his kneecaps are of precious silk (*pavoloki*), and his boots are of gold, set with precious pearls". The other characters, their clothes and tents are described in the same manner. Digenis's horse is "white, precious stones are entwined into his mane, and among the stones there are golden bells", "the horse started to prance and the bells to ring sweetly". The characters in the story jump on their horses and "fly like hawks". Digenis gains victory over the enemy troops: "He descended upon them like a strong falcon and slew them as a good mower cuts grass". Into the epos are incorporated letters, among others Maksimiana's love letter: "O radiant and overbright sun, glorious Devgenij, you rule over all... the courageous and powerful, like the month of May among all the months... thus you shine among us." There are also prophetic dreams and sentimental experiences: the mother of the girl abducted by Amis has "the root of her heart torn out", she compares herself to a reed, and so forth. This exuberance of language was reflected in many monuments of the early literature.

10. Side by side with the historical romances were also translated ideological didactic novels, in which instructions in the form of a homily, a fable or an aphorism were added to the main theme.

The first of these didactic stories is "Akir the Wise" (in the West: Achicar or Ahicar). It had already originated in Assyria in the 7th century B.C. It is translated, possibly, from the Syrian version, but perhaps from the Greek. The subject-matter combines numerous aphorisms with a fabulous adventure theme. Akir, councillor of King Sinagrip of Niniveh, fulfils difficult tasks imposed upon the king by the Egyptian Pharaoh (for instance, to build a castle in the air: Akir lifts young boys into the air, who are carried in baskets by tamed eagles; the boys demand building materials which the Pharaoh cannot hand them). With this is linked the story of Akir's disciple who mendaciously reports on him to Sinagrip; Akir's instructions to his pupil contain aphorism-proverbs: "A sparrow in the hand is better than a thousand birds in the air", "When gall becomes sweet, the stupid will learn wisdom" ,and so forth.

Very old, too, is the tale of *Stefanit i Ichnilat* ("The Crowned and the Tracer"), which originated in India about the 5th century B.C. and which reached Greece through a series of Eastern translations. Under its Arabic name it is known as "Kalila and Dimna". It was translated from Greek in Bulgaria; there were two translations, one of which reached the Eastern Slavs probably in the 12th–13th centuries. The main theme of the story is the fate of the two jackals who falsely accused the bull before his friend – the emperor lion. At first the bull dies, then also the two jackals. The whole story is full of moralising fables, the heroes of which are animals: wolves, foxes, ravens, elephants, monkeys. Individual motifs from these fables entered into literature and especially into popular tales about animals.

Very interesting is the third didactic novel *Varlaam i Ioasaf* ("Barlaam and Josaphat"). This is a Christian version of the story of the Buddha, written in

India about the 6th century A.D., revised in Byzantium through the medium of translations into Eastern languages. Thus Buddha becomes "Josaphat", an Indian prince who is brought up in isolation so that he will not have the opportunity of getting to know the miseries of this world; but during his first walks he comes across a funeral, a sick man and an old man, and under the influence of these impressions becomes an ascetic. He is guided by the hermit Barlaam. Josaphat is forced to struggle against his pagan father, but finally, on ascending the throne, brings his country to Christianity. Among Barlaam's instructions are included purely Christian sermons and a few remarkable parable-fables. Many literatures of the East and West used the following tale: a traveller, pursued by a unicorn, hides from him in a ravine; but at the bottom of the ravine there lies a dragon, so that the traveller can only cling to the brink of the ravine by grasping the branch of a shrub which threatens to give way. Suddenly, on the sprigs of the shrub, he notices honey made by wild bees and begins to taste it, forgetting about the unicorn and the dragon and the instability of the shrub. The traveller personifies man in general; his position between the unicorn (sin) and the dragon (death) is a symbol of the transitoriness of human life; the honey stands for secular delights which make mankind forget sin and death and the frailty of all earthly things. Some stories from the novel entered into the *Prolog*, and were used by old writers (Kiril of Turov). The popularity of this work is attested by later translations and by the use made of its stories by writers of the 19th and 20th centuries.

11. The utopia, of Greek origin, translated probably only in the 13th century, occupies a place of its own. The "Story of the Indian Kingdom" is a fantastic tale about the allegedly ideal theocratic state of Prester John, in India. The riches of this state, its size, population and nature are described in a fabulous manner. This utopia was undoubtedly meant to contrast the picture of an ideal Christian state with European and Byzantine disorder. The story was translated from Greek into Latin, and from Latin – probably in Dalmatia – into Slavonic. The fabulous descriptions of the narrative had some influence on legends and epic works.

To the same utopian literature belong two other monuments which had influenced the adaptation of "Aleksandrija". The first is "Zosima's Journey to the Rachmans". The anchorite Zosima penetrates into the land of the blessed, the "Rachmans" who live "without sin", without clothes, eating only vegetarian foods, knowing neither metals nor the notion of time, nor lies, and so forth. This utopia is translated from an unknown Greek (possibly Latin) original, which had originated on the basis of Jewish legends about a land of blessed and sinless people.

While this ascetic utopia is written in simple language, and in content incorporates the exuberant descriptions in "The Indian Kingdom", "The Tale of Makarij" combines both fabulous and ascetic motifs: the first part –the description of the journey of three monks – unites fantastic scenes of India's marvels (such as men with dogs' heads, men with three legs, the country of serpents) with sombre pictures taken from the descriptions of hell; the second part recounts the story of the ascetic Makarij who met the three wandering monks and talked with them of the "earthly paradise" barred to man, yet still existing. – The sources of this translation are also unknown; it is possible that in its present state the text is a compilation. Both monuments appeared in the North, although echoes of the legend of the Rachmans also exist in Ukrainian folk-lore. The translations are not earlier than the 13th century.

12. It may seem very strange that East Slavonic literature had no poetry. This is not quite so: certain poems after Greek models had already originated in the early period; two of them, perhaps, were written by St. Constantin-Cyril. There were such poems in Bulgaria, too. Some of them reached the Eastern Slavs; it is possible, however, that they themselves wrote poems. These were based on an equal quantity of syllables in every line (syllabic verse). But it is precisely in the 11th century that the process of omission of the unvoiced vowels of Old Slavonic (ъ and ь) was taking place. When these vowels disappeared in some positions, the number of syllables in individual lines changed, and the texts continued to be copied but were no longer accepted as rhythmic language. Here is an example:

Old text	After changes	Number of syllables
Азъ словомь симь молюся Богу:	Аз словом сим молюся Богу:	12-9
Боже вьсея твари и зиждителю	Боже всея твари и зиждителю	12-11
Видимыимъ и невидимыимъ ...	Видимым и невидимым! ...	12-8

("I pray with this word to God: Lord and Creator of everything created, visible and invisible.")

While being copied, such a text underwent further changes. The quoted lines are an acrostic: each line starts with a consecutive letter of the alphabet (А, Б, В, etc.); this characteristic allows us to reestablish better the original form of the poem.

13. It is interesting to note that the majority of the above-mentioned monuments, with the exception of only a part of religious literature (sermons), were simultaneously popular in the West through the intermediary of Latin translations, or even solely in these translations. The drifting apart of East and West in Europe took place only after the end of the 13th century. New links with the West, no longer accidental but organic, were formed among the Eastern Slavs only after some time: among the Ukrainians and Byelo-Russians in the 16th century, among the Great Russians in the second half of the 17th century.

Byzantium was the principal source of translated literature, but some monuments came also from the West, from the sphere of the Latin influence. Part of the monuments translated from Greek came from Bulgaria, but the number of these monuments is considerably smaller than scholars conjectured until 1900. To Rus' came also the works of the Bulgarian writers of the "Golden Age of Bulgarian literature" (the epoch of Tsar Simeon, until 926). In the Chronicle, one also comes across reflections of non-extant Bulgarian monuments or oral legends.

As mentioned, the number of translated monuments of Bulgarian origin is somewhat lessened by the new discoveries (V. Istrin and others) in favour of original East Slavonic, mainly Kievan translations. The peculiarities of language, especially the use of words unknown among the Southern Slavs, serve as evidence of East Slavonic origin of translation: *posadnik* – alderman, *grivna* – a money unit, *kuna* – a coin, *nasad* – ship, *tijun* or *tivun* – bailiff, *šelk* – silk, *žemčug* – pearls, *uksus* – vinegar, some name of places and people. According to the newest data, in Kiev Rus' were translated, among others: *Prolog*, the Lives of Andreas Salos and Josephus Flavius, *Pčela*, the Physiologus, *Devgenievo dejanie*, Akir, Cosmas Indikopleustes, one of the two translations of the Physiologus also originated there. The translation of Hamartolos' chronicle is in some measure linked with the Eastern Slavs but also contains lexical characteristics of South and West Slavonic languages.

Comparatively recently (after 1900), the West Slavonic origin of some monuments extant among the Eastern Slavs has also been established. They originated either during the Slavonic mission to Moravia (9th century) or in the period of the existence of Church Slavonic literature in Bohemia (10th–11th centuries). Here too one can make use of linguistic criteria (in particular Catholic terms: *m'ša* – liturgy, *papež* or *apostolik* – the Pope of Rome, *kostel* – Church, *Sv. Marija* – Virgin Mary, and words which are found only in Czech in later centuries and are not found in East Slavonic monuments); in some cases one can prove that the translation is made from the Latin. To the monuments of Western origin, besides translations from the period of the Slavonic mission and the Lives of its two leaders Cyril and Methodios, one has also to add such monuments as the "Liturgy of St. Peter" probably translated at the time of the mission), the Lives of the Western saints: the patron of Prague Vitus, Apollinary of Ravenna, Chrysogonus, and some others; probably one translation of the "Gospel of Nicodemus", the "Paterikon of Rome", some prayers which mention the Western saints and, finally, original works: the Lives of St. Václav (Wenceslas) (two Lives and one *proložnoje* Life) and of St. Ljudmila (*proložnoje*). Some borrowings from monuments or oral tales of Western origin may be found in the Chronicle.

From now on we shall deal only with original literature, and shall return to translated literature within the framework of each individual period, inasmuch as translated literature played a substantial role in the formation of the literary style of each period.

ST. SOPHIA CATHEDRAL IN KIEV (BUILT 1037-39) BEFORE THE REBUILDING IN THE 17TH CENTURY .
Drawing by a Dutch traveller (Westerfeld) on August 4, 1657: Entrance of Hetmann Bohdan Chmielnyćkyj and his troops in Kiev.

PERIOD OF STYLISTIC SIMPLICITY
(THE EARLY MIDDLE AGES)

1. CHARACTERISTICS

1. The characterisation of the style of early medieval works presents certain difficulties, for a variety of reasons. First of all, students of philological and sociological trends did not provide analyses of the style of individual works, indispensable for such a characterisation. Although the 11th-century monuments are comparatively few, some of them have a highly individual complexion, and thus one has to generalise on the basis of only a few examples. Moreover, some of the monuments are extant in such late versions (16th–18th centuries), that not only their language but partly also their style has changed. Finally, precisely in this early period, the Byzantine influences – influences of a very highly developed literature, as we have seen, accessible in translation, and which have undergone a complex evolution – are so strong, that local and temporal features are often effaced by the stylistic influences of other works at various stages of development.

Nevertheless, even from rather scanty material, certain characteristics emerge with certainty, and we shall investigate them. These features become more defined if we compare the works of the 11th century with those of the following centuries, mainly the 12th and the early 13th century. Unfortunately, we have no means of observing the stylistic evolution (or revolution – in the history of literature these often occur) step by step. We are forced to proceed not from the comparison of coeval monuments, but from the comparison of monuments separated from each other by a long span of time – "the peaks", as it were, of the literature of the 11th and 12th–13th centuries. Of course, once we have established that they are substantially different in style from each other, we can with complete certainty conclude that the boundary line runs "somewhere" between these peaks; but for the chronological establishment of this line we have in reality only one basic monument: the Chronicle. It is the Chronicle which obliges us to presume that the boundary runs around the years 1120–30. That the line of demarcation is no earlier one, is supported by the style of such monuments as "The Works of Vladimir Monomach" which had in part originated shortly before 1125, and "The Pilgrimage of Abbot Daniil", written shortly after 1108: these works bear the characteristics of the early style. For other evidence, we have to compare works separated from each other by almost a century; as, for instance, the sermons of St. Feodosij delivered before 1074, with the sermons of Kiril of Turov, from the second half of the 12th century; and the hagiographic literature of the end of 11th century with similar works from the beginning of the 13th century. One fact is undeniable – the style changed radically, it was "regenerated". This regeneration of style is not accidental: all the European literatures, including medieval Latin literature, went through a similar crisis on the border of the 11th–12th centuries. The literature of the Eastern Slavs, too, followed the same path, proving in this way its appurtenance to "European literature" as a whole.

2. A certain *sui generis* "monumentality" of style is the basic feature of 11th-century Kievan literature. It consists of the creation of a literary work with but few stylistic devices, a limited number and role of stylistic adornments, and a concentration of attention on the subject-matter. The main aim is a "factual" account of a certain theme. The consequence of this is a comparatively simple and lucid construction of a literary work. Having stated what he wanted to communicate, the author sometimes also sums up, putting his conclusion into an aphoristic formula which he places either at the head of the work or in the middle of it, sometimes repeating it several times. The attention of the author in every work or part is concentrated on one thought and only reluctantly does he deviate from it: the delivery is "monothematic".

3. But it is precisely this monothematic treatment which results on the one hand in simplicity of syntax but on the other in frequent obscurity of composition. When the author (for instance in Nestor's Life of St. Feodosij) has to handle varied material, or (as in Vladimir Monomach's "Instructions") express several different thoughts, he is not particularly concerned to put these elements of his work into strict order: for him they are all concentrated around the basic idea, around the theme of the work (in the most extreme case around a few themes). That is why individual elements of the narrative simply follow each other without transition and, apparently, without connection. In the text digressions with the terminal formula: "Let us return to the above-mentioned" are typical. The syntax also reproduces this, as it were, "paratactic" simplicity of composition: sentences simply follow each other abruptly, sometimes partly repeating each other; the subject or complement in successive clauses is repeated ("Go to *town* and I shall tomorrow leave *town* and set off for my *town*", etc.). Frequently, the name of the *dramatis persona* is also repeated, as in the Chronicle or in St. Feodosij's Life. Quite often also the content itself is repeated, of course with some variants. Successive clauses are linked by the conjunction *and* which is sometimes repeated several times.

4. Among the characteristic features of the style of this period belongs the use of set formulas: among them texts from the Holy Scriptures and formulas probably used generally in the colloquial of that time, as well as "self-repetitions" of the author. Stylistic adornments are few. In the language of medieval poetics, the style is but "slightly adorned". Amplifications are rare. The basic stylistic devices are: 1) parallelism of neighbouring clauses: either syntactic parallelism or parallelism of thoughts, this being further strengthened by repetition of words; 2) less frequently alliteration which is often linked with the same repetition of words; 3) metaphors and similes which are not numerous and often traditional (arrows fall "like rain"; troops stand "like trees"; the hermit monk is a "*bogatyř*" (hero, he is "*chrabr*" (warrior), and so on). Developed symbology is still absent (Ilarion's "Discourse", built on Byzantine patterns, is partly an exception); 4) epithets neither numerous, nor often repeated, if we exclude the by-names ("Svjatopolk *Okajannyj*" – Svatopolk the *Accursed*, "Bonjak *Šeludivyj*" – Bonjak the *Mangy*). In general, the adornments do not expand into involved ornamentation which would obscure the simple order of thought or the visible lack of such order (see above).

5. The main ideological features of early literature are on the whole a Christian optimism, a joy that Rus' became worthy of joining Christianity at the "eleventh hour", just before the end of the world. Optimism obviously considers this unification through baptism as a guarantee, a pledge of salvation. That is why notes of ascetism are weak, and more than once we encounter the theory of "salvation in this world" by way of "petty deeds" (charity, repentance, prayers, etc.). There is faith in the possibility of the harmonious co-existence of the sacred sphere and the "world", of Church and State. In the field of politics, the ideology is "imperialistic" – the conception of a tribal and dynastic unity of the State is dominant, in spite of the fact that reality by no means revealed such unity (echoes of tribal frictions between the Poljane and the Drevljane, or the Kievans and the Novgorodians can still be heard in the Chronicle; conflicts between Kiev and Černigov, the independent political life of Polock and Tmutorokań, etc., are more real).

Side by side with these ideological "constants" we also come across considerable ideological differences: the tribal and political frictions and conflicts have already been mentioned; alongside these there are the different attitudes towards the Greeks, their political and religious aspirations (grecophilism and grecophobia are on the whole rare); sometimes particular stress is laid on the importance and rights of town populations; there is also a growing awareness of the social contradiction between poverty and wealth.

6. Notwithstanding the fact that it is works of religious content which are mainly extant (with the exception of the Chronicle and Vladimir Monomach's Works) we cannot doubt the existence of a literature of secular colouring (N. Nikol'skij). This has been lost as the result of an unorganised but efficient Church "censorship": in the libraries of the monasteries manuscripts of religious content were mainly preserved; the copyists, usually monks, followed the same principle when selecting the works to be copied. The 11th-century literature, as we know it, is the literature of a Christian country. From the point of view of the authors known to us, Christian culture was the only one conceivable. The pagans, in general, disappear from the sphere of interest of literature, though translated works (chronicles) impart enough information about the ancient pagan world. And only accidentally do we come across traces of Slavonic paganism in monuments, a paganism which receded into the past, but by no means without leaving traces.

2. SERMONS

1. Original sermons are distinguished with difficulty from the enormous store of translated homiletic literature. Moreover, the majority of sermons are difficult to date. Only the author's name and an occasional mention of political and cultural events and relations point to the time of their origin.

2. To the sermons of the 11th century belong first of all two sermons by the Novgorod Bishop Luka Židjata (the name does not, however, prove his Jewish origin). Unfortunately they are models of the "catechist sermons", i.e., a dry and brief enumeration of the Christian's duties. Sermons before the confession bore the same character. This is a special literary genre, of little interest to the historians of literature and, on the whole, inappropriate for the characterisation of the author as a writer.

3. We know more about St. Feodosij (d. 1074). To him are attributed eight sermons (fragments from others are in his Life), one prayer and two epistles to Prince Izjaslav (against the Latins: the epistles almost certainly are *not* the work of Feodosij and were written in the 12th century). It is known from Feodosij's Life that he wrote in a very abrupt tone to Prince Svjatoslav, comparing him to the usurper Cain, and that he delivered "numerous" sermons to the people. But only the sermons addressed to the monks are extant. They consist of reminding the monks of their duties, beginning with "outward" duties (going to church) and ending with "inward" duties (work, patience, humility, etc.). These are "moral" instructions. The sermons are written in a simple language, metaphor being employed as the main means of clarifying thoughts. Individual expressions, mainly traditional, are now metaphorical: "The heart burns", "The soul melts", "The death of sin" (sin = death), "To shake off sorrow". But sometimes Feodosij develops metaphors into entire scenes: one's attitude towards spiritual struggle (*podvig*) should not differ from one's attitude towards physical labour: "If one works in his field or vineyards, then – when he sees how the fruit grows – he forgets the toil in his joy and prays God that the fruit may be collected" – "If we are not given clothes or a coat or something else indispensable we grieve about it deeply, but when we waste time, we do not think about it and do not grieve about it" – "When the marching draws near and the trumpet blows, none can sleep: but does it become the Soldier of Christ to be lazy? He [the soldier – D. Č.] for a small and transitory fame forgets his wife, children, and property... even his head [life – D. Č.], he cares of nothing but to avoid shame. But as he is only mortal himself, so his fame ends with his life. But with us it is not so. If we resist in the struggle against our enemies, then as victors we shall win infinite fame and esteem ourselves worthy of indescribable honour."

Feodosij also formulates his views on the nature and significance of monkhood: "We must feed the poor and the wanderers by our labour, and not remain idle, moving from one cell to another." His Life throws a similar light on his convictions.

Feodosij uses the liturgy and the Holy Scriptures (which he often quotes), as well as a number of translated Greek sermons and the monastic statute.

4. Alongside the catechist and didactic sermons, there is one sermon-panegyric in "high style" which has come down to us. It is the "Sermon on Law and Grace" by the Metropolitan Ilarion, the first Kievan (not Greek) who for a short time had been Metropolitan during the reign of Prince Jaroslav the Wise (about 1057). This sermon combines devices of the lofty style of Byzantine sermons (and probably imitates some of its individual models, one of these is known) with the "monothematic" treatment, characteristic of the time. Its theme is Rus' baptism and, in connection with this, the glorification of the princes who had worked in favour of Christianization: St. Vladimir and his son Jaroslav-Georgij. The extensive sermon, many times longer than any of Feodosij's sermons, begins with a contrast between the pre-Christian state of humanity and Christianity. Judaism is the pre-Christian state. It is not quite clear why Ilarion speaks about Judaism and not about paganism: it is possible to see here some intimation of Judaic influences in ancient Rus', but these are not known to us, thought the higher stratum of the neighbours and rivals of the Kiev principality – the Khazars – professed Judaism. It is rather improbable that Ilarion wanted to juxtapose the dependence on the Greek Church and the independence of the Kiev Metropolis (this is the opinion of Soviet scholars). But this juxtaposition enables him to give an outline of Christian teaching, emotional rather than dogmatic. Judaism meant the domination of Law over Man; Christ, having freed Man from subservience to the Law, established the dominion of Grace. Ilarion develops this contrast between the Old and New Testaments in a series of antithetic metaphors: moon – sun, shadow – light, the night's coolness – the day's warmth; from these metaphors he passes on to the ideology of Christianity: hopelessness changed into hope of eternal life; slavery to law (this image in a country where serfdom was still reality is very effective) into a filial attitude to God. – From this antithesis Ilarion passes on to christology: here too we have a contrast – between the two natures of Christ, the divine and the human. This contrast is brought out (in seventeen antitheses) in a depiction of the entire earthly life of Christ. For instance:

as a man he was swaddled	as God, He led the Magi with a star;
as a man he lay in a crib	as God, He received adoration and gifts from the Magi

or:

as a man you were put into a grave	as God Thou hast destroyed hell and freed the spirit,
as a man you were sealed in the grave	as God Thou hast freed Thyself [from the grave – D. Č.] leaving the seals untouched.

In the second part of the sermon Ilarion passes on to Rus'. Every country glorifies its teacher, Christianiser, apostle. That is why "we too must, within our power, praise with our *feeble* praises Him who achieved the *great* and the miraculous" (traditional topos) – Prince Vladimir, whose conversion to Christianity is ascribed not to Greek sermons but to divine vocation: "The eye of merciful God implanted into his heart an under-standing of the vanity of pagan faithlessness, and the pursuit of one God." Ilarion describes the joy of the land in the light of Christian faith, concluding:

> Christ has triumphed,
> Christ has conquered,
> Christ has ascended the throne,
> Christ has become celebrated...

Returning to Vladimir, Ilarion depicts his virtuous life after baptism and his successes in christianising Rus', and addresses him as if he were present: "Arise from your grave, you who are worthy of honour, cast off your sleep: for surely you are not dead, but asleep until the universal resurrection." Ilarion exhorts him to look at his son and his family who lead a Christian life – in this way he finds an original form for glorifying Prince Jaroslav – and invites Vladimir to look upon Kiev which flourishes under the rule of Jaroslav:

> Look at the city radiant in its eternity,
> Look at the flourishing churches,
> Look at the spreading Christianity,
> Look at the city shining with the light of holy icons,
> (the city) fragrant with incense,
> (the city) ringing with praise and divine songs.

Ilarion concludes with a new series of antitheses, contrasting the state of the inhabitants of Kiev before and after baptism:

Rejoice, prince-apostle, who resurrected us dead from the malady of idolatry	for we revived thanks to you, and came to know Christ's life.

Then:

being blind from devilish falsehood	thanks to you we saw the light of triple-sunned divinity.
being speechless	thanks to you we began to speak and now from young to old we praise the one and only Trinity.

The sermon-panegyric ends with a prayer.

From the above-quoted excerpts the main stylistic devices of Ilarion can be seen: antithesis, parallelism, repetition, apostrophe (besides Prince Vladimir, Ilarion also addresses the city of Kiev). The language is slightly rhythmical (syntactically), for instance:

> ратныя прогони,
> миръ утверди,
> страны укроти,
> гладъ угобзи,
> боляры умудри,
> грады разсели,
> церковь Твою възрасти, etc.

("Beat off (the enemy) troops, strengthen peace, pacify (the neighbouring) countries, satisfy hunger, make the boyars wise, found cities, let your church grow.")

Ilarion also uses rhyme, as it seems – not accidentally: *jasno i veleglasno; vižd' cerkvi cvětušči, vižd' christianstvo rastušče; izyde jakože i vnide* ("brightly and loudly; look at the flourishing churches, look at the spreading Christianity; he left as he had entered."), and so forth.

The main tendency of the work is the glorification of Christian Rus', but Ilarion also adds to it the glorification of the princely dynasty, mentioning the (pagan) forefathers of Vladimir as well. Ilarion uses a fair number of compound words which originated in Church Slavonic under the influence of Greek, for example: *blagopriziranije, ravnoumnyj, ravnochristoljubec', mnogoplodně* ("a merciful look, equally wise, equally loving Christ, rich in yield"), etc.

It ought to be noted that the delivery of the sermon demanded quite a feat of oratory on Ilarion's part. Testimonies of a similar rhetorical art exist only from the second half of the 12th century.

Ilarions's "Sermon", which is extant only in later redactions (beginning with the 14th century), was extremely popular: its influence can be seen in Ukrainian literature (beginning from the Volhynia Chronicle of the 13th century until the 17th century), as well as in Muscovite literature

(Lives and eulogies, 15th–16th centuries) and in Serbian literature (even in the 13th century in the Lives of the Princes) where copies of the "Discourse" have also been preserved.

Ilarion is also credited with other sermons; one of them is of interest whether or not it is from his pen – "A Word to a Hermit Monk", extant in South Slavonic copies. It too contains a series of antitheses, apostrophes to the listeners or readers, and striking metaphors. The comparison of the hermit's life amidst nature with the life of birds singing the glory of God is quite outstanding: "In their ears there was no noise of the town, no shouting of people; the odious songs of a whore did not reach their ears, they did not see how countries wage war one against another... in their eyes there was only the swaying of the trees, (in their ears) the rustling of the branches, the songs of birds singing each its own song. That is why they (the hermits) did not know sorrow, they cast off sorrow by abandoning the world."

5. A certain number of sermons extant in later manuscripts can with certainly be ascribed to the 11th century. Especially those "Homilies" which speak of the recent baptism of Rus'. Such, for instance, is "The Homily about one who loved God" (it is possible that the word *christoljubec* meant a lay Christian), in which we are told about the Russian pagans' worship of *Perun, Chors, Sima-Regl, Mokoš,* and reminded about customs linked with the worship of *Rod* and *Rožanice*. There are also other "Homilies" of similar content (collected by Mansikka and others). – Two homilies by Grigorij, probably Bishop of Belgorod, combining instruction against drunkenness with exhortation towards "a Christian life" are undoubtedly ancient. – Also probably ancient are instructions with a social colouring. One of them is especially interesting: "About Dives and Lazarus", where the tale from the Gospels is used but very striking picture of the life of a rich man of that time is given. It is possible, however, that the details of the description are taken from Byzantine literature. The rich man

> lived on this earth luxuriously,
> walked in purple and in silk,
> his horses are well-fed pacers,
> are proud of their golden harness,
> his saddles are gilded,
> the slaves in front of him are numerous,
> he is (clad) in silk and golden pearls,
> and those behind him in necklaces and bracelets...
>
> . . . .
>
> at dinner (there are) many servants,
> the plates are chased in gold and silver,
> there is a multitude of different dishes:
> grouse, goose, crane, hazel-hens, pigeons

(there follow the names of some dishes still unexplained, e.g. *trtove* – probably tarts).

> the cups are of silver and large,
> the tankards and bowls are gilded,
> there is much to drink – mead, kvas, wine,
> pure mead and mead with pepper,
> revelry goes on the whole night with psalteries and pipes.

There are also sermons-eulogies of St. Feodosij and St. Kliment, the patron of Kiev.

Even this short outline of some of the anonymous sermons shows how varied the types of old Russian sermons were, and how varied were the themes touched on by the preachers.

3. HAGIOGRAPHIC LITERATURE (THE LIVES)

1. The original hagiographic literature is also orientated toward old Christian models and, to a still greater degree, is but a complement to the literature of translated Lives, among which there are some first class works from the point of view of composition and style. Besides the Greek Lives, monuments of West Slavonic hagiography were also known: the Lives of St. Cyril and Methodios, and the Lives of the Czech saints – Prince Wenceslas (Vjačeslav), and Princess Ljudmila. It was probably the latter two which led to the first original East Slavonic Lives – those of St. Boris and Gleb and St. Feodosij. One can detect in these monuments echoes of Czech Church Slavonic hagiographic literature, and even direct reference to it; while Nestor – the author of both Lives – also reveals in his third work, the Chronicle, a knowledge of Czech Church Slavonic literature.

The 11th–century Lives to a great extent possess the character of objective historical monuments. If we speak, therefore, of the influence of other hagiographic monuments upon them, it is not their reproduction which we have in mind, but their influence upon the form of the works. Unfortunately, foreign influences were also reflected in the content of the original Lives and in the choice of material which was thought worthy of mention: if something was said about an "official" saint, this was an indication for the Kievan author that a similar event from the life of a local saint deserved attention and mention. The Life of St. Feodosij had been written before he was a recognised saint, and already for that reason the author had to be "modest" and careful in his exposition.

A fact difficult to explain is that there are no Lives of Prince St. Vladimir and Princess St. Ol'ga, nor even of the founder of the Kiev-Pečerskij monastery, St. Antonij. We can merely guess the existence of such Lives in the past.

2. The Life of Boris and Gleb, the so-called *Čtenije* ("Legend") – in contradistinction to the non-hagiographic narrative about their death, the so-called *Skazanije* ("Tale") about which we shall speak later – was written by Nestor. The historical background of the Life is that after Prince Vladimir's death (1015), one of his sons – Svjatopolk – wishing to eliminate any possible pretenders to the princedom, first sent assassins against his brother Boris who, although at the head of his retinue, refused to offer any resistance and was killed; and then against his very young brother Gleb who was killed on the Dniepr. A third brother, Jaroslav, Prince of Novgorod, set out against Svjatopolk and, after a long struggle, expelled him from Kiev. Shortly after their death the brothers began to be worshipped as saints, gaining at the end of the century their formal recognition by the Greek Church: they were the first Russians to be canonized. It must be remembered what significance the existence of saints (or even the relics of foreign saints) held for every country in the Middle Ages. The Life starts with a prayer, an exhortation for God's help in the work which the author is undertaking in spite of "the coarseness and foolishness of his heart"; he refers to his sources (the tales of the *Christoljubcy*) and asks the reader to pardon his ignorance. All these are topoi, the commonplaces of medieval literature. There follows an introduction, shortly expounding the history of the human race from the Creation down to the author's own times. In the "last days" God felt the wish to unite Rus' also to the Christian world. The first part of the Life itself recounts the baptism of Prince Vladimir and of Rus', with no mention of the role of the Greeks. Only subsequently does the narrative deal with Boris's youth, his love of books and prayers, his wish to follow in the steps of "God's saints". Of Gleb, "a child in stature but a man in wisdom" (topos), Nestor speaks as of a friend of Boris and almoner. The characterisation concludes with a comparison with the saints whose names they had received at their baptism (Roman and David). Then the murder of the two brothers becomes the main theme, already known to us from other works. The account of the assassination of the two brothers seems to tally with the facts; the deviations from the Chronicle's account are insignificant: the state of mind of the two brothers, who know in advance the danger which awaits them, is rendered in the form of a prayer. Svjatopolk is dealt with very briefly and the author of the Life does not occupy himself with historical events: Svjatopolk "fled not only from the city, but also from his country to foreign lands, and thus ended his days"; and Nestor informs us of his "evil death" only as of a rumour. Then comes the conclusion, containing a description of the "miracles" which take place at the graves of the saints or after prayers to them; a description of the removal of their remains to Kiev and of the construction of a church dedicated to them. The stories of the miracles are united into a coherent whole and end with a discourse on the significance of humility and with praise of the saints. Here too the author mentions himself – "sinful Nestor" – as collector of material and author of the Life.

The narrative is very dexterously constructed, the material very ably distributed. Scholars have often wondered why Nestor, who was probably acquainted with the story from the Chronicle (or the *Skazanie* which we shall study further) effaces all concrete features as though deliberately. Even Kiev and Vyšgorod are mentioned by name only once, and are subsequently alluded to without being named; there are also no names for the assassins, not even for the avenger of the brothers' death. Jaroslav is mentioned only in the appendix; nor are the names of principalities and of the Pečenegs given (they are simply *ratnye* – warriors). This is particularly noticeable when comparing the Life with other accounts of the brothers' assassination. Nestor has been reproached for "depriving" the story of "individuality" and "colour". In reality, this is explained by the genre of the tale – a "Life" is written not only to recount facts but also to instruct; moreover, it is written not only for the fellow-countrymen of the saints but for all Christians. Thus Nestor places the events within the framework of the universal history of Christianity. It is also possible that he had in mind specific foreign readers – the Czechs; it was precisely in 1095 (about the time the *Čtenie* is supposed to have originated) that some of the brothers' relics were transported to Sázava monastery in Bohemia, the centre of Church Slavonic culture in that country.

But then Nestor enriches his story by pointing out parallels to the Lives of other saints, especially Wenceslas of Bohemia. Putting prayers into the mouths of the brothers, he tries thus to express their psychological experiences; he renders these, for instance, in this fashion: Boris "was going to his brother (Svjatopolk), not thinking anything evil in his heart; but the latter, accursed, not only planned evil against him, but had already sent evil in order to destroy him. The blessed (Boris) was rejoicing on his way that his elder brother would ascend the throne of his father, while the accursed one grieved having heard that his brother was on his way to see him". This antithesis of states of mind occurs in several places.

Nestor in his "Reading" also provided the basis of an ideological interpretation of the worship of the brothers: in spite of all their passivity, they are "strugglers" for peace on Russian soil, a peace which can be built only on certain definite moral foundations. Nestor sees these foundations in Christian morality, approaching an understanding of this morality as "not to oppose evil with force": Boris refuses to raise the mailed fist against his elder brother; Gleb, it is true, flees from danger, but also eschews resistance; in this light Jaroslav's struggle against Svjatopolk appears as an act violating the principles of Christian morality and is, therefore, mentioned only *en passant*.

3. Nestor showed himself perhaps an even greater master in a much longer Life, the Life of Feodosij, the manuscripts of which were even more widely circulated (the oldest manuscript dates from the 12th century). Nestor had entered the monastery only after Feodosij's death (1074) and collected oral stories about him, including stories of his mother (as related by one of the monks), a nun in one of the Kievan convents.

This Life also starts with "commonplaces" – a prayer of thanks that God has thought him worthy to be the biographer of saints and a request to pardon his lack of education and "uncouthness". The Life itself is divided into two parts; the oldest manuscript devotes about seven pages to the youth of Feodosij, and about thirty-three to his life in the monastery. The accounts of miracles are short: there are three miracles in all (three pages).

The entire story is subdivided into short chapters, episodes. In the first part there are fourteen episodes shedding light on the life and mainly the character of Feodosij in his youth: the characterisation of the young Feodosij and his mother is very striking and psychologically convincing. The orphan child from the family of one of the Prince's officials is depicted partly by traditional traits (love of study and of the Church, etc.), but his character becomes more vivid in the individual episodes of his life: his youthful religious passion for the image of Christ – Man and Sufferer – is expressed in the fact that Feodosij tries to wear modest clothes "below the dignity" of his position; in his attempts to work in the field together with the slaves; or to bake the Host for the Eucharist (perhaps the influence of the Life of Wenceslas of Bohemia); to wear "chains" on his body; and, finally, in his attempt to flee to Palestine where "Christ the Saviour walked in His flesh". The mother struggles against her son, but the gentle youth shows himself stubborn when it comes to his religious faith. Finally, he flees to Kiev where he is received into the Pečerskij monastery by its very founder, St. Antonij. The mother finds her son there, but he proves the victor, and she enters a convent in the same city of Kiev.

The second part (over forty episodes) depicts Feodosij as monk and abbot of Pečerskij monastery. Here the material collected by Nestor serves not only to characterise Feodosij's personality but also his ideology. In person, Feodosij remained constant: gentle in his attitude to the brotherhood of the monastery and, in the high position of superior of a famous monastery, whose support is sought by princes, he is as modest as ever: he wears simple clothes (resulting in a comical misunderstanding); he labours like any monk, chops wood, spins wool, helps to bind books... He does not punish sinning monks, does not reproach them, takes back those who flee from the monastery. But he shows himself adamant when it comes to conflicts with "the powerful of this world": he not only defends the monastery's interests, but also openly expresses his opinion in conflicts between princes, accusing verbally and in writing the usurper Svjatoslav; refuses to attend a princely banquet: "I shall not go to Beelzebub's feast, and I shall not take part in a banquet full of blood and slaughter." And here too, not only according to the account of the Life but also according to all the historical data, he proves – sometimes after a long struggle – the victor.

A series of episodes together with Feodosij's words as rendered by Nestor, illustrate his monastic ideology (corroborating the data of his sermons), as an ideal uniting a moderate ascetism with productive labour and the use of its fruits for helping "the poor, blind, lame and sick" for whom the monastery, during his term of office, built a hospital. The monastery was not rich at that time: Nestor depicts several cases of extremity when there were no stocks of food and even no wine and bread for the liturgy and no lamp-oil for the following day. And Feodosij is against economising: either he forces the monastery's steward to dispense the stocks to the brotherhood or gives away even the last to the needy. But the monastery's friends always come to the rescue: they are either unknown or at times depicted by Nestor as palpable messengers of God. In truth, this unexpected help to the monastery is the principal theme of the episodes which Nestor describes as miracles, on the whole very rare in his story.

From the point of view of style, Feodosij's Life is a very complex work. Its language is simple and smooth, sentences are short, stylistic embellishments are few. The language contains folk elements (the embryonic

Slavonic article *-tъ, -ta, -to* is in reality "the nominal determination"). But there are quite a number of literary influences: apart from the Holy Scriptures, there is the influence of the paterikons, and of the Lives of Wenceslas of Bohemia and Sabbas of Palestine who was the staunchest partisan of the same alliance of moderate asceticism and productive labour as Feodosij. Non-historical elements in the Life are very few. The vocabulary of the Life is interesting together with certain formulas related to the military terminology of that time: the monks are "mighty heroes"; the cross is "a weapon"; Nestor speaks of "the helm of salvation", and so forth. Similar images may be found in the sermons of Feodosij himself. There are many traditional comparisons from religious literature: Feodosij is the shepherd of his spiritual flock, "an angel on earth and a heavenly man"; the boyar's son who went into the monastery "fled from the world like an antelope from the entangling nets". There are simple but vivid antitheses: thus are contrasted the flesh and the spirit of man, the external and the internal. Moreover, in the Life of Feodosij, Nestor retains, up to a certain point, the same principle as in "Reading" – he seldom calls places and people by name, not even the town in which Feodosij was born. As no parallel source is available, this peculiarity of hagiographic style is particularly regrettable.

4. To hagiographic literature also belongs another story entered in the Chronicle under the year 1074, after the infoimation about Feodosij's death. Later this story found its way into the Pečerskij paterikon (IV, 4, 1) with slight modifications. But it is its original version which is extremely interesting. The story is often called "The Tale of the Four Monks of the Monastery of the Caves". I prefer to call it "The Tale of Isaakij", after the name of its protagonist.

Its subject matter derives from a very definite tendency on the part of its anonymous author. It is a story about "the gifts of the Holy Spirit", pledged by Christ to the Apostles and playing an important role in the whole of hagiographic literature. The story about St. Isaakij is in fact devoted to the monks of the Pečerskij monastery who possessed these very gifts. The tales devoted to the first three monks are very short – they are of the type of the paterikon stories (compare II, 3). The first three monks were endowed with various "gifts of the Holy Spirit": the first, Demjan, with the gift of healing; the second, Jeremij, with the gift of prophecy, "the discrimination of spirits" (i.e. the ability to apprehend whether a man has good or evil in mind), and of solace; the third, Matfej, with the gift of vision – the spiritual world appeared to him in graphic pictures. We are told about Isaakij's fate in a detailed way, but again in the style of the paterikons rather than that of the Lives. Having given up his wealth, Isaakij, a worldly merchant, entered the Pečerskij monastery in the days of Antonij and there led an austere and secluded life: never leaving his cave, taking food only every other day, he slept sitting upright and but a short time; and he wore a hair shirt – one which clung especially close to the body. One day, after several years of such acts, he was sitting in darkness at night when he suddenly saw a dazzling light. Two fair youths came near to him and, pointing to a third youth who was approaching, they said: "Behold Christ. Bow deeply before him." Isaakij failed to realise the satanic temptation, he bowed to the alleged Christ and found himself in the power of devils who, having mocked him, left him half-dead. After a long convalescence, Isaakij completely changed his mode of life. He started to live outside the cave and to do dirty manual work; after some time, signs began to appear in him which are considered the manifestations of saintliness: fire did not burn him, wild birds had no fear of him. "Not wishing for fame among the people" he pretended to be feeble of mind (the first case of *jurodstvo* among the Eastern Slavs, see VI, 3, 8) and inside as well as outside the monastery he committed acts for which he was even beaten. But now the demons were powerless against him and they themselves confessed it: "You have defeated us, Isaakij." Isaakij admitted that the demons had led him astray by appearing before him in the image of Christ and of angels when he "was not worthy of such a vision", but now he recognised them in whatever form they showed themselves. He ended his days in the monastery as a righteous man.

This story is also in the style of the paterikons and even reminds us in individual parts of the tales of old translated paterikons. Neither is its slant alien to that of the paterikons. Isaakij was tempted by the devil, for the most austere ascetism does not in the least guarantee the zealot the acquisition of the "gifts of the Holy Spirit". And this "ascetic pride" was fatal to him; the old Christian literature more than once condemned the ascetic's certainty that he had already obtained such a degree of perfection as to be worthy of beholding Christ. If one follows the trend of thought of the story in detail, one can see that the story of Isaakij is aimed at excessive ascetism linked with the absence of humility. It was in fact Isaakij's withdrawal from seclusion, his self-abasement in performing manual labour, his *jurodstvo* which gave him that very gift, the absence of which had almost ruined him: the gift of "discrimination of spirits" (see above).

IV

PART OF A FRESCO IN ST. SOPHIA CATHEDRAL
IN KIEV
One of the daughters of Prince Jaroslav the Wise
(Elisabeth or Anastasia?)

V

PLASTIC REPRESENTATION OF A SAINT FROM THE ST. MICHAEL
MONASTERY (11TH CENTURY) IN KIEV

Probably St. Nestor, according to the legend killing a heathen gladiator.

The story is written without stylistic adornment, but ably, and its slant is outlined in descriptive images. The tale of Isaakij is one of the most interesting examples of the Old Russian art of story-telling. It is so complete in itself that it may without hesitation be considered an independent work, regardless of whether it was circulated as a separate work or written by one of the chroniclers specifically for inclusion in the Chronicle. Later, it found its way into the Kiev-Pečerskij paterikon and was divided into four separate stories; this, it must be admitted, does not render incomprehensible the orientation emerging from the story of Isaakij as a whole. The story of Isaakij in its original form may be considered the embryo of the later original paterikons.

5. I have already mentioned that there are no Lives of the saints who were of importance in the history of Christianity in Rus', especially of Princess Ol'ga, Prince Vladimir, and St. Antonij of Pečersk.* Traces of the first two are preserved partly by the Chronicle, partly in an original and undoubtedly old compilation of no later date than the 12th century – "In memory and praise of Prince St. Vladimir" (previously falsely ascribed to the monk Jakov). But the traces in both monuments are so faint that it is impossible to recreate, even approximately, the content of these Lives. There are later redactions (16th century) of the Life of Vladimir, of obscure origin. The Kiev-Pečerskij paterikon refers to a Life of Antonij as one of its sources, but it is not improbable that this was merely a chronicle of the monastery in the days of Antonij rather than a genuine "Life" of the saint himself: whatever the case, the paterikon quotes passages which, in most instances, concern persons other than Antonij.

There are also extant ancient *proložnyje*, short Lives of Ol'ga, Vladimir, Boris and Gleb, which were incorporated into the composition of the translated Prologue (see II, 3). These "miniature" monuments have neither historical nor literary significance.

4. THE TALES

1. A peculiar feature of the original literature of the Kiev period is the almost complete absence (among extant monuments) of literary narratives with fictional themes and heroes. Two 12th-century tales by Kiril of Turov are an exception, whereas several imaginary heroes (Digenis, Akir, Stefanit and Ichnilat) are found in translated works. The very conception of fictional literature subsequently disappears completely in Muscovy, to reappear only in the 17th century.

2. Quite a number of tales existed as independent works. First of all

* Pečerskij Monastery = the Monastery of the Caves.

there were the narratives about the foundation of churches (one story, only a few lines long, probably dates from the end of the 10th century); then came the popular tales about miracles which later entered into the composition of the Lives (they were very popular until the 17th–18th centuries). Four stories of St. Nicholas's miracles, which originated before the beginning of the 12th century, were also original works. All these and other minor tales have no great historical or literary significance.

Special interest attaches to the story – also extant as part of the Chronicle – of the siege of Korsun' (Chersonese), in the Crimea, by St. Vladimir, and assigning his baptism to this place (the so-called "Korsun' legend"). To all appearances, it suffered a considerable evolution before its inclusion in the Chronicle and some of its elements remain controversial to this day.

However, there are three stories of historical content which are of both historical and literary interest.

3. The first of these is extant in two variants – one exists independently as *Skazanie* ("Legend") and is a story of the assassination of Boris and Gleb; the other – shorter – entered into the composition of the so-called "Chronicle of Nestor" and thence, with various changes, into other chronicles. Its historical background is already familiar to us (III, 3, 2). Both stories had either a common source or, very probably, the short story (the one from the Chronicle) can be considered a shorter version of the *Skazanie;* the opposite theory – that the "Legend" is an enlarged version of the story included in the Chronicle – is less probable. We shall examine only the *Skazanie*.

Skazanie is one of the most vivid works of the 11th century. Its contents fall into chapters not marked in the manuscript, but which present, as it were, separate scenes.

Skazanie starts with the story of Prince Vladimir's death. Then Boris is made to pronounce a stylised jeremiad:

> Woe is me, the light of my eyes,
> the radiance and glow of my face,
> the bridle of my youth [has been taken from me]
> the science of my ignorance!
> Woe is me, my father and lord!
> to whom shall I turn,
> at whom shall I look?
> Where may I delight in good education
> and instruction of your wisdom?
> Woe is me, woe is me!...

Already scenting danger from Svjatopolk, Boris consoles himself with pious reflections, e.g.:

> Everything passes and is lighter than a spider's web.
> What did the brothers of my father and my father gain?
> Where is their life and the fame of this world,
> And the purples and silks,
> the silver and gold,
> the wines and meads,
> the sweet dishes and swift horses,
> and the beautiful and great buildings,
> and the numerous properties,
> and the incalculable tribute and honours,
> and their pride in their boyars?

All this had disappeared. Reflecting upon his fate, Boris wavers between self-pity and the thought that were he killed, he "would become a martyr to the Lord". – The scene changes again: Boris has halted at the river Alta; most of his retainers, having discovered that he refuses to offer any resistance, forsake him. Early in the day, he reads the morning-service (from the psalms read at this service the author of *Skazanie* has selected those parts appropriate to the tragic situation). The murderers break into the tent, hack Boris with spears and pikes, and leave his few retainers to reflections as stylised as the "lament". – A new scene then shows Svjatopolk thinking that he ought to eliminate all his brothers, otherwise they

> will chase me away,
> and I shall be far from the throne of my father,
> and longing for my country will consume me,
> and I shall be shamed by censure,
> and another will take my princedom,
> and my courts will become empty...

He sends for Gleb who sets out for Kiev sailing a boat along the Dniepr. On his way Gleb receives the news of his father's and brother's death and laments over them. Finally, his boat meets that of the assassins: "the oars fell from everybody's hands and everybody grew numb with terror". Gleb – still a child – implores the murderers to spare him: "not to cut an unripe ear", "a green twig". His implorations do not help, neither does a prayer for his kinsmen, including Svjatopolk. Gleb is slain by his own cook "like an innocent lamb". – Somewhat briefly (but in greater detail than in the Life) we are told of Jaroslav's victory over Svjatopolk, of the latter's flight pursued by none, and of his "evil death" in the wilderness between Poland and Bohemia.

4. The narrative of the Chronicle often literally corresponds to that of the *Skazanie*, but omits some stylistic adornments (for instance, the laments). Moreover, the story is interwoven into the account of historical events, though it is made to stand out on its own.

Skazanie is an extraordinarily vivid work. The lyrical monologues – the laments – are remarkable. The selected texts from the Holy Scriptures are used successfully. Traditional themes regarding frailty of this world are also employed. The characters are successfully drawn, especially the very young Gleb, and Svjatopolk with his attachment to the goods of this world. We often find alliterations (especially frequent in the first lines of the Chronicle's story and to which there is no correspondence in *Skazanie*). The author is familiar with hagiographic liteiature, he mentions several Lives, especially that of Wenceslas of Bohemia. The great number of transcripts of the *Skazanie* (about 200) testify to its success among readers.

5. The story of the "sorcerers" is very simple in form, yet the author successfully renders the adventurous theme of the tale. Inscribed in the Chronicle under the year 1071, the story undoubtedly lacks any annalistic character; for here three tales with a common subject-matter but relating to different and partly undeterminable years are linked. The common theme is provided by the sorcerers who can prophesy the future but do not know their own fate – a theme already known to antiquity. The story is composed of three episodes of unequal length. The first of the sorcerers mentioned in the narrative appears in Kiev and prophesies natural catastrophes: "The Dniepr will flow backwards and countries will change place" (!) – but one night he himself disappears. The second case is told in detail: in the North-East, in the Rostov region, during a famine two sorcerers accused many women of hiding food in some mysterious way. And thus they ruined many women. But the *vojevoda* of the Prince of Kiev arrested them, and finally hanged them, and their bodies were eaten by a bear. The third episode recalls a "migratory" anecdote (there is also some similarity to an episode from the "Aleksandrija"): in Novgorod, the sorcerers carried along with them the entire population, and only the body-guard remained faithful to the prince and the bishop. Then the prince, hiding an axe under his coat, approached a sorcerer and asked: "Do you know the future?" The sorcerer answered that he knew everything. "And what is going to happen today?" "I shall perform great miracles." Then the prince, pulling out the axe, cut off the sorcerer's head and the people quietly dispersed. Three stories of different character and origin are here linked into one by their common theme and tendency. All the three episodes are very successfully recounted.

6. Also very interesting is the great history of Prince Vasil'ko of Tere- bovl' (Western Ukraine), inscribed in Nestor's Chronicle under the year 1097. It is rather improbable, though possible, that it was taken from the local chronicle of the prince; but in all likelihood it originated as an independent story written by one Vasilij, probably a priest in the house of the prince, who accompanied him during all his misadventures. The beginning and the end of the story are difficult to determine exactly, as they are not simply added to but "worked into" the text of the Chronicle – a symptom of the approaching new literary period.

Prince Vasil'ko took part in the peace talks between the princes in Kiev. An energetic and ambitious prince who later himself told the author about his grandiose plans, he was a dangerous rival to Prince Davyd of Vladimir in Volhynia, and the latter persuaded the Kievan Prince Svjatopolk to remove Vasil'ko from the political arena. The author tells us of the plans of Davyd and Svjatopolk in the form of a conversation between them – yet another of the "indirect" methods of representing the psychic life. The following story of Svjatopolk's invitation to Vasil'ko, and their meeting with Davyd, is also told in the same fashion. Vasil'ko is the guest of Svjatopolk. Svjatopolk then leaves the room and "Davyd speaks not, listens not, having treachery and fear in his heart". Finally, he too leaves. Vasil'ko is put in irons. The author – again in the form of a dialogue between Svjatopolk and the boyars, and Davyd – represents Svjatopolk's vacillations until, finally, he agrees to blind Vasil'ko – the usual Byzantine method of liquidating political enemies, then still rare in Rus'. The scene of the blinding is described tersely and powerfully, and the author here reveals the rare ability indispensable to every epic story, namely the ability of slowing down the narrative: he holds the reader's attention at every moment of the terrible scene. At first the attackers try to fell Vasil'ko; this does not at once suc- ceed; then they press a board against his chest; the first blow misses the eyes; the knife cuts into the face; first one eye is gouged out, then the second. As tersely, yet slowly, is recounted the further fate of Vasil'ko who is taken to the capital of Davyd's principality. The author accom- panies Vasil'ko and describes his talks with Davyd against whom the coalition of princes started to wage a war. During the narrative of this war, the end of the story of Prince Vasil'ko imperceptibly disappears.

7. These historical tales belong to different types. They vary also in style: they are artistically embellished in *Skazanije*, simple and straight-forward in the other two, but very delicately contrived in the story of Vasil'ko. Of interest are the devices which the authors reveal to use the psychological experiences of their heroes – prayers, monologues (including the imitation of laments), dialogues. The art of narration had achieved a high level, and it is very sad that other monuments of this genre are undoubtedly lost to us, especially if they were stories with fictional heroes. If such existed, they must have disappeared from literary circulation during the Moscow period of evolution. Some monuments of this type may be found even in the 12th–13th centuries.

5. THE CHRONICLE

1. The ancient chronicles are not only historical monuments but also literary works of high artistic value. The 11th-century Kievan chronicle, known under the conventional title of "Nestor's Chronicle", is of special interest to us. A second annalistic monument of the same time is the Novgorod Chronicle. Both are extant only in later transcriptions, beginning from the 13th century. Moreover, their principal parts entered into the composition of later versions.

2. The Kiev Chronicle covers the period from the 9th until the beginning of the 12th century. It is self-evident that one man, already known to us as the writer of Lives, could not be the sole author of such a work, the real chronicler, i.e., recording events yearly. But the Chronicle does not just present yearly inscriptions, for its text is a kind of literary ency-clopedia, into which are incorporated stories and sagas already known to us; contemporary items concerning events mainly in the Kiev, but also the Novgorod, Černigov and other principalities; documents (treaties with the Greeks, Prince Jaroslav's "testament"); notices of deaths and births in the Prince's family probably taken from the ecclesiastical register of the family's prayers for the dead; and a number of items, probably of oral origin, such as the stories which allude to the story-teller, but also anonymous ones, for instance, about events in the principality of Tmuto-rokań on the shores of the Sea of Azov. The authors also used literary material, translated Byzantine chronicles and apocrypha and, very prob-ably, written and oral West- and South Slavonic sources. Some of the excerpts and quotations included in the Chronicle are easily distinguish-able (as is the case with individual stories); to isolate the others and to determine their sources, long and difficult research is necessary, and it is not yet completed.

In broad outline the content of the Chronicle is as follows: it commences with the story of the confusion of tongues during the building of the Tower of Babel, and the origin and settlement of tribes and peoples, especially the Slavs. Here is inserted the legendary tale of the Apostle Andrej's visit to Kiev and Novgorod. The historical narrative starts in 852 (in the Chronicle the years are counted from "the beginning of the world", i.e. 5508 B.C.). In 862 the Varangian Princes were summoned to Novgorod. Then follows a yearly narrative sequence, with occasional omissions of considerable spans of time (for instance 867–876, 888–897, etc.). It is mainly the history of Kiev Rus' which is related, and news of the creation of the Slavonic alphabet as well as of the mission of Cyril and Methodios is communicated under the year 898 – to all appearances, this passage is of West Slavonic origin. The texts of two treaties with the Greeks are inserted in the story of the 10th century. In its major part, the story is here composed from sagas already known to us. A rather special place is taken by the story of Princess Ol'ga's baptism and by the tribute paid to her. The story of the baptism of Rus' under Vladimir (989) is very extensive and comprises a number of variants of the legend about this event: the story about the "trying of various religions" by Vladimir's messengers; the Greek missionary's sermon delivered to Vladimir (an enormous work which tells briefly the whole of ecclesiastical history and makes use of apocryphal literature); finally the story of Vladimir's march against the Greek colony of Chersonese, in the Crimea, and its subsequent baptism. Then again the yearly narrative is taken up; it is sometimes very bare in content (between 998–1013 only the deaths of various members of the prince's family are recorded). Under 1015 and the following years, the familiar stories of the assassination of Princes Boris and Gleb, and of the war of Jaroslav against Svjatopolk are noted. Then follows the annalistic narrative. Under 1037 we find the tale of the building of the Church of St. Sophia in Kiev and a eulogy of Prince Jaroslav the Wise. Until 1043 there are only short entries; then follows, taking us up to the beginning of the 12th century, a long story with excerpts from individual literary works already known to us in part. Also related here are: the foundation of the Kiev-Pečerskij monastery (1051); the death of its abbot, St. Feodosij (under 1074); the finding of his relics (under 1091); individual stories of events in remote Tmutorokań. The narrative is uneven, very detailed about some events, concise about others no less important. It is broken up by individual items and also by longer excerpts from various works (for instance, the sermon about "divine punishments").

The end of "Nestor's Chronicle" varies in different manuscripts and shows that the text was revised at least three times: one version ends with the year 1110 and contains a note by the copyist, and probably the author, of the final pages – Silvester, abbot of the monastery of Vydubiči, near Kiev, who worked in 1116; but in all probability the text reached then the year 1113; in other manuscripts (the so-called "Hypatius Chronicle") the text reached 1117 and differed from the first one in many ways.

3. The question arises: who worked on the Chronicle – and how and when – besides Silvester and Nestor who is named as the author of the Chronicle in the Pečerskij paterikon of the beginning of 13th century? Many scholars have occupied themselves with this question, referring at the same time to the Novgorod Chronicle and also the later Northern chronicles. The Polish historian Długosz, who wrote in Latin in the 15th century, used a chronicle unknown to us, which also helps in determining the genesis of "Nestor's Chronicle". Among the scholars who have studied the Chronicle, much has been done by the historians; among the historians of literature, valuable research has been done primarily by A. Šachmatov, followed by his pupil M. Priselkov, and in part by the Soviet scholar D. Lichačev, and others. In the following outline I shall give a brief account of the results of Šachmatov's research, which is, to date, undoubtedly the most authoritative.

There are a few criteria for the establishment of the individual chapters of the Chronicle on which various authors worked. Two criteria are fundamental: contradictions or differences between individual parts of the Chronicle, and the presence of passages the end and the beginning of which are obviously by different hands.

Thus, in some cases, individual characters are treated in the Chronicle as living persons. Under 1044, Prince Vseslav of Polock is mentioned as "still" living, whereas his death is reported in 1101: consequently in 1044 and in 1101 different authors worked on the Chronicle. Under 977, we are told that the grave of Prince Vladimir's brother Oleg is "now" still near the town of Ovruč, while under 1044 we are told that in that year his remains were transported to Kiev. Consequently, the author who described the events of 977, when Prince Oleg was killed, and the author who described the events of 1044 were different persons. There are several such cases of contradiction.

There are also diversities in the style or character of entries. Thus, beginning from 1061, events are dated precisely (day and month), whereas after 1073 such dating stops. Under 1066-7, we are told about events in Tmutorokań, about which there are only legendary items in the other parts of the Chronicle. There are also differences in ideology in the Chronicle's individual parts.

The breaks in the Chronicle are also very significant. It is hardly conceivable that the Chronicle was written before the acceptance of Christianity. But, after a more or less coherent narrative sequence of events under 1037, we find a eulogy of Prince Jaroslav and the story of his preoccupation with ecclesiastical and cultural life. After that year there occurs a certain pause in the narration. A fresh segment of coherent text begins anew only from 1044. There is another break in 1073 when even the news of St. Antonij's death is not recorded, whereas the Chronicle otherwise speaks in great detail about events in the Pečerskij monastery. As mentioned already, events in Tmutorokań are reported under 1066–7. Thus we can presume that the first adaptation of the annals dates from 1037 and is somehow linked with the construction of the Church of St. Sophia – probably with the establishment of the first Metropolitan in Kiev (in the opinion of A. Šachmatov, and on the supposition of D. Lichačev, the first draft of the Chronicle included the history of Christendom in Rus' until 1037). From 1044 the annals were kept in the Kiev-Pečerskij monastery, probably by that same monk Nikon who in 1061 fled from Prince Izjaslav's anger from Kiev to Tmutorokań, where he recorded local events. In 1068 he returned to Kiev and in 1073 he either left Kiev again or died. Only in 1074 does the chronicling of events start anew, again in the Pečersk monastery, with stories of which the year 1074 is full (Feodosij's death, the story of Isaakij). Subsequently, there was probably a break in 1093; in a Novgorod chronicle we find the preface to the Kiev Chronicle, which can be dated from this year. Further adaptation continues, again in the Pečerskij monastery, and ends with 1113. It is probable that the author of this adaptation is, in fact, Nestor whom the Pečersk paterikon calls "the author of the Chronicle" (IV, 4, 1 ff). In 1113 Vladimir Monomach ascended the throne of Kiev and the manuscript was then being worked on in the monastery of Vydubiči, founded by Vladimir's father, either by Silvester or by someone else.

This does not answer all the queries about the origin of the annalistic text, for every later chronicler could not only continue to make entries in the Chronicle, but also shorten, change, or amplify the old text which fell into his hands. To establish the original aspect of previous versions according to the copy of Silvester is not easy. We are helped here, i.a. by the Novgorod Chronicle, the beginning of which contained the same material as that of the Kiev Chronicle, only in briefer form. Moreover, we may presume that the Kievan Chronicle was an enlarged version of the old short text rather than that the Novgorod annals were a shorter version of the former.

4. We shall not linger on the involved questions of individual authors' work on the Chronicle. To determine the extent of their contributions to the text, we are helped by their ideology which we may deduce from several fragments of the Chronicle. While the first author is interested mainly in the question of the baptism of Rus', the second author's attitude (after 1044) to the Greek Church hierarchy and the Greeks in general is apparently quite critical; in particular, he tells of the foundation of the Kiev-Pečerskij monastery without mentioning Greek participation. He expresses definite political views on the absolute necessity of the peaceful co-existence of particular princes; he sympathises with the townsmen in their conflicts with the princes. And the author of the 1093 version, as may be seen from the extant introduction, is interested in

social questions, while national ideology is also greatly stressed: he regards the princes as born leaders in the struggle against the inhabitants of the steppes, he is a partisan of the "good old customs". The subsequent author, Nestor, is known to us from his other works. The Lives written by him testify to his knowledge of Czech Church Slavonic literature and we may therefore attribute to him those fragments in which the influence of this literature is discernible: the story of the invention of the alphabet; the eulogy of Princess Ol'ga (in which the panegyric of the Czech princess St. Ljudmila is echoed), and a number of others. One may also evidently add to these the excerpts from the Byzantine annals (Hamartolos); the account of the settlement of peoples, the Slavs in particular; as well as some corrections of the old text (extant in the Novgorod Chronicle), the treaties with the Greeks inserted in the text, and much else. The last version, compiled in the monastery of Vydubiči, included in the Chronicle new material about the activity of Prince Vladimir Monomach, especially concerning his policy of reconciling the hostile princes. Further material sympathetic to Monomach exists in the second version, extant in the Hypatius Chronicle (see above).

5. It is obvious that the varied composition of the Chronicle is reflected in the variety of styles in which its component parts are written. However, throughout the entire Chronicle, we find a series of features common to all the authors or superimposed on the old texts by later versions. In any case, some parts of the Chronicle show great literary ability.

In the later parts of the Chronicle we also find sections reminiscent of the sagas of its earlier parts (see above, I, 8). They call these to mind by the rhythm of the language, the breaking up of the speech into short syntactic units, and the use of alliteration. Such, for instance, is the fragment in the story of the internecine war of 1097, when the Polovtsian khan Bonjak, the ally of Prince Davyd of Vladimir in Volhynia, divines the issue of the campaign:

и яко бысть полунощи,	и-б-п
и вставъ Бонякъ	и-в-б
отъѣха от вои,	о-о-в
и поча выти волчьски	и-п-в-в
и волкъ отвыся ему,	и-в-о
и начаша волци выти мнози;	и-в-в
Бонякъ же приѣхавъ	б-п
повѣда Давидови,	п
яко побѣда ны есть на Угры заутра ...	п-н-н

("And when midnight came, Bonjak arose, rode away from the troops and started to howl like a wolf; and a wolf answered him with howling, and many wolves started to howl. On his return Bonjak told Davyd that they would gain victory over the Hungarians the next day.")

Such excerpts, always brief, are quite frequent. The authors of the Chronicle are much addicted to aphorisms and adages which are put into the mouths of the characters acting in historical events. The Novgorodians inform Prince Svjatopolk of Kiev, who wants to send his son to reign over them: "If your son has two heads, send him' (1102); before the battle of the princes, they say: "We shall either die or live"; in preparing for the march: "Prepare the road and pave the bridge"; the uncle of Prince St. Vladimir, Dobrynja, declares after the victory over the Volga Bulgarians: "They all wear boots, they will not pay us tribute; let us rather look for those who wear bast shoes" (*lapotniki*) – (compare with the above examples, I, 5). This is the style of the annalistic anecdotes of all periods and these anecdotes are probably derived from an oral tradition. The chroniclers, in general, like to begin or end a story with similar sentences, putting them into the mouth of collective groups ("the people", soldiers, princes). Thus, before the march, the people express doubts as to its success: "If only you [prince – D. Č.] collected 8,000 of them [soldiers – D. Č.] ... but our land has been impoverished by war and conscription"; at an assembly at Lubeč the princes "say to themselves: why do we ruin the Russian land?"; sometimes the sentence develops into an entire "address" – according to the Chronicle, one such was delivered by Prince Vladimir Monomach at a meeting of princes near the Lake of Dobolsk: "I am surprised ... that you pity the horses...; and why don't you think that the peasant will start to plough, that the Polovtsian will come and shoot him with an arrow and seize his wife and children and his entire property; thus you pity the horses but do not pity him [the peasant – D. Č.]?" Such a speech, of course, is merely an enlarged aphorism. And such speeches – in rare cases perhaps historical in content, though of course moulded into a certain form of literary expression by the authors of the Chronicle – are not few.

A very characteristic feature of the Chronicle – on the whole much more strikingly represented in the annalistic texts of the 12th–13th centuries – is the division of the narrative into dialogues between the protagonists. This adds greatly to the vigour of the exposition, and "dramatises" it. These dialogues, as well as the speeches, are an invention of the chronicler himself.

A further feature of the style of the Chronicle is characteristic of the epic narrative of all times and peoples, namely, the use of rigid, constant formulas in the description of set situations. In the Chronicle, the beginning of a battle is usually marked with the words: "To hoist the flag"; casualties of war or of a single battle are usually "countless"; the battle (*sěča* or *bran*') is either "ferocious" or such "as was never seen before"; the princes gather "many and brave" soldiers, "innumerable" warriors; the troops return from their campaign "with victory" or "with glory and great victory"; on their way back from the campaign "they wipe off their sweat"; pitying the dead, they "wipe off their tears"; to provoke enmity between princes is "to throw a knife between them", and so forth. In set form are also certain expressions which are found only once in the Chronicle: a bloody battle is characterised by the words: "Blood ran down the valleys"; about the Greeks we read: "The Greeks are deceivers even to this day". Vivid and picturesque metaphors and similes are frequent: a numerous army stands "like a forest" (recall the end of *Macbeth*), arrows fall in battle "like rain"; the sun shines through mist "as if made of blood"; Prince Svjatoslav (10th century) "walked lightly like a leopard"; Bonjak, having attacked the Hungarians, "drove them together as a falcon the jackdaws", etc.

Of interest are individual descriptions of events, mainly military. Such is the account of battle in 1024: "And during the night there was darkness, lightning and thunder... And the battle was ferocious, and when there was lightning, weapons glittered, and there was a mighty storm and a ferocious and terrible fight." Or the description of the fate of the prisoners taken by the Polovtsians in 1093: "Suffering, mournful, weary, numb with cold, hungry, thirsty and unhappy, with thin faces, blackened bodies, in a foreign country, with dry tongues [possible alternative reading: "among giants" – D. Č.], they go about naked and barefoot, their feet pricked by thorns...", etc.

In general, the art of the chronicler consists in embellishing factual events: what could have been said in two words the author of the chronicle amplifies, he delays the telling, and by this very device animates the narrative.

6. The language of the Chronicle is also of interest. In all probability, later scribes strengthened the Church Slavonic elements in the text. But even these later copies preserved a number of old local words: *grivna* (necklace, later a monetary unit), *gridnica* (hall), *skot* (in the sense of "treasure"), *meduša* (a wine-cellar), *pavoloki* (silk), *komon'* (horse), *kotory* (internecine wars), etc. Some of these words still exist in East Slavonic, especially in the Ukrainian, dialects. The syntax is also noteworthy and also, in part, the morphology (for instance, the use of the dual number, the forms of descriptive future, locative without preposition, etc.).

7. The Chronicle also possesses great significance for the determination of the repertoire of literary works at the disposal of the Kievan reader of the 11th century: we have already mentioned the use of translated Greek and West Slavonic sources, it is also possible to deduce the use of lost Bulgarian works. There are also signs that lost monuments of East Slavonic literature were used – especially the Černigov and perhaps a West Ukrainian chronicle. But, of course, it is the determination of various local legends which is very important, for example the Tmutorokań legends which had also possibly been written down.

8. Of great complexity is the question of those facts which the later chroniclers preferred to pass over in silence and of which there is no mention in the older copies. A comparison of Nestor's Chronicle with the Novgorod annals shows, for instance, that later versions eliminated mention of princely dynasties other than of Rurik's. Reference to Kiev's links with the Western Church is also probably omitted – we are aware of such links from other sources. The Chronicle also passes over in silence the links with the Bulgarian Church. The question of these omissions is not yet definitely solved.

9. The Chronicle provides ample material for the characterisation of the chronicler's *Weltanschauung* and, indirectly, that of his contemporaries. First of all, the chronicler presents a specific conception of the historic development of Rus'. In spite of some elements of grecophilism and a one-sided dynastic point of view, this conception consists of a conviction that Rus' was capable of independent political existence. In addition, the majority of the authors of the Kievan Chronicle upheld the idea of peaceful coexistence and cooperation among separate principalities and princes, and also the idea of social justice for the urban and partly the rural population. True, these ideas are not a political program – the chroniclers too often take up the standpoint of a religiously coloured optimism: they are convinced that success, especially military victory, is given by God, and this very fact testifies to the righteousness of the victors. The chroniclers believed in the possibility of the realisation of their ideals, but the end of the century had already brought some disillusionment.

10. The Novgorod Chronicle has come down to us in its early mid-12th-century version. Its first part (extant only in fragments) is undoubtedly older than the corresponding parts of Nestor's Chronicle. We find in it a whole series of items which are undoubtedly older than the corresponding excerpts in the Kievan Chronicle: we may therefore rightly assume that the Novgorod text, very similar to – but shorter than – the Kievan, has preserved the original versian of the Kievan entries.

In the Novgorod annals, Prince Oleg (9th–10th centuries) is called only *vojevoda;* in the hands of the Kievan chronicler (Nestor?) was the text of the treaties with the Greeks, in which Oleg is called "prince" – the chronicler accordingly changed the text. In general, it is easy to show by comparison of the two texts, that it was not the Novgorod chronicler who condensed the Kievan text but the Kievan chronicler who, on the contrary, expanded the Novgorod text. The Novgorod annals preserved stylistically a more archaic quality than the corresponding parts of the Kievan text. Of interest, for instance, are the verbal riddles (a characteristic trait of style of the Scandinavian sagas, cf. I, 8). On the whole, the Novgorod Chronicle is written in concise, unadorned. "lapidary" style. The Novgorod chroniclers continued their work in the same style in the following centuries.

Allowing for some exceptions, the monuments incorporated in the Novgorod Chronicle may be regarded – when compared to those in the Kiev Chronicle – as purely historical records rather than as monuments of literature.

6. THE PILGRIMAGE OF ABBOT DANIIL

1. Two works of Kievan literature, especially from the very end of its first period, demonstrate vividly the individualities of two writers and familiarise us with the process of their literary work. These are "The Pilgrimage of Abbot Daniil" and the works of Prince Vladimir Monomach.

Choženie palomnika Daniila ("The Pilgrimage of Abbot Daniil") is among the most popular works of the old literature: it is extant in no less than a hundred copies dating from the 15th–19th centuries. The comparatively minor differences between the versions signify the faithful preservation of the original form of the work.

Pilgrimages to Palestine started shortly after the acceptance of Christianity, but in other cases all we know is the bare fact that a pilgrimage had taken place. At the Holy Sepulchre, Daniil met inhabitants of Kiev and Novgorod. The Life of St. Feodosij provides the motive for such pilgrimages, the wish to see the actual country in which Christ the Saviour "walked in the flesh". Daniil, however, decided to present to his contemporaries – and, as we can see, bequeathed to his heirs – a detailed description of Palestine at the beginning of the 12th century, a description of great value from the archaeological point of view, and set by the author in a religious and emotional framework.

Daniil was abbot of a monastery, probably in the principality of Černigov, and he organised his journey on a grand scale. He was accompanied by a complete retinue, he employed guides everywhere. Baldwin himself – the King of Crusaders – took Daniil with him on a journey and, during the Easter Service at the Holy Sepulchre, placed him next to himself. Daniil was allowed to enter places in Palestine to which access was normally prohibited.

2. Daniil starts his account with characteristic commonplaces (topoi) – he does not want to be like the "idle slave" of the Gospels who failed to increase the talent of his master. He wants to make use of his pilgrimage, to depict it to the faithful so that from reading him they might think they had really been to Palestine. In addition, he asks his readers to forgive his poverty of wit. Already this introduction shows that Daniil is a talented and well-read writer. He gives detailed and exact descriptions, possible only because he had kept a diary during his journey, jotting down the length of a road, the dimensions of architectural monuments and various other details. Moreover, he adds comments to the description of his visits to various memorable places; these show his familiarity not only with the Gospel-stories but also with those of the apocrypha. It is probable that he prepared himself for his pilgrimage by reading the relevant literature.

Daniil was in Palestine between 1106 and 1108, and his "Pilgrimage" was probably written shortly afterwards.

3. To recount the contents of the "Pilgrimage" is almost as impossible as to recapitulate any contemporary guide-book. Daniil describes his sea-voyage to Palestine and mainly, of course, the country itself in which he attempted to see everything that in his opinion deserved attention. He visited Jerusalem and Galilee, saw the Dead Sea and the Jordan, as well as those hills with which the events of the Gospels are linked. The principal content of the "Pilgrimage" comprises a description of the Holy Places, of places memorable in the mortal life of Christ, as well as of places linked with the events of the Old Testament, followed by a description of monasteries and churches. He does not, however, forget the surrounding country and its nature. References to people whom he met are rare, but he does allude to Arabs as well as to West Europeans, to his fellow-countrymen and his guides, and to King Baldwin.

The descriptions of the Holy Places are most frequently linked with allusions to stories from the Old and New Testaments, including apocryphal stories. These were usually local tales, the historical material having been supplemented by various pious legends which had in part originated from the wish to show to the traveller something worthy of attention on all sides. Daniil briefly retells such legends. In the majority of cases his literary sources may be discerned. Thus, describing his visit to Golgotha, he mentions that beneath Christ's tomb lies "Adam's head" – "blood and water from Christ's ribs dripped on to Adam's head and washed away the sins of the whole human race" (this is from the apocrypha "About the Holy Cross"). Daniil also saw the well, near which the Archangel Gabriel appeared to the Virgin Mary for the first time (from Jacob's Gospel); he visited the place where Christ was tempted by the Devil; he saw the tower in which David wrote the Psalms; he ate fish from the Sea of Galilee which Christ had particularly esteemed, etc.

Daniil's descriptions of architectural monuments are not successful: in the majority of cases the author confines himself to an indication of their dimensions, and to an emotional characterisation with the help of such words as *marvellous, beautiful, awesome, indescribable,* and so forth. Here is his description of the Church of The Resurrection in Jerusalem: "It is constructed wonderfully and artistically, and its beauty is inexpressible; it is apparently rotund; it is awe-inspiring, and on the outside it is adorned with mosaics marvellously and indescribably, and its walls are covered very beautifully with tiles of costly marble!"

The descriptions of nature are much more vivid. The Jordan reminds him of the River Snov' in his homeland: "The River Jordan flows rapidly, its banks are very steep on one side, and low on the other. Its water is muddy and sweet to the taste, so that it is not unpleasant to drink this sacred water, no one falls sick from it, and it does no harm. The Jordan is just like the River Snov' in width and depth, but it flows very unevenly and rapidly. Its meadows are exactly like those near the Snov'." – "In width, the Jordan is exactly like the River Snov' at its estuary. On this side of the River [the place of Christ's baptism – D. Č.] there is a small wood, and along the banks of the Jordan there are a great many trees similar to willows, but not willows. And above the Font, along the bank of the Jordan, there are a great many reeds, but not like our reeds... and much osier. And here a multitude of animals live – there are wild boars, a countless number of them, and many leopards. And there are lions on the other side of the Jordan, in the rocky hills..." He describes the environs of Bethlehem: "And this land near Bethlehem is very

VI

THE MURDER OF THE PRINCE, ST. GLEB

Illustration to the "Skazanie". From the so-called Sil'vestr Manuscript (14th century).

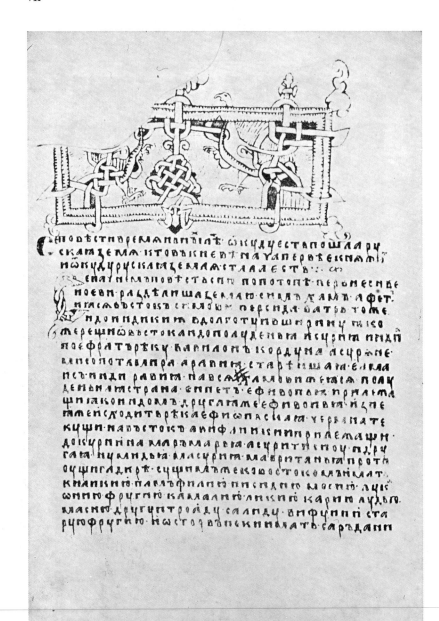

**THE FIRST PAGE OF THE SO-CALLED LAURENTIAN MANUSCRIPT OF
THE OLD RUSSIAN CHRONICLE (1377)**

The upper left corner is torn off.

beautiful and mountainous, and on the slopes grow a great many fruit trees, most beautiful olive trees and fig trees and various others, and many vineyards, and in the valleys are cornfields." He also describes the wilderness and deserts – such is the road from Jericho to the Jordan: "All the way it is flat, all is sand, the road is very difficult, many cannot breathe from the heat and die of thirst. Not far from this road is Sodom [the Dead Sea – D. Č.], and from this sea stench and hot air emanate, as from a burning stove, and it consumes the earth with this evil-smelling heat." The neighbourhood of the monastery of St. Savva is as wild: "Here is a terrifying and very deep ravine [river bed – D. Č.] without water, with very high walls of stone; upon the stone walls there are perched the cells [of the monastery's monks – D. Č.] which God marvellously and terrifyingly supports at such a height." He dwells also on the description of the country and on its economic possibilities: agriculture, horticulture, cattle-breeding.

4. All these descriptions, as well as the infrequent characterisations of people, are, in the majority of cases, linked with the expression of emotions: Daniil walks along the banks of the Jordan a long time "with love"; he and his retinue kiss the place of Christ's Transfiguration "with love and tears"; at the first glimpse of Jerusalem "no one can refrain from shedding tears at the sight of this land which they had awaited with such longing, and of these Holy Places where Christ walked for our Salvation". And the "Pilgrimage" concludes with a picture of general rejoicing at an Easter service at the Holy Sepulchre. Daniil proceeds with a lamp kindled by the sacred fire, "with the greatest joy, having been enriched by divine grace, holding in our hands gifts and the sign of the Holy Sepulchre, illuminating with them all places: we walked rejoicing as if we had found some rich treasure". He also mentions the mood of others: "Prince Baldwin stands in awe and in great humility and tears flow from his eyes as if from a spring"; "All the people sing at the Holy Sepulchre: 'Lord, have mercy on us'!" – "with great joy and revelry, having seen the sacred light of God" [on Easter Day, in the Church of the Holy Sepulchre, light falls from the skies – D. Č.]. "And he who did not see this joy on that day, will not believe the narrator."

In all these descriptions, the use of comparison to make accessible to the reader everything seen and experienced by the pilgrim, alternates with a refusal to describe what is "inexpressible" (*hyperoche*).

5. The richness of Daniil's language and his erudition must also be noted.

In spite of the use of literary sources, Daniil's language bears clear traces
of the spoken language of his country: the use of the embryonic article (as
in the Life of St. Feodosij): -tъ, -ta, -to in all inflected forms of words is
noteworthy; and in the choice of vocabulary, Church Slavonic elements
somewhat recede before the East Slavonic. Unfortunately, the sometimes
inexact observation of the old orthography by the copyists partly with-
holds from us the lexical and even stylistic peculiarities of this interesting
work which – properly speaking – stands on the border of *belles-lettres*
and "scientific" (in the 11th-century sense) literature.

7. WORKS OF PRINCE VLADIMIR MONOMACH

1. Prince Vladimir Monomach (1053–1125) – the son of Prince Vsevolod
and of a Byzantine princess related to the Monomach family – is the
only 11th-century writer whose Collected Works have come down to us.
True, they have been imperfectly preserved in the so-called Laurentian
copy of the Chronicle, and they are not extant in their entirety. To this
day there is still the question whether they were already incorporated
into the Chronicle in the 12th century, or whether the 14th-century copyist
(the Laurentian copy was written in 1377) transcribed into his own version
the already defective manuscript which had been inserted into the manuscript which he was copying. There are many obscure places in the extant
text, and scholars have indulged in many conjectures (including some
unnecessary ones).

The Collected Works consist of the "Instruction", of a political letter
to Prince Oleg of Černigov, and of a prayer; it is not clear whether the
autobiography of the Prince, which is included in our text, belongs to his
"Instruction" or whether it was written as a separate work.

2. Like the "Pilgrimage" of Daniil, the works of Vladimir Monomach
are of interest to us because they show, among other things, the character
of the author's literary work. They contain many quotations from the
Holy Scriptures, possibly from the *Paremejnik*, and signs of his acquin-
tance with other works – with one of the sermons by Basil the Great (from
the *Izbornik* of 1076); with *Šestodnev;* with some of the apocrypha; and
possibly with the "Physiologus". There is no doubt that some of the
successful proverbial phrases also have literary sources. We must presume that the Prince noted quotations for himself, and possibly collected
them over a long period. Only on the basis of some kind of diary could
he have compiled the list of his numerous campaigns (about 80) which

are enumerated in the autobiography. His Prayer (or Prayers, for it is not clear whether this is a single work) is a compilation of Church prayers. All this shows us the Prince as a man of letters. His "Instruction" is written in the form of precepts for his children (it is possible that he was inspired by examples of such instruction in the *Izbornik* of 1076), but he assumes that it will be read or "heard" by other people as well. The letter to Prince Oleg of Černigov is also obviously intended for a wider "public" to whom Vladimir wants to show the peaceful character of his policy.

3. The "Instruction" was written shortly before 1125, the year of Vladimir's death. Characteristically, it was written according to a rather sustained austere plan: after a preface (with an apology for the weakness of the work – a topos), and after a religious and moralising introduction, with quotations from religious literature, there follows advice of a secular character, mainly political: initially concerning the duties of a prince as a ruler and *vojevoda*, then giving moral advice of universal interest. There follows the autobiography which may belong to the "Instruction", for it as it were illustrates the advice of the Prince by examples from his personal life.

The first part consists of quotations from the Psalter, the main theme being the damnation of sinners and the salvation of the righteous. Further advice relates to spiritual discipline: "Mastery of one's eyes, reticence of tongue, humility of spirit, subordination of the flesh to the spirit, suppression of anger, purity of thoughts, the endeavour to perform good deeds." This part is concluded by an emotional tribute to God for His gifts, for the beauty and harmony in the organisation of the universe, and for His demanding so little of men: instead of "seclusion, monkhood, fasting", "three minor acts" are sufficient: "repentance, tears, and prayer" (this reminds us of the *Izbornik* of 1076). The Prince asks his reader to fulfil at least half of these demands, and especially to pray.

Secular advice is sustained in the spirit of Christian humanity: helping the poor, justice, leniency of judgment, faithfulness to promises, respect for the clergy and the aged, care of the sick, attendance at funerals, indifference to earthly goods. This is followed by entirely secular counsels: frugality, personal attention on the Prince's part to all princely and domestic duties, hospitality, defence of the people against despotism and, finally, "knowledge" (the example of Vladimir's father who knew five languages). All these counsels are motivated in part spiritually (by "fear of God"), in part ethically (all people are equal); on part practically (by the necessity of avoiding blame and winning praise). The secular advice is concluded by a programme of the Prince's day.

4. Then follows the autobiography. It enumerates the Prince's campaigns which led him not only to Eastern but also to Central Europe (Glogau); and relates his "labours" in hunting and the dangers experienced by him (hunting at that time was an essential element in winning lands, and in the culture of the country). Vladimir only briefly mentions affairs in connection with the administration of the country and his endeavour to be always just and merciful.

5. The letter to Prince Oleg Svjatoslavič was written after the battle in which one of Vladimir's sons perished (1096). Monomach reminds his reader that all men are mortal and that, with the Last Judgment in mind, people should endeavour to keep good relations among themselves. Then follows a concrete request to free the wife of the dead prince, who had been taken prisoner.

6. The Prayer is addressed to Christ, the Virgin Mary and St. Andrew of Crete (it is possible that these are separate works), and is a compilation of Church prayers. Monomach intertwines with it requests for himself and for the State.

7. The literary character of all these works is beyond doubt. Precepts for children were one of the favourite forms of Byzantine literature. Monomach, married to an English princess, might have known of the existence of similar works in the West. There already existed the brief instruction of Jaroslav the Wise, inserted into the Chronicle as his "testament"; and "letters" were a traditional literary form. But it is the sustained poetic tone of Monomach's works which is remarkable. Typical are his reflections on the beauty of the world, cast in the form of a eulogy of God's grace: "By Thy skill, o Lord, the various animals and birds and fishes are adorned; and we marvel at the miracle of how Man was created from dust; and how human faces are so distinct that if the whole world were gathered together, none of them would look the same, but each one – thanks to God's wisdom – would have his own likeness." "And we must also marvel how the celestial birds come from Irij [*irij* – the country to which migrating birds are said to fly in winter – D. Č.]... and do not remain in one country but... disperse over all countries, according to God's command, so that they fill the woods and fields... And Thou

Lord, hast taught these heavenly birds – at Thy command they sing...
and at Thy command, though they have voices, they become silent." –
Vladimir finds picturesque and vivid expressions for the simplest thoughts.
Describing a journey along the Dniepr on the banks of which stood
hostile Polovtsians, he writes: "Their mouths watered at the thought of
us, as they stood by the ferry and in the hills"; imagining how Oleg
looked at his dead son, Vladimir writes: "And you saw him, flesh and
blood, faded like a young flower"; advising the princes to remain in
their inherited principalities, he clothes this thought with the image: "to
eat one's forefathers' bread"; the request to free his dead son's wife, who
had been taken prisoner, is expressed in this manner: "My daughter-in-
law must be sent to me... so that I may embrace her, and weep with her
over her husband... instead of singing wedding songs – for I have seen
neither her wedding nor her happiness... and, the mourning over, I
shall settle her here, and she will perch over her grief like a turtle-dove on
a withered tree." We find here also a reflection of the imagery of folk-
poetry, with which we are not closely familiar, as well as of literary
imagery, together with the evidence of Vladimir's own poetical gifts.

The language is also interesting. With the exception of the prayers,
Vladimir's works to a certain degree replace the Church Slavonic
vocabulary by that of the spoken language, certain traces of which remain
to this day in Ukrainian.

Vladimir's works are also notable from the historical point of view
because of their portrayal of the lively personality of the Prince, whose
pacific policy and endeavours to soften the social differences of his day
are known to us from other sources too. Bookish and literary influences
are of no less interest to us than his ideology, which reflects that of his
day as embellished by Christian ideals.

8. THE *IZBORNIK* OF 1076

1. The difficulty of throwing light on many questions of Old Russian
literature is best illustrated by the so-called *Izbornik* ("Miscellany") which
is extant in the original manuscript of 1076.

Its content is extremely varied. There is an introduction on the benefits
of reading; three different "Precepts" by parents for children; excerpts
from the Scriptures ("The Book of Wisdom" and "Sirach"); a sermon by
Basil the Great; St. Athanasius' answers; and, finally, collections of
various proverbial phrases. There is a certain community of theme in
the material of the *Izbornik*: it is a compilation of religious and moral

advice for laymen. The content reminds us somewhat of the works of Vladimir Monomach, written later (see above). Much space is devoted to the necessity of charity to the poor (a separate story on this theme – "The Charitable Sozomenus" – is even included in the miscellany); together with this we have warnings against opposing the "powerful" of this world, and also warnings against drunkenness. There is a certain systematic planning in the arrangement of the material.

2. The *Izbornik* attracts attention by the very strong East Slavonic elements in its language ("full vocality" form of words, ж instead of the Church Slavonic жд, ч instead of щ, etc.*). But monuments of undoubted Bulgarian origin had also undergone similar changes somewhat later (for instance the Kiev manuscript of *Zlatostruj*, 12th century). A second feature, unusual in translated works, is evident – the multitude of individual adages collected in the "Miscellany", and a certain number of passages in individual stories where adages are syntactically rhythmic and rhymed; they also contain alliterations. Here are examples of such sentences:

кыимь путьмь идоша,
и коею стьзею текоша.

("By what road they advanced and which way they took.")

старейшааго деньми почьтити не лѣнися,　с-п
и покоити старость его потъщися　　　п-с-п

("Do not be slow to show respect to the old man and try to give peace to his old age.")

днесь бо растемъ,
а утро гинемъ.

("For we grow up today and perish tomorrow.")

даждь мокнуштюму сухоту,
зимному теплоту

("Give a dry shelter to him who is wet, and warmth to him who is cold.")

хранися от пития,
осквьрняеть бо молитвы твоя.

("Beware of drunkenness, it profanes your prayers.")

* In declination instr. masc. and ntr. ending in -ъмь or -ьмь instead of -омъ or -емъ.

At prayers:

Не смѣшаи словесъ своихъ съ простыми словесы,   с-с-с-с-с

вѣды, яко богу събесѣдникъ еси . . .   с

("Do not mix your words [at prayer – D. Č.] with everyday words, knowing that you talk with God.")

Or the appeal to pray when admiring the beauty of nature:

Егда же възриши нощью на небо и на звѣздьную красоту,

                                            в-н-н-н-н

молися владыцѣ богу добрууму хитрьцу.   в-д

Заутра же освѣштаемъ припади къ творьцю своему,   п-т-с

давъшууму ти сь день на приложение животу.   д-т-с-н-н

("When at night you look at the sky and the beauty of the stars, say a prayer to God, the wise artist. And in the morning, in the light of the day, bow to your Creator who gave you the gift of this day to lengthen your life.")

In some cases entire fragments are syntactically rhythmic, for instance this appeal for charity to the poor:

> алчьнаго накърмі, . . .
>
> жадьнааго напои,
>
> страньна въведи,
>
> больна присѣти,
>
> къ тьмьніци доиди,
>
> виждь бѣду ихъ
>
> и въздохни . . .

("Feed the hungry, give water to the thirsty, receive the wanderer (into your house), visit the sick, enter the prison, look at their unhappiness, and sigh.")

In addition to those cited in the examples quoted there are alliterations based on repetition of the same words. There are also cases of identical beginnings in a number of phrases (anaphora). Sometimes, a number of adages on the same theme form, so to speak, "a chain of aphorisms" (e.g. about reading books), bearing in poetics the special name *priamel* – gnomic chain.

One should note also the selection of sayings with beautiful and vivid imagery: "Avoid flattering words as crows who would peck out eyes of your spirit"; "A dark cloud hides the beauty and light of the sun, an angry thought destroys the beauty of prayer"; "Do not linger in the slime of sin until you suddenly disappear in it." There are a number of effective antitheses: "With your feet walk slowly, with your spirit hurry rapidly to the gates of Heaven"; "Fulfil the will of God in little things, He will fulfil yours for eternity."

There are complete picturesque descriptions, for instance that of Paradise (in the "Story of Sozomenus"); a realistic presentation of a drunkard; and especially the scenes from the life of the poor: "When quenching your thirst with a sweet drink, remember him who drinks water warmed by the sun"; "When you repose in a well-protected room and hear the sound of heavy rain, think of the poor who now lie beneath the falling drops as under falling arrows"; "When in winter you sit in a warm room... sigh, and think of the poor who bend over a small fire, – their eyes are sore from smoke, they warm only their hands, while their backs and all their bodies shiver in the cold."

3. We find in the *Izbornik*, for the first time, a series of proverbs, later also repeated in Old Russian literature (in Vladimir Monomach, in the "Supplication of Daniil", etc.), for instance: "Sloth is the mother of evil"; "A fruit-tree is recognised by its fruit"; "Do not abandon an old friend, a new one is no match for him"; also phrases which later recur in the epigrams of the 16th–18th centuries in the Slavonic literatures: the world is "a turning wheel" which raises some high and lowers others into the depths; or "He is not poor who possesses little, but he who desires much."

4. It is not surprising that the individual works included in the *Izbornik* were later copied, up to the 19th century (the New York Public Library has an 18th-century manuscript of the "Story of Sozomenus" which is not very different from the original of the 11th century).

The question arises whether or not the *Izbornik* – or at least its individual parts – is an original work of Kievan literature. This is quite possible. The Greek originals of all the works included in the *Izbornik* are unknown to us. But even if such originals were to be found, the translator would have to be recognised as a master of words, and the translation – to a great degree – as an independent re-shaping of the translated material. The *Izbornik* is also of interest as an example of the philantropic ideology in old Rus', and as a model of Christian demands on the layman. The following parts of the *Izbornik* might have been original: the introduction on reading (which refers to St. Cyril, probably the Slav missionary); then the "Precepts from Father to Son";

"Advice to the Rich"; and perhaps also *Stoslovec* ("A Hundred Sayings") ascribed in the text to Gennadius, although no such work exists among the works of the Byzantine writer of that name.

9. THE QUESTION OF THE OLD RUSSIAN EPOS

1. We have already encountered indications of lost monuments in Old Russian literature (chronicles, Lives). Obviously, there must have been more of them. But the old writers did not quote their sources, and only in certain cases (most helpful to the modern scholar) did they even vaguely mention that they had borrowed their material elsewhere.

Every possible opportunity to prove indisputably the existence of one or another monument, is therefore particularly important. Occasionally one may come to certain conclusions as to its content. As far as its form is concerned, if there are no quotations, it is of course impossible to make any conjectures.

The question of the Old Russian epos is especially interesting. Epic works glorifying historical or fictional heroes (these latter occasionally turn into historical personages after some time) have existed and still exist among all nations. There are, however, no extant monuments of the East Slavonic old epos, with the single exception of "The Tale of Igof's Campaign" and later monuments deriving from it. The situation here is not however entirely hopeless: until recently, epic songs had been preserved in most diverse parts of Great Russian territory, especially in the extreme north. They bear the popular name of *stariny* (or artificially – *byliny*). Among their heroes we find names which occur in the chronicles: Prince Vladimir; Dobrynja (according to the Chronicle Vladimir's uncle); Aljoša Popovič (in the chronicles Aleksandr Popovič). The events described in the *stariny* refer to a remote past: they speak of the "Kievan Prince", of the struggle against the Tartars.... Consequently, it seems useful to deal with the question whether their origin is really linked with such ancient times. Research in this field has yielded appreciable results only in the works of the so-called "historical school", the main representative of which was Professor Vsevolod Miller. In the first place one has to answer two questions: 1) Is it true that the *stariny* – even though changing their form – have existed continuously from the 11th century down to the present day? 2) How is it that, while mainly narrating events in the southern principalities, they came from the Ukraine to North Russia? And only then can we deal with the third question: 3) What can be established about the original form of these works?

2. The first question may be answered more or less satisfactorily: on the one hand – by reference to the heroes mentioned in the old monuments; on the other – by the discovery of individual, even though quite fragmentary, manuscripts with a content already reminiscent of the modern *byliny*, dating from the 18th, 17th and even 16th centuries. The second question is more involved; but new evidence is continually being found in local literatures of the existence of legends about the same heroes in the Ukraine and in Byelo-Russia, where there are no *stariny* now. Even in the West, where such evidence – it is true – is confined to isolated instances, it nevertheless exists for the whole period from the 13th to the 18th centuries. One must assume that the *stariny* were forced out of their country of origin, the Ukraine, in the 16th–17th centuries by the appearance of a new aspect of the epos, the so-called *dumy*. The *stariny* are extant in the North, where they penetrated probably quite early, and underwent modifications, the last of these most likely in the 16th–17th centuries; and, like much of ancient culture, they have been preserved only in survivals which reached the popular masses among whom the *stariny* still exist to this day. The *stariny* of Northern (Novgorod) origin could, of course, have come to the Great Russians directly from Novgorod.

The existence of epic songs in the Kievan period is testified primarily by "The Tale of Igof's Campaign" which mentions the poet of ancient times, Bojan. In his songs Bojan celebrated "old Jaroslav" (Jaroslav the Wise, of course); "the courageous Mstislav" (Mstislav of Tmutorokań, of whose single-handed combat with Rededja the Tale tells us the same story as the Chronicle under 1022); "the beautiful Roman Svjatoslavič" (the Chronicle speaks very little of him). The Tale originated shortly after 1186. The 13th-century Galician-Volhynian Chronicle also mentions "the famous singer" Mitus, and recounts how after one successful campaign the princes listened to a song in their honour (*pěsn' slavnu*). Długosz also mentions such songs. Moreover, similar epic songs also existed among the Byzantines, the Scandinavians and the Polovtsians. Traces of the epic tradition also seem to exist in the Chronicle. Ecclesiastical literature, too, mentions poets, *Pěsnetvorcy* ("creators of songs") (for instance, Kiril of Turov speaks about the celebration of heroes by singers – this, however, may be merely an imitation of Byzantine literature).

3. If we turn to an analysis of the contemporary *stariny*, juxtaposing their evidence with data from the chronicles, we can establish a number of thematic cycles, three of which are undoubtedly linked with Kiev.

a) The first cycle deals with Vol'ga or Volch(v) Vseslavič; we are told of his miraculous birth without a father; of his childhood, and how from his very birth he bore arms, of his skill in hunting, his ability to transform himself into various animals; his conquest of the "Indian Kingdom" – how he penetrated into it in the guise of an ant with all his soldiers also having been transformed into ants, finally of his meeting with the peasant-hero, Mikula. The chronicles preserve some accounts, analogous to these tales, of three princes whose names remind us of that of a hero of the *stariny:* there had also long existed stories about Princess Ol'ga and her skill in hunting. Prince Oleg (9th–10th centuries) was considered a magician (*veščij*), and the Chronicle recounts his miraculous conquest of of Constantinople (with the aid of boats placed on wheels); the name of Prince Vseslav Polockij is reminiscent of the patronymic of the *starina's* hero, whereas the Chronicle and "The Tale of Igof's Campaign" preserved a series of tales about Vseslav reminiscent of the hero of the *stariny* about Vol'ga: Vseslav is born "by magic", i.e. without a father (like several heroes of Slavonic and Western legends); he is capable of "self-transformation", like Vol'ga of the *stariny;* he succeeds in conquering, not the "Indian Kingdom", it is true, but Kiev. The motif of the child-hero is also to be found in "The Tale of Igof's Campaign", in which the soldiers of Kursk are surrounded by weapons from their very birth... Some motifs of the *stariny* are reminiscent of translated epic works: Digenis is a child-hero; Alexander the Great is born "by magic"; the "Indian Kingdom" is the theme of the *Povest'* already known to us (see II, 11). The *starina* about Vol'ga's meeting with Mikula is undoubtedly of Novgorodian and later origin. The *stariny* about Vol'ga-Volch are obviously a very complex conglomerate of old local and borrowed epics.

b) Several themes are linked with St. Vladimir. He is called "Vladimir, the beautiful, dear sun" (Vladimir, *krasnoje solnyško*), the "sweet" prince who entertains heroes. Prince Vladimir's banquets are also mentioned by the Chronicle and even by foreign sources. But in the *stariny*, he is only the centre of a cycle of epic tales and, as a personality, is also sometimes endowed with negative features.

Among heroes bearing historical names, one must note first of all the "Chronicle" uncle of Prince Vladimir – Dobrynja, the *posadnik* of Novgorod. He performs a number of feats in the *stariny:* he slays a dragon, and frees Vladimir's niece, Zabava Putjatična, from it; he finds water for Prince Vladimir, he bathes in the river Pučajna where bathing is forbidden and dangerous; finally, he becomes a match-maker and finds a wife for Prince Vladimir. The first four themes are undoubtedly linked with the role of Dobrynja in the baptism of Rus' – water and bathing are the symbols of baptism. According to the Chronicle, the Kievans were baptised in the river Pučajna; the dragon is a symbol of paganism (as in many Lives); the *vojevoda* Putjata (cf. the patronymic of the girl saved from the dragon by Dobrynja) had taken part in the baptism of the Novgorodians. Dobrynja also appears in the role of match-maker in the Chronicle and in stories about Prince Vladimir's wedding: in subject-matter these legends call to mind the German "Nibelungen-Lied".

c) Less colourful are the *stariny* whose origin and ancient themes may be linked with Vladimir Monomach. Vladimir Monomach himself became completely identified in the *stariny* with Prince St. Vladimir. The tales about the hero whose name can be found in the chronicles, namely the tales about Aljoša Popovič (in the Chronicle – Aleksandr), refer to the times of Monomach. Incidentally, it has been recently proved that these tales had existed as epic legends before entering the chronicles. Aljoša killed Tugarin Zmejevič, a semi-fantastic creature who became friendly with Prince Vladimir's wife and spent much time at the court of the Prince. It is easy to recognise in Tugarin the historical Polovtsian Prince, Tugor-khan, whose daughter was married to Svjatopolk, Mono-mach's predecessor on the Kiev throne; in 1096 he waged war against the Russian princes and was killed in battle against Monomach. In the chronicles, Aljoša is also referred to as a later Rjazan' hero (13th century). Moreover, one detail of the description of Aljoša's battle with Tugarin is reminiscent of "Aleksandrija". Thus in the *starina* and in the chronicles there are a series of themes superimposed on the original theme. A little known *bylina* is linked with Vladimir Monomach himself. It is the *bylina* about "Gleb Volod'evič" who frees the boats captured by the Princess of Khersonese: in this case, the hero's name stands for both Vladimir and the Novgorodian Prince Gleb who, in 1077, had indeed waged a campaign against the Greek city of Khersones in the Crimea, where trading vessels were being detained. In this case, too, there is in the *starina* a later theme, but the event itself is basically preserved as it was. More *bylina* themes may be related to the times of Vladimir, especially the Novgorod *bylina* about Stavro Godinovič, an actual Novgorod envoy who was detained by Monomach and who, according to the *starina*, was set free by his wife who had disguised herself in men's clothes: the details are taken from fables.

d) The absence of any *starina* linked with Jaroslav the Wise seems strange. It is possible that his times are depicted in the very picturesque *starina* about

Solov Budimirovič. From the description of the boat in which he arrived at Kiev, and from references by the Varangians as to where he came from, Solov Budimirovič was a foreign poet who, after a number of adventures, married in Kiev – inevitably – the niece of the only prince mentioned in the *stariny*, Vladimir. It is possible that this is the Varangian hero Harold the Bold, who married Jaroslav's daughter, and to whom is ascribed an old Scandinavian song of how a "Russian girl" rejected him. – It is even more probable that Jaroslav had already appeared not in a *starina* but in an oral work of a different type – an "ecclesiastical poem" about "Jegorij Chrabryj": here Jegorij – St. George (the Christian name of Prince Jaroslav) comes to Rus', saves it from dragons (St. George – the dragon-fighter) and from wolves, clears the course of the Dniepr, and frees from captivity his sisters "overgrown with bark". A number of episodes are taken from the (apocryphal) life of St. George; but the liberation of Rus' from wild animals is of course the symbol of cultural work; the freeing of the Dniepr route – the work of Jaroslav who had united in his hands the Kiev and Novgorod principalities. He indeed freed his sisters from Polish captivity, where they had found themselves during his struggle with Svjatopolk, and where they had become "overgrown" with a "Catholic bark" (frequent symbol of sin or heresy). If this supposition is correct, then the authorship of such a song ought rather to be ascribed to the clergy who, as in the West, took part in the creation of epic works. The participation of clerical authors in the composition of a number of songs about Dobrynja – i.e. about the baptism of Rus' – is also very probable.

4. A most complex question is that of the favourite hero of contemporary *stariny*, Il'ja Muromec. In the first place, it must be said that until the 18th century his name was alternatively read as Murovec, Muromic, Muravlenin, Murovlin, etc. This enables us to regard him not as a native of Murom – in the 11th century a completely isolated town in the North-East – but as a hero of one of the Černigov towns, Murovsk or Murovijsk The reading "Muromec", however, makes it possible to link his origin with the "Murmansk coast", i.e. to look upon him as a Varangian. In any case, he is also mentioned in Western sources (the German poem *Ortnit* and the Scandinavian *Tidrekssaga*). There is a complete cycle of various fabulous motifs connected with Il'ja. We have already mentioned his struggle against his son and the obscure origin of this theme. It may be assumed that the oldest themes linked with the name of Il'ja are: his liberation – on the way from Murom to Kiev – of the town of Černigov from "the hordes", his victory over the "Brigand-Nightingale" sitting on twelve oaks on the river Smorodina (there is such a small river in the Černigov region, and there is also a village of Nine Oaks). Il'ja brings Nightingale to Kiev where he either kills him or, according to other variants, sets him free; later he liberates Kiev from The Idol of the Heathen". The first two themes are already geographically linked with

Černigov which in the 11th–12th centuries was an important political center rivalling Kiev – the very name of this subsequently half-forgotten town in contemporary *stariny* already indicates their ancient origin. Later chronicles mention a famous brigand of the time of Vladimir. "The Idol of the Heathen" as well as the "hordes" may symbolise any of the 11th–century nomad tribes.

5. We may distinguish in the Chronicle a number of passages with typically epic themes, and a characteristic style (many alliterations, epic formulas). Such passages, as well as those in "The Tale of Igof's Campaign" in which its author mentions or narrates past events, can give us some indication of the further subject-matter of the old epos and even about its style. One theme is alluded to in the Tale and retold in the Chronicle: the struggle of the Tmutorokań Prince Mstislav against the Kasogian giant Rededja. In the Chronicle this story contains many alliterations. The short fragment in the Chronicle relating the death of Roman Svjatoslavič (1079) also has an epic quality: according to the Tale he was celebrated in song by Bojan. The Chronicle retells a saga of epic character extant in modern Ukrainian fairy tales, referring it to the time of St. Vladimir. This saga – about the Kožemjaka who gains victory over the Pečeneg giant in single combat – is, as it were, a variant of the story about Mstislav.

6. It is difficult to say anything definite about the style and form of the original works of the old epos: the *stariny* bear unmistakable traces of later revisions, mainly linguistic. Extant epic fragments in the chronicles and in "The Tale of Igof's Campaign", and the quotations from the works of Bojan preserved in the Tale, almost rule out any suggestion that the old epos had a verse-form. In the language of the *stariny* a certain number of old words, rarely or never employed elsewhere, have been preserved: such are *šolomja* (hill); *stol'nyj grad* (capital); *polenica* (heroine); *iskopyt'* (hoof-mark); *dorog rybnyj zub* (a walrus' tusk). Even more pointers to the *stariny* may be found in the descriptive details: the heroes shoot arrows from bows and fight with spears and swords; the prince rides to collect tribute (the ancient *poljud'je*); the landscape is that of the southern steppes, though the *stariny* have been preserved in the north. A few other features extant in the *stariny* probably belong to the old epos: their existence is confirmed either by "The Tale of Igof's Campaign" (see IV, 7), or by parallels from the epos of other peoples. These include the use of "the ornate epithet"; parallelisms; and antitheses – like the device of introducing the epic theme ("this is not a cloud… this is the army", etc.). Finally, also, epic repetitions are very common in modern *stariny* as they have proved valuable in aiding the memory to retain a large work. Particularly characteristic of the *stariny* is the repetition of descriptions (mounting a horse, shooting from a bow, etc.). In the contemporary *stariny*, moreover, there are many elements taken from fables.

7. In any attempt to characterise the style of Bojan's works on the basis of the quotations from the 11th-century poet in "The Tale of Igof's Campaign", we can say but little: Bojan obviously used to insert into his "songs" similar proverbs or phrases. His style was terse and full of stylistic devices. Sometimes the symbol completely obscured the real meaning (in one of the quotations from Bojan, in "The Tale of Igof's Campaign", we have *only* "falcons" and "jackdaws" instead of the "Russians" and their "enemies"). Bojan's undeveloped metaphors are reminiscent of the Scandinavian *kenningar* (cf. I, 8 and IV, 7, 3). In "quotations" from Bojan we find sound imagery (horses neigh beyond Sula; glory rings in Kiev; trumpets blow in Novgorod), and comparisons taken from nature (falcons, jackdaws, and other birds). In these quotations there are rhythm and alliteration (*truby trubjat*) and syntactic parallelism. These passages from "The Tale of Igof's Campaign", and probably the major part of the reminiscences about Vseslav, are, though undoubtedly revised, the only surviving fragments of the ancient epos (cf. IV, 7).

8. There is every reason to believe that the old epos was a court-epos, with its own specialised singers – this is confirmed by the Tale's reference to Bojan. The epos was delivered – as testified by the Tale – to the accompaniment of *gusli*. It is not clear whether we are to understand by this a stringed instrument of the violin type (the modern Yugoslav *gusle* are later than the *gudok* of the Great Russians), or rather of the zither type, which is also to be found in illustrations in the ancient manuscripts having preserved its name among the Great Russians to this day. The *stariny* are now executed without musical accompaniment. One can hardly speak of "singing" in the contemporary sense of the word, the rendering being rather a "recitative". Any further conjectures as to the manner of execution of epic "songs" in the past belong to the realm of guesswork. But there is no ground for total pessimism. Research into modern Slav folk-verse and the rhythm of old epic works ("The Tale of Igof's Campaign" and perhaps fragments from the Chronicle) may help to bring nearer to solution the many still obscure questions concerning the old Russian epos. Investigation of the subject-matter of the *stariny* is also far from being finished.

10. VARIOUS WORKS

1. All the 11th-century monuments are of interest, even if they are without purely literary value (in the later periods these will concern us less and less). For indeed, non-literary monuments – especially the ancient ones – are sometimes of significance to the historian of literature, as they may for instance indicate how far those representatives of an epoch who were not professional writers were capable of expressing their thoughts. Occasionally, we also find in such monuments stylistic devices of a certain artistic merit: set turns of phrase and expressions, metaphors, "commonplaces", and even euphony and alliteration (viz. in Oscan-Umbrian inscriptions or in Old Frisian laws). As to early Russian non-literary monuments, it is primarily their lexical aspect which is of interest to the literary historian, for it reflects that struggle between the local and the Church Slavonic tongue which was indeed an essential feature in the development of Old Russian literature.

2. We must mention first of all the *prayers* and other *liturgical texts* (eulogies or panegyrics, services in honor of saints, etc.). A few prayers have been preserved: alongside those compiled by Vladimir Monomach, there are three prayers extant, ascribed to St. Feodosij; while a number of prayers enter into the composition of other works (sermons, and so forth). In the 11th century there lived in the Kiev-Pečerskij monastery a monk by the name of Grigorij, "a composer of church songs", and there is reason to believe that it was he who wrote some of the oldest extant "songs", eulogies and services. The services include those to Prince St. Vladimir and to St. Feodosij, and those on the occasion of the transfer of the relics of Boris and Gleb, and of St. Nicholas. Another writer was Metropolitan Ioann I (after 1007), a Bulgar rather than a Greek, to whom are attributed "readings" in honour of St. Boris and Gleb. A eulogy of St. Feodosij, written shortly after 1096, is preserved in the "Kiev-Pečerskij Paterikon". In the Chronicle and in "The Legend of the Murder of Boris and Gleb" we find "eulogies" (panegyrics) and "macarisms" to Boris and Gleb, and to Princess St. Ol'ga. We also find fragments of certain works of the same type in the enigmatic "In Memory and Praise…" (see III, 3, 5). The very powerful impact of the Greek (original or translated) liturgical literature is indicated in all these works, with the exception of the eulogy of Princess Ol'ga in the Chronicle, which shows signs of the influence of a Latin eulogy – that of Princess St. Ljudmila of Bohemia (an influence which possibly derived from a lost Church Slavonic translation). The language of these works is strongly rhythmical, occasionally we find (probably accidental) rhymes or euphonies; there are no alliterations. Here are some examples:

Boris and Gleb:

дает а исцѣленье:
хромым ходити,
слѣпымъ прозрѣнье,
болящимъ цѣлбы,
скованнымъ разрѣшенье,
темницамъ отверзенье,
печальнымъ утѣху,
напастнымъ избавленье . . .

("You are both healers: you make the lame walk; the blind to see; to the sick you give health; to the chained – freedom [from chains – D. Č.]; you open [the gates – D. Č.] of the prisons; you solace the sorrowful; you free the poor [from poverty – D. Č.].")

St. Feodosij:

апостолъ и проповѣдникъ,
сый намъ пастырь и учитель,
сый намъ вождь и правитель,
сый намъ стѣна и огражденіе,
похвала наша великаа и дръзновеніе . . .

("He is an apostle and a preacher; he is our shepherd and teacher, our leader and ruler; he is a wall and a defence for us; our great glory and the one who gives us courage [before God – D. Č.].")

The rich and beautiful imagery of these works is entirely metaphorical. Thus, God and Christ are the sun; grace is the light of sun or the spring of water; saints are stars, torrents, shepherds of spiritual flocks, labourers in God's vineyards. In spite of the "quotative" character of liturgical literature, we can praise highly the literary art of its authors-compilers.

3. The *epistles of the hierarchs*, exclusively Greek, are of much smaller literary interest. The Slavonic version of the text, however, is attributable to the hierarchs' Slav clerks who, as we know from the practice of the Southern and Western Churches, were often the true composers of the epistles, working from

only a rough draft provided by their superiors. Such are some 11th-century epistles "against the Latins". These are merely an enumeration of often very insignificant differences in the teaching and practice of the Southern and Western Churches. They are testimony not to the "formalism" of Kievan Christianity, but to the decadence of Greek theological science, although not among even its best representatives.

Much more noteworthy is the *letter* to Prince Vladimir Monomach from the Metropolitan Nikifor (1104–1120). In addition to a brief eulogy of the Prince for his pious way of life, this letter contains an exposition (of ancient origin) of the psychology of the period: the soul is endowed with three main faculties – intelligence, passion and will (Greek *logistikon, epithumētikon, thumoeides*) which are served by the five senses: sight, hearing, smell, taste, and touch. By means of this introduction the author probably wanted to awaken the interest of the Prince in his further request not to trust too much in "hearing" – evidently meaning denunciations – for this is a doubtful source of knowledge through which "the arrow pierces" the Prince, "harming" his "soul". One must re-cognise the ability of the author and the translator to expound abstract thoughts simply and clearly; but one must also wonder at the capacity of the literary language of that time to provide a medium for the transmission of such thoughts.

4. To the literary compilations one must also add the composition of the so-called *Chronographs*, i.e. surveys of universal history based on the Holy Scriptures, on translated Greek chronicles (Malalas, Hamartolos), and on Russian sources. It seems that the first attempt at such a compilation had already been made in the 11th century. This non-extant chronograph was probably compiled – as can be judged from later monuments of this kind – mainly on the basis of Hamartolos. The Kievan chronicler, however, under 1114, seems to have used a chronograph into which the Malalas Chronicle also entered.

5. The *legislative monuments* have no purely literary significance. These are in the first place *Russkaja Pravda* (i.e. "Russian Law"), the composition of which is attributed by authoritative tradition to Jaroslav the Wise; as well as Church "statutes" ascribed, one, on safe grounds, to St. Vladimir, and a second, with very little justification, to Jaroslav. The "Russian Law" also has 11th-century supplements added by the successors of Jaroslav. Of particular interest here, from the literary point of view, is the language, almost entirely free from Church Slavonisms; the simplicity of the syntax, free from any considerable Greek influences; and especially the vocabulary, though its terminology in certain particulars is not entirely clear to us to this day. Of course, the cultural and historical significance of the legislative monuments is enormous.

6. A number of letters on birch-bark, some of which date back to the 11th century, have recently been found in Novgorod and other towns. Like the earlier inscriptions on various objects, these letters of course provide in the first place material for the characterisation of the spoken language of the locality in which they are found. The possibility that some of them may provide at least

minor literary and folk-lore material is not ruled out (one of the later inscriptions contains, for instance, a riddle translated, as it appears, from the
Greek).

As already mentioned, the beginning of the 12th century marks the
beginning of a new period in Kievan literature, characterised by a
considerable change in style and a concomitant evolution of ideology.

THE AGE OF ORNAMENTAL STYLE
(12th–13th CENTURIES)

1. CHARACTERISTICS

1. The period beginning with the second quarter of the 12th century has much more pronounced features than the 11th century. Kiev still stands at the head of the literary movement, but next to it Novgorod begins to play an important role, and later other cultural centres also appear. The grounds for dating the new period of literary development from the 12th century are of purely literary character. The shifting of the political centre of gravity, on the one hand, to the West (Galič), on the other, to the North-East (Suzdal'), would not in itself be sufficient reason for demarcating the line of literary development; the new centres continue the Kievan tradition and even use the works of Kievan authors.

2. Some 11th-century literary characteristics are replaced by new ones. Instead of the monumental simplicity of the 11th century, we find in the 12th century a *variety of ornamental adornments* in style, adornments which sometimes conceal entirely the leading thought of the work. Some works have already lost their thematic center, and the plot of each individual work itself is no longer so simple as it had been a century earlier. For various reasons, memories of the past are characteristic of the chronicles; we find similar reminiscences, also inserted for various reasons, in the "Life of Aleksandr Nevskij" and "The Tale of Igoŕ's Campaign". We also find imitations of "the singer of old times", Bojan, and such digressions as Jaroslavna's "lament". Similar digressions also appear in monuments with a more or less sustained thematic character (like the "Kiev-Pečerskij Paterikon"). Sometimes the whole construction of the work has a "mosaic" character. In the Hypatius Chronicle, on almost every page, one can feel behind the author a literary tradition providing him with rich material (especially in Prince Daniil's biography). Deviations from the main theme no longer have that character of clumsiness, which marked the digressions of 11th-century literature. The complexity of the narrative belongs to the very essence of the style of the age. Borrowings are not included as independent fragments, but are revised by the author in the spirit of his own style; that is why it is much more difficult to isolate the component parts from the works of the 12th and following centuries.

3. A fundamental change comes with "symbolism". Symbolism is one of the basic characteristics of the new conception of the world. From this point of view, the whole of reality appears as a token of something else, of a higher existence which is not given to us directly and which is in general inaccessible to us. Symbolism is not alien to any style, not even to the most "realistic" one; but it now acquires exceptional importance (as later in baroque and romanticism), for the man of the Middle Ages seeks behind or "under" every being precisely the more essential, the deeper, the more stable and "true" existence. The symbolic conception of the world is undoubtedly the most essential feature of the literature of the 12th–13th centuries.

The literature of this period does not confine itself to simple similes and metaphors. If only one extant work of this time provides theoretical (and rather weak) evidence of the symbolic *Weltanschauung* (Klim Smoljatič's epistle), the authors of other works of various genres very often provide developed symbolic imagery: a battle is the symbol of a banquet or a wedding; spring is the symbol of rebirth. The sermons of Kiril of Turov and "The Tale of Igof's Campaign" are full of such symbolic imagery. Reality is sometimes not represented at all, not even named: it is entirely replaced by its symbol. The symbol often does not serve to convey what it symbolises, but is in itself the very aim of literary expression.

In some cases the complexity of the metaphors reminds us of one of the stylistic devices of the old Scandinavian literatures, the so-called *kenningar*. In 11th-century literature they hardly ever occur. It is still impossible to determine whether this device penetrated into 12th–13th-centuries literature (and in what way), or had been transmitted from earlier works which, however, are not extant (cf. IV, 7).

4. In the same way, style in general becomes an aim in itself – it is not only a means to an end, but it also has independent value. Adornments sometimes occupy nearly the entire structure, and behind it the real subject disappears, at least for a time. It is sufficient to mention the historical ornamentation of Svjatoslav's speech in "The Tale of Igof's Campaign", which over a long period drives the intention of the "golden speech" into the background. In its original form "The Supplication of Daniil" too, probably had no "pivot", served no particular purpose, and had nothing to communicate to the reader. The same traits are preserved in certain *stariny* dating from this period.

That style had become an aim in itself can best be seen from the fact that the historical subjects are of much less significance. The entire "Tale of Igof's Campaign" is devoted to the unsuccessful war of two appanage princes. On the occasion of the erection of a wall in the monastery of Vydubiči, a sermon-panegyric is delivered which is constructed with the whole weighty apparatus of rhetoric and erudition. The chronicles elaborate in a minute way descriptions of petty and everyday events. Here it is not so much the "decline" of political life which is responsible, as the absence of any particular interest in the choice of inherently important themes.

5. The wealth of adornments is characteristic. Such is the abundance of alliteration in "The Tale of Igof's Campaign", the multiplicity of metaphor in the sermons of Kirill of Turov, and the extension of demonology in the hagiographic works (while in the two Lives of the 11th century demons are only mentioned in passing). Of interest is the appearance of new stylistic embellishments. Such include primarily hyperbole, which plays a considerable role; such is the wealth of epithets, some of which are fixed (*epitheta ornantia*), one of the favourite epithets being "golden" (and its compounds).

Complex syntactic constructions also characterise the new style.

Unfortunately, we possess too few monuments of this period to be able to judge to what extent originality and the endeavour to provide something new, something out of the ordinary, were valued. But these features will be discerned in the most accomplished works of that period.

6. In the realm of ideology we should note, on the one hand, the increase of ascetic moods, together with the fact that, on the other hand, "the world" is becoming more powerful, more independent, more conscious of its attraction and its might. The world begins to intrude behind the walls of the monasteries, to say nothing of ecclesiastical life in general. That is why the ecclesiastical writers see little hope for the chances of Christian life "in the world". This pessimism even increases when the Tartars gain victory over Christian potentates and princes. The representation of the joy of the newly converted Christians, who had joined the Christian world at "the last hour", is replaced by gloomy pictures of reality, even to an image of the earth trying to shake from its surface the sinful human race (Serapion's sermons).

It is interesting that the political and economic decadence does not accordingly render the representatives of the "world" more modest. On the contrary, within the limits of their miniature spheres of influence, they now pursue their egoistic secular aims, paying no heed at all to religion and morals. The world is now represented in literature in considerably more vivid colours, with stress on its luxury, riches, colours, and gold...

The harmony between the sacred and profane spheres is disturbed and hardly anyone believes in its possibility at all.

7. It is noteworthy, however, that the influence of Byzantium does not decrease. True, already in the 11th century there was enough translated Byzantine material. The 12th century uses partly the same material as the 11th, but does it with more artistry. It is quite possible that the influence of Byzantium played a considerable role in the very change of style. In any case, the 11th and the beginning of the 12th century were in Byzantium and in the West a period of transition to the "highly ornate" and "amplified" style. This process of transition took place both in Byzantine literature and in the Latin literature of Western Europe, as well as in the national languages where such already existed. This literary transition among the Eastern Slavs merely proves that the Eastern Slavs were part of the all-European world of letters and underwent the same processes. Important influences from the West were possible among the Eastern Slavs mainly through Byzantine mediation.

2. SERMONS

1. The number of sermons which we can ascribe with certainty to East Slavonic authors is not great. It is true that there are works by several authors whom we can identify. The number of anonymous works which we can establish as belonging to the 12th or 13th centuries, according to their content or on the basis of formal criteria, is insignificant. Among anonymous sermons or "pseudo-epigraphs" (i.e. sermons mistakenly ascribed to other authors, for instance, to the Church Fathers), there is undoubtedly a certain number of original East Slavonic sermons. Unfortunately in the last few decades research into them has made no advance at all.

2. Kirill, Bishop of Turov, a writer of the second half of the 12th century, was the most talented preacher. His extant short Life stresses his ascetism and ecclesiastical education. It has been proved (Vasilij Vinogradov) that he used Greek sources in the original. Besides sermons, he also wrote epistles to princes, now lost; tales; Church songs; and prayers (on these works see IV, 12, 1). There is no doubt that not all of his sermons are extant; there are also others ascribed to him with some probability. Unquestionably his are the sermons delivered on the eight consecutive Sundays beginning with Palm Sunday. Their content is throughout linked with the events which the Church mentions on a given day. As these are the events of Christ's life – the Passion, Crucifixion, and Resurrection – the sermons bear a clearly expressed Christological character. In vivid images Kirill reminds his audience of the Gospel Story, uniting it with dogmatic discourses expressed always in symbolic form. The cycle is concluded by a sermon on the oecumenical councils which laid the foundation of Christology.

3. The exposition is extremely varied. Sometimes Kirill confines himself to symbolic imagery (for instance, Spring as the symbol of the Resurrection). Sometimes he dramatises the sermon, introducing into it, for example, "laments" (The Virgin Mary's and Joseph of Arimathea's on the Body of Christ); conversations (for instance, that between Christ and the lame man in the Pool of Siloam, or between the blind man cured by Christ and the Jews); speeches (the angel's discourse to the woman bearers of myrrh); panegyrics (for example, on Christ's Ascension, on the Fathers of the Oecumenical Councils, etc.).

Kirill's sermons are not wholly original. In the majority of them he uses two or three sermons by Greek preachers, mainly John Chrysostomos. But he never copies; he either shortens or lengthens the exposition, omits what has little concern for his listeners (for instance, reference to navigation) and, on the other hand, adds such adornments as appeal more to the minds and hearts of the audience. He emerges victorious from his competition with the Greek preachers, having produced a number of works in the best rhetorical style.

4. Kirill constructs entire sermons in symbolic imagery. Christ's Resurrection is symbolised in a broadly drawn picture of spring, with comments on every single image – for instance: "Today the sky has been illuminated, it shook off the dark clouds like a veil, and proclaims with its transparent air the glory of God – I do not speak about the visible skies, but about the spiritual Heaven, about the Apostles... who came to know the Lord and to forget all sorrow..." – "Today the sun rises high, its beauty and joy warm the earth; Christ, like the sun of truth, rose from His tomb and saves all who believe in Him." – "Today all the sweet-voiced birds of the Church choirs, building their nests, rejoice – that is to say, the ecclesiastical hierarchy: bishops, abbots, priests, and deacons, each sings his own song to the glory of God." Kirill speaks of gardens and rivers and fishermen, of flocks and shepherds, of apiarists and bees – for him everything serves as an element of symbolic imagery.

Another of Kirill's favourite devices is the dramatisation of the narra-tive. He uses it, for instance, in the sermon about the healing of the lame one in the Pool of Siloam. The prostrate one bemoans his fate, imagining his destiny: "I would call myself dead, but my stomach demands food, and my tongue is dry from thirst. I would call myself alive, but not only am I unable to rise from bed, but I am powerless to move... I am a living corpse, this bed is my grave. I am dead among the living, living among the dead..." Having described in detail his life and his expectation of help, his hope that someone may take him to the Pool, the lame man concludes: "I have no property to pay the man who would take care of me... There is no man who would serve me without scorning me... There is no man who could take me to the Pool." Christ answers this with another speech, into which Kirill puts the Christian teaching of divine providence, of man and of Christ's becoming Man, this being an act of charity to sinful mankind: "Why do you say, 'There is no man'? I am become for you this man, I, generous and charitable, and I have not broken My promise given when I became Man... I renounced for you the sceptre of the higher kingdom and wander in the lower, as a servant; I did not come (here) in order to be served, but in order Myself to serve... I became Man, to make man God... Who else serves you more faith-fully? – And you say, 'There is no man'!"

Short excerpts cannot give a complete idea of that rhetorical art with which Kirill develops these and other thoughts to render them graphic and understandable to his listeners. Elsewhere he uses a form of speech already known to us from other examples, namely, laments.

Antithesis is Kirill's favourite stylistic device. It is especially appro-priate in depicting the dual nature of Christ, the divine and the human. The author develops, in much more detail and more vividly, a series of antitheses reminiscent of similar examples in the "Discourse" of Metro-politan Ilarion (see III, 2, 4). But Kirill uses antitheses everywhere. He also uses syntactic rhythm, especially frequent in enumerations: of

Christ's charitable acts, of the effects which Christ's Resurrection had on earth and in heaven, etc. In other passages Kirill constructs series of similes, for instance a comparison of Christ to the Good Samaritan, and so forth. Occasionally the rhythm of the language is stressed by a verbal rhyme (*vъspěvajut* :: *rydajut, obchožu* :: *poslužu*, etc.). There are no alliterations.

Attempts to discover echoes of folk-lore are hardly justified. The sermons of Kirill analysed above are examples of rhetorical and learned sermons. True, he mentions "singers", juxtaposing them with the historians, but there is hardly any question here of popular epic song. Kirill's laments are of Greek and not Slavonic origin (the lament of the Virgin Mary is an imitation of a similar lament in Greek literature).

In any case, Kirill's sermons cannot be considered models of themeless rhetoric; they give in a rhetorical form a sufficiently clear and impressive exposition of the foundations of Christology.

5. A number of further sermons in different style are also ascribed to Kirill of Turov. There are no grounds for rejecting his authorship in all these cases, for every preacher changed his style depending on the type of the sermon and the character of the audience. Neither are there grounds for rejecting Kirill's authorship in the case of compiled sermons.

Kirill's sermons had extraordinary success. They were incorporated into various collections together with the patristic sermons – the highest form of recognition on the part of the compilers of these miscellanies. They were extant in copies and printed editions until the 18th century. They also reached the Balkan Slavs, and in the Ukraine we find imitations of Kirill's work even in the 17th century.

6. Another famous 12th-century preacher was Klim (Kliment) Smoljatič (this name does *not* prove his origin from the town of Smolensk). In 1146 he was elected Metropolitan of Kiev, the second Slav after Ilarion, but the election was not confirmed by the Constantinople patriarchate. One of his theological treatises (see IV, 12, 2) has been preserved in a revised form. Two works are attributed to him with only partial probability: the sermon-eulogy to the Holy Fathers, and a panegyric composed in the style of the *akafist*. Only the monastic life is represented very vividly: the monks are compared to eagles and falcons "which ascend into the clouds of life without sorrow"; but the life of "this world" is represented very negatively, in general without concrete features.

7. Another type of sermon which has come down to us is a Černigov

sermon of the second half of the 12th century. It is an anonymous sermon "On princes". The author exhorts the princes to be of peaceable disposition, referring to the example of the Černigov Prince David Svjatoslavič (d. 1123). "Hearken, princes! Why do you oppose your elder kinsmen, why do you wage war and bring heathens [Polovtsians – D. Č.] against your brothers [kinsmen – D. Č.]? What did Boris and Gleb suffer from their elder brother? Not only the loss of power, but also the loss of life. Whereas you cannot suffer even words from your brothers and on account of a petty offence you commence a mortal enmity..." – "Shame on you, who fight against your own kinsmen! Stand in awe and cry before God, otherwise your malice alone shall lose you [heavenly – D. Č.] glory."

8. Georgij's sermon from the monastery in Zarub was written no later than the middle of 13th century. This is consequently an ascetic work in which "Christian music" – i.e. "the beautiful, sweet-sounding Psaltery with which we ought to entertain ourselves before the Lord, Christ our God" – is opposed to secular culture, to the vagabond minstrels (*skomorochi*), musicians and singers" who are listened to for pleasure. This is a vindication of "simplicity" and an attempt to introduce ascetic elements into the life of "the world". More moderate are three moralising sermons by Moisej, probably the Bishop of Novgorod (d. 1187).

9. Yet another type of pure panegyric – moreover, in praise of a secular personage, the Kievan Prince Rjurik II Rostislavič – enters into the so-called Hypatius Chronicle under the year 1200. Moisej, abbot of Vydubičy monastery, voices gratitude to the Prince who had erected a wall to protect the church of the monastery against settling. The abundance of adornments is noteworthy; there are here both "commonplaces" (a request to forgive the author's "crude intellect") and comparisons of Rjurik's words and deeds with sunlight, moonlight, the glitter of stars and time, eternally true to the laws of the Creator, and of Rjurik's soul with a microcosm, etc. Alongside these are mentioned popular legends showing why the Church to that day has been saved from subsidence (the Church itself moves away from the edge of the precipice, it is hanging on a golden hair lowered from heaven). Rjurik was probably given a copy of the Chronicle.

In the panegyric of the patron saint of Kiev, St. Kliment, dating probably from the 12th century and on the whole poorly preserved, we have an encomium which combines religious and political motifs (the supremacy of Kiev).

10. The sermons of Serapion, Bishop of Vladimir, belong to the very end of the period. A monk of the Kiev-Pečersk monastery, he became Bishop of Vladimir (Suzdal') in 1274, and died the following year. There are extant five sermons certainly delivered by him, partly in Kiev, partly in Vladimir. All these (plus two which can only be doubtfully ascribed to him) are devoted to the theme of "Divine punishment", which the author sees in natural calamities: earthquakes, heavenly phenomena, the plague (1230), a flood in Durazzo (1273), the Tartar invasion. Divine punishments chastise men for their sins. In addition to common everyday sins, Serapion mentions as a sin the persecution of putative witches and sorcerers. The theme of divine punishment is intensified into a foreboding of the end of the world. "The earth, firmly anchored and immovable, now moves at the command of God, shaken by our sins; it cannot abide our transgressions." God "now shakes and sways the earth; He wants to shake off the many lawless sins from the earth, like leaves from a tree." Repetition is the one basic device of the sermons. Serapion enumerates human sins in rhythmically constructed phrases; beginning with Christ he enumerates the teachers whom men have ignored, and he also enumerates God's punishments:

> We saw the sun fade
> and the moon darken
> and the stars dim,
> and now our eyes an earthquake behold...
> . . . .
> And against us a cruel people came,
> who seized our cities,
> laid in ruins our sacred churches,
> slew our fathers and brothers,
> dishonoured our mothers and sisters...

In a later sermon Serapion further amplified his enumeration of God's punishments. Nevertheless, men were still no better. Serapion is also fond of beautiful comparisons – between sinners and animals or sick people; between waverers and a swaying reed; between the listeners' hearts and a corn-field in which he unsuccessfully sows God's word.

The Metropolitan Kirill's instruction to priests was written some time later. In it the Metropolitan exhorts the shepherds to take care of the souls of their flock, "The whole world is not worth one human soul". Therefore priests must first of all take care of their own souls, to enable them successfully to lead the many.

11. Even the comparatively few extant models of sermons show that in the 12th and 13th centuries the genre had been a viable part of ecclesiastical life and a fertile field of literary creation. The variety of its forms proves the sermon to have been a very fruitful literary genre. One cannot in the least agree with the views of the old scholars who saw only one possible object for the sermon – moralising instruction; their attitude towards other aspects of the sermon, in particular the Christological sermons of Kirill of Turov and towards panegyric sermons, was therefore entirely negative. From the historical point of view the 12th and 13th-century sermons must be judged quite differently. Not only were the moral instructions of Serapion indispensable, but so too were those sermons which endeavoured to communicate the bases of Christian teaching, at least on broad lines. Moreover, the notable stylistic ability of some authors exerted quite an influence on style in other fields of literary creation.

3. THE TALES

1. Rather few independent and original stories are extant from the 12th and 13th centuries. Besides the short tales which found their way into the *Prolog* and represented in most cases merely adaptations of other versions, often translated, stories were added to the old compilations of miracle tales, etc. A numer of stories in the collection of the miracles of St. Boris and Gleb belong undoubtedly to the 12th century. But two stories by Kirill of Turov and a few historical narratives are primarily of literary interest.

2. The stories of Kirill of Turov are symbolic tales. Their subject-matter is not entirely original – the theme of the first is to be found both in the East and the West, the second is taken from "Barlaam and Josaphat".

Both tales are written after the same pattern. Following an exposition of the plot – and Kirill does not compress the narrative – there comes a detailed explanation of the symbolic significance of the story. The first tale tells about a resourceful landlord who entrusts the protection of his vineyard to two men, one blind, the other lame. Together they see and hear everything, but neither can steal anything; the blind man cannot see, and the lame one cannot flee. Yet they found a way out: the lame man sat on the back of the blind man and showed him the way. The symbolic explanation is this: the landlord is God; the blind man, the body; the lame man, the soul. Sin is possible precisely because the body and the soul join forces for evil. The connection of this story with ecclesiastical and political events are doubtful. The parable was probably derived from Greek sources, with the object of instructing one and all. It is a miniature didactic novel.

The second story is more complex. Its plot is taken from "Barlaam and Josaphat". A certain Tsar feared neither God nor men. However, a revolution (to use a contemporary term) forced him to flee his kingdom. Wandering about, he found his way to a cave full of arms, where there was a man, poorly clothed but making merry with a woman over a bottle of wine. The explanation is much longer than the story itself: the State is man's body; the Tsar, man's soul; the cave in the mountain is a monastery; the arms are spiritual arms; the happy man is a monk (the woman, of course, is also interpreted in spiritual terms). The explanation is further followed by a eulogy of monastic life.

The language of the tales is not so florid as in Kirill's sermons. The main stylistic device appears to be a certain degree of syntactic rhythm. The author also uses parallelisms and antitheses. Kirill supplements his source (in the second story) and enlarges the narrative. All the details are explained symbolically.

3. The two historical tales are, so to speak, preparatory essays to the Lives. They have been preserved, nevertheless, by the Chronicle.

The first story deals with the assassination of the prince-monk, Igoŕ of Černigov, by the Kiev populace in 1147. The text is included in the annalistic history of Izjaslav II, then Prince of Kiev. But omitted from the story are the dialogues, common to the Chronicle, and significant elements of clerical style. The negative attitude towards the Kievan population, apparent in the story, differs on the whole from what we find in the rest of the Chronicle. Prince Igoŕ, captured by Izjaslav, takes monastic vows. But the inhabitants of Kiev, remembering also the conflict provoked by the captive of Prince Vseslav of Polock, decide to kill Igoŕ. The author places pious reflections in the mouth of Igoŕ. There follows a narrative of the course of events which ends with Igoŕ's death. Certain expressions echo the story of Boris and Gleb. The tale ends with a typical hagiographic conclusion: Igoŕ "discarded the clothes of mortal man, donned the long-suffering and incorruptible attire of Christ, Who also crowned him with a martyr's crown".

4. The second tale is better preserved. This concerns the murder of the tyrant Prince Andrej Bogoljubskij, who transferred his capital from Kiev to Suzdal', where he lived in the village of Bogoljubovo. He was killed by his own boyars who were dissatisfied with his autocratic policy. A member of his *entourage* described this event, immoderately praising the Prince's devoutness and virtues. The tale is written in hagiographic style. Very graphic are the descriptions of the truly luxurious buildings constructed at Andrej's command; his virtues are depicted in the same florid style. The story ends with a tribute to the Prince, comparing him to Boris and Gleb. It is realistic in detail, full of texts from the Holy Scriptures and of *clichés* from eulogies of the martyrs. The Prince is made to recite prayers and pious thoughts. The final sentences are in the style of the *akafist*. The Kievan chronicler incorporated into the Chronicle, unchanged, this story of the enemy of the Kiev principality, undoubtedly taking into consideration its historical value.

5. There are a few more historical tales extant in the chronicles. Some of them have been preserved separately, as, for instance, the story of Batu's death. The existence of others may be conjectured with some probability, though the traces of them are unclear in the annals. Some of the shorter tales are interesting as testimony of the beginning of literary life in the provincial centres. Even provincial Turov, whose Bishop, Kirill, probably preached in Kiev, where the Turov bishops usually lived, has given us a story about the miraculous salvation of the monk Martyn after his prayer to Saints Boris and Gleb.

But it is still obscure whether the specific characteristic of later Muscovite literature had then already originated. This characteristic consisted in writing only of real events – an original "pathos of reality" – and for a long time hampered the rise of original tales. On the other hand, it may be that "the censorship" of subsequent centuries expurgated the stories with fictional heroes, making an exception of a small number of works like "Akir the Wise" and "Digenis"; though it is possible that the copyists accepted their heroes as being historical personages too. In any case, such works as Kirill of Turov's stories were exceptional for that time.

6. The redaction of the translated novel occupies a special place. In spite of the fact that the material was borrowed, the translated novel must be considered an original monument of the early period. The so-called "Aleksandrija, 2nd redaction" originated in the 13th century from the pen of an unknown author. The narrative, it is true, is a compilation. The author created a vast and original work on the basis of the translated

"Aleksandrija". He used the translated Chronicles of Malalas and Hamartolos, and a series of pious works, including apocryphal ones ("The Revelation of Methodios of Patara" [of Olympos] as well as "The Story about the Indian Kingdom", the "Physiologus", *Pčela*, and stories of Zosima's and Makarij's travels). A number of fantastic details concerning the miracles of Eastern countries are taken from these monuments and introduced into the description of the campaign of Alexander the Great. On the other hand, all the themes of the implacability of fate and the transitoriness of all earthly things, are stressed: "He who seeks vanity's fame passes like a shadow and soon perishes". It is interesting that the author makes an attempt to represent the change of character, the evolution of his heroes; the Persian King Darius, rival of Alexander, as well as Alexander himself, gradually subdues his pride, and Alexander at the end of the novel recognizes the futility of earthly life and becomes a pessimist.

The vivid imagery and the interesting adventures made this version, which was included in the so-called Hellenic Chronograph, an especially popular monument. "Aleksandrija, 2nd redaction" is the first attempt at an original didactic novel which six centuries later produced among the Eastern Slavs such works as the novels of Dostojevskij, and Tolstoj's "Resurrection". The pessimistic notes of "Aleksandrija, 2nd redaction" are noteworthy; they are, on the whole, characteristic of the period. But the ideology of the work differs essentially from the chivalrous ideology depicted in the Kievan Chronicle and in the biography of Daniil of Galič (see IV, 5). The mood of "Aleksandrija" was to gain the ascendancy in the future.

4. HAGIOGRAPHIC LITERATURE

1. Hagiographic literature is represented first of all by one of the most notable monuments of the period, the "Kiev-Pečerskij Paterikon". It is interesting in that we know the history of its origin – a rare case in Old Slavonic literatures. The monument, which had originated between 1215–1225, is extant in two versions: one being Arsenij's version, revised in Tver' on the initiative of Bishop Arsenij in 1406, and Kassian's version, composed in the Kiev-Pečersk monastery in 1462. Fortunately, both editions sufficiently well preserved the original text, only supplementing it with new material.

The origin of the Paterikon at first formed the theme of its framework. Simon, Bishop of Vladimir-Suzdal' (1215–26), having a sudden yearning

AN ICON OF THE MOTHER OF GOD FROM THE SVENSK MONASTERY
(NEAR BRJANSK)
Next to the Holy Virgin St. Antonij of Pečersk (right) and St. Feodosij of
Pečersk (left). End of the 13th century.

CHURCH ON THE RIVER NERLJA IN THE PRINCIPALITY OF VLADI-
MIR-SUZDAL' (1165)

for the Kiev-Pečerskij monastery, where he had previously been a monk, addresses a letter to another monk of the same monastery, Polikarp. In this letter, Simon tries to persuade Polikarp to renounce his intention of becoming a bishop. He proposes that Polikarp should instead occupy himself with literary work, and sends him as a model his own earlier stories about the life of the monks in the Kiev-Pečerskij monastery (nine stories about eleven monks). He adds to each story a short "instruction" for the ambitious Polikarp. The latter follows Simon's advice and, in the form of a letter to Akindin, the abbot of the monastery (1214–31), imparts to him eleven further stories (about thirteen monks). These two series of stories compose the Paterikon in its original form. Both the above-mentioned versions contain a number of addenda from various sources. We must presume that the completed text had already originated in the 13th–14th centuries, as the additions are on the whole identical in both redactions. In Arsenij's redaction, the instructions to Polikarp are omitted; in both versions the following are added: Nestor's Life of Feodosij; the eulogy of Feodosij; the story of Isaakij from the Chronicle – here divided into four separate tales –; the story of the foundation of the Kiev-Pečerskij monastery, also written by Simon; a note on Polikarp's death; and a pseudo-Feodosij epistle against the "Latins". Fortunately, the language remained very archaic, so that probably no linguistic revision was made: the religious monument demanded exactitude in transmission.

2. The Paterikon is not a "collection of Lives", as it is often said to be. Like the translated paterikons, it is a miscellany of stories about isolated episodes from the lives of pious monks; it also contains stories about "fallen" monks, which end – with one exception, it is true – with the reformation of the fallen. Also included in it are very short tales (one is of just a few lines). These stories differ from the Lives first of all in that their authors do not attempt to write a description of the *whole* life of the hero. The Paterikon is not divided into "Lives", but into *slova* (chapters). And the form of Simon's and Polikarp's letters is undoubtedly a literary form, for Polikarp writes to Akindin, though they both live in the same monastery.

The writers obviously did not expect that all the heroes of their stories would become canonized saints; the word "saint" is found but rarely. Their official recognition as saints took place in the Ukraine only in 1643, and in Russia in 1762.

The translated paterikons and, in part, the tale of Isaakij served as models. Moreover, both authors used monuments which have since been lost, namely, the Rostov annals, the Chronicle of the Pečerskij monastery, and the Life of Antonij which, possibly, also bore the character of monastic annals. Thus we learn once more about the existence of non-extant monuments.

3. The subject-matter of the stories is varied. Every story serves as a basis for a "moral", sometimes clearly expressed, sometimes only implicit. It is possible occasionally to date the stories, when they mention abbots, princes, or familar historical events. The majority of the stories which can be dated concern the 11th and the beginning of the 12th century.

The stories are distributed according to a fixed scheme: after the tale of Onisifor, to whom Antonij – having appeared to him in a vision – promised salvation for all those buried in the monastery's crypts, there follow two stories about martyrs to the faith, and then stories of various content. Of particular length and interest is the story of the Prince-monk Nikola the Pious, a descendant of the Černigov princes. The last stories of Simon are devoted to instances of temporarily "fallen" monks: among them the miserly Arefa, who was given credit for giving as "alms" the gold which had been stolen from him; then Tit and Evagrij, who are constantly fighting one against the other; Jevagrij is an example of a monk "fallen", as he did not reconcile himself with Tit until his death, whereas Tit repented. The story of Afanasij already tells about the "fall" of the entire monastery, when poor Afanasij died and the monks did not even bother to bury him "as he was very poor and had no belongings in this world, and was therefore disdained"; two days later Afanasij was resuscitated, and lived another twelve years.

Just as varied are Polikarp's stories, which, in a number of cases, have the character of complete novels with diverting plots. Such is the story of Grigorij, whom Monomach's brother Rostislav in a moment of youthful mischief-making ordered to be drowned. Before his death Grigorij predicted a similar death by drowning to Rostislav, which indeed occurred; this is narrated in detail by the Chronicle (1093) and mentioned in "The Tale of Igof's Campaign". Almost a complete novel is the story of Moisej the Hungarian, who, having fallen into Polish captivity in 1015, struggled for many years against the temptations put in his way by a rich and eminent Polish lady who had fallen in love with him. Another story is that of Prochor, who, during the famine at the end of the 11th century, distributed to the poor ashes instead of salt and taught the hungry to bake bread out of orach. The story of the painter Alipij is interesting from the cultural and historical point of view. The tale of Nikita reminds us of the story of Isaakij; to Nikita there also appeared a demon in the guise of an "angel of light" and imparted to him learning, oratory and even the gift of prophecy. Nikita, too, contrived in the end to save himself from "the devil". To the temptation of demons there succumbed also the monk Fjodor, to whom the devil revealed a "Varangian" treasure hidden in the monastery. Fjodor was saved from temptation by his friend Vasilij; he even forgot the place where the treasure was hidden. The son of a Kievan prince, who wanted to get his hands on the treasure, tortured both friends.

The introductory story about the foundation of the Kiev-Pečerskij monastery is rather mysterious. It is the only instance in the entire early Kievan literature when we meet the Varangians, fleeing to Rus', as bearers of Christian cultural traditions; they make an important offering to the monastery. We are also told here how the Greek architects who built the monastery church first came to the monastery; they set off for Kiev at the invitation of unknown personages, according to the story either the then deceased Antonij and Feodosij, or angels.

4. The literary shaping of the stories is uneven. It is possible that both authors simply copied out certain passages from their sources. Stylistically some excerpts recall the Chronicle; others, the stories of the assassination of Boris and Gleb. In any case, both authors attempted to write a broad narrative, enlivened with details and digressions. It was especially important for them to provide a characterisation of the experiences of their heroes. Both of them, and Polikarp in particular, attempted this by introducing dialogues into the narrative (for instance, Nikola the Pious disputes with his Syrian doctor, who tries to persuade him to renounce his severe ascetic life which is threatening his health; Moisej the Hungarian argues with the Polish lady in love with him, and so forth). Still more successful are the monologues of some of the zealots, often cast in the form of prayers. Both authors also made moderate use of texts from the Holy Scriptures. Other means of psychological characterisation are metaphors and similes, especially favoured by Polikarp: "He was pierced by the arrow of envy"; temptations are "spiritual animals" or "a fire" from which "bones crack"; asceticism "purifies" man "as fire purifies gold". Prochor is characterised by Polikarp as a man who "marched easily along his way"; lived "like a bird"; while he even carried the *loboda* (orach) collected for baking bread "as though flying on wings". Occasionally we come across proverbs. Polikarp sometimes prefers to employ literary turns of phrase; he seems to be embarrassed by the "vulgar" word *loboda* (orach), and he avoids it by referring to "the grass which I mentioned earlier". The exclamations are also in a lofty style: "This the Lord has created to His glory!", and so forth.

5. Polikarp, and less frequently Simon, do not fear digressions and deviations from the main theme of the story, always ably merging them into the basic thread of the narrative. Polikarp interweaves into his story of Fjodor and Vasilij the legend of the devils who helped the saints to build a church. In another instance he tells the legend of Feofil, who collected his tears in a pitcher. Before his death an angel appeared to him and brought him a bowl containing a fragrant liquid; these were the tears which Feofil had not managed to drop into his pitcher and which had fallen to the ground where he dried them with a kerchief. Both stories are migratory legends.

A number of digressions and passages belonging to the basic theme of the stories provide most valuable cultural and historical material. The Christian Varangians, the patrons of the monastery, have been already mentioned. In other stories we find a Syrian and an Armenian doctor. Also characterised are princes, often with very negative features; judges; and the population of Kiev. Books and libraries are mentioned as well. There are also allusions to events in Polish history. We learn most, however, about the life of the monastery itself, especially about the period of the decadence of communal life in the monastery. At that time the monks had their own private property; proprietary inequality reigned in the monastery. Alongside the monks who remained loyal to the legacy of Feodosij (productive labour and charity) we find some who are selfish, egoistic and malicious. Both authors speak out about these manifestations of the decadence of monastic life.

6. The ideological colour of the Paterikon is also linked with the characterisation of the negative traits of the monastery and the "world". Demonology, little represented in the 11th century monuments, now plays a great role. Temptations, temporarily successful or entirely unsuccessful, appear in the majority of stories. Both authors' attitude to the world is strongly negative. They consider retirement from the world and severe asceticism as the only road to salvation, although now we also meet a number of monks of whose ascetic accomplishments nothing is said (Prochor, the painter Alipij). In some parts we also find warnings against a too severe asceticism and the concomitant "ascetic pride" in one's deeds. Several passages are devoted to Feodosij's prescriptions; work and charity are highly valued, but they now seem to be considered the concern of a few. The whole tone of the stories is opposed to the "secular life" against the influence of which even monastic walls are of no avail.

7. In addition to the sources mentioned by the authors themselves, the Paterikon also uses translated hagiographic literature. We find here a complete range of themes concerning the "gifts of the Holy Spirit": among the ascetics there are miraculous healers, seers who "recognise spirits", who are not burned by fire, and who exorcize devils. All these are themes from the old hagiographic literature. A number of tales remind us of certain stories from the Lives and the paterikons (see above, 5). However, the Paterikon undoubtedly retells stories which belong to the monastery itself and which had originated there long before Simon and Polikarp presented them in a literary manner. We do not find any direct borrowings from hagiographic literature. Obviously, the authors' selection of material from the legends current in the monastery played an important role here. As one of the stories states, this selection was made on the basis of the similarity between the material of monastic legends and that found in "classical" hagiographic literature. What was recounted in the latter about recognised ascetics and saints could also be told about local zealots and about unknown and unrecognised ascetics. This criterion of selection undoubtedly deprived us of very valuable material. Some such legends not included in the Paterikon have probably been preserved in popular tradition, perhaps to this very day. Unfortunately, folk tradition usually deprived the local legends of their hero, and substituted a well-known saint.

8. The stories of the Paterikon, especially those written by Polikarp, are among the best examples of the art of psychological characterisation in ancient literature. They also show that it was possible to combine an ornate style with the communication of substantial content. This "substantiality" of the Paterikon's stories was responsible for their great subsequent popularity. In the baroque period printed editions started to appear – with some changes of text, it is true. In the 18th–19th centuries the texts of the Paterikon were also subjected to Synodic censorship which expurgated those passages which were deemed "inclining to temptation".

9. The Life of Avraamij of Smolensk is unfortunately obscure on the basic question of the character of the saint's deeds. The Life is extant in two redac-

tions, a long and a short one; the manuscripts of both are no older than the 16th century. The author is thought to have been Efrem, a pupil of the saint, and thus the Life must have originated no later than the middle of the 13th century, as Avraamij lived at the end of the 12th century. It is not definitely established which version is the older. The distinguishing feature of the longer one consists mainly in the "adornment" of almost each phrase with well-chosen quotations from the Holy Scriptures, the Church Fathers, and hagiographic literature. Moreover, "topoi of modesty" are added at the beginning and in the middle of the Life, with a prayer at the end. All these may belong to the 13th-century stylistic embellishments, but it is possible that they are later additions.

In both Lives the contents are almost literally identical. Unfortunately, the author is deliberately vague. Avraamij leads a monastic life in one of the monasteries near Smolensk. His erudition and the severe ascetism of his life are particularly stressed. When he becomes a priest, his sermons provoke the displeasure of the abbot, and he is forced to go to another monastery in Smolensk itself. But here, too, though his sermons enjoy great success among the young, he is accused of heresy and reading "books of mystery'"(*glubinnye knigi*) by the clergy and even by the congregation. Though the Prince exculpates him, he is forced to live in his former monastery, is forbidden to deliver sermons and, it seems, even to officiate at divine service. When, after Avraamij's prayer, a drought is ended, the ban is lifted and he becomes a priest in one of the Smolensk churches, where he lives many years, teaching the faithful and any who come to him. He dies after being a monk for fifty years.

References in the Life to Avraamij's thoughts concerning the next world and the Last Judgement, the announcement that the icons painted by him also depicted eschatological themes, the mention of "books of mystery" – all these make the conjecture that he preached the imminent end of the world quite probable (possibly in the year 6700 "after the creation of the world", i.e. in 1192). But this is merely speculation.

Whether we regard the longer or the shorter text as the original one, we must admit that the author wrote in a clear style, at times vividly (the image of the saint, the judgment on him, etc.). He was undoubtedly familiar with the Lives of Feodosij and Savva of Palestine, and also – if the longer version was written by him – he must be considered well versed in the Holy Scriptures and the Patristic works then translated.

10. In addition to these Lives, a number of other hagiographic works originated at that time, for instance, the stories about the saints' miracles, supplementing the old Lives (see IV, 3, 1); then there are a number of short Lives, the "*Prolog*" – Life of Aleksandr Nevskij, the Lives of the Novgorod saints Varlaam of Chutyn' and Bishop Arkadij, and also of the Rostov saints, Bishop Leontij (written in the 12th century) and Bishop Isaja (d. in 1274). These are interesting as early monuments of literature in the North and North-East. To the same period belong the "*Prolog*"-Lives of Vladimir Monomach's son, Prince Mstislav, and probably of Kirill of Turov. Their literary importance is small.

5. THE CHRONICLES

1. The chronicling of events continues in both Ukrainian and Great Russian territory. From the literary point of view, the chronicles from the Kiev and Galicia-Volhynia principalities are the most interesting. The main source of our knowledge of these is the so-called Hypatius Chronicle which contains three different annalistic monuments and which had reached the North. Its popularity is testified by the fact that it is extant in five copies, after one of which it has been named. Here are brought together the Kiev Chronicle of the 12th century, which ends in 1199; the Galician annals, recording events from 1205 to the 1260's; and the Volhynia Chronicle which reaches the year 1289 (in the manuscripts erroneously given as 1292).

The second part of the annals is not a chronicle proper, but a biography of the Galician Prince Daniil Romanovič (see § 11, "Biographies").

2. The Kievan Chronicle is a complex conglomeration of various elements. Its last editor was probably the abbot Moisej of Vydubiči. Some passages form coherent stories. There also seem to be traces of non-annalistic tales.

The most characteristic trait of the Kievan Chronicle is the dialogue form in which the narrative is sustained. The *dramatis personae* express their intentions in speeches, which are further communicated by their ambassadors. For instance:

"There came news from friends in Černigov, 'Prince! do not go anywhere ... they want to kill you...' Hearing this, Izjaslav ... sent ambassadors to Černigov ... and told them, 'We planned a big campaign and ... swore an oath; we shall consolidate our oath once more...' But they answered, 'Why swear an oath without meaning?' ... And they refused to kiss the Cross. Izjaslav Mstislavič's ambassador asked them, 'Is it a sin to kiss the Cross in mutual love?' ... And Izjaslav told his ambassador, 'If they refuse to swear an oath ... tell them what we have heard'. And Izjaslav's ambassador told them, 'Information has come to me that you are betraying me ... Is it so, brothers, or not?' And they could not answer...'"

Sayings of proverbial type or historical anecdotes stand out in great number among the speeches. For instance, a certain prince renounces the Kursk principality: "I would rather die with my *družina* in my own country ... than have the Kursk principality." The witticism about armies standing on both sides of the Dniepr is repeated in different

words: "They have no wings" – "You can't fly across like a bird."
Prince Volodimirko of Galič, who is reminded by the ambassador from
the Kievan Prince of his oath "to kiss the Cross", answers ironically:
"This little cross". As for sayings of the proverb type:"Peace lasts until
war, and war until peace"; "You dug a pit and fell in it yourself"; "Evil
will perish evilly." Though some of these phrases are taken from religious
literature, the entire colouring of the Kievan Chronicle has, on the whole,
a secular and military character.

3. An especially vivid characteristic of the style is the use of set formulas
when describing events, particularly military ones. Such formulas change
somewhat, but their sense remains the same. The beginning of a campaign
starts with the words: *zaratilisъ, ispolčilisъ* ("they armed themselves,
they prepared themselves"); the prince "mounted the horse". The prince
"heartens his followers" with a speech, which is sometimes rendered in a
few words. Before the battle the music-signal is given: "They blew the
trumpets", they started "to beat the drums and blow the trumpets",
"they beat the tambourines", "trumpeted into the trumpets", and so
forth. Before the battle "they raise the banner", "they show the banner".
The prince is first to "break a spear", i.e., attack the enemy. The battles
are described with various details; in particular, we find traditional
formulas: "They fought strongly"; "stones from the fortress" or "arrows"
fall "like rain", etc. The battle is compared to Doomsday; certain
descriptions mention the clatter of arms, the voices of the soldiers, the
groans of the wounded, the dust raised by the horses, and even some
mysterious voices. After the battle the troops return home either "with
glory", "with great glory and honour", or "having achieved nothing".
The prince dismounts from his horse, the warriors occasionally "dry
their sweat" or "dry their tears", thinking of the casualties. There are
also similar formulas for events of a non-military character.

4. The ideology of the Kievan Chronicle combines various elements; this
is best seen in the motivation of events which includes egoistic, patriotic,
chivalrous, and religious factors. The basic conceptions of chivalrous
ideology are "honour" and "offense"; an offense is vindicated, "ignominy"
which is "worse than death" has to be "washed from oneself". But, quite
frequently, one also encounters purely egoistic formulas: "I want to get
Novgorod by truth or deceit". But "hope is placed in God", "let God
(or "the Saviour" or the "holy cross") judge between us". And even in
case of defeat, they are conforted by the thought that "God in His power

gave victory to our enemies, but honour and glory to us". But, fighting very often for their own petty egoistic interests, the princes frequently consider themselves "the guardians of the Russian land" (by which is usually understood only the Ukraine or even the Kievan principality alone) or the guardians of "the Christian people" ("Allow us, o Lord, to sacrifice our lives for the Christians and the Russian land and join the martyrs"). All the themes merge into one, for example in such words as: "God did not commit the Russian land and Russian sons to infamy. Now, brothers, ... let us hope that God will allow us to win honour in these lands, in the face of foreign peoples!"

One must note that the Kievan Chronicle is one of those comparatively rare annalistic monuments of the old period in which one can sometimes trace efforts to give a characterisation of the hero not only externally, on the basis of his deeds, but "internally", deducing at least some acts from the man's character and linking them with his entire personality. Thus is characterised, for instance, the Galician Prince Vladimirko as *mnogoglagolivyj* (talkative), egoist and cynic; in the old Chronicle, man is characterised only by his deeds, less frequently by his opinions (Vladimir Monomach); in later chronicles the heroes are usually represented by hyperbolical traits; next to them appear "villains". Only in the 16th century do we find exceptions, but already without any regard to historical truth. Princes, however, are not the only "heroes" of the annalistic narrative: sometimes we also meet the population which views the plans and enterprises of the princes either sympathetically or unsympathetically. And the views of the population are usually rendered in speech form, "We follow you with children, as you wish", etc. It is remarkable that the Chronicle twice (in 1188 and 1190) mentions the Crusades in warm words, comparing "the Germans" to martyrs for Christ's faith. Thus, the assertion that the Eastern Slavs were unaware of the Crusades or that they did not consider them a positive historical event, is incorrect.

5. Certain devices are found only sporadically. Such, for instance, is the "rhythmized" language as in the history of Prince Igof's campaign of 1185 (these passages are possibly taken from another monument). Alliterations are also rare. Occasionally we encounter parallelisms in the representation of various events, especially happenings among the troops on both sides before battle; secular events are mentioned but rarely.

Some excerpts in different style are in all probability insertions. Such are "the obituaries" of princes, entries about events in princely families, and a small number of individual stories. Under 1147, the assassination of the Prince-monk Igoŕ of Černigov by the Kiev population is recounted; under 1175, the murder of Prince Andrej Bogoljubskij by conspirators. Both stories are composed in a style which is reminiscent of that of the Lives (see IV, 3, 3–4). Very picturesque are the pages devoted to the life of Prince Rostislav of Kiev in 1168, and this story bears the characteristics of religious style. Short laments have also to be noted as deviations from the style of the military tales. In such insertions we find quotations from the Holy Scriptures and compound words: *blagoumnyj* (noble-minded), *vysokoumie* (highmindedness), *paguboubijstvennyj* (pernicious and deadly).

6. The second part of the Hypatius Chronicle, as already mentioned, consists of the biography of Prince Daniil of Galič, in only some copies divided into years, like the other chronicles. It ends about 1260. The subject-matter is mainly a complex story of the Prince's struggle for the throne of the Galician principality, in particular with the Hungarians, followed by a complicated story of internal strife and external conflicts of the principality, especially with the Tartars, Poland, and Lithuania, but also with West European powers.

7. The style of the biography is the most complex in the literature of the period. The author is a professional writer (possibly one of the officials of the Prince's chancery, probably the *pečatnik* himself, i.e., the Prince's Chancellor, Kirill); he favours involved constructions and rare, bookish words; he stresses his literary devices. One of his most consistent stylistic devices is the *dativus absolutus*, which he uses with extraordinary lavishness.

For instance:

> Не дошедшимъ же воемь рѣкы Сяну,
> сосѣдшим же на поли воружиться,
> и бывшу знаменію сице надъ полкомъ:
> пришедшимъ орломъ и многимъ ворономъ,
> яко оболоку велику,
> играющимъ же птицамъ,
> орлом же клекьщущимъ
> и плавающим крилômы своими
> и воспромѣтающимъся на воздусѣ,
> якоже иногда и николи же не бѣ . . .

("And the soldiers did not reach the river Sjan, and dismounted from their horses to arm themselves, and there was such an omen over the troops: there came eagles and numerous crows like a great cloud, and birds played in the air, eagles screeched and floated on their wings and turned somersaults, as never before at any other time.")

As in the Kievan Chronicle, there are a great number of dialogues. There are, of course, many historical anecdotes and aphorisms: a certain prince, an enemy of Daniil, says, "If only I had ten soldiers, I would march against him"; Daniil speaks of Tartar military tactics: "The Christians get strength from space, the Tartars from constriction"; or "One stone breaks many pots"; "there is no honey without killing the bees"; and, with an effective harmony: *Dněstr zlu igru sygra Ugrom – gr-gr-gr* (the Dnestr played a bad joke on the Hungarians).

The author is fond of by-names and the characterisation of the *dramatis personae* by epithets.

In Daniil's biography, too, the fixed formulas of the Kievan Chronicle are preserved, only here they are often developed and, almost in every case, somewhat changed: "Stones fell from the towers like heavy rain"; "Arrows poured on the town like rain"; "They threw spears and fire-brands like flashes of lightning"; "They threw stones at them like a violent hail." Likewise vary the descriptions of battles, in which the author devotes much space to individual soldiers, primarily, of course, to the hero of his biography, Prince Daniil. A central place is also given to him in the description of non-military events.

Adornments of style are numerous. These include, for instance, the use of rare and obsolete words which are immediately explained: *vsja okrestnaja vesi, rekomaja okol'naja* (neighbouring villages). The author is fond of abstract expressions; instead of "they were chased" he writes: *nyně že izgnanie bystъ na nichъ*, and so forth. He likes the play of words; see above *Dněstrъ zlu igru sygra Ugromъ*; or *bojarin bojarina plěnivše, smerdъ smerda, gradъ grada* ("One boyar conquered another, the peasant conquered the peasant, the town [defeated] the town"). Rhythmized language is rare, alliteration still rarer.

8. The composition of Daniil's biography is of interest. Undoubtedly, the author used various sources and material; but the unity of style, for example, the extraordinary frequency of *dativus absolutus*, proves that the entire work was written by one and the same hand.

The biography starts with a poetic introduction devoted to memories of the past; first the lately deceased Roman of Galič, Daniil's father, is mentioned:

приснопамятнаго самодержьца всея Руси,
одолѣвша всимъ поганьскымъ языкомъ,
ума мудростью ходяща по заповѣдемъ Божиимъ:
устремил бо ся бяше на поганыя яко и левъ,
сердитъ же бысть яко и рысь,
и губяше яко и коркодилъ,
и прехожаше землю ихъ яко и орелъ,
храборъ бо бѣ яко и туръ . . .

("Lord of the whole of Rus', of revered memory, victor over all heathen peoples, living with his wise mind according to God's will, he rushed against the pagans like a lion, wrathful like a lynx, he destroyed them like a crocodile, passed through their lands like an eagle, was courageous like an aurochs...")

Following this the author recalls the times of Vladimir Monomach, who "drank the water of the Don from a golden helmet", and the past of the Polovtsians, thus obviously transmitting fragments from a Polovtsian epos. One can only speculate why the biography suddenly comes to an end, without a proper close. Many scholars have tried to isolate the individual component parts of the biography of Prince Daniil. The uniformity of style of the whole biography (insignificant fragments excepted) repudiates such attempts.

9. The biography of Prince Daniil is continued in annalistic form; this is the chronicle of his nephew, Vladimir Vasil'kovič, Prince of Volhynia.

Prince Vladimir is a copyist who has copied books himself. The story is written by a scribe. The style is less *recherché*, but the devices are on the whole the same (there is no *dativus absolutus*). A number of scenes and dialogues are presented in literary form, either dramatically or in the form of a witty anecdote.

The eulogy of the Prince, written on the news of his death, is especially pompous. This is again a complete biography in which we are told of the Prince's building program and literary occupations, of his administration, his wars, and his art of hunting. Some passages are imitations of Metropolitan Ilarion's "Sermon on Law and Grace" (see above, III, 2, 4).

In many places the language has an ecclesiastical flavour. For the first time in annalistic literature is there such a great number of compounds like *mnogocennyj* (of great value), *blagopochval'nyj* (praise-worthy), *dobrovonnyj* (aromatic), *mnogoderznovenie* (great courage), and so forth. But there are also pages written in a simpler language, which almost evoke *genre* pictures. There are a few conversations couched in riddles (see above, I, 8).

The conclusion consists of only a few pages devoted to events after Vladimir's death.

10. The other annals of that time are much less interesting from the literary point of view. First of these are the Novgorod chronicles. It is supposed that Vladimir Monomach's son and grandson, who ruled in Novgorod, occupied themselves with the continuation of annalistic entries. The Chronicle has reached us in a later version. Ideologically, the content of the Novgorod Chronicle has a more religious colour than the Southern annals. On the one hand, the entries were probably made by the clergy and possibly at the episcopal court; on the other hand, the dynastic point of view is entirely absent and the attitude toward the princes as the elected organisers of administration and military leaders is very often violently critical.

But the Novgorod Chronicle is a purely annalistic monument with no literary aspirations. The dry and clear style makes no use of literary adornments, and the historian of literature is confronted with a lack of interesting material, the more so that the chronicles avoid coherent stories. The language is noteworthy for its strong dialectical flavour.

11. The principality of Suzdal' was a new political centre, which became especially strong under the rule of Prince Andrej Bogoljubskij (1157–1175). We have no literary monuments of the early period; the golden age of the principality's culture is evidenced mainly by the extant monuments of architecture. But the so-called Laurentian Chronicle (MS. 1377) contains, from the year 1111 to 1205, a number of items from the South and from the Suzdal' principality, and between 1206–1305 reports from other North-Eastern principalities (Rostov and Tver'). In the 12th century, it seems that the authors used the annalistic records of South Perejaslavl'. In the 13th century, the Chronicle was obviously kept in Rostov too, but was revised for the last time in about 1305, in Tver'.

All these are merely remains of the literary activity in the 12th–13th centuries. The Laurentian Chronicle stands midway between the Southern and Novgorod Chronicles. We find in it coherent stories, partly about old times (for instance, the legend of the origin of the enmity between the Kievan and Polock princes is retold). We also find here necrologies of princes (especially 13th century), panegyrics in honour of princes and bishops (beginning of 13th century), and stories of the assassination of princes by the Tartars (Michail of Černigov, Vasil'ko Konstantinovič, and Roman of Rjazan'). The style has a clerical quality. The fruits of literary activity in Suzdal' also include the story of the assassination by conspirators of Prince Andrej Bogoljubskij in 1175 (cf. IV, 3, 4), which found its way into the Kievan Chronicle. But in

general, the Laurentian annalists considered themselves purely chroniclers, and in most cases they give dry accounts of events.

The Laurentian Chronicle was undoubtedly revised in the 14th century,
probably by the copyist himself, Lavrentij. This revision, however, belongs to
14th-century literature. Moreover, one of the copies (the Radziwiłł copy, after
the name of its previous owner) contains a few hundred miniatures of great
cultural and historical interest. These were painted in the 15th century and are
not without Western influence (cf. also VI, 7, 1).

12. Parts of the old North-Eastern entries have been preserved, not in the
Laurentian Chronicle, but in other, later ones (for instance in the so-called
"Simeonovskaja" Chronicle, a 16th-century manuscript). Likewise, some
chronicles (those of Novgorod and the so-called Voskresenskaja, see VI, 4, 3)
preserved fragments of the Kievan Chronicle of the 13th century.
　In later annalistic monuments, remains of the 13th-century Rjazan' Chronicle
are preserved, with characteristically sharp criticism of princely rule. We find
fragments of the Galician Chronicle of the 12th century in the Kiev annals. The
Polish 15th-century historian Długosz used some chronicles unknown to us.

Moreover, we find in the chronicles, especially the Kievan and Galician,
traces of the use of another literature. Alongside the inevitable quotations
from the Holy Scriptures and imitations of them, we encounter the influence of the translated Chronicles of Hamartolos and Malalas, possibly
of "Aleksandrija", but especially of the tales of Josephus about the
Jewish war. All these monuments are used mainly as sources from which
certain formulas for the description of events, individual metaphors,
images and comparisons can be taken. The author of Prince Daniil's
biography sometimes quotes his sources: Malalas, some other chronograph, and Homer (there is no quotation from Homer in his poems).

Only rarely do we come across insertions, fragments wich differ in style from
the remaining text. In the Kiev Chronicle there are such fragments – the already
mentioned stories of the assassination of Prince Igor' of Černigov in 1147, and
of Prince Andrej Bogoljubskij in 1175, and Moisej's sermon. Moreover, "The
Tale of Igof's Campaign" (1185) differs greatly in style from the remaining
parts of the Chronicle, and in particular contains a lyrical representation of
Igof's experiences in Polovtsian captivity. In the biography of Prince Daniil of
Galič, the story of the assassination of Michail of Černigov by the Tartars differs
from the style of the author, whereas the stories of the battle on the river
Kalka and the capture of Kiev by the Tartars are perhaps derived by the
author from other sources but are so rewritten by him that we do not notice
any stylistic difference from his own stories. In the Novgorod Chronicle there
is inserted a description of Prince Aleksandr Nevskij's life, divided into
several parts; in the Laurentian Chronicle the insertions are the above mentioned obituaries and panegyrics and, perhaps, the stories of the murders of the

princes. But it is possible that all these separate stories are by the author of the annals.

The 12th–13th centuries mark a dividing line in the history of chronicling. After that time annals fall into two widely different types: the purely annalistic, of little interest to literature, and the artistic versions of historical tales.

6. THE REMAINS OF THE EPOS

1. A number of epic themes belonging to the 12th–13th centuries can be reconstructed on the basis of modern *stariny*. It is true that the epic themes relating to these centuries in the majority of cases have no heroic character. It is possible that a certain number of monuments have been lost; from the middle of the 12th century the links between individual principalities become increasingly weaker and therefore of smaller interest to all Eastern Slav tribes. Only the struggle against the Tartars has been reflected in the older epic monuments (where the names of other hostile nomads are replaced by the name "Tartar"), and has led to the creation of new ones.

2. The epic works linked with the West-Ukrainian principalities were a new phenomenon. In one way or another, two heroes lead us to Galič. Both are representative of a new type of "hero" – the knight.

According to the narrative of contemporary *stariny*, Djuk Stepanovič – whose name and patronymic already point to the West (Djuk – Duke, Stephan – a popular Hungarian name) – came to Kiev from "Galič-Volynec", from "rich India". Strictly speaking, he is characterised only as a rich man; when his tales are doubted in Kiev, a delegation is sent to his country – and proves unable to describe the magnitude of Djuk's riches.

Side by side with him appears Čurilo Plenkovič (a name preserved in Galician popular songs, in Ukrainian local names, and by the Polish 16th–17th-century writers, Rej and Klonowicz). Like Djuk, he is a knight, but of less noble character. He is of the Don Juan type; the description of his riches and beauty ends with a light romantic motif: when he was a *čašnik* (cupbearer) at the Kiev Court, the princess herself could not take her eyes off him so that she cut her hand with a knife. A love-affair with a married woman costs him his life.

Both "heroes" appear together in the *bylina* devoted to the quarrel about their riches. For three years, they must display themselves in a new costume every day and then jump across the Dnepr on horseback. Djuk is the victor.

Some details in the description of Djuk's riches are taken from "The Tale of the Indian Kingdom" (the Western translation dated no earlier than the second half of the 12th century – see II, 11). There are also some similarities between these *byliny* and the descriptions of the luxury of princely courts and buildings in the Galicia-Volhynia Chronicle.

3. The fantastic *bylina* about Michail Potok, the dragon-slayer, is probably an altered version of the Bulgarian tales of St. Michail of Potuka, also a dragon-slayer, whose remains were solemnly transported in 1206 to Trnovo – which could have been responsible for the popularisation of the legends about him in Rus'.

Of obscure origin are a further number of *byliny* in which the names of the heroes have a ring of the Galician historical heroes: Prince Roman, *voevoda* Dunaj. Concerning some of the Galician princes and heroes there exist oral Ukrainian tales which do not appear in the Chronicle; the date of their origin is unknown.

4. With the Tartar invasion are linked some *stariny* of a very different character (in their modern form), which originated somewhere on the territory reached by the invasion. Such are the *stariny* about Kiev's invasion by "Kalin-tsar" who is overcome by Il'ja Murovec; about the invasion by Batyga, in whom one cannot fail to recognise Batu (Russian Batyj), who is overcome by Vasilij Ignat'evič. The heroic victory over the Tartars, the "happy ending", is, of course, a later alteration of a historical ending. An effective beginning remained in the *starina* about Vasilij Ignat'evič: the lament of the Virgin Mary over the imminent loss of Kiev.

Several variants of the *starina* about the "Kama" carnage where the Tartars appear twice (as in the *stariny* about Kalin-tsar), correspond to historical truth (the invasions of 1223 and 1237); (*Kamskoe*, of course, instead of *Kalkskoe*, from Kalka) all the Russian heroes perish in battle as punishment for their pride and arrogance.

These *stariny* are also centred around Kiev, but it is not impossible that they originated elsewhere.

5. The Novgorod *stariny* are the most perfect from the point of view of form. Two of them can be dated back to the 13th century. Both are about "Sadko – the rich merchant". Only the name of Sadko, the

ST. DIMITRIJ CATHEDRAL IN VLADIMIR
(Principality of Vladimir-Suzdal', 12th century).

FRAGMENT OF A PLASTIC REPRESENTATION

Abraham (left) receives the three angels (representations of two of them are preserved). From the St. George Cathedral in Jurjev (Principality of Vladimir-Suzdal'). 12th century.

posadnik (mayor) and builder of one of the Novgorod churches, is historical. We are told in one of the *byliny* how Sadko the singer has become rich, having won a wager with the Novgorod merchants that there was a fish with "golden fins" in the Novgorod lake Il'men. Sadko lost a second wager, that in the course of three days he would buy all the goods on the Novgorod market, but he still retained a great enough fortune to remain a "rich merchant". The content of the second *starina* is quite fantastic: during one of his business-trips, Sadko visits the kingdom of the "Sea King", who is so pleased with his singing that he wants to give him one of his daughters in marriage. But, on the advice of St. Nicholas, Sadko chooses the worst of all the brides offered to him and does not touch her during the wedding night. In the morning he wakes up in Novgorod and, in gratitude to St. Nicholas, builds a church named after the saint. The *starina* is full of original features which do not recur in the remaining *byliny* tradition. In contrast to the majority of the *stariny*, this one is a "mercantile epic", the appearance of which in Novgorod, a merchant republic, is understandable. Individual motifs may possibly have originated from the fable tradition, but several, including the figure of the "Sea King" himself, have no parallel in Slavonic fairy-tales or in the fables of neighbouring countries.

The second group of Novgorod *stariny* deals with Vasilij Buslaevič, representative of Novgorod's adventurous youth. In the first *starina* we are told of his years of dissipation and of his fights with the inhabitants of the city; the second tells of his journey to Jerusalem where he meets his death while performing fearless deeds, heedless of the warnings of the pious. It is possible that the actual type of Vasilij Buslaevič belongs to the 13th or 14th century, but it has been convincingly shown that later, in the 16th century, at the time of Ivan the Terrible's struggle against Novgorod, songs about Vasilij Buslajevič were transformed into "broadsides" which represented Tsar Ivan under the name of Vasilij Buslaevič (Šambinago). It is impossible now to isolate the older elements from the type of the hero and from the subjects of *stariny* devoted to him (cf. VI, 11, 2).

There are still a few *byliny* belonging by virtue of their subject-matter to the "mercantile epic". They are probably linked with Novgorod.

6. A number of local sagas and legends extant partly in chronicles, partly in contemporary oral East Slavonic tradition, probably date from the same time. In particular, the Ukrainian legend of the child-hero, Michajlik, who, having quarrelled with the Kievans, leaves the city carrying off on his spear the "Golden Gates" – one of the most famous old-Kievan monuments – is obviously linked with the destruction of Kiev at the time of the Tartar invasions. A boy-hero named Michail, son of one Daniil Lovčanin, is mentioned in the *stariny*. But here, too, as in several other *stariny*, a *definitive* decision about the origin of modern prose or song legends is impossible.

7. A serious question arises: to what degree can the only extant historical epos of the 13th century, "The Tale of Igof's Campaign", give us an idea of the epic form of that period? The Tale stands too much on its own for us to reach a final conclusion, on the basis of this unique example, about the form of works lost to us. In any case, judging from the Tale and the biography of Prince Daniil of Galič, one can only speak about the strong tendency towards exuberant descriptions. The *stariny* about Djuk Stepanovič and Sadko, and partly also that about Čurilo, are closer to certain parts of the Hypatian Chronicle than to the Tale. A detailed study of the style of these monuments and a comparison with the style of the *stariny* may throw some light on this question.

7. THE TALE OF IGOŔ'S CAMPAIGN

1. "The Tale of Igof's Campaign" (*Slovo o polku Igoreve*) is the monument to which most research has been devoted and which to this day is still obscure in many respects. Not because the authenticity of the work may be doubted (on this point see 13), its manuscript having been burned during the Moscow fire of 1812. The great number of unsolved questions linked with the Tale arise from the fact that it is in many respects an exceptional monument. Its language and, to a considerable extent, its style can – with a great degree of probability – be included in the history of the development of Kievan literature. The style of the Tale can be linked with the culture and art contemporary with it. But the Tale is the only example of a genre of which (with the exception of the Tale itself) we have only insignificant remains included in works of another type (the chronicles) and which undoubtedly have suffered great changes. Moreover, the Tale is a monument of such high poetic standing that it is impossible to suppose that it may be considered *typical* of its genre – the secular historical epos. Thus, in spite of the undoubted links of the Tale with the preceding, contemporary and subsequent literature, we are forced to study it as a work *sui generis*, and we shall dwell with special attention on its original traits.

Unfortunately, the Tale was copied from a manuscript which was later burned, and was printed in 1800 when palaeography was as yet poorly developed. Moreover, the manuscript (probably from the end of the

15th or beginning of the 16th century) was undoubtedly distorted during the process of copying: its spelling reflected the peculiarities of the South Slavonic orthography which had reached the Eastern Slavs (cf. V, 1); the scribe, obviously of Pskovian pronunciation, imported into his copy features of his native dialect (mixture of *s* with *š*, *c* with *č*), and moreover made mistakes in the text, which he only poorly understood. All this leads us to the conclusion that in the text available to us there are many obscure places; most of these, however, have been elucidated by scholars.

2. The subject-matter of the Tale is simple in the main; it is the campaign of the Novgorod-Seversk Prince Igoř Svjatoslavič in 1185 against the restless nomads – the Polovtsians. The campaign ended, after an initial victory over the Polovtsians, in the cruel defeat of Igoř's army. The army was almost entirely destroyed; Igoř himself fell into captivity from which he later succeeded in escaping. One of his sons, who also found himself in captivity, married a Polovtsian princess and returned home even later. We are familiar with this campaign in sufficient detail from the Hypatian and Laurentian Chronicles.

The basic scheme, in accordance with which this factual material is distributed, is quite clear; the Tale begins with a short introduction and ends with a brief conclusion. The main content can be divided into four parts. 1) To begin with, the history of the campaign is expounded, up to the final defeat of Igoř. 2) Then the narrative takes us to Kiev where Prince Svjatoslav tells the boyars of his ominous dream and, learning of Igoř's defeat, pronounces a speech, "The Golden Word", addressing himself to various appanaged princes and exhorting them to fight against the Polovtsians. This "Word" of Svjatoslav merges imperceptibly into a speech by the author himself. 3) The following section is clearly distinguished; it is the "lament" of Igoř's wife, Jaroslavna, over her husband. 4) Then follows the story of Igoř's escape from captivity. The Tale has a brief conclusion. The whole story is not very long – about sixteen pages of modern print.

If the plan of the entire work is clear, in the individual parts a truly poetic "disorder" reigns; this was probably intentional. The "lament" alone is divided into four separate "stanzas" beginning with the same words, "Jaroslavna weeps..." In the remaining parts the author continually proceeds from one theme to another, from the description of contemporary events to reminiscences of the past, or to representation of scenery, or to the expression of his own feelings, or even to quotations from the 11th century poet Bojan, or to allusions at times obscure to us.

All the attempts to "correct" the vagueness of the plan by various transpositions of parts of the text are questionable and unconvincing. Scholars of recent times have refrained from such attempts.

3. The obscurity is further intensified by the main stylistic peculiarity of the Tale, a peculiarity which is found but rarely in the chronicles of the 11th–13th centuries. Instead of an exposition, a rendering of events, the author presents the reader with complexes of metaphors. Moreover, the real significance of the metaphors is rarely explained (and then usually after the metaphor), and is often revealed only by an allusion, or not at all. Thus Bojan "recalling... the fights of olden times, it was his wont to loose ten falcons on a flock of swans; and the one swan whichever was overtaken was the first to sing a song". The explanation follows: "Bojan did not loose ten falcons on a flock of swans, ... but laid his own magic fingers upon the living strings, and they would of themselves sound forth the glory of the princes".

More often the meaning of the metaphor is revealed only by an allusion: Igoŕ addresses the army – "I wish... to break a lance on the edge of the Polovtsian land ... I wish to lay down my head, or else to quaff of the Don from my helmet". It is clear to the reader that Igoŕ is exhorting the warriors to a campaign the issue of which is unknown. Or the reminiscences about the battles of bygone years: "On the [river – D. Č.] Nemiga they threw sheaves of heads and thresh with chain flails of Frankish steel; on the threshing floor they lay down life and winnow soul from body". Here only the words "life" and "soul" show that this complex of metaphors denotes battle and the death of soldiers. "Alone" – it is said of a prince – "thou didst let fall the pearl of thy soul out of the valiant body through thy golden necklace": the word "soul" shows that death is indicated.

But very often the metaphors are not elucidated at all. Of another prince's death during battle, it is said, "He fell under scarlet shields upon the bloody turf as it were upon the couch with his beloved" – the image of death as a marriage or a wedding is found in the epics of various nations. "Prince Igoŕ dismounted from his golden saddle, but only to a captive's saddle" – a metaphor of defeat and captivity. "Vladimir stopped his ears in Černigov morning after morning", – even in the context of memories about discussions of former times, the metaphor is not quite clear, and has been explained in various ways. Or, "Vseslav cast lot for the coveted maiden. Craftily leaning on his spear, he leaped to the city of Kiev, and touched with the spear-shaft the golden Kievan throne" –

from the Chronicle story of Vseslav we know that in 1068 he had for a short time seized the Kievan princely throne. The metaphor "city = maiden" can be found in the folk-lore of various peoples. Quite obscure is yet another excerpt devoted to memories of Vseslav. In Polock the bells of St. Sophia's would ring in the morning for him, but he already heard the matin-bells in Kiev". Though we know that Vseslav was a Polock prince, it is difficult to give a satisfactory explanation of this metaphor.

In some ways the metaphors of the Tale remind us of those verbal riddles which we occasionally find in the chronicles (cf. I, 8). They also recall a special device of Scandinavian poetry, the so-called *kenningar*, i.e., conventional metaphors in which the very mysteriousness of the obscurity is valued; notwithstanding the considerable bulk of extant Scandinavian poetry, some of the *kenningar* remain enigmatic to this day. The similarity of the metaphors of the Tale with the *kenningar* of Scandinavian poetry does not reside in the individual figures of speech, but rather in the very principle of using conventional, obscure and unexplained metaphors. Like the *kenningar*, the metaphors of the Tale are frequently composed of two terms and replace definite nouns: for example, "ten swans" – fingers; "steel chains" – swords; "scarlet wine" – blood; "coveted maiden" – town; and so forth. Also frequent are verbal metaphors, of this kind: "to winnow soul from body" – to kill; "to touch the throne with a spear" – to ascend the throne, etc. But at the end of the 12th century, any influence of Scandinavian poetry was hardly possible. Citing quotations and sayings from Bojan, the Tale thus reveals that this device had *already* been used in the 11th century (probably all the memories of Vseslav are linked with the poetical works of his contemporary Bojan). The metaphors of the Tale continue this old tradition (cf. I, 8).

"The Tale of Igoř's Campaign" also uses omens, dreams, and forebodings as metaphors. Svjatoslav's dream reminds us even more of verbal riddles and the *kenningar*. Here is the beginning of this dream, as narrated by Svjatoslav: "Early this night... they were clothing me in a black shroud upon a couch of yew, they poured me blue wine mixed with sorrow. They dropped upon my chest large pearls out of the empty quivers of the pagans. And they caress me, and the beams of my gold-domed hall are already without roof-girder..." The meaning of further omen-metaphors have remained obscure to this day. Nature is full of auguries; for instance, before the campaign Igoř's army sees an eclipse of the sun – an evil omen. In reality, this took place on May 1st, 1185, *during* the course of the campaign. The Tale transposes it to the eve of the campaign, in this way stressing the heroic determination of Igoŕ to undertake the campaign despite the evil omens. Before Igoŕ's defeat: "The next day, very early, bloody dawnings announce the break of day. Black clouds come up from the sea; they would fain veil the four suns, – and within them blue lightnings quiver"; and "The earth groans, the rivers flow turbid, dust covers the fields". And after the news of the defeat is received, "and trees have shed their foliage for evil!"

The metaphors of the Tale are not always so involved. Very often the metaphor simply consists in replacing an ordinary word, the name of an object, by its symbol. Bojan is a nightingale, the Polovtsians are crows or jackdaws, the heroes of the Tale are falcons, and so forth. The whole of Nature is symbolically portrayed: animals, sun, moon, mist, dust, dawn, and twilight. The Tale also uses equivocal metaphors, based on the dual function of the Slavonic instrumental case – the latter denoting both a real attitude and a comparison. For instance, we are told of Prince Vseslav: "*skoči otai ljutymъ zvěremъ*", "*a samъ vъ nočь vlъkomъ ryskaše* ("he leaped secretly like a wild beast"; "at night he coursed like a wolf") – these sentences may be understood as an assertion that Vseslav was a werewolf and turned into various animals, but they may also be interpreted as a comparison of the rapid campaigns of Vseslav with the leaps of a "wild beast" or "wolf".

The metaphors and the symbolism of the Tale are sometimes difficult to elucidate, as we often have no knowledge of the real facts which the author communicates merely by a metaphor (cf. the examples above about Vseslav). In other cases, for instance before the campaign, when Igoŕ "proved his mind with firmness and sharpened it by the courage of his heart", the metaphor hints at two processes of preparation of arms for the battle: "proved" and "sharpen", the basic metaphor being the "mind" (*um*) = sword.

4. Hyperbole is another favourite device used in "The Tale of Igoŕ's Campaign". The author represents princes as cosmic forces. Prince Svjatoslav "with his powerful hosts... set his foot upon the land of Polovtsian, trod down hills and ravines, muddied their rivers and lakes, dried up torrents and swamps; like a whirlwind, he snatched the infidel Kobjak... from the great Polovtsian iron hosts, and Kobjak fell in the city of Kiev, in the hall of Svjatoslav". Or Prince Vsevolod of Suzdal' "can stir up the Volga with oars, and pour out the Don with helmets". The regiments of the Černigov prince "vanquish hosts with war-whoop, sounding the glory of their grandsires". The soldiers of other princes "swam in blood in their gilded helmets"; this is an intensification of the usual in the military tales – "blood filled the valleys". And here too, as in the metaphors, reality is hidden behind imagery.

5. The same function of replacing reality by an image is performed by the mythological elements of the Tale. In other monuments mythological elements appear only incidentally and are at once either rejected by the authors or incorporated by them into the system of Christian *Welt-anschauung*. Thus, the pagan gods are mentioned in the sermons, though these latter are directed against faith in them (cf. III, 2, 5). In the Chronicle, prophetic predictions and omens are narrated, and parallel examples from Christian literature are quoted. According to the Chronicle only "ignorants" (*nevĕglasi*) believe that during an eclipse "the sun will devour" some mythological creature (serpent or wolf). In the Tale we more than once find representatives of lower mythology: Div, Dĕva-Obida; Prince Vseslav is a Proteus, a werewolf. Beside these the Slavs are "grandchildren of Dažьbogъ", Bojan is the "grandson of Veles", sun – "Chors", etc. The use of the names of pagan gods in the poetry of the Christian era has an analogy, it is true, in Scandinavian poetry and in the Latin poetry of the Middle Ages. But, most probably, the expressions "*grandchildren* of Dažьbogъ", "*grandson* of Veles" point to the author's euhemerism – a popular conception in Christian literature that the pagan gods are the product of superstition, and are, in fact, simply ancient kings and heroes mistakenly regarded as gods. This point of view is expounded in "Book of Wisdom" (14, 16 f.), in the translated Chronicle of Malalas (II, 7) and repeated in the Chronicle in the speech of the Christian missionary before Prince Vladimir; later it is expressed in the Chronicle once again (in 1114, in the Hypatian Chronicle), and it can also be found in the translated Menaeum of the 11th century (*Codex Suprasliensis*). Furthermore, the imagery of the lower mythology, outside the Tale too, easily coexisted side by side with Christian conceptions, just as "demons" did.

8. Metaphor and hyperbole represent only the most striking feature of the Tale's style. But we also encounter in it the use of diverse tropes and figures of speech. Some of them are striking in their richness. Thus, an extraordinary role is played in the Tale by euphonic devices: alliterations and the harmony of sounds within words. In this way, for instance, is described the initial victory over the Polovtsians:

С зараніа въ пятокъ потопташа	п-то-потопт-
поганыя плъкы половецкыя	по-по-кы-по-кы
и рассушясь стрѣлами по полю	по-по
помчаша красныя дѣвкы половецкыя	по-кы-по-кы

("From dawn on Friday they trampled the infidel Polovtsian hosts and, scattering like arrows over the plain, took captive fair Polovtsian maidens.")

The combination of the sounds *p* and *t* is to render the sound of the cavalry's trampling (a similar euphony had already been employed by Virgil). Another example is the memory of the tragic death of the young Prince Rostislav (1093) who was drowned in the small flooded river Stugna:

не таке ти, рече, река Стугна,	т-т-р-р-сту
худу струю имѣа,	у-у-стр-у-ю
пожрѣши чужи ручьи,	р-у-ру
и стругы ростре на кусту,	стру-р-стр-у-у
уношу князю Ростиславу	у-у-ю-р-ст-у
затвори Днѣпръ. Темнѣ березѣ (etc.)	т-р-нѣ-р-т-нѣ-р...

("No such words come about the river Stugna: meager of its own stream, having swallowed up other brooks, it did draw off their boats amid the bushes on both sides, lock the Dnepr up for the young Prince Rostislav. – On dark bank...")

One can see here what seems a deliberate selection of words alliterating with the name of the river Stugna – *struju, strugy*... Alliterations and euphonies within individual phrases are usual, for instance:

... пороси поля прикрывають	по-р-по-пр-р
... князи ... сами на себе крамолу ковати	к-с-с-к-к
... се ли створисте моей сребреней сѣдинѣ	с-с-с-с
... понизить стязи свои,	н-зи-с-зи-с
вонзить свои мечи	н-зи-с
... единъ же изрони жемчюжну душу	же-з-же-ю-ж-у-у-у
изъ храбра тѣла чресъ злато ожереліе	з-ра-ра-ре-з-же-ре

("Dust covers the fields – The Princes... to forge discord against themselves – what have you done to my silvery grey head? – lower your banners, sheathe your swords – alone thou didst let fall the pearl of thy soul out of the valiant body through thy golden necklace.")

We come across frequent paranomasia:

трубы трубятъ	—	trumpets are trumpeting
свѣтъ свѣтлый	—	the light is light
мосты мостити	—	to bridge a bridge
пѣвше пѣснь	—	singing a song, etc.

The choice of words is quite often (see above) determined by euphonic considerations. Harmonies of rhyme (*homoioteleuton*) are rare and probably accidental.

One must also add to the euphonic elements of words a certain syntactic rhythm of the language. However, all attempts to find in the Tale some kind of verse measure have failed: it is not, of course, verse, but a somewhat rhythmic, cadenced prose.

7. If we turn our attention to the imagery used in "The Tale of Igoŕ's Campaign", the first thing that strikes us is the considerable amount of auditory and colour imagery.

The author himself, as well as Bojan, "sings" songs of Gothic maidens in the Crimea; songs of virgins on the Danube are also mentioned; the author refers to the laments of wives of dead soldiers and to the lament of the drowned Prince Rostislav's mother; the lament of Jaroslavna is one of the component parts of the work. There are mentioned the war-cries of soldiers and the cries at the beginning of the battle – the Polovtsians with their war-cry even "barred the fields", whereas the Černigov soldiers with one war-whoop "vanquish hosts". Before the campaign "praises ring"; during the battle the soldiers "roar like aurochs"; the inhabitants of the town of Rimov "wail" under the blows of Polovtsian sabres; during the battle "spears clatter", sabres and swords rattle when banged against helmets, trumpets blow before the campaign and emit a "mournful sound" after the battle, horses neigh, carts creak. The author hears even the peal of "Russian gold" in the hands of Gothic maidens in the Crimea; he depicts the peaceful life recalling the cries of the ploughmen; church bells are also mentioned. Especially remarkable is the frequent mention of the voices of nature. Animals and birds appear very often (mention of animals and birds is frequent in the Chronicle from the end of the 11th century): nightingales, crows, jackdaws, the cuckoo, eagles, woodpeckers, river birds, wolves, foxes, aurochs, horses – every animal has its own voice, and for every voice there is a special verb. The whole of nature resounds: "the night moans with thunder", "the earth drones" or "knocks", clouds draw near with lightning and thunder. To these are further added mythological and metaphorical sounds: "Div" cries from the top of the three, *"Děva-Obida"* splashes her swan's wings in the sea, Russian earth (here personified) groans, glory "rings" ("glory" or "praise" here means not only a song of praise but also, for instance, "glory of the forefathers"). The author and the *dramatis personae* "hear" the sound of events remote in space and time. In this context, the abundant usage of euphonic and onomatopoeic stylistic devices is not surprising.

The colours are also very vivid; they are partly real and partly symbolic. The epithets "golden" and "silver" are very frequent; everything referring to princes is connected with gold – their helmets, saddles, stirrups, arrows, thrones, the roof of the castle, and so forth. The epithet "red" is also frequent; the shields of the Russian army and the standards are red. The variant – blood-red – gives the epithet a horrific shade: a blood-red dawn presages defeat, "blood-red grass" is an indication of a bloody battle, "blood-red wine" is a metaphor for blood; other variants are "purple" and "fiery". The black colour is used in connection with obscure and evil things: crows are black, so are clouds, the soil after battle, loosened by the horses' hooves, and the shroud in Svjatoslav's ominous dream. Blue is, of course, employed in connection with the sea, but sometimes it appears as an ominous symbol: "blue wine" and "blue lightning". "Silver" is again a positive symbol: the "silver shores" of the river Donec, which helped Igoŕ in his flight, the venerable silver hair of Prince Svjatoslav... The grey colour (like its variants *sizyj* and *busyj*) has no special significance; the wolf and the eagle are grey.

8. The art of psychological characterisation is worthy of mention. It is true, psychological experiences are in most cases conveyed in terms of their external manifestations: the protagonists sing, shed tears, moan and cry. But the author includes in his work three lyrical monologues: Prince Svjatoslav's speech, with an appeal for peaceful relationships between the princes, and a united struggle against the Polovtsians; the thanksgiving speech of Prince Igoŕ to the river Donec; but especially Jaroslavna's lament, original for the fact that she is not lamenting the deceased prince but complaining of separation from him and that her address to the sun, wind, and the river Dniepr bears rather the character of "amorous incantation". The Princess turns to the river Dniepr with the words: "float back to me my beloved, that I may not at morn send him my tears down to the sea". The author was able to fill these three lyric monologues, quite different in tonality with a vividly expressed emotional content.

By the use of metaphors, taken from military life or from nature, the author can represent not only the external but also the psychological aspect of his heroes. Of such are the soldiers' hearts "tempered in turbulence", or Prince Igor's spirit "sharpened his mind by courage of the heart", or the designation of Igor's brother who took part in the campaign of Prince Vsevolod as *buj tur* (courageous aurochs). Or, in the mouth of Prince Vsevolod, the characterization of his Kursk soldiers: "And my men of Kursk are glorious warriors: swaddled under trumpets, cradled under helmets, nursed at the spear's point. To them the roads are known and the ravines are familiar; bent are their bows, open their quivers, sharpened their sabres. Like grey wolves in the fields they roam, seeking honor for themselves and glory for the Prince". And the very composition of the Tale comprises elements of similar artful psychological characterisation. Let us recall, for instance, that the author transposed the eclipse of the sun – an ominous presage – to the eve of the campaign in order to stress in this way Igor's intrepidity and his thirst for military feats. The author says himself, "The Prince's mind was ablaze with eagerness and the omen was dimmed by his craving to taste the great Don..."

9. "The Tale of Igor's Campaign" has a number of features in common with the style of the Chronicle. The main feature is the use of aphorisms and set formulas. Some of these are repeated in the Tale as "refrains". To these belongs the formula "seeking honour for themselves and glory for the Prince"; then "and the Russian land is already beyond the hill"; or in two variants of the Tale about nature's compassion for human sorrow "the grass bends in sorrow, and the tree is bowed down to earth by woe" (on another occasion the first part of the formula is replaced by another – *unyša cvěty* (flowers have grown), probably because the word *unyša* harmonises with the preceding word *unošu* (to the youth). Some of these formulas are introduced with the patriotic ideology in Svjato-slav's speech, exhorting to vengeance against the Polovtsians "for the Russian land, for Igor's wounds".

A few proverbs are ascribed to Bojan: "Neither a crafty man, nor a clever man... can escape God's doom"; "If it be hard for thee, head, without the shoulders, it is bad for thee, body, without the head" (cf. III, 9, 7). But we find also proverbs which are not ascribed to Bojan, for instance, "*Koli sokolь vъ mytěchъ byvajetъ, vysoko pticь vъzbivajetъ*" – here the rhyme is characteristic too, linking both parts of the two-term formula ("When a falcon moults, high does he smite the birds").

The Tale is linked with the style of the Chronicle also by the frequent introduction of speeches. Besides the already mentioned monologues, one notes Igof's address to the army; his conversation with Vsevolod before the campaign; the mention of the princes' conversation among themselves ("This is mine, and this is mine, too"); the reporting of women's laments in direct speech; the Polovtsian khans, while pursuing Igof, speaking among themselves (their conversation is typical speech in riddles).

10. In spite of the originality of the Tale – the only extant monument of the historic epos – it does not stand isolated either lexically or phraseologically. Only a very small number of words used are not to be found in other monuments of the same (or a close) period, and, moreover, a number of such words are completely *normal* derivatives of popular roots. A whole range of turns of phrase finds exact parallels not only in ecclesiastical literature, but even in the translation of the Bible, in which so many passages are devoted to military events. Quite a number of parallels has been found also in the contemporary East Slavonic folk-lore, primarily in the Ukrainian and Byelo-Russian. The similarity with contemporary folk-lore, however, is explained rather by the fact that the old historical epics contributed to its stylistic formation.

11. Various hypotheses have been advanced concerning the author of the Tale and, especially, concerning his origin. No one of those has been proved: neither the excessively high appraisal of the Kievan Prince Svjatoslav and the Galician Prince Jaroslav (Jaroslavna was his daughter), nor the great space devoted to Vseslav, the appanaged Prince of Polock (Svjatoslav's wife belonged to the family of Polock princes) allows us to link the poet *definitely* with any of these principalities. It must be borne in mind that it was very typical of the medieval "bards" to wander from the court of one ruler to another. The fact that the poet knew military and hunting life well, and that he was perfectly acquainted with the genealogy and inter-relations of princely families allow us to consider him most probably "a court poet". The Tale is indeed a work of "court" poetry. But it reflects also the ideal of peaceful life among princes, an ideal which found no reflection in the political practice of the rival princes. From this point of view the author of the Tale rose above the typical ideology of the princes of his time, as expressed for instance in the chronicles of the 12th–13th centuries. At a time when every annalist is chiefly preoccupied with the interests of his prince and his principality, the author of the Tale is conscious of the community of Eastern Slav tribes and their common political interests. In this respect the Tale is an ideologically important monument, though this ideology reflects rather that of a great Eastern Slav power. Not for nothing does the author of the Tale mention the two princes Jaroslav and Vladimir Monomach, who came closest to the realisation of this ideal. In general there are in the Tale elements of "historic romanticism", of attraction to the past, which appeared in the 12th century in the period of political and economic decadence in many fields of life; by this attraction can be explained also the names of pagan gods (euhemeristically interpreted). Here belongs, too, the appearance of Varangian names in princely families: *Rjurikъ, Ingvarъ, Rogvolodъ Malъfredъ*. By this same fascination with the greatness of the past are explained the unsuccessful military enterprises such as Igor's campaign; almost at the same time the Novgorodians made a successful raid on the Swedish commercial town of Sigtuna, which brought, however, no further effects; also, the attempt by Prince Jaroslav of Galič to intervene in Eastern politics is mentioned in the Tale. In general, mention of foreign countries is very frequent in the Tale – beside Polovtsians we meet Greeks, Moravians, Germans and Venetians (as Prince Svjatoslav's guests).

Typical of the Tale, too, is the ideology of chivalry, which is also vividly represented in the Kievan Chronicle (cf. IV, 5, 4). Interesting as well is the appearance in a literary work of a feminine figure, Jaroslavna, though not endowed with individual features. Mention is also made of Prince Vsevolod's "love and caress of the fair daughter of Glěb, his dear wife". A number of feminine figures, real and metaphoric, are scattered throughout the entire Tale. This fact, too, though in a small degree, causes the Tale to resemble the typical works of "court literature" of other nations.

12. Attempts have been made to find points of similarity between the Tale and the epic works of Western Europe. Only minor resemblances have been noted. This is not surprising, as the Tale stands on a quite different *genetic* step from comparable works of other nations. This is an epic whose historical content closely reflects reality. On the other hand, the Greek epos, and the songs of Icelandic *Edda*, as well as the *Nibelungenlied* and other German epic works, and the French *Chanson de Roland*, being all based on historical material, are separated from the events depicted by several hundred years and the historical occurrences therein are therefore distorted and enveloped by the trappings of the saga. Their form also belongs to an entirely different stage of development: they are either more archaic (*Edda*) or, on the contrary, are products of a very lengthy stylistic evolution resulting in a vast exposition of the content. Closer to the Tale in some respects are works in a more concise though florid style – *Beowulf* or, even more so, songs about the journeys of Charlemagne to Jerusalem, but these too are not "historical" in the same sense as the Tale. In the Tale only the prophetic omens and dreams are unreal; only the stories about Vseslav could be a basis for the development of epic fantasy out of the material of the Tale, and possibly also the metaphors in the description of Igor's flight, who, having overstrained his horse, runs "like a wolf" (*vlъkomъ*), "like an ermine" (*gornostajemъ*), *swims* "like a species of duck" ("*bělymъ gogolemъ*") across the river, bolts like a falcon (*poletě sokolomъ*). But owing to the scarcity of written epic works, we do not know whether such development was achieved later. Some hint at such development is given by the contemporary epos (*stariny*) and partly by fables.

13. Doubts as to the authenticity of the Tale do not stand up to criticism. Nor are the conjectures put forth by some scholars acceptable, that the Tale is an

18th-century forgery (A. Mazon) and that the author of the forgery had aimed at imitating the 14th-century monument *"Zadonščina"* (see V, 6, 8; actually only Mazon attempted to prove this hypothesis). *"Zadonščina"* was discovered as late as the 19th century, so that it must be assumed that the forger was familiar with the now lost copy of the work. But even were this granted, it is completely incomprehensible why the author of the forgery, having in his hands the manuscript of a work on the brilliant *victory* of the Moscow prince over the Tartars, found it necessary to transform it into a work on an *unsuccessful campaign* of two petty princes. Incomprehensible too is the inclusion of a great number of obscure passages in the text of the "falsification". Finally, knowledge of the Old Russian language was so scant in the 18th century that it is utterly impossible to suppose that any scholar or poet of that time could have produced a text containing no mistakes in the language of six centuries earlier, moreover consistently inserting traces of a later orthography and of Pskov dialect; in the Czech forgery of the 19th century, accomplished with the cooperation of V. Hanka who was very well versed in Old Czech literature, the historians of language found up to 800 mistakes. Some morphological forms in the Tale (for instance, the dual) correspond to Old Russian, but entirely contradict the 18th-century conception of this language. Parallels to the Tale in Old Slavonic monuments (to some extent still unknown in the 18th century), also make the assumption of forgery quite untenable.

A not less essential mark of authenticity is the poetic excellence of the Tale. The sceptics could not point out who, among the poets of the latter part of the 18th century, would have been capable of achieving such a forgery. The *"Zadonščina"* – which in Mazon's opinion was the model for the forgery – is a work poetically so weak (see V, 6, 8) that without the participation of a great poet the forgery would have been impossible.

The manuscript of the Tale, which was in the same miscellany as the Chronograph and the story of Digenis (which at that time was still entirely unknown), was seen by scholars whom it is impossible to suspect of the wish to support a forgery; it was N. M. Karamzin and A. Ermolaev who first recognised the manuscript as belonging to the 15th or 16th century.

The appraisal of "The Tale of Igor's Campaign" was given by A. Brückner in a felicitous phrase: the Tale is "a real and not an artificial pearl".

8. STORIES OF TATAR INVASION

1. Stories about events so important in the history of the Eastern Slavs, namely the Tatar incursions, have not, strangely enough, been preserved as individual works. Their existence in such form is highly probable, and even certain in one instance. But stories about the battle on the River Kalka (1123) and the capture of Kiev (1240) are only extant embedded in the chronicles, and the story about Evpatij Kolovrat only in the body of an involved story about the icon of Nikola Zarazskij or Zarajskij.

2. The story of the battle on the River Kalka is preserved in the Novgorod First and Laurentian Chronicles; it is also extant in not such a good state, intermingled with local news, in the Galician biography of Prince Daniil. The story in the Suzdal' Chronicle, of Kievan origin, is historic in content: the Tatars at first clashed with the Polovtsians who had asked the Russian princes for help. The Tatars on their side tried to convince the Russian princes that they had no hostile intentions towards them. In spite of this, some of the princes set out on an extensive campaign against the Tatars, but this ended in a major defeat with the destruction of the army and the deaths of most of the princes. The story is narrated in the usual annalistic style (reminiscent of the Kievan Chronicle) with graphic details: the army crossing the Dniepr in skiffs which cover the whole river; a number of princes defending themselves for three days against the Tatars in a "fortress" made of carts; the Tatars putting the captured princes under boards on which they arrange a banquet, the princes being crushed to death beneath the boards. In later texts information about the death of the *byliny* "heroes" in the Kalka battle is added.

In the biography of Daniil the main attention is devoted to his escape by flight; the chronicler completes the exposition by justifying the flight of the eighteen year old hero, and speaks of his courage.

3. The story of Kiev's capture has been preserved in particular in the Laurentian Chronicle and the so-called "Voskresenskaja" Chronicle. Some idea of the original details of the story (as usual, its form changes greatly in individual monuments) can be gained only by combining the tales from all the sources. Having taken Perejaslavl' and Černigov, Batu sends spies to Kiev who marvel at the greatness and beauty of the city. In Kiev at that time rules the deputy of Prince Daniil of Galič, Dimitrij. Batu approaches Kiev "and because of the creaking of his carts, the bellowing of camels and the neighing of his horses", nothing else could be heard. The Tatars destroyed the walls and entered the town: "And one could see the breaking of lances and the blows on the shields, and the flights of arrows darkened the daylight". The Kievans defended themselves on the *komary* (scaffolding) of the Church of the Virgin Mary, but the scaffolding collapsed under the weight of the people, and the town was finally captured. According to the biography of Daniil, the Tatars pardoned *vojevoda* Dimitrij "for his courage". According to the same source, the Tatars set out against the Hungarians, passing through the Western principalities on the advice of the said Dimitrij who wanted to "keep them away" from "the Russian land", which the author understands to mean only the Galicia-Volhynia principality.

In the description of the Tatar invasion one can see an imitation of the Holy Scriptures, but especially of the stories of Flavius Josephus.

4. A number of similar stories about the capture of other towns (Kozelec, Rjazan') are preserved in the Northern chronicles. But the most note-worthy independent work is the story about Evpatij Kolovrat (sometimes called *Povest' o razorenii Rjazani* – "The Story of Rjazań's Ruin"). It has clearly a compilatory character; it cannot be asserted positively that the author assembled it from various written sources, but the presence of several sources (possibly oral) is certain. Moreover, the style is mixed; one can note in it echoes of the old epic style, side by side with the style of ecclesiastical works, and with elements of the poetics of either court or popular oral literature.

The story is composed of four episodes. The opening is in the style of the annalistic narratives: in 1237 Batu sends emissaries to the Rjazan' Prince Jurij Ingorevič, demanding tribute; the Prince asks the Suzdal' "Great Prince" for help, but is refused; finally he succeeds in bringing to his side only some of the minor secessionist princes. Deliberations take place on how to satisfy Batu with "gifts". But the Tatar, getting his information from one of the Rjazan' boyars, learns about the beauty of Evpraksija, the wife of Prince Fjodor Jur'evič of Rjazan', who had been sent to him as one of the emissaries, and demands her as a concubine. The Prince of course refuses, and Batu orders him and the other emissaries to be killed. When Evpraksija learns about her husband's death, she throws herself down from the top of a high palace and falls to her death with her son in her arms. This is a typical local "etymological" saga, explaining the origin of the name "*Zaraz*", "*Zarazsk*" from "*zarazit'sja*" – to smash oneself to death (in reality an old name of a palace, probably "*Zarajsk*"). This romantic part is followed by the narrative of military events.

The second part tells about the unsuccessful campaign of the princes against the troops of Batu, about their defeat at the siege of Rjazan', the fall of the town and the destruction of all its inhabitants by the Tatars.

The third part is an epic story without definite historical basis. It tells of new battles against the Tatars, of the Rjazan' hero Evpatij Kolovrat who has come from Černigov and who, with a retinue 1700 strong, attacks the Tartars. The entire story is devoted to Evpatij's deeds and his single-handed fight against the Tatar hero Chostovrul (Evpatij in the story is a giant). The Tatars defeat him only with the aid of battering-

XII

АN ILLUSTRATION FROM THE SO-CALLED RADZJWIŁŁ-CHRONICLE

A copy of the Suzdal' Chronicle dating from the 15th century.
Representation of the expedition of Prince Svjatoslav against Constantinople (971).

XIII

FROM THE RADZIWIŁŁ CHRONICLE

The same manuscript as in plate XII. Representation of a military expedition.

rams (*poroky*). Amazed by the courage of Evpatij and his retinue, Batu sets the captured men free.

The last part tells about the arrival in Rjazan' of Prince Ingvar' Ingorevič. He visits the ruins of Rjazan' after the battle (i.e. the first one: no more mention is made of Evpatij), and buries the dead. Then follows his lament and prayer. After that he sees to the funerals of the other princes, finds the bodies of Fjodor Jurevič, Evpraksija and their son, and buries them in Zaraz.

The conclusion consists of an eulogy to the dead princes and the announcement of Ingvar' Ingorevič's accession to the throne of Rjazan'.

In the manuscripts, of which there are about seventy extant, this story is wedged into a narrative in ecclesiastical style on the icon of Nikola of Zaraz (or Zarajsk). Thus at the beginning, is narrated the icon's transference from Korsun' to Rjazan' and at the end, various miracles (of the beginning of the 16th century) and the history of Zaraz clergy (reaching the end of 16th century, in later manuscripts – up to the beginning of the 17th century).

These stories, it is true, are undoubtedly later additions, but it is quite possible that the very story of Rjazań's destruction underwent a revision. Moreover, it certainly did not originate immediately after Batu's victory as there are anachronisms in the list of princes. From the presence and absence of information on historical events, one can surmise that the story originated not earlier than in the seventies of the 13th century and probably not later than in the beginning of the 14th century.

5. The story, clearly a compilation, is rather unified in style. But the unified style is constantly broken by the alternation of secular-epic and church-didactic phraseology and even by their interlacing in one and the same sentence.

The epic style, it is true, is considerably less vivid here than in "The Tale of Igoŕ's Campaign" and even than in the Southern chronicles. There are sustained descriptions of battles in epic style. The heroes "drink the deadly cup" (the image of battle-revelry), the battle is described by the classical expression "and they commenced the fight courageously", "and the fighting was fierce and terrible". Batu's army is "a great and heavy force". *Jedinъ bъjašesja s tysjaščej, a dva so tmoju* is a quotation from the Bible ("one fought against a thousand, two – against a countless host"). Blood ran "like a great river". Rjazan' heroes are called *udalьcy i rězvecy rjazanskija* ("the daring and high-spirited men of Rjazan'").

Somewhat stronger is the epic colouring of the story about Evpatij. Seeing the ruin of the Rjazan' land, Evpatij "inflames his heart", attacks Batu's army and sets out to "slaughter them without pity". The Tatars stood "like men drunken or insane". Evpatij slew them so that "the swords became blunt"; here the notion of the single-handed Jevpatij is clearly mixed with that of the entire retinue ("swords"). The Tatars think that the dead have risen. The first captives from Evpatij's retinue tell Batu ironically that they had been sent "to honour you, the great tsar, to accompany you with honour, and pay you homage"; "But be not surprised, tsar, there is no time to fill the cups for the great Tatar army" (here again the image of battle as revelry). During Batu's consultation with his boyars, the latter call Evpatij's soldiers "winged" (cf. *šesto-krylьci* in "The Tale of Igof's Campaign"), and Batu himself turns to Evpatij: "You have served me well with your small *družina* (guard)". All this, and much else, testifies to the epic tradition in the story.

Traces of this tradition are somewhat weaker in the last part of the story. But here too, seeing the destruction of the principality, Prince Ingvar' "exclaimed piteously", "giving a signal to the army like a trumpet"; he finds Rjazan' soldiers (*udaƖьcy i rězvecy* is repeated here too) "lying on a waste soil, on feather-grass (*trava-kovyla*)", he sees that their bodies are being devoured by animals and torn by birds....

But the presence of traces of old epic tradition does not hinder the author from using the phraseology of religious literature as well. The Tatars are "godless" or "honourless". Batu is "disgraceful in his godlessness"; he is moved by "the lust of the flesh". The Rjazan' princes are "blessed"; they act in the awareness that they "have received" everything in their life "from God's hand". The Tatar victory is explained as "divine wrath", for "who can withstand" this? Prince Oleg Ingorevič, captured by the Tatars, "reproaches" Batu; "He called him a pagan (*bezbožnyj*) and an enemy of Christians", for which Batu ordered him to be killed, and the author compares him with "the first martyr Stephen". When the destruction of Rjazan' is related, churches are mentioned first of all. There are fewer such turns of phrase in the story about Evpatij's deeds, but his soldiers when captured at first announce themselves to Batu as Christians, "We are of the Christian faith". Again the religious element is strengthened in the story of Prince Ingvar''s journey to the Rjazan' land.

To the beginnings of the new style which obtained at the end of the 14th century, one must ascribe also a certain, though small, number of compound words: *tьmočislennyj* (innumerable), *krěpkorukij* (strong-handed), *derzoserdyj* (bold-hearted), *lьvojarostnyj* (enraged like a lion). To these one may also add the "chains of words" in the eulogy to princes:

„христолюбивы, братолюбивы, лицемъ красны, очима свѣтлы, взоромъ грозны, паче мѣры храбры, сердцем легки, къ бояромъ ласковы, къ приѣждимъ привѣтливы, къ церквамъ прилежны, на пирование тщивы, до господарскихъ потѣхъ охочи, ратному дѣлу велми искусны, къ братьѣ своей и къ ихъ посолникомъ величавы."

("Loving Christ, loving relatives, beautiful of face, clear-eyed, terrible in countenance, extraordinarily courageous, light-hearted [kind-hearted – D. Č.], gentle to the boyars, amiable to guests, solicitous about churches, lavish in banquets, enjoying pastimes worthy of princes, skilled in military art, majestic before their brother-princes and their emissaries.")

The combination of religious and secular elements here is worthy of note.

Especially characteristic is the constant mixture of both styles. Thus, before the first meeting with Batyj's armies Prince Jurij addresses himself to the princes: "O, my lords and brothers! If we received from God's hand all good things, shall we not suffer evil as well? It is better for us to buy life with death than be subservient to pagans." He is ready "to drink the cup of death" for Church and Christian faith, but also for *otčina* (here: native country). In this address the traditionally epic "death is better than life in captivity" occurs side by side with Christian reflections. Still more characteristic is the frequently reiterated addition to the purely epic formulas, of the Christian "for our sins"; blood flows like a great river "because of our sins"; the whole population of Rjazan' perished "and all this happened because of our sins". Prince Ingvar' laments over the dead like a war-trumpet, but "also like a sweet organ", and here again "because of our sins". After the lament, in which once more secular and religious elements are traditionally united, a Christian prayer is put into the mouth of the Prince.

Repetitions of the same expressions also belong to the epic style: *udalьcy i rězvecy rjazanskija, uzoročije rjazanskoe* ("courageous and keen men of Rjazan', the ornament of Rjazan'"), "to drink the cup of death", and so forth.

The large quantity of rhymes, or rather of identical endings in the same forms rhyming with each other (*homoioteleuton*) is original; it is possible that this feature goes back to oral epic tradition. The following are instances: *mnogich gražanъ pobiša, a iněchъ ujazviša* (they killed many citizens and wounded others); or *požegoša* :: *padoša* :: *isěkoša* (they set fire, they fell, they slew); Batyj *želaja Ruskuju zemlju poplěniti, i věru christianskuju iskoreniti, a cerkvi Božii razoriti* (wishing to conquer the Russian land, and uproot the Christian faith and ruin God's churches); *počtiti* :: *provoditi* (to show respect, to accompany); *presěkaše* :: *krojaše* (they slew, they slaughtered); *byvali* :: *vidali* (they were there, they saw) *otpustiti i ničemъ ne vrěditi* (to forgive and harm not); *otъ zverěj telesa ichъ snědajema i otъ množestva pticъ razterzajema* (their bodies devoured by beasts and torn by birds). On one occasion, the rhymes follow one after the other: *jazyk moj svjazajetsja, usta zagražajutsja, zrak opusněvajetъ, krěpostъ iznemogajetъ* (my tongue gets knotted, my lips are barricaded, my eyesight starts to fail, my strength withers). There is also here a certain rhythm, a certain cadence in the language, as for instance in *grady razoreny, cerkvi pozeny, ljudi pobъjeny* (the towns are ruined, the churches burnt, the people killed), etc. To the oral tradition may also belong such expressions as *sila-ratъ tatarskaja* (the Tatar armed force), *trava-kovyla* (feather-grass), *pravda-istina* (the truth), and so forth.

The combination of various stylistic elements appears also in the lament of Prince Ingvar'. There are the traditional expressions of lament: "I have been left alone in such misfortune. Why didn't I die before you?" – "Why will you not speak to me...?" – "My dear sun set too early; beautiful moons, they quickly disappeared; morning stars, why have you set so early?" – "Do you not hear my unhappy words?..." And here too are reminiscences from "the Virgin Mary's laments": "O, my land, o, my land, o, my groves, cry with me", and the ecclesiastical: "If God hears your prayer, pray for me, your brother..."

The prayer of the Prince's brother is sustained, of course, in liturgical style, with invocations to Boris and Gleb. But in the eulogy of dead princes secular and church elements are combined once more. However, this was already customary in the 12th–13th centuries for monologues of this type.

6. The story has been preserved in late manuscripts (since the 16th century), and therefore the problem of the original form of the work and especially of the time when the collation of its individual parts took place is difficult to solve. Some elements of style, in particular a number of compounds, appear to indicate the influence of the Chronicle of Manasses (V, 2, 3); hence it must be assumed that some additions and changes in the text of the *Povest'* were made not earlier than at the end of the 14th century. But the main question of the existence side by side of various styles in the story – the "military" and the church style – is especially difficult to answer. This could have happened during the original revision of the work, but the Church elements of style may also be later layers. Moreover, in the description of Aleksandr Nevskij's life (see IV, 11, 3) we have a similar case of the coexistence of both styles.

It is interesting to note that the name of Evpatij – "Kolovrat" – is not, according to all appearances, an East Slavonic name, in which case we would have expected "Kolovorot". Whether an historic personage of such a name – in all probability a new-comer from the Western Slav world – ever existed, we have no knowledge whatsoever.

9. THE SUPPLICATION OF DANIIL

1. This rather enigmatic monument is usually called "The Supplication of Daniil the Exile" (*Molenie Daniila Zatočnika*), as it is named in numerous copies – without exception of later origin, of the 16th, 17th and 18th centuries. These copies vary so widely in content that it is impossible to produce a collated text of the work. The place of its origin is also un-certain, possibly Perejaslavl', but it is not known whether South- or North-Perejaslavl'. Only the time of the monument's origin, tentatively estimated by past scholars as being between the 11th and the 13th centuries, can now, on the basis of its stylistic complexity, be referred to the end of the pre-Tatar period. The 11th century, as the time of origin, can be excluded.

Copies of the monument exist under two different names: *Slovo* ("The Speech"), the shorter, and *Molenie* ("Supplication"), the longer version. The relation between the two is also a subject of controversy; for our analysis of the work it is indifferent whether the *Slovo* is a shortened version of *Molenije* or *Molenie* is an enlarged version of the *Slovo*.

2. Both monuments are written in a form of a petition to a prince, the author being often designated as *Zatočnik*, i.e., prisoner or exile; some-times this word is explained even as referring to a whole category of people. The old histories of literature strove to solve the problem of the author's biography and clarify the content of his supplication. In reality, it can hardly be doubted that the form of supplication is only a literary fiction similar to the supplications of Western literatures of the Middle Ages and of the literature of Byzantium (Theodore Prodromos or Michael Glykas). In reality, like the Western and Byzantine parallels, the "Suppli-cation" and "The Word" devote only a short space to the actual appeal for the prince's mercy, sustained on very general lines, while they devote considerable space partly to the apotheosis of princely rule and partly to various advice and instruction – not at all relevant within the frame of an entreaty. This glorification of the prince and the instructions are given in the form of a collection of aphorisms, feebly linked together. This reminds us of such a translated monument as the Ecclesiast, Jesus Sirach, *Pčela* (the "Bee"), or other florilegies, and the *Izbornik* of 1076.

Beyond doubt, the monument was not written for a particular prince, but for the reader, whoever he was. This form, however, served for the later revision and expansion of the monument. Every copyist, in the measure of his literary ability and erudition, allowed himself to enlarge the collection of aphorisms with supplements taken from oral or written tradition. Thus there found their way into the text aphorisms from various other literary monuments, the name of the prince, geographic data which gave rise to speculations as to the place of Daniil's imprisonment or exile, and finally – transposed to the work – the migratory legend about the fate of the petition, thrown into a lake by the author and swallowed by a fish which found its way to the princely table, thus reaching its destination.

3. Turning to the literary aspect of this monument, we are struck first of all by the extreme variety of its subject-matter. There are in it variants of the texts of the Holy Scriptures: "I thirst for your love as a deer for a source of water"; "Heavenly birds do not sow, do not reap, but hope for God's charity"; "Everyone sees a mote in the eye of another, but does not see the log in his own", and so forth. The authors simply quote the Scriptures: "Solomon says", "David says" (Psalter) and, without giving the name, they quote Job, Sirach, the prophet Isaiah; they mention figures from Biblical history, for instance King Hezekiah; in one instance they glorify the prince with words taken from the "Song of Songs". Among other quotations found by scholars are quotations from the *Izbornik* of 1076, from the Physiologus, possibly from "Akir the Wise", etc. Such quotations as one from Theophrastus obviously came from a *florilegium*. Besides these, there are proverbial phrases taken from chronicles or historic narratives inaccessible to us: the words "I would rather die than have the Kursk principality" are ascribed to another prince than in the Chronicle; there is a variant of an annalistic saying by Prince St. Vladimir, "You shall not gain good men [advisers or 'voevody' – D. Č.] with gold, but, with the help of men you shall gain gold and silver and cities"; an aphorism ascribed to Svjatoslav Igorevič (10th century) is quoted from an unknown source; the Polovtsian khan Bonjak is mentioned, and many other such.

The selection of aphorisms seems to be exclusively literary; according to all appearances there are no folk-proverbs, at least none such as appear in contemporary oral tradition. But there are kindred ones: a man is drowned not by a ship but by wind; rust is iron, and sorrow is man's spirit; the sea cannot be emptied with a spoon (*upolovneju*); "I ate neither butter from sand nor milk from a billy-goat" (a similar saying can be found in 17th-century Polish literature). Similar are also "secular parables", for instance, "Crayfish is no fish, hedgehog no animal, he who obeys his wife no man". Of traditional type are also "geographical" witticisms: *Komu Pereslavlъ, a mne Goreslavlъ*, and a number of other adages from different sources, added by later copyists. The themes of a number of didactic aphorisms are found also in later literature, "It is better to drink water with the princes than mead with boyars", or references to people thinking of the misery of others and forgetting their own (cf. stories from the Chronicle about sorcerers, III, 4, 5). There are, as it seems, allusions to fables, "It is better to cook iron than to live with a bad wife" – this appears to be an allusion to a fable concerning the soldier who cooked soup from an axe (already in Czech literature at the beginning of the 18th century). The entire cycle of aphorisms about bad wives is probably of later and literary origin.

Only in general terms can a scheme for the distribution of the aphorisms be established – the original plan was probably effaced by additions and revisions. After the invocation to the prince and the appeal for his "favour" sustained in general terms, follows a glorification of princely rule in similar aphoristic form: "Gold is the adornment of women, and you, o prince, are that of your people"; "The helmsman is the head of the ship and you, o prince, are the head of your people"; "Psalteries are tuned by fingers, and our realm by your rule", and so on. The general instructions to the prince which follow are characteristic of those times when it was considered that the personality of the ruler in some measure determined the whole life of the nation. Therefore "the education of the ruler" is a favourite theme. In the opinion of the author, a prince must first of all have "wise" counsellors, the author hinting that he too could be such an adviser. Then follows in the majority of copies, as mentioned, a motley mixture of aphorisms. Some of these are clearly taken from the "cycles" of other monuments, about bad wives and monks without the calling. One passage, of obscure origin, breaking from the gnomic style, describes the scene of a tournament or a circus contest.

A whole series of aphorisms refer to such social problems as the position of the poor in society, the oppression of princely officials, of rulers, and the rest.

4. The style of the "Supplication" is rather elegant. The introduction starts with an invocation to "brothers", reminiscent of the beginning of "The Tale of Igof's Campaign":

„Вострубим убо, братие, аки в златокованную трубу, в разумъ ума своего, и начнемъ бити в сребреныя арганы - во извѣстие мудрости, и ударим в бубны ума своего, поюще в богодухновен- ныя свирѣли, да восплачются в нас душеполезныя помыслы.‟

("Let us sound forth, O brothers, on our spirit, as on a trumpet of gold, and let us play on a silver organ – on the knowledge of wisdom, and let us strike the tambours of our spirit, playing on the God-inspired reeds, so that thoughts beneficial to the soul should weep within us.")

This is a very artifically constructed invocation with a parallelism running through (musical instruments and spiritual faculties). The majority of further aphorisms are constructed on the already familiar scheme (see I, 5) – two-term formulas of the type: *ich že bo rizy světly – těch i řeči čestny* ("The discourses of those are respected whose garments are beautiful" – of course said here ironically). Sometimes both parts of the formula are linked by rhyme:

Добру господину служа, дослужится свободы,
а злу господину служа, дослужится болшие работы.

("He who serves a good master, shall gain freedom; he who serves a bad master, shall gain much work.")

Occasionally we find alliterations which also stress the construction of the aphorism, for instance:

Богатъ мужь возглаголеть,	м-воз
вси молчать и слово его до облакъ вознесуть;	в-м-воз
а убогъ мужь возглаголеть,	м-воз
то вси на него воскликнуть . . .	в-н-н-вос

("When a rich man speaks, all keep silent and praise his words. When a poor man speaks, everybody shouts at him.")

In this last aphorism there are quite a number of other euphonies too, typical of aphorisms and proverbs, especially the repetition of the same words. There are also in the "Supplication" a few "chains of aphorisms" (see above the three sayings about the significance of princely rule) – *priamel* (see III, 8, 2).

Even if a great number of sayings from the "Supplication" cannot be considered original – the wisdom of the proverbs is usually not popular but translated – nevertheless this monument with its secular colouring is especially interesting to us, as one of the rare secular monuments of the old period.

10. ADAM'S SPEECH TO LAZARUS

1. Still more enigmatic is "Adam's Speech in Hell to Lazarus" (*Slovo Adama vo adě ko Lazarju*). This monument, extant in four defective manuscripts dating from the 15th to 18th centuries, but its content can be established from the extant parts. It is a story based on "The Gospel of Nicodemus" which relates the descent of Christ into hell. In all probability, the monument dates from not earlier than the 13th century.

Its subject-matter is that of "The Gospel of Nicodemus" developed in a number of scenes. This is the only *original apocryphal writing* of East Slavonic literature (Bulgarian literature knows original Bogomil apocrypha). The Word starts with a joyous song of David in hell, when he learns of Christ's birth and of the approach of the moment of "hell's destruction"; then follows the conversation of patriarchs and prophets. When Lazarus's resurrection comes near, Adam sends through him his repentant supplication to Christ on earth. Only fragments of the conclusion are extant – Christ's descent into hell and the liberation of the righteous.

2. Not only is the content of the Word interesting, but also its form – its rhythmic language and its abundance of poetic imagery. The beginning has only been preserved in a poor state; the introductory verse is somewhat reminiscent of the beginning of the "Supplication of Daniil". Then starts David's song:

> "O warriors, let us sing joyously a song today,
> let us leave tears and rejoice!"
> – says David, sitting in the pit of hell,
> laying many-eyed [sic!] fingers on live strings,

and he struck a melody on the psaltery and said:
"The joyous hour has now come,
the day of salvation has come!

I hear already the shepherds,
playing in the stable [where Christ is born – D. Č.],
their voices pierce the gates of hell
and come to my ears.

I hear already the stamping of Persian horses
on the backs of which the Magi bear gifts to Him [Christ – D. Č.]
from their kings – to the King of Heaven,
Who is born now on earth...

And Him, o friends,
we have awaited many days...

The Virgin-Mother envelops Him in swaddling clothes,
Him who Himself envelops the sky with clouds
and the earth with mist..."

The prophets complain:

And who from among us can
bear Him a message?
The gates are of brass,
the columns of iron,
the locks of stone,
strongly sealed...

Adam also complains – he and his descendants

have been in sorrow and disgrace for many years...

I saw Thy divine light only for a short while,
and now I have not seen for many years
The most brilliant sun,
I do not hear the storm blowing...

We so not see yet, o Lord, Thy light-giving sun,
and Thy beneficial light,
grief has enveloped us,
we grieve over our sorrow...

3. The imagery reminds us of "The Tale of Igof's Campaign" and of some other works of the old period. The singer lays his fingers on "live strings"; we come across words of the same stylistic stratum: *obida* (injustice), *tuga* (sorrow), *družina* (guard, friends). The antithesis of Christ – the infant, whose mother "envelops Him in swaddling clothes", and Christ – God, who "envelops the sky with clouds and the earth with mist", repeats the imagery of Joseph of Arimathea's "lament" in one of the sermons by Kirill of Turov. Characteristic, too, is the great number of monologues in the extant parts of the Word.

This mysterious monument is evidence of the originality of the lost monuments of the old period. Like "The Tale of Igor's Campaign", "Adam's Speech in Hell to Lazarus" is the only example of a type now lost, namely, the original apocryphal "religious poem".

11. SECULAR BIOGRAPHY

1. Secular biographies belong to a genre which disappeared later, and are usually not isolated as a special group of works. We have already come across two such biographies, that of Prince Daniil Romanovič of Galič preserved in the body of the Hypatian Chronicle (in some of the copies in an altered form), and the obituary of his nephew, Prince Vladimir Vasil'kovič of Vladimir in Volhynia. The latter's biography could not even be sub-divided into years and was placed as a whole in the same Hypatian Chronicle under one year. If we turn to the older annalistic tradition, we are struck by the completeness of the story about Prince Izjaslav II of Kiev (1146–54) in the Kievan Chronicle, which is included in the same Hypatius Chronicle. It is hardly possible, however, to isolate from the Chronicle any individual biographical work devoted to Prince Izjaslav.

Biographies of secular personalities differ from annalistic narratives mainly by the fact that the subject is brought to the forefront of the historical narrative, and all the events are recounted from the point of view of this person's participation in them. The second feature is the absence of strict adherence to chronological arrangement. The author of Prince Daniil's biography even apologises in one place (under 1251) to his readers for the absence of chronological pattern. In its original form, preserved in some copies of the Hypatian Chronicle, the text not being divided into years, the chronology was determined only by vague expressions such as "after some time" (*vremeni minuvšu*), etc. Moreover, Daniil's biography has a special "introduction" with reminiscences of

the past and picturesque borrowings from epic narratives. The biography
has come down to us in an unfinished state; Prince Daniil died in 1264,
while the biography breaks off a few years before that date (exactly when
is not certain).

2. In the Laurentian, Novgorod and Pskov Chronicles another bio-
graphic monument is extant; it has also been preserved in two separate
later copies – "The Life of Aleksandr Nevskij", the Prince of Novgorod
and then of Suzdal' (d. 1263). In the Chronicles the Life is rather clumsily
divided into separate parts and placed under different years. The existence
of other copies enables us to form a clear enough conception of the older
form of this monument.

Like Daniil's biography, the Life of Aleksandr has an introduction
devoted to memories of the past. Here, too, Prince Vladimir Monomach
is mentioned. This introductory part begins with a portrayal of the
"Russian land": "O, most brilliant and beautifully adorned Russian land!
You provoke astonishment with your many beauties: with numberless
lakes, rivers and springs in hallowed places, with steep mountains, high
hills, groves, pure fields, with marvellous variety of animals, innumerable
birds, large cities, beautiful villages, gardens, monasteries and Church
temples, with terrible princes, respected boyars, many magnates; you are
full of everything, o Russian land, O orthodox Christian faith!" Then
follows a dry enumeration of neighbouring countries, bordering on the
Eastern Slav Principalities. The author then passes on to memories of
bygone years, in particular of Monomach's times which he did not know
well enough to avoid anachronisms. Beyond Jaroslav's epoch the author
sees only decadence (*bolěznь krest'janomъ* – grief for the Christians").

This introduction has been considered by some scholars, without
sufficient grounds, as the beginning of the lost monument "The Tale of
the Ruin of the Russian Land". In both separate copies of the Life this
Lay appears as the introduction to the Life, and stylistically it is very
close to it.

Then begins the account of Aleksandr's life. He is the son of Prince
Jaroslav of Suzdal' and Princess Feodosija. The author compares him
with the Biblical Joseph the Beautiful in looks, with Samson in strength,
with Solomon in wisdom, and with the Emperor Vespasian in military
successes (Vespasian conquered "the Jewish land"). In other sources he
is also compared to Achilles and Alexander the Great, and it is possible
that such comparisons were included in the biography itself. Then
follows the testimony of the ambassador of the Teutonic Knights, that

he never saw such a "king among kings, or prince among princes"·

Then begins the narrative about the military feats of Aleksandr as Prince of Novgorod. The first clash is with the Teutonic Knights, the commander of which assembled "a great army and filled many ships with his regiments", came "breathing a martial spirit" and sent envoys to Aleksandr to tell him that he intends to conquer his land. The Prince says his prayers to God, "strengthens the spirit of his warriors" with a speech and sets off on the campaign. Then follows the story of how one of the warriors, a baptised Finn, Pelgusij, sees during night-watch the ship on which Boris and Gleb sail, to help "our kinsman Aleksandr". The battle is narrated in epic style, the feats of six warriors are described, but mainly those of Aleksandr himself who "made a sign on the face" of the enemy commander "with his sharp spear".

The ruin of the palace built by the Knights on the Novgorod soil and the liberation of Pskov, which had been seized by them, are briefly narrated.

The next war is described in more detail, though the enemy – the Swedes – are not named. The army of Aleksandr is compared to the army of the Biblical David, and the battle takes place on a frozen lake. Aleksandr says his prayers before the battle, remembering the victories of Moses and Prince Jaroslav the Wise. "At sunrise both sides met and there was a cruel fight, the crackling of broken spears, the rattling of striking swords, so that the frozen lake began to move and the ice could not be seen, covered as it was in blood" – this is entirely in the style of annalistic narratives. Eye-witnesses saw angels in the air helping the Novgorodians. Aleksandr returns home, and is triumphally met in Pskov by the populace and the clergy, who "sang songs and glory" to the Prince. The author reminds the Pskovans not to forget Novgorod's help.

There we are briefly informed about a few victories over the Lithuanians.

Next comes the exposition of Aleksandr's relations with the Tatars who had not reached Novgorod, but whose rule Aleksandr had re-cognised. The name of Aleksandr became famous in all countries "up to the Egyptian Sea and Arabian mountains, on the other side of the Varangian (Baltic) Sea, and as far as Rome". But "at that time a certain powerful king appeared in the East and God subjected to him many peoples". This Tatar "king", hearing of Aleksandr, commands his presence and his submission.

Aleksandr goes to the Horde, the "Tatar women" frightening their children with his name. Batu releases Aleksandr "with great honour".

Aleksandr rebuilds Suzdal', destroyed by the Tatars, where his brother was prince.

There follows a short note about an embassy from the Pope and Aleksandr's refusal to embrace the Catholic faith. There are some more separate entries, ending with the news of Aleksandr's death on his way back from the journey to the Horde (from "the other tribes"), and a short "lament" of the author: "Woe to you, unfortunate man, how can you write about the death of your master, how is it that your eyes do not fall out together with your tears, and your heart does not break from bitter sorrow?"

The story of Aleksandr's funeral is sustained in ecclesiastical style. Before he died Aleksandr became a monk. A quotation is cited from the sermon of the Metropolitan Kirill at the funeral, "the sun of the Suzdal' land has set". The "miracle" at the funeral is related, when the deceased Aleksandr himself took from the hands of the Metropolitan the manuscript of the prayer which it was customary to place in the hands of the deceased.

3. The characteristic features of the Life's composition are its introduction and its conclusion, as well as the absence of any chronological data (the delegation from the Pope is referred to as having happened "at some other time"). The Life differs from the annalistic narrative mainly by the silence over events from the hero's life which might have appeared derogatory; nothing is said about his recognition of the Tatar rule, though this recognition had a positive significance, as the collection of tribute by the princes saved the population from constant Tatar raids. Much is passed over in silence; thus no allusion is made to the fact that Aleksandr became Prince of Suzdal' at the end of his life. Neither Germans nor Swedes are named – they are simply "the enemy". This "depersonalisation" reminds us of the style of the Lives of the Saints. But on the whole, even the "nameless" events in Aleksandr's Life are historical.

The style of the work is mixed, but elements of the style of military tales from the Chronicle dominate. The style is reminiscent of that of the Kievan Chronicle in a number of expressions. But there are also many elements of religious character in the tale: before the battle prayers are put into the mouth of Aleksandr; on individual occasions the work recalls Biblical events and quotes texts from the Scriptures; the significance of princely rule is also characterised by Biblical texts, and the miracles connected with Aleksandr's battles are recounted. Church and secular elements of style are often combined in one and the same sentence. Sometimes we come across ecclesiastical epithets (pious, etc.) in the text sustained otherwise in annalistic style. The comparison of Aleksandr with Vespasian follows directly after comparisons with characters from the Bible; in one instance the story of the victory ends with the words "he returned with great glory", in another – "he returned praising God", and so on. Several fragments of liturgical character give the impression of insertions made in the text. Some scholars therefore have thought that the Life, in its contemporary form, is a Church version of a purely secular text. There is no need, however, for such a hypothesis. The mixture of styles could have originated under the pen of the author himself. A similar mixture of styles is characteristic of "The Story of Rjazan"'s Ruin" (see IV, 8, 4).

Among the peculiarities of style one has to point also to an element of epic style not characteristic of the chronicles, namely, the story about the participation of individual heroes (partly historical personages) in the battle against the German Knights. Of interest in the vocabulary of the Life is the small number of compound words characteristic of the Church style. Noteworthy too is the use of expressions into which words of one root enter: *svĕtlo-svĕtlaja zemlja Russkaja* (in the introduction), *pobĕždaja nepobĕdimъ, v carjachъ carja... v knjazъjachъ knjazja, vidĕvъ takoe videnie,* etc. The language on the whole is rather simple.

4. The appearance of the genre of secular biography is not altogether incomprehensible. The biographers could have proceeded direct from models of the short princely "obituaries" in the chronicles. Examples of lay biographies existed also in Byzantine literature, as early as the 10th century. In the 13th century this genre develops especially in Serbian literature, where it continues for a few centuries and, in the 15th century, exerts considerable influence on Russian literature. It is interesting that in the Byzantine, and still more in Serbian, literature of secular biographies the authors make abundant use of the stylistic devices of the Church Lives. These were used also by the author of the obituary biography of Prince Vladimir Vasil'kovič. Only the biographer of Prince Daniil almost never employed the Church style.

In recent times a conjecture was made that the author of Aleksandr's Life and of Daniil's biography was one and the same person. Reasons for such an assertion are far from sufficient. The compositional similarity (the presence of a similar introduction) can be explained by the identity of the genre; the stylistic differences between these two monuments are very great; and above all the most vivid linguistic feature of Daniil's biography, the use of the *dativus absolutus*, is absent from the Life.

The Life of Aleksandr exerted considerable influence on later literature, but it proved to be insufficiently religious in tone and was subsequently replaced by Church texts, real Lives, and no longer biographies of the prince, who meanwhile had been canonised.

12. VARIOUS WORKS

1. Neglected by scholars are the *Prayers* of this period. Among them the first place in stylistic perfection is occupied by the prayers of that master of pulpit oratory – Kirill of Turov, which have been in practical use right up to the 20th century. They are prayers for all the days of the week, three or four prayers for each day. They are accompanied by eulogies to the saints and then by pious eschatological reflections (on death, Last Judgement and future life). The prayers are framed in extremely pessimistic tones, the basic motif being the complete unworthiness of man; they are beautiful examples of the religious lyric. The entire collection takes up about a hundred pages of contemporary print.

From the 12th century is extant the "canon" to St. Ol'ga – a panegyric in which eulogies to the Princess are linked with eulogies to Christ and the Virgin Mary. The author of the "canon" is also believed to be Kirill. Vivid imagery is characteristic of the literature of both prayers and eulogies. The author compares Princess Ol'ga to a "wise bee", to a dove which after baptism flies on wings silvered by christening onto the palm of virtue. He brings "flowers of praise" to Ol'ga; the sins of men are "collectors of taxes" sitting at the "heavenly gates", and so on. The imagery, however, is mainly traditional.

2. The *epistle* of Klim Smoljatič (after 1147) is a purely theological treatise, extant, however, only in its revised form, and is only one of the epistles written by him. The author justifies himself against someone's accusations that he had quoted Homer, Aristotle and Plato. Kliment says that he has read at the court of Prince Izjaslav II an epistle addressed to himself by one Foma. The epistle transports us thus into a little known sphere of 12th-century literary life, indicating the use of Greek literature, at least in translations or *florilegia*, and the interest in epistles of a theological nature at the court of the Prince of Kiev (Kliment mentions also his ecclesiastical and political epistle to the Prince of Smolensk).

The subject of the epistle consists of symbolic explanations of individual passages in the Holy Scriptures which, in Klim's opinion, modelled on that of Greek theological writers, contain not only a "literal" but also an "inner", deeper meaning. One can see traces of the use of theological literature and works of the type of the "Physiologus" as well as of apocrypha. The symbolic explanation of the Holy Scriptures was not at that time a dominant trend in Greek theology.

XIV

AN ANGEL FROM THE PICTURE OF THE LAST JUDGMENT. FRESCO
FROM ST. DIMITRIJ CATHEDRAL IN VLADIMIR

(Principality of Vladimir-Suzdal', 12th century).

"Kirik's Questions", a Novgorod monument of the 12th century, is devoted to practical problems of ecclesiastical life. Here bishops reply to a number of questions asked by Kirik (a Novgorodian monk) and others; among those answering them is mentioned "Klim", probably Kliment Smoljatič. The questions refer to various difficulties encountered in the course of clerical life.

3. We become acquainted with the literary life of the beginning of the 13th century from another extant epistle, an instructive compilatory *letter* of one Izosima (in whom Sobolevskij sees Simon, one of the authors of "Kievo-Pečerskij Paterik"), addressed to Anastasija, probably Princess Verchuslava-Anastasija. This is an example of a private instructive letter; the author first cites examples of saintly women who can serve as models to his "spiritual daughter", and then reminds her of the Last Judgement, using for this part of the letter a translated sermon.

4. To the field of *scientific literature* belongs, first of all, Kirik's chronology (see above, § 2). The Novgorodian author gives chronological dates for Biblical and world-history.

Interesting from the literary point of view are attempts at compilatory world history, the "Chronographs", the "Hellenic and Roman Chronograph" composed on the basis of translated Chronicles of Malalas and Hamartolos, of Biblical books and apocryphas; the latter has not reached us in its first redaction. The second redaction originated in the 13th century, in the North-East, and here, to the original composition of the chronograph, "Aleksandrija" and Josephus are added. A further "Chronograph", a later historical compilation, is an outline of mainly Jewish history from Adam to the ruin of Jerusalem.

The *Tolkovaja Paleja* (Old Testament stories with Commentaries) is an enigmatic work. The time and place of its origin are unknown, the possibility that it originated in Bulgaria cannot be excluded, and it dates from not later than the 13th century. This is an exposition of Biblical history up to David, with critical notes derogatory to Judaism. The author uses the "Hexaemeron" and the comments of Theodoret of Cyrus. The method of interpretation, possibly the original work of a Slav author, is symbolic. Somewhat later "The Words of the Holy Prophets" appeared in the Ukrainia and Byelo-Russia; in a certain sense this is the continuation of *Tolkovaja Paleja*, based on the material of the prophetic books of the Old Testament.

These monuments have a stylistic interest, too, as they retain very few elements of the "heavily ornate" style in which some monuments of the end of 14th–15th centuries were written.

5. Of slight literary interest is the description of a *journey* to Palestine at the end of the 12th century by a Novgorodian, Dobrynja Jadrejkovič (who became a monk and later a bishop known to us under the name of Antonij). It is written dryly and colourlessly and is interesting only as an archaeological and linguistic monument.

6. The "*Epistles*" *of the hierarchs* belong to the field of official Church literature. One ought to note the epistle of Feodosij, probably "Fedos the Greek", to

Prince Izjaslav (Izjaslav II, 12th century) which very superficially enumerates the "unorthodox" features of "Latin" education and life. A more interesting author is Metropolitan Kirill II (ca. 1243–80) who, after the Council of 1274, edited a "Rule" with an instructive introduction.

The *gramoty* (records), increasingly numerous, are interesting chiefly as monuments of language. They provide comparative material from which can be judged the differences between the literary and the spoken language (cf. III, 10, 6).

V

THE PERIOD OF SPIRITUAL STRUGGLE

1. CHARACTERISTICS

1. The 14th and 15th centuries were very significant in the spiritual life of the Eastern Slavs. At that time some of the basic trends of later spiritual and cultural development became manifest and partially unfolded, but a final definition was still lacking. Moreover, at the end of the 15th century the opposing currents clashed more sharply than ever in practically all the spheres of cultural life. In literature, however, these spiritual struggles were perhaps less acute than elsewhere. This lack of clarity in the literary scene could be partly explained by the fact that in the two following centuries the representatives of that current which emerged victorious had carried out a "purge" in the sphere of letters. In some instances literary monuments were simply cast aside, and we have now – as will be seen – only the most inoffensive and insignificant relics of certain literary tendencies. In other cases, literary monuments were subjected to an adaptation that blurred their "untimely" elements, and deprived them of their individual character. This "censorship" – though only partly deliberate – was accompanied by other factors which always contribute to the loss of ancient literary monuments, for example, changes in literary taste, and loss of interest in the content of works of a specifically topical nature.

2. The literary style of the 14th-15th centuries seems primarily to have been a direct continuation of the heavily ornamented style of the late 12th-13th-century literature of Kiev. We have here the same abundant embellishments and the retention of a number of artistic devices; the same mixture of East Slavonic elements and Church Slavonic vocabulary and phonetics. The literary genres also appear to have remained the same. The only striking feature was the decline of the original sermon. Individual works of the Kievan literature continued to be copied, and continued to exert their influence in the literary life. The manuscripts of the Kievan works which have come down to us are in many cases not later than that period, and the boundary between the 13th and 14th centuries – purely from the stylistic point of view – appears much vaguer than other lines of demarcation between periods of literary history. Nevertheless, certain basic differences do enable us to draw these lines, even though, like all other boundaries in histories of literature and most of the divisions in the cultural sphere in general, they still fail to provide either an exact chronology or a final decision as to whether a monument belongs to one period or the other.

Alongside the standard of literary history, there are also some extra-literary ones, of which at least one – language – shares in determining the characteristics of style. Other criteria are in the realm of geography, politics and intellectual history, and these are of great importance when defining time-limits of a period.

3. The geographical-political criterion is fully significant only in later literary development, namely in the transfer of the centre of literary life from Kiev and the rest of the Ukrainian region, to the North and North-East, to the Great-Russian area. In the 11th-13th centuries the role of the Great Russians in East Slavonic literature was small and hardly creative. The attempts to date the beginning of north-eastern literature with the Kievan Paterikon and Serapion's sermons, are very dubious. Only a small part of the Paterikon originated in the North-East, and even the author of that part – Bishop Simon – was not only a former Kievan monk, but also a local patriot of Kiev (cf. IV, 4, 1). Bishop Serapion, also a Kievan monk, spent only a short final period of his life (two years at most) in the North-East, and only some of his extant sermons were delivered there (cf. IV, 2, 10). The first work of importance which belongs to north-eastern literature is the biography of Aleksandr Nevskij (IV, 11, 2–4).

In the 14th century, however, the literature of the North-East stands on its own feet, even though it still leans to a certain extent on the Kievan literature of the 11th–13th centuries. But in addition to the geographical frontier (which undoubtedly was ethnographical as well as cultural), there now emerges a political one. The Ukrainian and Byelo-Russian territories now come under the domination of Lithuania or Poland. The literary community breaks up, and when the peoples meet again – as late as the 16th century – they are speaking completely different languages, both literally and metaphorically (cf. VII, 6).

However, inside the Great Russian area also political life gave a new character to the whole of our period, including literature. The political context of the time comprises a curious combination of the struggle between appanaged principalities, and the simultaneous resistance to Tartar domination, a resistance gravely impeded by the princes' feuds. In the internal struggles all means are ruthlessly applied: even the support of the Tartars is not scorned but, on the contrary, sought. Tver' and Moscow are, with varying success, the main pretenders to overlordship. Literature devotes considerable space to these political themes, even though it substantially understates the real situation. After Moscow's final victory some of the local patriotic literature (e.g. the Tverian) falls victim to the "censorship" already mentioned. On the other hand, ecclesiastical writers especially stress the Christian character of "Rus'" and only reluctantly speak of internal discord in the "Christian" camp.

Curiously enough the role of victorious Moscow in literature is rather insignificant; even the "Muscovite" writers are partly foreigners (Kiprian, Camblak, Pachomij – see V, 5, 2–4, and 4, 9). Moreover, even the panegyrical epos about the Muscovite Prince's victory over the Tartars in 1380 is written by a man of Rjazan' (IV, 6, 5), and as late as in the 16th century the theory of "Moscow – the Third Rome" emanates from the pen of a Pskovian monk (VI, 7, 4).

Even more important appears the ever growing separation from the West, predominantly conditioned by political developments, and first by the Tartar rule which had somewhat weakened the bonds with Byzantium. In 1453 Constantinople fell to the Turks, but already before this it had to some extent forfeited its influence through the attempt to effect a union with Rome. Economic decline too weakened relations between the merchant republics of Novgorod and Pskov and the West. There were still, however, attempts to forge political links with the Lithuanian State, especially on the part of the appanage principalities of Tver', Rjazan', Novgorod and Pskov, but these failed because of Moscow's opposition. And Moscow, on the basis of denominational dissentions with "the Latins", now developed an ideology that seemed to rule out absolutely any link with the West. Nevertheless, in reality the help of Western technology was frequently sought.

4. Questions of language are the most pertinent to the study of literary development. The literature of the Kievan period used a relatively pure Church Slavonic both in translations and in many religious works, as well as Church Slavonic with an admixture of local vernacular elements (e.g. the chronicles). The Church Slavonic was then not as different from the colloquial language in Kiev, as it was from the spoken Great-Russian in the 14th–15th centuries. This parting of the ways was intensified in the Russian by a number of linguistic processes: changes in declension (corruption and shedding of the dual, shedding of the vocative, of the old palatalized forms, like *na berezě*, etc.); changes in conjugation (loss of the aorist and the imperfect, of the dual, etc.); changes in syntax (for instance the local dative and the locative becoming usable with prepositions only), besides changes in the actual vocabulary. All this resulted in the fact that the literary language now appeared to be a much more artificial language than before, thus, from the end of the 14th century, becoming subject to the influence of reforms by the new Bulgarian linguistic school of Patriarch Euthymios of Trnovo (i.e. the so-called "Second South Slav Influence", the influence of the Bulgarian literature following Christianization being known as the "First").

Euthymios's reform aimed at combining the old spelling with the Bulgarian pronunciation of the 14th century (the conventional differentiation between the ъ and the ь, which had phonetically fallen away in Bulgaria, the abandonment of the *j* ("jotation")) – Mapia instead of Мария; the Church Slavonic spelling of the groups ръ, рь, лъ and ль, in such cases as the Church Slavonic плъкъ – Russian пълкъ, which was then pronounced in a more Russian manner as полк. Likewise even "jus" – ѫ was introduced, which as early as the 11th century had no separate sound among the Eastern Slavs. By making a still more pronounced distinction between the written and the spoken languages, this artificial orthography prepared the way for the influx of archaisms, Church Slavonisms and a number of other stylistic devices. Once the written language became *fundamentally* different from the colloquial one, nothing stood in the way of the florescence of these artificial style-elements.

5. Church Slavonisms and (Russian) archaisms were now used in the vocabulary without any reservation. In many cases the Church-Slavonic words only now ousted the Russian forms that had frequently been used in literature in the past; thus instead of вожь, бологo, норовъ, сборъ (or съборъ), etc., there appeared since that time only вождь, благо, нравъ, соборъ, etc.

The already present inclination towards a heavily ornate style advanced now without hindrance and was buttressed by the influence of translated works of South Slavonic literature (e.g. Manasses's Chronicle, cf. V, 2, 3) or original compositions (e.g. Camblak's, cf. V, 3, 4). To be sure, this development should only partially be ascribed to South Slavonic influence; in considerable measure it was the result of inherent processes of Russian literary development.

Thus, there now appeared in literary works in great numbers, words, forms and constructions which had never had such circulation before. These included: 1) compounds (*composita*), partly taken over from the old "High Style" literature (e.g. the Service of Menaea and Chrysostomos's sermons), partly adopted from works which had recently become available (Manasses), and partly spontaneously created by a writer in any given context (compare for these three types: *dobrozračnyj, l'vojarostnyj, volkoubijstvennyj* ("good-looking, lion-like ferocious, wolf-killing"); 2) The use of participles (present participle in the Church Slavonic form with *šč*), and participial constructions became very popular; 3) Ornamental purposes were also served by pleonastic expressions of various kind (*s molitvoju i moleniemъ* – "with prayer and supplication", *skoroobraznymъ obrazomъ* – "in a speedy way", etc.) These in many cases stimulated the use of popular conjunct words (*put'-doroga*, etc.); 4) Pleonastic expressions related to paronomasias of various kinds, e.g. *edinъ inokъ, edinъ v'ъedinenyj i uedinjajasja...* (roughly: "A secluded hermit secluding himself in solitary seclusion"). Among these there are also such conjunctions which link words according to the sound only, without any semantic relationship, like *učenie i utěšenie* ("study and solace"); 5) Epithets, substantives and verbs, often form word-chains; 6) In such word-chains synonymic expressions are often joined together leading to a kind of word play; 7) Concrete ideas are frequently replaced by abstract constructions. Instead of "they had fallen" (*pali* or *padoša*), we find *padenie bystъ imъ*; instead of priest – *svjaščennikъ* – *sušča sanomъ svjaščennika*, and so on; 8) All this leads to the use of complicated and archaic syntactical constructions (in addition to the participial constructions, e.g. *dativus absolutus*); 9) Finally, forms which had already been lost by the colloquial language (the aorist, imperfect, even the dual, etc.) are also used freely.

The consistency of these basic features of highly ornate style in individual works (the relative "height" of style) depends, of course, on the author's craftsmanship and the type of work itself. But already "layers" of language, differing sharply from one another, are used for the individual portrayal of character, *milieu* and situation (cf. for instance V, 4, 7 and 5, 4).

The literature of the 14th–15th centuries shows such a profuse and assiduous application of artistic devices of poetry – topoi, tropes and figures of speech – that there cannot be any doubt as to their *deliberate* use. Whether there existed at the time systematic treatments of "poetics and rhetoric", or whether writers worked out a style of their own on the model of translated literature cannot be established now. Moreover, there are from that period copies of the concise treatise by Choiroboscos (II, 8). Mention is made, too, though unfortunately without exact references, of the Russian "epistolary guides", which had been used as models of good style in the Middle Ages.

All these poetical devices – many examples of which we shall encounter while carrying out concrete analyses – created a very complex style. The danger of such a style, mainly the loss of the real value of the content, was made less acute in the 14th century by the presence of a number of current ideological problems.

6. The "Second South Slav Influence" consisted not only of the dissemination of certain orthographic and stylistic usages. No less important was the "Hesychasm" introduced and spread by the Southern Slavs and also directly from Byzantium. This was a mystic current which had become prevalent especially at Mount Athos, in the 13th century, and around which extensive controversies had developed. The basic principle of the Hesychasm was the attempt to replace the ritual side of Christianity by the *inner* life. This inner life was understood by the leading figures of the movement (Gregory the Sinaiite – 13th–14th century; Gregory Palamas – 14th century, much could also be traced back to Simeon "the New Theologian" – 11th century) as the path of mystical exercise. With their mystical views, based on a Christian-Platonic theological and philosophical system, they offered concrete directions for mystical exercises. The goal of the mystical inner life is the approach to the Divine Being, and the means towards this they saw not in asceticism, usually understood as external mortification, but in contemplation; they believed that "spiritual action" required as the first step complete purification of the soul from all "mundane" thoughts and interests, and "inward calm" (Greek: ἡσυχία). The thoughts of the mystics should, therefore, be constantly directed towards the Divine Being. Prayer was the traditional Christian form of such a mental attitude, but the Hesychasts did not think of "prayer" as being an external uttering of words, but rather as inward action. They therefore urged "spiritual prayer" (*umnaja molitva;* in modern language, *duchovnaja molitva*). At the same time they advised certain external conditions for

this intellectual activitiy, namely, remaining in darkness, bowing the head, and holding the breath. In such a way a mystic could, if not achieve "union" with God, at least receive "divine light" into his soul.

The objections of the Hesychasts' opponents were directed against their theologico-philosophical views on one hand, and against "the technique of mystical exercises" they had developed on the other. Naturally, both these doctrines were, from the Christian point of view, fraught with grave dangers. The ultimate aim of the Hesychasts was, however, not mystical experience as such, but the creation by means of such an experience of a "complete Christian man" who could both be Christian and act in the world. Their final goal, as with all the real mystics, was not calm but action.

It need not be pointed out how much this current contributed to the resuscitation of the inner life of Russian Christians, although the theological and philosophical teachings of the Hesychasts were only partially understandable.

7. It is still not clear to what extent the Hermit movement – an indigenous Russian movement of the 14th–15th centuries was prompted by Hesychasm. It could have emerged spontaneously from the internal situation in Russia, in the same way as similar processes began at the time in the West contemporaneous with Hesychasm yet outside its influence.

The Hermit movement came into being as early as about the middle of the 14th century. Some monks who took the spiritual duties of their station seriously, and often too laymen who experienced a call to the monastic life, left the populated regions and wandered into the solitude of northern forests to lead there the life of a hermit. Undoubtedly, they had before them the example of the ancient anchorites of the Egyptian desert. They encountered many difficulties; the long and cold winter; the wild beasts; the lack of spiritual community and of ministry of the soul. All this was somewhat different from the situation in Egypt. But with determination the hermits willed their departure from the world, for they believed that only in this flight was it possible to discover opportunities for the spiritual struggle. Judging by scanty references in Lives of the Saints, in chronicles and records, this movement drew thousands of undoubtedly superior men who aspired to Christian ideals.

It is possible to list the number of reasons and motives which led to the beginning of this movement: the spectacle of Christian lands ruled by heathens (the Tartars); the hopeless political struggles and frictions; the decay of monastic life; the secularisation of the Church; the difficult economic conditions and oppression in social life. All this, however, only partially explains the Hermit movement, and then only in its externals. The movement gained momentum, and individual ere-mites reached the Far North (Lake Ladoga, the Solovki Islands and the Murman coast). The colonization of the North, advancing along parallel lines, created new dangers for the hermits. Together with Russian peasant-settlers, they were often viewed as foes by the Finnish population which had suffered from Russian agricultural colonization; they were fought as competitors by the peasants; they rendered themselves suspect and were persecuted by the princely administration which followed in the settlers' footsteps. But most of all, they were torn out of their seclusion and became once again involved in mundane entanglements.

By the end of the century, and in the 15th century, the movement already had centres and monasteries. These, however, could not retain the monks within their walls, for the ascetics left them to settle in seclusion even if still in the vicinity of monasteries. Only there could clear signs of Hesychast influence be discerned in the hermits' ideology (see V, 4, 6 and 11), but consistent Hesychast ideology does not emerge until the end of the 15th century.

The foundation of monasteries by hermits marks a revival of monastic life. The popular reverence for the hermits develops a new ideal of Christian life which in the beginning is purely ascetic, but begins to assume a somewhat clearer outline in the eyes of the people only at the end of this period.

The literature of the Hermit movement unfortunately leaves much that is not clear. This literature is not large; there are few legends, almost without exception brief, and often showing little understanding of the movement; a few treatises emanating only from the movement's later stage; and merely accidental references in works of other sorts. The pertinent works have been edited either very badly or not at all. In spite of the lack of clarity for us of the spiritual context of the Hermit movement, this should be considered as the most significant religious movement of Old Russia.

8. Even more vague for us are the two sects or "heresies" of the 14th and 15th centuries. No substantial monuments of these sects are extant because of ecclesiastical "censorship". By supplying tendentious accounts this censorship has also substantially distorted the image of the sects.

The first sect emerged in the 14th century at Novgorod. It is known by the mysterious name of *strigol'niki*. No light is shed on the views of the sect by etymological explanations of the word as derived either from the Russian *strič* (to shear) or the Latin *striga* (witch). From vague allusions and from the literature which was perhaps connected with the sect (like the collection of patristic sermons – *Izmaragdъ*) we can see only that the *strigol'niki* had raised the charge of simony against the official Church. We do not know, however, whether these allegations referred to serious shortcomings of religious life or were directed at local conditions or at the Greek Orthodox Church in general or were merely objections of rigorists against customary Church levies. It can only be said with certainty that in Novgorod at that time there was real interest in ecclesiastical conditions, and that there appeared men who – to some extent – had freed themselves of clerical authority. Any assumptions of a connection with West European trends (e.g. with the Flagellants) are unfounded.

We know slightly more about the other sect which likewise emerged in Novgorod at the end of the 15th century, but also extended to Moscow. These sectarians received from their adversaries the name of *židovstvujuščie*, i.e. Judaizers. The sect was brought to Novgorod from Kiev.

A number of works of these heretics are extant (see V, 2, 5). They are in fact translations of Biblical texts and scientific works from the Hebrew. This presumably formed the basis for the assumption that the *židovstvujuščie* had come near to Mosaic faith or even became converted to it. Such a theory sounds improbable simply because of the fact that its members included many priests and gentlemen of the Great Prince's court. If we consider the charges against this "heresy", the following general points do emerge: the denial of Christ's divinity; a sceptical approach to icon-worshipping and religious ritual in general; the repudiation of prayers to saints, and for the dead, together with a high appraisement of the Old Testament (it is for this reason presumably that they wanted to translate it from the original). All these characteristics remind us of certain trends of Hussitism, which gained a foothold in Hungary in the 15th century and also found some response in the Ukraine. A number of scholars argue – though without sufficient grounds – that almost all the charges of the sect's enemies amount to slander, and that the *židovstvujuščie* were merely influenced by the Renaissance, had advanced scientific interests and perhaps only wished to gain further knowledge from Jewish sources. The "heresy" became so widespread that it could only be suppressed with great effort.

The existence of both sects, and especially of the *židovstvujuščie*, points in any case to grave religious ferment. Moreover, the combatting of heresy confronted the Orthodox Church with the serious problem of ecclesiastical authority and Church-State relationship.

9. If we view relations between Russia and foreign countries in the 14th–15th centuries, we must first of all take into account the considerable weakening of links with Byzantium; even the knowledge of Greek was by then a very rare accomplishment. Curiously enough, after the marriage of Great Prince Ivan III with a Byzantine princess (1472) there became noticeable in Moscow a certain merely nominal acceptance of Byzantine tradition which was confined to court ceremonial and the like. There was no spiritual connection with the culture of the Empire which had declined in the meantime, and links with the West became even weaker. Use was being made of Western technical knowledge in architecture, art of warfare and medicine, but generally foreign experts were brought to Russia. Novgorod's diplomatic and trade relations with the West only occasionally brought in their wake the knowledge of Latin. Even this knowledge, however, was not being applied to making acquaintance with Western *culture*. The West became an unknown and uncomprehended enemy territory.

The abortive attempt of a union between the Roman Catholic and the Greek-Orthodox Churches in the 14th century (the Ferrara-Florence Council) played an essential part in the creation of an unbridgeable gulf between Russia and the West; the Russians themselves did not even follow the authority of the Greeks.

The spiritual communion with the West – which until then found its expression at least in a number of parallel or convergent manifestations – appears to have broken down completely in the 14th century. The Hesychast movement seems to be the last spiritual phenomenon having even slight parallels with similar Western processes.

10. The multiplicity of spiritual currents in the 14th and 15th centuries in Russia entitles us to describe this period as one of spiritual struggle. Although some spiritual movements of the time seem now both insignificant and incomprehensible, nevertheless all together they form the essential context of that period which, after all, led to the creation of a new literature (its connection with the Kievan literature is far looser than it may appear), of a new religious culture and of a new political power. All things considered, we have a variety of viewpoints from which to assess those forces which eventually triumphed, and which, during the

16th and 17th centuries and possibly even later, were to become the controlling forces in Russian literature.

2. TRANSLATED AND BORROWED LITERATURE

1. The translated literature of the 14th and 15th centuries is more limited in its range than that of the earlier period. Now, it was merely a question of completing what already existed, rather than the laying of new foundations. There were external factors, too, limiting the Southern Slavs' access to literature for translation. The Tartar rule had closed the borders, even if not completely, at least as regards cultural relations with other countries. At that time the Southern Slavs suffered no less serious blows from the Turks than had their Eastern brethren from the Tartars, and their knowledge of Greek declined considerably. An important section of the Eastern Slavs – the Ukrainians and the Byelo-Russians – found themselves within the frontiers of the Lithuanian State, and their literary life progressed from now on along completely independent lines without exerting a noticeable influence on Great Russia. The Mount Athos monasteries became a new and highly important centre of translating and copying activity. As will be seen later, the translated and borrowed literature in this period played a very significant literary and cultural role.

2. Religious literature experienced an important expansion through the translation of Biblical books not yet available in a Slavonic version. This happened at the end of the 15th century when Old Testament texts were needed in the struggle against the sect of the so-called *židovstvujuščie* (see V, 1, 8), and when it was found that some of these did not exist in Slavonic. Thus there came into being translations of the historical books of the Old Testament. Not only the Greek, however, but also the Latin (and even – as an aid – the German) renderings were used for translations. The Bible thus compiled of old and new translations is called "The Gennadij Bible" (1499) after the initiator of the complementary translations, Metropolitan Gennadij. But this translation is very bad in some parts, as a number of words and phrases which were incomprehensible to the translators were merely transliterated and not translated at all. Thus, for instance, *protivu castra* – Latin: *contra castra*; *otъ arse* – Latin: *ab arce*; and even *eisъ* – Latin *eis*, etc. It is obvious that such passages remained completely obscure to the reader. It may be assumed that here we find one of the first examples of a translation considered merely as a pious deed and not taking the reader into account.

In addition some texts of the New Testament with commentary (*Učitel'noe Evangelie*) were translated; especially noteworthy is that of Patriarch Kallistos, one of the Hesychasts (see V, 1, 6). There also appeared at this time some liturgical texts in honours of the saints.

Little is known about the translations of sermon-literature, because these are difficult to date; probably about this time was translated a collection of sermons by Basil the Great (*Slova postničeskie* – Sermons for Lent). Next to the enlarged redaction of the sermon-collection by Chrysostomos,

one should note, too, the beginnings of "collected sermons" in which some
new translations were included (cf. V, 2 and 9), especially the individual
sermons of the Hesychasts, either translated or taken over from Bulgaria.

The rise of the translation of theological tracts is significant of the period.
The translations are very diverse and mainly relate to ascetic literature; many
of these are directed against the purely external expression of asceticism; and
it was these works which were either written by the Hesychasts or were re-
commended by them for reading. A very important event was the South
Slavonic translation of the Greek-Orthodox basic mystic work – the *Areo-
pagitica* (a 6th-century work falsely ascribed to St. Dionysios the Areopagite
of the 1st century.) The text with a commentary by Maximus the Confessor
was used for this translation. The latter's treatise "On Love" was also
translated. About this time too there were probably rendered into Slavonic from
a Greek translation the works of Cassianus, a Latin writer, who has left us
an eye-witness account of the life of ancient eastern hermits and some considerations on monastic life. Also translated were the works of Simeon the New
Theologian, who was considered a forerunner of the Hesychasts and who had
placed inner life above mortification of the flesh. Other translations of the
period included the works of Isaac the Syrian, which enjoyed great popularity
as late as the 20th century (they were referred to by Dostojevskij), and then a
series of works by the Hesychasts: Gregory the Sinaiite, Palamas, Kabasilas,
Patriarch Kallistos, and of the Bulgarian representatives of Hesychasm:
Theodosios and Euthymios of Trnovo. Of importance also are the renderings
of a commentary on the *Climax* by Michael Psellos and of a didactic *Dioptra*
by Philip the Monk. Hagiographic literature was also enriched. It seems
that a newly compiled paterikon text had been borrowed from Bulgaria.
And again there appear among others Lives of the Hesychast saints, Gregory
the Sinaiite and Theodore of Edessa.

At that time a new "Prologue" text (cf. II, 3), the so-called "*stišnyj*" (from
"*stich*" – verse), also came to Russia from the Balkan Slavs. In this "Prologue"
the legends were somewhat wider in scope than in the old text and (in the
Greek text) each Life was prefaced by an epigram in verse. The Greek verse
is rendered in prose in Slavic. This text was not widely disseminated, but it
did have an influence on the writing of legends in Russian.

Apocryphal literature too was enriched by means of translations. To them
belonged a new version of the "Evangile of Nicodemus", translated from the
Greek, and also the explications, presented in the form of dialogues, of various
theological questions (e.g. "The Questions of John the Theologian" and
"The Questions of Bartholomew to the Virgin"); and the fantastic Solomon
Legends, parallel to the legends of Merlin in occidental medieval tradition.
It is not always possible to date exactly the translations of the apocrypha.

---

3. Scientific literature is represented less richly. The *Enchiridion* by Epictetus
the Stoic was translated in the 14th century. Scientific literature appears now
in more modern Bulgarian translations: first the two new *šestodnev* (Hexaemeron; see II, 7): the one by Severianus of Gabala (4th–5th centuries), the other
a Greek Hexaemeron-poem by George Pisides (7th century), which is more
a song of praise. The Greek verses were probably rendered into prose by a

Bulgarian. More chronicles became known such as that of John Zonara. This primarily offers factual information and, though mainly dealing with ecclesiastical history, also records lay history from ancient times to the beginning of the 12th century. Zonara's chronicle is also extant in an abridged form.

Far more important was the Chronicle of Constantine Manasses. This was written in the 12th century, covering the time up to the beginning of the preceding century, and was translated in Bulgaria. Ecclesiastical events – for him, too – are the main subject-matter; nevertheless, he devotes adequate space to secular and military affairs. Manasses wrote in a florid style which is rendered well in translation. The tradition of the military tale in the manner of Josephus has here been retained and enriched. Typical of the style of translation are hyperbolic epithets, many of them compounds. Some of these were apparently made *ad hoc*, because the translator often had to resort to unusual word-forming devices to render Greek compounds. The following are examples of such compounds: *čelověkoubijstvennyj, gorьkoserdyj, lьvojarostnyj, mnogoblagodarstvennyj, mnogopobědnyj, mnogožalьnaja skorpija, skorogněvlivyj, svěrepodychanie, světopitatelьnyj, tigropardus, tjažkošumjaščij, zvěroprogonitelь, zlostraža,* and so on (men-killing; bitter-hearted; lion-like ferocious; manifoldly grateful or deserving great thanks; much victorious; many stinged scorpion; given to flying into a rage; wild breath; light-nourishing or nourishing as the light; tiger-leopard; loud noise-making; beast-repelling; evil guarding). Some epithets are tautological in connection with the relevant noun, e.g. *mnogovozdychannyja stenanija* ("heavily sighing groans"). Epithets often vary, as *derzorukij* and *krěpkorukij,* or *čelověkosnědivyj, krovojadnyj, mjasoědnyj lev, serdcesnědivyj medvědь, surovojadecь,* etc. ("bold-handed, strong-handed, men-eating, blood-eating, meat-eating lion, heart-eating bear, raw-meat-eating"). The recurrence in these examples of names of animals and of the word "animal" is indicative of the comparison between man and beast – also often used by Manasses.

Manasses played with synonyms like *dolgoleten i star, blagoobrazen i dobrozračen* ("of many years and old, good-looking and beautiful"). The translator merely explained some words by *sirěcь* – "that means".

The characterisation of historical figures is colourful throughout: "the mad dog, the robber of men, angry and wrathful, breathing murder", "boar-like", "like an ancient and hoary eagle that has neither features, talons nor beak". Another hero is "like God's Paradise from which flow four rivers, those of Justice, Wisdom, Courage, and Temperance" (the four virtues of Plato's philosophy). Maximus the Confessor is "the Nile of Orthodoxy flowing in gold streams"; in another passage he is referred to as "the Nile flowing with silver streams". Names are treated etymologically, thus, for instance, the name *Lev* denotes the qualities of a good ruler, while the bad one is designated as *zvěroimenityj, zvěro-obraznyj,* etc. ("with beastly name, wild beast-like").

Personifications of countries, towns, etc. appear very frequently.

Exclamations are frequent: "Alas!"; "O, The allperceiving Sun!"; "O, Sun and Earth!"; or as rhetorical questions, "And what then?" The writer's reflections as, for instance, observations upon the omnipotence of gold, are introduced (perhaps following the model of the Greek tragedy) with such exclamations: "O, thou Gold! ..." or "O, Envy! ...", etc. Elsewhere, there are passages full of feeling and sensibility. There are, however, instructive precepts as well: "O player, such is your play – the wheel of life!" (referring to the wheel of fortune).

The battle scenes are picturesque and follow the old tradition of heroic tales. "He drew his sword and covered the earth with corpses as if with sheaves, and made seas of flowing blood." Battles are the harvest: "The harvesting and cutting sword and the sickle were outstretched —— and men were harvested like ears of corn." Armies are depicted by the lustre of their arms; the number of the host is like that of sand on the sea-shore. The sea also offers further symbols to Manasses. We often encounter in his work pictures of the stormy sea, which, with one exception, stand for political events. Other natural phenomena are also employed as symbols.

The purpose is always a moralising-Christian one and the Bulgarian translator appended to each chapter brief notes on Bulgarian history. Among those, in one passage, he describes the then capital of Bulgaria as the "New Constantinople". This occurs in a sentence that hints at Trnovo as being the Third Rome: "This had happened to old Rome, but our New Constantinople thrives and expands, consolidates and grows young; may it flourish until the end [of times – D. Č.]." Such style and content created a new school in Russia.

To the other essentially historical works belong the secular biographies of the Serbian kings, a genre that developed in Serbia in the 13th century and had also found a Bulgarian exponent. The genealogical work (the *Rodoslov*), based on such biographies, became known and set the example for the Russian *Stepennaja kniga* (see VI, 10, 3). The Serbian biographer's style was as highly ornate as that of Manasses.

Among other scientific works mention should be made of the translation of the two remaining parts of "The Fount of Knowledge" (*Pēgē gnōseōs*) by John Damascene. The "Dialectic" (Introduction to Philosophy) and the "Grammar' had by now been added to the earlier translation of the "Theology".

4. Narrative literature was also enriched. Both the most important novels of this period dealt with well known themes, the history of Alexander the Great and the Deeds of Troy.

The new redaction of the Alexandreis which became known in the 15th century was of Croatian (Dalmatian) origin. It brought together the pseudo-Kallisthenian and the Italian versions. In this adaptation the Christian motifs are more strongly stressed. Alexander is a monotheist and worships the One God in Jerusalem; he also acknowledges of the vanity of all human things. On the other hand, he is also a sage (as already in *Pčela*), but didactic sentences are placed not only in his mouth but also in those of his adversaries. The third characteristic of this so-called "Serbian Alexandreis" is the romantic and sentimental motif that comes especially to the fore in Alexander's relations with his Persian wife Roxana, as well as in the adventures of her father, the Persian king Darius. Roxana too is depicted in a romantic vein. She voices a "lament" at Alexander's grave: "O, Alexander, emperor of the whole world, you have abandoned me in this foreign land and have gone down

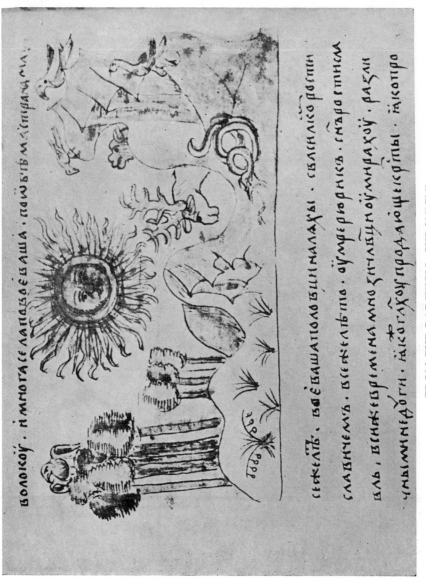

FROM THE RADZIWIŁŁ CHRONICLE

The same manuscript as in plates XII and XIII. A landscape (in the text of the year 1152).

A FIGURE IN PRAYER
From a fresco of the 12th century (Novgorod).

like the sun! O, earth and sun, mountains and hills, sea and gorgeous trees of the fields, cry now with me, pour streams of tears, fill the seas, drench the ... mountains that are poisonous to me". And then Roxana commits suicide.

The Deeds of Troy now became available in a new variant as part of Manasses' Chronicle. But here it was a foreign composition, riddled with Western elements; it may have been translated or compiled in Dalmatia (from the Latin). The narrative, as un-Homeric as that of Malalas, is maintained throughout in a fairy-tale style with extensive use of the dream motif. This new rendering (*Pritča o kralech*) does include numerous facets of Western court culture which were in many cases misunderstood in translation. We encounter here tournaments, balls, coats-of-arms on shields; the concepts of *honneur* and *courtoisie* are clumsily rendered as *čest'*, *dvorba, dvorščina* and *služba*, while the *belle dame* appears as *dobraja gospoža*, and love scenes are rendered in a very clumsy fashion. The translator, however, succeeds in finding good idioms for the military aspects of chivalry. Achilles looks on a good horse, "like a falcon eyeing a bird"; "from the days of his youth" Priam cannot "kill a sleeping warrior", etc. Didactic motifs are translated very poorly, and only the final phrase, "Thus God humiliates the proud..." is in the moralising tradition. Psychological motifs are much less extensive than in the Serbian Alexandreis.

At the end of the 15th century there appeared from the West the translation of the Tale of Troy by the Sicilian writer Guido de Columna (second half of the 13th century). This was combined with the *Pritča o kralech* and survived until modern times. The South-slavisms allow us to assume a South Slav intermediary. Guido de Columna attempted to write an historical novel in the true sense of the word. Fundamentally, Guido's novel (in 35 books) has as its foundation the same tradition concerning the alleged participants in the war, Diktys and Dares. This tradition had already appeared in the earliest Slavonic translation, in the Chronicle of Malalas. But this rendering describes events more extensively than the Homeric poems (which had also been substantially enlarged from the Greek tragedies and other traditions) and discards the mythological element (i.e. the gods' part in the contest) but retains the fabulous material. The translation is probably the work of a Ukrainian or a Byelo-Russian; there appear words like *izradca, valki, treba, voljat, djakujut,* etc. (traitor, wars, necessary, they elect, they thank). Furthermore, the translation is described as "Russian", which was impossible in 15th–16th century Moscow, since the written literary language was never referred to as "Russian". It is not impossible that the East-slavic text was based on a South-slavic original (there are many South-slavic peculiarities in it). In any case, the work of Guido de Columna came to Russia: it is cited in Moscow in 1537.

The narrative includes both the prelude to, and the aftermath of, the war (the Argonauts' voyage, etc.), and it thus became a further source for the knowledge of classical mythology in Russia. The chivalric aspect of the work, the attempts at psychological characterisation, especially in the love elements, were scarcely appreciated by the Muscovite reader. Guido's novel contains, however, a strong strain of moralizing, albeit in the spirit of knightly morals, in which many sentimental and psychological elements appear (the heroes weep, Achilles is unable to sleep because his love for Polyxena conflicts with his military duties, etc.). But the battle scenes still recall the old formulas of the 11th–13th centuries, for they have older sources in common. Thus, before the battle begins, speeches are delivered to the troops, the arms are gilded and the silks are embroidered with flowers. The soldiers are likened to flowers – an unusual metaphor in Eastern Slav tradition. The battle is marked by the clangor of arms, the earth is dyed red with blood, the fighters "breathe the fire of boldness (*jarostъ*)". Nor are traditional expressions lacking: the warriors gird themselves for battle (The Tale of Igor's Campaign), "to mount a horse (*na konь vschoditъ*)", the troops "roar like lions", the air is filled with clamour and groans. Rather unusual, though brief, are the descriptions of the time of day, especially of the dawn. Poetic pictures of heroes, and particularly of heroines, although not new, are less awkwardly handled than by Malalas.

Guido's work was quoted by the 16th-century writer Tučkov, and later by Ivan the Terrible. It was also used by writers of the 17th century, the authors of works on the interregnum, etc. In 1709, by command of Peter I, Guido's book was printed, being mistakenly considered as a historical work.

As far as style is concerned, this novel substantially enriched the old elements of East Slavonic stylistics. Moreover, it assisted authors in varying further the traditional formulas of style; regrettably the new elements in the content exerted no influence.

A new Bulgarian translation of the "Stefanit and Ichnilat" romance (II, 10) also became known at this time.

It appears that from Dalmatia, too, came the curious tale of the "Twelve Dreams of Šachaiša (or, of Mamer)". Most probably this possibly oriental story reached the Slavs through an unknown (non-extant) Greek version. The tale relates the twelve dreams of Šachaiša, the king of the town of Iriin, and their meaning as expounded by the sage Mamer. All the dreams are viewed as latter-day omens; and so "when that evil time comes", a general transformation will set in – "the upside-down world" in which not only will social relations be reversed but also "the elements themselves will alter their habits... the sun and the moon will darken and the stars will fall... the years and months will shorten, and the world will then come to an end". The eschatological feeling undoubtedly corresponded to the aftermath of Tartar invasions, and we do not find here any Christian view of the end of the world.

A tale concerning the atrocities of the Wallachian (Rumanian) Prince Drakula (the historic Vlad Cepeš) was also translated from a West European account and was probably disseminated most widely during the continuous waves of terror unleashed by the Great Princes of Muscovy, primarily under Ivan the Terrible.

5. A separate, and not at all clearly defined group of translations belongs to the work of the *židovstvujuščie* (see V, 1, 8).

There have come down to us no writings of this sect, whose beliefs and spiritual origins are still uncertain, which would give an insight into their teachings. Nevertheless, we learn something about their interest in the Bible and in scientific literature. The works ascribed to the members of the sect are all translations from the Hebrew, but it is questionable whether all of them belong to the *židovstvujuščie*. It cannot be ruled out that some of these were translated by Jews themselves for the use of their co-religionists who did not understand Hebrew any longer (G. Florovskij) as, for instance, the translation of the Psalms, by Fjodor the Jew, in the form of a Jewish prayer-book. Moreover, some of these translations were certainly made in the Ukraine or in Byelo-Russia; among the Great Russians they were merely copied and sometimes slightly altered lexically.

Translations which with great probability may be ascribed to the *židovstvujuščie* are the renderings from the Hebrew of the Biblical books of Esther and Daniel, and the Slavonic translation of the Pentateuch (the Books of Moses) corrected in accordance with the Hebrew original. The *židovstvujuščie* presumably had also worked on other biblical books not yet extant in Slavonic. Such activity would correspond to the interests of Western Protestants (the Hussites). Nothing is learned, however, of the sect's views, and equally little can be derived from the translations of scientific literature. To the latter belongs the Lunar Table, "The Six Wings" (*Šestokryl*) which presumably served originally for calculating the date of Easter but was later employed for mystical ends (for foretelling the future?). The other works are philosophical: the Logic, presented under the name of *Aviasaf*, but in reality the work of the Jewish philosopher Moses Maimonides (d. 1204), "The Philosopher's Aims" by the Arab philosopher Algazali (1059–1111) – a prolegomenary work, and finally the pseudo-Aristotelian *Secreta Secretorum* (*Tajnaja Tajnych* or *Aristotelevy vrata*), an Arabic work which is a kind of treatise on physiognomy and character allegedly written by Aristotle for Alexander the Great. The Slavonic translation was prepared from the Hebrew original with additional material from Maimonides, the Arab physician Alrazi (Rhazes, 9th–10th century), the Greek physician Galen (2nd century A.D.), and another still unknown source. Hence, the Slavonic version also includes dietary and medical instructions. The translations vary: the ponderous language of the Logic can be contrasted with the general clarity of the *Secreta Secretorum*. In all the renderings, the attempt is discernible to replace the old terminology (going back as far as the translations of John Damascene) by new philosophical and scientific (mathematical and medical) terms. This was successful in some measure, but did not enjoy much popularity. On the other hand, it is possible that some Ukrainian and Byelo-Russian elements and, through their intermediary, Polish as well, had entered Russian literary language through the translations of the *židovstvujuščie*.

The cosmography of the *židovstvujuščie* has not been sufficiently studied. It envisaged the system of the world according to Ptolemy, but followed an Arabic source which had altered the details of the Ptolemaic system. The translation, made from Hebrew, employed the same terminology as the other works of the *židovstvujuščie*, and is probably of Ukrainian or Byelo-Russian origin (as too are some of the afore-mentioned works, primarily the Logic and the *Secreta Secretorum*).

Moreover, these works were known in the West. The *Secreta Secretorum* was translated into Latin in the 13th century at the latest. There was also a French version in the 13th century. A Czech translation existed in the 15th century, and in the 16th, a version by Bavor Radovský. The Latin translation was already printed in the 15th century. Maimonides' Logic and Algazali's book also appeared in Latin early in the 16th century. An Arabic cosmography by Al-Bitrogi – which in some respects is reminiscent of the cosmography of the *židovstvujuščie* – appeared in Latin print in the first half of the 16t hcentury. Thus the selection of translations by the *židovstvujuščie* corresponded to the interests of the late Middle Ages in the West and of the Renaissance.

6. The sources from which translations were made were still mainly Greek. Through the intermediary of the Southern Slavs (the Croats) translations from Latin were added, and the *židovstvujuščie* turned to Hebrew literature. Translations made at Mount Athos are often of uncertain origin, i.e., it is not always easy to ascertain to what Slav nationality the translator belonged. In any case, during this period, Russian literature was being enriched by translations of original works not only of the Bulgarians, but also of the Serbs and Croats. Polish influences do not yet seem apparent, but there is a flow, even if of very limited extent, to the Great Russians of the newer Byelo-Russian and Ukrainian literatures. The languages, especially in the scope of their vocabulary, have become so different, that it is possible to discern in such works obvious traces of Great Russian redactions.

3. SERMONS

1. Sermons rapidly decline as a literary genre in the 14th–15th centuries, to disappear almost completely in the 16th century. This happened, of course, because practically no preacher recorded and handed down his sermons in written form. At all events, from this period there are extant only the sermons and instructions of three high churchmen, in which it is not always possible to draw the line between sermon and epistle. And it is very interesting to note that all three were foreigners.

2. The only epistles without literary embellishment are the work of the Bulgarian Metropolitan Kiprian (Cyprian) (1389–1406); these he sent primarily to priests on various occasions. His expectation of the end of the world in the year 7000 (1492) is of some interest.

3. Some of the works of Kiprian's successor – Metropolitan Fotij (Photios) the Greek (1409–1430) – should also be considered as sermons. These are three sermons for different feasts, two on Evangelical texts, three on Divine punishments (hunger, drought and Black Death); his epistles are also extant. It is unlikely that Fotij himself wrote his works in Russian Church Slavonic; he probably composed them in Greek. They are without much ornament but are very interesting from the point of view of cultural history. The Metropolitan in his writings speaks against the superstition of trial by combat (*pole* – i.e. duel), and Hesychast influence can be seen in his recommendation of uninterrupted prayer. His main stylistic device is the metaphor. Hence, the already traditional parallelisms of Christ's Resurrection and the spring, of the spiritual shepherd and the ship's captain, appear in a more original guise: as a man from whom various streams flow;the grades of spiritual completeness are represented by a ladder (climax) – slavery, hired labour, sonship of God. All that is traditional and probably borrowed.

4. A preacher of completely different stature was Gregory Camblak, a Bulgarian from Rumanian lands, or a Rumanian, who was Metropolitan of Kiev before 1416, and delivered there many sermons which are of some significance for Ukrainian literature. To Russian literature he is of interest because his sermons, not only those of the Kievan times, but also those he delivered both before and after in Moldavia, are extant in Russian copies, and in the 16th century appeared in the *Četji Minei* as a collection of nineteen sermons.

Camblak's sermons are representative of the high oratorical style, and scholars are wrong to couple the author's name with that of Pachomij the Serb (see V, 4, 9). Camblak's sermons are full of tension and contain rather little moral instruction, being more concerned with dogma. But in general they convey information to the listener or reader; for instance there are tales concerning the lives of the saints, and it appears that they were able to move the listener emotionally, which, after all, is one of the aims of a sermon.

About twenty-six works of Camblak are extant; these include two hagiographical tales and a biography of King Stephen of Serbia, also presented in hagiographical style. We encounter sermons partly devoted to saints (St. George, the Apostles Peter and Paul, St. John the Baptist, the Prophet Elias, the Old Hermits, etc.), and partly to certain days in the Church calendar, while specific questions are the subject of others. They are composed in a variety of ways, several being in the form of panegyrics. In others (on Good Friday), laments (*plač*) are introduced; thus, as in the case of Kirill of Turov, there are laments of the Virgin and of Joseph of Arimathea. For Holy Thursday, Camblak devises his sermon as the prosecutor's case against Judas, addressing the latter directly. Camblak also makes John the Baptist speak to Herod. In other cases he develops any given theme in a rather systematic fashion. Thus in the sermon about the dead (*ob usopšich*) he develops the theme "We are but guests and wanderers here..." (Peter's First Epistle) with the picture of this world's worthlessness, for it is but shadow, grass and dream. He does this to show the way towards a better life of virtue. He returns to the same theme in the sermon on the monastic life where, as additional motifs, he makes use of other ideas (monks as bees who collect honey from the flowers, i.e., from books, and so on). The sermon delivered five days before Christmas is interesting from the psychological point of view, because Camblak speaks here of the "Heart's Betterment", and attempts to make the meaning of the liturgy clear to his listeners.

Nevertheless, it is impossible to deny the predominance of rhetorical elements in all his sermons. Here belong exclamations directed to the listener and apostrophizing him or other persons and objects. "O, Sun!... O, Moon!..." are traditional appeals in supplications. Camblak, how-ever, as stated already, in one of his sermons speaks directly to Judas; in another, he makes God speak to the Prophet Elias, and elsewhere, he asks rhetorical questions. Characteristic, too, are the repetitions of similar exclamations or questions; but he uses this device with moder-ation; repetition is generally used only three to five times. Thus in the sermon on the day of Jesus' entry into Jerusalem (Palm Sunday): "Once again the... Saviour enters Jerusalem, and once again (there are) miracles! Once again the promise of the Resurrection, and once again the dead arise!" (Lazarus). Camblak then asks who taught the city's inhabitants to receive Christ in such a festive way: "Who made them do so? Who taught them to receive Him in such a way? Who suggested to them to call Him that...? [David's Son – D.Č.]" (five times *kto* – "who"). Longer word- or sentence-chains appear rarely, as for instance:

> At night the rich man is devoured by anxiety, –
> how he can purchase much at a low price,
> how he can build for such an amount houses of two and three storeys,
> how he may well distribute [his estate] among his children,
> how he can furnish his estates and property,
> how he should plant his garden,
> how he should increase his herds and flocks,
> how he should rig out a ship,
> how he should load his purchases,
> how he should go on a long journey...

At times such chains are linked with *homoioteleuton* (rhyme), as

> *oružija oplъčajutsja,*
> *mečeve obnažajutsja,*
> *slugy podvizajutsja...*

> ("Arms are being prepared for the campaign,
> Swords are being drawn,
> Servants are toiling...").

In the panegyrics, epithets are accumulated but not in overlong chains. Interesting are the metaphors and comparisons; Camblak often develops a rich symbolism which enters into the details of a picture. Thus he ascribes symbolic meaning to details in John the Baptist's life: his food – honey, his drink – water, are easy to explain; camel-hair is a "philosophical (*ljubomudrennoe*) ornament", and leather stands for valour. There is an explanation of the Cross. Its four points are equated to the four confines of the earth, to the four elements, to the four seasons, to the ship's cruciform mast, to Moses who extended his hands cross-wise in prayer, and so on. And now the Cross is for us "the banner, and the spear, and the shield, and the sword, and the bow, and the good quiver filled with arrows certain of reaching the mark, and the armour, and the helmet ...". Some of the metaphors are paradoxical, as, for instance, the comparison of St. George's body covered with wounds to the earth bedecked with flowers.

Camblak's language contains compounds which accumulate in some instances, such as *blagopristupnyj, sъpostradatelьnyj, posětitelьnyj, blagousrъdnyj, blagokazatelьnyj, neprerekatelьnyj*, etc. ("easily accessible, compassionate, visiting, eager in goodness, showing the good, incontrovertible"). All types of abstractions are used, though their number is not overwhelming. Participial constructions are not excessive for the normal usage of the period.

In any case, Camblak's sermons were an important factor in the development of the 16th century literary style (cf. VI, 1).

4. LIVES OF THE SAINTS

1. Lives of the Saints represent an important and extensive type of literature in the 14th and 15th centuries. The preponderance of the religious element in cultural life is one of the basic reasons for th extent of this religious genre. Its predominance is undoubtedly connected with major upheavals both external (the Tartar yoke) and internal (the rivalry of the seceding principalities for supremacy). But not without significance were infiltrations from Byzantium and the Southern Slavs. The impact of Tartar domination in Russia was enhanced by Turkish advances in the Balkans and finally by their seizure of Constantinople. The Christian Orthodox world was retreating before the heathen along the whole line. This general pressure could not remain without consequences; for that reason alone Hesychasm found a very suitable ground for its development.

It is regrettable that the Lives of the Saints have been only inadequately examined as works of literature. V. Ključevskij appraised them as a purely historical source, E. Fedotov as a source for the history of Russian piety, and N. Serebrjanskij confined his interest to the legends of prince-saints. Ja. Kadlubovskij was the only scholar to devote to them studies within the more exact meaning of literary history. R. Jagoditsch made important methodological suggestions for research into their style.

2. Metropolitan Petr (Peter; 1308–1325), who transferred the Metropolitan See from Kiev to Moscow, was the subject of a factual and unornamented saint's legend written in 1326 at the instigation of the Muscovite prince by Bishop Prochor (d. 1327). This serves at the same time as a eulogy of the Suzdal' principality, the city of Moscow and Prince Kalita, and is therefore the first example of a politically coloured Life. Later (before 1400) it was rewritten in an ornamented style by Metropolitan Kiprian (Cyprian; 1389–1406).

The Life of the Bishop Ignatij of Rostov (d. 1288) is merely a list of miracles and a panegyric which probably originated in the 14th century.

3. Other Lives which make use of the treasures of popular lore came into being in the 15th century.

Preëminently such is the Life of the Rostov Bishop Avraamij, who is depicted as a champion against the heathen. Avraamij meets the Apostle John, who gives him a wand with the aid of which the Bishop succeeds in smashing the idol of Veles. The angered devil hides himself in Avraamij's washing vessel, but Avraamij shuts him up there while he lays a Cross over the utensil. The devil, set free by accident, takes revenge on Avraamij. Impersonating a warrior, he denounces Avraamij before the prince, claiming that the bishop had found a treasure-trove and thus built a monastery. In a debate with Avraamij, the alleged warrior has to concede that he is, in fact, a demon. Following this, the prince gives a munificent donation to Avraamij's monastery. As far as history is concerned, Avraamij is totally unknown.

A very simi ar but far more detailed legend refers to a historically known Archbishop of Novgorod, Ioann. Ioann locks the devil in a washing bowl, while making the sign of the Cross over the vessel. He releases the devil, however, on condition that the latter take him to Jerusalem in one night. The devil turns into a horse and carries Ioann to Jerusalem and back. But the Archbishop does not fulfill the pledge he had given the devil, to tell no one about the ride. After Ioann tells someone in the course of conversation that he knows of a man who succeeded in reaching Jerusalem in a night, the devil begins taking his revenge. Time and again he appears in woman's clothing near Ioann's cell and smuggles in articles of feminine attire. The people decide to depose the Archbishop, convinced of his being a whoremonger. He is placed on a raft which is set loose on the river Volchov. The raft, however, floats upstream, towards a monastery. This convinces the people that Ioann is innocent; the devil is disgraced and begins to howl. At a later date, a historical motif was attached to this legend. The successful warding off of the siege of Novgorod by the Suzdal' army was ascribed to Ioann, who had ordered an icon of the Virgin to be brought to the city walls, whereupon the Suzdal' men were blinded, and in utter confusion could be struck down or taken prisoner at will by the Novgorodians, while "the rest fled".

These legends were rewritten by Pachomij Logofet (see below – 10) in his heavily ornate style.

A third legend which, as it appears, was only related orally in a Novgorod monastery and never welded into compositional unity is – in its original form – the Life of Michail of Klopovo (about 1470). He was an aged man who suddenly appeared in a monastery and led his life in utter silence, and made prophecies by symbolic action: the raising of one arm indicating sickness; of the other, death. Later he was thought to have been a representative of the *jurodivye*-type (cf. VI, 3, 5), which he definitely was not. The legend considers Michail a supporter of the Muscovite prince. It is characterised by its popular language and some idioms reminiscent of folklore, and was subsequently rewritten in many ways (VI, 3, 4).

4. The master of hagiography was Epifanij "The Wise" (*Premudrij*, or even *Premudrějšij*) who lived at the turn of the 14th century. He had chosen his heroes, St. Stefan of Perm' and St. Sergij of Radonež, for their spiritual qualities. Epifanij's Lives are vast works for which he collected material with great diligence. His style, however, is not that of a narrator, but one of the most ornamented of the period. Nevertheless, he strives hard to prevent this exuberance of style from obscuring the content and thus nullifying the didactic aim of his works. Their composition is highly artistic too; his style, of course, is not of his own creation but is based on his literary studies. Since little of his life is known to us, however, it remains questionable to what extent he had been subject to Southern Slav influence. Perhaps he had been to Constantinople and Mount Athos. Before 1379 he must have come to a Rostov monastery, where he made the personal acquaintance of Stefan of Perm'; he died before 1422. Undoubtedly his roots were in the Rostov principality; at any rate, he does not conceal his hostility towards Moscow.

5. Epifanij's Life of Stefan of Perm' was probably written shortly after the Saint's death (1396). The subject-matter, broadly speaking, is not very complicated. Stefan was born at Ustjug in the North, the son of a cleric (probably not of a priest). He studied diligently and went to a Rostov monastery because there was a large library there. Epifanij praises not only Stefan's ascetic exercises but also his zeal for study, for he also studied "secular sciences" (*vněšnjaja filosofija*). Credence should be given to Epifanij's statement about Stefan's knowledge of Greek. Stefan spent whole nights in conversation with well-read monks whom "he ardently questioned" about what interested him, acting both as "interlocutor and interrogator". He decided to make use of his knowledge of Finnish ("Permian") for missionary activity, for, being born a northern Great Russian in a town surrounded by a Permian population, he must have known something of that language. Stefan coined a new alphabet suitable for Finnish, presumably being guided by the idea that every language and especially every divine service should also have an alphabet of its own. This part is followed by some of Epifanij's thoughts on the Permians, and then he goes back to the story of Stefan's life. Stefan departs on his mission, blessed by God and by the bishop. An instructive discourse on the significance of the mission is placed in the bishop's mouth. Stefan

"went into the land where the Holy Apostles had not made any journeys on foot,
went into the land in which Apostles did not wander,
which has not been reached by the Apostles' promulgations and sermons,
where there had been no trace of worship of God and knowledge of God,
where the name of God was not pronounced in any way,
where the idols are being worshipped,
where sacrifices are being made in the service of deaf idols,
where prayers are offered to carved images of deity,
where beliefs are held in magic, and witchcraft, and devil worship, and other
where infidels speak foreign tongues.   [diabolic delusions,
where uneducated and misguided people live."

A prayer by Stefan is followed by the description of his missionary work and the perils involved in it. He wins a small circle for Christendom, but his enemies increase as well as their "malice, grumbling, scorn, calumnies, blamings, disapprobations, molestations, abuses and evil tricks". On one occasion, during a sermon, they "surrounded him on all sides [armed] with clubs (*oslopy*), and threatened with many curses to kill him". Another time Stefan's foes "heaped a multitude of dry straw bundles around him and the fire was brought, while it was planned (*vъschotěša chotěniem*) to burn the servant of God". But again nothing was done to him. Meanwhile he erected a small church in which he could conduct divine service. He was also shot at with arrows; and when he burnt down a temple of idols (*kumirnica*), Stefan was attacked with cudgels and hatchets, but again he was not put to death. A homily about the futility of idol worship is placed in Stefan's mouth in order to indicate that many of the local population became reconciled to Stefan and then allowed themselves to be baptized. Also those who did not receive Baptism paid visits to his church and were impressed by the beauty of the service. The non-baptized members of the peaceful nations did not know what they could do against Stefan: "He has a bad custom (*obyčaj*), he will not start a fight ... should he have dared to start a fight we would have torn him to pieces a long time ago (*rastrъzaa rastrъgnuli*). ... But as he has patience we do not know what we can do to him." "He spoke no evil word to any of us, and he neither turned away from us, nor fought us, but suffered everything gladly." Meanwhile, Stefan had translated the "books" (the Book of Hours (*Horologium*), the *Oktoechos*, the Psalter, and evidently the Gospels), which are extant only in parts. He also taught the Christian youth to read and to write.

But now there emerges a formidable adversary, the Finnish sorcerer Pam. Epifanij gives a detailed report with humour and in popular terms of the certainly invented war speech by Pam. The sorcerer speaks in rhythmical and rhymed speech: "O, fellowmen of Perm'! Do not abandon the gods of your fathers, do not forget sacrifices and the worship of gods, do not depart from ancient customs, do not avoid the old faith." (*ne ostavlivajte*:: *ne zabyvajte*:: *ne pokidyvajte*:: *ne pometyvajte*). Epifanij makes Pam develop arguments that would sound convincing to the sorcerer's Permian listeners: nothing good has ever come from Moscow, but merely "burdens, and heavy tributes, and violence, and stewards, and accusers and overseers". The Christians have only one God; the Permians many, and "many gods, many helpers, many supporters", at the hunt "in water, ... in the air, ... in marshes, in oak-woods, in groves, in meadows, in brushwood, in thicket, in birch forests, in fir-wood, in copses and in other woods". Then follows a similar enumeration of objects of the hunt; and the reward of the hunt, the furs, are of value to Moscovite "boyars and high officials". And furs can also be sent "to the Horde, and to the false [Tartar – D.Č.] Tsar, to Constantinople, and to the Germans, and to Lithuania, and to other States and countries, and to the far-away peoples". Moreover, Permians are able to engage in single-handed fight with the bears "while among you, many men, numbering up to a hundred or two, set out against a single bear, and frequently bring back one bear, but sometimes return without a single one, bringing nothing with them, after having exerted themselves in vain". Lastly, the gods help the Finns to learn everything that happens far away. Stefan challenges Pam to join him in an ordeal, to walk through flames. But when the fire is lit, Pam withdraws in fear. "He falls to the ground . . . and prostrating himself at [Stefan's] feet, announces his guilt, declaring his inability to go through with the contest, and reveals his falsehood." This happens three times; similarly Pam thrice refuses to dive through the ice on a river. This element of treble recurrence is reminiscent of fairy-tale style. But Epifanij does not allow the sorcerer's conversion. Pam departs, convinced that "your teacher Stefan had in his childhood and youth learned from his father how to cast a spell on fire and water by magic and witchcraft . . . I have, however, learnt in my life many evil crafts . . . but this one I do not know . . . I have not acquired this from my father (*u batka svoego*)". And he runs away "like a stag".

The Permian Christians send Stefan to Moscow to bring a bishop from the Metropolitan. But the Metropolitan ordains Stefan himself Bishop. Thus he returned alone; "he went to receive a bishop, and came back and did not bring with him [the bishop], he returned alone not bringing anyone with him, he went to bring a bishop, and suddenly he became Bishop himself!" But he

neither indulged in flattery	nor exerted himself,
neither urged.	nor gave money in bribes,
neither made promises.	nor gave anything to anyone,
and nobody received anything from him for the ordination, neither a present	nor bribe money, nor a reward.

Epifanij now sets out his main observations about the mission; first he voices praise to God for His "calling of the people" to Christianity, and then turns to some thoughts on the Permian alphabet, written in the spirit of the literature concerning the first Slav mission. This defence of the mission in the native language is probably one of the last examples of this kind in Russian literature. Moscow knew only the policy of Russification, and but a few decades later there commenced the struggle against the independent Permian Church, to which Stefan's translations for the most part also fell victim.

Epifanij ends his observations with a glorification of Stefan, and then relates the story of the Saint's journey to Moscow before his death. It is worthy of note that the Life contains no account of his miracles.

For the conclusion, Epifanij found a traditional but nevertheless very impressive form – the laments (*plači*). In an obviously deliberate imitation of popular tradition, he frames the lament of the Permians in the form of the wailing of children over their dead father, while the lament of the "Permian Church" becomes a widow's dirge for her husband (an imitation of Ilarion's *Slovo*, see III, 2, 4: "Every land praises its Apostle...", etc.). After a prayer for the prosperity of the Permian Church there also comes a third lament – "The Lament and Eulogy of the Monk Who Penned This".

6. Epifanij's second Life is devoted to Sergij of Radonež, known as "the greatest Russian saint". Again, it is well arranged, but it has not yet been properly edited for the purpose of hagiographical studies. Some of the texts published (Archimandrit Leonid, N. Tichonravov, *Čet'i-Minei*, the Nikon Chronicle) are obvious revisions of Epifanij's original with the versions rewritten and augmented by Pachomij the Serb, and possibly by others as well. The outline of the whole, however, probably originates with Epifanij, and for the most part, it is possible to discern easily those sections which reproduce his original faithfully. Only the song of praise (panegyric) at the end of the Life raises some doubts as to its authorship, but in my view it belongs mainly to Epifanij, though I propose to use it with great care in what follows.

Sergij was born about 1319 and died in 1391. He is the most important representative of the Hermit movement, which is to be discussed later (11). His Life was written shortly before Epifanij's death (i.e. about 1420).

Epifanij opens the Life with a preface in which he describes *inter alia* his method of work. He had made notes to put away "for memory and use", and when, twenty years later (i.e. about 1411), he learned that no one had been working on Sergij's Life, he commenced his work, though "for many more years" he was delayed in the progress of the work by various doubts.

Sergij was born at Rostov, the son of the boyar Kirill and his wife Maria. Even before his birth there occurred a miracle which, according to Epifanij, was a portent of Sergij's subsequent holiness. During the Angels' Song in the liturgy, a child's cry was heard thrice in the church attended by Sergij's mother. Inquisitive women began immediately asking each other who had brought a child with her; the men too asked their wives the same question after the service. But it transpired that the cry came from a child still in the mother's womb, namely from Maria's child.

After his birth, the child was christened Varfolomej (Bartholemew). He was a weakling but never cried, and he would take no nourishment on the days of fast. At the age of seven, he went to school where, in contrast to his two brothers, the work was very hard for him. However, the comprehension of his studies finally "came [to him] not from men but from God". When the boy was once sent to look for a missing foal, he encountered an old man who accompanied him back to his parents and blessed him; after this the boy became a good pupil at school. He was now like an old man (a topos: *puer-senex*); he fasted and prayed and did not play with other children. This story is followed by young Varfolomej's prayer.

In 1328 and 1329 the Rostov principality sustained two heavy blows: firstly, a devastating Tartar raid, and secondly, a Muscovite invasion. Epifanij does not spare any colour in depicting the reign of Muscovite terror. The Rostov principality "was deprived of... power and princely rule, of property and greatness, of honour and splendour, and everything was transferred to Moscow". Kirill with his family fled to Radonež – a small town in the neighbourhood of Moscow. Varfolomej remained as he had been before, being known for his "peace, neekmess, taciturnity, humility, absence of wrath, unadorned simplicity, and equal love... for all people". His brothers had married, but already Varfolomej wished to become a monk. However, only after the death of his parents did he give his hereditary portion to one of his brothers; the other, whose wife had died in the meantime, had already taken the vows and assumed the monk's name of Stefan – it was this brother whom Varfolomej persuaded to go with him into the wilderness. They built a chapel in the woods in honour of the Holy Trinity, which was consecrated by a priest. Here, at first, the brothers led a common life. Later, however, Varfolomej remained alone after Stefan, who could no longer support the hardships of their life, went to Moscow where he subsequently became an abbot. Epifanij thus describes life in the wilderness, "A life full of worries, a hard life: afflictions from every quarter, shortages everywhere; and great lack of food and drink and other necessities, since in the neighbourhood of this abode there were neither villages nor farms nor men dwelling; there were neither man-made roads in any direction nor a passer-by nor a visitor, but on all sides forest, and wilderness everywhere".

In this solitude Varfolomej was visited by an abbot who conferred upon him the monk's habit. Only now did he assume the name of Sergij. After a prayer placed in the mouth of the saint and an imaginary conversation between the newly cowled monk and the abbot, Epifanij begins

the description of Sergij's "spiritual struggle". Who can describe –
Epifanij exclaims – "his solitude and his courage, and the constant
prayers that he unceasingly addressed to God: his warm tears, the cries
of his soul, the anguish of his heart, the nocturnal vigils, the serious
songs, the uninterrupted devotional exercises, standing for long periods
and reading aloud, the frequent genuflections, the hunger, the thirst,
the sleeping on the ground, the spiritual poverty and the want of everything...". An in addition to this come the horrors of the wilderness:
"the attacks of the devil, the visible and invisible combats and wrestling,
the horrors of demons, the diabolic apparitions, the terrors of solitude,
the fear of unforeseen emergencies, the sudden appearance of wild
beasts and their ferocious attacks...". Demons appear to the saint
as robbers in an attempt to persuade him to abandon the place. At
their third attempt the difficulties of a hermit's life are conveyed to
the reader in the words of the robbers, who conclude their speech with,
"Run away in haste from here, before thinking it over"; but the holy
man remains.

This is followed by an episode which shows Epifanij's narrative art
at its clearest; it is the story of St. Sergij's life of friendly companionship
with a bear. "There were, as already mentioned, many wild animals in
the wilderness at that time; some of them went about howling in packs,
others in small groups of two or three, or even singly; some of them
passed by in the distance, but others approached the holy man, stood
round him and sniffed him. One of the animals, and its name was
'Arkuda' which means [in Byzantinic Greek! – D.Č.] a bear, got used to
being near the reverend man. When the holy one saw that the animal
approached him not with evil designs, but merely to receive a morsel of
food, he would bring a slice of bread out of his hut, and place it on the
stump of a tree or a block of wood. When the animal came (as was its
custom), it would find the food ready, take it in its mouth and go away.
But at times there was not enough bread, and the beast coming would not
find his slice; then the bear, however, would not depart for some time,
but would remain standing looking hither and thither in expectation,
like a wicked creditor who wishes to collect his due. But when there was
only one slice, the holy man had to divide it into two, so that he could
keep one half for himself and offer the other to the animal.... But often
there was no daily bread whatever; and when this happened both went
hungry, he and the animal. Sometimes the holy man neglected himself
and went hungry, for when he had only one piece of bread he threw it
to the animal, preferring to eat nothing on that day and go hungry rather

than make the animal suffer and go without food. The animal came not once and not twice, but for a long time every day, in the course of many years."

The "spiritual deeds" of the saint, who "directed his soul with secret thoughts towards aiming at the richness of eternal virtues", are told relatively briefly. Sergij did not wish for a quiet life but "to maintain relations with God alone, and to belong to the Almighty with his aspirations; and approach Him in order to become enlightened by His grace". As will be shown later (infra, 11) this is a somewhat limited and vague formulation of the Hermit movement's mystical ideas.

Subsequently, the Life is divided into comparatively short chapters. The saint returns to the world, or rather the world comes to him. Other hermits appear in Sergij's abode, wishing to enter upon "the narrow path"; they set up a community which provides for itself by manual labour, while Sergij diligently exerts himself for the good of the hermits. He succeeds in obtaining from the Perejaslavl' bishop permission to build a monastery, and become its abbot. For a long time there were only twelve monks at Sergij's monastery, but their number began to grow. In the end, the monastery no longer experienced shortages, but Sergij – even as abbot – continued to wear poor-man's clothes and to work physically, so that a peasant who came to the monastery to see him refused to believe that this was the abbot who had become so famous. Brief stories of three miracles follow: in the wilderness Sergij finds a well which the monastery needs; he brings a boy back to life who, according to his words, however, was not dead but merely frozen stiff; he heals a possessed boyar. The description of statute of "communal life" set up by Sergij, and the story of a conflict with the monks, in which Sergij, not wishing to press his own case, left the monastery, founded a new one and only after repeated supplications by the monks returned to his original abode, actually concludes the description of Sergij's activities as abbot.

The following chapters, which deal mainly with the foundation of monasteries from that of Sergij, in view of their style, can hardly be ascribed to Epifanij. These dryly written narratives are only interrupted by the description of two political episodes and some visions; they, too, cannot be considered with complete certainty as being by Epifanij.

The political events consist of two meetings between Sergij and the Moscow Prince Dmitrij (who later acquired the surname of "Donskoj"). The Prince visited Sergij's monastery before his campaign against the Tartar Khan Mamai (1382). Sergij blessed him and grieved over the

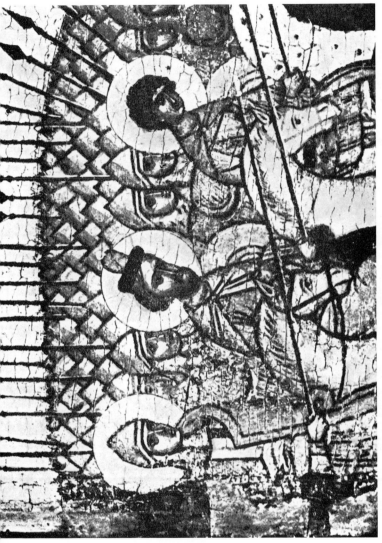

A FRAGMENT FROM A NOVGOROD ICON (CA. 1460), REPRESENTING A BATTLE OF THE NOVGORODIANS WITH THE SUZDALIANS

In the centre of the Novgorod troops, from left to right, the saints, Princes Aleksandr Nevskij, Boris and Gleb, the invisible protectors of Novgorod (in the sky – not visible on our fragment – an angel fighting against the Suzdalians is also represented).

ST. STEFAN OF PERM TRAVELLING TO MOSCOW

He passes the Monastery of St. Sergij of Radonež. An illustration in a manuscript of the 16th century.

many about to die in the war. It is worthy of note that here there is no mention of reports – current in later Muscovite chronicles and stories – that Sergij predicted victory to the Prince and sent two monks to join his troops. These two anecdotes should be considered nothing but tendentious political reporting, especially the one concerning the impossible participation of monks in a war. The other contact of Sergij with the political world was the Church authorities' abortive attempt to move him to the acceptance of the Moscow Metropolitan see. Muscovite chronicles give further details of Sergij's share in politics as an agent of the Moscow princes in influencing the other princes to accept their over-lordship, and even exerting pressure by a means unusual in the Eastern Church – that of the interdict. These statements are obviously deliberate political lies and contradict Epifanij's account, which described Sergij's single journey to Moscow as something unique in his life. It is significant that Pachomij, always ready and willing in the service of the authorities, should say nothing of these tendentious reports.

The three visions related in some of the chapters of the Life's final section are the appearance to the saint of the Virgin accompanied by two Apostles, and two visions of the monastery's monks. One of them, while serving Holy Mass, saw an angel at the altar taking part in the liturgy. Another monk saw fire emerge from the chalice at the time of consecrating the Communion sacrament; the fire swept over the chalice, rolled into a ball and entered the vessel from which the saint communicated. The two last visions are both typical light-visions of the 14th century, for the Hesychasts had taught of "divine light" as a real substance; this also had its parallels in the West, e.g., the vision of the Blessed Suso.

Sergij's Life ends with a eulogy of the saint and a prayer addressed to him. These belong among the most splendid works of their kind, but possibly are a rewording of Epifanij's original. Even so, they glitter with long rows of synonyms and long chains of epithets, but differ from the body of the Life by a certain poverty of subject-matter.

7. Epifanij's literary art need not be discussed in detail after the above exhaustive description and quotations. There is a certain amount of originality in the composition of his works. In both saints' Lives the chapters of subject-matter alternate with sections containing instructional material for the reader, such as prayers and thoughts ascribed to the saint, appropriate instructions by bishops and abbots, and the writer's

own treatises (e.g., the chapter on the Permian alphabet). Thus Epifanij's Lives serve two purposes simultaneously: they convey information about subject-matter and edify at the same time.

Prefaces to both Lives provide evidence that Epifanij was also a student of topoi, for they include a great number of commonplaces. (In the following quotations, references to Stefan's Life are abbreviated "St." and to Sergij's "S."). Firstly, there are the topoi of the introduction; the author says, in describing the factors which moved him to write the work, "It is well to hear or to record from memory the life of the venerable man; this has a salutary result and renders considerable service to both listeners and narrators" (St.); "It is right to conceal the secrets of kings, but it is (also) correct and necessary to voice the works of God" (S.); "When something is not written down, it is given up to oblivion" (St. and likewise S.). In both Lives, Epifanij gives the same quotation from Basil the Great and the same pithy sentence, "I am writing on hearts not parchment." The author writes so as not to be "an unfaithful servant"; he is "tormented" and "possessed" by "the wish" to tell the story (St.); he is "overcome" by the desire to write; his desire is "unquenchable" (S.). Secondly, a rhetorical question is also a topos in its own right: what should be written about? (known in medieval poetics as *addubitatio*). "Whence should I begin so as to tell listeners in a worthy manner of his work and deeds?" (S.); "What should be remembered first?" (S.). Thirdly, the invocation of Muses – or of God, among Christian writers – is a further topos of a works' opening. Epifanij has in both legends prayers with an appeal for God's assistance, namely in that of Sergij at the beginning (S.) or at the end (St., S.) of the introduction. Fourthly, the promise to relate at least "a few of the many things that could be told" (St., S.) is also a topos (*ex pluribus pauca*). Connected with this is, fifthly, the "moderation" topos, containing many formulas of humility: the "inability" to present such a theme in a worthy way (St., S.), the realisation of his "uncouthness" (St., S.) and "unworthiness, lack of wisdom and ability" (S.) – which, also appearing in the body of the work (S.) in most exquisite style, convey a direct impression of fine irony. Epifanij, however, uses this topos as a metaphor, too, as in "A great and heavy load cannot be carried in a small can" (S.). Sixthly, there are the excuses and requests for the readers' indulgence (*captatio benevolentiae*) with the request to pray for the success of his work (S.); these seem rather belated when reading the already finished composition. And further, Epifanij's excuse that he had not studied, had not visited Mount Athos, and did not know Plato and Aristotle (St.), or that he had visited many a place without profiting from it (S. in the eulogy); – all that is again a topos. Seventhly, topoi appear also in the body of the Lives. Sergij, even in his youth, had been like an old man (*puer-senex*); and there are, also, the descriptions of the wilderness (S.), the ethnography and topography of the Finnish lands (St.). Eightly, the references to his sources: the eye-witness reports (St., S.) the autopsy (St., S.) are also enlarged topoi. Ninthly, Epifanij at the end of his works uses the topoi of the conclusion: a prayer (St., S.), a panegyric (S.,), a renewed apology (S.). His "laments" represent perhaps an original East Slav topos too (St.), but he does not confine himself to one lament but provides three at the same time; he is an artist of language carried away by his own literary technique. In any case, it is impossible – though this is often done – to consider all these topoi as an expression of the author's personal sentiments.

8. The whole construction of Stefan's Life is exceptionally harmonious. A framework is provided by a personally coloured introduction and the author's lament – again with personal motifs – at the end. A second frame, as it were, is that of the narrative about Stefan's years of youth and his death; a third – of general observations on the country of Perm' at the beginning of the legend and on the Permian alphabet at its end. The extensive central section is the mission's history. The whole scheme is as follows:

> Introduction
> The Saint's Early Life
> The Permian Land
> The Mission
> The Permian Alphabet
> The Saint's Death
> The Laments.

The legend of Sergij has a purely chronological plan, though it has not consistently been carried out.

Both saints' Lives are composed in ways which help Epifanij in his task of preventing the narrative from becoming excessively concise and dry. These are methods which allow him to sustain the plot's development and include the repetition of the same action; tradition, especially folk-lore, enables him to use treble repetitions (the story of Pam and Sergij's cry in his mother's womb). In other instances he splits a general idea into separate subordinates (Pam's speech, the description of animals in the wilderness). He also inserts dialogue into his narrative (the conversation between the old man and Varfolomej; Sergij's talks with monks and with devils, and Stefan's conversations with Pam). In various ways he enhances the interest when, for instance, he produces the *dénouement* at the very end (as in Stefan's return without a bishop since he has become bishop himself, and then when the New Testament parable of the vineyard is related – only at its end instead of the "workers" of the Scriptures there appear "the people of Perm' "). Epifanij raises the tension by using the element of surprise when, for example, in the incident with the bear, and in the description of the life of the Finns he speaks of their peaceful disposition which makes it impossible for them to attack a man first. In the last case he applies the old method frequently used of presenting foreign life as peculiar and incomprehensible (of this type are passages in the Nestor Chronicle about the Apostle St. Andrew's amazement at the Novgorod bath-houses) – an old artifice known now under the name of *ostranenie*. All these methods serve the purpose of slowing down the tempo of the narrative. Moreover, Epifanij uses many tropes and figures of speech; as in the antitheses, God has in his power "to grant light to the blind, speech to the dumb, children to the barren, word to the wordless, voice to the voiceless" (St.). Many monks are "the first at beginning, the last in wisdom, the first in number, the last at work" (St.). Sergij summons the monks "not to the meal, not to drink, not to rest, not to sloth, but to patience . . . and to every grief and affliction . . . to work and to fast, to spiritual deeds and to many tribulations" (S.). A further antithesis is provided by the character sketches of Sergij, and of his brother unable to stand the life in the wilderness. Metaphors are numerous, both in long chains and in a developed form. Thus, the comparison of the abbot and the skipper (S.) and of a missionary and a farmer who "had uprooted the thornbush of idolatry in the land of Perm', ploughed with their sermons as with a plough, sowed the seeds of written instructions in the furrows of their hearts . . . from which there grew the ears of virtue which the Permians cut down as if with a sickle . . . bound the sheaves that bring good to the soul, dry them on the barn floor of temperance, thresh them with flails of patience, and store them in the granary of the soul . . ." (St.), or the comparison of the Permian Church after Stefan's death with a widow (St.), and so on. Epifanij loves epithets and builds long chains of them in many passages; here his synonymic system merits real admiration. He also uses compounds, only a few of which however are new: e.g. *blagokrasnyj, beloobraznyj, blagolistvennyj,* and some others ("good-beautiful [which reminds us of the Greek *kaloskagathos*], white-looking, with beautiful foliage"). The play with synonyms often leads to tautologies and pleonasms: "will instruct and enlighten" (S.); "translated and rendered" (St.); "inexorable foe and opponent and antagonist" (S.). Preference for word-chains also makes Epifanij resort to gradation (climax) – "to find, to search, to chose, to ordain bishop, and to despatch to Perm'" (St.). He often uses rhetorical questions: "How should I call you?" (St., the author's lament); "What good can ever come from Moscow?" (St.); and rhetorical exclamations, "O virtuous woman, who became mother of such a child!" (S.). For hyperbole Epifanij employs mainly the method of comparing his heroes with saints, prophets, Samson, and so forth (St., S.) He pays special attention to the sound value of the words; we encounter, therefore, in his works all means which intensify linguistic euphony. Chains of words (examples: *supra*, 5, 6), and chains of brief sentences (*ibid.*) are numerous. Anaphorical constructions are rarer: in one of Stefan's prayers fifteen sentences begin with the word *Gospodi* (vocative of "Lord"); in the account of the mission's beginning in March , the word *marta* (genitive of "March") is anaphorically repeated ten times, etc. To serve the same purpose Epifanij resorts time and again to similar word roots (paranomasias, etc.), e.g., "to make my unreasonableness reasonable and my inability ability" (S.); *naseliti selitvu i vozgraditi gradec* ("to populate a village and to found a citadel" – S.); *edin edinstvovati* ("to be alone in loneliness" – S.); "adorned it with every adornment" (St.); *s molitvoju i moleniem* ("with prayer and orison" – St.); or – in the struggle against Sergij – "the devils wanted to shoot him (*ustrělit'*) with the arrow (*strěla*) of sin, but the venerable man shot (*strěljal*) at them with many arrows (*strělami*), while shooting (*strěljaja*) at darkness from his righteous heart" (S.). In the Life of Stefan, repetitions of words and paranomasias cover long periods; in such cases alliterations naturally emerge. Elsewhere, they appear only accidentally, as in *sušča sanomъ svjaščennika, učeniju i utěšeniju, strělamъ smertonosnym suščimъ* (St.: "who was a priest according to his rank, teaching and solace, the arrows were lethal"). In Epifanij's writings rhymes (*homoioteleuton*) appear far more frequently than in those of any other religious writer of Old Russian literature, and sometimes they cover long periods. Even the customary similar suffixes of the verbs, because of their abundance, can only be viewed as a deliberate artistic contrivance. Thus, for instance (only short examples are given here): *k zemlě ... neprochodnej i bezgodnej* (St.), *blagovětstvovaniju rugaetsja, věrě christianskoj nasměchaetsja* (St.), *omračenie prosvětiti i moe nerazumie vrazumiti* (S.) ("in

the impenetrable and barren land; he derided the Gospels, he mocked
the Christian faith; to lighten the darkness and to make my lack of
wisdom wise"). Entire sentences are repeated, especially where internal
parallelism appears in the narrative as well. Thus, to show that Stefan
decided upon a completely new field of missionary activity, Epifanij
enumerates the countries in which each Apostle had worked according to
tradition, and every sentence ends with the same formula, "But he had
not been in the land of Perm' ".

Epifanij was also capable of playing with words of various lexical
strata, resorting sometimes to popular words as, for instance, in Pam's
speech, as well as in some ironically coloured passages.

All in all, Epifanij displays a high degree of craftsmanship in his art.
His descriptions are vivid and the instructive interpolations are lucid.
He achieves this clarity together with his "high" and "heavily ornate"
style. Even if his Lives do not deal with exceptionally profound problems, nevertheless he is able to convey to his readers certain definite
ideas; these ideas are neither flat nor misstatements involving a corruption of Christian faith. And though there may be some doubts about
Epifanij's "erudition", his deep reading is beyond dispute. He knows
the Chronicles (and imitates many a passage), the Holy Scriptures, and
a number of saints' Lives of which, significantly, he mentions not only
the Life of St. Feodosij, but also that of St. Savva (Sabbas), whom
indeed Feodosij wished to imitate. Epifanij thus uses literature not
indiscriminately. It is worthy of note that he knew the writings of the
Moravian Mission; at least those of Černorizec Chrabr concerning the
Slavonic alphabet. Epifanij's contribution to hagiographical literature
becomes even more outstanding when contrasted with the Lives of the
Saints written in the two following centuries. He compares favourably
with the later writers, not only on ideological grounds but also as a
reporter, because his brief information – for he considered more would
be too cumbersome for his ends – about names, chronology and events
stands up to historical criticism. Epifanij's command of the language,
even if not compatible with the taste of our times, should be valued
highly.

9. The next writer of the Lives of the Saints already shows the path
of decline. He is Pachomij Logofet, or "the Serb". Pachomij was a
Serbian professional writer of excellent literary training, but lacking
individuality. Assumptions that he had been influenced by Hesychasm
are not substantiated by his writings. After spending some years at

Novgorod in the bishop's service (he arrived there no earlier than 1429), he was invited in 1440 to the monastery of Sergij of Radonež – the "Troicko-Sergievskaja Lavra". In 1461–62 he worked in Moscow, and in 1462–63 at the White Lake (Beloozero) monastery. He died at the age of 76, before 1484. In all these places he had been a diligent author who wrote many Lives of the Saints, religious tales, eulogies and divine services for Saints' Days.

Pachomij enjoyed great popularity among his contemporaries and, curiously enough, also among scholars, who, time and again, attempted to ascribe to him almost every anonymous monument of the 15th century. Only his cooperation on the chronograph appears probable (see below, V, 10). Pachomij had conscientiously fulfilled his assignments everywhere; while in Moscow he represented the pro-Muscovite point of view, and while in Novgorod the anti-Muscovite. In all, he wrote ten Lives of the Saints, six tales (*skazanie*) and eighteen eulogies.

The recasting of various Lives in the "new style" belongs to Pachomij's most important work. Unfortunately, he also revised Epifanij's Life of Sergij by removing anti-Muscovite barbs. However, even Pachomij could not go so far as to introduce into the work an account of the political deeds attributed to Sergij by Muscovite chronicles. It is likely that there had not yet been any tradition about such deeds of the saint (see also above, 6). Pachomij also wrote the Life of Metropolitan Aleksij – Sergij's contemporary and admirer. His Life of Varlaam (Barlaam) of Chutyn' was popular at Novgorod. He edited the legend of Ivan of Novgorod, and at the White Lake Monastery he wrote a new Life of its founder, Kirill (Cyril).

In all his redactions, Pachomij introduces no new material except accounts of the working of miracles. At times he omits factual information or distorts it at will; he compensates his readers by enlarging on eulogies and stylistic ornamentation known as "word-braiding" (*pletenie sloves*: Epifanij). He acquired excellent command of Church Slavonic; there are few Serbisms, though at times Russian forms are too precise. His "word-braiding" is reminiscent of Manasses' in his intention, but certainly not in his execution. While Manasses has something *definite* in mind – an allusion to a characteristic of the person described, to an event, and so on, for every single epithet, every single metaphor, and every single compound, Pachomij uses his ornaments for unqualified praise or for equally unqualified adverse criticism of a person, without however enlarging in any way on the material itself. Manasses' style is concentrated; Pachomij's extensive and lacking in content. In the exuberance of adornment, too, he is far behind Epifanij. His artistic means are mostly those which are suitable for undefined subject-matter, like exclamations, "O, your great miracles, Emperor Christ!"; "O, your indescribable help, you Purest of All [the Virgin]!", etc. Comparisons are mainly drawn with good and bad Biblical characters, of whom nothing definite can be said. He has not very many compounds, but includes frequent epithets created *ad hoc*; those are not too copious, so that sometimes the impression is derived of *oxymōron* (*radostotvornyj plač* – joy bringing tears). There also appear like endings (*homoioteleuton*), mostly verb suffixes (*pochvaljajušče* :: *poslušajušče* :: *ugoždajušče* – "praising, listening, serving", etc.). Pachomij occasionally accumulates participial constructions, thus making long sentences vague. But only in eulogies does his style reach full development. He himself sets his task – at the beginning of the Life of Metropolitan Aleksij of Moscow – as "binding wreaths of praise"; facts are of little interest to him.

10. Pachomij was assigned to write the Life of Kirill of the White Lake, the outstanding representative of the most important spiritual trend of the period – the Hermit movement. Pachomij had worked on the Life in the monastery founded by Kirill, and in this case at least he described actual happenings (written about 1462–63).

Kirill of the White Lake (d. 1427) was a Muscovite who had worked in the service of a high dignitary. He became a monk in one of the Moscow monasteries, the abbot of which was one of Sergij's pupils. He used to spend his time in fast and prayer; he also met Sergij. Pachomij speaks of Kirill's *jurodstvo*, "in which he wished to conceal his virtue", and of his posing as a madman. Kirill had also "the gift of tears", because he could not even eat bread without weeping. For a time he had been an amanuensis, but later preferred to work in the bakery. He became a recluse, but as many visitors used to come to him he left for another Moscow monastery. There, however, during a divine service he heard the voice of the Virgin ordering him to go North. From the window of his cell he a saw a column of light in the north, and considered this a confirmation of the order. He left with the monk Ferapont for the White Lake. There they discovered "a very beautiful place" where Ferapont, not being able to endure "the narrow and hard life", founded a monastery in a less secluded area. This monastery (*Ferapontov monastyr'*) subsequently became the centre of opposition to the hermits' spiritual heirs.

Dangers of life are mentioned: a falling tree, a forest fire, a landlord sending robbers to Kirill as he suspects him of possessing money, peasants wanting to set fire to his cell because they saw in the hermit a future monastic landlord. Three monks from Moscow and two peasants come to join Kirill as his first disciples. He organises their life into a "communal "one, even water not being allowed to be kept in the cells, silence being compulsory as well as a strict fast and the complete prohibition of wine. Through some incidents Kirill's personality is also shown. He tells a monk who has insulted him, "All were wrong about me; you are the first to realise that I am a sinner." Kirill is opposed to monastic possessions, because he considers them harmful to monastic life. In his letters to princes, Kirill puts forward a number of moral and social demands. He can be considered the founder of the ideal of monastic poverty: his own monastery, however, did not observe this precept.

Pachomij in many ways misunderstood Kirill's aims, and passed over in silence some aspects of his activity.

11. Hagiographical accounts of other hermits whose lives belong to the same and an even earlier period (see V, 1, 9) remain unpublished, and their nature can only be assessed on the basis of quotations by scholars who had access to the manuscripts (Kadlubovskij). Their composition is determined by the normal course of a hermit's life: escape from the world, years of solitude, and then a return to the world, which actually comes back to them when settlers assemble in the surrounding area, escaping from the difficulties of life in the central areas of Great Russia. For those people, the hermits are primarily spiritual leaders, but often cultural and economic leaders as well.

But far more important are the invariably scant references to the hermits' mystical life and their ideology. The spiritual life of the hermits is "the spiritual combat", the struggle to attain to God, and "the search for Him". The three basic steps of Christian mystics are to be found in the Lives. The first step is "the purging of the spirit", (*očiščenie uma, zritel'noe očiščaja* – Greek: *katharsis*) – "The soul is uplifted, the heart purified from all passions" (*serdce očiščaja ot vsěch strastnych mjatež*). The second is the "illumination" (Greek: *phōtismos*) – "The light of divine wisdom (*logos*) is being collected in his heart"; "and God's splendour (Greek: *doxa*) is being perceived"; and thus one becomes "the chosen receptacle of the Holy Ghost". The visions of light reported in the Lives of Sergij and Kirill are external manifestations of spiritual experiences. Though there is no direct evidence of the third step along the path of the mystics (Greek: *henōsis* – union with God), "the search for God" in any case points to striving toward such communion. But the Lives keep silent on this point (see, especially above: Sergij, 4, 4). The reasons for this are many: the language needed for such a purpose had not yet been developed, while, moreover, the accounts did not originate from those who had successfully entered upon the path of mysticism. Mystic literature was scarcely, if at all, represented in Old Russia.

The hermits' mystical theory, as far as it is possible to judge, is, of course, a kind of Christian Platonism with a strong admixture of Hesychast teachings. In any case, "God's splendour" and the divine light belong to its basic concepts. The most frequent evidence of Hesychast influence is offered however by translated works (see above 1, 6).

12. Pachomij also wrote a popular saint's Life, the – for him – typical tale of Varlaam of Chutyn'. Before Pachomij, this saint, who at the end of the 12th century had founded a monastery in Novgorod, was celebrated by only a very brief Life. Pachomij turned it into a hundred-page version, only one-third of which is devoted to the saint, while the remainder deals with miracles at his grave. The whole tale is formed of a colourless account of the saint's ascetic life and of three miracles ascribed to him. These miracles were the unmasking of thieving monks, the prediction of a snow-fall in summer, and the raising to life of a dead man whom Varlaam himself described as having only fainted; it was therefore properly a healing. Hence, all the miracles show Varlaam as the carrier of the gift of the Holy Ghost (the charismatic gift). In Pachomij's life this ideological aspect is fully obliterated. Moreover, the expansion of the legend is devoid of any special ornamental qualities – compounds are few, as are metaphors and similes; impressive sentences are also absent. A certain "high style" is noticeable in panegyric passages alone.

The ornamentation of Pachomij's legends (both of Varlaam and of Moscow Metropolitan Aleksij) is very inferior to that of Epifanij or the Chronicle of Manasses.

5. SECULAR BIOGRAPHY

1. The tradition of secular biography (cf. IV, 11) seems to have by now reached full development. But already by the end of the 15th century the interest in this type of literature had waned. Besides, some of the works of this kind were suppressed for political reasons. We possess thus only a few relics, mostly fragments or re-told tales incorporated in the body of chronicles, while other profane biographies had been recast in the style of the Lives of the Saints.

2. The characteristics of this genre are only partly perceptible in the biography of Prince Dovmont-Timofej of Pskov. He was a Lithuanian prince who fled to Pskov in 1266, was baptised and became Prince of the city; Pskov, like Novgorod, being a merchant republic, had its princes elected. As Pskovan prince he launched many victorious campaigns against his homeland – Lithuania – and against the German Knights. He died in 1299. At Pskov, he was later revered as a saint and acquired a "prologue" legend. His secular biography, however, is extant in the first Pskovian Chronicle (1265); this is stylistically rather colourless. It contains historical data conveyed in the matter-of-fact style of a military tale. The embellishments consist of imitations of the Nestor Chronicle (the baptism of a heathen prince modelled on the picture of Vladimir's conversion), and of Aleksandr Nevskij's biography (see IV, 11) from which many turns of phrase are bodily transferred, especially from the panegyrical part.

3. Far more significant are the biographical works of Tver', which disappeared from literary life after Moscow's victory over the city.

A biography was devoted to the Tverian Prince Aleksandr Michajlovič (d. 1339). Its contents are reproduced in part in the so-called Nikon Chronicle, but its original form cannot be reconstructed.

The second biography, of Prince Michail Aleksandrovič, is not extant as a whole. Two fragments – the introduction to the life story and the epilogue in the form of a eulogy – have survived in the *Tverskoj Sbornik*, the "Tverian collection" or Tverian Chronicle (see V, 6, 2). But the centrepiece, which deals with the Prince's struggle against the Muscovite princes, is missing. Its contents, again, are retold in the Nikon Chronicle, and some passages may be regarded as quotations. The final part, it appears, is re-told fairly accurately by the IV. Novgorod Chronicle. There is also a kind of preface to the biography which, it seems, did not belong to it originally.

The introduction of the Tverian Chronicle is marked by very complicated sentence structure. After a long opening sentence and a statement that the work is written to save the name of this "great autocrat" from "the storm of forgetfulness", there comes a passage in which, probably for the first time, appears the dynastic ideal in a form later used in Muscovite literature – the whole princely family being regarded as one uninterrupted line in which generations (*stepeni*) change, but which descends directly from Rjurik to Michail.

The story of the Prince's life, in so far as extant, deals with both his youth and education and is characterised by its consistently secular tone. The author places in the forefront of his aims the intention to show how much of "courage of valour" (*mužestva chrabrosti*) Michail "had shown on earth". Only afterwards does he turn "especially" to the Prince's belief in God. His adolescence is also described in a secular vein: he "spent time in a dignified way (*blagočinno*) with his *družina*"; at the same time his respect for the clergy is also stressed. The Prince's activities are described in general phrases which are beautiful, if rather vague. Under his reign "peace and liberation of Christians from their fetters" held sway, "and they enjoyed themselves in joy (*radostiju vrzadovalisja*) and their foes were covered with shame", this, on the whole, being hardly true. Michail conquered "many towns", "the non-rebellious with love, and the rebellious with the sword". The Prince's internal policy was also successful. Defects in government and judiciary disappeared, and this is told with a religious-moralizing stress. The description of his death is, on the other hand, handled in a more concrete and rather dramatic way, dialogues and prayers being used as adornments. The Prince is taken ill at a banquet in honour of a Byzantine mission; before he dies he wishes to become a monk. Although his retainers are against this, no one dares to say a word or raise any objections, for he was "a terrifying man, and his heart was like that of a lion". The cowling ceremony is narrated in a lyrical vein. The biography ends with a customary Russian topos – the lament (*plač*) by the Prince's son and heir; it shows practically no traces of popular tradition except the general idea of the loss of a father, the question of who would console those surviving, and the development of the concept that the dead can never be seen again. The lament goes thus: "O my father, my father, the most sweet and beloved lord, the dear light of my eyes, the good teacher and the guide of my youth! I had always rejoiced seeing the brilliant beauty of your angelic face. But who is now to comfort the sorrow of my greatly bereaved heart when I am cut off from your sweet and inexhaustible love? Now, I shall no longer see my good and beloved father; I shall neither greet your venerable and splendid grey head nor enjoy your beautiful speech, nor hear your calm instructions and your kindly voice." Such was the language of educated circles.

The style of the extant sections is much higher, on the whole, than these rather unpretentious passages. The author loves compounds, and among them the newly-formed *svjatoučitel'nyj, bratonenavidstvo, drugoljubec, studoslovec*, etc. ("teacher of saintliness, fraternal hatred, a friend's friend, reviler"). There also appear abstract words and rare locutions turning the concrete into abstract. Speeches and rhetorical questions abound. The most characteristic feature, however, is the preference for often impenetrably long sentences with participial construction; in one, a fifteen-line sentence, there occur eleven participles.

Suggestions have been made in support of Epifanij's authorship (V, 4, 4) of this work, but the style is utterly different from that used by him in his Lives of the Saints. Moreover, the introduction to the biography in the *Tverskoj sbornik* says it was written in 1455, a long time after Epifanij's death.

4. The biography of Prince Boris Aleksandrovič of Tver' (1427–1461) has come down to us in a better condition, though in only one copy lacking the final section. The Prince also ordered the writing of a Life of his great grand-father Michail Aleksandrovič. Boris Aleksandrovič had indeed done much to raise Tver''s political significance; his biography obviously pursues political aims, but it fell into oblivion after Moscow's final victory (1486) and its copies were probably destroyed deliberately. The author calls himself "Monk Foma (Thomas)", but beyond this we know nothing of him.

The biography has a singular construction, consisting of five more or less independent narratives of panegyrical character. Presumably it was written during the Prince's lifetime, thus before 1461 and probably not later than 1453, the events related not extending beyond 1450. The end of the final tale is missing, the narrative abruptly ceasing in the middle of a sentence.

The first tale is a eulogy connected with the Florence-Ferrara Council. The author's personal praise is linked up with the probably imaginary eulogies of the Prince by the Byzantine Emperor, the Patriarch of Constantinople, and by various eastern princes of the Church taking part in the Council. Nothing is reported of the Council itself, which aimed at union between the Eastern and Western Churches. The author compares Prince Boris with Moses, Joseph, Solomon, Augustus, Tiberius, Justinian, Theodosius, Constantine, Leo the Wise, and "the book-loving" Ptolemy. These comparisons constantly recur in all the six sections. Significantly, Boris is described as the heir of St. Vladimir and is likened time and again to Jaroslav the Wise. Boris's fame "from East to West", and even as far as Rome, is emphasized throughout and is the theme of most of the glorifications by participants in the Council (three of these eulogies are missing in the manuscript). Much of this work resembles Ilarion's sermon (III, 2, 4) and Aleksandr Nevskij's biography (IV, 11), and a long quotation is woven in from Camblak's sermon for Palm Sunday ("Who had taught them [the princes of the

Church – D.Č.]..." etc.). The author even expresses the wish that God should command "the whole world" to belong "to this Land promised by God" – the Tverian principality. The second part deals with the Prince's building activities and includes valuable historical data unknown from other sources. Such information is also given in other parts of the work. The third part speaks of the great fire which afflicted Tver', and of the Prince's subsequent order to build the city anew. The fourth part is devoted mainly to Boris's alliance with Vasilij the Blind – Prince of Muscovy – in the latter's struggle against Prince Šemjaka. The fifth part is a record of the Prince's wars, including his reconquest of the town of Ržev from the Lithuanians. This is followed by a number of entries of purely annalistic value, being provided even with dates. The final part was perhaps not definitively revised.

The biography is really well composed and is clearly narrated. Contextually, it is secular throughout. From the point of view of biographical composition, the continually recurring references to earlier histories are of interest; in addition to the already mentioned St. Vladimir and Jaroslav the Wise, the old princes of Tver' appear also. The lay character of his reign is always brought to the fore. Foma mentions the Prince's civic buildings, his martial deeds, his valour which expressed itself, for instance, in his taking first the sword from the Polish king's gifts and paying no attention to the gifts of gold and cloth (the report about Svjatoslav I in Nestor's Chronicle was in similar vein). The author also speaks of the magnificence of the princely court, where the Prince "had commanded the courtiers to appear before him in beautiful brilliance". The Prince is at times described as "Tsar", the title reserved for the Byzantine Emperor and the Khan of the Golden Horde. References to Vladimir and Jaroslav are probably allusions to Boris's over-lordship among the East Slav seceding princes. In addition it is emphasized that even Tamerlan's heir had sent him rich gifts.

The biography is written in a profusely ornamented style, though by no means as complicated as that of the Tverian Chronicle. And therefore these two monuments could hardly be ascribed to the same author, as some scholars (Šachmatov) think. Ornaments of style are highly individual. The "joy" of all at the Prince's deeds is used by Foma as his main theme: *radost'*, *veselie* are repeated time and again. Metaphors are few: the Prince is compared to the sun which radiates "golden rays", to the moon, to the morning star, to the light of dawn, to a constellation, as well as to a "high-flying" eagle – but he also appears as a military captain who is both the shepherd and lamb of Christ's flock. Elsewhere,

Lithuanian enemies are "wolves", disobedient citizens "shut their ears like a deaf viper", etc. The author loves the play of words. Firstly there come synonyms which he marshals in pairs: "artistry and artifice" (*chudožestvo i chitrost'*); "wise and clever" (*premudryj i razumnyj*); *dobrolěpen i dobroviden* ("beautiful"); "famous and praised", and so on. Also he often uses paranomasias and figures of speech, e.g., *děla dělaše* ("to carry out deeds"). The same word is repeated in various places ("art" – *chitrost'* – five times; "blessed" – five times; alongside the four times repeated "peace" – *mir* there appears the verb "to live in peace" – *mirstvovati;* next to the thrice used "love" – *ljubov'* there is the neologism for the adjective "loved" – *ljubestvenen* as well as the normal *ljuboven*, and again *Ljublin* – the name of a town founded by Boris; alongside "gifts" – *dary* used three times, the verb "to give" is used twice, etc.). Besides, Foma very often uses antithetical pairs of words together: the Prince is famous in the *East* and *West*, he grants *honours* to those who surrender and *punishment* to those who do not yield; he attracts into his *proximity* those who are *afar*; he conquers *many* in *few* [wars]; he fetters the *proud* and places the *humble* next to him on the throne. Foma himself, in his work, "began at the *bottom* and reached *high*", while he and his readers only *heard* of rulers of the past but *saw* Boris, and so on. On a few occasions only, the antitheses are of a different type, e.g.: "He had not conquered one, and rises against the other." Some of Foma's antitheses are strict formulas, and he interpolates the topos everywhere in his work: he himself is "the uncouth illiterate", his tongue "is indolent and poor of words", his "texture" is "poorish", for the Prince he can afford only "twopence" worth of his praise, but he "brings forth all he has"; he wishes "to pay his debt", and not be like "an unfaithful servant". He is tormented by the desire to eulogize the Prince; he is writing for the future, for the "newly born children" who will not see Prince Boris; the prince has "the wisdom of an old man in a youthful body", etc. These topoi are distributed throughout the whole work instead of appearing, as was the custom, at the beginning. Ecclesiastical style is rarely used (to this style perhaps belongs the topos which originated in Ilarion's *Slovo*: "Each land praises its hero, but we..."). As against this there are stylistic reminiscences of chronicles of the past and of Aleksandr Nevskij's biography; these traits are noticeable in the vocabulary with *zaratišasja, vsjadu na kon'* ("prepared himself for war, mounted a horse") in the meaning of "embark on a campaign", *v silě tjažčě, priide vъborzě*, ("with heavy host, speedily came") etc. Some of the passages remind us of the phraseology of "The Tale of Igor's Campaign": one of Boris's foes escaped: *poběže negotovymi dorogami* (literally, as in the Tale); in the glorification of the prince as "a friend of justice and reservoir of thought" it is stated: *šestosloven esi imenem, sedmotyseščen esi smyslom*, vividly recalling "Jaroslav Osmomysl" in the Tale ("He ran away along unmade roads; your name is sixfold, your reason seven-thousand-fold – an expression as unintelligible here as in "The Tale of Igor's Campaign"). Some of the battle-scenes closely resemble those of the old chronicles: "The armies were like a flowing river and the waving sea, and they shone like fires seen burning from afar", or "Some fired cannons, others catapults, and others threw stones, and some let loose showers of arrows", and when cannons fired "it was so terrifying that from this mighty thunder many people fell to the ground" – only the cannons are new here. A number of scenes are very impressive, as, for instance, the Prince's incognito appearance even though he is recognised by all, or that of the arrival in Tver' of the blinded Prince Vasilij of Muscovy, and many other instances. The author also endeavours to describe the psychological movement, and does so in a rather skillful way, first with Prince Boris's speeches and then with his prayers presented as thoughts ("He spoke to himself"). But all too often Foma uses the outward symptoms of the mood he is describing – everybody is "weeping" and "sighs from the bottom of the heart", "tears are streaming like a spring of water", and so on. He does not forget the people – "the sons of Tver'"; the Prince addresses them as well, and their mood is periodically described. Foma makes little use of the artistic devices typical of the period. Thus compounds are neither numerous nor original, and hyperboles and hyperoche few. On the other hand, he has many pretty sentences, partly borrowed from the Scriptures, but also in the form of proverbs: "The father when chastising loves too"; "What has happened cannot be undone"; "The shepherd is silent and the ewes conquer the wolves" (sic!); and to explain the many misfortunes during Boris's rule: "A great man has to stand great trials", beside the ecclesiastical: "Purified as gold in the melting-pot", etc. Popular vocabulary is deliberately avoided, with the exception of a few sentences put into the mouth of the *Muscovite* Prince.

    The author is considerably well-read: he knows the Nestor Chronicle and perhaps also the Kievan, a number of Lives of the Saints, the Life of Aleksandr Nevskij, the sermons of Ilarion and Camblak, and perhaps also those of Kirill of Turov. He quotes the *Aeropagitica* and very frequently – sometimes incorrectly – the Holy Scriptures. It may well be that "The Tale of Igoŕ's Campaign" was also familiar to him. In any

ST. SERGIJ AT HIS HERMITAGE

He is surrounded by bears and wolfs. An illustration in a manuscript of the 16th century.

ST. KIRILL BELOZERSKIJ

Between 1420-1430. Icon which is attributed to one of Kirill's monks and probably
is a portrait.

case, Foma's work belongs to the stylistically most interesting products of the 15th century. Moreover, he adroitly links the rich embellishments with the varied and clearly expounded historical subject-matter.

5. Completely different in its external splendour, coupled with utter disregard of content, is the Muscovite secular biography of Prince Dmitrij Donskoj: *Slovo o žitii i prestavlenii Velikogo Knjazja Dmitrija Ivanoviča*. This not very extensive work must have been composed after the death (1389) of the successful Prince who had become famous as a result of his victory over the Tartar Khan Mamai (1380). According to its style it can hardly be dated before the middle of the 15th century.

The biography provides evidence of a change in literary taste: the disappearance of interest in subject-matter and the growing preoccupation with form. This work, as it were, forms a bridge to the hagiographical style, while contextually remaining largely secular. Dmitrij's descent from St. Vladimir and his kinship with St. Boris and St. Gleb are stressed, and his childhood and adolescence are depicted as those of an ascetic. His reign is described in vague terms: "During his government the Russian land blossomed as the one [land] once promised to Israel"; "And his name was hailed from the East unto the West, from sea to sea, from one end of the world to the other". Those who envied him goaded the infidel Khan, Mamai, against him. The Khan invaded Russia so that he might erect mosques in the place of churches, and impose Tartar officials instead of the princes. After a victory over a small Tartar force on the river Voža, Dmitrij hears that Mamai himself "filled with evil lawlessness" is marching against him. The Prince prays to the Virgin and makes a speech to the princes and nobles (the army is not mentioned). Then "he became as indomitable as Abraham", and advanced with the aid of St. Peter (Moscow's metropolitan-saint), like Jaroslav the Wise against Svjatopolk. Then follows a brief description of the battle: "Both hosts approached each other like great clouds, the arms flashed like lightning on a rainy day, the warriors fought hand to hand, and blood streamed in the dales, and the river Don flowed mingled with blood, the heads of the Tartars lay about like stones, and the corpses of the heathen were like a felled wood" (an imitation of Nestor's Chronicle). Some saw that angels helped the Christians... After this victory: "All bowed beneath his hand; even the renegades and rebels of his realm (*carstvo*) all submitted".

This is followed by a glorification which, although very impressive, bears little relation whatsoever to Dmitrij or his life: "He was the father of the world, and the eye of the blind, the foot of the lame; ... the high-soaring eagle; the fire that consumes disbelief; the bath that cleanses from dirt; ... the refuge for those who work for God; the trumpet to rouse the sleepers; the peaceful captain..."! etc. – this being copied out in its entirety from eulogies of saints, but having there a symbolic meaning which is totally absent in this instance. The glorification, in turn, is succeeded by some more passages concerning Dmitrij's rule, in which Christian and ascetic virtues are in the forefront once again. The instructions given and the arrangements made by the Prince before his death represent a factual chapter of the biography; these are followed by the traditional final topos – the widow's lament, which is of great beauty. The lament is in the form of questions: "Why did I not die before you?... Whither are you going, treasure of my life? Wherefore do you not speak to me? My pretty flower, why did you wither so early?... My sun, you are setting too soon; my beautiful moon, you are waning too soon..." etc. A section of this lament repeats word for word the lament of Prince Ingvar' in "The Tale of Rjazan's Ruin". Then comes the author's lament, very long and equally impressive in parts, but here catachresic (false) metaphors (*katachrese*) and similes likening the prince to Old Testament patriarchs, Adam, Seth, Enoch, Israel, Joseph, Moses, above all of whom the author places Dmitrij, show that once again the hagiographical style had led a too bold stylist astray. Next comes a quotation from Ilarion's prayer. Each land praises its apostle, "the land of Kiev with surrounding towns praises St. Vladimir", but "the whole Russian land" sings the praise of Dmitrij. Finally, there is added a request to the Prince: may he, in the name of the author – who feels himself incompetent – praise the dead before God, in a fitting manner, and pray for "all the people of your realm (*carstvo*)".

This biography, with its preponderance of ecclesiastical style while dealing with a lay personage, shows perhaps that the author lacked feeling for this type of writing, and here possibly is an early sign of a coalescence between the world and the church, numerous examples of which occur only in the 16th century. The secular biography becomes virtually extinct with the works of the 14th–15th centuries. And the *Žitie* of Dmitrij Donskoj was rewritten later as a proper hagiographic Life.

6. THE TALES

1. There had been many attempts to single out various independent tales from the body of the 14th and 15th century chronicles. Such a procedure is open to many doubts, as the tales in question could well have been specifically written for the chronicles. Therefore we shall confine ourselves in this section to *definite* interpolations in the chronicles or to tales extant in separate manuscripts. Even in the latter case, however, the question must be asked whether a tale had not been extracted from the chronicle at a later date, being considered as having a special interest. An example is provided by the tale of the murder of Prince Michail of Černigov in the camp of the Golden Horde, which about this time was expanded on the basis of annalistic entries and turned into a saint's Life.

2. The story of the assassination in the camp of the Golden Horde of Michail Jaroslavič, the Prince of Tver' (14th century) at the instigation of his adversary, the Muscovite Prince Jurij Danilovič, is an independent tale. Naturally, it has a strong anti-Muscovite colouring, and it is difficult to say whether this is not without exaggeration. The Prince is shown very competently as a totally disinterested partisan of Russian interests, and his murder, as well as the six days' martyrdom before the assassination, is told with gruesome details (he is trampled upon, his corpse for a long time is denied burial, etc.). Tales of the assassination of princes already known to us (of Boris and Gleb, Andrej Boguljubskij, Michail of Černigov, and perhaps the story of the blinding of Vasil'ko) are used here.

3. The second tale again deals with Tver', and the version extant in the Tverian Chronicle is certainly the more ancient one (V, 7, 2). At the time of the rule of Prince Aleksandr Michajlovič (d. 1339) there came to Tver' (in 1327) a Tartar official, Ševkal, apparently with the intention of slaying the Prince and laying waste the land. He drove the Prince from his palace and took up his quarters there himself. The citizens complained to the Prince against the misdeeds of the Tartar, but he ordered them to be patient. Following an insignificant incident (the Tartars tried to deprive a deacon of his horse while he bathed it, and in answer to his cries the citizens began to gather; whereupon the Tartars took up arms), the assembly of the population (*věče*) was summoned. All the Tartars in Tver' were killed, so that only their horse guard, being outside the city, could carry the news to Moscow and thence to the Horde. Subsequently, a punitive expedition was led against Tver' by Ivan Kalita, the Prince of Muscovy.

The tale was probably written shortly after the events, with the intention perhaps, if not to escape, at least to mitigate the Tartars' vengeance by describing the uprising as *unorganised*. It is also likely that the tale was only rewritten after 1455, when the Tver' Chronicle was compiled.

4. It is not surprising that the great victory over the Tartars in 1380 – which did not, however, prevent them two years later from delivering a devastating blow against Moscow – found a reflection in literature; three works are devoted to the victory at *Kulikovo Pole*.

Firstly, there is the narrative in the chronicles (e.g., in the IV Novgorod Chronicle). Here, the description is meagre. Khan Mamai advances against Moscow with the aid of Oleg, Prince of Rjazan', and the Lithuanian Jagajlo (Jagieɫo). Prince Dmitrij with his cousin Vladimir of Serpuchov and two princes from the West – of Polock and Brjansk-after prayers and with the Metropolitan's blessings, takes the field against the Tartars. On September 8th the battle is fought beyond the Don, on the banks of river Neprjadva. The vanquished Mamai flies and is defeated yet again by the Tartar Khan Tochtamyš, who occupied Moscow two years later (cf. 9). Mamai himself escapes further westward to the Crimea, and vanishes there. The description of the battle is given in regular annalistic style.

5. Much more interesting is an epic work, the so-called *Zadonščina*, written presumably somewhat later, and whose author is one Sofonija of Rjazan'. This designation is used perhaps to remove the blot acquired by Rjazan' for supporting the Tartars. *Zadonščina* is extant in six copies of the 15th–17th centuries, all of which are very poor, and three of them are, moreover, incomplete. The many attempts to reconstruct the original text have so far been unsuccessful.

The work is an obvious imitation of "The Tale of Igoŕ's Campaign". Its imitative character is especially obvious because the *Zadonščina's* author misunderstood many passages of the Tale and had clumsily used many borrowings. Some passages were also mutilated by subsequent copyists (all the manuscripts, as already stated, are very poor). Thus, right at the beginning of *Zadonščina*, as in "The Tale of Igoŕ's Campaign", references are made to Bojan, "who laid his fingers on the living strings". Similarly, there are mentioned the princes referred to in the Tale, but the author of *Zadonščina* has Igor' instead of the "beautiful Roman" – a little known figure from the Tale. *Zadonščina's* heroes also "armed their spirit with their strength" (after the Tale, but changed), and they "filled themselves with war-like spirit" (both works). [In subsequent references "The Tale of Igoŕ's Campaign" is abbreviated as *IT*, *Zadonščina* as *Z*, and variants as *V*.] Instead of Bojan, it is the nightingale (*Z*) which called the lark. With changes in the names of towns, also imitated is the description of martial feeling in the countryside before the campaign begins: *Komoni ržut' za Suloju, zvenit' slava v Kyevĕ, truby trubjat' v Novĕgradĕ, stojat' stjazi v Putivlĕ (IT)* – *Koni rɔžut na Moskvĕ, zvenit slava po vsej zemli Russkoj, truby trubjat na Kolomnĕ, v bubny b'jut v Serpuchovĕ, stojat stjazi u Donu velikogo na brezi (Z)* (IT: "Horses neigh *beyond Sula*", Z: "*in Moscow*"; IT: "Glory rings *in Kiev*", Z: "*in whole Russian land*"; IT: "Drums beat *at Novgorod*", Z: "*at Serpuchov*", IT: "standards are raused *at Putivl'*", Z: "*on the bank of the great Don*").

Some of the expressions are frequently reiterated; but by this time most of them have become prosaic – the two princes of Brjansk and Polock speak like the heroes of "The Tale of Igoŕ's Campaign", saying they "would like to drink from the Don out of their helmets" (Z. supplements "swiftly flowing Don"), but while the princes in the Tale say that they are the sons of the same father, *Zadonščina* adds the grandfather and great-grandfather too. Jaroslavna's beautiful lament is imitated, but divided among three boyar women. The list of fallen boyars is inserted in the description of the first defeat; at the end likewise, to the detriment of the general impression, there comes a long enumeration of the fallen warriors from each town. A number of passages had not been understood by the imitator, thus the foxes "who bark at the red shields of Igoŕ's host" (IT) become foxes who "bark at bones" (Z), though they are hardly animals that seek their food on battlefields and moreover are made to bark *before* the battle when there are no bones whatever! The cuckoo, too, in *Zadonščina* "calls because of human corpses", the innocent bird being automatically appropriated from "The Tale of Igor's Campaign" and put in the place of eagles and ravens. The word *šolomja* (hill) is misunderstood as well, and the author of the *Zadonščina* turns the Tale's sentence: "O, Russian land, you are already beyond the hill", into the meaningless: "O, Russian land, you were already under King Solomon" (*šolomja* — *Solomon*). The mythical Div of the Tale which gives its ill-omened cry from a tree-top is also misunderstood as in *Zadonščina*: "Div calls under Tartar swords" – whereas in the Tale saddled horses of a prince stand by "in front", i.e., in the direction of the Don, in Z. the horses of Prince Dmitrij's allies also stand "in front", this "in front", however, being, further away from the Don than Dmitrij's forces, and so on.

The content of the *Zadonščina* is simple. After recalling Bojan, the story opens with preparations for the campaign by Dmitrij and his cousins; the Novgorodians regret that they are unable to come and aid them; the princes "of the whole Nordic land" gather. After Dmitrij's speech to the princes (the army is not mentioned), there comes the description of the princes of Brjansk and Polock setting out to war. Then the first battle is recounted in brief; here too appear the two monks allegedly attached to the prince by St. Sergij of Radonež; the country mourns, the widows of the fallen boyars lament. Now follows a conversation between Prince Vladimir of Serpuchov and Prince Dmitrij Bobrok, who throw their reserves into the battle, and victory is won. The grief of the fleeing Tartars and of their wives in their homeland is described. Only here does the imitation of "The Tale of Igoŕ's Campaign" end, and then follows the conclusion, prosaic throughout, that speaks of the fate of Mamai whom the Italian mocked in the Crimea, and the enumeration of the dead.

It does not follow that *Zadonščina* should be described as "a plagiarism"; standards of literary originality in the 14th century were quite different from those of the present time. However, even by the old standards, *Zadonščina* is a work of little value as it slavishly copies the artistic devices of *one single* monument. This, according to the terms of medieval poetics, should be described as a "centon", i.e., a work compiled out of passages of another.

The only original elements are the shedding of the mythological allusions of "The Tale of Igoŕ's Campaign", Svjatoslav's impressive speech, and the transposition of the Tale's various parts. Dmitrij's war is treated, in many passages, as a struggle for the Christian faith. In a number of places the author uses a device of modern folk poetry – rare in the Tale – the negative parallelism: "And the grey wolves came from the Don's estuary. ... These are not grey wolves but Tartars", and "Then the geese cackled on the river Meča. ... These are not geese ... but ... the infidel Mamai", etc. Use of ornamental epithets is also more regular than in the Tale. In any case, it is symptomatic that the work apparently was little liked and was not very well understood by the copyists. This presumably, however, was not because it was thought weak poetically but rather for its too poetical character; the exceedingly complicated use of metaphors made it difficult to understand. Moreover, *Zadonščina*, being a secular work, lacked religious justification, a thing which in the 14th century mattered a great deal.

Many passages from *Zadonščina* are certainly beautiful in themselves; this beauty, however, can only be appreciated when "The Tale of Igoŕ's Campaign" is not known. The impossibility of the assumption that the Tale is but an imitation of *Zadonščina* (see IV, 7, 13) is even more strongly supported by aesthetic criteria than by any other argument. Those who have no feeling for the differences in the aesthetic values of both monuments ought not to engage in the study of literary history.

6. The third work devoted to the *Kulikovo Pole* is the so-called "Story (*Skazanie*) of the Mamai Battle". The first version was probably produced in the 15th century, but it is difficult to see clearly through the many layers of later (16th century) additions and changes. The *Skazanie* is in the genre of the military tale and, though following the plan of an annalistic narrative, it contains a number of unhistorical additions, such as the night-time review of troops by Dmitrij Donskoj and Dmitrij Bobrok when they attempt to determine the outcome of battle by various omens (e.g., fire in both camps, rumbling of the earth and the voices of beasts and birds) reminiscent of an episode in the Nestor Chronicle (1097). The battle opens with a duel between the monk Peresvet and a Tartar giant, which likewise reminds us of the old Chronicle (1022). There is an attempt at psychological characterisation of the *dramatis personae*; this is very one-sided, but graphic. Research has yet failed to establish at what stage the various unhistorical changes in names and details were made, and when religious motifs were strengthened (the replacing of Jagiełło's name by that of the long-deceased Olgerd, of the name of Bishop Gerasim by that of the as yet not appointed Metropolitan Kiprian, details of Dmitrij's visit to Sergij of Radonež, etc.). Scenes and pictures introduced into *Zadonščina* under the influence of old chronicles are varied here in a very poetic way, as, for instance, the picture of the battle-banquet in the introduction: "Strong winds arose then. ... The Russian Great Princes rose to their feet and, following them, marched ... the boyars filled with success, to drink a chalice of mead and to eat grapes; nay, not to drink the chalice of mead and not to eat grapes, but to attain honours and famous names in posterity." Similarly changed are the descriptions of the army in the old style: the helmets glitter like the morning dawn, but plumes on helmets are like the blazing fire, etc., instead of the simple ancient formula: "the army (or the arms) shone". Unfortunately, as stated already, the time of the origin of the present text is still disputable (cf. also V, 9, 3).

7. The victory over Mamai had at first a merely moral significance. As little as two years later, Mamai's vanquisher and successor, Khan Tochtamyš, appeared before the gates of Moscow. Prince Dmitrij saved himself by flight; the city was taken and burned down by the Tartars. Reports of these events are contained in the chronicles. One of these is materially different from the general tendency of the chronicles to ascribe the principal role to the prince.

These accounts, however, speak of the valorous but abortive defence of Moscow by its citizens, and even mention one of them by name, "Adam the Weaver (*sukonnik*)". Narratives of this kind should be viewed as a definite literary contribution of the commonalty; stylistically it follows the pattern of a military tale.

8. Tochtamyš in turn is routed by Tamerlan, and the latter then enters Russian territory (1395). The chronicles contain two accounts of Tamerlan's campaign which, in fact, hardly touched Russia proper. Russia's salvation is ascribed to the miracle-working of the so-called "Vladimir" Icon of the Virgin. The ecclesiastical style of this section and Tamerlan's legendary biography lead one to assume that the chronicles had originally contained at least portions of a separate tale dealing with Tamerlan.

9. A separate and unusual work is the tale about the capture of Constantinople by the Turks in 1453. The author of this tale signs himself "the much-sinning and lawless Nestor-Iskander [Alexander]" who came to the Turks as a child, became a Mohammedan, and took part in the capture of the Imperial city. There is no plausible hypothesis as to the personality of the author. A. Orlov thinks he was a Slav who fell into captivity only as an adult, embraced Islam and subsequently concealed his origin. This sounds very probable, as conversion to the Mohammedan faith would have been held much against him. Other scholars argue that erudition in Christian literature and knowledge of Slav and perhaps Greek writings should not be credited to Nestor-Iskander himself, but to a later editor of his work. At any rate, it is very strange that day-by-day events in the Turkish camp and the city are recounted with great accuracy, for after all the author could not have been on both sides at the same time.

The narrative opens with the foundation of Constantinople, which is recounted with historical names and details. Later a legend is woven into the account. At the foundation of the city there appeared an eagle which seized a snake and carried it aloft. Bitten by the snake, the eagle fell to the ground where it killed the snake. In this the author sees a symbolic prophecy of the city's fate: it is to be taken by a foreign nation, and then freed again. After theological observations supplied with texts from the Holy Scriptures, there follows the account of the siege. Day by day, the author in minute detail describes the position on both sides, as, for instance, the number of cannons and their dimensions, the activities of the besiegers and the conversations of the Turks, as well as – on the other side – the restlessness in the besieged city, the speeches made to the populace and army by the last Emperor, Constantine, and even private conversations between the Patriarch and the Emperor, and

so on. Most beautiful are the passages written under the obvious influence of Josephus and of the 12th–13th century chronicles containing the
well-known formulas: "On the fourteenth day, the Turks, after completing their godless prayer, began to blow trumpets and to play organs
and to beat the drums, and after bringing up cannons and many
arquebuses, they started firing at the city and shot from arquebuses and
from countless bows. ... And a great and terrible battle took place.
From the thunder of guns and arquebuses, and from pealing of bells
and from the sounds of screaming and weeping of men, women and
children in the city, it seemed that skies and earth had become one
and trembled both; and one could not hear what another was saying.
Then the roar and the cries and the screams and the wailing of men, and
the bursting of cannons and the pealing of bells merged all in one
terrible sound, like heavy thunder. Furthermore the smoke thickened,
rising from many fires and the firing of cannons and arquebuses on
both sides and covering the whole city, and one could not see another
nor distinguish with whom he fought, and many died of the fumes of
gunpowder." The traditional picture is only slightly altered by the use
of firearms. Elsewhere it is taken from Josephus almost word for word:
"On the thirtieth day ... from both sides of the city walls corpses fell like
sheaves, and their blood flowed along the walls like a river. From the
cries and roar of people on both sides and from the wailing and moans
in the city, and from the ringing of bells, and from the clamour and flash
of arms, it seemed that the whole city was upside down, and the city
moats were full of corpses to the brim so that the Turks ascended the
walls as if by steps and fought on. The dead had become for them a
bridge and a ladder to the city. Likewise, all the rivers and the coast
near the city were filled with corpses, and their blood flowed like strong
rivers. ..." Others turns of phrase are equally reminiscent of the same
literary origin; the Emperor's speeches are not very remote from the
orations in Josephus.

An ill omen forms the conclusion. A great flame emerges from the
Dome of St. Sophia and rises to the sky; then a rain of blood falls on
the city, and it is enveloped in darkness. This is understood, in both
camps, as heralding the fall of the Imperial city. The Turks press into
Constantinople and, after prolonged fighting, in which the Emperor
falls, conquer the city completely. Now pious observations follow.
This was the punishment for Byzantium's sins, and there are exclamations:
"O, how great is the power of the barbs of sin! O, how much evil does
crime bring forth! ..."

The Turks show themselves magnanimous victors; murder, robbery and violence are forbidden in the conquered city, and when the head of the Emperor is found it is handed over to the Patriarch for burial.

The final section consists of the prophecy of the future, with quotations from Methodios of Olympos, Leo the Wise, and the Prophet Daniel – a new Emperor will come from a "blond" people, and the author explains this, from the similarity of the sound, as "Russian" (*rusyj* – blond; *rusy* – Russians).

From the stylistic point of view, the work is typically heavily ornamented, even though its embellishments are only in the form of numerous epithets, word-chains, and the frequently varied use of the formulas of the old military tales.

The narrative found favour in Moscow, because its conclusion corresponded to the idea of "Moscow – the Third Rome". The prophecy of Constantinople's liberation by the Russians and some scriptural quotations are perhaps additions made by a subsequent editor. If this was so, it would have had to happen shortly after the work's completion for as early as 1512 Nestor-Iskander's account was included in the Chronograph in its present form.

10. Another tale which, through a typical misunderstanding, was regarded as a Life of a Saint in the 16th century is the story of Petr of the [Golden] Horde (*Petr Ordynskij*). It was in fact a broadsheet written with a definite purpose. The tale originated in the Rostov district, possibly only after the loss of independence in 1474, and was written in order to set out and establish the rights of the new ruler, the Great Prince of Muscovy, to Petr's succession in certain areas.

The first part relates the adoption of Christianity by a Tartar prince, who, under the influence of the Rostov bishop's sermons, moved his residence there and, deeply impressed by the beauty of the churches and of the divine service, received baptism. While, during a falcon-hunt, he was asleep on the shores of a lake, the Apostles Peter and Paul appeared to Petr in a dream and gave him two sacks of gold and silver. Petr bought land for a church and laid out its boundary with gold and silver coins (an apocryphal motif). Later, Petr was buried near his church, and a monastery was erected there.

The second part of the tale (omitted in the later, hagiographical, version) is the genealogy of Petr's descendants (down to his great-grandson) with recurring references to proprietary relations of Petr and his monastery, the rights being conferred by Rostov princes and envoys of the Horde. Petr's great-grandson saves Rostov from a Tartar invasion.

The tale is very vivid and contains interesting details. There is also a number of smaller accounts in a similar vein, about other Tartars who became Christian. This tale contains an important anachronism: Petr's monastery had already been in existence before the time which is given in the tale as the date of its foundation. This conclusively proves its later origin, i.e., not before the middle of the 15th century, as stated already.

The origin of this tale, however, is not characteristic. The author and his patrons obviously had as their only aim the furnishing of proof for their claims. Who would disdain having the written formulation of one's claims presented in good literary form? The subsequent fate of the tale is interesting; for, in the 16th century, a hagiographical work emerged from it. This was a result of the spirit of the time, when in Moscow a rare hope had become a universal conviction, namely that the Muscovite State, which in reality was anything but Christian, was a kind of Christian Empire in which the whole culture in one form or another served the interests of Christendom, and that everything of cultural value created hitherto (including literary works) possessed a sacred character. Such was the fate of many other secular biographies (cf. V, 5, 2 and 5), and an identical course was taken, with even less justification, in the case of the tale of Petr Ordynskij (cf. VI, 1).

11. Only one brief tale, which significantly comes from a Novgorod principality on the outskirts of the Russian area, has a non-historical content. This is the story of the mayor Ščil. The name is historical; Ščil was a monk who early in the 14th century built a church in the vicinity of Novgorod. In the tale, however, he appears as mayor (*posadnik*). The "pathos of reality" seems to have reached such a stage by the end of the 15th century that an imaginary person could not become the hero of a tale, and resort had to be made to a historical name.

This is a tendentious ecclesiastical work which is meant to illustrate primarily the Church's rejection of usury. Ščil is a usurer (but his rate of interest reaches only half of one percent per annum!), and, because of this, the Novgorod bishop – who is also supplied with the historical name of Ioann – refuses to consecrate a church built by Ščil. Ioann orders the mayor to lie down in a coffin, whereupon it sinks into the earth. Ščil is delivered from hell, after his son has ordered many masses for the dead (*sorokoust*) in forty churches of Novgorod. This probably is meant to show the need for requiem, and is presumably directed against the Novgorod heretics who denied the need of prayers for the dead (V, 1, 8).

This brief work is actually the only tale of the 14th–15th centuries which warrants the name of a short story in today's meaning of the term.

12. Two works which may be described as historical tales and deal with events of contemporary political strife (V, 1, 3) appear right at the end of the 15th century. These, however, are obscure on three points. First, they come from an author unknown, and apparently not ranking very highly spiritually; second, their political and ecclesiastical tendencies are harbingers of the darkest currents which were to dominate Russian life for centuries after that time; third and finally, they have not yet been critically edited.

The first is "The Tale of the City of Babylon" (*Skazanie o Vavilonĕ gradĕ*). It was not, however, until the 16th century that it acquired a framework that indicated reference to the State of Muscovy. In its original form, the story was presumably simply an attempt on the part of one of the Byzantine dynasties to substantiate its claims to the throne by alleged inheritance of the Babylonian coronation regalia of King Nebuchadnezzar. The possible Greek prototype is unknown, but in the 12th century a pilgrim from Novgorod (Dobrynja, cf. IV, 12, 15) had apparently heard at Constantinople a tale of the Babylonian regalia, which were reputed to be there.

The narrative is in the form of a Byzantine Emperor's epistle; the texts call him Lev, Levkij, Vasilij, etc. The Emperor despatched three envoys to Babylon (for a reason not stated), a Greek, a Georgian (*obežaninъ*), and a Russian (*rusinъ*); the Emperor with his army accompanied them part of the way. The ruins of Babylon were full of snakes, and a great dragon lay around the city. A ladder which was there, bearing an inscription in three languages and showing the way, enabled the envoys to cross the dragon. They then reached a church containing the burial place of the three saintly youths (see the Book of Daniel). From there a mysterious voice directed them to the palace, where they discovered the crowns of Nebuchadnezzar and his consort and an inscription to the effect that these crowns were destined for the Emperor (Lev, Vasilij, etc.) and his consort. The envoys took the crowns and the various jewels, and left the city. While crossing the dragon, the Georgian fell on it, and it woke up and hissed; whereupon not only the mission but the army, too, fell as if dead. The envoys recovered, however, reached the Emperor, and gave him their spoils. He presented them with most of the precious stones and had himself and his wife crowned with the two crowns.

A later framework is formed by the addition of a fairy-tale story at the beginning, dealing with Nebuchadnezzar and also explaining the fall of the city, the presence of the dragon and the snakes. Actually the "epistle" already presupposes this narrative, because otherwise the presence of snakes and of the dragon, which appear in the epistle without any explanation, could hardly be understood. At the end, a legend was added to the effect that the Babylonian regalia were presented by a

Byzantine Emperor to Prince Vladimir Monomach. In this way "Holy Moscow" became linked with Babylonian imperial tradition, which, according to the Bible, could be called anything but Christian!

The origin of this crude fable, which is, moreover, told in a very obtuse style, is not clear though there exist many Oriental and European parallels with some of its motifs. The mission's composition could only be of Russian origin. The Georgian is presumably a representative of the third Greek-Orthodox country; a representative of the fourth, a Syrian, refused to participate. The most reasonable assumption is that a Russian scribe had written down an oral Byzantine legend. Nevertheless, it is worthy of note that this slight work should have played such a role in the later ideology of Muscovite absolutism.

13. A legend, similarly crude in content, though far more artistic in its literary execution, originated at Novgorod with the prime object of buttressing, not the political, but the ecclesiastical claims of the city. This is "The Tale of Novgorod's White Episcopal Mitre" (*Povest' o belom klobuke*). The origins of this monument are clearer. This is a forgery, besides being a pseudo-epigraph, ascribed to Dmitrij Gerasimov, the well-known translator from Latin. The sources of its first part are known; these were the *Donatio Constantini*, the spurious western work on which the Popes had based their claims to secular power, and the apocryphal legend of the Emperor Constantine extant at the time in Slavonic translation. The author of the *Povest'* also claims that he had learned its content in Rome from the "Latins", who, for the most part, "conceal" the fate of the white mitre "with shame".

The subject-matter of the *Povest'* is as fabulous as that of "The Tale of the City of Babylon". The white mitre worn by Novgorod Archbishops, as distinct from the other bishops, is said to be the same which the Emperor Constantine – whose conversion to Christianity is told with fantastic detail – had presented to Pope Sylvester. But when the Western Church "fell away" from the Orthodox, the "heretical" Pope wanted to destroy the mitre. He was stopped by an angel who said to him, "Was it not enough for you to deny Christ's holy faith? ... Now, you wish even [!] ... to destroy ... the sacred white mitre." Thereupon the mitre is sent to Constantinople, whence, as the city was about to be captured by the "Hagars", it was transferred to Novgorod; this was foretold by an angel to Bishop Vasilij (a historical figure – Archbishop, 1330–52). The tale ends with the description of the festivities for the arrival of the Constantinople Patriarch's embassy which delivers the mitre to Novgorod. Later, it received a framework consisting of an epistle to the "Latins", and a writing (ascribed to Archbishop Gennadij) on the use of the "holy mitre" during divine service.

The narrative gives a minute description of the different phases of the wanderings of the "holy mitre", where all its moves are preceded and accompanied by visions, appearances of angels and similar miracles. The ecclesiastical style is fluent and ornate.

The purpose of this work certainly was the advancing of a claim by the Novgorodian Church to a Roman-Byzantine tradition. By the end of the 15th century, when Novgorod became a dependancy of Muscovite princes, the Archbishop personified all that was left of the city's independence. Therefore, only episcopal insignia appear in the tale, and mention is made too of the gift of a rod from the Constantinople Patriarch to the Novgorodian Archbishop (which, in fact, was donated by the Moscow Metropolitan in the 14th century). It is significant that here, though only in the first part in connection with the *Donatio Constantini*, ecclesiastical power is linked with secular. The author, who obviously freely invented the content of the later parts, forgets this motif in the course of his narrative. In the 16th century the tale was transferred to the mitre of the Moscow Metropolitan. In the end, at the Council of 1667, it was declared apocryphal.

7.   THE CHRONICLES

1. After the end of the 13th century we have either handed-down chronicles from the north and north-east, or at least traces of lost annalistic monuments in other works. The oldest chronicle manuscript is the Laurentian Chronicle of 1377; it also contains the oldest copy of Nestor's Chronicle; and its continuation which goes up to the year 1309. The text, however, was partly revised in the 14th century. This redaction, which probably comes from the pen of the copyist Laurentius (Lavrentij), deals with the princes of Suzdal', and especially with Jurij Vsevolodovič; the description is mainly an imitation of the panegyric style of the Chronicle of Nestor.

2. Of far greater literary interest is the Tverian Chronicle (*Tverskoj sbornik*), which has not survived in full and is extant only in a Byelo-Russian copy preserved in the Ukraine. It is merely a compilation made as late as the 16th century, in which even entries for the same year are copied twice from different sources. The actual Tverian Chronicle begins, it appears, with the year 1247. The annalist, in any case, wrote later, making use of a number of other chronicles. His contribution goes up to the year 1399, and was apparently not available in full to the 16th century compiler. Anyway, the first part reaches only the year 1375, the narrative being picked up again in 1382 and then continuing without interruption. The Chronicle devotes much space to matters both spiritual and temporal, while at the same time attention is paid to world history. It embodies also some complete stories, and at least one of these seems to have been an *independent* tale (see V, 6, 3). Another work partly extant is the second part of the Chronicle, which opens with the year 1402 and bears a separate title. This is the biography of Prince Michail Aleksandrovič of Tver'. According to the author's introductory words, he had been commissioned by Prince Boris Aleksandrovič of Tver' to compose a *panegyrikon* (*čest'*) on his great-grandfather, Michail Aleksandrovič. Of this panegyric, however (see about it: V, 5, 4), merely the opening section is extant; this is preserved in the body of the Tverian Chronicle. Prince Michail had fought Moscow bitterly for the primacy among the Russian seceding principalities; his plans were thwarted by the Tartar grant of a charter (*jarlyk*) to the princes of Muscovy as "Great Princes". It is permissible to assume that relevant sections had been expurgated from the Chronicle as a result of Muscovite intervention after Tver''s loss of independence.

In any case, the description of Michail's rule is incomplete and the style of the other sections is uneven. Beside brief factual reports of events, there are traditional formulas of old annalistic writings, like the prince's orations to the army: "Let us set out, O warriors (*družina*)!" and "Men are being cut down like grass". Archaic or local words are explained in the text as in Daniil's biography. There are also the equally traditional idioms of religious phraseology, like "because of our sins", and new demonological motifs, e.g., the devil being an "all-too-clever fighter" who entraps men in his "secret" or "hostile nets" (*sěti, mrěža*). Here, too, the author does not forget world history; he reports at least the capture of Constantinople by the Turks (where the word "Russian" is used instead of "Christian"). In many passages there are reminiscences of the heavily ornamented style in which Prince Michail Aleksandrovič's biography is written (see V, 5, 4). These are, for the most part, compound, abstracts and participial constructions, which make many a sentence unduly long.

3. From the point of view of literary history, other chronicles of the period are worthless, although they are of great significance as historical sources.

Chronicle writing is continued especially at Novgorod. Alongside the continuation of the I. Novgorodian Chronicle, about the middle of the 15th century,
two other annalistic works come into being: the so-called I. Sofia Chronicle
(*Sofijskij vremennik*, about 1432) and the so-called IV. Novgorodian Chronicle
(about 1450).

The basic characteristics of the style of all these monuments are roughly
identical. There are running entries, without any stylistic adornments, and
brief sentences in which mention is made of speeches at stormy popular
meetings. The assumption of scholars that these entries render the style of
speeches as actually delivered cannot be substantiated. The language partly
reflects the vernacular and partly that of the chancery, known from Novgorodian legal documents.

In the IV. Chronicle there appear passages that are reminiscent of the highly
ornate style of the literary works of the period, as for instance the description
of a storm in the year 1421 (written about 1450): "At midnight, there occurred
a great concussion in the skies. A huge cloud came from the south, letting
loose terrible thunder and lightning; fire shone from the skies so that no man
could look up and [the cloud] came and stood over the city, and the rain-
carrying cloud (sic! *tučenosnyj oblak*)* changed into a fiery picture so that
people thought that in the clouds there were the fire and flames which
burn sinners. And people were frightened by the anger, and were afraid, and
everybody shouted: 'God save us!' " The rather clumsy play with synonyms
(*ogn'*, *plamja*; *tuča*, *oblak*; *ubojašasja*, *strach*, *užasošasja*) indicates the author's
intention to imitate the heavily ornate style. Or elsewhere: "And there had
been in the district (*volost'*) ... shouts and cries and bellowing and cursing
(*klič*, *rydanie*, *vopl'*, *kljatva*) of all people about our government and our city,
because there had been amongst us no pity and no just justice." Foreign
words, explicable by Novogorod's vigorous foreign connections, also appear.
Time and again there are compounds especially characteristic of the new style:
tučenosnyj, *plamenovidnyj*, *samoizvol'nyj*, etc. (rain-carrying, fire-like, self-
willed. But, on the whole, all these ornamental devices are merely occasional.

It is ideologically interesting that the IV. Novgorodian Chronicle
does not confine itself to local news; and the intention of the author is
obvious: to make it into an "all-Russian" chronicle.

4. Chronicle writing also began at Pskov about the middle of the 14th
century. Here, too, annalistic activities were carried on very intensively.
There were probably three (A. Nasonov) original versions of the Pskovan
chronicles, which were also diligently copied (the latest edition could be
collated from no less than twenty-four manuscripts). However, these are
stylistically plain; they lack embellishment and report merely local events.
Only isolated episodes are reported in more detail.

5. Muscovite chronicle writing starts at the end of the 14th century. The
most ancient chronicle has not come down to us, but it can be seen from
remnants extant in other chronicles that it did not represent in any way the

* Osl. *toča* = rain.

THE ARCHANGEL GABRIEL FROM AN ICON OF THE ANNUNCIATION
FROM USTJUG (12TH-13TH CENTURY)
Later in the Cathedral of the Assumption in Moscow (Uspenskij sobor).

HEAD OF AN ENGEL FROM THE PICTURE OF THE LAST JUDGMENT
Attributed to Andrej Rublev. Cathedral of the Assumption (Uspenskij sobor) in
Vladimir-Suzdal'. Ca. 1408.

standpoint of the Muscovite principality striving for primacy. Moreover, it depicts Moscow's adversaries – Lithuania and Tver' – with a certain amount of sympathy. It is therefore safe to assume that this Chronicle was the work of the Metropolitan's circle, as the then holder of the See, Kiprian, held the view that he was the head not solely of the "Muscovite" but of the whole "Russian" Church, and in accordance with this position remained politically neutral in the struggle of the princes for supremacy in Western Russia. But after Kiprian the character of the Muscovite chronicles changes; they want to be "all-Russian" and to represent, at the same time, the Moscow point of view. Thus, much material with a variety of origins accrues in them, and the authors attempt to give a biased interpretation of the facts at their disposal. The first redaction came into being during the days of Kiprian's successor – Fotij, 1423; but it can only be discerned in the body of later chronicles. In 1463, there appears a new redaction, which treats its material to a great degree in a didactic manner. Šachmatov, as early as 1904, assumed the existence of further redactions of 1472 and 1479. This has been confirmed by the later discovery of other manuscripts. The 1479 version marks a novel approach: the author "improves" upon the material in many ways, e.g., he distorts accounts of events to suit the Muscovite point of view. Moreover, he introduces rhetorical interpolations which either substantiate the Muscovite attitude or are directed against Moscow's adversaries, e.g., Novgorod. The annalist becomes a pamphleteer. In any case, not all the sources of the 1479 version are well known.

The Moscow, Novgorod, and Pskov chronicles are continued, while with the loss of independence of the appanaged principalities other chronicle writing comes to an end.

6. The inter-relationship of the chronicles is different from the order as set out above. The Laurentian Chronicle (1377) formed the basis of the Moscow redactions of 1409 and 1429. The new versions of the Novgorodian Chronicle were influenced by the Muscovite annals. The Tverian (1455) Chronicle made use of both the Novgorodian and Muscovite records. Obviously, many other sources were also used for each chronicle, and every annalist rendered the adapted material in his own style.

8. TRAVELLERS' TALES

1. A very popular literary genre in the Middle Ages was the description of real or imaginary travels, Marco Polo and Mandeville providing examples of each type. In Russia, however, there is but a scant representation of either type. In fact, most accounts of travels are only bad guide-books, although, because of their references, they possess at times certain archaeological and historical significance.

2. The Novgorod literature has three works of this type, all of which are rather insignificant from the point of view of literary history.

About 1348–49, one Stefan *Novgorodec* (Novgorodian) accompanied by eight companions paid a visit to Constantinople. His account is hardly more than a rather dry list of churches and monasteries with notes fully understandable to eye-witnesses alone. Apart from ecclesiastical buildings, he includes only brief descriptions of the ports. In some passages, the author displays a certain tendency to add hyperbolic embellishments; in the Studion monastery "the icons, heavily adorned with gold, shine like the sun".

Two other descriptions of Constantinople refer to more ancient works, no longer extant. These are accounts of the 14th century: *Skazanie o Car'gradě* ("The Tale of Constantinople") and *Besěda o svjatynjach Car'grada* ("The Dialogue on Constantinople's Shrines"). The *Skazanie* is a guide-book to the city "for those who go to Constantinople". The *Besěda* is written in the form of a dialogue between an Emperor and a Patriarch; this, however, does not make the content any more lively. Particular stress is laid on the destruction wrought by the Crusaders in 1204.

3. Commissioned by the Muscovite bishop Pimen, who had to travel to Constantinople in 1389, was a description of the journey by a member of his suite – Ignatij Smoljanin (presumably a native of Smolensk). He describes the Ukrainian steppe with its fauna, then the Tartars of the Crimea, whose friendly hospitality he stresses, Azov and finally Constantinople. In addition to a dry enumeration of the city's holy places and mention of the legends connected with them, as well as brief scriptural texts, Ignatij relates the only political event he had witnessed at Constantinople, the struggle between the supporters of two pretenders to the Imperial throne – John II and Manuel II. Manuel wins in the end with the aid of the "Romans", i.e., the Crusaders. Ignatij vividly describes the riots during which John's partisans by night "run through the city on horseback and on foot, with unsheathed weapons in hand, holding the arrows ready and the bows strung". In similarly vivid vein he tells of Manuel's coronation. Ignatij lays particular emphasis on the fact that the first to greet the new Emperor at the coronation were members of the grave-diggers guild (a reminder of the Emperor's mortality). And this part of the narrative enjoyed such popularity among the readers that it is extant in manuscripts as a separate tale.

4. Not lacking in interest is the description of travels to Constantinople and Palestine by Zosima, a monk of Sergij's monastery (1420). Zosima copies Daniil's account (III, 6) but, in contrast to him, displays an intolerant attitude toward members of other religions. He takes note of many things outside the ecclesiastical sphere, and relates some legends that do not occur in other authors. The style is factual and dry.

In 1466 A Muscovite merchant, Vasilij, journeyed to Palestine by the land route. His account is merely a monotonous list of what he had seen, with the rarely used epithets: "great", "beautiful", etc. With one exception, he does not retell any legends, but merely mentions them. It is doubtful whether this account was written with any literary aim.

5. Most interesting are the descriptions of travels which led neither to the Imperial city nor to the Holy Land. The first is an account of the journey of the Muscovite delegation to the Florence-Ferrara Council of 1447. The anonymous author combines the list of stopping-places with brief remarks on what he saw. The delegation travelled across Germany by way of Lübeck, Nuremberg, and then Venice. The description shows that at this time the occidental and Muscovite cultures had hardly anything in common. Therefore the account is built on hyperoche: "not to be understood", "not to be described", "to tell of this is impossible and inconceivable" (sic!). In fact, the author is unable to tell a story; he offers not even disconnected details but merely utterly disjointed remarks, while his art of description confines itself to the epithet *čudno* (marvellous). The same applies to his "description" of Italy. Palaces, gardens, fountains, a hospital, a library, sea trade at Venice, are merely mentioned but not described. That such a valueless account was copied and read, supplies evidence of the absolute divorce from the West.

The slightly clearer description of a Christmas pantomime adjoined to the account can hardly be by the same author.

The brief notes about the return journey are probably by yet another author, and these are no better.

A further writing is the account of the performance of an Annunciation play at a Florentine monastery. The minute report of scenic arrangements and of the play's content is probably due to the limitations of the theme. This is much more elegant and better presented than the reports of other travellers.

A theological account of the Council is a polemical treatise against the Latins and contains hardly any information on foreign lands.

6. Probably the most interesting work of this kind is the description of his travels to India by Afanasij Nikitin, a merchant of Tver'. It is merely an unrevised notebook which deserves attention more for its content than for its literary form. Its significance for literature is strongly overemphasised by modern scholars. Nikitin's work is entitled *Choženije za tri morja* ("A Journey Across Three Seas"). He set out from Tver' in 1466 to travel to Persia by the Volga with a Muscovite embassy and two merchant ships. Near Astrachan' they were robbed, and Nikitin continued his journey, without merchandise, to Persia, and thence to India. He spent three years there (1469–72), and set off to return to Russia by way of the Persian Gulf, but on the way he died before reaching Smolensk. The manuscript, presumably intended for further revision, contains many sentences in a number of oriental languages; it was obviously not written for a Russian reader. The manuscript found its way to Moscow and became incorporated in the chronicles (under the year 1475); in this way it reached the reader.

Nikitin's descriptions are certainly influenced by "The Tale of the Indian Empire" (II, 11), but as far as can be proved, his reports correspond on the whole to reality. In the thirty-odd page account of his travels, Nikitin is obviously unable to describe all he has seen; moreover, he had visited only parts of India, namely the North- and Middle West.

Nikitin mentions, even if in brief sentences or as mere references, the customs, dresses, castes, fairs, gods, holidays and prayers (he had been to the predominantly Mohammedan areas), the weather (the tropical rain), beasts of burden (including elephants), the art of warfare, etc. Many things he merely alludes to.

Of particular splendour are the accounts of the buildings and the festivals, much of the colour for which he had found in "The Tale of the Indian Empire". It is significant that Nikitin employs few Church-Slavonisms, and both from the point of view of vocabulary and syntax his language is rather simple. A few examples will render the character of his style. He had visited the pilgrimage site at Buddha's birthplace – Parvati. "For a whole month I wandered with the Indians to Buddha's House. And the House [probably a temple – D. Č.] is very great, like half of Tver', [built] of stone, and Buddha's deeds are sculptured thereon . . . how he performed miracles, how he appeared to them in many shapes: first he appeared in human shape, then as a man with an elephant's nose [proboscis – D. Č.], and for the third time as a man but with an ape's face, for the fourth time as a man but looking like a wild beast; he always appeared to them with a tail, and he is carved in stone, and the tail is over two yards long (v sažen'). The whole Indian land comes to Buddha's House, to see the miracles. . . . In Buddha's House, however, the Buddha is hewn out of stone, very great, and the tail is above him, and his right hand is raised and outstretched, like Justinian's, the Emperor of Byzantium [on a giant statue at Constantinople – D. Č.], and in his left hand he has a spear, and he is naked. . . And before Buddha stands a very great steer, and it is made of black stone and gilt all over, and [the pilgrims] kiss its hoofs and shower flowers upon it, and shower flowers upon Buddha." Or the Sultan's departure for the hunt: "The Sultan goes out to the hunt with mother and wife, and with him [there are] ten thousand men on horseback, and fifty thousand on foot, and 200 elephants in golden armour, and he is preceded by 100 trumpeteers and 100 dancers and 300 ordinary horses in golden harness, and behind him [follow] one hundred monkeys. . . And his court is very wonderful, everything is wrought in gold, and even the last stone is engraved and beautifully painted with gold, and in the courtyard he has various utensils. And the city of Beder is guarded at night by 1000 men of the city's governor, and they ride about on horseback and in armour, and each of them has a torch." The Sultan visits a Muslim feast: "The Sultan's robe is embroidered all over with sapphires, and on the cap – a large diamond, and the quiver of gold with sapphires, and he has three sabres beaten in gold, and the saddle of gold, and before him a runner dances ... and behind him go numerous runners, and behind him goes a tame elephant fully clothed in damask, and it presses the people back and has a large iron chain in its mouth and presses back men and horses, so that no one should approach the Sultan." In such accounts the numbers alone are exaggerated, and these, moreover, Nikitin must have got from the Indians who are lovers of large numbers. But of a completely fabulous character is, for instance, his account of the Kingdom of Apes: "And the apes go about at night and steal hens and eggs, and live in the mountains under stones. And these apes live in forests, and they have a Prince of Apes (*knjaz' obez'jan'skyj*); and he goes about with his host; and they complain before their prince against those who interfere with them, and they come into town, destroy courtyards and kill people; and their army is, as it is said, very great, and they have their own language, and bear many children; and when a [child] is like neither the father nor the mother, they throw it on the roads; and the Hindus take them and teach them all kinds of manual craft, and others are sold, so that they should not run back, and they teach others to dance." It must be admitted that Nikitin adds here "as it is said". Or: "There is a bird and its name is *gukuk*, and it flies by night and cries: "gukuk"; and any roof it alights upon, there a man will die; and whoever attempts to kill it will see fire flashing from its beak."

At the end of the manuscript there is a prayer by Nikitin who grieves that he is cut off from the Christian world, does not know when holidays occur, has no books (these had been taken away from him by the pirates), cannot return to Russia, and he asks God to help him to regain the right path.

Nikitin's own fate is mentioned in the work only as far as it deals with his journey to Persia. In India, on one occassion an attempt was made to steal his horse, and on another to get him to adopt the Mohammedan faith. Only once does he express his longing for home.

It is impossible to say how Nikitin wrote his book. Some discrepancies can now be seen as, among other things, he does not clearly define the various lands. He says in one passage that there are no horses in India, but subsequently an immense number of horsemen appear.

In any case, the work shows how at that time a man, though not a professional writer, could nevertheless master difficult material. With contemporary writers, he shares the preference for magnificent pictures, representing thus the taste of the reader.

7. Mention should also be made of yet another work which belongs to the category of imaginary travels and has no high literary qualities. This is the epistle of the Novgorod bishop, Vasilij (1331–52), to the Tverian bishop Feodor, incorporated in the I. Novgorodian Chronicle (1347). Here the question is raised whether paradise had survived. Referring to apocryphal literature and to his own impressions of Jerusalem, Vasilij believes he can prove that nothing created by God could disappear. And the ships of Novgorod reached paradise which was on a high mountain, as they had reached hell beyond the Icy Sea. This narrative is one of the first definite appearances of folk-lore in old Russian literature.

9.   HISTORICAL SONGS

1. In the 14th century epic poems begin to appear in a new form, that of "historical songs", in which events of history are presented in a quasi-realistic version. First of all, it is now easier to identify historical personalities, and, moreover, the old heroes, the *bogatyri*, are no longer there. However, strict limits of time may hardly be drawn with certainty. As we shall see, even the events of the 16th century are presented in the form of *stariny*, and eventually the heroes reappear with new functions (cf. III, 9; IV, 6 and VI, 11). Here, too, it is only possible to speak of the retention of the old themes in modern poems.

2. More restricted in many respects than other historical poems are the songs about the Tverian struggles of the year 1327 (cf. V, 5, 2). The songs probably entered into Kirša Danilov's 18th century manuscript collection and were written down as a rare epic song in the 19th century. The first, probably the older, version describes how Tsar Azvjak Tavrulo-vič (Uzbek), sitting on a golden stool,

> *sudy razsuživaet,*
> *da rjady razrjaživaet*

("judges and rules"), a formula similar to that of "The Tale of Igor's Campaign". Azvjak distributes Russian towns among his boyars. The absent Ščelkan – in whom it is not difficult to recognise the historical Ševkal – on his return receives at his own request "the old, rich Tver'", together with the two brothers, "the courageous Borisovičes". At Tver', Ščelkan oppresses and worries the people; the "peasants" complain to the Borisovičes and present gifts to Ščelkan, but gain nothing. Then a peasant "cleaves" Ščelkan "in twain". The change of name, i.e., the reference to "peasants" rather than to town populace, is the result of centuries of tradition. The Borisovičes were probably the really existing Tverian boyars Štetnev, called Borisovič after family ancestors.

The versions written down in the 19th century enrich with fairy-story details the content of the song in which Tsar Vozvjaga Tavroljevič takes Azvjak's place. To retain Tver', Ščelkan stabs his son and drinks a cup of his blood; Ščelkan's sister lays a curse upon him and foretells his death "on the sharp spear, on the steely knife".

3. Surprisingly, no songs are known concerning the most famous and, in addition, victorious battle against the Tartars – the battle of Kulikovo Pole in 1380. Some scholars (Šambinago) attempt to single out from later manuscripts of the *Skazanie o Mamaevom poboišče* (see V, 6, 6) a number of passages which are reminiscent of the popular epos. Among them, for instance, is the description of the Tartar giant Telebej:

> His height is three fathoms,
> his width is two fathoms,
> between the shoulders – the stretch of arms of a good man,
> and his head is like a beer cauldron,
> and between the ears – an arrow's length,
> and his eyes are like drinking cups,
> and the horse under him is like a mountain.

This reminds us of descriptions of giants in the *stariny*. The following passage sounds even more impressive:

> Льется кровь богатырская
> по седельцам по кованым,
> сверкают сабли булатные
> около голов богатырских,
> катятся шлемы злаченые(...)
> добрым коням под копыта,
> валятся головы многих богатырей
> с добрых коней о сыру землю ...

("The heroes' blood flows onto the beaten saddles, the steel sabres glitter over the heroes' heads, the gilded helmets fall under hoofs of good horses, heads of many heroes mounted on good horses fall to the damp earth".) This passage also contains ornate epithets from Russian folklore. One should not see here, however, relics of a 14th-century song; it is much more likely that such passages had entered the manuscripts in later centuries under the influence of *stariny*.

4. It may well be that the impact of the battle of Kulikovo Pole on contemporary epic songs, and particularly on a number of *stariny*, expressed itself in the introduction of the Tartars instead of earlier nomadic tribes, and possibly too in the incorporation into the songs of the successful outcome of the encounter. On the other hand, there is hardly any doubt that a fable and a song about Kulikovo Pole were only written later under the influence of the *Skazanie* (see V, 6, 6).

10. THE SPIRITUAL CRISIS OF THE 15TH CENTURY

1. From the 12th century one crisis follows another, changing more and more the fundamental premises of East Slav life. The material foundations of the Kievan Empire vanish in the 12th century; for its eastern trade the West finds new routes opened up by the Crusades. The political decline of the small principalities, disintegrating in inter-necine struggles, is a symptom of a more profound process, not its cause. And the literary flourish of the late 12th and 13th centuries is but a twilight.

Night falls with the Tartar invasion. It is easy to speculate whether, by merging all their strength, the Eastern Slavs could have retained their independence against the nomads. However, a certain cultural supremacy might have been maintained, as the monasteries and the intellectual life were not interfered with to any great extent by the invaders. But such was not to be. Doubtless, the spiritual powers of the land were inadequate, and there is no need to seek for further explanation when consideration is given to the various subsidiary causes: the considerable weakening of relationships with Byzantium – the only potential spiritual metropolis of Eastern Europe; the almost complete severance from the south-western (Ukrainian) and western (Byelo-Russian) principalities; the weakening of the material resources of the potential maecenases – the princes; and lastly the struggle of the princes among themselves, now conducted with Tartar assistance. All this could only strengthen among thinking Christians that feeling which had already arisen in the 12th and 13th centuries, namely that "the world was in a bad state", and that escape from this world offered the only opportunity for remaining religiously and even morally pure.

In 1463 Constantinople fell to the Turks. This appeared to the Eastern Slavs, after all they had heard before about Turkish incursions into the Christian Balkans, as indicating that the fate of the Christian world was now sealed. Moreover, after the Byzantines had – for political reasons – welcomed proposals of union from Rome, they were no longer considered the safe bulwark of Christianity.

All these were surely only the subsidiary causes of the profound spiritual process that found its ultimate expression in the great crisis of the 16th century. One of the most penetrating students of Russian intellectual history (G. Florovskij) admits the existence of "an enigma": why – he asks – for centuries did the Eastern Slavs not develop an independent spiritual culture as well? He has in mind the more restricted field of theological culture, but this can be applied to all fields of intellectual culture. Even Soviet scholars who, after all, see "dialectical materialism" as a key that opens all doors, are unable to offer any plausible explanation of this phenomenon. However, the fact remains that the Eastern Slavs, when left culturally alone and having to be self-dependent, were unable to develop a high-ranking independent culture.

2. The first attempts at a spiritual renascence, which neither have found a definitive expression nor are fully clear to us, came from the sectarians (cf. V, 1, 8, and 2, 5). In their fight against the Church hierarchy they tried to cleanse and transform the Christian faith; possibly they went too far (we do not know this for certain) and perhaps, under foreign influence, they went about it the wrong way. The very fact that this movement emerged in two phases and certainly did not attract the worst people, is most significant. Their attempt to forge a link with new eastern cultural spheres could have opened fresh vistas of development. Whatever survived of their activities was at least an extension of the cultural sphere towards the "secular sciences" (even though in reality this could be later considered as pseudo-science). In other words, without accepting the religious teachings of the *židovstvujuščie* it was still possible to enlarge considerably the compass of culture by means of the avenues discovered by the sect, the Arabic and Jewish scientific literature.

3. Alongside, there developed another movement which undoubtedly was the most significant of the times from the point of view of spiritual history. This was the Hermit movement of the 14th and 15th centuries

(V, 1,7 and 4, 11). Too few literary relics of this movement have come down to us to permit its assessment as a complete whole. Even if the movement extricated men from society and led them into solitude, and if its representatives were apparently only concerned with their own spiritual well-being, nevertheless, its best exponents – men like St. Stefan of Perm', St. Sergij of Radonež, St. Kirill of the White Lake, and even their admirers such as Epifanij the Wise or the famous 15th-century painter Andrej Rubljov (a monk of one of the monasteries founded by the followers of Sergij of Radonež) – show that it had created spiritual and cultural values which opened new roads and pointed to the future.

4. Rather problematic, but nevertheless significant, appears the influence of Hesychasm – a spiritual movement developed in Byzantium in the 13th century (cf. V, 1. 6). It remains uncertain, however, to what extent this movement had exerted a serious spiritual influence, in spite of the translation and distribution of Hesychast literature. The connections between the early Hermit movement and Hesychasm are doubtful, but the latter's subsequent influence – from the early 15th century – cannot be denied. Nevertheless, it is rather difficult to say which aspect of Hesychast teachings and practice had exerted that influence. Because of its theological-philosophical ideas, the movement could prompt understanding and interest in serious theological, ethical, philosophical and aesthetic problems; it could have played a part too as the bare "technique" of ascetic life. How far its influence went in the first direction can hardly be determined. A later manifestation of Hesychasm came, it seems, about the end of the 15th century, but by then it was already too late. Hesychasm was brought to nought and worn down and smashed in the exactly same way as were the other spiritual movements of the time; all of them were destroyed by the same political power, dull-witted and uncomprehending.

5. Nil Sorskij is the writer who was both the last significant representative of the Hermit movement and of Russian Hesychasm. He was born in 1433, and his secular name seems to have been Nikolaj Majkov. That he described himself as "peasant" (*poseljanin*) is most likely but an inflection of the modesty formula (a topos) or, at the utmost, an indication that in his youth he had worked on the land. Anyhow, he was not of peasant origin; he had served as an official at court, though for a short time only, because at an early age he was cowled in Kirill's monastery on the White Lake. But he did not stay there for long either, leaving for

Mount Athos where he studied Hesychast teachings at close range and acquired the Greek language. After his return, he settled down in the vicinity of Kirill's monastery on the River Sorka [not Sora]. He soon became known widely as a theoretician of the hermits, and this is shown both by his correspondence and by the attempts of high Church officials to seek his counsel on various occasions. He took part in a number of Councils; the first definite report of him is reference to a statement made by him at the Council of 1503 that monasteries should not need to have any possessions of land and peasants, and that "monks should live in solitude and nourish themselves by the toil of their hands". To reinforce the opposition to Nil, Josif Volockij (see below, 5), who had already departed from the Council, had to be brought back. With this contemporary references to Nil end. It is characteristic that this ascetic, deeply revered by contemporaries and by following generations, never became the subject of a Saint's Life.

However, Nil is the only hermit to leave a literary legacy behind; this is of great value and is extant in many manuscripts, yet to be edited properly. Even if Nil's tracts – the "Instruction" (*Predanie*) for his disciples, the great monastic statutes, numerous letters, a prayer, and some translations, the extent of which is not yet fully known – in no way belong to the history of literature but to the history of Russian theology, nevertheless they should be considered, for they played a significant role in the spiritual crisis which determined the outlook of Russia's whole life and culture in the 16th and 17th centuries. His purely literary works, the Lives of the Saints revised by him, unfortunately also remain in manuscript.

Nil's writings deal only with the road toward spiritual perfection of man, and primarily of the one who has chosen the ascetic's "narrow path". This means that his writings are above all intended for monks. To be sure, Nil is no supporter of the great monasteries; monks should live, two or three together, in small retreats, they should support each other in their spiritual struggles and nourish themselves by the labour of their hands. He is also against the pompous splendour of monasteries and churches. Poverty is the hermit's normal condition, and he does not need any riches for giving alms, because his alms should consist of spiritual help "with the word".

On the path of spiritual struggle one should be led first and foremost by Holy Scripture. In contrast to most of his countrymen, however, Nil does not hold all religious writings to be equally authoritative. First come the Holy Scriptures, in the more narrow meaning of the word.

They have to be studied to be understood, and only accepted in accordance with reason (*razum*); many questions are not touched upon at all in the Scriptures, and thus guidance from an experienced ascetic should not be cast aside, even when it is difficult to discover a safe guide. Nil warns against the belief in and following of everything that can be found in religious literature. But one should not see "rationalism" in that; here is merely a healthy critical method presumably brought by Nil from Mount Athos. His hagiographical work also included the restoration of texts from which subsequent additions and inventions had to be expurgated. A later charge made against Nil was that he had deleted references to miracles in the Lives. But, surely, this is merely the application of the same critical method which made him warn against believing in apocrypha and pseudo-epigraphs. Almost invariably stories concerning miracles after a saint's death are later additions to the Life, and thus any attempt to establish the original text would naturally lead to deletion of subsequent additions that often, by mentioning historical names or events, give direct or indirect indication of the date of their origin.

In his works, Nil attempts to provide that leadership for the spiritual struggle for which, as he puts it, it is difficult to find a safe guide. His advice deals with the "purification" of the soul of its passions, and Nil describes this process with great psychological finesse, following the model of Patristic and Hesychast writings. Most men, even the ascetics, live according to their "emotional will". The passions take control of men; not all at once, however, but by degrees. Nil gives five such degrees in the process of the passions mastering human will (John Climacos gives six). These are: 1) introduction of the image *(prilog)*; 2) combination (*sočetanie*), i.e., retention of the image by will; 3) union (*složenie*), i.e., the act of being carried away by the image; 4) taking into captivity (*plěnenie*), i.e., the impossibility of liberation from passions raised by the image; 5) constant excitement of the original passion, only this can really be called passion (*strast'*). His next task is to show the means by which man can free himself, at each stage, from the development of passion. In a similar way, following again the writings of the ascetics, Nil lists the individual passions, of which he gives eight: immoderate eating and drinking, unchasteness, covetousness, wrath, immoderate grief, pusillanimity, arrogance, and pride. These are analysed in turn, and methods of combatting each are suggested. Significantly, Nil regards the last two as the most dangerous, and discerns in them the origin of what would now be described as the "power complex." With great finesse, Nil analyses all these passions and the means with which they may be fought. Passions are condemned because they lead a man away from his object, namely spiritual perfection, and because they create obstacles in his spiritual struggle. Nil mentions the traditional tools of the ascetics in this struggle, above all prayer and fasting. But he violently opposes the traditional conception of both. Prayer must be first of all "spiritual prayer" (*umnaja molitva*) and not external expression in a defined ritual. Inner feeling and not the voicing of set words constitutes the prayer, and thus the vocal expression (*pěnie*) often distracts people from spiritual activity. "He who prays with the mouth and neglects the spirit prays in the air." One ought to pray to God alone, and not to angels or men (this apparently refers to prayers addressed to saints). What Nil has to say about fasts and other ascetic exercises points in the same direction. Here too everything "corporeal" is for him but a way, a means for spiritual perfection. "Material actions are but foliage, and spiritual ones are the fruit!" Hence, he develops ideas about fast that directly contradict the strict monastic regulations. One must only beware of immoderate drinking and eating, and of revelry, but otherwise one ought to eat "according to one's need". There are actually no forbidden dishes; he who refuses tasty meals "neglects the good created by God". Commenting on the meaning of this passage, a supporter of Nil's says: Fast can even be dangerous, for those who hold fasting to be a virtue, have fallen into the devil's power; in their heart there grows the seed of self-satisfaction, from which emerges "the internal Pharisee". Moreover, attention should be paid to the physical capabilities of each man because "wax requires a different treatment than copper or iron". In place of strict asceticism, Nil suggests ascetic exercises in accordance with individual capabilities as well as menial tasks, conversations (on spiritual subjects, of course), meditations on death, and above all spiritual prayer. Although Nil describes a day in the life of an ideal hermit, he leaves in fact to each one of them the free choice of selecting his own way. No harmless activities are prohibited, and the hermit should act according to circumstances (*ašče prilučitsja*). Nil even concludes his monastic statutes with the words, "If anyone knows better and more profitable means he should act as he thinks fit, and we shall rejoice to see it." On the whole, his system of thought is animated by the feeling of freedom. Only one aspect of the spiritual struggle stands steadfast for him as the "crown of all", and that is the spiritual prayer (*umnaja molitva*).

Here, however, we enter upon a field in which Nil closely approaches the practice of the Hesychasts. This is a certain technique of praying which is connected with holding the breath and the concentration of the spirit in the region of the heart. It leads to a condition of esctasy (*izöstuplenie*), in which man "holds everything mundane as ashes and dust", and perceives the light "which the word does not possess". Nil quotes the words of Isaac the Syrian, "I perceive within myself the Creator of the world". This means "to commune with God (*priobščat'sja*) in so far as man's inner capabilities will allow". Thus we encounter in Nil, besides the first two steps of the mystic path (purification and enlightenment) the third one also, union (*henōsis*).

Nil's ideas are not original; one finds them in Church writers to whom he also refers, namely, John Cassianus (4th-5th century), John Climacos (6th century), Maximus the Confessor (6th century), Isaac the Syrian (7th century), Gregory the Sinaiite (14th century), etc. Nil, however, is not a compiler but a writer who assimilates and works upon the ideas of others and then expounds them in his own words, even if with many quotations.

The very fact that he presents them shows that he did not at all wish to withdraw completely from the world. Writing to a monk, Kassian, he himself says, "I cannot bear to hold secrets in silence." He wishes to transmit his spiritual experiences to others, "for the benefit of the brethren", even if "this is both unwise and foolish". Political questions are of no interest to him, and he condemns political activities by monks. He feels compelled, however, to enter the Church-political sphere. His appearance at the Council of 1503 has been mentioned already. As he demanded that monks "should win their daily bread and all their other needs through their right occupation, menial tasks and labour", the possession by monasteries of estates populated with peasants was for him both unnecessary and harmful. For "we ought neither to have, nor wish for, nor achieve the unneccessary". Moreover, earthly wealth "is possession won by force from someone else's work", and when a monastery is endowed with such an unjust gain, it is not "to our benefit", the reason being that administration of property distracts monks from their final aim – the spiritual struggle. Possession of property "ensnares" monks into relations with the world. Philanthropic activities of the monasteries, which become possible with property, are unnecessary: alms of monks should not be material, but should be in the form of "help to a brother in need through the word, to alleviate his sorrow with spiritual contemplation."

Another question raised by Nil before public opinion was that of the persecution of heretics, at that time the *židovstvujuščie*. In contrast to the ecclesiastical hierarchy, who wished to extirpate the heretics by means of secular justice, i.e., fire and sword, Nil confined himself merely to a declaration that heretics "should be alien to us", and saw a way of influencing them not by force but by giving a personal example to them (among others holding such an exceptional view was the Metropolitan of Moscow). With his respect for the spiritual powers of mankind, Nil wished to convert the heretics.

These two problems of worldly affairs with which Nil was particularly concerned were not made into hard fought issues by him, but only by his successors, Nil himself having died in 1508.

6. Although Nil's writings are not truly literary works, his style deserves attention. He is an excellent stylist and succeeds in expounding the most difficult problems in simple language. His style, however, is not lacking in ornaments. When presenting spiritual problems and reformulating the thoughts of his masters, as well as when translating, Nil had to work out a terminology for the exact rendering of ideas. In other instances, however, he resorts to rich synonyms, as for example in *trud*, *rukodělie*, *rabota* (perhaps: effort, manual work, labour). Elsewhere, he arranges synonyms mounting to a climax. He does not use many compounds, but among them, it seems, there are some neologisms, like *zloljutstvo*, *zloobrazen*, *ljuboprepiratel'nyj*, as well as the traditional ones: *mimochodjaščij* [*mir*], *mimoidoše*, *skoroletajuščij*, etc. ("angry and furious, angry-looking, fond of arguments, the transitory world, to pass away, quick-flying"). His speech is often lightly coloured with rhetoric; he praises silence and rejects debate (*ljuboprepiratel'nye slovesa*). As shown already, he is not opposed to didactic speech, and he often presents his orations in the form of sermons. For instance, he uses series of rhetorical questions: "When we see the naked bones we say to ourselves: 'who is this, an Emperor or a beggar? a famous or an infamous one? where is the beauty and the enjoyment of this world? is not everything here but ugliness and stench?'", and so on. Nil frequently resorts to metaphors, especially to make his conceptions clear, for example "one stabs oneself with the knife of despair"; one collects texts of Scriptures as "a dog gathers crumbs from under his master's table"; passions are "the waves which rise against the soul"; passion "steals" our success. He who follows the example of the great saints "takes over the flag from the hands of the warriors, from the race of giants," etc. Often whole chains of metaphors are used: "The heart is the preserver of thought; the spirit

the helmsman of the feelings; the thought, a quickly-flying and impudent bird;" or the metaphor concentrates on one idea: "the fatal end approaches; the hatchet is at the root of the tree; the felling of my barren soul is prepared; the harvest will not be put off, the sickle is sharpened, the harvesters are ready to seize my soul full of the weeds of sin, and cast it into the eternal fire". Elsewhere occur metaphorical juxtapositions: the spiritual prayer is the favorable wind; the spoken prayer, the helm that is needed only when no wind blows; a traveller knows where his resting place is, and for how long he may rest; man does not know when he will die. There are also metaphorical parallels: the art of reading and singing if once acquired cannot be forgotten; so too with spiritual activity. Man knows what burdens can be carried by a mule, a camel or a donkey (the names of foreign animals suggest the assimilation of the image from a foreign source), and thus a man alone can decide the burden (asceticism) he is about to place upon himself. Developed metaphors occur also. Moreover, it is in imitation of Byzantine prototypes.

7. On the other hand, there were monks representing a different trend which could be described only in a strictly limited sense as "spiritual". The first significant name is that of Pafnutij Borovskij (d. 1477) whose Life is at the same time a program. It was Josif Volockij (1439–1555), however, a disciple of Pafnutij, who became the leader of the movement. He was born Ivan Sanin, a nobleman; at an early age he became a monk in Pafnutij's monastery, and after the latter's death, its abbot. While abbot, he undertook journeys throughout Russia in disguise in search of a monastery with an exemplary Rule. But soon after his return, he left the monastery and went to his homeland, to Volokolamsk, where he laid the foundation of a new monastery (after that he was also known as Josif Volokolamskij). This monastery was endowed with magnificent gifts and was most luxuriously appointed. From the outset it had a number of monks from the best families. Nevertheless, the Rule was very strict; life was hard, even though certain classes of monks enjoyed a number of privileges. The monastery developed extensive philanthropic activities, and helped starving peasants in the vicinity. Josif wrote letters to the estate-owners to persuade them to treat their "subjects" better. He believed that by such means he could care for the souls of men, both rich and poor, as well as for the alms-giving monks.

As a writer, Josif has left behind extensive works. These include his monastery's statute, the collection of sixteen epistles under the title *Prosvetitel'* ("The Enlightener") – in which he mainly deals with the heresy of the *židovstvujuščie*, and several epistles. Also important are some statements of his disciples which, generally speaking, faithfully define his beliefs. Josif's works are compilations only. They consist of hardly more than quotations from religious writings, in which, in contrast to Nil, he shows no difference whatsoever. In exactly the same way he quotes from Lives of the Saints and the Gospels. For him Nikon's (11th century) *Pandecta* (the Ascetic's Guide) are *bogovdochnovennye pisanija* (God-inspired writings), and he even goes as far as to say that "civil laws are equal to those of the Prophets and Apostles, and to the writings of the Holy Fathers".

However, this selection did not play a very significant role. It seems that Volockij's only aim in his writings was to enforce certain definite demands; this is not difficult in a monastic Rule. Except for minor sections, this work is only a casuistic ordering of all questions of monastic life. The main theme is *blagočinie* – "decorum". Fear is the mainspring to which Josif appeals: "fear of God", fear of death and fear of punishment. The rules themselves are not very exacting, but strict adherence to them is demanded. In spite of the mention of "iron fetters", punishments are not very severe. The monastery is compared to the palace, and God to the Emperor. Josif himself saw this orderliness embodied in the "Autocrat at the Palace". Even spiritual advice is presented in the form of counsels on physical bearing: "Press your hands together, place your feet together, close your eyes and collect (concentrate) your spirit." The rules which one scholar (Fedotov) has described as norms of Muscovite *kallokagathia* apply generally, even to laymen: "Step softly, let your voice be measured, your speech decent, drink and eat quietly ... be sweet in your answers, don't exaggerate in conversation, your face while speaking should be alight so that those with whom you are talking may rejoice." In the monastic Rule it is laid down, "Above all, we care for bodily beauty and propriety, and only afterwards for inner security (*chranenie*)." Most of the rules for monks and laymen alike are prescriptions for external behaviour. Thus, for instance, he writes about fasting to a layman: "Three days a week – Monday, Wednesday and Friday – dry food, bread or white bread with water or kvas. But when this is impossible, a dish or two cooked without fat. When, however, on Mondays, Wednesdays or Fridays, there falls a feast of the Lord, of the Gospels or a holiday – all dishes are allowed. Everything is also permitted – even on Mondays, Wednesdays and Fridays – including meat, curds, wine, and, according to our custom, mead, on the following occasions: twelve days after Christmas until Epiphany [6th January

– D.Č.], the week after the "Pharisaic Sunday"*) the week around Shrove
Tuesday, the week after Easter, and the week after Whitsun". ... "And
on those days of fast, when it is impossible to fast as written down
here, alms should be distributed according to means... For you it
would be enough to give a *grivna* on each of such days, and otherwise
give alms according to what you can afford." Or: "And on the great
fasts eat dry bread and white bread in the first week, and every five
days raw vegetables – cabbage, kvas of bread or of honey. Likewise,
on Mondays, and Wednesdays and Fridays, throughout the whole period
of the fast, and on Tuesdays and Thursdays – food cooked with fat
and honey as may be needed, and on Saturdays and Sundays even
caviar and giblets." Thus the whole year is regulated. The following
sentence shows what significance Josif attached to these rules, "He
who however does not keep the fast on Wednesdays and Fridays is
like the Jews who crucified Christ."

Prayers are ordered likewise, that is, the oral ones, with instructions
for how many prayers should be read, and how many genuflections and
obeisances should be made; all this is laid down precisely.

The *Prosvětitel'*, which unfortunately is our most important source
of information about the *židovstvujuščie* heresy, certainly contains much
that is untrue, but which the author himself obviously did believe.
Josif demands the death penalty for the heretics. "To slay a sinner and
a heretic with the hands or with prayer is all the same." To kill a heretic
means "to make the hand holy". Josif wants the same penalty for both
the repentant and the inveterate heretic, for one cannot know how true
the repentance is. He does not believe in the possibility of converting or
convincing them. And the penalised innocent merely profits by this, for
he, as an innocently suffering righteous man, may expect to be rewarded
in the Kingdom of Heaven. Josif wants, with God's help, to oppose the
stiff-necked "heretics" and their "devilish tricks", i.e., he advocates the
complete extirpation of their views by all possible means. One should
even pretend to be their fellow-believer in order to win their confidence.

Josif's views concerning monastic possessions are closely bound up
with his assessment of secular power. This power appears to him to be
boundless. "The Tsar in his conduct is equal to all men, but his power
is equal to that of God." Josif quotes this from a Byzantine writing
by one Agapit (I. Ševčenko). "Thou, Lord, hast been appointed from
above, as God's right hand, as autocrat, ruler and supreme lord of all

* This is the Sunday on which the Evangile according to Luke 18 is read in the
church.

the Russias, for God has chosen thee to take His place on earth, and has raised thee to His [!] throne and placed thee upon it." In theory, the Church is above the State, but the secular ruler is the defender and guardian of faith and of the Church. Therefore, to Josif heretics are like criminals (thieves and robbers). In heresies he sees the reason for the Empire's decline. It seems to him that secular and ecclesiastical powers should coalesce. The secular power should see to the implementation of ecclesiastical laws, and the secular ruler should be the highest court of appeal in Church matters as well, for "the Court of the Tsar is not judged by any other Court".

In Church matters, utility becomes Josif's only criterion. This principle, nevertheless, is a most dangerous one, a force indeed destroying all religious and moral foundations. In Josif's writings this is even more fraught with danger, for he no longer draws a distinction between the needs of the State and the Church. It might well be, as some scholars wish to prove, that Josif had at first attempted to place the interests of the Church before those of the State. His disciples and followers took over completely his later views on the identity of Church and State, and from the historical point of view, Josif emerges as the partisan of this identity. He condones all interference by the great prince (whom he already describes as "Tsar") in ecclesiastical affairs, such as the deposition of bishops (even on political grounds) and the settling of differences within the Church. With the needs of the State he justifies the necessity of the holding of monastic property. Admittedly, the note of philanthropy appears in his statements; rich monasteries can also give rich alms. But of far greater importance is the next point, "If monasteries have no estates, how can an honourable and noble man become a monk?" And "if there should be no reverend *starec* [here are meant, however, representatives of high society – D.Č.], whence will come [candidates] for the Metropolitan throne, for archbishoprics, or bishoprics, or any other honourable appointment? And when there are no noble and dignified *starcy*, then faith will be shaken." One can hardly doubt the authenticity of such a formulation. A number of Soviet scholars see Josif's "merit" in this formulation which surrenders the Church unconditionally to the State, and carries the theory of Muscovite autocracy to its final conclusion. It can be stated, unfortunately, that these formulations provided the very basis of the most profound spiritual crisis which Moscow experienced in the following centuries.

It must be added here that Josif should not in any way be identified with his followers who worked after his death. He certainly did not possess that boundless optimism which is so characteristic of them. In his writings the assumption is made that the Tsar might be a "disbeliever". And "such a Tsar should not be obeyed". Such a "refractory Tsar" is no "servant of God, but of the devil, and not a Tsar but a tyrant (*mučitel'*)". Josif, however, did not consider the question who should decide whether a Tsar was a "disbeliever" or not, when all one could do was to supplicate (*umoljat'*) the Tsar, but not contradict him.

8. It is not necessary to say a great deal about the literary aspect of Josif's work. He is a compiler, whose whole art consists in the apt selection of quotations and passages (some of which were totally misunderstood). His language is plain and clear. But it is his ideology that raises many questions. It is quite wrong to consider Josif as a conservative. He is primarily an innovator, and a particularly bold one; the "reactionary" is usually the most zealous innovator, and this time and again is the case in Russia. Josif had contributed much to the ideological grounding of the theory of the "service State" (*služiloe gosudarstvo* – Russia in the 16th century)*; his idea is the idea of service, of a society that he had identified with the State. When he uses this idea of service to the State, he forgets the basic tenets of Christian *Weltanschauung*. Thus all men harmful to the State, and even those who *might become* harmful, should be destroyed, and the Church offers a willing hand to this work of destruction. A great deal has been written on the "superfluous man" in Russia of the 19th century; in 16th century Moscow all men were "superfluous", the State alone was "necessary". The basic lines of Josif's concept of the world are novel throughout and do not even appear in the ideology of the Byzantine Empire, to which earlier scholars tried to trace back the ideology of Josif and his adherents. All citizens have duties but no rights – this basic tenet of the conception of a State held by Ivan the Terrible is already implicit in the ideas of Josif.

Another characteristic of Josif's ideology is the total indifference to matters of culture. Here, indeed, he is conservative. His views are the same as those of many representatives of the Middle Ages expanded to absurdity. Admittedly, there were not many such. The old alone should be preserved, for all new ideas are either superfluous or false. For him,

---

* "Service government": a governmental organization which arose in 16th-century Moscow; a government, in which each individual serves – in some way or other – the interests of the state (the features of the "service government" are described in every textbook of Russian history).

the task seems to be the dissemination of old concepts and not the creation of new values. Even his own innovations he views as "old". Josif's writings are only compilations, as an earlier scholar, Chruščov, has noted. But by the oblique exposition of the old (for every repetition of spiritual values is necessarily an exposition at the same time), he lays the foundations of an entirely new ideology. In the 16th century this point of view is heightened. And one hundred years later even Greek travellers found in Russia a variant of Christianity that astounded them by its uncommonness and singularity.

Of course, beneath this surface there had also been a different spiritual life, and it is partly due to Nil's school that such a life had been preserved. At any rate, with the end of the 15th century, a completely new chapter was opened in the spiritual and literary history of Russia.

11.   VARIOUS WORKS

1. The adoration of new saints brought with it the need for the inclusion in divine services of special prayers addressed to them. Hymns of praise, and eventually complete liturgies, had to be composed. About this time there also appeared liturgical works in honour of locally revered saints. Since the earliest times there had been good models for these in the form of the liturgical Menaea (II, 2) – the symbols and idiom of which could be imitated, and which could even provide ready-made formulas for adaptation. This actually happened. It is true that foreigners, men like Grigorij Camblak (V, 3, 4), and especially Pachomij the Serb (V, 4, 9), were those who had created the most complete models in Russia. Compared with the old Menaea, the new literary techniques did not exert great influence. This field, however, is wide open for research, the objective difficulties of research being far too great, and in most instances works of this character being extant in later redactions only, which are either abridged or expanded and are remodelled in their lexical content. Pachomij's art is the easiest to assess, for many of his works have been well preserved. As with his hagiographical writings, his skill consists in the use of ornate speech with considerable reduction of the subject-matter (the Lives).

A number of special services (e.g., consecration of priests and deacons) were now written or reworded in Russian form. These, of course, are even closer to the liturgical tradition.

2. An important source of both ecclesiastical and social history are the epistles of the hierarchs, which have come down to us from this period in relatively large numbers. These, however, are of incidental importance to literary history, as they contain only scant factual information, being mainly a sequence of definite turns of phrase providing the epistle's framework. A certain sameness of form implies the existence of epistolary guides or other „epistolarium". It is probable that the writers took over these forms from more ancient epistles.

Of special significance are the few epistles dealing with the "heresies" (see V, 1, 8). Unfortunately, they do not enable us to define the characteristics of these heretical movements.

The epistle of the Bishop of Rostov, Vassian Rylo, to Great Prince Ivan III (1480) occupies a special place. This letter was dispatched to Ivan when the Muscovite armies stood on the river Ugra undecided whether to join battle with the Tartars or not. In his epistle (*Poslanie na Ugru*), Vassian attempts to influence the Great Prince to fight the Tartars. He draws Ivan's attention to his responsibilities to his subjects, who expect him to do battle, and to his responsibility to God who gave him power. In conclusion, the bishop refers to examples from history concerning both religious and lay wisdom (a quotation from Democritus, borrowed from *Pčela*). For the last time, a prince of the Russian Church speaks here of his right and duty to admonish secular rulers, adding that they should heed such admonitions (cf. III, 3, 3). For no particular reason, this letter is considered as the ideological basis of Muscovite absolutism, merely because of the pompous title given by Vassian to the Great Prince. Simply the reference to the ruler's duties to his subjects makes such an interpretation impossible.

3. Collections of sermons were now being not only copied but also revised and even newly compiled. Probably about this time there were included in the collections popular works of Slav preachers translated from the Greek (the sermons of Kirill of Turov, and those only ascribed to him, a number of anonymous sermons, etc.). *Zlatostruj, Izmaragd*, as well as other collections were dealt with in this way. In addition to sermons, adaptations were also made from didactic works of various kinds, special attention being paid to local themes such as superstition, drunkenness and exploitation of the poor. Special stress was laid on the reading of the "Books", i.e., the Holy Scriptures and religious literature. It appears that *Izmaragd* was used by the *strigol'niki* for purposes of propaganda (V, 1, 8).

4. Theological literature was enriched by original tracts. The works of the main exponents of both the opposing movements at the end of this period have already been discussed (V, 10). In the last years of the century, there appeared from Pskov a treatise concerning the number of times "Hallelujah" should be chanted during a divine service – twice or thrice. This was presented in the form of a narrative legend, "The Life (*Žitie*) of Saint Evfrosin". Actually, this is not a legend at all, but a tract in favour of singing "Hallelujah" twice. It tells of a pious ascete, the monk Evfrosin, a historical personality (d. 1481), and of his opponents – the priest Iov and the deacon Filipp who had abandoned his spiritual ideals – and of the people who are actively participating in the strife. The arguments of Evfrosin – the victor in the debate – consist only of indisputable statements and terms of abuse, while the case of his adversaries is not stated at all and their wickedness, wrathfulness and "infidelity" are depicted in terms at least partly borrowed from Manasses. In depicting the character of Evfrosin use is made of idioms reminiscent of Hesychast writings. A tract against the "Latins" – the Catholics – originated in Moscow after the Florence-Ferrara Council (*Slovo izbrano ... na latynju*), but probably not earlier than the 60's. In this work, theological arguments are almost totally

absent. It is merely an apologia for the independence of the Russian Church from the Byzantine, which, at the Council, had entered into union with the Church of Rome. The significant part of the work is a panegyric eulogy of Great Prince Vasilij II, who is described in a wealth of exquisite epithets (compound) and who is compared to the most pious rulers of all times. There is not sufficient evidence to prove the theory of Pachomij's authorship of this work.

5. Considerable progress was made in the 15th century in works of chronographic character. The Chronograph of that century encompasses a description of Slavic history. In addition to the Russian chronicles and the material taken from the old Chronograph (see IV, 12, 4), there also appear data from Manasses and from the Serbian biographies of princes. The oldest biography made use of came into being in 1431, and it is therefore impossible to consider the new Chronograph as having originated before the 40's. The Russian sections now show the influences of Manasses and of the richly ornamented Serbian biographies. The writer's approach is an ecclesiastical one. At the beginning of the 16th century (1512) this rendering was replaced by a new work.

Probably in Pskov, there originated in the second half of the century the chronographical Palaea which bridges the gap between the Old Testament and the Baptism of Rus'; under Vladimir, Kiev became "the second Jerusalem".

6. Legal documents are now of linguistic importance only. These include deeds, treaties (with foreign countries too), the Pskovan codex (*Sudnaja gramota*) of the 15th century, and the Muscovite *Sudebnik* (code) of 1497. These show evidence of the expansion of the chancery language, which is much closer to the vernacular than to the literary language of the time.

7. The tables for the calculation of Easter are, of course, outside the field of literature proper. Until the end of the 15th century, such tables went up to the year 1492, which was the year 7000 "after the creation of the world". With the conclusion of the official Church tables many had perhaps linked the idea that the end of the seventh millenium would be "the end of the times" and thus the end of the world. Some scholars hold the view that an eschatological feeling was *prevalent* at that time. We lack, however, any convincing witness to the broad dissemination of such a feeling. The character of Russian 17th–18th-century spiritual life (see VII, 7) is transposed into the past, and attempts are made to discern an eschatological panic or "psychosis" in the 15th century. At any rate, the Easter Tables which appeared in Russia at the end of the 15th century have for us, if not a literary and historical interest, at least a certain importance in the field of spiritual history. These tables were almost simultaneously prepared (or received from abroad) by two factions, by the Orthodox and by the *židovstvujuščie*. It is possible that the Lunar Table of the *židovstvujuščie* – *Šestokryl* (see V, 2, 5) was linked with the problem of the Easter Tables. The "paschalia" for the following centuries have brought in their wake a spiritual tranquillity which was even consolidated by the uninterrupted progress of time after 1492!

About the end of the 15th century there appeared a Greek-Russian conversation book which is also not without importance for the history of the literary language.

VI

MUSCOVITE LITERATURE

1. CHARACTERISTICS

1. Russian literature cannot be described as "Muscovite" until the 16th and early 17th centuries. Although some works were written in Novgorod or Pskov, and even at Murom and other provinces of the Muscovite State, their uniform style was fundamentally determined by Moscow which now, in contrast to its lack of literary productivity in the past centuries, not only supplied the lion's share of literary output, but also became the leading force. The Muscovite literature of the period is however entirely divorced from the writings of the rest of Europe. It has a character of its own, and its features bear no resemblance whatsoever to those of the contemporary late Renaissance and Reformation in the West. But certain parallel phenomena may be discerned perhaps in the striking rhetorical features of numerous Muscovite works which are reminiscent of the style of so many Western European writings of the time. Muscovite rhetoric, however, lacked the fundamental traits of both the Renaissance and the Reformation – conditioned in each of the two Western movements by different intentions, namely the striving toward clarity of composition and precision of expression. If comparisons were to be drawn with Erasmus or Luther, not only would the vast divergence between Muscovite and Western literatures be apparent, but so would their existence on quite different planes, the criteria being not according to value but according to art. Similar too, is the case of the relation to the literatures of other Slav peoples – Poles, Czechs, Croats, and even Ukrainians and Byelo-Russians, who have few purely literary monuments from the 16th century. In fact, the literature of none of them has anything in common with the Muscovite, either in content or form!

The fact that various influences reached Moscow from the West is not in contradiction to all this. Such influences were confined mainly to technical culture (the art of warfare and printing) and fine arts, not excluding icon-painting. In the literary sphere (see chapter VII, 2), such influences were of no consequence at all.

2. First of all, the relative significance of poetic ornament had grown still further in comparison with the already ornate style of the 14th and 15th centuries. It appears, moreover, that writers considered ornamentation as their proper and only task. Methods were not new; we know them already: compounds, participial constructions, word-chains, the piling up of synonymic expressions, antitheses easily formed with antonyms (words of opposite meaning), hyperbolic expressions of praise or censure, deliberate use of pronounced Church-Slavonisms. All this was apparent before, but now it is often intensified still further. Characteristically the subject-matter becomes further obscured by these embellishments, and even acquires a different meaning. Quotations, which are not required to bear any relation to the subject, have in part an ornamental purpose as well. The number of set formulas has increased; anything not abstract, even when transformed by luxuriant embellishments, seems to be of no importance. Even the main direction of these writings is hardly discernable (cf. below, 5).

The works are often no more than variations on familiar themes. This is mainly linked with the basic ideological tendencies of the period.

3. The ideology of the 16th–17th centuries is, to a great extent, conditioned by political changes in Eastern Europe. The many appanaged principalities were by now replaced by a centralised Muscovite State. The principalities still in being (some survived until the end of the century) were purely nominal political entities. The question that now arose was what form this centralised State should take. This was settled by will of the Muscovite Great Prince, later Tsar, in favour of absolute autocracy. The Church, through its representatives, had renounced all its claims to any form of influence, even a moral one, while its power was no longer a subject of discussion. However, this apparently did not satisfy the autocrat; the slightest attempt to enforce his authority as religious adviser or monitor, or even reluctance to proffer the expected answers to the ruler's questions often cost the Muscovite Metropolitan his see, and in one case his life. Between 1505 and 1584 there were nine Metropolitans; of these six were deposed, and one subsequently murdered. Representatives of local dynasties and boyars probably deserved persecution more than those who actually suffered; there could be no question of "local separatism" of the former seceding dynasties, and among the boyars any too outspoken counsellor could be banished. Ivan the Terrible, however, resorted to different methods. His attempts to justify his persecutions with his political aim, the final centralisation of the State, could not conceal the fact that his system of terror could result in nothing but moral deterioration in the country. He did not confine himself to the ruthless punishment of the allegedly guilty ones; he exterminated whole families including women and children, servants and serfs. He decimated the populations of once flourishing cities. And all this with complete abandonment of all moral restraint. For instance, mass rape and acts of savagery toward the women of not only the "guilty" but also of peaceful subjects appeared to him a very suitable means of holding in check the population, which, however, did not offer any resistance at all. The horrors of the interregnum, as described, for example, by Avraamij Palicyn (VI, 13, 4), are certainly the result of Ivan's times.

4. Moral decline, which was the inevitable result of the feeling of lawlessness was, however, not the greatest evil bred by the 16th century. Indifference towards new cultural values was much more perilous. This we have already observed in the case of Josif Volockij (V, 10, 8), but this attitude, in an even more intensified form, had now become a universally accepted dogma. The general belief of the time was that all possible and necessary values had already been found and that they existed in Russia. The only thing worth striving for in the cultural sphere (and especially in literature) was the collecting, safeguarding, and, at the most, the presenting of the legacy of the past in different forms. In reality, a fair amount of the new found its way into Russia, but this could only appear disguised as the "old". This explains the sameness of content of the overwhelming majority of works; it is evidence of spiritual stagnation. As all the subject-matter handed down from the past was regarded as inviolable and "sacrosanct", form alone could be "perfected". But into these new vessels nothing but old wine was poured. And thus there came into being quite a few works which belong merely to the "pathology of literature", for the new is rendered as the old, and the old as the new. And how can the traditional be preserved when it is no longer possible to distinguish it from the new?

5. Such an ideology did not fall on untilled soil. Already the disciples of Nil Sorskij had begun to speak out. The 16th century is characterized by the great number of polemical works, and in some writings of various

genres there are concealed polemical intentions. The greatest tragedy is that the controversialists – the adherents of the "new" and defenders of the "old" alike – have scarcely openly touched on the basic problems of the times. Both sides speak in the name of the "old", and almost without exception they speak of incidental matters; perhaps they were short of words. Only rarely is it possible to discern in their often passionate speeches vague references to the two main problems of the times. These speeches consist mainly of debates as to whether new cultural values ought to be formulated, or whether the old (frequently merely alleged to be so) should alone be preserved; or, to what extent the preservation of the old was necessary. A second theme, more in keeping with the period, is the necessity for spiritual (Christian) freedom as an absolute prerequisite for cultural creation; this is barely discernible through paeans of praise and words of abuse, through attacks on non-existent heresies or the defence of those to which no one had any objections. Only those who believed that not merely spiritual freedom but perhaps the spirit itself was alto- gether superfluous and therefore harmful speak in a slightly clearer vein. When 16th century writers attempt to express the two basic problems, they speak only of definite political or ecclesiastical-political questions from which all essentials are completely forced out. Thus almost the entire 16th-century literature ends up a blind alley.

The political and eccesiastical-political antitheses were resolved, however, not through ideological polemics but by force. This perhaps explains the terrifying picture of a country which laid claims to world authority but in which hardly any problems can be seen. The seekers are merely pushed to one side, either by force or by being ignored.

6. But all this says nothing about the value, or lack of it in Muscovite literature. Not only had it striven toward its literary ideal, but had partly attained it. The style of some monuments has a perfection which, un- fortunately, bears no relation to the subject-matter (this particularly applies to the works of Metropolitan Makarij's circle – cf. VI, 10). It is significant that the written language is not on such a high plane as before and does not keep aloof from the vernacular; elements of the spoken language penetrate into some works (e.g., *Domostroj*). At the same time, the chancery language, gradually acquiring definite form, also extends its sphere (in the Chronicles, for example). Other monuments acquire a distinctive character through their many-layered linguistic structure (e.g. Metropolitan Daniil, Tsar Ivan the Terrible). Other authors vary their style according to the type of writing (Kurbskij). Finally, however, there emerges a colorful literary language which is occasionally employed for stylistic purposes. In most cases it remains unregulated and becomes a problem later on.

It is important to notice the infiltration into the literature of elements of folklore. This happened partly as the continuation of a process that had commenced in the preceding century – namely, the introduction of folk-lore traditions into the Lives of the Saints (V, 4, 3) and into other types of literature, and partly through deliberate or unintentional application of stylistic methods of folklore to works of literature.

7. In the past it was sometimes asserted that the character of the Muscovite 16th century depended on Byzantium, as a result, among other things, of the Byzantine marriage of Great Prince Ivan III. This is hardly the case. There can be no question of the intensification of Byzantine spiritual influence. Byzantium's spiritual legacy (even if only in part) was taken over by the Western Renaissance. Even the influence of the Hesychasts did not increase at the end of the 15th century. Moreover, the Muscovite 16th century was only the intensification of some characteristics – by no means positive – of Byzantine court manners and political practice. What came into being, owing to such intensification, was, as in other similar cases, but a "pseudomorphosis", now the pseudomorphosis of the "Second Rome". The decline of Byzantine influence is adequately indicated by the translated literature.

8. By the end of the 16th century the dynasty had died out (Tsar Fedor). The prudent reign of the last Tsar's brother-in-law, Boris Godunov, failed to avert the grave social crises which were the result of the 16th century. Neither the usurper, the False Dmitrij, nor the Tsar elected by the boyars, Vasilij Šujskij, could resolve the intricate social conflicts still further aggravated by Polish and Swedish intervention. This period, *Smutnoe vremja* (not quite correctly translated as interregnum, for during most of the time there had been lawful or unlawful rulers), ended with the election of Michail Romanov, the founder of the new dynasty. His reign (1613–1643) does not introduce any new trends into literature. Allmost all that was written was still in the 16th century tradition (cf. VI, 13).

9. It is curious that the art of book-printing in 16th-century Moscow was limited to the abortive attempt of Ivan Fedorov (1561–64). He succeeded in printing only the Gospels and the Acts of the Apostles. His printing press was destroyed by a mob, and Fedorov escaped to Lithuania where he continued his activites among Byelo-Russians and Ukrainians. The brief 1561–64 episode has no significance in the history of literature.

2. TRANSLATED LITERATURE

1. Newly translated literature was not extensive and was, in the main, completely haphazard. This is a sphere where the "pathological" character of literary development is shown at its clearest. The best example of what had to be done and of what could be done without much effort is provided by Prince A. Kurbskij who, after his flight to Lithuania (1564) produced with a few collaborators numerous and extensive translations from the Church Fathers (Chrysostomos, the Damascene) and a number of compilations. Also he took care to translate the newer scientific literature. To be sure, he translated Greek works from the Latin. He showed, however, that it was possible to create something new even if based on the "old". In Moscow, no such attempt was ever made.

Nearly all these translations (with the exception of those by Maksim Grek, see VI, 9) were made from the Latin or from the German. Or they originated from unknown sources, sometimes by way of Western and Southern Slav neighbours. A purely arbitrary selection of translated works cannot give grounds for assuming that these were in any way suited to breach the wall that separated Moscow from the rest of the world.

2. Early in the century, in conjunction with the struggle against the *židovst-vujuščie* (V, 1, 8) translations were made of anti-Jewish works by Nicolaus de Lyra and by "Samuel the Jew". In 1535, a psalter-commentary by Bruno Herbipolensis (of Würzburg) was translated. About the same time Muscovite literature was enriched by a translation of Augustin's *De civitate Dei*. All these were translated from the Latin.

3. Even more haphazard were translations from scientific literature. Actually, the translation of the Latin *Lucidarius* (Russian: *Lucidarij*) can hardly be included under the heading of "scientific" literature. This popular and "vulg-arised" presentation of theological questions was first composed in the 11th–12th centuries; but though later revised in the West, it remained in its essence a mixture of obsolete, fantastic, and superstitious information on natural science and theology. ... The translation, moreover, was extremely clumsy, the translator having merely transliterated a number of words (hence, there appear in the Russian text such words as *gelisteri* – German: *gelbe Stier*; *ader* – *Natter*; *lintvorm* – *Lindwurm*; *slongi* – *Schlangen*, etc.). Next came "The Herbal Book", translated in 1534 and considered as a work on medicine, under the title "The Pleasantly Cool Garden of Health" (*Blagoprochladnyj vertograd zdraviju*). Of geographical works, the two which reached Moscow mainly by accident were translated, a description of the Moluccas (!) and a brief report about the church of Loretto in Italy. Both translations were made before 1530. An idea of the extent of Muscovite scientific literature may be given by mention of the follow-ing translations which were made at the beginning of the century; the trans-

lation of Donatus' Latin Grammar, which originated at Novgorod; and possibly also of a compilation "On Astronomy: from translations from the German", extant in 17th-century manuscripts, which contains merely geographical data and references to observable movements of the sun and moon (A. Sobolevskij alone considered the translation as a Novgorodian work of the 16th century).

4. Equally haphazard are translations of tales. Their sources are in part unknown, and they may perhaps be partly the result of the re-writing of foreign prototypes.

The Tale (*Povest'*) of Basarg the Merchant is a fairy tale which brings together a variety of migratory motifs. A merchant of Constantinople comes to a country in which the King "of the Latin faith" threatens him with death unless he solves some riddles. Basarg's seven-year old son solves the riddles, kills the king and ascends the throne. At the end of the 17th century this tale was revised with Basarg's son becoming a Russian merchant, Borzomysl. In this new version there appeared some motifs of the transfer of foreign (in this case, Roman) Coronation regalia to Russia (cf. VI, 4, 2 and V, 6, 12). The story survived in folk literature in an abridged form and with stress on fairy-tale elements until the 18th century. It may have exerted an influence on the *stariny*. The primary source was presumably Greek.

The Tale of Tsarina Dinara goes back to an unknown Georgian (less likely Greek) source. It relates unhistorical victories over the Persians of the historical "Iverian" (Georgian) Queen Dinara. Presumably, in this tale, Dinara takes the place of Queen Tamara (12th–13th centuries), who in fact did win great victories over the Persians. The narrative is written in the splendid style of a military tale.

From the West – via Novgorod – came the popular German morality play, "The Dialogue (*Dvoeslovie*) between Life and Death" by Nicolaus Mercatoris. Its theme is the power of Death, which carries off all rich, famous, and venerable people. From Russian sources, the dialogue became expanded with quotations from ecclesiastical literature. In the 17th century it was turned into a tale, "Life" being replaced by a valorous hero (*udaloj molodec*). The subject-matter was of consequence to the religious song about *Anika-voin* (*Anika* – Greek: unconquerable; *voin* – warrior).

5. By the end of the 16th century and in the early 17th century there appeared newly translated tales which, as chap-books, enjoyed great popularity right into the 20th century .

The first of these is the history of Bova, the king's son (*Bova Korolevič*). The primary source was the Italian romance of chivalry about "Buovo d'Antona." This reached the Byelo-Russians in the 16th century and passed from them to the Great Russians, probably through a Croat (Dalmatian) translation or adaptation. Names became Slavonicised, many Italian ones remaining misunderstood. In this tale, Russian literature again comes in contact with the occidental (the Buovo romance was also known in France and England). The plot concerns a Royal son who has to fight for his inheritance because his father has been killed by his wife Meretrys or Militrisa (Italian: *meretrice* – whore). Buova has to flee his country; he visits various lands and everywhere experiences many adventures. He wins the love of a princess – Družnena or Družneva (Italian: *Drusiana*), takes part in tournaments and, in fact, lives the life of a Western knight. In the end, he receives Družnena's hand and the throne of his father. The chivalrous features of the life of occidental knights first become blurred in the Great Russian version, which, moreover, follows Russian literary tradition in many ways. The second Russian version (17th century) introduces into the romance folk-lore elements from Russian fairy tales. In the 18th century this apocryphal version was printed and achieved great popularity. Radiščev and Puškin wrote poems about Bova, both in a political vein. In popular lore, "Bova" very rarely appeared as one complete fairy-tale, but details of the romance exerted an influence on fables and the *stariny* (e.g., supplying some motifs and names).

The second narrative is presumably an adaptation and not a proper translation of an oriental fairy tale connected with the Persian "Book of the Kings" (*Shâh-Nâme*). It reached Russia through the Cossack armies. The tale *Uruslan Zalazorevič* (later Eruslan Lazarevič) deals mainly with two episodes concerning the hero Rustem, as told by *Shâh-Nâme*; other Persian names are also retained in the text. Among many other adventures, Uruslan vanquishes Tsar Kirkous (Persian: Kejkaus) and, unknown to himself, fights his own son (Persian: Zorab). Numerous other adventures are pure fables. "Uruslan" was also influenced by the tradition of the military tales; like "Bova" it was printed, became a chap-book and influenced literature (Puškin's *Ruslan i Ljudmila*) as well as folk fables and the *stariny*.

At the beginning of the 17th century – again by way of the Byelo-Russians – there appeared the didactic tale of the "Seven Wise Men", a tale popular both in the East and the West. It probably reached the Byelo-Russians via Western Slav renderings from Latin. It is in the form of a collection of short moral tales (cf. "Stefanit and Ichnilat", see II, 10). In order to save a prince who has slandered his stepmother, each of the seven sages tells the king a story with a moral; the stepmother, on her side, answers each of the stories with one of her own. The story of the seven sages and individual novellas taken out of their context acquired exceptional popularity, and one of them became a folk fable.

In 1608–9 a translator in the diplomatic service rendered from the Greek Aesop's Fables, popular throughout Europe, and added as an introduction a biography of Aesop (probably of the 12th century). The Fables revived the tradition of "Stefanit and Ichnilat" (II, 10) and of biography – that of "Akir the Very Wise" (II, 10). The language of the translation is not always clear and also contains some Polonisms. Some of the fables (there are about 140 in the book) influenced Russian fairy-tales concerned with animals.

6. Translated literature had a certain significance for the indigenous literature. Scientific works brought some, mostly abortive, additions to scientific terminology. The long tales, especially those of the 17th century, exerted an influence on Russian narrative art by their plot and individual motifs; to be sure, this influence was largely confined to the "lower", predominantly popular, strata of literature.

3. HAGIOGRAPHIC LITERATURE

1. The 16th century Lives of the Saints provide evidence of this genre's decline. They are still numerous; and revisions of older works (see VI, 10, 2) are even more plentiful. But many of the legends are entirely divorced from tradition. On the one hand, there now emerge "apocryphal legends" in which folk-lore material is linked with the name of one saint or another; and on the other, there appears a series of revisions and new legends which because of lack of subject-matter become merely exercises in stylistics, or replace facts by fabrications. Some legends replace the description of the spiritual life of a saint by his economic and political achievements, others, on the contrary, fall into a kind of nihilism (the Lives of the *jurodivye*, see below, 8). This colourful picture is symptomatic of that religious and ideological crisis through which Russia passed, and which had been undoubtedly deeper than it may have seemed later.

2. Russian life appears at its most serene when we read the legends of the Josif school. The most important Lives of this school are those of Josif's teacher, Pafnutij Borovskoj (d. 1477), and three legends by Josif himself. The propriety which, above all, Josif demands of his monks, also dominates the style of these legends. The most important elements of their ideology can be read between the lines.

Pafnutij's Life by Josif's brother is not an important work of literature, but some of it is very significant. We learn nothing of the saint's inner life; strict asceticism is hardly brought to the fore. Pafnutij breaks with the hermit tradition when he lays the foundations of his monastery in the vicinity of a town – Borovsk. The monastery receives rich gifts; the monks work and so does Pafnutij. Strict discipline rules the monastery, and its inmates approach Pafnutij with fear. He is as strict with the monks as he is with laymen. Pafnutij was closely related to the Muscovite princely family, and Ivan the Terrible is said to have been born after prayer to this saint.

3. The most interesting of the Lives about Josif Volockij is the one written at the behest of Metropolitan Makarij and included in his Reading Menaea, even though it was composed at a time when Josif was not yet spoken of as saint. The author describes himself as a partial eye-witness but complains that he could collect hardly any material. In fact, this extensive legend is devoid of real content. It is written with moderate embellishments which fully take the place of concrete facts. Moreover, little is said – and then only in passing – of Josif's spiritual path, whereas much space is devoted to his ecclesiastical-political and political activities.

HEAD OF AN ANGEL FROM A FRESCO IN THE CATHEDRAL
OF THE ASSUMPTION IN VLADIMIR

15th century.

THE PRINCE ST. MICHAIL OF ČERNIGOV
Icon of the 15th century.

According to this legend Josif was born in 1440, a pious child of pious parents; at the age of twenty he entered Pafnutij's monastery. His life there is related in general terms only: "He was obedient without questioning ... and accepted the sayings of the *starec* [Pafnutij] as if coming from the Lord." We learn later that he possessed the art of preaching in church. "Josif had purity of tongue and quickness of eye, and sweetness of voice and emotion in preaching; there was none like him in those days." He also persuaded his parents to take vows themselves, and for fifteen years he looked after his crippled father whom he was allowed to take into his own cell. Three years later Pafnutij died, but before his death he urged Great Prince Ivan III to make (!) Josif abbot. While abbot, Josif decided to introduce communal life into the monastery. He found, however, no support among the monks, and so departed secretly with some of them to wander in search of an ideal monastery. Kirill's monastery on the White Lake made the greatest impression on him. The author of the Life lays particular stress on the external order and discipline in this monastery. On his return home, Josif remained abbot for a short time only, and then retreated into the forest near his native town of Volokolamsk (1479). His life as a hermit, however, was certainly brief; the author anyhow does not attach much importance to it and does not speak of it in detail. On the other hand, he refers to a rich benefactor – the seceding prince of the region who donated land for Josif's monastery. A church was erected with the prince and the boyars taking part in the building. As early as 1484 the foundation stone was laid for a stone church, which, when finished, was splendidly appointed.

The narrative which follows is a description, restricted to general terms, of monastic life in which strict discipline and communality prevail. According to the author, who hardly touches upon the monks' spiritual life but goes into details of external facts, some of the monks make one thousand, two thousand or even three thousand obeisances a day; their dining room is not heated; in church each monk stands in a place assigned to him, and so forth. The legend's report of complete equality among all monks in Josif's monastery is contradicted by his Rule, according to which each monk is allowed to chose one of the three grades of ascetic life, and upon this depends his diet and dress. Stories of miracles also belong to the spiritual sphere; these are unpretentious. During divine service a simple-minded monk sees a dove hovering over Josif's head. The appanaged prince appears to have died, and the boyars are already beginning to lament his demise (the only lyrical passage in the Life); Josif then appears, and upon learning that the prince expired without the last sacraments, he begins to pray. The prince wakes up, confesses, receives communion and dies. Neither Josif nor the legend's author dares to describe this as a raising from the dead.

Much more space is accorded to Josif's activities "in the world". Gifts of estates to his monastery commence immediately after its foundation. Shortly afterwards we encounter Josif in his relations with the Great Princes of Muscovy. These apparently go back to the days of his abbotship in Pafnutij's monastery. The accounts are very typical; Josif considers the Great Prince as the supreme arbiter in all questions. When the seceding prince falls ill and orders himself to be cowled, Josif asks the Great Prince "what his commands are"; the Great Prince forbids such action, and therefore the ceremony is abandoned. St. Feodosij acted in a totally different way in a similar case in the 11th century! The heresy of the *židovstvujuščie* is then dealt with in general terms; and Josif's polemics against them are mentioned only briefly, the main emphasis being placed on the fact that Josif by letter influenced the Great Prince (Vasilij III) to imprison even the repentant heretics for life. When Josif hears of this decision, "he praises God". The new appanaged prince demands gifts from the monastery. Josif appeals to the Great Prince, and as a result the monastery comes under Muscovite jurisdiction. Protests against this are made by the competent Novgorod archbishop, whom Josif had not informed of his action (being prevented, according to the Life, by circumstances). In Moscow, of course, this quarrel is settled by the Metropolitan and the Great Prince against the Archbishop's interests. The author passes over in silence the rather disagreeable details. Josif is also depicted as a philanthropist. Once when he surprises a thief who wished to steal grain from the monastery, he not only does not punish him but even helps him to take the stolen property away. During a famine the monastery takes care of many peasants and children, cuts down the food of the monks, lends money to permit the acquisition of more grain, and so on. Josif also takes part in political affairs, as when he engineers a reconciliation between the Great Prince and his brother.

Before his death, Josif writes a letter to the Great Prince asking him to chose his successor from among nine candidates. According to another version of the same Life, he makes the monks select a candidate whose election he asks the Great Prince to confirm. Anyhow, both in the above mentioned letter and in his testament, he asks the Great Prince to take care of the maintenance of the monastic statutes. This, in any case, indicates the acceptance of the absolute identity of temporal and ecclesiastical powers by the author of the Life and most likely by Josif himself as well, as both documents are probably authentic.

At the end, four miracle stories are appended. Two of these relate the "punishment miracles": two monks who doubted the worth of the monastery and transgressed the Rule are stricken with lameness as a penalty.

The fluent language of the Life is moderately embellished. Striking and typical for the time (see VI, 10, 2) is the author's tendency to replace descriptions by general turns of phrase, even where he must have been familiar with the facts.

4. The miracle tales included in the Life and some other stories probably formed the basis of the Volokolamsk Monastery Paterikon (Kadlubovskij). But certainly the work was never completed, as no capable man of letters lived in the monastery.

By the end of the 15th century, the Lives of St. Zosima and St. Savvatij – the founders of the Solovki Monastery – had been written and re-written many times. Only in the 17th century were they incorporated into a Solovki Paterikon together with some other monuments.

5. The legend of Petr and Fevronija – a saint's Life built around motifs of fairy-tales – was written by an unknown author whom many, without adequate proof, take to be Ermolaj Erazm (VI, 12, 3). The content briefly is as follows: Prince Pavel of Murom has a wife who is visited by a dragon in the form of her husband. When Petr, the prince's brother, learns of this, he decides to slay it. Meanwhile the dragon tells the wife that it is to meet its death at the hands of a man named Petr by the sword of Agarik. Petr realises that it is he who is meant; the sword alone is still lacking. Acting upon the instructions of a miraculous youth, Petr finds it walled up in a church. Petr kills the dragon but becomes covered with ulcerous sores from its blood. In his search for a physician, Petr's envoy reaches a house in the Rjazan' principality, where he finds a girl – Fevronija, working alone at a loom. The girl answers the envoy's questions with riddles which she solves herself, she also performs the difficult tasks imposed upon her by Petr. The girl is ready to heal him, but when he comes she demands that he marry her in return. This Petr promises to do. However, after the cure is accomplished by his anointing himself with a liquid medicament, he does not fulfil his pledge. But the girl has cunningly ordered him to refrain from rubbing the liquid on one part of his body, and from this spot ulcers start spreading again all over him. So, he has to turn to her again for assistance. She heals him, and this time he carries out his promise and marries her. Thus far, it is a "fairy-tale

of the wise maiden", known the world over, coupled with some epic motifs (the dragon's blood). The second part of the work, however, links hagiographic elements with some political ones. After the death of his brother, Petr becomes Prince of Murom. Immediately intrigues arise against the peasant princess. She is denounced before the prince for taking breadcrumbs away from meals (it is not said for what purpose). When the prince wishes to investigate this, he finds thyme in Fevronija's hand (cf. the Miracle of the Rose of St. Elisabeth). But subsequently voices are raised again against the princess because of her low origin, and the boyars demand that the prince send her away. Petr, however, does not wish to part from his wife, renounces his throne and leaves the country. A number of episodes are introduced into the account of their journey. These are partly moralising, and in part deal with miracles. Meanwhile, at Murom, strife breaks out amongst the boyars, each of whom wishes to rule. The prince is therefore recalled, and rules right-eously and justly for a long time. In their old age both Petr and Fevronija enter monasteries (their monastic names are David and Evfrosinija). They ask to be buried in one coffin, and they pray to God to let them die simultaneously. When the prince feels death approaching, he sends word to Fevronija. She, however, is still busy with an embroidery for a Church and wishes to finish her work. Only after the prince's third exhortation (n.b. the triple repetition so typical in fairy-tale), she sticks the needle into the still unfinished embroidery and dies. They are both buried in their respective monasteries, and the coffin originally prepared for them remains empty. But on the following morning their bodies are found in the coffin in the Church of the Virgin's Nativity in the town. Later (probably in the 16th century) an introduction and eulogy were added to the legend.

The Life is written without any particular adornments, but is told very well, in a succinct way with well-composed speeches and dialogues. There is no doubt that the author took advantage of some local legends with certain objects; for instance, an unfinished embroidery in a church with a needle still sticking in it was probably a relic existing in the church mentioned. There is no historical evidence concerning the protagonists of this Life. But the author either did not notice or preferred not to notice that his whole legend bore not a trace of religious spirit. We do not know whether or not he deliberately worked apocryphal material into his work. But the tale of the wise maiden, which was known throughout the ancient world, is merely repeated in the Life's first part with even the same riddles which the maiden poses and the same difficult tasks she has to perform (to make a garment out of a handful of flax). The Life recalls the Scandinavian sage of Ragnar Lodbrok, since the same motifs are joined in it: the battle with the dragon and the tale of the "wise maiden." Nevertheless, any genetic connection should not necessarily be assumed. This Life supplies interesting evidence of the penetration of popular lore into literature and of the decline of religious thinking. But there are also political motifs significant for the spirit of the times, such as that a state cannot exist without a prince; and the stress on the legality of a lower-born consort of the prince is perhaps an allusion to the many wives of Ivan the Terrible, while the latter is perhaps alluded to in the account of a prince who leaves his state. It is not known where the legend originated; in any case, it provides an excellent example of Muscovite 16th-century literature.

6. A historically known saint, Antonij Rimljanin (the Roman) – who is mentioned in the Novgorod chronicles as being an abbot between 1117–47 – acquired a stylistically similar apocryphal Life. Antonij's veneration as a saint began only about the mid-16th century. His Life was probably composed in connection with his canonization in 1598. This Life, however, is a definite forgery, as the 16th-century author signed the work with the name of Abbot Andrej, an alleged disciple of Antonij's; all the author did in fact was to write a historical tale.

The story of the legend is as follows. Antonij was a Roman, born of Christian parents at a time when the city "had fallen away from the Christian faith". Surreptitiously his parents taught him the "true faith" and the Greek language. After their death, Antonij placed his property in a cask, threw it into the sea, and went into the wilderness where he became a monk; there he prayed on a rock on the seashore. But a storm carried the rock away across the seas first to the River Neva, and then along the Volchov to Novgorod. There Antonij learned the Russian language and subsequently disclosed his origin to a bishop; the bishop gave him land on which to build a monastery. Antonij is known to be the founder of this monastery (1117). Some time later Novgorod fishermen hauled up a cask containing valuables and tried to appropriate them, but Antonij proved to the judge that the silver, gold and crystal church vessels were his, for it was he who had thrown them into the sea so that they should not be defiled by the "heretics". Thus, he acquired the means to erect stone buildings for his monastery.

The Life makes use of various local legends. The rock on which Antonij had prayed and his staff as well as his picture were known in Novgorod from the 16th century on. All the rest is invented, mainly on the basis of misunderstood historical evidence concerning the separation of the Churches and the foundation of this particular monastery. French enamelled icons, were preserved in Novgorod as Antonij's gift; these, at any rate, had their origin in the 12th–13th centuries and bore Latin inscriptions. This was probably the foundation of the tradition that Antonij was a foreigner. It cannot be argued with certainty whether the Life, doubtless of Novgorodian origin, reflected the theory that the "true faith" had passed from Rome to Novgorod (Antonij himself and his church-treasures are symbols of this), so that we would have here a certain Novgorod parallel to the concept of "Moscow as the third Rome".

Antonij's Life, being a deliberate forgery, once again shows the disintegration of religious feeling and thought.

7. In the same way, religious decline is shown by the 1537 redaction of the Life of a Novgorodian saint, Michail of Klopovo (see V, 4, 3), written by Vasilij Tučkov, a Muscovite official. Tučkov had, of course, no new sources for the political colouring with which he enriched the Life. Here, Michail appears as an enemy of Novgorod and a partisan of the Muscovite princes' interests: "Unless you temper the wrath of the well-wishing Tsar Ivan Vasil'evič, you will suffer much need", etc. In addition, the author composes long speeches for the saint, intensifying the miraculous elements and expurgating any stories reminiscent of Novgorod's independence. The pompous style and the allusions to secular literature – not only to authors like Homer and Ovid, but also to Hercules, Achilles and the Trojan war – cannot conceal the fact that here once again we are confronted with a deliberate forgery.

Even worse is a product of the Smolensk literature – the Life of a fictitious saint, Merkurij, who, having saved Smolensk from Batu (in fact, Batu had never been near Smolensk), returns to the city carrying in his arms his own head cut off by a Tartar, and dies there. This is a migratory legend, known in Greece and in the West, as well as among the non-Christian peoples of the East, linked to Smolensk probably without even the existence of relics of a saint bearing the name of Merkurij. Later, literary revisers of the Life strengthened the apocryphal motifs even further, but did not attempt to give it any religious significance.

The religious decline is also shown by the fact that about this time various compositions which were by no means representative of hagiographic literature entered this genre. The biography (*žitie*) of Dmitrij Donskoj must have gained this distinction because of its ecclesiastical style (V, 5, 5). A genealogical tale about Petr Ordynskij could only be regarded as a saint's Life because of the general inclination to view all writings as "sacred" (cf. V, 6, 11).

8. In contrast, evidence concerning the *jurodivye*, a typical 16th-century phenomenon, is very inadequately preserved. This phenomenon represents a significant stage in the development of Russian piety. The *jurodivye* are "fools in Christ", "the saintly fools". Although they are frequently considered as a typically Russian expression of devoutness, it ought to be mentioned that many saints of this nature were already known in Byzantium; and as far back as the old paterikons there had been sporadic evidence of the pious hermits' "folly". One of the Byzantine legends – that of Andreas "*Salos*" (the Greek epithet for this type of saint in the 8th–9th centuries) – was already available to Slav readers in the 11th century. Later the Life of St. Simeon *Salos* (6th century) also appeared in translation. St. Isaakij (III, 3, 4) practised this particular type of asceticism for a long time. But otherwise this expression of piety appeared no longer among Ukrainians and Byelo-Russians, and remained confined to Great Russia. In the West, some features of this type were manifested by a number of Spanish saints and even by devout Protestants (e.g. the Swabian Pietists). The two main characteristics of this type are, on the one hand, the simulation of madness – the "fools"; and on the other, a spiritual struggle against the world by means of "folly" with apparently senseless actions. For the *jurodivye* were by no means real fools, and this differentiates them from the madmen revered in the Muslim East. They merely simulated "folly" in order to escape worldly fame. And their apparently senseless actions were intended to reveal the vanity, transience and emptiness of the "world". They appeared significantly at the very places where the "world" had become too strong and powerful, and its splendour and brilliance had tempted Christians to forsake the paths of religion, and where Christianity, devoid of content, had become a mere convention; and so they appeared in Constantinople, and in Russia in the rich mercantile cities of the Novgorod region and Moscow.

The Lives of the *jurodivye*, as already stated, are badly recorded, scarcely edited and merely adapted in a pious manner. As early as the 16th–17th centuries the "censorship" of church was active, and thus we have no Lives at all of some of the *jurodivye*, and of others either later redactions or modern adaptations.

The Life of St. Prokopij of Ustjug, who lived in the 13th century, was recorded in the 16th century. Because of its many anachronisms, this legend is almost certainly unhistorical and is clearly of the 16th and not of the 13th century. According to the Life, Prokopij was a foreigner "from western lands, of Latin language, of German state". At Novgorod, he recognised true faith in the beauty of the church arrangement and divine service. Baptised by Varlaam of Chutyn' (12th century!) "he took up, for the sake of Christ, the life of the *jurodivye*", and then in order to avoid the worship of the people he fled to the West "in search of his long lost fatherland" (probably the celestial *patria*). The only reward he received for his folly was molestation, reproach, and blows and pushes. He remained in the "great and splendid city" of Ustjug where he led a life typical of the *jurodivye*. He was homeless, he slept on a garbage heap or on the church steps, but at night he prayed for the town and its people. He took alms only from the pious, and not from the rich. He prophesied the fall of Ustjug "by fire and water". No one believed him, but then stones rained down near the city (the fall of meteors that actually took place in the 16th century). The Life stresses the fact that Prokopij was not a real madman. At night, during a great frost he visited the cleric Simeon and prophesied that the latter's son would be a saint; this son is supposed to be St. Stefan of Perm' (V, 4, 5) (an anachronism). At Simeon's house, Prokopij is represented as a merry and laughing guest. As stated already, the Life is not historical and, in contrast to Byzantine legends, tells nothing concrete about the saint's "folly".

In the 15th century there were two *jurodivye* at (northern) Rostov, then an important city. The Life of St. Isidor (d. 1474) contains passages borrowed word for word from other Lives of the *jurodivye*. Like Prokopij, he is said to have come "from western lands, of Roman family and of German tongue". He made his home in a hut in the marshland; no one believed his prophecies and he was persecuted and mocked. Ioann the Merciful (*Milostivyj*) (d. 1581) is also said to have been a foreigner. In the early 18th century a Latin psalter, allegedly his property, was found in his coffin at Rostov.

In Moscow there were many *jurodivye* whose cult originated in the 16th century. St. Maksim (d. 1433) was canonized in 1547 but has no Life. Vasilij the Blessed (*Blažennyj*) – the famous Moscow church where he lies buried is usually called after him – died about 1550 and in 1588 was canonized. He is better described by oral tradition than in the panegyrical Life of him, which is written in ornate style, without any concrete subject-matter and full of anachronisms (Ivan the Terrible is reproached with his sins and cruelties in the year 1570!). Ioann the Great Cope (*Bol'šoj Kolpak*) was living at the end of the 16th century (after 1584); he dwelt mainly in Rostov, whither he had come from the Far North. A water-carrier by profession, he built himself a cell in Rostov in the vicinity of a church and there practised strict asceticism. He spent the last years of his life in Moscow, and was interred in the same church as Vasilij.

The Pskovan Chronicle contains an episode from the life of Nikola, a local *jurodivyj*. When Ivan the Terrible arrived at Pskov in 1570, after days of unbridled terrorism, and the city had given him a festive welcome, the Tsar was approached by Nikola who "urged him with terrible words to put an end to the great shedding of blood". Ivan began his punitive measures of the innocent town by ordering the removal of the great bell from the Church of the Trinity. But then, "in accordance with the saint's prophecy", his best horse died, and Ivan withdrew without "great bloodshed". The popular legend gives details of the Tsar's visit to

Nikola. The latter provided the Tsar with raw meat, whereupon Ivan said, "I am a Christian, and eat no meat in Lent." "But" – Nikola is said to have retorted – "you drink Christian blood!" The same thing was anachronistically said of St. Vasilij, who apparently in the same year offered the same dishes to Ivan at Novgorod and after the Tsar's reluctance to partake of the meal had shown him the soul of martyrs slain by him rising to heaven (Vasilij, however, died at Moscow about 1550).

The meaning of the reverence for the *jurodivye* is better shown in the reports of foreigners (e.g., Fletcher) and in popular legends than in saints' Lives. Foreign travellers speak of many *jurodivye*, often naked, with long hair and wearing iron chains around their necks, who wandered about the towns uttering warnings. Those against whom the *jurodivye's* attacks were directed, accepted their prophetic words as entirely deserved by sinners. A naked *jurodivyj* incited the populace against Godunov who was virtually in charge of the government under Tsar Fedor (1584–1598). Fletcher says, "Next to the monks, the Russian people particularly honour the *jurodivye* . . . who, like political broadsheets, attack the shortcomings of the nobility, whom no one else dares to criticise." But Fletcher thinks that in some cases even they were liquidated for "too sharply abusing the Tsar", and the Tsar here is Ivan the Terrible! Whereas Fletcher takes note of the undoubtedly important political aspect of the reverence for the *jurodivye*, more serious motifs also appear in the popular legends, the origin of which can probably be ascribed to the 16th and, at the latest, the 17th centuries: here the *jurodivye* are Charismatic men whose main characteristics include, above all, the three "gifts of the spirit" – the ability to discern the soul, the gift of prophecy, and the gift of visions (cf. the tale of St. Isaakij – III, 3, 4). The legends that deal with St. Vasilij Blažennyj have been recorded. In his youth, when a cobbler's journeyman, he scorned, and at the same time pitied, a merchant who had ordered a pair of boots but who was about to die (this motif was used by L. Tolstoj in his story *Čem ljudi živy*). As a *jurodivyj*, Vasilij acted in a seemingly senseless and even wanton way: he stoned the houses of the pious (according to another version – the churches) and kissed the walls of houses where blasphemy was practiced (another version says "of the pot-house"). But there was point to all this because in front of the houses mentioned first, stood the devils who were not allowed to enter, and near the second, guardian angels were weeping because men were singing within. He threw a stone at an icon, because a devil was painted on it under the Virgin's image (cf. Leskov's *Čertopisnye ikony;* the same motif recurs in his *Zapečatlennyj angel*). He destroyed wares at the market, because the vendors were swindlers (Andreas *Salos* did likewise). He gave alms not to a beggar but to a merchant who, being ashamed to beg, was going hungry in secret. He recognised the devil in the guise of a beggar who had given earthly happiness in return for alms . . ., and so on. Miracle-tales about Vasilij are part of the tradition. Also traditional are the incidents related above. These are to be found in popular legends (the Afanasjev collection); they are also encountered in the West where, however, they are based principally on the motif of "Christ (or an angel) wandering through the world". Some of the other motifs go back to the legends of the Byzantine *saloi*. In the tales of Vasilij Blažennyj the popular legend rises considerably above the official hagiographic writing of the 16th century, which suppressed the oral tradition because hagiographers "appointed" by the official Church lacked any comprehension of the old Christian idea of the Charismatic Man and his complete divorce from the "understanding of the world". The Church at this time allied itself with the State; and, even more, it sold itself and subjected itself to the secular power (cf. also VI, 10).

9. A Life of Metropolitan Filipp (b. 1507; Metropolitan 1566–69) was written down at the Solovki Monastery after 1590, and was probably rewritten only in 1601. Neither version has been published, and it is impossible therefore to speak of this monument in greater detail. According to the account of the historians, Filipp – a son of the most noble Kolyčev family – became a monk in 1539, and abbot of the Solovki Monastery in 1548. As a result of the intervention of Tsar Ivan the Terrible and following an election by the Council, he took up the appointment as Metropolitan of Moscow on the condition that the Tsar would allow him to exercise the ancient right of the spiritual power to intercede for the persecuted (*pečalovanie*). A year later, however, there came a new, and in fact the greatest, wave of terror, when the Tsar with inhuman cruelty and deliberate display was perpetrating his bestialities. Filipp at first attempted to plead with the Tsar, and then publicly attacked him during divine service in the Cathedral. As a result he was removed from his See in 1568 (the charge of "sorcery" was among the accusations), and was garrotted by a confidant of the Tsar in the monastery where he was held captive.

Filipp's sermon about the Tsar's powers and the dialogue with Ivan in the Life are, of course, the work of its author, who shows a considerable gift of rhetoric. However, the speeches consist in part of quotations compiled from the same writing of Agapit (I. Ševčenko; cf. V, 10, 7) as

was used by the theoreticians of unlimited absolutism; only the selection
of quotations was different.

10. Tsar Ivan the Terrible, in his capacity as a writer (cf. VI, 7, 8), also
composed hagiographic works (songs of praise and hymns in honour of
saints). Of the same character are the works of the son of Ivan whom the
Tsar fatally injured in a fight (1582). One of the legends by the Tsarevitch,
that of Antonij Sijskij, contains a description of a storm at sea, which is
typical of the 16th-century hagiographic style:

Закоснѣвшу же ему и не пришедшу скоро в монастырь нѣкыхъ
ради великихъ нуждъ монастырскихъ, коснящу же ему время не
мало тамъ, но внегда же изорудовати потребы монастырьскыя,
восхотѣ въ монастырь возвратитися и не возможе морскаго ради
треволненія и вѣтренаго ради противнаго належания, понеже
воздуху уже премѣншуся, во глубокую сѣнь преложшуся, и морю
возгремѣвшу, волны яко горы ношахутся и вѣтреному дыханію
противну велику возбраняющу, и лды уже на морѣ плаваше
великыя, и не дадущу ему возвратитися во обитель пакы блажен-
наго и сицеваго ради залогу нужнаго, и озимѣти Геласіе сему
тамо, и не пріити ему въ монастырь на преставленіе преподоб-
наго...

("He stopped there and did not go at once to the monastery, being
[preoccupied] with various needs of the monastery; and he remained there
for a long time and after settling the monastery's affairs, he wanted to
return to the monastery and could not, because of the turbulence of the
sea and the resistance of the wind because the weather [*vozduch*] changed
in the meantime and it became very dark, and the sea was threatening, and
mountainous waves arose, and the strong blowing of the contrary wind,
prevented [him], and great floes of ice swam on the sea and did not allow
him to return to the monastery though this was desirable because of the
sacred and most important circumstances. And thus had the said
Gelasij wintered there and did not go to the monastery, while the saint
departed for home.")

Such is the rendering of a simple sentence in the original which merely
says that the monk Gelasij could not return to his monastery because of
a storm at sea! In this short passage we find all the features of the style of
the period: nine participles, seven datives absolute, and the play of
synonyms (monastery – *monastyr'*, *obitel'*; wind – *větrenoe naležanie*,
větrenoe dychanie; to prevent – *ne dati, vozbranjati;* circumstances – *nuždy,*

potreby; etc.). The long sentence can be easily and simply broken down into three separate ones, but nevertheless the construction remains artfully dense. Concrete words are replaced by abstract constructions (cf. above, the synonyms for the word "wind"). And a minor incident in the Saint's life, an episode that deals with a person of only secondary importance, gives the author the opportunity to draw an impressive picture with perhaps symbolic significance of the storm as an image of "the world" including nature. In other parts of the Life we find passages reminiscent of Holy Scripture and references to parallels from other Lives of saints.

This is a further intensification of the high style, even when comparisons are drawn with the style of Epifanij and Pachomij the Serb.

4. THE TALES

1. The narrative literature of the 16th century is very meagre. The fabulous stories of the preceding century acquired great popularity; this applied especially to those that could serve for the justification of one or another political point of view. The Novgorod tale of the White Mitre (V, 6, 13) serves now for the glorification of Moscow, as the Muscovite Metropolitan now also wears a white cowl. But a genealogical work that can hardly be termed a literary work is appended thereto. As Moscow is now raising claims to being the Third Rome, the memory of the ancient rulers must be kept alive. Some further connected tales can be singled out from the annals. These, however, have no particular literary significance; only one Pskovan tale of the end of the century has strongly pronounced individual traits. It is also worthy of note that various old tales now enter into the category of hagiography, for Russia's whole past is perceived as "sacred history". A number of skilful descriptions can be found in the annalistic or pseudo-chronicle works (*Kazanskij letopisec*). The tales (cf. VI, 2, 4–5) are merely translations which presumably appear to readers as accounts of actual events! The "pathos of truth" reigns supreme over 16th-century literature, more than over any other period of Russian literary life, except that phase of Soviet literature when writers were only allowed to report reality (cf. also VI, 7, 3, end).

2. The transformation, extension, and rounding off of the two fictional works concerning the city of Babylon and the White Cowl belong to the 16th century. The reason for the supplements (which in the absence of critical editions of the text can only be defined with probability) is to supply the Muscovite State with all sorts of historical links. It is here attempted to connect Moscow with one or another ancient tradition, either genealogically (see below, 3) or ecclesiastically (the Tale of the White Mitre); or ideologically, which was then the same as ecclesiastically ("Moscow – the Third Rome"), or in the realm of power politics ("The Tale of the City of Babylon", "The Tale of Monomach's Coronation Regalia"). For only such derivation of its claims could give the Muscovite State real greatness and incomparable splendour. An "inferiority complex" could be discerned behind all this if political and propagandist motifs had not appeared all too often as the basis of these traditions created *ad hoc*. Propaganda, however, had exerted influence within the country only; attempts to carry it abroad (e.g., Ivan the Terrible's genealogical claims against foreign lands) were of course doomed to failure.

3. The tale of the Princes of Vladimir (*Skazanie*) contains the fabulous genealogy of the Muscovite princely family (the princes of Muscovy bore for a long time the title of princes of Vladimir [Suzdal"]). This is the genealogy of the Rjurik dynasty.

The tale begins with the Biblical Flood and the Tower of Babel. This is followed by a list of great rulers of the past, beginning with Egypt ... The Rjurik family is made to descend from Roman Emperors on the basis of utterly fantastic conjectures. After the death of Julius Caesar, his brother Augustus succeeds to the throne. He is crowned in Egypt and assumes the power of the Egyptian pharaoh and of the Persian Emperors. Augustus conquers the whole world. He sends his brother Prus to the Vistula, and Rjurik is a descendant of Prus. From Rjurik descend the princes of Vladimir (cf. VI, 10, 3). At the end of the tale it is stated that the Kievan princes received the regalia of Byzantium (this tale is also extant as an independent work) and, after his victory, received from the Emperor Constantine Monomachos (both anachronistic and untrue) the Cross of Christ, the Emperor's Crown, and the Pelerine (or the shoulder coat: *barmy*) as well as the box of carnelian (*serdolik*), "out of which the Emperor Augustus had derived great joy" (a hardly understandable passage). "From that time onward the princes of Vladimir had themselves crowned with the Imperial Crown."

This legend is certainly a 16th century invention. The principal item of the "regalia" is a Byzantine prince's cap subsequently made into a "crown" by the addition of a fur rim and a cross on top. Monomach's "regalia" played no part in the coronation service as late as the coronation of Prince Dmitrij (1498), who was subsequently removed from the line of succession to the throne, was imprisoned and died in prison.

Stylistically the tale is not unwieldy, even if long lists of names form part of it; these names, at least some of them, are taken over from the chronographs. The vocabulary is ecclesiastical, with few compounds. Striking are several anachronisms and mistakes; these are made not only in world history but in Russian history as well (e.g., the non-existant Great Prince Vseslav Igorevič, etc.), which should have been known well enough by the old "erudite" (*knižnik*) who had read the chronicles.

The tale appears for the first time in 1523. The attempts to back-date its origin to the 15th century (after 1480) and to consider Pachomij as its author, are not convincing.

4. That the art of story-telling was not entirely extinct is best shown by local Novgorodian and Pskovan tales which, though included in the chronicles, have, nevertheless, a polished character.

The Novgorodian tales date from the end of the 14th and early 15th centuries; some of them, recounting the prophecies of the ruin of Novgorod, stand out when compared with the laconic style of the chronicles. The most detailed of them is the tale of Ivan the Terrible's destruction of Novgorod in 1570. This tale is, however, stylistically as dry and matter-of-fact as the rest of the Novgorodian chronicles.

5. Far more interesting are the two Pskovan tales.

The first is the "Tale of the Taking of Pskov" by the Muscovite Great Prince Vasilij in 1510. The story begins with recollections of the days when Pskov was a free city "ruled by no prince, and living at its own will". But the mercantile republic was by then already under the protection of the Muscovite Great Prince. The events of 1510 begin with Prince Vasilij's betrayal "with cruel guile" of the treaty which the Pskovans have honoured. During a conflict between Pskovan citizens and mayor (*posadnik*) the Great Prince, to whom the Pskovans have complained, time and again delays negotiations, and in the end orders the arrest of the richest and most influential citizens. They are carried away from Pskov and their property is given to Muscovites. Those left behind in Pskov "could do no more than weep"; and as they are "devoid of reason and merely youngsters", they decide to offer no resistance to the Great Prince. Pskov's independence comes to an end with the removal of the bell which tolled for the assembly of the towns-people. After the exposition there comes the lyrical part: "And now the Pskovans cried bitterly. How did their eye-balls not drop out together with their tears? [borrowed from

Aleksandr Nevskij's biography]. How was it that their hearts were not torn out by the roots?" [reminiscent of Digenis]. After this the author gives vent to his mood in the form of a lament (*plač*) for the city; this imitates Biblical prototypes: Jeremiah's lament and the book of the prophet Ezekiel, from which is taken the picture of a great eagle (17,3) which robbed the city of Pskov "of the three cedars of Lebanon, [the city's] beauty, opulence, and children". The image of the sacking of the city is adapted from Serapion's sermons (IV, 2, 10) with an admixture of local factual colour (i.e., decline of trade, departure of foreigners, etc.). And at the end there appears the picture of banished Justice (popular in the West since the 14th century): "Justice had gone to heaven ... injustice had remained on earth" (*pravda – krivda*). This image had already appeared in the *Tolkovaja Paleja* (VI, 11, 4); it reached this monument from the Apocrypha of Solomon's Judgement.

The tale is rather colourful from the point of view of style, which ranges from that of the Bible and the embellished sermon-style of Serapion down to the factual style of the annalists, characteristic of the Pskovan Chronicle. The author visibly seeks his bearings in the works of the literature of the 11th–13th centuries. Significant are the paranomasias: *sdumav dumu, dve voli ... izvolili, žalovati žalovanjem* ("thinking thoughts, two wishes fulfilled, to bestow a favor"); repetitions of words: in one sentence, for instance, there appear thrice the various forms of *posylati* ("to send"), twice *volja* ("the will"), etc.; there is also repetition of prepositions, characteristic of folklore: *ot Filippa ot Popoviča ot kupčiny ot pskovitina* ("from the Pskovan merchant Filipp Popovič"); indigenous epithets appear as well, as in *polonjanaja věst', žalobnye ljudi* (the tidings of captivity, the sorrowing people), etc.

The monument is embodied in the First Pskovan Chronicle, which also contains a brief report of the same events in which the prince of Muscovy is described as a predecessor of the Anti-Christ. The tale deals in much greater detail with the prince's breach of the agreement, but views the events as God's punishment for Pskov's sins.

6. The final Pskovan tale comes from the days following the siege of the city by the Polish king Stefan Batory in 1580–82. The *Pověst'* differs from a contemporary annalistic account which sharply condemns the policy of Ivan the Terrible toward Pskov by its pro-Muscovite orientation.

The tale explains Batory's attack on the city (actually an incidental part of his campaign against Moscow) as being by request of the Livonian Germans and at the instigation of the "traitor" – Prince Kurbskij "and his allies". The Virgin herself helps the inhabitants of Pskov during the siege; on the intercession of Pskovan saints (Prince Dovmont, Nikola the *Jurodivyj*, and others) she gives advice to the Pskovan gunners; later she comes to succour Dmitrij of Salonika whose icon was damaged by a Polish cannon ball. From a deserter the Pskovans learn of the existence of Polish mines, which they destroy. Pskov is defended by the populace, including women and monks, and by the many religious processions. Relief from Moscow can fight its way through the Lithuanian lines, but the Papal Legate, Antonio Possevino, "with Ichnilat's treachery (see II, 10) and ... with the cunnings of the fox", wants to prevent peace from being made. Moreover, the author considers the Papal Legate to be a Lutheran; and such also, in his view, is Batory himself – an obvious sign of the complete indifference that held sway in the 16th and 17th centuries to everything that was happening in the West. After Batory takes his leave, his Chancellor continues the siege of the city. He sends an infernal machine, which is described in fantastic terms, to the *vojevoda*, Prince I. Šujskij, but this is dismantled by "a master". Meanwhile peace is signed at Moscow, and with the account of the arrival of the news of the conclusion of peace the siege ends, and so does the tale.

This story, like its predecessors, supplies evidence of the literary culture acquired in the meantime by Pskov. It is obviously influenced by Aleksandr Nevskij's biography (or later hagiographic legends about him), by the *Alexandreis*, by the Tale of the Rout of Mamai, by Manasses, by the Kazan' Chronicle, and by "Stefanit and Ichnilat" (many of these works had been incorporated in the chronographs). The composition is somewhat unusual. Chronologically arranged, it is divided into short sections, which bear strange titles; often these titles merely indicate the particular character of the section, as for instance "The Essential" (*Suščee*), "The Lamentable" (*Plačevnoe*), and so on. The sometimes dry narrative is enlivened by individual scenes and rich ornaments. Epithets are especially numerous, and among them particularly the compounds: Batory is *vsegordelivyj, mnogogordelivyj, vysokogordelivyj* ("proud above all, manifoldly proud, highly proud"). Some of the compounds appear to be new, viz.: *blagozdravie, gordonapornyj, gradoukrěplenie, zlouserdnyj, mertvotrupy, molebnosoveščatel'nyj, udobovschodnyj*, and even treble compounds: *chrabrodobropobědnyj*. ("good health, proudly advancing, town fortification, eager in evil, dead corpses, asking advice, easy to ascend, valorous-good-victorious"). Compounds are often used for the construction of paranomasias, e.g.: *mnogokrěplenija krěposti, zlozamyšlennoe umyšlenie, mudroumyšlennyj um, smirennomudrostiju umudrjašesja, ada-*

ST. SERGIJ OF RADONEŽ
An embroidery of the 16th century.

THE MOTHER OF GOD APPEARS IN A VISION TO ST. SERGIJ, ACCOMPANIED
BY TWO APOSTLES

An embroidery of the 16th century.

manta tveržae utverdišasja, etc. ("manifoldly fortified fortress, evil intention, wisely-thinking mind, becoming wise through humility, fortifying themselves stronger than diamond").

The compounds of which the first particle is identical are heaped on in some sections (*mnogo-* seven times, *svjat-* and *svjašč-*, *bogo-*, etc.). The author also uses many tropes and figures; metaphors are abundant: Batory is "a raving beast", the "unsatiated snake", the "evilly gifted viper (*aspid*)", the "roaring lion". Some metaphors are developed still further. Next to the traditional images of the military tale, there appear new ones: the Polish army storms the city like a "dark smoke", it "flows towards the city like flood waters" and like "surging sea waves"; the enemies "shine against the city with their sabres like many lightnings", they "submerge" the Pskovans "with rifle-balls as a great rain cloud floods with countless drops" and "kill Christians as if with poisoned teeth of a snake", the Pskovans die "as stalks of wheat torn out from the ground", or like ants. The comparison of Batory to a snake is carried to considerable lengths: he opens his mouth "like insatible hell"; "he flies to Pskov speedily and joyfully like a great evil snake hurrying from a huge cave, and throws his terror upon the city like fiery sparks and dark smoke". In this context, Batory's army is depicted as "snakes and scorpions", and so on. When the Pskovans caught with hooks affixed to poles those Polish soldiers who were trying to blow up the city walls, this is likened to a duck hunt with hawks in "inlets [of rivers and sea]" and then the defenders "picked the sweet prey of their [the Poles'] bodies ... like the white vultures". Rhetorical devices are also employed; there are apostrophes by the author, speeches and letters of varied styles; occasionally there appear adages mostly influenced by literary sources. The spoken language, so typical of the Pskovan chronicles, is evident on rare occasions only; on the whole, the Muscovite style of splendour predominates.

According to entries in a cypher, the author appears to have been a painter (*zograf*) by the name of Vasilij. He must have been a well-read man. He quotes the Holy Scriptures, and his numerous animal similes seem to indicate the influence of Manasses through the intermediary of the Chronograph. In other respects, too, the influence of the old Kievan literature so important in the literature of Pskov may be discerned here also.

5. THE CHRONICLES

1. The writing of annals was approaching its end. It did not cease altogether, but there were changes in its character. Chronicles came nearer to chronographs, that is to say, they became synthetic expositions of history in which the material was not arranged according to dates but following the pattern of connected historical developments. In accordance with this, the material was now often no longer arranged chronologically, but divided up into separate chapters. These frequently bore separate titles, and this became even more important as whole monuments were now being written into the chronicles. After the Muscovite chronicle redaction of 1479 there was a new feature: the authors no longer allowed themselves merely omission or "stylisation" of facts when recording them; they went further, to the extent of actual forgery (M. Priselkov, cf. 5, V, 7).

2. The Novgorod and Pskov chronicles continued to be compiled, on the whole maintaining their specific character, but connected long tales often appeared in the text. Essentially, with but a few exceptions, there wese not independent works, but original constituent components of the chronicle.

The so-called second Novgorod Chronicle recounted in great detail the period of the punitive expedition of Ivan the Terrible against the city (1571–72). Subsequently, ecclesiastical chronicles were the only ones to be written. One of them (the so-called Third Chronicle) extended almost to the end of the 17th century.

The Pskov chronicles were also continued, even in the 17th century. Under the year 1510 we find a complete tale about "the capture of Pskov" by Moscow (see VI, 4, 6).

3. Of much greater interest are the Muscovite chronicles, and especially the "Nikonian" (named after Patriarch Nikon, of which there is an extant 17th-century copy), the "Voskresenskaja" (named after the Voskresenskij – Resurrection – Monastery to which a copy of the same work had also been donated by Nikon), and L'vov's Chronicle (named after its first 18th-century editor, L'vov). All these have only partially preserved their annalistic character, which they derive from the old chronicle literature.

The most extensive Nikonian chronicle originated first as a compilation about 1540; it dealt with events up to the year 1520. Later, the following additions were made: up to the year 1543 the same material as in the Voskresenskaja Chronicle; an independent work for the years 1534–53; and a chronicle of Ivan the Terrible (see below, 4) which extended even farther. The Nikonian Chronicle includes complete monuments of a wide compass. The passages from old annals are in most cases merely copied out with a changed vocabulary, but this, however, often alters the meaning. In addition to known monuments, the Chronicle includes otherwise unknown writings. Moreover, numerous recollections of old epic tradition are adapted either from folklore or from unknown sources, the result being that the Nikonian Chronicle is of particular significance for research into ancient epic tradition.

The Voskresenskaja Chronicle is less extensive in scope and, for the earlier periods, is but a compilation of the Muscovite Chronicle in the 1479 redaction, of Novgorodian chronicles and possibly also of the Hypatius Chronicle. It deals with events not later than the year 1541, and was subsequently brought up to 1560.

L'vov's Chronicle is also a compilation of the period which, in addition to various chronicles, also turned for material to the chronographs. The first redaction presumably covered the period up to 1533, and was later completed to 1560.

Each of these chronicles is extant in several copies. About 1570 the Nikonian Chronicle was incorporated into a profusely illustrated world history (see VI, 10, 5).

4. The Nikonian Chronicle (as, in part, the Voskresenskaja Chronicle too) contains a separate work which describes the events of 1534–53 and has a special title: "Chronicle of the Reign of the Tsar and Great Prince, Ivan Vasiljevič ..." [the Terrible] (*Letopis' načala Carstvovanija ...*). It opens with a minute description of the last days of Ivan's father, Vasilij III (the tradition of the biographies is followed here: the Lives of Daniil of Galič and of Aleksandr Nevskij begin with references to the heroes' fathers), and then proceeds with the account of the principal subject – Tsar Ivan himself, whose childhood is dealt with first. The Tsar's private life is described in great detail, but the main theme, however, is the capture of Kazan'. The Chronicle in general bears an official character, with the use of literal adaptations from numerous records and dispatches, thus representing the chancery style of the age. The typical rhetorical style flourishes in the speeches of the Tsar and Makarij; these bear hardly any traces of authenticity and must have been the handiwork of the author. In the battle-scenes there appear some elements of the old military narrative style, and some events (e.g., Vasilij's death) are recounted with an admixture of strong lexical and some phraseological elements of the vernacular. This confusion of styles is noticeable in some monuments after the late 16th century. Of ideological significance is that the struggle against Kazan' is justified primarily as being in the interests of Orthodoxy.

In the chancery style are written lists of officials or reports such as the following: "In accordance with the estimates (*smĕta*) of the treasurer (*kaznačej*) for everything – with gold, clothes and vessels ... 48,000 roubles (*rublev*)", or the account of a reception of a Tartar princess at the Moscow palace: "And when the Tsarina, Fatma Sultan, came to the palace, the Great Princess had ordered Ogrofena Ivanovna Volynskaja together with the young boyar women to greet her at the sledge; and when the Tsarina ascended the stairs, the Great Princess had ordered...", etc. All speeches, including those of the young Tsar himself and of the dying Vasilij III, follow the Church rhetorical style. This is also the case with prayers and some accounts, as for instance of the enmity of the Tartar Tsar who "roaring like a lion threatening the hunter, and wishing to seize the divinely protected power of Great Prince Ivan, had boasted that he would destroy the Virgin's inviolable possessions [Moscow – D.Č.]"; or – Ivan "arms himself with piety and the joyful hope of Christ's mercy". In these passages there are numerous compounds. There are also turns of phrase of the military tale, e.g.: "to drink of the chalice of death" (to fight); "arrows flew like rain", "and it had been an evil and terrible battle"; "rose in the stirrups" (embarked on a campaign); "blood flowed through the valleys", and so on. There are, too, elements of the vernacular, as in *Ogrofena* (*Agrafena*), *guži, vprjaženy, mindal'naja kaša;* gerunds like *spěšači, nesuči;* and commonplaces like *chlěb i sol', čtoby ... pjadi ne otstupala*, etc. ("harness, harnessed, almond groats, in haste, carrying, bread and salt, so that she did not yield a single step").

5. The so-called Kazan' Chronicle is actually not a chronicle within the strict meaning of the term. In most manuscripts it is entitled "The History (*Istorija*) of the Kazan' Empire". This work is, as it were, on the boundary between historical narrative and historical novel. In both content and style it is one of the most interesting monuments of the period. The *Istorija* enjoyed great popularity; and this is best seen from the fact that there were ten redactions of the work, and that there are two hundred extant manuscripts. Here the rhetorical style is primarily combined with that of the military tales (especially of Manasses and of Nestor-Iskander's tale, see V, 6, 5) as well as with folklore elements.

The work is mainly devoted to the capture of Kazan' (1552) and the preceding events. The author, who claims to have been a captive in Kazan' for twenty years (this is perhaps an echo of Nestor-Iskander), presumably wrote his account well after 1560. Nothing more, however, is known about him. In any case, he appears as a man well versed in letters, who draws extensively from them without slavish imitation.

The work contains a legendary story of the foundation of the city in 1172 in a region called by the author "Russia" and populated by snakes and a two-headed dragon (cf. The Tale of the Babylonian Empire). The history of the Tartars and the Turks is related briefly but realistically, with special attention to the relationship between Kazan' and Moscow since the 15th century. Three quarters of the "History" is devoted to the reign of Ivan the Terrible. Šig-Alej, the Muscovite candidate to the Kazan' throne at that time, was unable to maintain his authority. This was followed by the Muscovite intervention, and the city fell in 1552. The author seems to be well informed about the political life of Kazan'. It is significant that, on the whole, he depicts the Tartars with a certain amount of sympathy: they are "valorous", they fight and die "laudably", and so on. Tartar women are spoken of with even greater sympathy, and characteristics of the life of Russian princesses (laments) are attributed to them. Nevertheless, in the author's eyes, the Tartars are always "heathens" in contrast with the "Christians", namely the Russians. Russian warriors call to each other, "Speed to the godly work, Christ is going to help us unperceived!" At the same time reference is repeatedly made to the old princes, and even to Svjatoslav Igorevič, St. Vladimir, and Vladimir Monomach (with a spurious narrative of his fight against the Greeks). The legend of "Monomach's Regalia" (see VI, 4) appears here, and Moscow is, for the author, not only the "Second Kiev" but also the "Third Rome".

Elements of purely rhetorical style are slight. Compounds, which are not numerous, are mainly taken over from Manasses (thus the Volga is *zlatostrujnyj Tigr* – "the gold-flowing Tigris"). The play of synonyms appears occasionally: Prince Čapkun, whom the writer makes responsible for the conflict between Kazan' and Moscow, is *l'stec, prilagatej, pagubnik, smuščenik* ("liar, slanderer, destroyer, sower of confusion"). Speeches and laments are for the most part chains of brief exclamations and questions: "What shall we do?", "O, mountains, cover us!", etc. Only abstract words are in the rhetorical style, e.g., *pobĕditel'stvo* instead of *pobĕda* (victory); instead of "men fell" – *padenie ljudem;* instead of "fire" – *sila ognennaja; kričanie* for *krik* ("shouting"); participles are also numerous. In contrast, descriptions of battle scenes are full of expressions going as far back as Manasses or the even earlier chronicles. The warriors "fill themselves with martial spirit", or are like "a leopard with warlike fury", "the flag is shown as a sign of victory", the warriors' cry is "thunderlike", "the chalice of death is being drunk", corpses lie "like mountains", blood flows "like a river". Occasionally there are original metaphors: the Russians attack "like a river which cannot be halted", the Tartar host is like "the sea in a storm", etc. One cannot with certainty determine the origin of the many comparisons of people with animals; only some of these are reminiscent of Manasses, but they are also numerous in the chronicles. Thus the Russians fly "like eagles or hungry falcons", they, fight "like lions", they run "like deer", they swarm upon the enemy "like bees"; a Tartar tsar gnashed his teeth "like a wild ferocious beast, and whistled menacingly like a horrible great dragon"; he "devoured" his dignitaries as an animal swallows sweet grapes. Manasses, Nestor-Iskander, or popular tradition could all equally account for the origin of the soothsayers' omens. Elements of popular speech also appear: *pčelisto, rybno, nudma, osoka, pogreb, vekšica,* etc. ("rich in bees, rich in fish, compulsory, sedge, cellar, squirrel"), and the popular epithets of adornment: *čerleno vino i medy sladkie, krasnye ženy, děvicy krasnye, čistoe pole velikoe, koni dobrye, velikij grad Moskva, temnaja nošč' osennjaja, terema zlatoverchie, straži krěpkie,* etc. ("red wine and sweet mead, beautiful women, beautiful maidens, wide clear field, good horses, the great city of Moscow, dark autumn night, gold-roofed palaces, strong guards"). Many expressions taken over from popular poetry are frequent, e.g., *Kazan'-rěka, zemlja-mati, star da mal, poěchati daleče v pole, nošč' jako jasnyj den', vo edinoj sračicě bez pojasa, vozmu pticu borzoletnuju... da poslju ot mene ko otcu mojemu i materi, zvoniti vo vsja tjažkaja,* etc. ("the river Kazan', mother-earth, old and young, to ride far into the field, night is like a clear day, in only a shirt and without a belt, I take a speedily-flying bird ... and despatch it to my father and mother, all the heavy [bells] peal").

The vocabulary in such folklore expressions is sometimes Church Slavonic (cf. above, *nošč', grad, sračica*), and even the morphology is older, as for instance in the case of the frequently used *dativus absolutus.*

After the women's laments and the battle-scenes the most ornamented passage occurs in the description of the Tsar's entry into Moscow after the victorious Kazan' campaign. This again reminds us, on one hand, of the imagery of the old chronicles (Daniil of Galič, 1251), and, on the other, of modern epic songs (the Curiosity of women in the Čurilo-Song).

The work is unfortunately unreliable in several respects as a historical source, since it relates many legends including Tartar ones; moreover, it attempts to bring many features into line with subsequent developments (e.g., the participation in the campaign of boyar and princely families that had later fallen into disgrace).

The Kazan' Chronicle influenced a number of later works, as for instance the Pskovan account of the siege of the city by Stefan Batory (see VI, 7), and numerous tales of the interregnum.

6. Later – after 1576 – there came into existence another "History of the Great Prince of Moscow", the sole hero of which is again Tsar Ivan. It could be described as a subsequent "secular biography". Here the hero is painted in such dark colours that the "History" would deserve to be called a libel were not most of its contents a true representation of events. This work came from the pen of Ivan's erstwhile friend and collaborator, Prince Andrej Kurbskij (1528–1583), who was also an important military commander in the battle for Kazan'. Kurbskij had much intercourse with Maksim Grek (VI, 9). After the breach between Ivan and his circle of the 50's, the Prince managed to escape to Lithuania in 1564; there he devoted himself to further studies and, in the course of years, translated many works from the Latin language. He learned Latin in Lithuania. His translations included the Church Fathers, amongst them the Dialectics and Theology of John the Damascene (by then, the old translation – II, 5 – had become obsolete), Lives of the Saints, a more modern book on Logic, and others. He also compiled a new anthology of religious literature, the *Novyj Margarit*. Kurbskij had become a polemical writer as well. He sent a number of letters to private individuals, containing warnings against Catholicism and Protestantism. He drafted a brief history of the Council of Ferrara, and he warned his readers against the use of the Apocrypha and of Skorina's Slavonic Bible prints. The direct influence of Maksim Grek is often noticeable here, as well as, to a certain extent, Kurbskij's Latin studies. The "History" also came into being in these years. Lexically, it bears many characteristics of the author's new environment.

The motives behind Kurbskij's desire to write include, among others, his wish to instruct future generations in the pursuit of good and the avoidance of evil. The "History" is arranged as the story of Tsar Ivan's development. Kurbskij explains this by the circumstances of his life, first of all by his parentless childhood spent among men who encouraged his evil passions. The Tsar improved under the influence of the priest Silvestr. The struggle for Kazan' forms the climax of this stage in Ivan's life. Kurbskij, who himself participated in the campaign, devotes the greater part of the first section to this event. This is followed by an account of the wars in the West. He says that, immediately after the capture of Kazan', Ivan fell under the influence of bad counsellors, including the "most cunning monks" of the "Josif School". Their opponent – Maksim Grek – and Josif's follower – bishop Vassian Toporkov – are depicted in dialogues with the Tsar. Toporkov is said to have advised Ivan as follows: "If you wish to be an autocrat, don't keep any counsellor who might be cleverer than yourself. .... In this way you will govern firmly and have everybody in your hand." After the death of Ivan's first wife, Anastasia (1560), there came a decisive turn for the worse; under the influence of slanderers, he broke with Silvestr's circle, and started his atrocities. A shattering account of these atrocities, although often confined to the mere enumeration of those executed, forms the second part of the "History". The third part, almost an independent work, is the biography of a pious hermit, Feodorit, the missionary to the Lapps, whose clash with Ivan cost him his life.

The "History", on which, no doubt, Kurbskij spent a long time, is excellently constructed. The language has only minor elements of the Ukrainian Church Slavonic, while Kurbskij in his letters of the same period consistently makes use of numerous Ukrainian words. The style of the "History" varies from section to section. In the first part we encounter the strict formulas of the military-tale style, though with some slight changes ("arrows like rain", etc.). The second part is a simple narrative enlivened only with pathetic exclamations and apostrophies to the readers: "Hark, I diligently pray, to this bitter and solemn tragedy!", "In this way has he [the Tsar] ... paid ... for the services and kind actions", etc. The third part (Feodorit's life) approaches closely the style of the Lives of the Saints. Ornaments here consist mainly of rhetorical elements which can be seen more clearly in Kurbskij's epistles. The work ends with an epilogue, in which, with words full of pathos, Kurbskij speaks of the Muscovite State as the Empire of the Anti-Christ in which the Tsar's role is that of the "inner dragon". But the impact of the work, as probably intended by the author himself, is in its entirety. The deliberate tracing of the Tsar's development and its explanation, however, are not convincing, even more so as Kurbskij lays stress, next to the evil influences, on Muscovite tradition and on the character of the princely family of Moscow. Nevertheless, Kurbskij's view of the period strongly influenced a number of 19th-century scholarly descriptions of the times of Ivan the Terrible.

6. TRAVELLERS' TALES

1. In the 16th century many Russians visited foreign lands, even countries of Asia Minor and Egypt. The travel literature of the period, however, is meagre and has no literary importance. Such, for instance, is a description of Mount Athos, a dry composition compiled at the command of Metropolitan Makarij (see VI, 10).

2. In 1558, an embassy was sent to the Christian Churches of the East. It returned in 1561 after visits to Constantinople, Mount Athos, Jerusalem, and Egypt. Vasilij Poznjakov, a member and later leader of the mission, left behind a brief and colourless account of this journey. He made use of the Tsar's epistle and the reply thereto by Patriarch Ioakim, of the description of Jerusalem then available in translation (see VI, 2), and of some notes of his own. Significantly, Poznjakov speaks of the representatives of the western Church, whom he had met in Jerusalem, as "heretics" and "the accursed ones" (*okajannye*), and of their divine service as "devilry" (*běsnovanie*).

3. A compilation, based on Poznjakov's account, was prepared at the end of the century by Trifon Korobejnikov, who had gone to Constantinople in 1582 and stayed there and at Mount Athos until as late as 1593–94. This contains only insignificant additions to Poznjakov's material; among other things, the description of the journey through Lithuania and Wallachia and some minor remarks about Constantinople. The accounts of Jerusalem, Sinai, and Egypt are taken over from the other work. This work, of hardly any literary interest, acquired great popularity and went through many printings even as late as the 19th century.

7. POLEMICAL WRITINGS

1. The political-religious crisis of the 15th century reached its climax in the following century. The opposition to the Muscovite idea of autocracy with its merging of Church and State, though not ideologically weak, had no political backing. Hence its opponents, like Kurbskij and Artemij, chose to flee without putting up a fight. Even great political entities, like the Republic of Pskov, could offer no effective opposition within Russia, and saw possible though not desirable victory over Moscow's claims only in "secession (*otojdem*) to Lithuania or the Germans". Even the religious works of the followers of Nil Sorskij are not well preserved; presumably some of them were deliberately destroyed, and others were intentionally no longer copied by the adherents of the victorious Josif faction. The literature of local opposition certainly declined with Moscow's destruction of the seceding principalities and free cities. There are only trifling remains (see above VI, 4, 5–6), for the most part extant in local chronicles. In spite of all this, the relics of the political writing of the 16th century are fairly numerous. In any case, it is not possible to agree with the assertion of Soviet scholars (D. Lichačev, I. Budovnic) when they praise this type of writing to excess and wish to place it above contemporary western literature, in fact above the writings of the Reformation, that is to say, above Luther, Erasmus, and the others. However, Russian political writing from the very outset was restricted by certain limited assumptions. The point is that being already severed from

the Byzantine literary tradition, unable to discover links with the ancient past, and lacking a renaissance, Russian political writing did not have the ideological richness of the Ancients and also of the Christian – even Patristic – literature. Indeed, debates over truly fundamental issues occur but rarely (as for instance in Fedor Karpov). These issues mostly appear as having already been solved by Christian Orthodoxy, though in the majoity of instances there is no clear appreciation of what these decisions had actually been. Polemics remain confined to problems of contemporary and rather parochial shortcomings (monastic property) or even to personalities (evil tsars, metropolitans betraying the Church, and the private lives of the debaters themselves).

2. There is no doubt that the most outstanding political writer amongst those opposed to monastic property was Prince Vassian Patrikeev (born about 1460), a relative of Great Prince Ivan III and perhaps the greatest writer of the 16th century. Like his father, Prince Vassian ranked among the first dignitaries and military commanders. As the result of the conflict at court about the end of the century over the question of the succession, both he and his father were forced to take monastic vows and were imprisoned in a monastery on the White Lake (1499). From there he later went to Nil's hermitage and became his most zealous disciple. After the death of Nil and of Ivan III, Vassian was allowed to move to Moscow and rose to great importance at the court of Vasilij III. Then, that is before 1525, he spent much time in the company of Maksim Grek (see VI, 9). However, Vassian's influence failed to overcome the party of Josif Volockij, which by this time already held sway at the court. The unscrupulous Metropolitan Daniil accused him of heresy, and Vassian was declared guilty after a most unfair trial. He was banished to the monastery of his enemies at Volokolamsk, and died there shortly afterward.

Undoubtedly, Vassian was a representative of a certain political trend, and he skilfully blended the Christian and political points of view. When he enjoyed influence at court, he was so successful that Josif Volockij was forbidden to reply to his political writings (Varlaam – a close supporter of Nil's faction – was then Metropolitan). But the extant writings of Vassian illustrate only those of his political views dealing with attacks on the autocratic rule of the prince; and this aspect played only a secondary role in his polemical writings.

Not all of Vassian's writings have survived. He refers to his "eleven manuscripts (*tetradi*)", which are unknown to us. The first traces of his collaboration, and possibly of sole authorship too, are noticeable in the writings, which apparently appeared in 1503, of the *starcy* concerning the struggle against the heretics. In that year, together with Nil Sorskij, Vassian was present at the Council. While Josif Volockij demanded the execution of all the *židovstvujuščie* and even of the repentent heretics, the *starcy* wrote, "Unrepentant and unyielding heretics should be thrown into prison, but the Church of God with open arms receives the repentent ones and those who renounce their heresy, because Christ came to discover and save the lost ones." Josif quotes Moses, the Apostle Peter who with his prayer struck Simon Magus with blindness, and St. Leo, the bishop who tied a sorcerer to himself with the omophorion and stood with him in the fire until the sorcerer was burnt to death while the Saint remained unharmed. The *starcy* replied thereupon that when God wanted to destroy sinful Israel, Moses interceded with God on the people's behalf. "And you, Master Josif, are praying that the earth should swallow those unworthy heretics or sinners." The *starcy* added, "And why, Master Josif, do you not wish to test your sanctity– that is to say, to bind [a heretic] with your cloak until he burns to death? Then, we would receive you as one of three youths who had emerged from the fire [cf. the Book of Daniel – D.Č.]" ... "Do understand that there is a vast difference between Moses and Elias and the Apostles Peter and Paul – and your own self." The message ends with an appeal for brotherly love, mercy, and God's patience.

The works definitely written by Vassian include the following: 1) "The Introduction" (*Predislovie*), against Josif; 2) "The Reply (*Slovo otvětno*), against those who condemn the truth of the Gospels"; 3) "A collection" (*Sobranie I*), against Josif which contains excerpts from Nikon's *Pandecta* (11th century), coupled with the author's own remarks; 4) A second "collection" (*Sobranie II*), a dialogue mainly on the question of ecclesiastical tradition; and 5) A new redaction of the *Nomokanon* which constituted the basis for the charges that led to Vassian's condemnation.

The fundamental questions dealt with by Vassian are not numerous. He has merely to deal briefly with the issue of heresy, for the heretics' fate had already been decided in accordance with Josif's views. Two main problems still remain unsettled – those of the ecclesiastical life and of monastic property. The question of right to religious instruction and political issues are dealt with by Vassian only in passing.

As to heresy, Vassian repeats the ideas developed in the epistle of the *starcy*, "God's mercy will save all; it will bring to penitence and to right understanding all sinners, including the publican, the whore, and the renegade, and all those who have sinned"). The punishment of the heretic should not be death (*ne v glavu*). Repentent heretics should be taken back into the Church.

At first (in the 1st Collection and the Dialogue), Vassian wished to discuss the arguments raised by Josif and his followers in support of their views. As stated before (V, 10, 7–8), they made indiscriminate use of passages from the Scriptures and of any works at all including saint's Lives and the Apocrypha. Vassian holds as conclusive the Holy Scriptures alone. As to the many examples in the Lives which supply evidence of land holding by saints and monasteries, Vassian did much critical work subsequently confirmed by modern scholars (A. Pavlov). Vassian went to the oldest manuscripts of the saints' Lives available to him and failed to discover there the tales referred to by Josif. This, in Josif's view, was tantamount to the "spoiling" of legends – a thing he had already accused Nil of doing – and the "profanation" of the saints. In reply, Vassian argued that transgression of Gospel law by the disciples of Josif constituted in fact such a desecration of the old sacred tradition; their true veneration could only be expressed by adherence to the commands of the Gospels. That Vassian's textual criticism convinced his opponents is shown by the fact that at his trial no direct reference was made to any of the stories which he had proved to be of later supplementary character. In fact, most of the stories rejected by Vassian were *miracle*-tales, and it has been argued therefore that he had denied the miracles performed by the saints. This forms the essential part of the charges laid against him at the 1531 trial. He was even accused of denying the miracles of Metropolitan Iona, not yet canonized, and of a man (perhaps a monk) of Kalazino. Vassian merely retorted that he did not know whether Iona or the Kalazino man had been workers of miracles or not. It is easily understandable that Vassian rebelled against Josif primarily for having allowed himself to be revered as a "saint and prophet" in his lifetime.

However, for Vassian it was far more important to develop his ideas on the nature of real piety. Firstly, he rejects the inordinate concern with the adornment of Churches, which makes them into playhouses (*sen' pozoriščnaja*). Church ornaments could be destroyed by fire or pillaged by barbarians and thieves, but what is given to the poor "cannot be stolen any longer by the devil". The whole embellishment of divine service is superfluous too; "The voice of prayer lies in the tenderness (*umilenie*) of those praying; he who perceives truth sees humility not in the loud clamour of the chant and exhortation." Josif's ideas are based upon "human commandments" and thus piety based thereon is no more than "the words and the externals (*vněšnij obraz*)". One ought to live according to the precepts of the Gospels, following "the commandments of Lord Christ", while the monks of today live "contesting the Lord's laws". Monastic life must be that of "poverty, alms giving, and all kinds of brotherly love and compassion"; it must be "inexhaustible open-handedness and the well of mercy" shown towards all men "both bad and good, righteous and unrighteous". This is "the spiritual healing"; and when this is not implemented, one turns into a "deaf snake". Therefore, Vassian opposes the formalism of Josif's Rule. The basis of "spiritual healing", both for one's own self and for others, should be the study of the works of the Prophets and Apostles and of the Gospels; all this can advance spiritual development.

Less interesting are Vassian's attacks on the way of life of the monks and high churchmen. With his peculiar skill of formulating his thoughts in a succinct way, Vassian sums up his attacks in one sentence. When speaking at the trial, he says ecclesiastical dignitaries "want only feasts and landed property, and to gambol and carouse with thieves".

Of course, in Vassian's views not all property is the outcome of theft. But this appellation applies at least to the property of the clergy, for it results in the permanent plunder of the monastery's peasants. At the same time it leads to a "spiritual spoliation" of the monks themselves; for they are being deprived of the tranquillity they need for the spiritual struggle, they are no longer independent of mundane entanglements and are deprived of the possibility of implementing the precepts of the Gospel. What Vassian has to say is not very original. Some passages seem to be more vivid paraphrases of what is to be found in the writings of Nil, and especially of Maksim Grek. Vassian's arguments revolve, above all, round the concept of "the commands of the Gospels".

"Where are there recommendations in the Holy Scriptures in Apostolic and Patristic tradition for the excessive acquisition of property by monasteries; that is to say, where is one [ordered] to win populated estates and to enslave our brethren, Christians, and to obtain from them unjustly both gold and silver?" Instead of distributing property among the poor "we [the monks] constantly travel about towns to look to the hands of the rich; we flatter them in many ways and show ourselves cringingly obliging to them so that we may receive from them an estate or a farm, or silver, or occasionally some cattle." All this results in the enslavement of the peasantry by monasteries: "We are possessed by gold and by greed, but our poor brethren, who live in the countryside, have burdens imposed on them by us in a variety of ways; we burden them with one fraud upon another, with one usury upon another, and we never show them mercy. And, when they cannot pay the interest, we mercilessly take away their property, their poor horses and cows, and then we expel them as unclean, together with.their womenfolk and children, far beyond our boundaries." This is almost identical with what Maksim Grek says (cf. VI, 9, 2). The saints, however, had acted in a completely different way: "They toiled with their hands and gained, according to the Commandment, their bread by the sweat of their brow. They neither looked to other hands nor nourished themselves on Christian blood, nor did they assemble treasures on earth for themselves by usury, as it is being done today by the alleged workers of miracles" (an allusion to Josif). The monks of the present day have many "Church estates and properties, and they invent for themselves countless varieties of clothing and meals, but they take no care whatever for the Christian brethren who perish from cold and hunger". "We vex our brethren and rob them, we sell Christians and mercilessly torture them with whips, and we throw ourselves onto their bodies like wild beasts."

Rich monasteries are also in many ways involved in the affairs of the world. Firstly, they lend money on usury, they take care to sell their grain at a profit, "they keep it for so long as to sell it at a time of shortage, in order to obtain a better price". The peasants – "Christians, our brethren" – are being sold (together with estates). A property-owning monastery must engage in litigation; "we exhaust ourselves in juridical processes" against poor people for the return of loans, and with neighbours over the question of boundaries of estates. In addition, according to Josif's Rule, the monastery is the judge over its peasants, but "if it is a sin to torture Christians inside [the monastery] it is also a sin outside the monastery". Thus, property-owning monasteries are "transgressors of the law"; they "desecrate" the tradition of the saints by an unseemly way of life. And Vassian describes the doctrine of monastic property as "a new heresy". Christ ordered us to turn the other cheek, "but you [Josif], opposing this command, are doing everything contrary to the law; and what are you then if not Anti-Christ, that is to say Christ's foe?"

In passing only, Vassian deals with two more questions, one of which was of great significance for the future development of literature. This is the issue of the right to religious instruction. Josif's followers denied the right of "laymen" (meaning here *non-bishops*) "to preach the way of salvation". One of them (Nil Polev) wrote to a monk who had dared to express his opinion about the deposition and imprisonment (on political grounds) of the Archbishop Serapion of Novgorod, "You are undertaking tasks that are beyond your station; you are but the foot and you are passing judgment on the head." Vassian, however, following Nil in this respect, determinedly defended the right and moral obligation of any Christian (even non-clergyman) to instruct others. Josif's followers, as will be seen later, conceded this right only to the Tsar apart from the bishops (see below, 4).

The only issue on which Vassian expressed political views is the problem of autocracy. As the misfortunes of a state are often caused by the intellectual weakness (*malomyslie*) of the Tsar, Vassian urges that the ruler should discuss (*dumati*) all questions with the boyars. This was certainly the political watchword of the old parties still accustomed to feudal usages. However, Vassian's demand for strict separation of ecclesiastical and worldly authorities applies to problems of *Church*-policy. Monks (and thus bishops as well) should not "interfere in mund-ane affairs"; monks who are striving for such wordly authority "are not lovers of God but trouble-makers (*gnéviteli*)". Vassian acknowledges that power is granted to the Tsar by God, but he is perhaps the last writer who, in this connection, makes no reference to the "sacred character" of the Tsar's *power*. "Worldly entanglements" are, to his mind, matters of indifference to the Church. This sharp division of ecclesiastical and State spheres, amounted, in the period under review, to a defence of the in-dependence of the Church, because then, really since the days of Metro-politan Daniil, the entire authority was in the hands of the State.

A knowledgeable scholar (Nevustroev) ascribed to Vassian, without any grounds, a parody which bears the significant title: "The Advice (*Izvět*) of Josif of Volokolamsk to the Muscovite Great Prince on how dependent princes should be conquered, and the whole Russian land united and expanded in all directions."

It is odd that Soviet scholars should insist on trying to discover "concealed" political motives behind Vassian's polemics; even his defence of monastery peasants evokes from these "socialists" nothing but ironic smiles! From these quarters, too, he is charged with lack of Christian charity towards his adversaries; but this perhaps has some justification. However, Vassian perceived developments which he saw as portending the decline of true Christianity, and against these he fought with polemic writings. For this reason too, his style is worthy of note. He writes in the rhetorical style of propaganda, which can be seen especially in his habit of apostrophizing Josif and his readers. His exclamations belong to the same type: "Who will not weep about this? Who will not rend his garments on seeing the influence of such darkness and gloom upon our reason!" In all his works of other types, namely in the Speech (*Slovo*), the tract (*Sobranie I*) and the Dialogue, he tries to write terse, clearly constructed sentences and to present impressive formulas using neologisms such as *prestupar'* ("transgressor"), *pišči* (plural; not used elsewhere: "meals") and popular words: diminutives of the words "village", "horse", "cow" (*derevniška, lošadka, korovka*), and especially paranomastic antonyms: *ne čudotvorcy a smutotvorcy* ("not miracle- but trouble-makers"), *ne zakonopoložitel' a zakonoprestupnik* ("not law-giver but violator of laws"), *ne pravila a krivila* ("not law but sacrilege"), and so on. These quotations show that he also used expressive imagery, even though his concrete descriptions are always very brief; he prefers formulas to images. He attempts to justify the political tenor of his writings: "For this reason you call me shameless and loose of tongue, and you condemn me. But what can I do? I, enlightened by the Scriptures, must preach the road of salvation to all people."

Vassian was condemned not only by his opponents; the court ruled likewise on the charges of heresy. This was the most tragic episode in Vassian's life. Under Metropolitan Varlaam he was entrusted with the examination of the *Nomokanon*. Metropolitan Daniil did not approve of the resulting work, for in his sources (Maksim Grek helped him with the translation of Greek texts) Vassian failed to find any confirmation of Josif's views concerning monastic property. Therefore he was accused of the "destruction" of "sacred books" (*razmetal svjaščennuju knigu*). He was said to have deleted a number of rules and to have replaced them by "the views of Greek sages: Aristotle, Homer, Philip, Alexander, and Plato". False witnesses were brought against him, for all the witnesses of the fact that he had been entrusted with the examination of the *Nomo-kanon* had died in the meantime, with the exception of a bishop who denied it. The prosecution also produced spurious translations from the Greek, and in these the uninhabited land which monks tilled themselves now became "estates", in the Russian meaning of *sela*, i.e., "villages". Vassian was also charged with holding a really unorthodox view on Corpus Christi; this, however, did not play a prominent part in his condemnation. He bore himself with great dignity before the court (Soviet scholars hold this, too, against him!); he defended himself and his views, but declared that he was willing to let the Metropolitan improve on his work (*a čto ne gorazdo, ty ispravi*). The uneducated Metropolitan probably thought that he was being laughed at. The dangerous adversary was therefore condemned and disappeared from literary life. Banished to Josif's monastery at Volokolamsk, according to Kurbskij's account, he was there "tortured to death" by the monks; this was probably not true. In 1545 Vassian was no longer alive. His burial place was in keeping with his secular rank of prince.

3. Of the whole 16th century the most interesting man of letters is the almost forgotten Fedor Karpov, whose writings have received little attention to date. Karpov was in the diplomatic service, and because of his knowledge of Latin was often entrusted with negotiations with foreign envoys, mostly western, including Herberstein who has left behind a description of Russia at that time. It appears that in 1536 Karpov fell into disgrace. Some of his letters to Maksim Grek are extant. According to these, for a certain time he took an interest in astrology; he called it the "art of arts", and said, "I believe that the delights of astrology (*zvězdozakonnaja prelest'*) are very necessary and useful to Christians." Maksim wrote four brief tracts against astrology in reply and, following up Karpov's enquiry about a passage in the Book of Esdras (III, 6, 47–54), gave an explanation of it. "My mind is weary," Karpov wrote, "since I have reached the depths of doubt. With great hope I pray you to give me that medicine that will sooth my mind. Though I am ashamed to trouble you, I do not wish to keep silent, for my wisdom-seeking mind cannot keep still. It wishes to know that which it does not possess; it seeks to find that which it has not lost; it desires books which it has not read; it longs to overcome that which is unsurmountable." This bantering, elegant style does not prevent Karpov from developing fundamental ideas; and he was the only man of letters of the century to do so.

Unfortunately, we know only Karpov's answer to an otherwise unknown letter of Metropolitan Daniil (see VI, 8). This reply was written before 1539. We gather from it that the Metropolitan had to decide on the issue of patience (*terpěnie*), as indicated in his notes (also not available to us), or was asked directly what he had to say against patience as the basis of life. This subject was also the theme of Daniil's letters of condolence (VI, 8, 5; similar advice had been given by Filofej in his letters of of condolence; see below, 4).

Karpov is the only 16th-century Russian writer to draw a sharp distinction between the ecclesiastical and secular spheres. He does not wish to deny the importance of patience for a monk, nor does he want to diminish its significance for a man living in the world, for such patience helps him to bear misfortunes. He believes, however, that the life of a State cannot be built around patience; for if it were the essential foundation of relations between man and man, "the strong would then oppress the weak", and the weak would have to suffer without offering resistance. If it were possible for men to be governed by patience alone, princes and laws would be superfluous; judges also would be unnecessary, for "patience would pacify all and sundry". No form of government could be organised then, and life would be in a state of chaos (*bez činu*). In the life of a state, human relationship must be based on *pravda*. *Pravda* means "Law" to Karpov; this is clear from his exposition, for the word can also mean "Justice". Karpov quotes the ancient definition of *pravda* – Law (modern: *pravo*): Law is the granting to each of his own (*suum cuique tribuendi*). Where Law rules, patience loses its importance. In a world where servants, arms, horses, beautiful clothes, and money are won by force, only he who has nothing can resist everything; but even he may be ravished by force. Thus, "the cause of the people will be ruined by prolonged patience". For patience (here *dolgoterpěnie*, a word that until the 20th century has always been used to denote the "great virtue" of the Russian nation), "without Law and *order*, wrecks society (*obščestvo*)." Everything that the people achieve is brought to nought. Moreover, "because of this, evil customs are introduced into the State and, because of their poverty, men become disobedient towards their rulers".

Therefore, each state must ("according to Aristotle", Karpov adds) "be governed by rulers according to the ideal of Justice, and not according to the dogma of patience". The State is necessary for men, because they live in "that great sea in which so many disastrous storms arise". And the rulers *(načal'nici, gosudari, cari)* must "justly *(pravedně)* care for everyone according to his nature, and defend the innocent, punish those who cause harm and annoyance, remove the totally incurable from the midst (*srěda*) of the good". Thus is harmony established among people. The ruler should be like the harp-playing King David who tuned the strings and, by touching them, achieved the "harmony of sweet sound". This comparison between the ruler and the artist presumably also has its origin in Aristotle. Karpov, however, is not in favour of formally applied Law. The ruler must also encourage his subjects "to virtue and good deeds", offering them rewards, mercy, and the right to speak for themselves; but as for the wicked, the ruler should improve them by punishment and should only "exterminate" those who do not wish to partake in "the medicine of betterment" (here again, there is an allusion to Aristotle). The ruler should not suffer oppression, and should not allow his subjects "to live under the heavy slavery of patience"; he should also have regard for human weaknesses. Here, Karpov refers to the Scriptures and to the fact that the ruler bears the responsibility for his government before God.

The scheme of historical development briefly indicated here is Christian, but with a modern tinge. At first, men lived under the "Law of Nature" (*zakon estestvennyj*), then under the Mosaic Law, and now – "in the Age of Mercy" – under the Law of Christ. Thus, at all times, men had lived "under a Law".

Finally, Karpov deals with the mercy (*milost'*) of the ruler; for his mercy the ruler can be loved by all. Mercy without law, to be sure, is laxity, just as law without mercy is tyranny (*mučitel'stvo* – the customary translation of the Greek *tyrannis*). These two destroy the state and any society; "but mercy, guided by the Law, and the Law, tempered by mercy, preserve the state of a ruler for a long time."

The letter is beautifully set within a framework. At the beginning there are long elegant formulas of courtesy, which were certainly meant in irony, for Karpov praised Daniil for those virtues the complete absence of which became apparent immediately after his elevation to the metropolitan throne. At the end there is appended an historical-political appraisal which is introduced by the pessimistic sentence, "I believe the end of time is approaching." Karpov says that he is not writing in times such as those when "the song birds made the author's writings sweet", but in the cold of winter, probably metaphorically meant. Karpov ironically describes the contemporary scene as the "Golden Age," for everything, rank, love, friendship – he says – can be obtained for gold. Even if the first of the Apostles, Peter, were to appear with the Teachings of Our Lord but without anything of material value, he would find doors closed against him everywhere and would be spurned. As we can see, the theme of Dostoevskij's "Great Inquisitor" here makes its appearance already. The world is full of evils: lechery, fraud, malice and ingratitude; "The evil man offers poison in return for honey, punishment for fruit, fraud for good deeds." "There is now strife everywhere." And Karpov quotes in translation Ovid's description of the Iron Age:

> *vivitur ex rapto; non hospes ab hospite tutus,*
> *non socer a genero; fratrum quoque gratia rara est.*

Thus, in reality, the Golden Age is but the Iron Age. The enumeration of vices is also reminiscent of the immediately following lines in Ovid. Greed rules everywhere. He who took the cloak also wants the shirt; he who stole a sheep also wants to take the cow. But this is not limited to robbery only, for man "wants to tear his neighbour from this life".

Karpov expresses the hope that the Metropolitan "has realised by now what perilous and unhappy paths were being trodden by the crippled feet of the secular government and the whole of mankind". ...

Unfortunately, it cannot be said with certainty which period Karpov has in mind, and whether the miseries he remarks are of a purely personal or political character. Under Vasilij III there had indeed been moments that could give rise to grave doubts, even among the supporters of absolutism, as to the unlimited power of the Tsar. And this uncertainty prevailed during the regency of Vasilij's widow, Elena (1533–38), and of the boyar clique.

But for all that, Karpov has left for us one of the most interesting and at the same time most perfectly constructed writings of the 16th century. Maksim Grek called Karpov (especially when addressing him in his writings) a man gifted with much understanding and true faith, a man most marvellous, most loved, most dignified, and most wise. Kurbskij, at a later date, refers to him as "the wise man". It would be hardly correct to describe Karpov as a "Westerner", even though he had perhaps read Aristotle (in Latin of course), for this philosopher had also enjoyed high prestige in Byzantium; he does quote Ovid, who was not a "modern" Westerner but an ancient one! Karpov has two quotations from Aristotle (Ethics, X, 10), and two allusions to the same chapter. It is probable that he relied on Cicero and Thomas Aquinas's commentary on Aristotle's Ethics, published in Venice in 1519. Nevertheless, he directs his thoughts to Russian problems. He is simply an intelligent, educated man, who saw the essence of state not in the deceptive brilliance of outward show, but in the building up of state life on certain fundamental Laws. The majority of his contemporaries thought otherwise; the Tsars and other rulers, too, had different ideas on the subject, even though there was no lack of attempts to create written Law. The consequences of the 16th-century situation became apparent in the following century (in the period of the interregnum).

It was not only Karpov who considered problems of Law and Justice; *pravda* – the Law – also played a great role in the writings of "Peresvetov" (see § 7), as well as in a work, the *Skazanie o Petrě* ..., probably rightly considered as a piece of polemical writing directed against Peresvetov. The same theme is also prominent in a short story, *Povĕst' nĕkoego bogo-ljubivago muža* ..., written before 1563; this shows the corruption of the rich by injustice as illustrated by the story of its hero, a Tsar, who above all "loved Law and Justice (*sud i pravda*)" but who, in the end, began to oppress his subjects. Peresvetov and the author of the last-mentioned work both emphasize the motif that appears in Karpov's works: beggars and outlaws cannot be the mainstays of any strong state. Peresvetov, however, links Law with *groza* (strength, cf. § 7); nor do he and the other writer draw a distinction between Church and State. Karpov's writing enjoyed little popularity, and later generations would not be able to understand these ideas of his.

4. Compared to Karpov's writings, the famous "circular epistles" of the Pskovan monk Filofej are rather primitive products of great but ineffective diligence that consisted of collecting and copying quotations with the addition of a few commonplaces. The effective formula of Filofej's writings, "Moscow – the Third Rome" – which was possibly not invented by him (V. Malinin) – hardly suffices to make him into a "famous writer" or "thinker", as Soviet scholars want to regard him; and the remainder of his work contradicts the appellation of "a progressive man" current in the same circles.

A number of Filofej's writings are extant: letters of "condolence" to the Pskovans, presumably after the abolition of their special rights in 1510 (VI, 4, 5), and to a boyar who had fallen into disgrace, of an unknown date. Neither, by any strech of the imagination, deserves the description of letter of "condolence", for in both of them Filofej declines to use the clergy's right to intercede with the prince on behalf of sufferers. Moreover, the second letter is no more than a slight revision and extension of the first; the changes are so trifling that it may be rightly assumed that both were copied out of the same epistolary guide (see V, 1, 4). The contents consist of extracts from the paterikons and Lives which give instances of the righteous suffering, but Filofej declares that those seeking consolation are rightly punished by God (in accordance with *jus talionis*), and even when they suffer without cause, such suffering has definitely been imposed by God in His Love. In the message to the boyar, there also appear new motifs: the secular power, the ruler, should be obeyed with faith and submission, otherwise disaster will threaten mankind "both in this and in the next life". But we learn from a Pskovan Chronicle that, "at a later date", Filofej, "with great courage" interceded with the Great Prince to help the persecuted. A further writing of his is directed against the measures taken by the Pskovan government during a plague (probably 1521/22), such as the closing of the infected streets and houses, the prohibiting of visits to the sick by priests, and the provisions for burial of the dead outside the city walls. Because Filofej considers that this pestilence also is the Lord's punishment, he has to disapprove of all these measures.

Indeed, he is able to produce religious arguments against the ban imposed on the priests, but against the other restrictions – by no means new in Pskov – he can only argue that they would provoke derision and mocking amongst the city's neighbours, including the heathen (!). Three further writings of Filofej's are addressed to various people interested in astrology. Instead of the theological arguments advanced by Maksim Grek, he is only able in the first brief message to draw attention to the fact that the Scriptures "forbid investigation of this [i.e., astrology] not only by us commoners, but also by tsars, bishops, and all the high officials". In order to confirm this, he produces quotations from Sirach (under the false name of Solomon), from the un-canonical Third Book of Esdras (the quotation is not suitable at all, for there is no enquiry into nature, but into the future of the Jewish people), and from the apocryphal "Vision of Zacharias", which in fact declares as taboo all inquiries into natural phenomena, besides a number of passages from the Holy Scriptures, which in part have no bearing on the subject. – The second, a very brief message, confines itself to references to the (alleged) decisions of the Councils against "the astrologers and astronomers (!)", and also against "marmeania" (ἡ εἱμαρμένη – "the fate" of the Stoics; the word occurs in early Russian literature, for instance in Hamartolos) and against "mafimaty" (mathematics too!). Filofej considers all this as "Greek lies" (basni), from which nothing but blasphemy emerges and which must be thrust aside "like snakes"! The next work deals with the question of "bad and good days" and is worked out in greater detail. It opens with a comic blunder: Filofej gives a variant of the modesty formula, which starts by saying Ellinskych borzostej ne tekoch (roughly: "he has not run with the Greek speed"). However, he copied it wrongly; in his introduction it was elen'skoj borzosti which simply means "with the speed of a deer" (A. Sobolevskij). Then comes a reasoned argument. All days are created by God, and thus none of them can be evil; the hour of his birth cannot determine the status of a man, and so on. Filofej admits here that with the aid of a lunar table (Šestokryl) it is possible to reckon the periods of darkness of the moon and the sun. The second part of the message deals with errors of the Catholic Church, and the whole suddenly ends with the assertion that "our lord is the only Christian Tsar in the world" and that "all Christian Empires found their true aim and united themselves (snidoša-sja) in the only Empire of our Lord in accordance with the Books of the Prophets", which, however, Filofej forgets to quote in this context. "Two Romes have fallen, the Third stands, and there will be no Fourth." This is followed by a picture from the Apocalypse. And "he who rules ...

should not place his hopes in gold and passing wealth, but in God alone." The conclusion returns to the basic problem of the epistle.

The sudden appearance of these formulas raises the question of their origin. A thorough student of Filofej's works (V. Malinin) argues that the author copied them from an unknown source. Some sections of the epistle are literal extraxts from known works. These formulas do not seem to originate from Filofej's mind alone. As early as in Manasses (V, 2, 3) Constantinople is linked with "primeval" or "lost" Rome. Some of the writings of Patriarch Kallistos (V, 1, 6 and 2, 2) to his Bulgarian friend Theodosios (Feodosij), known in Russia in a Slavonic translation, describe Constantinople as "the new Rome", to which "the more ancient Rome" surrendered its supreme authority (*stariišin'stvo*), as to the "second" Rome. And, in a note, the Bulgarian translator of Manasses called the capital of Bulgaria "the second Imperial city" (Constantinople). All that Filofej had to do in this case was to insert "Muscovy" instead of "Bulgaria". It is also possible that he found the formula "Moscow – the Third Rome" in some earlier source which is unknown to us. We should not necessarily believe in this compiler's own art of invention!

Filofej's fame rests, however, on two epistles to the Great Princes, to Vasilij III (probably after 1511) and to Ivan the Terrible (after 1533). Some scholars think that the second letter was also intended for Vasilij III, but this appears highly improbable. But even if the names of the addressees are changed, the appraisal of the writing will still remain the same.

Both messages are not long and contain, among others, the same thoughts that we have already encountered. The Great Prince of Muscovy (whom Filofej calles "the Tsar") rules in the "Third Rome" and is the only Christian lord. The advice not to pay heed to gold and riches is repeated here too. The Tsar is given the title of "The Holder of reins of the Divine Holy Throne of the oecumenical apostolic Church". Filofej also recalls the forefathers of the Great Prince, St. Vladimir and Jaroslav. The subjects on which Filofej addresses Vasilij III are at least partly religious: he calls upon the Great Prince to fight immorality (homosexuality), but at the same time asks him to introduce "the true sign of the Cross" to replace the "Greek" form which many laid on themselves. Filofej does not forget to remind the Tsar of the inviolability of ecclesiastical property, with reference to the rulings of the Fifth Oecumenical Council – the decisions of which have not survived at all. The second epistle, after long verbatim borrowing from the *Climax* and extracts from the Apocalypse, opens with a reference to the "secession" of the Byzantine Church (union with Rome), and again repeats the idea of "the Third Rome" – which adheres to Orthodoxy, but where "the good deeds have decreased in number and injustice has grown". The message again has a practical aim: the Great Prince should put an end to simony (the selling of ecclesiastical offices). This section is copied with some minor alteration from the *Nomokanon* and from Metropolitan Kirill's decisions (13th century). The message ends with a passionate exhortation.

A further writing on simony is also ascribed to Filofej. However, this is presumably someone else's compilation based on the last-mentioned work.

The writings of Filofej may also be considered eschatologically. Such an approach is justified by the long quotations from the Apocalypse and also by some turns of phrase. And when to his formula "The Third Rome now stands" he adds the words "and there shall not be a Fourth one", he probably wishes to remind his addressees of the "approaching end" of the world. However, both the recipients of the epistles and later generations understood this sentence, which might be an Apocalyptic warning, as a prophecy of the "Eternal Kingdom". Even if the "theory" of "Moscow – the Third Rome" was a misunderstood apocalyptical allusion, the fault lies with Filofej's literary shortcomings, for his famous writings are anything but clear.

It is very difficult to decide whether this compiler, who might have coined a few well-sounding phrases of fatal portent, can be taken seriously as a writer. One thing is certain, however: his famous sentence may not be described as a "cohesive and clearly formulated *theory*" (I. Budovnic).

5. The letters of the Novgorodian Archbishop Feodosij, Makarij's successor in office (after 1542), however, are much richer in their content. Some of his epistles (fourteen are ascribed to him) are addressed to Ivan the Terrible. In the two letters before the Kazan' campaign, he reminds Ivan not only of his ancestors Igor', Svjatoslav (both of whom were heathens!), and St. Vladimir, but also of the Emperor Constantine. It is only natural that he should hail the expected victory of a Christian prince over the pagans. His later epistles are more interesting because in them (after 1547) he once again voices the ideology of Christian autocracy. The Archbishop begs the Tsar to fight crime. "No one but you ... can halt this desecration of the spirit and external turbulence." To deal with "external" unrest, the Tsar has been given by God "the sceptre of the kingdom of this world", "after the likeness of the kingdom of heaven". Feodosij also appears to yield to the Tsar the task of curing souls. "As the terrible and all perceiving eye of the heavenly Tsar sees the hearts of all men, so you, too, with your royal depth of mind, have great power rightly to exercise your good government. ..." "You should ... bear every sorrow with piety,

and those subject to you shall be spared all spiritual and bodily unrest", because "as the master of the ship is always on the alert, so too the all-seeing spirit of the Tsar firmly steers the ship of government, while he allows the streams of lawlessness to run dry". Feodosij also considers the Tsar as the supreme arbiter in the affairs of the Church, for, he concludes, "I am writing this to you, divinely-appointed lord, not in order to teach and instruct your penetrating mind or your noble wisdom, for it does not behoove us to forget our station and to presume so far, but [I write] as a disciple to a teacher, as a servant to a master". How different is this Feodosij from the 11th century Saint of the same name, who believed that it was proper for the clergy to instruct the ruler (and he was only abbot of a monastery), and for the ruler to heed such instruction. And as late as 1480 Vassian Rylo was still repeating the same formulas (see V, 11, 2)!

6. We cannot discuss here all the polemical works of the 16th century. There are many of no significance whatever, and others which advance original points of view but whose origin is however far from clear. Of this kind, for example, is the "Dialogue (*Beséda*) between St. Sergij and the miracle-worker of the Varlaam monastery, St. German", previously ascribed to Vassian. The anonymous author, who for his clumsy style alone could not have been Vassian, is not a representative of Nil's school. The author is opposed to monastic property, but he argues from the autocrat's standpoint: the Tsar should not share his power with the "unburied dead" (i.e., with the monks), for damage to political life would be the result. Amongst other polemical writings are those of Ermolaj-Erazm (see VI, 12, 4–5) already known to us, who, in a number of minor works, points out the importance of the labouring peasants and makes a number of suggestions as how their position might be improved. In his dry, matter-of-fact style, Ermolaj-Erazm yet succeeds in drawing vivid pictures; to support the prohibition of intoxicating liquor he presents realistic and shocking scenes of drunkenness. Two anonymous epistles are ascribed, without sufficient evidence, to the priest Silvestr. These emphasize the Tsar's responsibility before God, and advise him against arbitrary rule.

The tale of Drakula (V, 2, 4) was certainly also treated as a polemical writing, but it is difficult to say whether its heroes aroused enthusiasm or abhorrence.

7. The seven writings signed with the pseudonym "Ivaška Peresvetov" are the only ones which are concerned with the reforms carried out by Ivan the Terrible.

Until this time this writer is still a subject of debate. In his works, he gives some information about himself; he says that he came from Lithuania after service as a courtier in Poland, Hungary, Wallachia, and Bohemia, and he knows Turkey, though not from his own experience. The language of his writings hardly indicates that he was a foreigner (only a few Southern slavisms can be traced). The two "petitions" he sent to Ivan the Terrible use the form of petition (*čelobitnaja*) merely to offer advice to the Tsar, not in a general way as Daniil did (see IV, 9), but in concrete terms. The fate of Constantinople ("The Tale of the Turkish Tsar Magmet"; tales of the last of the Emperors, Constantine; the tale on "Greek books") and some other works are all written by the author with the same aim – to instruct the Tsar. It may well be that "Peresvetov" was a pseudonym; it is impossible, however, to accept the thesis that the works were only written at the time of the terror (*opričnina*), and thus after the fact attempted to justify some of the Tsar's actions in the guise of advice. Even in 16th-century Russia, the period of literary forgeries, hardly could such an ingeniously falsification come into being. Still more improbable is the theory that the Tsar himself was the author. Peresvetov's style has nothing in common with the individual style of Ivan. It can hardly be doubted that Peresvetov had been abroad, and the date of the composition should be placed between 1547 and 1555.

Peresvetov usually speaks of countries other than those in which he is supposed to have lived. He claims to know Constantinople well, and Turkey, and counsels the Tsar to follow the example of the Turkish Sultan. He enhances this advice by saying that the Sultan conducts his life in accordance with Christian books seized from the Greeks. Peresvetov's thoughts revolve round the word "justice" (*pravda*); allegedly, he says, foreigners praise Tsar Ivan but regret that there is no justice in Muscovy. When the Wallachian *vojevoda* Petr heard that "in Russia ... the Christian faith was good, perfect in every detail, and the beauty of the Churches great, but there was no justice there", he wept and said, "If there is no justice, there is nothing at all." According to Peresvetov, justice is at the source of the life of the State. He seems to vacillate, however, between the foundation of justice on the decrees of God and its foundation on the good of the state. Justice is "heart's delight for God", and "God loves not faith but Justice"; and there is a detailed argument in favour of justice consonant with the interests of the State and of the ruler. For Peresvetov the interests of ruler and State coïncide. The essence of justice is the existence of Laws and their strict observance. This can only be accomplished through the severity (*groza*) of the ruler. "Without this severity it is impossible to introduce justice into the state." In his unhistorical biography of the last Byzantine Emperor, Constantine, whose life is somewhat likened to that of Tsar Ivan, the author shows that Byzantium's decline was predetermined by the weakness of the Imperial power and by the Emperor's succumbing to the influence of his high officials. The criticism of the Byzantine "boyars" becomes in turn a criticism of those of Moscow. The measures adopted by the Sultan are to be the model of justice and severity toward officials who harm the state.

When the "true Christian faith" of Moscow is joined with "Turkish Justice", then Moscow shall become God's Kingdom on Earth.

Definite advice is given by the author as being from foreign sources; he places it in the mouth of the Wallachian *vojevoda* Petr and of the "philosophers". But primarily he praises the measures of the Turkish sultan, especially his persecution of unrighteous judges right up to their execution ("flaying alive"). Other counsels follow, in part, various foreign models: the fixing of salaries for officials, mainly for the judges; the disregard of wealth and origin when appointing to government and military offices (the author refers in this connection to Alexander the Great and Augustus); but, above all, the introduction of a permanent standing army and good care of the troops because "a wise Tsar makes the hearts of troops rejoice like a falcon's". To concrete points of political business belong suggestions for conquering the Kazan' realm, that "paradise-like little country"; to build fortresses on the southern border of the State; and to make Nižnij Novgorod capital in place of Moscow. Most of these counsels fitted into Ivan's program of government, since the Tsar particularly contested the relics of feudal independence, although mainly by measures destined to undermine the very foundations of the State. This was in line with the Tsar's conception of severity (*groza*). Peresvetov, however, goes even further; he thinks serfdom (*cholopstvo*) should be abolished in the interest of the military service. The Sultan had done this. "Enslaved men ... are not valorous, for the slave is not ashamed and does not worry about his honour." He says to himself, "I am a slave (*cholop*) and shall never acquire a different name." Very pointed comments on contemporary conditions in Russia are given by Peresvetov in the form of reported rumours from abroad. But the Tsar "should enlarge and defend the Christian faith and bring the unfaithful within the fold, he should raise the glory of God and introduce Justice into his realm to bring delight to the Lord's heart." Peresvetov did not raise the question whether the severity of the autocrat could always be compatible with justice. ... He had presumably written before the time when Tsar Ivan commenced to show his severity (*groza*) against his own subjects. At any rate, we see in the author a heterogeneous mixture of three not altogether compatible principles: justice, severity, and the religious foundation of the state, of which he offers no genuine synthesis.

The works of Peresvetov are written in a clear and vivid language with an inclination toward aphoristic embellishments and transparent images. Time and again he repeats the same idea; several brief sentences of only slightly varied content often follow immediately one after another.

Occasionally rhymes (*homoioteleuton*) occur in such sequences of sentences.

8. Tsar Ivan took a personal part in polemical writing. He was not only well read, but also a man of letters to whom are ascribed a number of panegyrics and prayers written in a lofty style. Also his private letters (to a man of his circle during the days of terror who had asked to be ransomed from Crimean captivity; to the monks of a monastery where a number of forcibly cowled dignitaries were held prisoner and in the Tsar's view were leading unmonastic lives, that is to say, they had been given too much freedom: both 1573) with their strong element of the spoken language, but with numerous well applied ironical and satirical remarks, show the Tsar as a man who could write skillfully. In contrast, the diplomatic dispatches, probably not written by him, are remarkable only for their abuse of the recipients. They contain far too many non-Great Russian elements. Nicely turned out, however, are his various directives and a petition to the Tartar khan whom, in an unusual political play, Ivan named "Tsar of all the Russias". This is written in a mock-obsequious vein which is highly effective (1575).

The man who moved the Tsar to a polemic defence of his policies was Prince Andrej Kurbskij (see VI, 5, 6). The Prince, immediately after his flight to Lithuania (1564), sent a letter to the Tsar. This letter's composition, its rounded Church Slavonic language (which, according to his own admission, Kurbskij "had not studied in his youth to perfection") are very artistic, its contents deeply moving. In a single letter (*epistolija*) Kurbskij puts down in compressed form some thoughts that he must have had in his mind for a long time past. The epistle is obviously meant as a parting letter which would not be followed by any further correspondence.

The letter is deliberately kept short, with repeated indications that the writer does not wish to say any more and that the addressee himself knows everything already. In this parting letter, Kurbskij wishes merely to remind Ivan of the fate of those persecuted by him, to call him to account before the Almighty's Throne. The letter is an indictment opening with a number of questions, as to why the Tsar had ordered many of his heaven-sent collaborators (*sil'nych vo Izraile . . . i voevod*) to be condemned on trumped-up charges. Only someone who does not recognise a higher judge than himself could do this. However, there is such a Judge, Christ, "the Judge between you and me". Then Kurbskij reminds the Tsar of the persecution to which he himself had been exposed and places against this his faithful military leadership in which he had known no defeat. He ends this part of the letter with another vision of Christ's Last Judgment, to which he summons the Virgin and all the saints, including his ancestor Prince St. Fedor Rostislavič (of Smolensk). The third section is even briefer; it contrasts the fate of those executed or persecuted by the Tsar, who "stand before God's throne" to witness against the Tsar, or those who "by day and night raise complaints" against him "from earth", with the life of Ivan today in the circle of "flatterers and table-fellows" who lead him into wickedness and who even sacrifice their children to him. This indictment, "wet with tears", Kurbskij wants to be laid in his coffin. Sentence shall be passed "when I appear with you for trial before my God, Jesus Christ". The indictment, probably the strongest ever written by a Russian exile against his persecutors, is a masterpiece of rhetorical style. Sentences fall like heavy blows, building up long climaxes in section after section. No word can be deleted as superfluous, none of the then so popular quotations are given, though some sentences remind us of familiar passages in the Holy Scriptures.

Unexpectedly, the Tsar replied to this letter. This answer – an immoderately long epistle, with page-long quotations and numerous digressions – contains charges against the boyars who had ruled in his childhood and who had neglected him. This could not refer to Kurbskij, for at that time he himself was but a child, only two years older than Ivan.

In this maze of defences and charges there are hidden some basic ideas. Firstly, the Tsar holds even advisory participation of the boyars in the affairs of government not only as superfluous but directly contradictory to the very meaning of autocracy. Secondly, he identifies his secular rule with spiritual-religious authority. He describes Kurbskij's "treason" as "apostasy from the honourable and life-giving Cross of Christ", and calls the Prince an "iconoclast", comparing him with the icon-destroying Byzantine Emperors. As to Kurbskij's "treason", in the Prince's view this was no more than a transfer of allegiance to another master, which was fully permissible according to feudal conceptions, and which Ivan allowed himself when it suited his ends. After all, he not only had foreigners amongst his body guard (opričniki) but also did not spurn the services of Ivan Peresvetov (see above, § 7). The identification of the Tsar's secular and ecclesiastical authority is apparently not very alien to Kurbskij himself, for does he not, admittedly ironically, call the Tsar in his letter "intercessor and defender of Christians" (christianskij predstatel')? Ivan merely reminds Kurbskij, quite correctly too, that it is he who is the legitimate autocrat (referring to St. Vladimir, Vladimir Monomach,

Aleksandr Nevskij, and Dmitrij Donskoj) and that therefore all his actions are lawful. "And we are free to reward our slaves (*cholopy*) and we are also free to punish them." Apparently to punish unjustly as well, for he raises this possibility in respect to Kurbskij when he assails the Prince time and again with the insane question why he "is afraid of undeserved death, which is not death at all but gain", for "if you are righteous and good, why should you fear to suffer injuries from me, the stubborn ruler, to gain thus the Crown of Life?" Allegedly "it is God's will to suffer whilst acting rightly." Ivan believes that by his treason Kurbskij had destroyed not only his own soul but likewise "the souls of all his ancestors!" Therefore he speaks of Kurbskij's canonized ancestor only with scorn and mockery.

Not until thirteen years later (1577) did Ivan send a second letter to Kurbskij from the same town, Wolmar, where the Prince's first letter had been penned and which in the meantime had been taken by Russian troops. Kurbskij replied as late as 1579 from Polock, just captured by the Poles. Now there came the second letter and also a third one, with the addition of an enclosure, a translation from Cicero (*Paradoxa*, 4 and 6) proving that an enforced flight does not constitute treason. Shortly afterward, the Prince also sent another, the fourth, letter to the Tsar. Kurbskij's second letter pours scorn on Ivan for the awkward form of his message, which the Prince calls *širokoveščatel'noe i mnogošumjaščee pisanie* ("a verbose and noisy writing"), unworthy not only of a Tsar but even of a common "poor soldier". The Tsar does not quote "brief words ... but superfluously ... whole books, lections and epistles. And at the same time [you speak] of beds and warm jackets, and chatter unceasingly, truly like a raving woman." The Tsar's letter evokes no more than "amazement and laughter not only among the learned and knowledgeable men but even among simple children", especially in a country "where not only grammar and rhetoric are known, but also dialectics and philosophy". Kurbskij rightly describes Ivan's accusations as nothing but an insult. The Tsar's second letter, which opens with his full title, contains nothing essentially new except still further charges against the boyars, accusing them now – the Tsar addresses them now as "ye" – of his wife's death in 1560; it is in parts as petty as the first epistle. The conclusion sounds somewhat conciliatory, while the Tsar leaves the final judgement to Kurbskij's own consideration. "And we are writing this to you, not out of pride and haughtiness ... but to advise you to amend, and to think of the salvation of your soul."

Kurbskij's subsequent letters deal in detail with a number of the Tsar's accusations, some of which are not worth refutating (e.g., the charge of sorcery), and in parts accuse the Tsar of new crimes; he is also able to hold against Ivan the latest Polish victories. Here the Prince also points out that Ivan's ancestors, too ("Your dynasty bloodthirsty from time immemorial"), "used to devour the bodies of your brethren and drink their blood". Kurbskij stresses here as well the literary weaknesses of the Tsar's second letter. He speaks of "tales of drunken wives" and says that "to swear in such a way befits only a drunken maid-servant". Kurbskij's stay in the Ukraine (Volhynia) strongly influenced his language in other works of the period. In his letters to Ivan there are only a few foreign words which would be unconventional in Moscow, like "parasites, maniacs, decrees", and a few other expressions.

Basically, Kurbskij's last letters offer nothing new. Most of all, they give us the astounding realization, noted by a modern scholar (V. Leontovyč), that Kurbskij's conception of secular power was no different from that of his adversary. The essence of the polemic is constituted by a personal question only – the moral judgement of Ivan's actions. Kurbskij's view that the ruler is subject to moral law appears to be in opposition to the Tsar's opinion that the ruler is free of any, including moral, obligations. Kurbskij yields a point in advance when he postpones the final settlement of the quarrel until the Last Judgement. The harvest of ideas in this polemic turns out to be quite meagre even if it may be of great interest to a historian or to a historian of literature.

As far as literary history is concerned, Kurbskij's letters are the best achievement of the Muscovite rhetorical school. This applies especially to the first letter; the subsequent ones are influenced by Kurbskij's studies in Lithuania. The epistles are composed with great clarity, each of them being built up according to a prearranged pattern. Only the discursiveness of Ivan's letters forces Kurbskij to resort to certain digressions to deal with non-essentials. The letters are marked by a great precision and conciseness of expression, aided by the sparing use of the stylistic devices so popular in 16th-century Muscovite literature, such as compounds, participles, long quotations and play with synonyms and antonyms. Kurbskij is simply a representative of Nil Sorskij's literary school.

In contrast, Ivan's letters are merely an evidence of his own individual style. They show primarily the great erudition of the Tsar, who, like Josif before him, sought to support his statements by quotations (which Kurbskij characterized well). His irony, and at times his biting sarcasm, appear only as an expression of unbridled rage. His ideology is smothered by non-essentials or suppressed. F. Karpov alone raised some essential points against this ideology, but unfortunately his arguments were squandered on such unfit subjects as Metropolitan Daniil.

8. METROPOLITAN DANIIL

1. Metropolitan Daniil (1522–1539) was the typical product of his times. Born presumably not later than 1480, he became, after Josif Volockij's death, the abbot of the latter's monastery at Volokolamsk, which was then perhaps the most famous monastery. When in 1521, in defiance of all canonical rules, a follower of Nil Sorskij – Metropolitan Varlaam – was deposed by the Muscovite Prince Vasilij III and made prisoner in a monastery, Daniil was appointed Metropolitan by the Prince, with equal disregard of ecclesiastical law. He showed himself a willing tool of Muscovite policy and of the prince's wishes. He showed himself ready to violate all canons and even general moral laws. He appeared as a false witness. and unjust judge at the trials of Vassian Patrikeev (VI, 7, 1) and of Maksim Grek (VI, 9, 1); as a perjurer in the case of the appanaged Prince Šemjačič, to whom he issued a safe-conduct for the journey to Moscow and then allowed his detention by the Prince of Muscovy; and as a violator of canon law both in the divorce of Vasilij III from his first wife (who was forcibly veiled), and at the Prince's second marriage, disallowed by all competent Church authorities; but this did not prevent Daniil from marrying the Prince personally. He completely surrendered his ecclesiastical powers to the Muscovite Prince, and for this he was exiled in 1539 when the boyar clique ruling the country during Ivan the Terrible's minority had him deposed, also illegally, and banished to the Volokolamsk Monastery where he died in 1547.

2. Daniil, however, was not without gifts as a writer and preacher; this is shown by his own compilation of sixteen sermons and fourteen epistles and thirty other extant letters. He was also an ascetic of the Josif Volockij type. His works are primarily devoted to negative criticism of the ways of the higher classes and offer a varied insight into the customs of the period. In addition to luxury, foppishness, extravagance, lewdness, and homo-sexuality, he also opposes the enthusiasm for astrology, the musicians and singers "goliards" (*skomorochi*), as well as the moral shortcomings of monks, the carelessness of priests, the ill-treatment of peasants by land-owners, etc. His ascetic ideas go so far that by reference to some passages in the paterikons, mostly misunderstood, he advocates self-castration. (These statements bear no relation to the later sect "*skopcy*".)

Daniil's works are marked by unselective quotation from everything he had read. In addition to the Bible and to patristic texts, he quotes religious works of various kinds, which he places on the same level as the Holy Scriptures, as well as the apocryphal books and pseudo-epigraphs, and so on. Moreover, at times he quotes inappropriately, i.e., without paying attention to the real connection with his context, and also quotes passages which, due to bad translation or inaccurate copying, have become fully incomprehensible. Nevertheless, his own text is clear throughout, although Daniil is rather fond of erecting constructions very complicated stylistically, with which he occasionally links plain and even vulgar vocabulary.

3. The way in which Daniil's sermons or "instructions" are constructed shows that, on the whole, they were hardly suitable for oral delivery. After an introduction – often very brief – there is a long string of quotations, and the whole concludes with the generally well worked out "instruction" (*nakazanie*). But one of his contemporaries, in conversation with Maksim Grek, maintained that "one cannot hear a single word of instruction" from Daniil. If this were to be believed, then Daniil's sermons were only intended to be read, and were probably written after his deposition from the Metropolitan See.

Daniil's works deal with various questions. A series is devoted to heresies, and in these he refutes Vassian Patrikeev's conception of Christ's Incarnation (cf. 5; Vassian believed that Christ's Body was different in nature from the human one). Daniil also inveighs against the *židovstvujuščie* (6, 7, 11), who no longer existed at the time. In his argument against these, he develops the teaching of Divine Providence and Wisdom and the theory of Christ's Incarnation. His later sermons are also directed against this sect. The attitude towards heretics (1) should be "based on love", and yet severe punishment and unethical measures should not be spurned; this applies in particular to the persecution of unrepentant heretics (8), against whom the strictest measures ought to be taken; and here Daniil draws no distinction between spiritual and temporal authority. He speaks then (3 and 4) about the necessity of following Church tradition and ecclesiastical ritual as closely as possible, and in this context he makes no distinction between dogmas and the less important rules of ritual. Thus he speaks in great detail in favour of making the Sign of the Cross with two fingers, and this later made his sermons very popular amongst the Old Believers (VII, 7). One of his chief arguments is based on a false quotation, another on a reference to a pseudo-epigraph (!). We have already characterised the stock of Daniil's quotations; the theological content of the sermons is mostly primitive, and some of the passages directly cause offence as for instance when he asserts (7) God to be "insidious" (*kovarstvo Božie*) in the measures which He would use to bring the straying back to the path of righteousness, or when he suggests immoral measures against the "heretics" or "evil men" in general (cf. incitements to animosity toward them: 1, 2). It must be admitted, however, that in the question of the persecution of heretics, Daniil slightly tempers the views of his master, Josif Volockij, although he, too, is inclined to place them on a par with common criminals, thieves, and robbers.

Further sermons deal with the moral shortcomings of secular life. We encounter general instructions about contempt of the world in a number of sermons (2, 9, 10, 12–16) in which Daniil dwells upon isolated issues to which his collection of quotations is also devoted, such as enmity among men (9, 10), divorce and adultery (14–16), etc.

4. The composition of most of the instructions is not very systematic. Rhetorically constructed word and sentence chains alternate, while the strings of rhetorical questions and exclamations are exceptionally long; there are also strong "realistic" separate scenes and descriptions, which belong to the most powerful aspects of his sermons.

Thus Daniil writes of the man who is a Christian (12): "He is a Christian who possesses truth and righteousness. He is a Christian who has in his soul humility, gentleness of character and simplicity ..." etc.; sentences opening with "He is a Christian" follow twelve times in succession. Elsewhere (13) he describes the seductions of this world: "What use is it to you to do what senselessly leads to loss and dissipation? What use is it to you to indulge, without moderation, in many sweet and appetising dishes and drinks? ..." etc., and these questions are repeated twenty times. Likewise he is fond of enumeration. "You are stealing by force gold, silver, clothing, houses, fields, serfs, horses, cattle and other things ...," "you are slandering, condemning, belying, teasing, accusing, burdening, calling many 'fools' ..." etc. (12). Or: "There are orders and arrangements ... [governing] Christian life: the offices and Sees of Metropolitans and archbishops, and bishops, and archimandrites, and abbots, and deacons, and archdeacons, and lectors, and singers, and the places of candlesticks and prayers", and so the enumeration continues (2).

The manifold description of particular sins is done in a similar vein. "You see the beautiful women, whores, or another woman-like pretty looking face, and you smell the bright and soft body, and you run after her to embrace, to kiss, to caress, to fondle, and being so shameless and aroused, you are seized with devilish love for her ... you become as befogged as any madly voluptuous stallion, and burning with lust as with fire, you hanker like a boar after his sow, sweating and foaming; and thus, jealous of those who have no reason, you subordinate decent behaviour to indecency ..." (12). Or the description of a dandy, "Great things you do to serve the whores; you alter your dress, you measure your walk, you wear red and exceedingly small boots, so that your feet suffer a great deal from the pressure of their points, you shine so, you gallop and snort, and neigh, making yourself just like a stallion" (12), "You wash and scrub your face; your cheeks are red and pretty, you make them glow, as if you were preparing some wonderful dish for eating. You make the lips shine, clean and very red; like some women who make their beauty artificially, so you, too, beautify yourself, rubbing and annointing your-self with aromatic salves, and making your body very soft so that it could seduce many ..." (12). He has a great deal of similar imagery.

Daniil's rhetorical style requires, of course, a certain rhythm introduced into the language. Apart from an occasional rhyme (*homoioteleuton*) he uses hardly any euphonic devices.

Daniil's criticism of morals was so forcible that he could hardly offer any positive advice to his readers. Passages such as the following occur very rarely (13): "When you want to enjoy yourself, go before the doors of your house and look at the skies, the sun and the moon, the stars and the clouds some of which are lower while others are higher, and spend your time in this way perceiving their beauty and praising their Creator – Christ the Lord. This is true philosophy." Elsewhere he advises the occupation of husbandry (13). His pastoral advice on the care of the soul confines itself to the need for peace. Simple, human feelings appear in-comprehensible to him, as when he attempts to convince parents that they should not grieve for their dead children. He opposes also the cutting of the beard, and repeatedly declares that even conversations between men and women are objectionable.

5. Daniil's epistles (the numbers are given according to Žmakin or Družinin) are addressed to various people, including monks (1, 5, 6, 7, 12), and in these last we encounter especially long enumerations of monastic virtues. He stresses most the need for constant attention to the inner life. In this context, however, he can still say nothing concrete about the "inner struggle". Moreover, he speaks of the external qualities of a

monk in great detail: of the "dryness of body", of the paleness of face, of
the poverty of dress; eyes should be lowered, the neck bent, the look quiet,
the gait soft and not vain, the voice measured; the monks should also be
able to cry often, to groan compassionately, be meek in a God-pleasing
way and shed purifying tears. Here, too, he gives realistic descriptions of
the deterioration of monastic life. Concrete instructions for monastic life
are also not omitted. He rejects a monk's complaint, without going deeply
into the matter, with no more than cold "words of consolation" to the
effect that a man is purified by suffering. Letters to secular persons (10,
11, 13, 14) primarily deal with chastity, and here he merely transposes
monastic laws onto secular life (it is not allowed, for instance, to touch
one's own body, all company should be avoided, one ought always to be
silent, etc.). Impressive pictures of the Last Judgment are used to fortify
his counsels. In only one epistle (14) does he speak of being animated by
"spiritual attention, temperance, and solicitude". Several writings which
Daniil did not incorporate into his collection are brief "messages of
comfort" (Družinin's edition); here he does no more than repeatedly
cover the same ground and reiterate the same idea: all misfortunes should
be borne with obedience and resignation, and "patience" is the only
healing measure he can suggest, for "be patient" or "suffer courageously"
(terpi doblestně) are repeated by him in practically every epistle (cf. 31).
Some of the writings are impersonal. One (9) deals with the "Fear of
God", another (8) with the Last Judgment (again in a very memorable
way), a third (4) with the vanity of worldly goods. Four epistles are directed to a (perhaps fictitious) bishop and proffer counsel as to execution of
his office, including his teaching. Daniil, however, closely defines the
extent of teaching activities with reference to the "sacred writings", which
he recognises as comprising not only the Holy Scriptures but also the
Lives of the Saints, religious canons, and in fact everything that had
been written down. Some other writings shed further light on Daniil's
personality; this material is of a rather unattractive nature.

The style of the epistles is varied. Here, too, there is no lack of long
quotations, rhetorical devices (chains of questions), and vivid imagery.
Typical, for instance, are his pictures of worldly possessions, with the
traditional enumeration of those destroyed by death: "Where are the
many possessions and countless riches of this man or that? Where is their
physical strength now? Where is their bold power? ... Where are their
eyes? Where are their loquacious tongues and eloquent speeches? ...
Where are their invory-inlaid couches and gold-embroidered beds? ...
Where are their sweet unadulterated wines and other fragrant liquors?

Where is the gallop of horses and the festive pleasures?" (27 questions). "All is ashes, dirt and dust, flesh and blood, grass and bloom, shadow and smoke." Elsewhere he enumerates sixteen "good deeds" (*podvigi*). The addressees are also repeated many times (*O dobryj druže!* – 5 times).

What a gifted eulogist of asceticism and poet of the vanities of the world! His life evidently corresponded little to his ideals.

6. To Daniil are also ascribed some monastic statutes in which he obviously follows in the steps of his master, Josif Volockij. Possibly his work too is a redaction of the *Kormčaja* (III, 10, 5) since many of the quotations used in his work appear to be taken from that compilation. A 16th-century miscellany also has some connection with Daniil; it contains fourteen systematically arranged instructions for monks, which include many reminiscences of Daniil's work. At any rate, both these latter works show evidence of Daniil's popularity among his contemporaries.

9. MAKSIM GREK

1. Totally different was the fate of that strange Greek, who, if not an actual member of Nil Sorskij's movement, nevertheless co-operated with Nil's followers and supported various views of that group. Later, together with Metropolitan Daniil, he became one of the writers revered by the Old Believers.

Maksim (his lay name was Michael) came from a Greek family of Trivolis in Albania. The year of his birth is not exactly known; presumably he was born around 1470. In the last decade of the 15th century, like many other Greeks, he spent some time studying in Italy at Venice, Florence, Padua, Bologna, and Milan. He also moved in the Italian humanist circles, sat at the feet of John Laskaris (who moved to Paris in 1494), heard the sermons of Savonarola (died in 1498) in Florence, and subsequently praised this enemy of the secularisation of the Renaissance. Homeward bound, in Venice he visited the humanist publisher Aldus Manutius (who printed Greek books there between 1494 and 1506). As he himself later admitted, Maksim had for a time been carried away by some aspects of the Renaissance (e.g., by astrology), but he remained a Greek Orthodox Christian, returned home and in 1505 or 1506 became a monk at Mount Athos. Besides the appreciative mention of Savonarola, only fleeting reminiscences of the Renaissance are discernible in his writings. In his view, secular knowledge ("philosophy") should remain but the servant (*raba*) of theology. He appraises the culture of humanistic

Italy as pagan; the Italians would have built heathen temples if the Pope had allowed them to do so. Nevertheless, he values the contributions of some of the humanists. In Italy, he learned to appreciate Plato and compares him with Aristotle, who was reigning supreme in Catholic theology. He also thinks highly of John the Damascene, who had actually been an Aristotelian. Maksim's fame as a scholar was considerable at Mount Athos, and when in 1515 the Muscovite prince Vasilij asked for a translator from Athos, Maksim was dispatched to Moscow, accompanied by a Bulgarian and a Russian monk.

Maksim arrived in Russia in 1518, never to leave the country again. In Moscow he was given two Russian assistants who knew Latin, and his translations progressed with their help. First, he translated a psalter commentary (a compilation of the works of fifteen authors) and when, after a year and half, he had completed this, and in addition translated for the Metropolitan a section of the commentary on the *Acta Apostolica*, he asked for leave to return to Mount Athos. But then the correction of a translation of liturgical works was entrusted to him by the prince. Maksim found many errors in the translation and in the copies. He also wrote many works, including one on grammar, in which he adapts the Greek pattern to the Russian. During this period, Maksim also wrote some works which show that in spite of the humanistic environment of his youth he was not inclined to introduce into Russia any elements of humanist culture. These consist of four tracts (addressed to F. Karpov) against the astrology which had been disseminated in Moscow by a German surgeon, Nicholas of Lübeck (presumably Blücher), a writing against *Lucidarius* (see VI, 2, 3) and a work against Catholic dogma (*filioque*). Some of these writings quickly made him enemies. At an early stage he was noticed by representatives of Nil's movement, especially by the bellicose Vassian Patrikeev (VI, 7, 2), and obviously it was they who interested him in the three subjects to which his Slavonic writings are devoted: a tract about monastic property, in which he supports Nil and subscribes to the views of Vassian; a tract in which he denies Moscow's right to claim to be the New Jerusalem as long as the old one still exists; and a tract in which he argues against the view that the Russian Metropolitan need *not* be appointed by the Patriarch of Constantinople. All this did not fit into the Church policy of the Muscovite government. When Daniil became Metropolitan in 1522, he was displeased with Maksim for refusing to make a translation for him; equally strained were his relations with the Prince since Maksim refused to recognise the ecclesiastical legality of the latter's divorce. He still did not know that, when in Moscow one is asked for an opinion, one should know what answer is expected. In 1525 Maksim was thrown into prison and shortly afterwards stood trial on charges of "heresy". This consisted in the fact that while correcting a liturgical manual he had made some grammatical errors which altered the meaning. He was also charged with political offences: that he had conversed with a nobleman who was in disgrace, and was also allegedly in touch with the Turkish envoys, who were presumably Greeks. The inexperienced Greek was also unaware that it was best not to speak openly to anyone, especially to foreigners, always suspect in Russia. The indictment then meant condemnation; nevertheless, Maksim denied various accusations and wished to explain his errors of translation by his inadequate knowledge of the language. As a heretic he was banished to the Volokolamsk Monastery (the above-mentioned nobleman was sentenced to death) where, as he later said, he was tormented by hunger, cold, and the smoke of stoves. He felt as an even greater affliction the fact that he was excommunicated and not allowed to go to Church or to write.

Then in 1531 there came the charges against Vassian Patrikeev (see VI, 7, 2). In addition to the offence for which Maksim had already been sentenced, i.e., heresy, which consisted of the "desecration" of sacred books (at the same time Maksim was also accused of having discussed heretical opinions), he was now charged with reproaching the monasteries and their miracle-working representatives for possessing property, and even with having engaged in sorcery! Maksim, who this time was dealt with by Daniil as if he had deliberately undertaken the improvement of books, had by now acquired a much clearer understanding of Muscovite methods, he acknowledged his "misdeeds" and asked for mercy. That Daniil personally was not serious about the charges is shown by the fact that he (later? – VI, 8, 5) made use in his works of Maksim's translations and even of the writings of Nil Sorskij. At any rate, this time the sentence was even more severe. Maksim was barred from the Sacrament of Communion and was put into irons. In reality, however, his fate was unexpectedly made much easier: he was sent to a monastery in Tver' where the uneducated bishop, Akakij, was a great believer in knowledge and allowed the imprisoned scholar to write. It was there that Maksim recommenced to write; his first works were against monastic property. Among others he wrote a dialogue between Filoktemon and Aktemon (Greek: Philoktēmōn and Aktēmōn), i.e., the supporters of property and the "have nots", and a whole series on the same subject. When in 1537 the Tver' palace (kreml') was burnt down together with a number of churches, Maksim wrote a dialogue between Bishop Akakij and God. In this, the Lord upbraids Akakij for his purely ritualistic conception of Christianity. Later Maksim wrote other works in which he praised Aka- kij's activities in the restoration of the burnt churches.

With the fall of Daniil, Maksim's position improved. The new Metro- politan, Joasaf, was no follower of Volockij and even possessed some of Maksim's works. When Joasaf was succeeded by Makarij (1542), Maksim attempted to seek permission to communicate, but as the ban had originated with Daniil – who was then still alive – this was only allowed, after Daniil's initial refusal, in 1543. In 1551 Maksim was moved to the Troicko-Sergievskaja Lavra, where the abbot, Artemij, was a follower of Nil. However, all attempts to obtain permission to return to Mount Athos, supported by monks of Athos and two eastern patriarchs, were of no avail. In 1553 Maksim was approached by the young Tsar, Ivan the Terrible, who in the following years wanted him to write against the "heresy" of Baškin. The latter's entire heresy amounted to the fact that he wished to have the advice of a priest on some problems of dogma which had raised doubts in him. Maksim evaded this assignment. About this time he wrote some epistles; a profession of faith; a number of polemic writings against the *židovstvujuščie*, against the Latins, the Armenians, the Mohammedans, and even against Greek heathendom; several works on the shortcomings of Russian life and against monastic property, corrupt- ion, superstitions, the recognition of the apocrypha, and other subjects. He also made a number of translations. Meanwhile fresh clouds gathered over his head. In 1553/54 his protector, Artemij, was also – without any justification whatsoever – accused of heresy (and of course found guilty; he fled to Poland where he proved himself an important defender of Greek Orthodoxy). However, Artemij was no longer abbot, having previously relinquished his office and withdrawn to his earlier hermitage. The friendship with Prince Andrej Kurbskij could not yet harm Maksim, because Kurbskij did not become a "traitor" until as late as 1564 and Maksim died at the Lavra in 1556. Maksim's subsequent veneration by the official church and later by the Old Believers led to the development of a saint's legend which experienced a complicated history.

How this foreigner, truly Orthodox and friendly to Russia, judged the state of things in the "Third Rome" can best be seen in one of the works of his later years. "I went" – he says – "along a difficult and grievous road and met a woman sitting by the wayside, her head resting on her hand and her knees bent and bitterly crying and hopelessly weeping, dressed in black cloth as widows are used to wear; and around her there

gathered wild animals, lions and bears, wolves and foxes." After long
hesitation she replied to the passerby thus: ". . . I am, o wanderer, one of
the noble and brilliant daughters of the Emperor of All, the Creator and
Lord of all the good things and all the perfect gifts showered upon
mankind. . . . My name, however, is not one name but many, for I am
called supremacy and might and mastery and government; my true name
which encompasses all these is Vasilija (Greek: *Basileia* – the Empire).
I have received this beautiful name from the Almighty, and those who
rule over me must be the bulwark and support of men, supporting them
and not being the cause of steady decline and permanent disorder. . . ."
"But many, not understanding my name, direct the affairs of their subjects
in a way unworthy of the tsar's title, and become tyrants (*mučitele*) instead of tsars; they dishonour me, and when they receive God's just
reward for their own stupidity and folly they are struck with horror and
faintness." After that Vasilija speaks of the crimes of rulers and complains that she now has no such protectors as the prophets and the saints
who used to reproach the rulers with their sins, and concludes by saying:
"And thus, I am sitting here as a widowed woman beside the road through
the desert, lacking such defenders and zealous champions. Such, O
wanderer, is my misfortune, worthy of many tears!"

2. We have enumerated Maksim's main works, and in manuscript there
are extant more than two hundred items ascribed to him, but some
of these are minor works. In part they have not been published, and the
two available editions are both incomplete and poor; moreover, one of
these is only a translation of Maksim's writings into modern Russian.
   In order to study Maksim's literary style some passages of his writings
in monastic property should be quoted. In his earliest work on the subject,
he praises the poverty of the Catholic Carthusian order. The conclusion
says, however: "At the Last Judgement, the Righteous Judge will not
acknowledge those who boast that they, in God's name, have performed
many miracles, have made prophecies and have exorcised devils. And
they will hear from the Judge, 'Stand back, you lawless people! I have
never known you.' Why does He not acknowledge them and why does
he expel them? . . . Because the Divine Paradise will not receive usurers
and the cruel ones who heap treasures on earth and who live on the
interest taken from beggars and the poor." In the dialogue already
mentioned between Filoktemon and Aktemon, Maksim sarcastically
repeats the arguments of those who advocate monastic property. When
Filoktemon argues that every monk is actually without property, for the

estates belong to "all jointly", i.e., to the monastery and not to individual monks, Aktemon-Maksim retorts: "This is however not different in any way from the instance when many live with the same whore, for should they be reproached each would answer, 'I do not sin, for she is the common property of all'." Maksim censures even more strongly the property-owning monks as he depicts before their eyes the conditions of their peasantry. "Dressed in soft garments, he shuts his ears, like a deaf viper (*aspid*), and his hands have forgotten how to give with love the alms to those oppressed by poverty. Alas, they are tortured with whips for the cruel usury, and, if they cannot pay it, they are deprived of their freedom and are sold as slaves, or all they have is taken away from them and they, the poverty stricken, are sent away empty-handed from their confines." It is impossible to compare the behaviour of today's monks with those of old times; "but will something so inhuman be related about righteous men? ..."

3. Maksim preaches the inner truth of Christianity. His point of view – which, however, is no more than a variation on a traditional Old Testament theme – appears most clearly defined in the significant dialogue between the Tverian bishop Akakij and God after the great fire of 1537. Akakij fails to understand why God has punished Tver'. "Thou, O Lord, art a witness Thyself, that I was never negligent in Thy divine hymns and Thine other beautiful divine services. I have always observed Thy holy feasts, I revered Thee with beautifully-voiced songs of honorable priests, with loud pealings of the euphonious bells and with the burning of much incense. I adorned beautifully Thine and Thy Mother's revered icons with gold, silver and precious stones. ..." God replies to the bishop: "How can you men complain of My just judgement? Instead of confessing your sins to Me, you anger Me even more with the sound of well tuned songs and bells, with the lavish adornment of My icons and with the burning of much incense before Me. Your gifts would be pleasing to Me, if you brought them in accordance with your property and your rightful work. But when you bring all this out of unjust and abhorrent usury, from the pillaging of the other people's estates, then My soul hates not only such offerings mixed with the tears of widows and orphans and with the blood of the poor, but is angry even more against them, for what they bring is contrary to My Justice and love of Mankind. That is why I am destroying your gifts with fire and giving them over to the pillage of the Scythians [Tartars – D.Č.]. ... My adornment, my crown forged of gold is the well-being and adequate care and nourishment of orphaned children

and widows while their lack of the necessities of life is a vexation and utmost desecration, even though sweet-sounding chants resound unceasingly in your shrines. What joy can I derive from these songs which reach Me together with the weeping and groans of the poor who are crying with unassuaged hunger," etc. Likewise, Maksim wrote to a monk: ". . . If you wish to please the Lord of all, do not adorn your outer hood with multi-coloured silk that will rot in the grave . . . but zealously adorn the spiritual hood of your inner man – the most venerable part of soul and spirit – with the pure teachings of divinely inspired writings, with sober prayers and with deeds acceptable to God."

4. Here we see the characteristics of the highly rhetorical, pathetic, and lofty, but at the same time lucid, style of Maksim. He writes mainly "speeches", irrespective of whether he speaks in his own name or in the name of the protagonists in his dialogues. He apostrophises not only real or imaginary people, but also objects and personified ideas. And in each case he wishes to make his views clear, and, indeed, he succeeds in so doing. Of the external ornaments of speech he has in common with his contemporaries the compounds and the participles. Athanasius the Great is for him the "beautifully-flowing Nile"; most of the compounds are equally traditional. In the fragments of the parable about "Vasilija", quoted above in 1, there are sixteen participial forms. It seems, however, that Maksim failed to master the play with Slavonic synonyms and Slavonic euphonic devices. His use of synonyms is often merely the variation of compounds, whereby one part of the compound is changed and the other retained. However, he can hardly be accused of repetition of the same words in the course of a whole section. Nevertheless, his style did not become tautological.

Very frequently he has extended images which could perhaps be described as "developed metaphors", and for which examples could be provided from the excerpts quoted above. But even here he has at times whole series of metaphors used to characterise various thoughts or ideas, when, for instance, the psalter is for him "weapon, defence, help, and orchard full of various fruit, a vessel filled with 'spiritual honey' ", and so forth. At times an idea is discussed in great detail by means of metaphors, thus God in His Trinity is compared to a triangle from which various conclusions are derived concerning Catholic teachings. The question of communion is also considered by means of a metaphor, which, however, is oblique. All instances of triplicity in the world are used by Maksim as proof of the existence of the Trinity and hence of the three parts of the soul; for example, the three parts of the tree: root, trunk, and branches; all this could be accepted, but then there are added the three parts of the day, three parts of the house, three parts of the sun: "the halo, the light, and the rays", which amounts to artificial division. The name "Babylon" is also used metaphorically for confusion, and so on.

5. This raises the question of Maksim's contribution to knowledge. This is not of much weight. To be sure, he wished to write down basic principles for the criticism of texts for his Russian contemporaries. Attention – he says – should be paid to the following: 1) whether a work belongs to a known writer; 2) whether the content everywhere corresponds with Church teaching; 3) whether there are any internal contradictions in the work. These in his times were by no means particularly modern principles for which Maksim would have needed humanist schooling. Factually speaking, he considers the Hebrew text of the Bible as "spoiled", and prefers that of the Septuagint which he considers as directly "divinely inspired". On the basis of his critical principles he offers a successful critique of some apocrypha, which however are among the most clumsy (The Tale of Aphroditian, a Bogomil writing, etc.).

The polemical writings of Maksim are in parts better than those current not only in Russia but in Byzantium as well. And thus, in one of his polemics against the teaching of the Catholic dogma, he actually speaks of important *dogmatic* differences, and not of the minutiae of western usage. Still, he holds Catholics to be Christians. His criticism of the Armenian faith is, however, very narrow-minded. The criticism of ancient heathendom can probably be explained by his Italian experiences, for the subject was quite irrelevant to Russia. He stresses the significance of the philosophy of Plato, Aristotle and Socrates ("the most venerable and truth-loving among the Greek philosophers"), but he speaks with hatred not only of Epicurus but also of the Stoics – and all this in connection with Christian dogma. And even if, on the whole, he correctly assesses the differences between dogma and ritualistic and cultural institutions, we encounter in his writings incomprehensibly violent sallies against various fashionable details of the life of his day. He is not only opposed to the cutting of the beard, which later brought him great popularity among the Old Believers, but also against the wearing of headgear that looked like the Turkish fez (*taf'ja*) and of "Turk-like" boots. He suggests that people wearing such dress, and even their families (!), should be forbidden to visit Church and be excluded from Communion! It is much easier to understand that on the question of the

persecution of heretics Maksim approached the point of view of Josif's
supporters; that he engaged in speculations about the impending end of
the world; or that he, like some of his contemporaries, came out in favour
of making the sign of the Cross with two fingers and of singing "Hallelujah" twice, even if he showed undue zeal in the last case.

Maksim's attitude to the "secular knowledge" is as follows: he allows
an interest in classical antiquity, but he completely rejects the other
branches of learning for "much that is dangerous and corrupting is
hidden therein" (philosophy = science). He suggests that secular writings
"be scorned", because they are "nothing but corruption". His concrete
criticisms are primarily directed against two "useless objects", the
dubious speculations of I. L. Vives (1492–1540; to whose other better
works he pays no attention). However, Maksim's final conclusions go
further than the question that Vives deals with. "One should not dwell
unnecessarily on things that are beyond our reason and understanding."
He goes to equal lengths in his verdict on the unscientific "*Lucidarius*"
(see VI, 2, 3): "Hold fast to the book of Damascene and you will be a
great theologian and natural scientist (*estestvoslovec*)"; "there is no virtue
in saying (!) or teaching anything but what is recorded tradition [the
Scriptures]." Maksim advises F. Karpov, who was interested in astrology, not to consider the beauty and order of nature too closely, lest his
faith be weakened! Maksim cannot be considered as a medium for
conveying information about Western science. He may have been the
first man in Russia to write on the discovery of America, but at the same
time he believed in the existence of cynocephalous people. His scorn of
science would have been harmless where some science already existed; but
in 16th-century Russia his anti-scientific attitude was a help to the most
sinister obscurantism.

In any case, it cannot be denied that Maksim was well versed in, and
appreciated, theological and especially patristic literature, and that in
addition to the Greek works he also knew Latin literature (he often quotes
Augustine, Jerome, Tertullian, and others). Certainly he was the ablest
theologian among his Russian contemporaries.

6. A minor writing by Maksim, the treatise on grammar (see above, 1)
is of importance to the history of literature; this exerted some influence
on the terminology of subsequent Slavonic grammatical works. It seems,
however, that Maksim's references to poetical works (he himself wrote
poetry in Greek) had no influence whatsoever on the writing of poetry;
lyric poetry being completely unknown in Russia at that time. Why

folklore, which certainly had its poetical forms, did not exert an influence can hardly be understood.

10. ENCYCLOPAEDIC WORKS — METROPOLITAN MAKARIJ

1. In the 16th century Moscow was already surrounded by a "halo". The Tartar yoke had been cast off and the last remnants of independence of the seceding principalities had gradually come to an end. A much greater impact, according to all appearances, was made by the victory over the Tartar rump-state of Kazan' and by the coronation of Ivan the Terrible as Tsar, whereby the claim to the succession of both Byzantium and the Golden Horde was formally confirmed. Attempts were made to enhance this external brilliance with a "spiritual" one. The claim of the Byzantine legacy was based on Moscow's resumption of the Christian tradition, and that to the succession of the Golden Horde, on the assumption of secular power. Literature, therefore, was now faced with the task of expressing both these claims in literary terms. There was a suitable man for this. Metropolitan Makarij (1542–1563) had already before, when bishop of Novgorod, laid the foundation of a work of encyclopaedic character that aimed at the glorification of the Third Rome.

Makarij (b. about 1480) was cowled in the monastery of Pafnutij Borovskij (V, 10, 7), and throughout his life remained under the influence of Josif Volockij. As metropolitan he did not have much time to devote himself to literary pursuits. Nevertheless, there have come down to us many of his epistles and speeches (incorporated in part into the chronicles). The speeches, however, seem to be the work of the annalist (cf. VI, 5, 4), and as far as the epistles are concerned we do not need to mention them when referring to "polemical writing", for Makarij steered clear of precise formulations, even though there is no doubt that his sympathies were with the supporters of Volockij. He did, however, perform another task; he became the initiator and organiser of various ecclesiastico-political and literary projects. Thus in 1551 there took place a Church Council which aimed at placing the Russian Church on firm foundations. By command of Makarij, investigations began into locally revered saints, while the Councils of 1547 and 1549 canonized a number of venerated "workers of miracles". Now, the Lives of the new saints had to be written. Already at Novgorod, Makarij had collected material for them, and the legends were presently written under his direction. These entered into the new "Reading Menaea". Even more important is another of his undertakings, the development of Muscovite historical writing.

Besides Makarij there were other men who took upon themselves the same or similar tasks. Special mention should be made of a friend of Ivan the Terrible (of his early years), the priest Silvestr, also a native of Novgorod. Ivan's adversary, Prince Andrej Kurbskij, apparently cherished similar ideas, to the execution of which he made claims in his translation activities (cf. VI, 5, 6 and 7, 8) after his escape. We know only a few of Makarij's actual collaborators.

2. The first and most important of Makarij's undertakings was the new Reading Menaea, on which he had already begun work at Novgorod where, in 1541, he left a copy in the Cathedral library. But at Moscow this work grew and expanded, for according to Makarij's plan he wished to unite all the "sacred writings" in the form of an encyclopaedia which would in fact make all other literature superfluous. Makarij himself maintained that he was collecting "all the books there are in Russia". The Reading Menaea of Makarij were basically different from the old works of this type, quite apart from their extent. The old Menaea were now supplemented by the texts from the two *prologs* and the paterikons, as well as by Lives of Russian saints – admittedly not by all of these, and not in their original form. Many were reworded, and many written afresh. Also included was a Life of Josif Volockij, who had not yet been canonized. The old Menaea also included a number of sermons, and now the "didactic" material grows through the incorporation, no longer of individual sermons, but of entire collections. Strange to relate, the Scriptures are not included; the Old Testament books are often replaced by accounts retelling them! In contrast, there are included not only the works of the Fathers of the Church, such as those of Chrysostomos, Basil the Great, the *Areaopagitica* with a commentary by Maximus the Confessor, John the Damascene, the *Climax*, and also works of Flavius Josephus, Cosmas Indikopleustes, and Slavonic writings such as the sermons of Kirill of Turov and of Camblak, the travel-tale of Daniil, the *Prosvetitel'* by Josif Volockij, monastic statutes, and so on. Even epistles and records of Russian princes found their way into these collections of "sacred writings"! With complete absence of any critical sense, Makarij and his aides included a number of apocrypha: "The Book of Enoch", "The Revelation of Abraham", "The Confessions of Eve", "The Gospel of Jacob", etc., though these were already on the list of proscribed books.

The compilatory work often proceeded in a rather mechanical fashion. Often two different Lives of the same saint were recorded one next to the other or on different days. As there existed two versions of the works of

Josephus, these were copied down in two different sections of the Menaea. Newly written and freshly revised texts fared worse, the redaction consisting in part in the smoothing down of obsolete or incorrect language, e.g., in the translations of Southern Slav origin. In most cases, however, this was done without reference to the Greek original and thus resulted in no more than distortion of the original meaning. Early legends were rewritten in the new pompous style, often with the omission of the subject-matter, but with an expansion of the prayers, eulogies, and tales of miracles; in most instances these sections of the Lives were rendered according to the same pattern. If there was no legend at all and nothing definite was known about the saint in question, then a Life was composed afresh on the basis of liturgical texts, usually from a service Menaea which contained some vague eulogy. In other cases use was made of a Life of another saint with the same name or of the same type; the result was of course a forgery, the new work being written according to a prearranged pattern with the addition of embellished eulogies. Worthy of admiration is the facility of the authors in producing such a "word-braiding" without any real content.

The work did not gain popularity; besides the Novgorodian version, only two other complete copies are extant. The work of Makarij's circle resulted in the complete Menaea in which all the days of the year are "filled". Certainly, it saved many of the old works from oblivion, but some of these were here retained only in a distorted form, so that the merits of Makarij would be very dubious. Unfortunately, only less than half of Makarij's Menaea have now been published (April, September, October, and, in part, January, November, and December). The manuscript consists of more than 13,000 large folios, which in modern print would be equal to thirty massive volumes.

3. The style of Makarij's circle can best be seen in another work, the *Stepennaja kniga*, the content of which has parallels throughout in the early chronicles. This is Makarij's second historical venture.

Stepennaja kniga carskogo rodoslovija ("The Book of Generations of the Tsar's Genealogy") is an extensive re-working of the chronicles. The dynastic idea emerges here in a form already implicit in the *Tverskoj sbornik* (see V, 6, 2 and V, 4, 3). The whole line of generation since Rjurik (who is said to have descended from Prus, a brother of Emperor Augustus) is an uninterrupted sequence of the legitimate rulers of "Russia". The line, of course, leads to the Tsar of Muscovy. Such a line could not be produced without forgery. The editor of the *Stepennaja kniga* does not fight shy of any change or distortion of facts to fulfil his task. In addition to the legitimate autocrats there also appear the metropolitans. In general, the religious aspect of history is everywhere strongly brought to the fore.

Besides the historical foundations of the prehistory of Russian tsardom, the *Stepennaja kniga* also contains masses of new apocryphal material, originating partly in sources lost to us and partly in folklore. In addition, in various passages there are interwoven instructions, religious epistles, eulogies, etc.

On the whole, the work is of great stylistic perfection, written throughout in the lofty style which is also characteristic of other works of the official Muscovite literature. The old tales are supplemented by historical or legendary parallels (the Bible, the Deeds of Troy, etc.). From the old chronicles much is simply taken over with little understanding, and this is at times ridiculously clumsily misinterpreted. Above all, everything referring to the existence of independent seceding principalities and to their internecine struggles is passed over in silence or explained away. Thus the legitimate successor of Jaroslav the Wise is not Izjaslav but Vsevolod, since in this way the "legitimate" line can be brought down to Vladimir Monomach, and so on. The author is not always successful in forcing all the material into his mould, especially as he interrupts his story to relate subsidiary events that bore a religious character or could serve for the glorification of Russia or of the dynasty. Some of the digressions have almost reached the status of independent works.

The author is far more successful in the stylistic aspects of his work. The main characteristics of his style are already known to us, as for instance the excessive number of compounds, some of which are created *ad hoc*, e.g., *bogopreslavnyj, carskoimenityj, bogostudnyj, vraždotvorno, skorosol'nik* ("magnificent in God, bearing the Tsar's name, disgraceful to God, awakening enmity, speedy messenger"). At times there appear, as it were, "double superlative" compounds, as in *preizobilovanno, mnogosugubnyj* ("exceedingly abundant, manifoldly double"). However, the majority of compounds are conventional. More original are the many neologisms: *naprasn'stvo, pjat'stvo, pozdravie* (for *pozdravlenie*), *nepravovanie, edinočastvo*, etc. ("the futile, fivefold, greetings, fraud, unity"). Instead of "warrior" (*voi*) we read almost invariably *voinstvo* ("troops"), and so on. Some of the neologisms cannot be understood even in their context; this shows adequately that the author exerted his efforts more for embellishment and thus for evoking a general impression rather than for conveying the subject-matter. Participial constructions flourish here as well, one being often inserted into another, thus causing the sentences to lose their clarity.

An example of how the simple and unpretentiously impressive style of the tales of the old chronicles is undergoing a change can be provided, for instance, by the account of the duel between Mstislav, Prince of Tmutorokan', and the Caucasian giant, Rededja (1022). The story, like most of the other sections, now receives a title: "Of the courage and valour of Prince Matistlav, and how he vanquished the strong Rededja." The opening reads: "It should also not be passed over, how once upon a time valorous (*udaloj*) Prince Mstislav, well-known for his courage, had accomplished a marvellous deed, [he,] the seventh son of Great Prince Vladimir, but brother of the great martyrs, Boris and Gleb, of the same mother (*edinomateren*) as Great Prince Jaroslav, who then ruled at Tmutorokan'." While in the Nestor Chronicle the story is rendered in a secular-epic style, here the battle scene begins as follows: "Not being afraid of force, and placing his hopes in God the Almighty and in the Virgin Purest of All as his supporters; and after God heard the prayers of his righteous father, Vladimir, and of his divinely inspired grandmother Ol'ga and of his miracle-working brothers, the martyr-sufferers, Boris and Gleb, he braced himself with faith and armed himself with hope, and he did not refuse to fight single-handed with the foreigner for the sake of all his men. ..." Thus a heroic saga becomes an icon picture.

The author is nevertheless able, without having any corresponding models, to evoke by his stylistic art impressive and beautiful images, as for instance the description of a vision said to have been seen in the town of Vladimir in 1491. "The people saw ... above the spire of the church a heavenly vision, as if a bright cloud spread itself or as if a thin smoke poured out, of a whiteness (*belostiju*) like the purest hoar-frost, and shone with sun-like brilliance (*solncu podobnoobrazno*) and in the thinness and brightness of this cloud there could be seen the resemblance of the image (*podobie obraza*) of the blessed and great Prince Aleksandr [Nevskij–D.Č.] rising on horseback up to Heaven. ..."

The book contains seventeen "grades" (generations) and ends with Ivan the Terrible. The last date mentioned is 1560. The whole of Russian history is depicted here as the history of "Holy Russia" and is identified with the history of the Tsar's dynasty, as it has already been described in the exceedingly long title, which refers to the history "of those in the Russian land who shone with piety, by God appointed holders of the sceptre, who, like the trees in Paradise, were planted by God ...", etc. And yet this whole sacred history is nothing but a forgery. The author himself cannot remain silent about the fact that he omitted whatever was "inconvenient" (*neudobnoe*); but he also added a considerable amount.

4. The protocols of the 1551 Council, known under the title of *Stoglav* ("A Hundred Chapters"), are also linked with Makarij's name. In this monument only the framework has a literary significance. The Council is represented as the handiwork of the young Tsar – Ivan the Terrible, who sets tasks ("Questions," 69 in all) before the Council and opens it with a speech. The aim of the Council was *to confirm the old tradition* (*predanie*). This confirmation of what was widely believed to be the old was achieved. On the whole, all this took the direction desired by the followers of Josif Volockij, but possibly attention was also paid to the still imprisoned Maksim Grek.

5. After Makarij's death, but following in his tradition, there originated a world history (12 volumes), illustrated with 10,000 miniatures, eleven volumes of which are extant. The first three volumes contain the text of the Chronograph; the following ones, the Nikonian Chronicle (VI, 5, 4). The revision is not very thorough, and the manuscript must have come into being not later than 1580.

6. A peculiar manifestation of the times is the so-called *Domostroj* (the author must apparently have had in mind the Greek title *Oikonomikos*). The *Domostroj* was supposed to lay down the traditional way of life, but only for the upper and middle classes, of the Muscovite population. In the absence of evidence, considerable doubts could be raised as to whether this tradition, at least in part, was but an innovation. In vain one seeks a model for the egoistic cynicism and the ritualisticly formal "piety" of life as shown in the *Domostroj*, both in the sermon literature and even in western works (A. Orlov) of this very popular genre (cookery books and directions concerning husbandry do not, of course, belong here). Not only the Spanish work of Gracian, the Italian of Castiglione, and the Polish version of the latter by L. Górnicki, but even the Czech works (Tomáš Štítný of the 14th century, the anonymous *Naučení rodičům* – "The Instructions to Parents" – in the 15th century, and Šimon Lomnický z Budče of the end of the 16th century) are totally different from this Muscovite work; the Western instructions are either a product of the refined court culture or are a serious treatment of moral problems inspired at least in part by true piety. In contrast, the *Domostroj*, planned at mid-century in Novgorod and later adapted in Moscow by Silvestr (see above, § 1) and supplied with an epilogue, is prosaic throughout. The first part deals with the implementation of Christian and State duties ("How the Tsar should be honoured"), the second with family life, and the third with husbandry. The monument forms a part of literary history because of its language, which in many respects comes close to the vernacular. It has many turns of phrase from the spoken language and contains in a number of sections (extant in some copies only) scenes from daily life (women's gossip; seduction of women), which only a Soviet scholar dares to compare with Boccaccio!

A single example should suffice to convey an idea of the conversational style and mood of the whole work (Chapter 38). "And when a single word alone has no effect on the wife, or the son, or the daughter, when this is not heeded or taken account of, and when they do not fear and do not do what the husband, or the father, or the mother teaches, then whippings should be administered according to the offence; beatings however should not be administered in the presence of others but in private in order to teach, and to say a word, and to show affection; under no circumstances, however, should there be anger between the husband and wife. And for an offence, do not strike on the ear, nor in the eyes, nor with the fist under the heart, nor push, nor prod with a stick and do not hit either with an iron stick or with one of wood; when such blows are struck either in anger or in sorrow many injuries result therefrom: blindness and deafness, an arm or leg may be dislocated, headache or toothache may result, and with pregnant women the child in the mothers' womb may also be injured. However, strokes of the whip should be inflicted carefully while the lesson is being taught; this is both reasonable and painful and awe-inspiring and healthy. And only for a great wrong-doing and for a regrettable deed, and for a great and fearful disobedience and similar fadings, should the shirt be taken off and a thorough beating administered with a whip in accordance with the offence while the hands are held; and a word should be said after teaching the lesson; but there should remain no anger, and other people should neither see nor hear this; and no complaint should be made. ..." A work of the late 17th century (Kotošichin, VII, 10) shows that the ideal of the *Domostroj*, at least at that time, was turned into reality.

11. FROM THE FOLKLORE OF THE 16TH CENTURY

1. Significant traces of 16th-century folklore have been preserved to this day. To all appearances the old epic was subjected about that time to a thorough revision, in which professional musicians and singers, "goliards" (*skomorochi*), took the main part. It is reported (by Olearius) that songs were sung at the court of Ivan the Terrible about the victories over Kazan' and Astrachan'. Even in this case we cannot be sure whether the songs we have today correspond exactly to those of the 16th century. We can consider the themes at least as old ones. These lays are described by scholars as "historical songs". The people appear to have drawn no distinction between them and the *stariny*, and they were sung by the same singers.

2. There also exists a theory that in a number of the early *stariny* the original thematic form is concealed under layers of 16th-century motifs. However, these new layers can be seen with clarity only in the case of the Novgorodian *stariny* about Vasilij Buslaevič. The two lays concerning this hero depict him as an arrogant man who assembled around himself in Novgorod a *družina* of loafers of the same ilk, and together with these, or even on his own, terrorised the citizens. Later he went to Jerusalem and on his return journey, because he ignored various interdictions, he died after jumping backward over a huge boulder. In these *stariny*, which contain numerous characteristics of old Novgorodian life, many motifs have been found which are also included in the legends of Ivan the Terrible, so that perhaps one should consider Vasilij Buslaevič as a caricature of the Tsar, and the *stariny* as being directed against him (S. Šambinago).

3. Nevertheless, most of the other songs connected with the reign of Ivan the Terrible have retained other characteristics of his times. Even his "surname" – "the Terrible" – had more the connotation of "terrible to the foe"; these enemies were in the beginning the Tartars, and only subsequently the princes and boyars, and the partisans of local independence (Novgorod and partly Pskov as well).

The songs glorify various episodes in Ivan's reign. First is the capture of Kazan'; the older version – the one recorded by Kirša Danilov in the 18th century – links this victory with the assumption of the Tsar's title; the versions we have today contain in parts humorous characteristics, too (the relics of a redaction by the *skomorochy*?), and treat primarily of the capture of Kazan's citadel by blowing up the walls with a mine (historical). The next, Ivan's second marriage to a Cherkess woman (1561), is a satire, even if its butt is not the Tsar himself but his Cherkess brother-in-law Ma[m]strjuk (in the songs "a Tartar"), who is killed in a duel with a Russian. In fact, Mastrjuk was executed in 1571. Another version replaces the duel by a successful battle with the Tartar army. The next song is obviously linked with the fact that three years before his death (in 1581) Tsar Ivan in anger mortally injured his eldest son and heir, Ivan. In the song, however, there appears Ivan's other son, Fedor, who later became Tsar. He is slandered by Tsar Ivan's favourite, Maljuta Skuratov (the name is historical), but at the last moment is saved by Nikita Romanovič Jurjev, the brother of the Tsar's first wife (who is referred to as being still alive, while in fact she had died in 1561). Jurjev was later the guardian of the weak-willed and pious Tsar Fedor. One other song, only once recorded (by Kirša Danilov), deals with the conquest of Siberia by the Cossack chieftain Ermak, and with the recognition of this conquest by the Tsar (1582). In the single extant version some events of the 17th century are mentioned, and therefore its origin, or revision, should not be dated before 1630. In some of the other songs which are connected with Ivan's name, the historical foundations are not so easy to perceive. In a number of them there are references to the Tsar's death and to the grief of the "princes and boyars."

The first three songs referred to have been written down in many ways and offer numerous textual variations, so that their original form is difficult to determine. The versions that have survived are reminiscent of the *stariny*, but the recurrent difference is in the metre.

4. The surgeon of Tsar Aleksij (1645–1676), the Englishman Collins, was the first to write down some fables about Ivan the Terrible, and more were recorded in the 19th century. Most of them use the various fairy-tale motifs of a good or evil tsar transposed onto Ivan. In one fable there can be discerned traces of the Tale of the Babylonian Empire; the Tsar's regalia are brought from Babylon by one Fedor Borma, and a similar-sounding name (Barma) also occurs in other tales about Ivan. This is obviously a reference to the Tsar's confessor, Fedor Barmin, who at his coronation (1547) carried the Tsar's regalia into the cathedral. The origin of this fable, at least, may be placed in the 16th century, when the name of this otherwise undistinguished man was not yet forgotten.

The songs and fables, with the exception of the song about Kazań's capture, are definitely not part of the court epos. They could also hardly be ascribed to goliards active in higher circles, and they are probably genuinely old works of folklore.

12. OTHER WORKS

1. Extant monuments from the 16th century are very numerous. To these belong, first of all, several liturgical works devoted to Russian saints, *akafists*, and divine services which are the sequel to the writings of Pachomij the Serb.

Among the authors were Tsar Ivan the Terrible and his son Ivan. There existed a number of writers whose activity was devoted either exclusively or predominantly to this branch of religious lyrical poetry: Grigorij of Suzdal', Markell Bezborodyj, the monk Michail. To the interregnum period belong the first work of this kind by Prince Simeon Šachovskoj.

2. There are also numerous extant epistles, many of which are by Metropolitan Makarij (VI, 10). The authorship of the speeches included in the chronicles and ascribed to his pen is often questionable.

3. Many treatises were written at that time on a variety of subjects. The monk Ermolaj-Erazm (about the middle of the century) is described as the author of some of the political, economic and theological treatises. To his pen certainly belongs *Pravitel'nica i zemleměrie* (The Art of Government and Land-Surveying), in which numerous economic and financial reforms were proposed.

Further works are devoted to theological questions. The list of them is headed by two tracts: *Istiny pokazanie* (the Evidence of Truth) and *Mnogoslovnoe poslanie* (the Discursive Epistle). Both were written by the same monk, one Zinovij Otenskij (after the Otenskij monastery, where he had been exiled after Maksim Grek's first trial in 1531; he died in 1568); both works are directed against Feodosij Kosoj's heresy. Of the latter, unfortunately, we know only from these polemic writings. Kosoj seems to have developed a rationalistic doctrine which is reminiscent of that of some radical Protestant sects (the Anti-Trinitarians of neighbouring Poland); he is alleged to have contested the teachings on the Trinity, the divinity of Christ, the Christian cult and ascesis, the worship of the saints, and the significance of the writings of the Fathers of the Church; but it is doubtful that he did not believe in the immortality of the soul. Zinovij's works contain not only a criticism of the heresy, but also a positive presentation of the Orthodox doctrine, wherein he refers not only to the testimony of the Scriptures and the Fathers of the Church, but also furnishes a system of proofs for every single point. On the whole, he follows the tradition of Nil and Maksim Grek; to be sure, he recognises the right of the monasteries to land-ownership. Moreover, religious polemics developed; in addition to the trials of heretics – which remain obscure to us in many respects (those of Matvej Baškin and others) – other creeds were fought. Ivan the Terrible not only took an active part in the persecution of heretics, but also engaged in private in oral polemics with the Papal nuncio, Possevinus, and with the Hussite Jan Rokyta in a solemn controversy, after which Rokyta was handed a written refutation of his opinions, which probably had been written by Ivan himself (it bears the signature "Parfenij Urodivyj", and it remains open to conjecture whether this was a pseudonym of Ivan, or whether Ivan had a previously existing work, which was perhaps originally directed against the *židovstvujuščie*, by this writer, otherwise unknown to us, copied). Further theological polemics arose in connection with the 1554 trial of the official Ivan Viskovatyj, who objected to the new symbolic method of icon painting. Viskovatyj's views are unfortunately known only from his depositions at the trial; they seem to represent correctly the orthodox opinions. He was sentenced, however, to a three year's Church penance.

A scientific treatise *Ustav* (statute) on military affairs appeared during the reign of Tsar Vasilij Šujskij in 1606 and was revised in 1620; it was printed in the 18th century. *Ustav* comprises, among other things, numerous data on the exact sciences (mathematics, physics, chemistry, mechanics), which are presented from the technical point of view. It is a compilation on the pattern of Western sources.

It is very problematic whether the compilatory rhetorical and cosmographical works extant in 17th century handwriting go back to the end of the 16th century, as some scholars maintain.

The second half of the 16th century, however, saw the appearance of the *Azbukovnik* (from *azbuka*, "alphabet") – a list of foreign words with explanations which, in some cases, are rather detailed but unfortunately not always lucid.

4. Beyond doubt, however, the most significant compilation of this period is the Chronograph, which was not only the most important source of historical knowledge, but also a school of literary style and a manual of political ideology of the 16th and 17th centuries. The older text (see V, 11, 5) was revised in 1512, and became popular in this form. The narrative ends with the depiction of the fall of Constantinople, to which three works at the end of the Chronograph are devoted: the story of Nestor-Iskander (V, 6, 9), a short tale, and a lament which outlines the causes for Constantinople's historical hegemony passing to Moscow (with reference to Manasses, see VII, 7, 4). The theory that Filofej participated in the revision of the 1512 redaction is not proved. Another redaction was made in 1633.

New material was used in the editing of the 1617 Chronograph. The last chapters describe the period 1534–1613. They are under the influence of the style of the old Chronograph and, through it, that of Manasses. The description of the interregnum greatly resembles *Inoe skazanie* (VI, 13, 3). The Trojan history of Guido de Columna (V, 2, 4) is used in place of the older text. The information about West European events is substantially amplified on the basis of the Polish Chronicle of Marcin Bielski and the Latin *Chronicon* of Conrad Lycosthenes (both of the 16th century). Naturally, the Chronograph now takes up the view-point of the new dynasty of the tsars, the Romanovs.

5. Among the legal monuments the 1560 revision of the book of laws (*Sudebnik*) must be singled out. In 16th-century Moscow the new chancery style was being developed, and was to play an important role in the evolution of the literary language in the 17th century. There arose, too, a new group of literati who, side by side with the ecclesiastical writers, were also later to play a significant role in literature. The chancery style was characterised by a certain closeness to the spoken language, though it still retained many Church Slavonicisms which were already alien to the every-day language at that time.

13. LITERATURE DURING AND AFTER THE INTERREGNUM

1. It is perhaps not accidental that literary activity ceased for a few years after the death of Ivan the Terrible. At least there is hardly any work which can be ascribed to the period 1584–98.

The only work which may be dated in the period preceding the inter-regnum is the biography of Tsar Fedor written in the hagiographic style of the time of Makarij. It includes the lament of the widow, Tsarina Irina, this Russian topos being modelled on the older tradition (Dmitrij Donskoj's *Žitie*).

2. The interregnum eventually produced many works, the overwhelming majority of which begin to appear only after 1612. These bring 16th-century literature to an end; they have all its merits, but also all its defects. The merits are the stylistic art with which the writers use the rich vocabulary and the exquisite stylistic devices. The defects are attributable to the overestimation of the form, which entirely overshadows the subject-matter. One marvels at the art with which the writers spin their stylistic cobwebs around futilities merely in order to avoid having to say the important things which they may want to conceal; sometimes they are quite unable to render the content, this having to be moulded into the strict formulas firmly laid down by tradition. Except for these formulas there is nothing else.

We wish to acquaint ourselves only with the most important works of this time, and we have chosen those which are especially characteristic.

3. The first story is preserved as the first part of the so-called "Other Story" (*Inoe skazanie*). It was probably written in 1606 (the events of the autumn of that year are no longer recorded). The most interesting events of the reigns of Fedor, Boris Godunov, and the False Demetrius are depicted only in quite general outline, while the legend of Tsarevich Dmitrij's assassination at Godunov's orders, the identification of the False Demetrius with Grigorij Otrep'ev, and so forth, actually form the main content of the Story. Everything, however, is entirely unsubstantiated and rendered with the fewest possible details. The information is always wrapped in such a cloud of commonplaces, beautiful turns of phrase, and erudite digressions that much of what the writer wanted to say does not reach the consciousness of the reader. There are exclamations like: "O woe! How can I not shed tears over this?" or "How can my right hand write with the pen about this? ...", and observations of this type: "The cunning always hate the good; and the cunning, when they achieve what they have wished, are more ruthless than wild beasts", etc. The characterisations of Boris Godunov, Otrep'ev, and others are mostly variations of the Manasses text, taken from the Chronograph. The text is adorned by effective compounds: *slavoběsie* ("greed for glory"), *kras-*

norazcvĕtaemyj ("beautifully blossoming"), *zlosovĕtnik* ("a bad counsellor"). The military feats are described in the same style. The part
containing a few concrete facts is the (inaccurate) account of the *starec*
Varlaam concerning the False Demetrius.

The writer is a partisan of the Šujskij family, and concludes his work
with a eulogy of Tsar Vasilij Šujskij, who reigned at that time.

4. The "Story" (*Skazanie*) by monk Avraamij Palicyn was written in
1620, after the interregnum. It seems that its legendary content derives
from the above-mentioned work. Here, too, the most important parts
are inundated by vague adornments, and the later events (after 1606) are
likewise expounded in a similarly vague form. But Palicyn speaks also
of the interregnum period proper and, though he has no models for the
description of the complete moral collapse and the unprecedented
barbarism, he finds, nevertheless, an impressive language in which to
depict the savagery of the times. He uses somewhat fewer compounds,
but just as many exclamations and instructions as the writer of the 1606
Story. Like the latter, Palicyn holds the view that such events are punishments from God, or at least happen with "God's assent". He can name
the reasons for this punishment. In the first place there is the "mad
silence" (*bezumnoe molčanie*) under Boris Godunov, as no one ventured
to tell the Tsar anything about the defects of his reign; then there was
Tsar Boris' tolerance of the "Armenian and Latin" heresies; Palicyn
considers as a particularly terrible offence the circumstance that under
Tsar Boris, at the time of the famine, the communion bread was not made
of white flour but of rye. He believes, moreover, that the Greek-Orthodox
subjects of the Polish State are heretics, and even more so the Poles,
whom he considers to be Lutherans (cf. the "Tale of the Siege of Pskov"
– VI, 4, 6).

In any case he was capable of acknowledging an impressive list of sins
still being committed by the generation living after the interregnum. He
passes over in silence, however, the fact that he himself "collaborated"
with the Poles for a time! Palicyn devotes a very long section of his work
to the siege of the Troicko-Sergievskaja Lavra by the Poles. He is
unable to illustrate his description in an effective way, for he substitutes
for concrete representation the petrified formulas of the old military
literature. He was, it is true, not in the monastery during the siege. The
numerous visions and miracles which are described fall into the pattern
of the hagiographic style.

5. The greatest artist of the meaningless description, the official (*D'jak*) Ivan Timofeev, is the author of a similarly bulky narrative of the interregnum – the *Vremennik* (Chronicle). His work, which, to be sure, enjoyed no popularity, comprises over 300 pages of manuscript. This chronicle is much poorer in content than even the two previous works. Here the material is literally smothered under the encumbrance of adornments. Among its extensive digressions there is included a short reflection on the duty of the author to describe what he had seen. He communicates, of course, a number of concrete details; he is, however, far behind the other writers in his ability to outline new facts with ready-made formulas. With Timofeev, the formulas usually radiate from facts to boundless considerations. For the simple description of Godunov's election as tsar, of his coronation and accession to the throne, he needs 24 manuscript pages, and coins sentences such as the following: "He was anointed with oil from a horn, he, from among all mortals, was crowned in exceptional splendour, and from that time on appropriated the name of the highest ruler, because he accepted at the same time the designation of tsar and prince, as was the habit at the anointing of the real tsar, the [anointing – D.Č.] which gave the privilege of taking possession of the most magnificent elevation; thus he achieved the aim of his secret wish, for he collected the honour of all the tsars, and usurped it all in his name." Timofeev even prefers to use vague abstract designations instead of names: thus Boris Godunov is introduced as "a kinsman of the Tsar [Fedor]", whose name has no etymology (he is able to find the etymology for other names of Greek origin), "because it is clear that he is not included by God in the Books of Life because of his damnable deeds;" this sounds the more grotesque as Timofeev had already mentioned Saint Boris earlier.

The story begins with Ivan the Terrible. All the three non-dynastic tsars (Boris, the False Demetrius, and Vasilij Šujskij) are portrayed from the view-point of the new dynasty as being the products of all evil. Timofeev could have given us more precise information about the events in Novgorod, for some time occupied by the Swedes. But unfortunately these references, too, are frequently incomprehensible.

The particular character of Timofeev's style is that his stylistic embellishments include only a few metaphors (mostly traditional) and in general few visual means of adornment. His artistic devices are two. The first is his vocabulary and the use of compounds, among which the ones created *ad hoc* are almost preponderant: *raboubitel'*, *zemoiznurenie*, *dragoveščestvie*, *lukopuščennyj*, *molebnopěnie*, *inoizbiennyj*, etc. ("the murderous slave, the exhaustion of land, precious things, shot from the bow, prayer song, he who was slaughtered at another time"). In some cases the sense of such compounds can be guessed only with difficulty, and some of them have a double meaning; similarly, several abstract words are difficult to understand, as the author seems to avoid colloquial words deliberately. His second device is the syntactic construction, which is also a means of adornment for Timofeev. He gives the impression of sublimity by the great number of subordinate clauses and participial constructions. Timofeev was capable of giving his speech a certain rhythmic structure, which was further underlined by an occasional rhyme.

Ideologically, Timofeev has the standpoint of Palicyn: disorder is the result of the destruction of the old rules of life.

6. Something distinctive is also offered by the story of Prince Ivan Chvorostinin who, as a young man, had played a questionable role at the court of the False Demetrius and held various high appointments under Tsar Michail Romanov; because of his closeness to the False Demetrius, however, and later because of his agnostic leanings, his career was interrupted by periods of disgrace and banishment. A gifted man of letters (he was also active in the field of liturgic and religious literature), he, too, wrote a description of the interregnum. This account obviously seeks to suppress the role of the author. The style is again lofty, certainly with a strong tendency to the style of prayers, with long series of rhetorical questions, and with quotations from the Scriptures. The account of the alleged conversations between the author and the False Demetrius and the Patriarch Germogen are rhetorical exercises, written with the help of Manasses' Chronicle. The autobiographical character of the work is, to be sure, a novelty. Chvorostinin's story was obviously written shortly before his death (1625), when he had become a monk.

7. One of the more noteworthy narratives is usually ascribed to the pen of Prince Katyrev-Rostovskij, whereas the authorship of the work is far from certain. One may consider as its author Sergej Kubasov, who incorporated this story into the chronograph which he himself compiled. According to an entry in the text, it was written in 1626. The story (*Povĕst'*) exists in two versions and surpasses all other in richness of material. Beginning once more with brief references to Ivan the Terrible, it depicts the whole march of events of the 1598–1613 period. Here, too, accurate details, with names and dates, alternate with the rhetorical parts – the series of exclamations, questions, and lyrical effusions. In any case, the attempt to bring out the factual information in spite of these adornments is worthy of note.

Again the embellishments are, to be sure, borrowed, and predominantly from the same source, the Trojan story of Guido de Columna. From this novel the author borrows many locutions, even when describing concrete facts; sometimes he partly changes the formulas which he finds there. Occasionally he also uses other sources. He prefaces individual scenes, mainly of battles, with descriptions of nature which are also borrowed. Such is his description of spring, in which we can hear the echo of the sermons of Chrysostomos and Kirill of Turov: "And winter is gone now, and the time comes when the sun, circumscribing the zodiacal circle, enters the zodiacal sign of the Ram, when the day becomes equal with the night and spring is celebrated, when the time that rejoices mortals begins, and in the air brightness lights up. When snow has melted and the winds gently blow and the springs flow forth in further streams, then the peasant lowers his plough [into the earth] and draws the sweet furrow and calls upon the fruit-bearing God; herbs grow, fields become green, the trees dress themselves with new foliage, the soil is adorned everywhere with fruit, the birds sing sweet songs, while now by God's providence and His love for men, every benefit for man's enjoyment ripens." Occasionally, the author uses rhymes and paranomasias (in the above quotation) and, moreover, the less common stylistic device, alliteration. The number of compounds is not great; in the majority of cases they are traditional. The conclusion characterizes the tsars after Ivan the Terrible, and Godunov's daughter. Here, too, the author draws his stylistic devices from Guido de Columna.

8. We shall pass over the further monuments which concern the inter-regnum – there are over twenty of them in all. Among these there are a few which originated in Novgorod or Pskov. Worthy of mention are a lament on Russia's fate (*Plač*) and a few monuments devoted to certain personalities; besides the hagiographic legend of Tsarevič Dmitrij, who was canonized under Tsar Vasilij Šujskij, there is also a biography of Patriarch Germogen, who died in Polish captivity, similarly stylised as a hagiographic Life.

One writing is devoted to the military commander, Prince Michail Skopin-Šujskij. Skopin-Šujskij fought with success against the second False Demetrius and against the Swedes, but died during a visit to Moscow. A female relative of Tsar Vasilij Šujskij is said to have poisoned him. This work, too, is written in the familiar ornate style. The sentimental colouring of some passages is remarkable; side by side with the laments of Skopin's mother and wife we have also the laments of Tsar Vasilij and the population. The writer owes to folklore his subject-matter and some motifs, as well as some expressions (*pir na veselo, jasnye oči*, etc. – "joyful banquet, bright eyes").

9. The most interesting biographical work, however, is the tale (*Povĕst'*) of Julijanija (or Ulijanija) Osor'ina (or Osorgina) written by her son Družina. The work is extant in numerous copies (about thirty). It had certainly been conceived as a secular biography, but was written in the traditional form of Lives of the Saints. The biographical details are exact, beginning with the information concerning Julijanija's parents (the Nedjurevs, from the province of Murom), and her piety, studiousness, and seriousness notable from her childhood: "She was gentle, silent, calm (*nebujava*), not proud, and she shunned laughter and every game." Married at the age of sixteen, she remained devout and gentle towards the servants ("she called no one by his common name", i.e., by the scornful diminutive). She used to sell her hand-work and secretly divided the proceeds in alms and bequests for the Church. When demons appeared in her dreams, St. Nicholas expelled them (a similar story is repeated once more further on). When famine broke out (probably in the 70's), she devoted herself wholly to the service of the hungry. She begged food from her mother-in-law and divided it secretly among the hungry; she cared for the sick, attended to the burial of the dead, and cared for the orphans. It was especially emphasized that she washed the sick and the corpses with her own hands. She conceived the idea of retreating into a convent, but as her husband forbade this, she gave up her intention, but spent the rest of her life in chastity and ascetic exercices: she slept on hard and pointed objects, and spent the greater part of the night in prayer. After her husband's death, during the famine under Boris Godunov's reign, she sold her goods and chattels, released her serfs and, with the servants who remained with her of their own will, she baked bread with a mixture of orach and bark. This bread seemed particularly tasty to the hungry among whom she distributed it, "and they did not know that her bread was sweet as a result of her prayers". At this time she lived in the district of Nižnij Novgorod. In 1604, after a short illness, she died. "And everybody saw around her head a golden halo, like the ones painted on the icons of saints." When eleven years later her coffin was opened at the funeral of one of her sons, her body was found undamaged, and the coffin full of sweet-scented oil which brought health to the sick. "I hardly dare to write this" – her son concludes his narrative – "as it is not proved", i.e., there had not been an official Church enquiry.

This story from the life of a pious woman of the middle groups of nobility contains several interesting features of the true religious feeling of the 16th century, unfortunately still arrayed in the traditional hagio-graphic phraseology, a devoutness which was represented not only by this woman. She connected asceticism and mortification of the flesh with a high estimation of good deeds, even with the sacrifice of her own standing and interests. Moreover, a certain indifference to the ritual duties may be noticed: the biography, so sparse in details, comprises two particular episodes which are devoted to her home prayers: she did not go to Church during a cold winter and went to divine service only after an admonition from the priest. During the second famine, too, she did not go to Church, thinking of the life of a saint to whom "home prayers had done no harm either". If we also observe that in her old age Julijanija practiced "perpetual prayer" and that she herself called her prayer "a spiritual prayer" (*duchovnaja molitva*), we may see in her and in her son and biographer the last expression of the piety of Nil Sorskij and of the Russian Hesychast school.

This biography, which, as mentioned, depicts the life of Julijanija in the style of a saint's Life, became somewhat later a proper hagiographic legend, with a pious meditation which was added, now to the beginning, now to the end, with numerous quotations from the Scriptures and with supplements. Julijanija is made to utter various pious instructions; her mortification is reinforced; her fastings are expressly mentioned (Friday, Monday, and Wednesday), as are the meals she provided for priests, widows, and orphans, and so on. The work thus became longer and more splendid (even though some words of everyday speech crept in), but much less impressive and less instructive.

10. To the interesting aspects of this literature belongs also the use of rhyme. We find rhymes in the *Skazanie* by Avraamij Palicyn, who included rhymed sectious in various passages. It is characteristic that Palicyn uses rhyming substantives as well as the rhyming verbs, which had frequently occurred earlier, as for instance:

> Исходяще бо за обитель дров ради добытия,
> и во град возвращахуся не без кровополития;
> и купивше кровию сметие и хврастие,
> и тем строяще повседневное ястие...

("And they left the monastery to get some wood, they returned to the fortress not without blood-shedding, and they bought rubbish and faggots with blood, and prepared with it their daily meal"). The number of syllables in individual lines varies (9–17) syllables, while nearly every line has four, less frequently three or five accents.

A narrative which is ascribed to Katyrev-Rostovskij contained poetry, which the writer himself designated as "verse" (*virši*). These verses consisted once of six, and another time thirty lines. The second passage likewise had substantive rhymes (4) and even one adverbial rhyme. The number of syllables is still more variable, from five to 17 (a 22-syllable line contained very likely a 6-syllable gloss). The number of accents in a line is also variable (2–6). Here is an example:

> Изложена бысть сия летописная книга
> о похождении чюдовского мниха,
> понеже он бысть убогий чернец
> и возложил на ся царский венец,
> царство Великие России возмутил
> и диядиму царскую на плещах своих носил...

("This chronicle book relates the adventures of a monk from the monastery of Čudov. Because he was a poor monk and put on the tsar's crown he brought the tsardom of Great Russia into confusion, and carried on his shoulders [sic!] the tsar's diadem").

The "Monk from the Monastery of Čudov", according to official tradition, was the False Demetrius; the author of the verse confuses the diadem with the mantle worn by the tsars (*barmy*).

These verses are not the only ones extant. The English schoolmaster, Richard James, had six songs written down for him in Moscow in 1619; these were songs devoted to various events after 1598, among which there are two laments of Godunov's daughter Ksenija, after the death of her father. The origin of these songs is not clear; it seems probable, however, that they are literary rather than folk poems. One song consists of 5-line stanzas. The first reads:

> Бережочик зыблетца,
> да песочик сыплетца,
> [а] ледочик ломитца,
> добры кони тонут,
> молодцы томятца.

("The shore moves, the sand scatters, the ice breaks, the good horses

AN ANGEL, SYMBOL OF MATHEW THE EVANGELIST
From the so-called gospels of Chitrovo. 15th century.

ST. FLOR AND LAVR, THE PATRONS OF HORSES
An icon from the 16th century.

drown, the young people pine away"). The song treats of the difficulties of military service in winter. The number of syllables in one line slightly varies here (6–7 syllables), elsewhere more (8–13 for instance). There are rhymes, though in other songs the endings are only assonances in part. Some of the songs also contain numerous euphonies and a few alliterations. Sometimes the number of stresses in a line varies but little (2–3 or 3–4).

We have here obviously the first attempts of the Russian poetic art. The knowledge of Ukrainian and Polish poetry has led from this "pre-syllabic" poetry to the development of syllabic poetry (see VII, 5, 4 and 6, 7). The Ukrainian influence is shown by the presence of Ukrainisms in the verses of the narrative by Katyrev-Rostovskij: *priklady, ugljadaem, bespriklado, pochoženie*, perhaps also *nezabytno* ("examples, we learn, without example, adventure, unforgettable").

Probably shortly before his death, Prince I. Chvorostinin, already known to us (cf. above, § 6), wrote in verse a collection of polemic poems against the Catholics (*Izloženie na eretiki i zlochulniki* – "Statement against heretics and evil blasphemers"), already entirely under the influence of the Ukrainian *virši*: the Ukrainian rhymes *ě*: :*i* (*porfiry*: :*měry*) and numerous strong Ukrainisms (*negolduet, zgoda, ofěra, ozdoba*, etc. – "does not respect, harmony, sacrifice, ornament") show this sufficiently. Traditionally Ukrainian are also the couplets linked usually by feminine rhymes.

11. The remnants of historical songs concerning these times are not numerous. In a form reminiscent of *stariny* are a few songs on False Demetrius (in the songs: Griška Otrep'ev); some refer to Tsar Vasilij Šujskij and his alleged banishment to Siberia (in reality he died in captivity in Poland). On the other hand, there are many songs on Skopin-Šujskij (see above, 8); after hyperbolic statements about his victories, these songs deal with his legendary poisoning. They are abundantly studded with material from other historical songs and even from *stariny*. Few mention the leader of the rebellious Cossacks, Prokopij Ljapunov, and only one mentions the national army which, under the leadership of a Nižnij Novgorod citizen, Minin, and Prince Požarskij, defeated the Polish troops.

And yet individual motifs of the interregnum found their way into the *stariny*. Thus, for instance, the Polish wife of the False Demetrius, Marina Mniszek, takes the place of other female characters, all without exception hostile and evil. Also Il'ja Muromec becomes now a *kazak* or a peasant.

VII

THE BAROQUE

1. CHARACTERISTICS

1. After 1613 the old tradition seems to have revived. Indeed old Russia appears to have been resurrected, even in an improved form in the first decades, without the terror of Ivan the Terrible, without the tension between Church and State (for Patriarch Filaret was Tsar Michail's father), even without great external dangers. The literary works, in spite of their dramatic political themes, seemed to follow in style along the old channel. ... However, this was no longer possible. The presence of foreign troops in Russia, chiefly of Polish occupation forces and the Ukrainians who showed themselves culturally alien yet "orthodox", the long stay of so many Russian prisoners in Poland (among their number Patriarch Filaret), taught, although perhaps to only a few, that everything foreign was not necessarily and entirely to be rejected. The opinion that certain practical, "technical" achievements of the West might perhaps do some good to Russia, too, seems to have been most important. The new ideas could partly penetrate more easily and be maintained, since the foundations of 16th-century life were so completely shattered. But it was almost 1640 before a general change towards the acceptance of elements from Western culture seems to have come about. The new Tsar, Aleksej, was undoubtedly a strong driving force in the stimulation of intercourse with the West; after his accession to the throne an intensive and extensive activity in translating began for everybody in the field of literature (see VII, 2). The majority of translated works enjoyed no great dissemination; they have come down to us in only a few copies, often in a single manuscript. But this is a symptom which has parallels in all fields.

2. This was not a revolutionary process, but a slow penetration of new trends. A door to the West had already been opened; until now it remains however scarcely utilised: this is the Ukraine and Byelo-Russia, with numerous schools and, since 1631, with the Kiev Academy (which at that time aimed at education not only for the clergy but also for laymen). The teachers came exclusively from the clergy. And they held two keys to Western education, Latin and Polish; instruction in Greek had just at that time greatly receded. It was from their ranks that the educated men, the teachers, writers and translators, were recruited. They seemed to be less dangerous than the orthodox Greek clergy. After a few decades this was tried on a considerably smaller scale with the Greeks and, only at the end of the century, with other foreigners (see further, VII, 6 and 8).

But the activities of the foreigners, the reading of translated books, perhaps also of the originals in foreign languages did not take place without awakening suspicions, fear and even despair. The selected leaders showed themselves much too often (frequently only in appearance) as corrupters: heretics, traitors, wreckers (it seems that spies were all they lacked then). The spiritual authorities watched the foreigners at work more suspiciously than the secular ones, and the people were even more suspicious. At the end of the century it was suddenly discovered that the "Third Rome" was the "New Babylon" and its master, "the defender of all Christians", was in fact the Anti-Christ. This was the first acute and deep ideological cleavage of the Russian people, which produced the *Raskol* (see VII, 7), not only an ecclesiastical but also a cultural schism. Then followed further fresh cleavages one after another during the next two centuries.

3. The literary West which penetrated into Moscow around 1640 was of course the literary West of *that time* – namely the Baroque. The new style came at first as a little heeded addition to the subject-matter, which was then the only centre of interest. Only in the 50's does the consciousness of literary style begin to awaken. And oddly enough, the new style finds in the old 16th-century style much that is not to be brushed aside but transformed and freshened. For the baroque style is just as complicated, as heavily ornate, as the Russian style of the 16th century. Similarly it does not reject opacity and obscurity and prefers devious to direct ways. Also in many respects the ideological traits of the Baroque did not contradict the Russian tradition. First of all, the religious motifs placed in the foreground of baroque literature appealed to the Russian reader. Also the symbolism and even its ideological foundation, the representation of the invisible world as concealed beyond the visible one, was common both to the Baroque and to the old Russian literary tradition. Nevertheless, for this very reason, the Russian Baroque was less pronounced; it brought in its wake seemingly little that was new. Only as school instruction developed was it possible to teach deliberately the basic features of the baroque style. But that came only at the end of the century.

4. Some features of the Baroque stand in opposition to the literary usage of Moscow; but not so its predilection for the grotesque, nor its wide scope and its taste for hyperbole as well as the inclination for the ever new, original, unprecedented. These could be replaced by the already traditional variations of the transmitted forms and formulas. Only with great difficulty did people get used to two particular aspects of the baroque literature: first, to the dynamism of the Baroque, to its predilection for adventure, tension, catastrophe, peripeties; dynamism was not only to be external in the Baroque, but often worked into the essence of things through the bold conceptual antitheses; secondly, the naturalism of the Baroque, its graphic quality, were frequently exaggerated into massive bluntness, coarseness and uncouthness. Above all it was felt in Russia to be intolerable and blasphemous when dynamics and naturalism were introduced into sacred spheres. In a strange way, the partisans of the essentially "old" – the "Old Believers" (see VII, 7) – showed themselves to be the most talented disciples of the Baroque; in their conception of the world, historical dynamism is raised to the Apocalypse.

The ideological influence of the Baroque was its weakest feature. Certainly this baroque ideology was not uniform; the various conceptions of the world held by its representatives had structurally only few common features. The dynamic character of the *Weltanschauung*, the concept of general changeability, found the usual expression in the traditional representation of the "transitoriness" of everything. On the other hand, as already mentioned, the apocalyptic feeling of the end of the century was also a new expression of the dynamic view of history. With still greater difficulty did the universalism of the Baroque find its way into the consciousness of the Muscovites, nor was historical thought prepared for a representation of unity in the flow of time (the Chronograph, even the idea of "Third Rome"). But for those men for whom existence remained confined within the sacred sphere (which, in itself, entirely absorbed all other spheres) it was impossible to apprehend that nature was an integral part of a universal unity of being. Nature remained for a long time beyond the horizon of the Russian mind. Universal syntheses were attempted only in the theological sphere (without success), or they appear as a *deus ex machina* in the translated, or at best, in the compiled works.

The baroque style pushed its way most easily into the external forms of life. In the 18th century there are to be found enough typically baroque men, with the internally conditioned wide breadth of vision and bold approach to problems of life, with the "spiritual adventures" and vacillation typical of men of the time. To the earlier representatives of this type belongs the already mentioned Chvorostinin, a high official and an exile, a free-thinker and a monk (see VI, 13, 6). Later, such men can be named as Patriarch Nikon, the peasant who became leader of the Church and almost shared the power of tsardom with the Tsar himself, the originator of the great schism and eventually an exiled monk; and at the end of the century there is Tsar Peter I himself, as well as many people of his entourage, all representatives of the same type. It is not necessary to think only of the baroque men from the Ukraine, then active in Moscow. Only with the greatest difficulty did the baroque style penetrate into the most zealously guarded Church; but there too the Baroque gained ground in church architecture, in icon painting and in the sermon – in the latter perhaps because it had to grow up anew on barren ground.

Nevertheless, for that reason too, the Muscovite Baroque was in some respects restrained or moderated, as its intellectual representatives were primarily clerics and appointed professional litterati, who usually have no great concern with externals. And the "new men" whom one is often tempted to see in this period (thus the Soviet scholars) were either Ukrainians belonging to the same circles, or men whose spiritual "renovation" was purely negative; they had been uprooted from traditionalism, and no more.

5. In literature, the Baroque expressed itself mainly in a fresh growth of literary genres. Poetry appears, original belles-lettres in the proper sense of the word are developed, the sermon is revived, the theatre is born, etc. Poetry, theatre, sermon, as well as the novella to a certain extent, are, however, only foreign growths transplanted to Moscow. Soon they firmly take root, never to disappear from literature.

Now the same features of baroque art flourish in all genres, though to different degrees. The breadth of composition replaces the universalism of the content. The abundant adornment is not new, but, by severing its links with tradition, it comes closer to the baroque paradoxicality and is capable of producing an impression of originality without in fact being original. Antitheses and metaphors increase in number, and the latter show a tendency toward compression into complicated allegories. At the end of the century there penetrated into Russia works of the *Symbola et*

Emblemata type, and it seems that the *concetti* are paradoxical thought constructions which formed the foundation of various writings. The idea was to astonish the reader with the unexpected, and to disturb, move and shake him with the extreme. This aim was probably achieved but rarely. The reader (or listener to the sermon, or to the theatrical performance) was too slow, the works represented the baroque style in a moderated form, and in part they were not sufficiently impressive (cf. VII, 9).

A typical feature of the Baroque, the variegation of language and the predilection for neologisms, pervaded Russian literature partly by chance and only partly by the authors' intention. The great number of foreigners among the writers and primarily among the translators caused the spread of Ukrainian, Byelo-Russian, Polish and Latin vocabulary, and occasionaly also of other elements of speech, into the written Russian. This profusion of barbarisms (foreign words) corresponds, on the other hand, to the use in literature of words of various linguistic levels; the vocabulary of the high Church-Slavonic style (which had already become partly archaic), the chancery language, the colloquial speech of various popular strata (and together with it at least a few elements of folklore) appeared now either separately in particular works or in an unsual combination in the same work.

6. The schools contributed greatly to the consolidation of the baroque style by instruction in poetics. The origin of educational centres is obscure: the first "Greek" school is said to have been founded by Epifanij Slavyneckyj (VII, 6), the "Latin" school by Simeon Polockij in 1664. Both were attached to the Moscow monasteries. Between 1682 and 1687 there existed a monastic school under the direction of Sil'vestr Medvedev (VII, 5, 8). In 1687 the Greek brothers Lichud set up a "Greek-Latin-Slavonic" Academy in Moscow. Its significance was limited by its purely clerical spirit. Journeys to Kiev to the Academy there were rare.

A considerably smaller role was played by the printing of books, which were gradually to become a permanent feature. Many translations were ordered for printed editions, but they continued to be disseminated in hand-written copies. Most of the printing was confined to books for divine service and a few official publications: the Code (1649), a guide to military art (1647), the works of Simeon Polockij (VII, 5), various pamphlets and text-books.

7. As with many other literary periods in Russia (for instance, Classicism), the Baroque was affected by an external evolution, and was interrupted by the so-called Petrine reform. The direct influence of this reform on the spiritual life of the Russians, especially on Russian literature, should not be overrated. The reform touched primarily the sphere of state-organization, among other things, the Army, various aspects of technical

science useful to the State, and the external form of life of a very limited class. Literature declined; at first literary activity was carried on predominantly by Ukrainians (VII, 6); they adapted the old religious themes in the more consistent baroque forms. Only thirty to thirty-five years after the first split, the *Raskol*, did the reforms bring about a new cleavage between the class which had accepted the new, external "Westernised" forms of life, and the great majority of the people who continued to live enveloped in the old traditional forms, which were, however, beginning to change and to disintegrate. Old literature now recedes into the background. The new, secular literature begins with works which belong to the "lower" literary genres, to the primitive adventure novels (VII, 11) so clumsy from the artistic point of view. They further increase the range of linguistic variegation: to the earlier barbarisms are added West-European – German, French, English, and even Dutch (thanks to Peter's stay in Holland) – and Italian words. The written language – even the spoken language of certain classes of the population – seems to be pervaded by the same variegation. This colourfulness is a grave problem as it seriously impedes literary development. Only gradually does there arise a literature of serious kind, of "high" style, which, in an often slavish imitation of the West, tries particularly to introduce the declining baroque style. This literature finds no popularity, even among the narrow educated circles; Kantemir, Trediakovskij, Lomonosov remain exceptions. And only in the '60's of the 18th century does literature become the concern of society; it is mainly a literature which represents a new, classical style.

The interruption of literary development, this unusual pause lasting several decades, was overcome neither by schools nor by the printing of books. Schools and book-printing were now devoted mainly to practical tasks which were ordered by the State. The building up of literature did not come within the scope of this.

Thus the new development of literature starts only about 1740. This new literature, though it had to start anew after a long interruption, created important possibilities for further development. It created "secular" themes and introduced new genres. It created, with the Baroque's characteristic predilection for experiment, the new technique of poetry. And it partly sanctioned the linguistic changes of the Petrine and pre-Petrine times. The Ukrainisms and Polonisms which had flooded into the Russian language in the 17th century could – thanks to the activity of the late baroque poets – partly keep their place in the Russian literary language. Also the West-European terminology of the

Petrine reform became to a certain degree part of the literary language; the vocabulary of the "technical" language had already declined somewhat before the '40's.

2. TRANSLATED LITERATURE (17TH CENTURY)

1. The 17th-century translated literature is astonishing in its variety, its haphazard choice of material, the frequently poor quality of its translations, the colourfulness of its language and, not least, in the limited popularity of the majority of the translations. All this is explained partly by the fact that the selection depended on the accidental recommendations and whims of highly placed personages (e.g., Tsar Aleksej, later his son Fedor), and that the intention was to have the works printed, even though this did not happen. But above all it is explained by the haphazard choice of the translators. Among these there were Russian officials who had more or less mastered Polish or Latin; Ukrainians, Byelo-Russians and perhaps also Poles especially invited from abroad for the purpose. Many of them scarcely understood the text to be translated, sometimes due to the specialised character of the work concerned; others did not find the Church Slavonic or Russian equivalents or simply did not know Russian well enough. And thus they frequently introduced numerous foreign words into their translation or produced a text very hard to understand. The role of the translator in the introduction of foreign words into the Russian vocabulary is very significant.

It was characteristic of the times that the translations were mainly made from Latin, German and Polish. The translations from Greek are insignificant.

2. Even theological works were translated from Latin. No substantial additions were made. Even some works by the Greek Fathers of the Church were translated from Latin; some fragments from the books of the Bible, too, were rendered from Latin and German (although after 1581 a well printed text of the whole Bible, published in Ostroh in the Ukraine, was available). Also translated were the Catholic mass and a few liturgical writings probably for purposes of information only. Moreover, the Lives of the Western Fathers of the Church (Augustin, Justinus) were also translated. From Latin were rendered anew the paterikons – the "Roman Paterikon" and *Historia Lausiaca*, though this was in Greek in the original (see II, 3). The tale of "Varlaam and Ioasaf", which was now certainly interpreted as a real hagiographic legend (see II, 10 and VII, 5, 1), was revised anew with the aid of the Latin text. The translations of the sermons of St. Bernard and of the *Imitatio Christi* by Thomas à Kempis might have been the most substantial enrichment of translated literature, had they been widely disseminated. Also translated were *De contemptu mundi* by Pope Innocent, the new didactic writings in baroque style by the Jesuits H. Drexelius (*Heliotropus*) and Stanyhurstus, and the collection of sermons by Mefret.

3. Especially copious, though at the same time very badly selected, were the translations of "scientific" literature, much of which was obsolete, and some completely unsuitable for Moscow.

Among philosophical literature must be mentioned the translation of Aristotle's "Physics", without a commentary, however; the text was hardly understandable. Also, the pseudo-Aristotelian *Problemata* were translated. A particular influence was exerted by Raymond Lull (13th–14th centuries), whose *Ars Magna*, in a later version, was brought to Moscow by an Ukrainian adherent of Lull – Bohomodlevśkyj (probably Andrej). The bold, universal, but rather abstruse system of the Spanish logician won support later – strangely enough – from the Old Believers. (It would be worth while perhaps to seek in the alleged Lullian writings the influence of Raymundus de Sabonde, a 15th-century follower of Lullus, who had exerted some influence in the 17th century.)

The exact sciences are further represented by the translations of the practical text-books of arithmetic and geometry. Astronomy was represented by Hevelius' description of the moon (1647, translated after 1670) including an exposition of the general astronomical sciences. Beside this work which was important but probably incomprehensible by itself, an important collection of information on comets by the Pole Niewieski (original, 1681) was also translated. The basic astronomical teachings were to be found mainly in the geographical works, which included the *Theatrum orbis terrarum* by Johannes Blaeu (1645) who, like Hevelius, expounded the Copernican system (in translation *Zercadlo* or *Pozorišče vseja vselennyja*). But at the same time numerous astrological works were translated which amounted to primitive superstition.

The descriptive geographical literature contained mostly accounts of various countries: Palestine (worthy of attention is the description of a journey by Nicholas Radziwiłł, known as *Sierotka*, Polish 1563), Persia, India, Algeria, perhaps China (only one fragment of a book about China by Athanasius Kircher is extant), Turkey, even Spitzbergen. The account of Olearius' journey to Russia was translated from the 1646 edition.

Nature apparently inspired little interest. Epifanij Slavynećkyj (VII, 6) translated the famous anatomy of Andreas Vesalius *Humani corporis fabrica* (1543); this translation is lost. Moreover, the scientific works by Albertus Magnus (13th century) and Michael Scotus (12th-13th centuries) were also translated. Also smaller fragments of translations from zoological works of descriptive character are known.

There was a greater interest in history. Slavinećkyj translated Thucydides (not extant?). The Polish "Chronicles" by Marcin Bielski (16th century) and Stryjkowski (17th century); a Czech history (possibly written in Polish); as well as fragments of Swedish history were all translated. There was even a rendering of Ethiopia's history by Hiob Ludolf (1681). Flavius Josephus, an excellent translation of whose work from the earlier period was still available, was rendered anew from Polish (1623). Baronius' Church history – representing the Catholic point of view – was also translated.

Noteworthy among the political pamphlets are the Polish ones by Frycz-Modrzewski (16th century) and Fredro (1664), and – translated from Latin – the emblematic book by the Spaniard, D. Foxardo Saavedra, *Idea Principis christiano-politici* (Latin, 1659), which aroused interest in later times, too.

The two tracts on the "seven free arts" (*mudrosti*) were popular accounts of the medieval *trivium* and *quadrivium*. One of these was a translation or a compilation; the second was probably a compilation from the Greek author Spatharios.

4. Among the works more closely connected with literature, we have to mention various text-books on "Rhetoric" (cf. VI, 11), which also contained the theory of poetic art; the plan of some of these is the same as of the later works of Lomonosov (VII, 14, 3). Some of them may have been compilations, i.e., not exact translations.

The classical poetic works aroused no interest; only Ovid's "Metamorphoses" were translated (into prose) from Polish. Beside this stand works chosen entirely at random: a Polish ode in honour of King Sobieski, a commentary on the political novel by John Barclay *Argenis*, a book about the "Four Last Things" (death, the Last Judgment, hell, paradise) possibly by the Polish Jesuit Boym (there were, however, a great many such works). Some of the theological works had, to a certain extent, an accomplished literary form, for instance, those by Drexelius and Stanyhurstus (mentioned above). There was also a translation of some other ascetic-poetical writing.

5. In contrast there were a considerable number of works of a practical nature, ranging from books on hunting, riding, horse and dog breeding, to economic, agricultural, medical and military works (a manual of the art of war by J. J. Waldhausen of 1631 was printed in 1647). There were also translations of cookery books, dream books, calendars and excerpts from "newspapers" (non-periodic broadsheets which existed then in the West), as well as various fragments of works of topical interest.

6. Belles-lettres were finally being translated by the end of the century, although at first only works which were already old and belonged at that time to the "lower" stratum of literature ("chap books", etc.).

Then we have the picaresque novels in which love motifs play a certain role, such being a great novelty at the time. We shall mention here only the most popular of them.

Petr Zlatye Ključi i korolevna Magilena derives from the French medieval novel *Pierre de Provence et la belle Maguelonne* via German and Polish versions. The Russian translation (1680) is a version of the Polish text (and includes a few Polonisms). Petr *Zlatye Ključi* (golden keys – his coat of arms) sets out as a knight-errant, falls in love at first sight with the Princess of Naples, Magilena, and wins her affection; the lovers become separated and, after long adventures, are reunited. The scribe can find no other words for the central love theme in the work than colourless expressions from the chancery language: Petr *preklonilsja na vsju ljubov*, he hoped for *zakonnogo braka*, also Magilena *pomyšljaet ... k supružeskomu delu* (completely bowed himself before love, a lawful matrimony, thinks about matrimonial affairs). The sentiments are described by external symptoms: tears, cries, etc. Some passages are put in a religious (Christian) vein. The passages concerning knightly virtues and customs are the most adequately rendered.

Of French origin, too, is the story of *Meljuzina*, likewise a medieval novel which came to Russia through Latin and Polish versions, and was translated in

1677 by an official, I. Rudanśkyj (presumably an Ukrainian), who wrote poor Church Slavonic, with numerous Polonisms and Ukraininisms. The content consists of a fable (in its French version utilised for genealogic purposes): Count Rajmund marries Meljuzina, who at times turns into a fantastic creature (half woman – half serpent). When her husband learns this and reproaches her, she disappears. Meljuzina bore six sons, all of whose appearance was extraordinary. The greater part of the novel is devoted to their adventures. The translator was able to render well the Christian, but only clumsily the knightly, motifs.

The story of *Bruncvik* descends from the Czech medieval poem *Štilfríd a Bruncvík* through the intermediary of the Czech chap book (1565). Only the second part was translated, namely the story of Bruncvik, who experienced various adventures in the company of a lion whose effigy later entered into the coat of arms *Regni Bohemiae*. The numerous fable-motifs of the story (the bird griffin – in Russian *nog*, multi-headed dragons, the liberation of a girl from a dragon, the miraculous sword, etc.) are reminiscent of the corresponding motifs in Russian fables, which have not, however, been utilised by the translation. The language is fairly correct Church Slavonic.

Another story is also certainly of Czech origin and translated through a Polish intermediary (the Czech and Polish texts however are unknown to this day). It is the novel of *Vasilij Korolevič Zlatovlasyj Češskija zemli* ("Vasilij the Golden-Haired, the Czech Royal Prince"). This unhistoric prince, son of an equally unhistoric king, lives in Prague; Bohemia is a dependency of France. The story of the prince is told with fantastic details; the French princess Polimestra refuses to marry him, but Vasilij shows himself a shrewd and cunning man and wins finally the hand of the proud maiden. Unfortunately, one cannot judge how the translation is related to the original, but a great number of proverbial expressions, the vocabulary and the phraseology of everyday speech (*pojlo, dvoriško, opočin deržat'*, *tert kalač* – beverage, small property, to rest, "a ground cake" – a metaphor with the sense of "an experienced man") allow us to assume that the translator had made additions of his own, and had used the vernacular,

The *Historia Apollonii Tyri*, renowned all over the world, is a medieval redaction of the Hellenistic tale and came to Russia again through a Czech intermediary. The subject-matter consists of a whole series of adventures, which deal at first with the incestuous relation of "Tsar Antioch" with his daughter, then with the fate of "King Apolonij", who is pursued by Antioch, lives through involved adventures, is separated at first from his wife and daughter and then finds them again after a long search. The translation is in a simple style and uses Church Slavonic vocabulary. The text is somewhat shortened, probably on moral grounds, but the erotic motifs (Apolonij's wedding) are sometimes well rendered. Another translation of the same tale formed part of the *Gesta Romanorum* (see further, § 7).

Besides this novel there were also a few other translations, all of which derive from the then obsolete West European works, and mostly go back directly to Polish versions. In part they were certainly for a time the reading-matter of the upper classes (there were even copies in the Tsar's library). Later, some of them were revised, in a few instances becoming part of the religious writings, in others of the real popular tales, a few themes being made into the first theatrical plays (see VII, 9). One can also observe their influence on the fable tradition, perhaps even on the *stariny*. And even in modern times there exist poetical versions of them (A. M. Remizov).

7. Larger collections of mainly short tales appear also in translation. They were mostly very old; this certainly was very often the case with the short anecdotal tales.

Aesop's Fables, already known in part, were translated twice (cf. VI, 2, 4). The German A. Vinnius in 1674 translated 133 fables with comments from German into Church Slavonic (with some mistakes). In 1675 P. Kaminskij translated 233 fables from Polish into a relatively smooth language including some Polonisms.

Velikoe Zercalo ("The Large Mirror") is a collection of short instructive stories, already assembled in the 12th century, which had grown into 2,000 stories by the 16th century (under the title of *Speculum Magnum*). Since 1621 Polish translations had repeatedly been printed. The Russian translation omitted many of the stories (there remained about 270) and also the comments. Many of the stories have a Christian and ascetic orientation.

More artistic were the *Rimskie dejanija* (*Gesta Romanorum* – "Roman Stories", which certainly had nothing to do with historic Rome), a collection of longer tales among which was that of Apolonij Tirskij (see § 6). The collection was made in the 13th century, and by the 16th century the number of stories had grown to over 150. The Polish translations retained only thirty-nine of them. The Russian edition of 1681 is compiled from the Polish edition of 1663 (lost), and probably through the intermediary of an (equally unknown) Byelo-Russian translation. The stories, many of which have a secular character, are accompanied by instructions. One of the best known is that of Emperor Evinian. This over-proud Evinian, while hunting once, had to enter a river; he took off his clothes and then could not find them. Meanwhile, however, an angel had assumed his shape, so that the real Emperor had to lead the life of a vagabond deprived of property and dignity, until he came to the realisation of his unworthiness and then could resume his position (cf. VII, 8, 8). The secular character of the majority of the stories contributed considerably to the popularity of *Rimskie Dejanija*.

Collections of smaller anecdotes included a humorous miscellany translated from Polish *Facecie Polskie* (1617 – "Polish Jokes)", with inserted verse and instruction, at a time when emphasis was put on the stories themselves, which were not only secular but also frequently obscene.

In the same way the translation of the Polish *Apophthegmata* by Beniasz Budny transmitted to the Russian reader the best-known anecdotes linked with the names of the ancient philosophers and historic personalities. There is no lack of instruction here either, but they are practical rather than moral.

These collections were much copied, individual stories were also singled out from them and printed since the 18th century as complete collections, or produced as single-page prints. Many individual themes and motifs have entered folk-lore, but, as is often the case with anecdotes, as many of them were already known from other popular tales or Byzantine tradition, the question of the influence on folk-lore is difficult to decide. In contrast to the chivalric character of the novel, the shorter stories are mostly of bourgeois origin. They have also descended in Russia into the lower stratum of literature. They were certainly often used up to the middle of the 18th century as "Examples" (*Exempla*) in the sermons, or provided themes for poetry (*Virši* = poems).

3. HAGIOGRAPHIC LITERATURE

1. Some scholars describe the 17th century as the period of "the decline of Russian piety", for indeed there lived in that century only a few pious people, who later were canonized. Also, there was little hagiographic activity. The legends were much copied, and by the end of the century the Old Believers had rewritten some of them substantially (for example Maksim Grek's Life).

2. Two large hagiographic works were, to be sure, produced by individual men. Since Makarij's Menaea were inaccessible, there were attempts to create new, more handy ones. Already in 1632 a monk, German Tulupov, concluded his Reading Menaea; they consisted of a collection of old texts, from which Tulupov, too, like Makarij, selected various legends of the same saints. But unlike Makarij's Menaea, Tulupov's contained exclusively hagiographic texts.

Somewhat later, between 1646–54, a priest, Ioann Miljutin, also created a Menaea. He zealously collected particular legends of Russian saints (his Menaea contained over 100 of them). Miljutin not only took care in collecting the texts, but also saw to it that the character of his work should be uniform. Thus he shortened and revised the texts of the legends both grammatically and stylistically.

However, neither of the two collections enjoyed any popularity. Only the printed work of the Ukrainian, St. Dmitrij Tuptalo of Rostov (VII, 6, 2), was able to replace all the other Menaea texts. The Reading Menaea of St. Dmitrij was, to be sure, under the influence of western hagiography.

The paterikon of the Solovki Monastery was also a compilation (VI, 3, 4).

3. Almost none of the individual 17th-century Lives have been published and in most cases have been only insufficiently examined. There were, first of all, new revisions of old legends (e.g. the legend of St. Metropolitan Aleksej by Pachomij the Serb). The new legends were frequently written with reference to original sources. But St. Dmitrij's work remained, as regards historical thoroughness, unique. Various smaller supplements to and improvements on old legends, even the omission of "offending" passages, the collection of new miracles which supplemented the old legends, were everywhere continued, without producing any significant result.

As already mentioned, the 17th-century Lives remained mostly in manuscript form; therefore the history of literature must content itself with these brief references based on scattered remarks made by the few scholars who have seen the manuscripts.

4. THE TALES

1. The Russian term *povesti* covers works of various kinds in 17th-century Russian literature, namely stories which, owing to their intricate plot, may correctly be designated as novels; tales which are no more than somewhat long fables; themeless genre scenes; parodies; even poems, etc.

In looking for their common characteristics, we may notice that most of those which have been referred to are in themselves by no means "common"; that not all of them bear an exclusively "secular" character throughout (the most typical novella *Savva Grudcyn* was even written perhaps by its author as a religious work, see § 2). The attempts to find in them a depiction of "new men" (thus the Soviet scholars) are not convincing (see below); the writers also often maintain the point of view of traditionalism. Perhaps the only common feature of these "novels" is that they depict fictitious heroes, this not being customary before then (V, 6, 11).

Their origin is also very obscure. In some of them one may find traces of subjects and motifs borrowed from translated works; we may presume in some a link with folk-lore, which is, however, unfortunately unknown to us for the period concerned; one can also think of the recording of actual happenings (*Frol Skobeev*, see § 3). Also the social class of both the author and reader is obscure. The difficulties of research are further magnified by various circumstances. As their text had no sacred character, the copyists handled it much more freely than they did religious writings. Thus the copies differed greatly one from another, making the work of the editor more difficult, and the published versions of the majority of the tales are most unsatisfactory. Dating is indeed difficult, and exact dating is often impossible. In endeavouring to fill up the literary "vacuum" under Peter I, the Soviet scholars are now attempting (on insufficient grounds) to shift the origin of some tales to this period (cf. VII, 1, 7 and VII, 11, 1).

In any case, the tales reveal the change in the interests of the reader, and we may assume with great probability the appearance of a new class of readers whom the writers took into account. This new class was composed of merchants, townsmen, and even peasants, who, until the 19th century, remained the consumers of this literature, as well as of the novellas written later, and who collected, copied and often revised the tales.

As mentioned, the question of the relation of the "original" tales to the translated ones is very difficult. We do not know which is to be dated earlier in Russian tradition, the translated tale or its "original" counterpart. Some novels have a migratory theme, so that we may assume that the original tale was based on an older oral tradition, even though a translated parallel to it exists. The presence of a similar story in modern folk-lore cannot help us, as it could have arisen on the foundation of a translated tale ("*gesunkenes Kulturgut*").

No matter how one regards the origin of the novella literature, it differs little in its subdivisions and nature from the store of novels of the baroque literature of other Slav countries and of the West. It certainly differs little from the works of the "lower" literary stratum which, because of the existence of the "higher" one, is called "bourgeois" and "popular". Moscow still had no artistic prose belonging to the "higher" stratum, and did not acquire it until the middle of the 18th century.

Most of the tales are very short. Naturally, the length of a work is in no way a token of its quality. It is, however, an important symptom of the degree of literary development. Let us recall the vast works of Old Russian literature. To a certain extent, recent scholars want to create a "great literature" out of the small and, from a literary point of view, unimportant works: if every one-page short story is designated as a novel, one can reach astronomical figures in Western European literature of the same time.

2. The tale of Savva Grudcyn is held in very high esteem. One speaks about its "realism", its erotic plot; it is called the "Russian Faust". All this is not so. The "novel" is quite archaic, and it is not entirely impossible that it was written simply as a story of the miracle of an icon of the Holy Virgin.

It originated not earlier than the end of the 1660's, as the Polish siege of Smolensk (1662–64) appears in it, and some later features are present in the vocabulary. The numerous copies (about eighty) differ greatly in detail one from another. However, the subject-matter and its development are always the same.

The content is as follows. The Kazan' merchant Foma Grudcyn has a son, Savva. He sends him to Solikamsk while he himself travels to Persia. Savva stops on the way in the city of Orel Solikamskij, where a friend of his father, Bažen, invites him to his home. Bažen has a wife who becomes corrupted by "the enemy of mankind – the devil" "into abominable and lecherous intercourse" with the young man. Savva "fell into the net of adultery with this woman and carried on insatiable lechery with this woman," "all the time he rolled like a swine in the dirt of lechery ... a long time, like a beast". However, when on the eve of a holiday Savva declines the advances of the woman, she gives him a love potion, "and as if a fire started to burn in his heart" he starts "to long in his heart ... for this woman". But she slanders Savva, so that Bažen sends him away from his house. One day Savva goes out of the town "for a walk because of his great sorrow and sadness", thinking only of this woman and thinking that he would be prepared to serve even the devil, if only the latter would reunite him with her. He then sees a handsome youth who introduces himself as a merchant's son, makes Savva sign a document in which Savva renounces Christ, and promises to Savva the woman's "love". Immediately Bažen invites Savva again into his house and the latter can again "roll in the dirt of lechery like a swine". The letters of Savva's mother and father, who have meanwhile returned, have no influence on him.

The handsome youth, now Savva's boon companion, reveals to him one day that in reality he is the son of an emperor and wants to show him the realm of his father. The author himself is amazed that Savva had not thought that "there was no empire so near the Moscow State". The magnificent city receives them; in the palace, the "Emperor" is seated on a richly adorned throne, and Savva hands him the already mentioned document. Some features of this realm of Satan are traditional, but prettily depicted are the dark-skinned guard at the gates, the winged imperial body-guard, and so on; Savva's new friend explains to him that they are representatives of various exotic races who belong to his father's empire.

In the meantime, Savva's father sets out for Orel to search for his missing son. On learning this, the Devil suggests to Savva a journey, which Savva is immediately ready to undertake. The journey constitutes the second part of the tale. Although in the course of the journey "a poor saintly old man" draws Savva's attention to the fact that his companion is a devil, Savva continues to wander further with the devil, allows himself to be enrolled in the tsar's army, performs heroic deeds and even becomes known to the tsar. Savva falls ill in Moscow; as he calls for a priest and confesses to him, the friendly devil abandons him and Savva is tormented by demons. Savva prays to the Virgin Mary, who appears to him in company of the Apostles Peter and John and tells him to visit a certain church on the feast day of the icon of Virgin Mary of Kazan'. During the service, the document signed by Savva falls from above. Savva is cured, becomes a monk and lives in a monastery for several more years.

This tale is distinguished by the fact that it relates so thoroughly the temptations of a *layman*. There is no trace of any psychological description; the whole plot is set in motion only by the Devil, and Savva is no more than a completely passive pawn. Moreover, he abandons his beloved without a word of protest and follows the devil even after he has learned who he is. Neither is Savva's salvation motivated; the Virgin

воⷮстыхъ оⷮца нашеⷢ҇ѡ , преѡ҇
сщеннагѡ архїепкпа а́леѯі́а
митрополи́та кіеⷡ҇вⷭ҇скаⷢ҇ѡ
и всеѧ́ роси́и , новаⷢ҇ѡ чюдоⷮбо
рⷮца . бⷧ҇гви оⷮче ∶
ль́ма оу́бо нѧ́же ѿ бⷤⷤе
ственыⷯ҇ мꙋⷤꙗⷤе , по∙
вⷧ҇сть хотѧ́ще пи́сати ,

TITLE-PAGE OF A COPY OF THE SAINT'S LEGEND OF THE SAINT, METRO-
POLITAN ALEKSEJ OF MOSCOW

Beginning of the 17th century. The lower right-hand corner is cut.

ST. VASILIJ BLAŽENNYJ (THE BLESSED), FOOL IN CHRIST

An icon of the 17th century. A typical icon composition of the departuring 16th century and of the 17th century, in the style of the so-called "Stroganov school" of icon painting.

Mary appears as a *dea ex machina*, without Savva's having uttered a single word of repentance. Also the "erotic motifs" are hardly mentioned. The author knows only one formula for love: "to roll in the dirt of lechery like a swine", which is repeated several times. On no account can one speak of the "delicate, lyrical (!) tones", as has recently been the case. One can designate Savva as a "new man" only if one can deceive oneself into thinking of 16th-century Russia as an idyllic state.

The language, too, contains only few lexical elements which are representative of the new period. There is an attempt to date the origin of the tale to the time of Peter I on the basis of two single words which only later appear in writing: but the words *ekzercicija* and *komanda* could have been known without being part of the written language as there had been foreign soldiers in Moscow (since the 16th century). The language is, on the whole, archaic and even made so deliberately. The depiction of a few traits from the everyday life of merchants is also no novelty (cf. *Domostroj*, VI, 10, 6). The conclusion, which compositionally belongs to the tale, too, comprises numerous formulas of the ecclesiastical language and makes one think of the author as of a spiritual or spiritually educated person who certainly was a "conservative".

3. In a quite different vein is the second of the best known tales – *Frol Skobeev*. It originated still later, as the action is set in the tale itself in 1680. The content is typical of a "picaresque novel". The hero, whom the author depicts with sympathy, is a man with no moral principles who enjoys the greatest possible success.

There lived in the Novgorod district a poor nobleman, Frol Skobeev, who was engaged in minor legal activities. When he learned that a rich landowner, a neighbour of his, a court official (*stol'nik*), Nardin-Naščekin, had a daughter Annuška, Frol decided "to make love to her". No mention is made of Frol's other motives, nor of Annuška's good looks, nor of any other erotic motivation. Frol begins by bribing Annuška's nurse (*mamka*). Then, as his sister is invited to visit Annuška, he accompanies her in the disguise of a girl and seduces Annuška with the help of the nurse. When the Naščekins leave for Moscow, he follows them with the intention of either marrying Annuška or perishing in the attempt: *ili budu polkovnik, ili pokojnik* ("I shall be either a colonel or a corpse"). Through the nurse he learns in Moscow that Annuška is to visit a sister of Naščekin in a convent. He borrows from a noble acquaintance of his (also a *stol'nik*) a good carriage and fetches Annuška. He marries her and awaits further developments.

In the meantime Naščekin learns that Annuška had not arrived at the convent. A "proclamation" is made of Annuška's disappearance. Then Frol sets out to the nobleman from whom he had borrowed the carriage, succeeds in extracting from him the promise that he will ask Naščekin to forgive them; otherwise Frol threatens to denounce him as an accomplice in the abduction. The angry Naščekin decides finally to forgive his daughter, for "what is done cannot be undone". He sends her his blessing, then, as the Tsar, too, urges reconciliation with Frol, he reconciles himself with him completely and makes him gifts of property and money. Frol ends his days "in great fame and riches".

Frol is designated by the author himself and by the characters as a "thief and a rogue" (*vor i plut*), but nevertheless the sympathies of the narrator are entirely on his side. There is no trace of love on the part of Frol; he considers the marriage only as good business. Annuška, however, feels towards him *žalost'* ("compassion", but probably to be translated, however, as "love"). But Annuška acts towards her parents not differently than does Frol. In order to mollify them she pretends to be ill and so on. On no account is Frol a "new man"; his aim, which he indeed achieves, is precisely the same kind of life as that of Nardin-Naščekin – the life of a rich landowner.

It is the author of the tale, however, who is a "new man". But his work may have been written only at the time of Peter I; words like "proclamation", "register" (*reestr*), "lackey", etc., point to this. Otherwise, the language is simple, with strong elements of the vernacular and with some vulgarisms. Also the readers whom the author had in mind certainly belonged to a new class which earlier had shown no interest in literature.

4. A demonological novella, a favourite genre of baroque literature, is the tale about the possessed Solomonija, daughter of a priest from Ustjug. Demons have held sway over her since her wedding night; they appear to her either as "handsome youths", or in their true guise, or as animals; and they live with her for many years. She has even given birth to devils' children. She is cured on the same feast day of the icon of Virgin Mary of Kazan' as Savva Grudcyn. The devils are quite corporeal, there is no question of any spiritual temptation of Solomonija. The tale probably reflects the popular conception of devils. From the literary point of view, the tale is quite weak, and its language is the somewhat simplified language of religious works. It is notable that the tale ends with a miraculous salvation; as in the novella of Savva Grudcyn, this is evidence of the new literary genre developing within the old framework (here, the miracle-stories).

5. The folk-lore tales seem to have been less successful; the two most interesting of these are extant each in a single copy.

The first, concerning Karp Sutulov, is a revised popular fairy-tale, known in the East as well as in the West. While the rich merchant Sutulov is travelling on business, three men aspire to the love of his beautiful wife Tatjana: a merchant, a priest and an archbishop. She invites them to her house, all at about the same time; pretending that her husband is returning, she hides them in chests. She brings these trunks, as containing precious things, to the *vojevoda*, and there allows the men to get out.

The story is ably narrated, with various artifices of the popular tale: triple repetition, which slows down the action, and climaxes. The literary art of the author includes the parodying of ecclesiastical speech. The language contains only a few popular elements, even in dialogue. In any case, the author intended to write the Church Slavonic of that time.

A love dialogue between *Molodec i devica* ("A Young Man and a Maiden") utilises the heavy erotic symbolism of folk-lore in the framework of a conversation piece which changes the "height" of its style according to the content.

The date and the origin of the *Skazanie o Kievskych bogatyrech* ("Story of the Kievan Heroes") cannot be determined. In this tale the heroes of *stariny* and otherwise unknown heroes of Prince Vladimir's suite undertake a campaign against Constantinople, where the enemies of Kiev, known to us from the *stariny*, serve the Emperor. These enemies are conquered, but the work ends with a friendly visit of Tugarin (III, 9, 3) to Kiev. The tale repeats literally several formulas of the *stariny*; it seems, however, to have been written by a well-read man who did not use any one particular *starina*.

6. The tale "*O gore zločastii*" ("Sorrow-Misfortune"), remarkable for its verse form, is extant in only one manuscript. Its content consists of the depiction of how misfortune pursues man. The long introduction speaks of the fall of man, of his evil life after the fall, and then of how ...

> И за то на них Господь Бог разгневался,
> положил их в напасти великия,
> напустил на них скорби великия,
> и срамныя позоры немерныя,
> безживотие злое, сопостатные находы,
> злую, немерную наготу и босоту,
> и безконечную нищету, и недостатки последние,
> все смиряючи нас, наказуя
> и приводя нас на спасенный путь.

("God became angry with them; for this the plunged them into great calamity, struck them with great sorrow and boundless ignominious disgrace, evil penury, enemy invasions, evil, immeasurable nakedness, infinite wretchedness, and extreme want, thus making us humble, instructing us, and bringing us on the way of salvation.")

A "young man" (*molodec*) is instructed by his parents; their daily instructions are not to drink, or allow himself to be led astray by beautiful women, to have no evil friends, not to be a deceiver, etc. Of course, the "young man" wants to live "as it pleases him". In the first place, he earns some money, but a friend makes him into a drunkard, and he is robbed. He is ashamed to face his parents and wanders abroad. He goes to a banquet, at which he sits sadly, and, on being asked the reason for his sadness, he replies:

> Укротила скудость мой речистой язык,
> изсушила печаль мое лицо и белое тело, –
> ради того мое сердце невесело,
> а белое лицо унывливо,
> и ясные очи замутилися, –
> все имение и взоры у меня изменилися,
> отечество мое потерялося,
> храбрость молодецкая от мене миновалася.

("Penury has tamed my talkative tongue, grief has withered my face and white body – that is why my heart is not joyful, my fair face sad, my clear eyes clouded, my appearance and my glance are changed, the honor I inherited from my father is lost, and my youthful courage has abandoned me.")

The "good people" give him advice: not to be proud, to submit himself to friend and enemy, to respect young and old, and in all things to be humble. The young man becomes rich again and decides to get married. He brags of his success in front of his guests and friends. Sorrow-Misfortune hears this and soliloquises: "I had already to do with men more clever and ingenious than you, but I am through with them." They struggled against misfortune until death overtook them and they could save themselves from it only in the grave. Misfortune appears to the young man in a dream, and again in the guise of Archangel Gavriil (Gabriel) and persuades him to live in poverty:

> Да не бьют, не мучат нагих, босых,
> и из раю нагих, босых не выгонят,
> а с тово свету сюды не вытепут,
> да никто к нему не привяжется. . .

("The naked and the bare-footed are not beaten and not tormented; the naked and the bare-footed are not driven out of Paradise; they are not pushed out of the other world into this one; no one will have anything to do with them [no one will enter into relationship with them].")

The young man squanders his property in drink and proceeds further on his wanderings. When he is on the point of committing suicide, Sorrow-Misfortune appears to him:

> босо, наго, нет на Горе ни ниточки,
> еще лычком Горе подпоясано.

("Bare-footed, naked, no thread remains on her [Sorrow], she is girded with a bast belt.")

Sorrow-Misfortune reminds the young man that he did not follow the advice of his parents "and he who does not listen to the wise instructions of his parents, has to learn from me, Unfortunate Sorrow." After that Sorrow-Misfortune follows the young man everywhere:

> Полетел молодец ясным соколом,
> а Горе за ним белым кречетом;
> молодец полетел сизым голубем,
> а Горе за ним серым ястребом;
> молодец пошел в поле серым волком,
> а Горе за ним з борзыми выжлецы...
> . . . .
> Пошел молодец в море рыбою,
> а Горе за ним с частыми неводами...

("The young man flew as a falcon,
and Misfortune behind him as a white vulture;
the young man flew like a grey dove,
and Misfortune behind him as a grey hawk;
the young man ran into the open fields as a grey wolf,
and Misfortune behind him with rapid hounds;
. . . .
The young man plunged into the sea like a fish,
and Misfortune went after him with tight fishing nets.")

Sorrow-Misfortune advises the young man "to kill and to rob"; the young man, however, comes to his senses, regains the "road of salvation," and goes into a monastery. Misfortune remains in front of the "sacred gates, she will not be able to follow the young man any more". Two lines of prayer conclude the work.

The character of this tale is highly controversial. It is considered a draft of a *bylina* or of a religious song. But surely it is the work of a writer, a "well-read man" (*knižnik*). It is of note that here, too, as in the tales of Savva Grudcyn and Solomonija, the unusual theme is worked into the framework of traditional moralising, this being intimated even in the title, "How Sorrow-Misfortune brought the young man to monkhood". The unusual form, however, resembles that of the *byliny;* the lines with an odd number of syllables have mostly four accents. The author took over a series of set formulas from the *byliny*. Still more important are the general features of folk poetry: the repetition of prepositions, viz.: *za pit'ja za p'janye, na zemlju na niskuju* (intoxicating drinks, on the low earth); double words: *ukrasti-ograbiti, rod-plemja, p'jany-vesely* (to steal-rob, race-tribe, drunk-merry); the popular synonyms: *nevesel ... kruči-novat, skorben, neradosten* (sad ... worried, full of grief, unhappy); the *epitheta ornantia*: *zeleno vino, dubovyj stol, beloe telo, jasnye oči, čistoe pole, jasnyj sokol, seryj volk*, and so on (green [new] wine, an oak-table, white body, clear eyes, open field, clear [dear] falcon, grey wolf); a few adages, perhaps proverbs: *gnilo slovo pochval'noe* (boastful speech is rotten), etc. In vocabulary and morphology the Church Slavonic elements are almost entirely non-existent.

Most striking, however, are the beautiful imagery, even when it is broken by less successful lines; the attempt at psychological characterisation; and the lack of otherwise conventional concrete characteristics of time, place and even names of heroes. This last makes this tale in verse the first attempt at "typification" known to us. The hero, as also the author, shows hardly any noticeable features of the new times. The figure of Sorrow-Misfortune is related to the popular conception of personified "fortune" (*dolja);* its role, however, is not clearly outlined, perhaps because the author reckoned with the generally known concepts. In any case Sorrow-Misfortune interfered in the fate of the hero only after his bragging, a theme which also appears in fairy-tales.

Of another tale in verse there has survived a single copy only of the final section (eleven chapters). As each chapter is marked with a letter of the Church Slavonic alphabet – and as far as possible opens with the same letter – it may be assumed that about twenty-seven chapters have been lost. The final section is the love story of a maiden (narrated in the first person) who in the end is married, against her will, to another man, but still continues the relation with her first lover. The imagery is, on the whole, primitive. The language is reminiscent of folk-lore in some of the turns of phrase; in a number of passages there are proverbial (non-rhymed) insertions; the Church Slavonic elements are very slight. The verse is rhymed; the rhymes are mainly verb-rhymes; the lines are irregular in length, and each of them usually contains two accents, rarely more. Here is an example – after the betrothal –:

> Любезной не знает,
> весточки ожидает.
> Отец мой поспешает,
> свадьбу понуждает.
>
> . . . .
>
> Стали из за стола вставати,
> Богу поклон отдавати.
> Руку мою принимали,
> жениху отдавали.
> Немилой ручку принимает,
> крепко зжимает.

("The beloved does not know, he waits for a word [from me]. The Father hurries and presses with the wedding. —— They began to get up from the table, and to pray to God. They took my hand and gave it to the bridegroom. The unloved one takes the hand and presses it hard.")

In an unusual way, the tale ends with moralising lines – an homage to tradition.

7. Of little interest are a few historical tales which transfer popular subject-matter onto some historic person or place or event. Let us take, for example, the tale of the foundation of Moscow, which appeared in the second half of the 17th century. Its versions are so varied that one may speak of three different tales.

One of these recounts that a boyar, Kučko (or Kučka, the name recurs in all the three versions) possessed estates near the river Moskva. His two handsome sons are taken into service by the Suzdal' Prince as courtiers; they have an affair with the Prince's wife and decide to kill the Prince. The Prince attempts to flee, but is caught by the murderers. The tutor of the Prince's son, however, escapes with the Prince's child to the Prince of Vladimir, who wreaks his vengeance upon the murderers and the Princess, and founds the city of Moscow on the site of Kučko's estate.

The author, who sought a connection with various types of chronicle and legend styles, created a typical slight historical adventure tale in a colourful style and with loosely connected parts. The love theme is rendered in the style of the tale of Savva Grudcyn, the language being deliberately made archaic, sometimes unsuccessfully.

8. Much more significant are the four stories concerning a contemporary event – the capture of the Turkish fortress of Azov on the estuary of the Don. Three of them must have originated after 1645. Azov was captured by the Don Cossacks in 1637. In 1641 the fortress was unsuccessfully besieged by the Turkish Sultan and the Crimean Tartars, but after the withdrawal of enemy troops, it was cleared of Cossacks at the command of the Tsar.

These events served as basic material for the four stories: first, for the almost unadorned "*historical*" story which depicted only the events of 1637; then for the "*documented*" story which depicts the 1641 siege; then a "*poetic*" story which renders the same siege in a very ornate style; and finally, after 1669, when the Cossacks fought against the Persians, a new redaction of the Azov tales in which the events of the years 1668–9 were transferred to Azov – this is the "*fabulous*" redaction (the classification is that of A. Orlov). We shall examine closely only the poetic version; it must be noted that the existence of four works in differing styles provides evidence of the developed sense of style of their authors, that is to say, these unknown writers were capable of presenting the same material in various styles. Moreover, at least three redactions must have originated in the Don district, that is, in the provinces.

The poetic Azov tale is introduced as a report of 1642 to Tsar Mikhail, but the content corresponds in no way to this form. After factual information concerning the Turkish and the Cossack armies, the poetic part starts. The author uses the older military tales and certainly, too, folk-lore. The description of the siege begins thus: "All our open fields are occupied by the Tartar hordes. Where we had open steppes, there appeared in one hour, owing to their vast numbers, large and inpenetrable forests. Because of their large armies and the riding of their horses, the earth began to shake and quake near Azov; and because of their great weight the waters of the Don stepped forth onto its banks. ..." The description of the enemy troops is even more in the style of the old military tales: "As if a big storm hung over us"; "the standards were like large clouds"; the trumpets sounded "as if terrible beasts howled above our heads with many voices". The red armour of the Turks "appeared like the dawn-glow" and their helmets glittered "like stars". An envoy comes to the Cossacks, addressing them in these words: "You are in the desert, escorted by no one, and sent there by no one; you move without fear, like eagles hovering in mid-air; you run like fierce lions in the desert ... you, sly inhabitants of the desert, unjust murderers and merciless bandits." The demands of the Turks are depicted with similar minuteness and flourishes. Just as detailed is the answer of the Cossacks, with some stylistic embellishments such as: the Sultan, "foul infidel, heathen dog, vicious cur, does not trust in God as his helper, but puts his trust in his transitory wealth; his father – the Devil – raised his pride to the skies, but for this God will pluck him from the heights and will plunge him for eternity into the abyss." In this speech the Cossacks complained, too, that they had no assistance from the Moscow Tsar. They refused to negotiate. Then follows the description of the Turkish siege of the stronghold, again with variations of the old formulas: the "standards flourish", they are "like many flowers"; "In the fire and smoke they could not see each other, on both sides there was fire and smoke. ... This is a real celestial storm with thunder and lightning." After the thorough and sometimes dry description of further enemy assaults follows a poetic lament to the Tsar. During the night there appear to many in their dreams the Virgin Mary and a saint (in other redactions they are instrumental in the victory), who encourage the Cossacks with a speech. After four months of inconclusive siege, the enemy troops retreat; they "flee with eternal shame, pursued by no one".

The tale ends with the Cossack offer to the Tsar to take possession of Azov. As already mentioned, this offer was rejected.

The tale elaborates old poetic material, the story by Nestor-Iskander of Constantinople's capture, the story of the rout of Mamai, Alexandreis, the Deeds of Troy, and also the Bible. As it is easy to perceive from the above-mentioned quotations, the old formulas have been taken over only contextually, the formulas are now varied and presumably blended with those of popular lore (open fields, dark forests, etc.). The language has rather few Church Slavonic elements. The tale is a successful attempt at reviving the old poetic tradition. Unfortunately, no other story of that time, dealing with events of the recent past, can be compared with it (the stories of the interregnum, the stories about the conquest of Siberia).

9. The satirical tales form a group of their own. The tale concerning the unjust judge Šemjaka was very popular. It seems to be derived from a fairy story; Polish origin, however, is also possible: one manuscript explicitly notes "From Polish Books". A poor peasant plucked the tail from a borrowed horse, fell from a suspension work (*polati*) on the child of a priest and killed him, tried to commit suicide, jumped from a bridge and killed an old man with his falling body. During the trial, he showed the judge Šemkaja a small bag. The judge, thinking that the purse contained money, passed an absurd judgement, that the poor peasant should keep the horse until a new tail grew, that he should beget a child with the wife of the priest, that the son of the man killed should jump from the bridge on the peasant. Thereupon the accusers waived their claim and decided not to press the carrying out of the sentence. The purse, however, did not contain money but a stone with which the accused wanted to kill the judge. The language of the story is simple; the interest lies only in the plot.

Much more artistic is the other famous story, extant in many variants. This is the law suit against a Ruff (*Erš*) accused by a Bream (*Lešč*). It is an ingenious parody of legal proceedings, written in the official language, with cunning answers by the accused, who was alleged to have crowded out the plaintiff in the Rostov lake. The linguistic art of the author consists in a clever imitation of the legal proceedings according to the 1649 code of Tsar Aleksej (this story was therefore written in the second half of the 17th century).

In some further tales we find equally clever imitation of ecclesiastical language. The language of didactic pamphlets is parodied in a dialogue between a fox and a cock, which ends with the fox, who had reproached the cock for his sins, devouring the "sinner". "The feast of drunkards" (*Prazdnik kabackich jaryžek*) is a parody on divine service; the author achieves a special effect by a mixture of Church language with deliberate vulgarisms.

There are some further satirical works aimed at monks and priests. It is futile to seek in them something like "anti-religious propaganda". Accusations of deterioration of spiritual standards could also come in 17th-century Russia from devout men, but still more so from the Old Believers. Interesting because of its vulgar language is "The Supplication of the Monks of Kaljazino", who complain to the Archbishop of Tver' about the "severity" of their abbot who does not allow them to drink and sets before them too little rich food. The "complaint" ends with a threat – written in rhyme – to quit the monastery.

Some satirical works deal with excessive drinking. Next to the Feast of the Drunkards there is a story also written in apocryphal style, of a drunkard who goes to heaven and of all the saints (Peter, David, Solomon, etc.) who do not want to admit him to Paradise; he reproaches them with their own sins which are greater than his. The Apostle John, who had written so much about love, lets the drunkard in. The above-mentioned Drunkards' Feast, like some other works, paints drunkenness in very gloomy colours, and might have been written with a didactic aim.

The most remarkable feature of the satirical tales is neither the content, which remains traditional, nor the ideology, which is non-existent, but the poetic form. In these satires there appears in its purest form that very characteristic which is at times apparent in some other tales of the period (Karp Sutulov, the Azov-tales, etc.) – namely the parody of language and composition. The anonymous authors imitate – frequently in a very fine way – the language of the divine service, of legal records, of diplomatic documents, and of religious literature. This should be considered only in part as evidence of the writers' inability to create a new poetic form. In the majority of cases, it is a deliberate and definite imitation of these genres and possibly of their subject-matter as well.

10. The two features, substantially new in Russian literature – the emergence of fictional heroes and the stylized parody of form and language – are very pronounced. Fantasy now breaks into literature, which so far (often unsuccessfully) had aimed at the presentation of reality alone. The "non-real" wins its place in writing next to the "real". And the elements of parody in 17th-century literature show not only the links of this literature with Western models which it is imitating, and with the poetic theory of the Baroque, which encouraged parody, but also are evidence of the fact that indigenous tradition (of the form and partly of the subject-matter too) was no longer inviolable and "sacred" for both authors and their readers. The scepticism of writers and readers should not be exaggerated, as it is by Soviet scholars. There is no doubt, however, that men who enjoyed such parody could not consider tradition too seriously, and that not all its aspects appeared equally important to them. This is a proof, if not of the emergence of "new men", at least of substantial changes in the psychology of certain circles. Unfortunately, this evidence is, as it were, purely negative, i.e., it tells us nothing of the *positive* ideals of these men with a different psychology, nor does it tell us whether they had any ideals at all. Positive evidence is to be sought elsewhere – and regrettably one does not find it in *belles-lettres*.

The variety of secular tale literature is naturally something quite new. Only few of them, however, are of a high standard. The majority are products which the author himself did not wish to be compared with works of old literature. And during the following century the tales are relegated to lower literary strata. To be sure, they still influence at times the novel of the second half of the 18th century. Even the meritorious novels of the 17th century suffer for the most part from unevenness of composition and language; the mixture of various layers of language makes them unpalatable for us, but even their contemporaries could hardly have been satisfied with them. There was need for either a decision in favour of a certain level of language or a clear-cut distinction between functions of the various levels. This need was met in the following century.

5. SIMEON POLOCKIJ

1. Baroque in a pure form was brought to Moscow by a Byelo-Russian, Simeon Petrovskij-Sitnianovič, known by the surname of Polockij, who was born in Byelo-Russia in 1629. He studied at the Kiev Academy, which at that time did not have an exclusively "clerical" character. "Poetics" were a branch of instruction at the Academy, as everywhere then, and mastering the poetic art was obligatory. In 1650 Polockij concluded his studies. He became a monk in Byelo-Russia, at Polock (hence his surname), and taught there at a school. He not only considered poetry a subject for study at school, but wrote verse himself. Thus, in 1656, he could greet with his own "metres" Tsar Aleksij, who visited Polock when it was occupied by the Russians. In 1659 he travelled with some pupils and clergy to Moscow and brought another greeting in verse to the Tsar's family. Also in Polock originated Simeon's first play, "The Dialogue of the Shepherds", a conversation in verse between two shepherds and the angel who brings them news of Christ's birth; at the end there is a "Hymn" probably sung by a choir. The verse ("Sapphic stanza", see § 4) flows smoothly; the language (with strong Ukrainian and Byelo-Russian elements) is concise. Similar dialogues, on the same theme, are extant in Ukrainian, Polish and Czech literature.

In 1663 Simeon was called to Moscow. Here he taught Latin and grammar to officials, and as chief clerk took part in the Council of 1667, which precipitated the schism in the Russian Church and which at the same time condemned Patriarch Nikon. Simeon wrote up the records of the Council. In the same year appeared his compilatory work *Žezl Pravlenija* ("The Sceptre of Government"), which contains a very sharp polemic directed against the Old Believers. The scholars of the Kiev Academy did not at all understand this opposition to the official Church; the Old Believers were for them merely "straying sheep" or "predatory wolves". Next he wrote a popular dogmatic theological treatise *Věnec věry* ("The Crown of Faith", about 1670) in which he tried to enliven the seriousness of the subject with subtle questions; then he composed various greeting-poems and elegies for the Tsar's family, became court preacher and tutor to the Tsar's children; Aleksej's successor, Tsar Fedor, was one of his pupils. Simeon wrote instructive poems for the latter and taught him the art of poetry. For the court theatre he wrote two plays, one of which,

"The Comedy of the Lost Son", appeared in print in 1685. Still earlier he had published a *Bukvar'* (in 1679, a first spelling book with a reader); he revised anew from the Latin the novel of "Varlaam and Josaphat" (cf. II, 10), which appeared in print; then he compiled two very extensive collections of his sermons, *Obĕd duševnyj* and *Večerja duševnaja* ("The Spiritual Midday Meal", "The Spiritual Evening Meal"), which also appeared in print (1681, 1683); his verse translation of the Psalter also was printed. Two enormous collections of poems, *Vertograd* ("The Garden") and *Rifmologion* remained in manuscript.

Polockij died in 1680. He was the first writer many of whose works could appear in print.

2. Simeon primarily used Latin literature as the basis for his works; he also read the works of the Greek Fathers in Latin translations. He often quotes in his works the Latin Fathers of the Church, particularly Augustine and Jerome, but also Hrabanus Maurus (9th century), Anselm of Canterbury (12th century), Gerson (14th–15th century), Baronius and Bellarmin (16th–17th century), and numerous lesser authors from Catholic literature. He became acquainted with Slavonic literature only to a limited extent. He was charged with Catholic views; however, he was not really a learned or implacable dogmatist and was able to maintain friendly relations in Moscow with the older Ukrainian, Epifanij Slavineckyj, who was opposed to Latin learning.

3. Dogmatic questions occupy a limited place, too, in Simeon's collected sermons. These, most of which he delivered at the court of the Tsar, are of a varied nature. The few existing printed texts seem not to have originated from the sermons which Simeon had delivered himself (the sermon of "a Shepherd (= bishop) who visited his Herd" and similar ones). The didactic sermons deal with the upbringing of children, which was connected with Simeon's activity in the Tsar's family; they deal with the imitation of Christ, the degrees of perfection, behaviour in church, superstitions. Numerous sermons are homilies, i.e., interpretations of texts from the Scriptures, mostly of an allegorical nature; also there are numerous sermons dealing with saints, in which the *Vitae* serve as examples of one or another virtue or virtuous mode of life (St. Sophia as widow, etc.), glorification often playing here a significant role. Simeon gives a few funeral sermons as models (sermons at the funeral of a soldier, a bishop, etc.).

Simeon's sermons are based, on one hand, on classical models, and on the other, on his Kievan studies. He was also familiar with the theory of the sermon of the Ukrainian preacher Ioannikij Galatovśkyj, demonstrated in his *Ključ razuměnija* ("The Key of Understanding", 1659, 1663, also reprinted in Moscow which Galjatovśkyj had visited). And with Simeon there begins in Moscow the reign of the baroque sermon, characterised by its artistic composition and the abundant use of stylistic adornments.

The plan of Simeon's sermon consists usually in a simple three-fold division, but this apparently simple construction is amplified in some instances by the technique of surprise and by individual unexpected turns. Simeon's range of themes is quite extensive; from the care of trees and the breeding of animals he passes to the education of men; or he depicts various professions in order to deal in the central part with the activity of a bishop, Chrysostomos serving here as his model; he also starts occasionally with a striking antithesis or with a eulogy, etc. In the central section, while the basic thoughts of the sermon are systematically expounded, Simeon gives great care to artistic transitions. Hence, in order to pass from the simple theme of the necessity of reading the Scriptures to further exposition Simeon employs a metaphor; the Scriptures are a spring, a spring can quench the thirst, but it can also become a torrential stream. Starting from this image, Simeon goes on to speak of the need and the dangers of reading the Scriptures. Or, in the sermon on the Apostle St. Peter, who is the rock, and St. Paul who is likened to a sword, he joins the two parts by the story of David's combat with Goliath. David has first hit Goliath with the stone from his catapult, then he cuts off his head with a sword, but Peter and Paul were the rock and sword of Christ, and so on. Metaphors help Simeon to develop his themes: when the Holy Scriptures are compared to a stone, a comparison with corals, magnets and diamond follows; or when the Bible is "God's House", this metaphor too is expanded: God lives in the soul of men, in the "visible Churches", in the "heavenly City", etc.

The real art of Simeon consists in the embellishments of his speech. He does not use an excessive number of examples, parallels, historical illustrations, etc. to enliven his exposition. He works with small ornamental devices. Metaphors are numerous, and in many instances he draws them from tradition (in the case of saints, for example, from Hymnology); some are original. A bad priest is a smoking candlestick, a darkened sun, a blind leader, a dog which cannot bark, etc. Simeon obviously takes some images from the "*emblemata*" of the period. He also employs hyperbole: the Christian zeal of the man of today is as far removed from the zeal of the martyrs "as earth from Heaven", and so on. Sometimes he raises his enthusiasm to a hyperoche: "No tongue could praise you in a worthy manner, no terrestrial spirit could sing of you, o Mother of God!" He is very fond of antitheses, harmonising them in long strings: "Bring forth the fruits worthy of penitence . . ; instead of evil fruit – good fruit, instead of lies – truth, instead of pride – humility; instead of avarice and greed – open-handedness, instead of dirt – cleanliness, instead of hate – love, instead of immoderate eating and drinking – temperance, instead of anger – peace, instead of indolence – diligence. ..." The antithesis is also raised to oxymoron: "Every sorrow here is sorrowless, every grief is griefless, effort is effortless, pain is painless, bile is sweet, fire is cool, arrows are blunt." He also uses gradations (climax), often in several stages. For further embellishment he uses exclamations, apostrophizing the person to whom the sermon is devoted, dialogue, and exhortations to the listener.

Simeon also makes liberal use of devices connected with individual words: inversions do not appear very frequently in his work, but he has an extraordinary liking for word-repetitions with which the long sentences are articulated, thus "He was a great High Priest, great because he was the shepherd of a great flock, great because ..." (the word "great" occurs another five times); "Everthing can be achieved with God by prayer" – and there follow nine short sentences all of which begin with the word "prayer". Thus parallelism occurs in a number of sentences; this effect Simeon is able to achieve elsewhere without resorting to word-repetition. Otherwise, in longer passages, he uses paranomasias: in a relatively short description (about twenty lines) of Christ's transfiguration, the words "light" and "lighten" occur six times each, as well as the words "illuminate", "illumination" and "light-like" (the Slavonic root *svět-*). He also applies individual paranomasias: *černěti i čermněti*; *orudija ... sut' oružija, ne učitelie, no mučitelie*; and also bolder ones: *dobrě i bodrě*; *glava ... prinesesja na bljude ... bludnoj Irodiade*; *množestvo sětej paučich, da nas naučit*, etc. (to become black and red; working tools are arms; not a teacher but a tormentor, good and merry; the head was brought in on a platter to the lecherous Herodias; a multitude of cobwebs, that he might teach us.) Rhymes are also relatively frequent, not only the customary verb-rhymes, but also noun-rhymes (*blato* : : *zlato*, *terpěnie* : : *spasenie* – dirt-gold, patience-salvation). Alliterations too are not lacking: *větru bujnomy vozvějavšu, vozmetajetsja prach ot lica zemli* (v-v-v), or *ta vsja slavy, jako solnečnyj svět, prevoschodit vsja pročaja světila světom* (V-s-s-sv-p-v-p-sv-sv) (when a violent wind blows, the dust from the earth starts whirling; this entire praise surpasses, like the sun's light, all other celestial bodies by its light). Especially characteristic of Simeon's language, which is almost entirely free from the Ukrainisms and Byelo-Rissicisms of his earlier years, are the compounds (*composita*), which appear not in hundreds but in thousands in both his of very extensive collections of sermons; among them, numerous compounds are created *ad hoc*, like: *volkoporažatel'nyj, zvěroobrazovatisja, korablelo-mitel'nyj, lžemertvyj, mnogokonniki, mjagkopostel'niki, ognekolesnik, ravnotvoritisja,* and even the four-fold compound: *bogoduchnovennocvěto-rodnyj* (the wolfkiller, to make oneself like a beast, the destroyer of ships, apparently dead, he who has many horses, he who has a soft bed, he who rides in a fiery carriage, to level oneself, inspired by God and producing flower).

These devices become still more frequent in the numerous adages which frequently appear in the concluding part of the sermon; among them there occur also real proverbs, like "There exists no Tsar who would not be God's servant"; "All things without God are quite useless"; "With time there comes also a change"; "Truth hits the eye", etc. Many of these sayings are certainly taken from old poetry or *Florilegia.* Thus Simeon also quotes occasionally a "saying of Horace".

Simeon did not say much that was new to his highly placed listeners, but he was capable of dressing his thoughts in a form which fully corresponded to the baroque taste, and of not deviating too much from tradition as far as content was concerned.

4. Simeon is of much greater significance in the history of Russian poetry. Even if only relatively few of his poems were accessible to his contemporaries, he transplanted the so-called syllabic poetry of the Poles, the Byelo-Russians and the Ukrainians to Moscow. Russian poetry followed his lead for eighty years.

The essence of syllabic poetry, as it was worked out in 16th-century Poland, consists in the equality of the number of syllables in every single line of a poem, or in the regular reappearance of lines of equal length. The lines were connected by rhyme, almost always in two consecutive lines. Under the influence of Polish poetry, the rhyme is exclusively feminine (i.e. one accented followed by one unaccented syllable rhyme: ´ –). In the long lines (often thirteen or fifteen syllables), as the rhythmic structure of the language does not appear distinctly enough, a caesura is used: the end of a word must always fall after a certain syllable, so that the lines are broken into shorter units. This type of poetry admitted multiple stanzas, and later, also a varied order of the rhyme. Following the model of Ukrainian poetry, the Great Russian syllabic poetry for a long time has used the rhyme *ě* :: *i* (ѣ :: и, *i*) (Ukrainian *ě* is equal to *i*).

An example from Polockij's "Dialogue of the Shepherds" will illustrate this system. God the Father sends Christ on earth:

и умилися милосердый отец,
видѣвши людей своихъ яко овецъ
преданныхъ смерти, кромѣ всея вины,
туне без цѣны.

("And the merciful Father took pity when He saw His men surrendered to death like sheep, without guilt, and to no purpose.")

This is the so-called "Sapphic stanza" which in syllabic poetry consists of three 11-syllable and one 5-syllable lines, the 11-syllable line having a caesura after the fifth syllable.

Polockij avoids the masculine rhyme (accent on the last syllable), this being considered "bad"; he very rarely employs the dactylic rhyme (accent on third syllable from the end: ′ x x).

5. All Polockij's poems are written solely in this verse-system, namely, the five smaller books of dedicatory poems (1665–76) and the two extensive collections, each of them comprising over a thousand poems, on which he worked in the last years of his life (some of these had undoubtedly been written earlier). To date, only a few poems have been published and no critical study of the collections has appeared. Simeon also wrote poems in Latin and Polish.

The first thing that strikes us in Simeon's poetic work is the variety of genres he represents. According to the ideas of baroque poetry, the greatest part of his poetic output was in the *nugae* genre (in Polish *fraszki*). These are epigrams, minor poems of varied content. We ought to regard them from our modern viewpoint. They are historical, religious, and quite naturalistic ballads, that is, smaller stories in verse; and the variety of their content can hardly be exhausted. The themes from antiquity are either historical or the particularly numerous religious ones, for instance, the theme of the grateful lion (from a Paterikon); of the sinful nun whose child was adopted by the Virgin Mary (there are later versions of this by Gottfried Keller and Maeterlinck); of a pilgrim brought home from Jerusalem by an angel in a few hours (a variant of the story of Ioann of Novgorod); of an icon of the Virgin, whose hand caught a pious painter and thus saved him from falling when the devil knocked down the scaffolding on which the painter was standing, etc. Simeon also produced realistic ballads, for example, a poem about a humble bishop who included the sign of his low origin in his coat of arms; or the one about the philosopher Thales, who, while observing stars, fell into a hole (from Plato). Such stories were often accompanied by short moral instructions, also in verse. There are also numerous satirical poems whose themes range from merchants, monks, and the detractors of education, to family life, the conduct of widows, etc. These satires either enumerate the shortcomings of a certain class of people (in merchants Simeon finds eight faults, all of which are different kinds of deception); or merely select some of the defects; or depict vivid scenes, like the conversation at night between a wife and husband: "This [woman] is dressed better than I; men pay her homage, while they pay no attention to me who am wedded to you ...", or "Why do you keep looking at that woman? What did you speak about with the maid-servant? You went visiting, tell me about that!" – or the complaints of women who feel themselves neglected. Simeon certainly did not need to observe much himself as he took his material for the satires in great part from earlier sources. Lyrical poems with any personal colouring certainly seem to be lacking in Simeon's work, with the exception of one poem which expresses his concern over the inadequate appreciation of poetry and the shortage of printing presses. A great part of his collections consists of epigrams in the proper sense of the word: short, pointed poems.

> Волхвы к немощным иже призывает,
>   врача небесна оные лишает.

("He who calls a sorcerer to the sick deprives them of the heavenly physician.")

> Яко цвет селный скоро отцветает,
>   тако человек век свой проживает.

("Just as quickly as a field-flower fades, thus man lives through his life.") This last epigram shows that Polockij sometimes used paranomasias: in the first line the syllable "-cvĕt-" is repeated, in the second "-vĕk-". In longer poems word-repetition or root-repetition sometimes appears throughout. In the ten lines of the epigram "Magnet", eleven words are repeated twice or thrice in consecutive lines. In the ten lines of the poem in honour of Tsar Fedor's wedding, the syllables "bog-, bož-" (God) are repeated six times, "blag-" – eight times, "dar-" five times, so that the whole poem becomes a tissue of similarly-sounding words, thus producing euphonic and semantic effects. The weakest are Simeon's festive poems, his "Odes" and "Elegies". Here he juggles with compounds almost as excessively as in the sermons.

But Simeon also paid his tribute to the poetic jests of the Baroque. His paranomasias approach the playful artifices of the Baroque. Simeon wrote many poems, however, which belong to the various types of this group. Poetic shapes are few: one poem is in the form of a heart, another in that of a star, two others have the shape of a cross. He also wrote poems with an "echo", in which various sentences of the poem echo each other, the last syllables of the preceding sentence giving the response. He wrote, moreover, a poem, both halves of which can be read separately, so that two further poems result. Another poem of his is still more complicated: the middle syllables of every line form the end of the line of the first poem and the beginning of the line of the second. This is how the beginning of the poem looks:

Надеждо	Ру	си	е привѣтство
Але	кси	е	же въ
	ца	ру	цѣ твои
Сего не	пре	зри	ащъ рабъ приносит
малѣй	ша	го	рѣ
	да	ру	цѣ свои

The first half sounds then:

> Надеждо Руси, Алексие цару,
> сего не презри малѣйшаго дару

("You, hope of Russia, Tsar Aleksej, do not disdain this smallest offering.") The second:

> Сие привѣтство, еже въ руцѣ твои
> зри, ащъ рабъ приносит горѣ руцѣ свои...

("This greeting, which is in your hands, resembles a servant who raises his hands to Heaven. ...")

Simeon also wrote so-called "macaronic" poems, in which various languages are mixed: Church Slavonic and Polish, or even Church Slavonic, Polish and Latin.

Simeon utilised numerous variants of the stanza in his poems, mainly in the Psalter-translations. We have mentioned already the "Sapphic stanza" as an example. The inner rhymes destroy the "normal" line sequence of the rhyme (see § 4). Thus, the so-called "leonine verses" which apparently have 15-syllable lines, like

Преходит время, а грѣховъ бремя тя угнѣтает,
    демонъ же смѣлый на тебе в стрѣлы яд свой впущает...

("The time passes by, and the weight of sins presses you down, but the bold demon poisons with his poison the arrows which he throws at you. ...")

This apparently 15-syllable verse had to be written differently for its correct structure to be visible:

Преходит время,
а грѣховъ бремя
    тя угнѣтает,
демон же смѣлый
на тебе в стрѣлы
    яд свой впущает...

They are then 6-line stanzas of the structure: 5a 5a 5b 5c 5c 5b (the small letters standing for the feminine rhymes).

The translation of the Psalter also offers a variety of stanzas. This variety certainly occurs in imitation of the numerous translations of Psalms already in existence (the most famous, a Latin one, by G. Buchanan, 16th century; the Polish one by Jan Kochanowski; the Czech by J. A. Comenius). However, deliberate imitation of the Polish translation by Kochanowski which some scholars claim to have discovered, cannot be proved. The translation in which, according to one tradition, the then heir to the throne, the future Tsar, Fedor, participated (the translation of two psalms is ascribed to him), enjoyed great popularity until the end of the 18th century (several of these psalms were set to music).

In spite of all his art, Polockij was far behind his Polish and many of his Ukrainian contemporaries. Simeon's poems produce the impression of a certain monotony, not because they do not correspond to our taste, but because he makes insufficient use of those devices which usually serve to enliven syllabic rhythms: he uses predominantly grammatical rhymes, in which similar morphological endings rhyme (compare above *ugnětaet* : : *vpuščaet*, *viny* : : *cěny*, etc.); he has no more than fifteen percent of non-grammatical rhymes; moreover, his sentence nearly always coïncides with his line, while enjambment is a particularly effective means of enlivening the rhythm in syllabic poetry (cf. our quotation above, § 4). The inexact rhymes are very rare, as are masculine and dactylic rhymes (less than one percent!).

But, on the other hand, Simeon (like the Ukrainians) admits occasional deviations from the syllabic pattern; he has lines which have one syllable more or one less than the normal lines. It must be admitted that when read, these lines do not produce any impression of lack of proportion in the meter as a whole; the adjustment is achieved by the placing of the word-accents. The author, who probably did not count the syllables of every line, might not have noticed this innovation himself.

6. Simeon Polockij also plays a role in the history of the Russian theatre. He certainly told the Tsar's family of the Ukrainian and Polish school theatres. According to the clergy, the "pious rulers" (Byzantines) frequented theatrical performances. Tsar Aleksej therefore decided to found a court theatre. Here, however, the Germans got in ahead and produced the first plays in 1672 (see VII, 9, 1). But Simeon himself wrote two plays, one of which has appeared in print, "The Comedy of the Lost Son".

This comedy consists of a short prologue, six scenes and an epilogue. In the prologue, Polockij in a few lines speaks of the benefits of a theatre, for memory retains "the plot" (*dělo*) better than "the word". The scenes represent the Gospel parable of the Prodigal Son. In the first scene the father parts with his son, who pretends to want to go abroad to study. In the second scene the dissipated life of the son is shown us: he drinks and plays dice. In the third, the servants quit the hero, for his money is all gone. In the fourth scene the monologues of the lost son form the main content. He takes the job of a swine-herd, enjoys feeding the pigs, but is driven away because a pig is lost. The fifth scene begins with the father's monologue, in which he speaks of his longing for the missing son, moreover in such words as baroque poetry usually used to describe the longing of lovers for each other. The servants tell the father that the son has returned; he is given fine clothes; the father orders a feast to be prepared; the other son, who has remained at home, speaks to the servants and to the father and expresses his dissatisfaction at his father's kindness; the father answers him in words from the Gospels. The concluding scene is a monologue by the son who thanks God for the forgiveness of his sins. In the epilogue the Gospel idea of God's goodness is linked with didactic themes, such as the commandment to the young to obey their elders.

The plot is weak, and the greater part is taken up with monologues which are occasionally good lyrical poems. Between the scenes there were performed (at least later) small "interludes", humorous scenes which were not written, however, by Polockij (these could be staged with various other theatrical pieces). An extant interlude deals with the same story of the "astrologer" who fell into a hole while watching stars which is also the subject of one of Simeon's poems (in the 18th century it was the theme of a fable by Chemnitzer).

The second play of Polockij is closely connected with a scene from the "Three Men in the Fiery Furnace" (the Book of Daniel), which was enacted in a Moscow church in the 17th century. Here the plot is even weaker. After a monologue by the Emperor of Babylon, Nebuchadnezzar, who is represented as a typical tyrant, his statue, to which everybody must make obeisance, is placed on the stage; anyone who refuses is to be put to death by fire. Nebuchadnezzar is encouraged by a flattering courtier. After a musical interlude (*musikii i likovstvovanija*) the three Jewish youths who refuse to worship the statue are thrown into the furnace. The Babylonians, enemies of the Jews, express in a song their satisfaction with the punishment. The youths, however, know no fear; and lo! – an angel descends into the furnace, makes a speech to them, and protects them from fire. They answer with a quotation from the Book of Daniel. Nebuchadnezzar releases them, at which the choir sings a laudatory song in praise of autocratic rule (!). After a conversation between Nebuchadnezzar and the youths, an actor thanks the audience.

This play is half as long as the first. Simeon was here certainly bound to the tradition of Church plays. The play has become more of a spectacle (*zrelišče*) than a genuine theatrical play.

Both Simeon's plays rank with those of the Ukrainian and Polish theatre which belong to the genre of comedy (not Mystery). Perhaps he was influenced by the plays already performed by the German company.

The language of both plays is somewhat nearer to the spoken language than that of Polockij's other works; the number of enjambments is also much higher than in his poetry.

8. Simeon considerably enriched Moscow's vocabulary. His poems seem at first to be a treasure house of names from ancient mythology and history. We meet in his work the Roman and Byzantine emperors, ancient gods, muses, planets, the Wheel of Fortune, ancient poets and philosophers (Homer, Demosthenes, Aristotle, Virgil, Ovid, Cicero, etc.). Even among the themes of his poetry we find unexpected motifs from Plato, Horace, Propertius, ancient fables, ancient anecdotes, medieval stories (the Bishop Hatto, known to us from Southey's ballad translated by

Žukovskij); one finds mentioned in his work various peoples and lands, precious stones, animals and birds, and so on. Yet all this is consistent with the baroque interpretation, explained symbolically, and expounded by Simeon in the sense of a Christian, even ascetic-monastic, *Weltanschauung*. The whole world – in space and time – is for him only a starting point for the individual metaphor and further symbolic exposition of reality. This symbolic exposition usually signifies, however, a return to tradition. The widening of the sphere of poetry is thus only an enrichment of the sphere from which a poet (and also a thinker) can derive his symbols. An enthusiast for education, Simeon was unable to bring about any cultural renovation (see VII, 15, 3), even under the most favourable conditions.

9. Simeon's disciples and successors were much less creative than their master. Sil'vestr Medvedev (1641–92), at first an official, then a monk, the favourite pupil of Polockij, worked in a printing house. Medvedev was connected with the entourage of the Tsarina Sofja, and worked for the founding of an Academy (University) in Moscow. In 1689 he was involved in a conspiracy against Tsar Peter I, arrested, and executed. In addition to prose works of a non-literary character, he also wrote fifteen epitaphs for his master, and all kinds of panegyric and occasional poems. His works are remarkable for the complex structure of the syntax (long sentences) and a considerable number of non-grammatical rhymes. Nevertheless, they are a sign of progress.

Another pupil of Simeon, Karion Istomin (b. about 1650–d. after 1717), also a monk and worker in the same printing house and later Secretary to the last Patriarch, left numerous poetical works (collections) behind him, of which only the few that have been printed are better known today. He wrote poems for two beautifully printed primers (1694 and 1696), in which his art consisted mainly in assembling in a short poem the names of objects starting with the same letter, each one being illustrated – a playful exercise which would perfectly suit a baroque poet. He then wrote verses for "*Polis*", a kind of popular exposition of civics and children's encyclopaedia, where in the same way he compressed his material into two- and ten-line epigrams. His congratulatory and occasional poetry became known during his lifetime. His poetic technique is weaker (masculine and inexact rhymes) than that of Simeon and Medvedev, and his vocabulary contains less Church Slavonic elements. The influence of his Greek teachers (the Lichuds) on his poetry has not yet been investigated, yet Greek literature of the time also seems to have been influenced by baroque poetry (cf. further VII, 8).

Poems were also written for their books by Fedor Polikarpov, the author of a three-language primer (Slavonic-Latin-Greek) and of a similarly arranged dictionary (both printed in 1703); and by the author of an "Arithmetic" (1704), Leontij Magnickij, who had written a long didactic poem on the use of natural sciences, mainly mathematics.

Syllabic poetry gained ground slowly but victoriously. Yet it was the

Ukrainians, later immigrants to Russia, who shaped its fate in a decisive way. They determined its development in the 18th century (cf. VII, 6, 6, and 13, 8).

6. THE UKRAINIANS IN MOSCOW

1. Simeon Polockij was not the first representative of Ukrainian scholarship in Moscow, as the earliest influences came from the Ostroh circle. The Bible printed there in 1581 now became known. Its influence showed itself perhaps in the verses included in the story of the interregnum, which is ascribed to Katyrev-Rostovskij (VI, 13, 7 and 10). The author explains the aim of his work in verse, as the Ostroh Bible and other Ukrainian texts were in the habit of doing. Ukrainian works exercised a still greater influence on Prince Chvorostinin (VI, 13, 6 and 10); his polemic poem is reminiscent of Ukrainian works compositionally and lexically.

The Ukrainian scholars from Lwów (L'viv) visited Moscow as early as the 1620's, to be sure, without achieving any success there. In 1624–5 the author of the excellent Church Slavonic-Ukrainian dictionary, Pamvo (Pamfil) Berynda, visited Moscow. In the following year came the other author of a smaller dictionary and grammar, Lavrentyj Zyzanij; he wanted to get his catechism printed in Moscow, but the Muscovite theologians found many deviations from their views in it; the deviations were in no way of a serious nature, but Zyzanij was suspected of "heresy". He was also held responsible for the alleged inaccuracies in the presentation of cosmological teachings. The catechism did not appear in print in spite of the readiness of the author to make changes. Two decades later, however, Ukrainian works began to be printed in Moscow, but mostly the old works of the Ostroh printing press. In 1644 there appeared in Moscow the *Kirillova Kniga*, in which many Ukrainian works (1588–1620) were reproduced in translation, either in entirety or in fragments.

The majority of the works of the talented Ukrainian polemicist, Ivan Vyšenśkyj (d. before 1625), are extant in manuscripts dating partly from the late 17th century. It is true that some copies are unusable, as they replaced the Ukrainian words simply with similarly sounding Russian words (instead of *musyt'- mučit, vmieš – směeš,' pragnul – pravdu, pyl 'nujut'- imenujut* (must-torments, you can-you dare, he wished-truth [acc. sing.], they take pains-they call). But in other manuscripts the correct translation is given. Later these works were used by the Old Believers who regarded the polemics against the Catholics and the Uniates as polemics against the hated Patriarch Nikon.

2. From the 1630's onward Kiev took over the leading role in Ukrainian cultural life. And in 1648, the manuscript of the work of a Kievan monk, Nafanail, was translated and printed in Moscow. In 1652 the treatise *Lithos*, written in Polish in 1644 and ascribed to the Kievan Metropolitan Petr Mogila himself, was also translated. In 1647 the Church Slavonic grammar of the Ukrainian, Meletij Smotryćkyj, was reprinted (it appeared in Byelo-Russia in 1618); it then played a role in Russian school teaching until the middle of the 18th century; it was still in the hands of the young Lomonosov (see VII, 14, 1).

As early as 1649 two monks, Arsenij Satanovśkyj and Epifanij Slavynećkyj, were summoned from Kiev to Moscow, where they devoted themselves to the translation of scientific literature. Slavynećkyj (see VII, 2) has particular merits. Those monks were not the only ones; other Ukrainians and Beylo-Russian translators were active in Moscow too. Slavynećkyj, an adherent of the "Greek" trend, regarded Simeon's activity with some misgivings. In 1650 the first Russian scholars went to Kiev, a visit which was repeated later only too seldom.

The Chancellor of the Kiev Academy, Innokentij Gizel' (1669), the Ukrainian theoretician of baroque pulpit oratory, Innokentīj Galjatovśkyj (1670), and later also Lazar Baranovyč, the bishop of Černyhiv, with whom Simeon corresponded, came to Moscow on brief visits during Polockij's stay there. Baranovyč wrote sermons and poems in Ukrainian and Polish. Galjatovśkyj's sermons produced enthusiasm in Moscow. All the visitors tried, too, to popularise their own writings and other Ukrainian printed works, and in this they were partly successful (see below § 6).

Under Peter I a much greater number of Ukrainian scholars and writers were invited to Moscow. Their literary output rose considerably above the activity of Simeon's Russian disciples. Their cultural influence cannot be too highly regarded. Distinguished scholars have formulated their thoughts on the Ukrainian influence even in paradox: the Russian literary language of the 18th century (they said) was created by Ukrainians (N. Trubeckoj); Peter I did not need to break a window into Europe, for one window was already opened – in Kiev (G. Florovskij). Indeed, though one does not want to place the Kiev Academy on the same level with West European universities, even if the former was not yet exclusively devoted at that time to the training of clergy, at least one should not forget that numerous Ukrainians had been at West European universities. Incomplete data (gathered only on the basis of printed sources) show that in the 16th–18th centuries the students of the German and Dutch universities included eight hundred from the Ukrainian areas. Even if half of them (which surely is too high a figure) were possibly Polish nationals, the number of four hundred is still impressive enough. And, moreover, the Ukrainian visitors to English and Italian universities are not included in the above figures, but we know at least many names of such visitors.

3. Among the most important Ukrainians in Moscow was Metropolitan Dimitrij Tuptalo (1651–1709), later canonized. He received the surname of "Rostovskij" after the scene of his previous activities, northern Rostov. The son of a Ukrainian officer, he had – like his three sisters – preferred monastic life to a secular career after his studies at the Academy. He wrote his main work while still in Kiev – the new "Reading Menaea" (Čet'i-Minei), which had appeared for the first time in Kiev in 1684 and were reprinted there between 1698 and 1705, and later in Moscow. Under the influence of the Polish hagiographic legends (1579) by Piotr Skarga, and using the Acta Sanctorum of the Bollandists, as well as other Latin and Greek literature, they were based, especially in what concerns the Slav saints, on an independent and scientific study of the sources. Thus St. Dimitrij anticipated in some aspects the results of the research of the 19th century. A significant work from the literary point of view, the Menaea have become a source from which Russian readers and poets could up to the 20th century learn of the lives of the saints. Dimitrij's early sermons were sustained throughout in an extremely luxurious baroque style, with extensive symbolic constructions and rich stylistic ornamentation. The sermons dating from his Great Russian period are written in softer, often sentimental or dramatic, tones. These contain long dialogues, for instance between Abraham and God, numerous apostrophizings of the audience, or of David and Chrysostomos. Among poetic devices he uses mostly parallels and antitheses. He depicts expansive scenes, as, for example, Christ's Birth, and the baroque "surprises" are invented with a gentle sense of humour. However, some of his sermons are written in a ponderous prophetic style, such as the famous sermon concerning banished Justice who cannot find refuge among any class except the poor, persecuted, weeping and moaning peasants.

St. Dimitrij was a writer by calling; he even asked that his manuscripts be laid with him in his coffin. He wrote numerous poems, too, among which there was no lack of typically baroque nugae. He was a master of euphony, and some of his poems are entirely constructed on a certain sound or syllable as on an organ-pipe. He wrote several religious epigrams and "wreaths" (cycles) of them, as well as Church songs which appeared as late as in the 18th century in the Great Russian books of songs; some of them have become popular. He was also active as a playwright. Many of his plays were performed in Rostov, among them certainly one about St. Demetrius of Thessalonica, and another about the Virgin Mary's Assumption, as well as a Christmas play. They belong among the best plays of the Ukrainian baroque; their rich language, including the use of various levels (such as the colloquial speech of the Shepherds, etc.), and the lively construction of their plots are especially remarkable. His theological treatise against the Old Believers stands outside the scope of *belles-lettres*.

Dimitrij was a man of wide culture; from the catalogue of his library we know that he read the current theological and philosophical literature of all schools (Bacon, Descartes). His diaries record his reading, but only fragmentarily.

Dimitrij's works were kept on being printed, his Reading Menaea until the 20th century. Unfortunately, in the process of publication, his exquisite, lively and beautiful Ukrainian Church Slavonic was "improved" and partly deprived of colour. Only a few sermons have been faithfully edited from the manuscripts.

4. There was another Ukrainian in Moscow, very productive in the literary field, Metropolitan Stefan Javorśkyj (1655–1722). He was "Deputy Patriarch", the See of the Patriarch being vacant from the time of Peter I until its abolition. Like St. Dimitrij, Stefan was on the whole an opponent of the too secular tendencies of Peter and especially of the Tsar's sympathies for Protestantism. Stefan reorganised the Moscow Academy after the fashion of the Kiev Academy. He certainly was less talented and learned than St. Dimitrij, a fact which is shown by his treatise "The Rock of Faith", which leaned heavily on Catholic theology. Stefan was a poet and a preacher. The formal influences of the Baroque weighed more pronouncedly in his works than in those of Simeon Polockij; to be sure, he lived at the time of the "late Baroque" which, as is well known, intensified the characteristic features of the baroque style. His Slavonic and Latin poems (among them a valedictory poem to his library) are richly adorned with metaphors and antitheses. His sermons are mostly typical *concetto* sermons; in most of them some rare image is introduced and is further developed. Thus on the text of St. John 20, 22, "Receive ye the Holy Ghost", the author constructs an entire sermon in which he makes the Holy Ghost appear under different forms for the various groups of his listeners: to the Tsar as a dove, to the "princes and boyars" as wine, to the artillery as fire, to the fleet as wind, to the "common people" as water, and so on. Or, when he designates the spiritual gifts as "medicines", he describes an entire apothecary shop (the Holy Church) with all its medicines. He likens the Virgin Mary to the Zodiac, and deals separately with every single zodiacal sign. He uses, of course, rhetorical devices, exhortations, exclamations, questions. He himself talks with the Saviour and lets John the Baptist debate with Herod. Besides, John addresses Herod as "Your Majesty!" Such modernisation of Christian notions is typical of him. Noah is "the first admiral", God "the celestial chemist"; he speaks of "the Lamb's coat-of-arms", of "the privileges given from the celestial chancery", and so forth. He extensively combines Christendom and Antiquity, and is especially given to illustrating his sermons with examples from ancient history and literature. However, he does not lack images full of expression, for instance, the world as a stormy sea. He also seeks Justice (правда-справед-ливость) in the world and does not find it in Moscow. The Tsar's banquet reminds him of Belshazzar's Feast.

Stefan also uses euphonic devices: rhymes, simultaneous word-sounds and paranomasias, placing special stress on unusual word-combinations: *myslenaja maslina* (m-sl-na-m-sl-na – "spiritual olive tree"). He also left a text-book of rhetoric, "The Rhetorical Hand", in which he made the pupils learn tropes and figures according to the various joints of the fingers.

Javorśkyj's library has been preserved; it shows the much smaller range of his interests, which are preponderantly confined to theology, antiquity, and later Latin literature.

Javorśkyj's works were also printed with lexical corrections. His baroque art influenced the Russian sermon until well into the times of Elisabeth (1741–62).

5. It was a third Ukrainian, Feofan Prokopovyč (1681–1736), who exercised the greatest influence on Russian literature. He came to Russia somewhat later than his two predecessors. The son of a burgess of Kiev, he studied there and in Rome, but brought home a strong predilection for Protestant theology. After being professor and "Rector" of the Kiev Academy from 1705 on, he was called to St. Petersburg in 1715 and became archbishop of Novgorod and an active collaborator of Peter I. He wrote many drafts for the latter, primarily a statute of the Synod and a commentary on the Russian Law of succession, for which he used contemporary literature of legal theory (Locke, Hobbes, Hugo Grotius).

After Peter's death he passed over to the opposition group, devoted much time to the struggle against his enemies, consorted a great deal with the foreign members of the Petersburg Academy of Sciences founded in 1725, and had a small circle of friends to which, in addition to V. Tatiščev (see VII, 15, 6), belonged the young A. Kantemir.

Numerous works from Feofan's pen have survived: besides a Slavonic and Latin theological treatise, one play, several poems and three volumes of sermons printed later (1765 ff.), two dialogues published only in the 19th and 20th century, and a Latin manual of poetics. In the 1765 edition a very one-sided selection of Feofan's sermons was made; they deal almost exclusively with political problems. Stylistically, they are distinguished by a terseness of stylistic devices and the use of almost exclusively rhetorical media; exclamations, invocations, antitheses and gradation (climax) appear here in full force. Possibly under the influence of Italian adversaries of the eccentricities of the baroque style, or perhaps under the influence of the Protestant theory of preaching, Feofan demands from the preacher above all a clear presentation of the subject-matter. In his treatise on poetics he does not mention poetic *nugae*, but among his own poems there are some emblematic verses on the border of such *nugae*. In these he plays with over-audacious metaphors, paranomasias and with oxymorons of the "Light of Death"; he also uses a great many euphonies. He translated, among other things, one of the most famous emblematic collections, *Princeps politicus* by Foxardo Saavedra. Among his Latin poems (Feofan wrote in Polish too) we also find baroque *nugae* (e.g. anagrams). His play "Vladimir" (1709) depicts Kiev's baptism, the comical figures of the heathen priests, Vladimir's vacillations before the final choice; it contains typical baroque panegyrics to Hetman Mazepa, to the Kievan Metropolitan, and to the Kiev Academy. Later there were some attempts to dedicate the play to Peter I, but without justification. Many scholars attribute to Prokopovyč the play "The Grace of God" (1728). This idea, however, must be rejected; the play had been produced in Kiev, with which Prokopovyč no longer had any links at the time, and the strong Ukrainian colouring of its language differentiates it from all writings by Prokopovyč dating from his later period. Prokopovyč's Latin poetics (*De arte poetica libri III*) was published at Mogilev in 1786.

Prokopovyč owes his important place in the history of Russian poetry to his treatment of syllabic verse in the last period of his life. First of all Prokopovyč abandoned the rhyming of consecutive lines. He introduced the scheme *a.b.a.b.* and even used the scheme of the octave taken from Italy *a.b.a.b.a.b.c.c.* (in the notable answer to Kantemir's First Satire).

Moreover, he increased the number of non-grammatical rhymes to forty per cent of the total number of rhymes; the number of enjambments is also considerable in some poems (in a fairly long one it comes up to thirty per cent, while masculine rhymes occur in only one poem of his which has obviously an "experimental" character; there are no irregular rhymes. Some "tonal" lines, with regular alternation of stress, may be ascribed rather to chance. Among Prokopovyč's poems there are also witty epigrams (he compares, for instance, the work on a dictionary with the forced labour of a convict; the theme is taken from Scaliger) and elegies (the lament of a shepherd after a long spell of bad weather – an allusion to himself – in which he alternates 10-syllable lines with 4-syllable ones). Most of his poems are occasional verse. The language is in many cases close to everyday speech.

The ideological influence of Prokopovyč, who was a genuine disciple of Western learning, proved much more important for Kantemir. Prokopovyč's personality and his ecclesiastical-political and purely political activity are quite variously judged. But in the history of Russian poetry a place of honour belongs to the slender output of this Ukrainian.

Prokopovyč's library, too, is known to us from its catalogue; it is a very rich and excellent collection – theology, literature, philosophy, law, history, even astronomy, are well represented. But Prokopovyč's erudition exercised a strong influence only in the field of theology, where his text-books, with a strong Protestant flavour, determined the nature of theological instruction for a long time to come.

6. Of no less significance were the Ukrainian and Beylo-Russian print-ed books. Those printed in L'vov, Kiev, Vil'na and other places were periodically introduced and then proscribed, though not always on sufficient grounds. Thus in 1627 the *Učitel'noe Evangelie* (a collection of sermons from Gospel texts, 1619, by the Ukrainian writer Kirill Tran-kvilion Stavrovećkyj) was burned in Moscow as "heretical". The following year all the "Lithuanian" books were forbidden and seized from the monasteries and churches; "Lithuanian" manuscripts were even taken from private persons. It is significant that the proscribed work by Stavrovećkyj (who only became a Uniate later) was used in 1682 by the Patriarch, who read sermons from it in church, and that in 1683 an un-known priest from the North-East compiled a collection of sermons (*Statir*) in imitation of the forbidden book, and that even in 1730 Sta-vrovećkyj's sermons were read in a Moscow church out of his book.

Berynda's dictionary, of little use to Great Russia, nevertheless played an important role in Moscow, and Great Russian copies of it were made. The works of the Ukrainian visitors to Moscow (see above § 2) were also widely disseminated. Galjatovśkyj's theory of preaching (*Ključ Razumě-nija* – "The Key to Understanding", 1659) was simply reprinted. Also one could often find in the hands of Moscow clergy Innokentij Gizel's guide to religious moral theory, *Mir s Bogom čelověku* ("The Peace between Man and God", 1661, 1678). The Kievan edition of the Kiev Paterikon also became known. Particular success, however, was enjoyed by the "*Synopsis*" (1674), a survey of Ukrainian history from Kievan times, with a fairly cursory sketch of Moscow's history; this work became a popular text-book and survived in numerous editions until the middle of the 19th century; it was translated into Greek in Moscow in the 17th century, as into Latin at the beginning of the 18th. Galjatovśkyj's collection of miracle tales, *Nebo novoe* (The new heaven, L'viv, 1665 and 1666) was translated by a monk in 1677 "into the Slavonic-Russian dialect"; that is how hard it was at that time for a Great Russian to understand Ukrainian-Church Slavonic. The popularity enjoyed by Ukrainian printings led to permission being granted for their sale in public. In 1672, the Kievan Cave Monastery opened a bookshop in Moscow, and after the same year Lvovian printings were sold there. The new Patriarch Ioakim (1674), however, suspected the Ukrainians of "heresy", forbade the sale of a number of books, and had some pages removed from others. The 1690 Council banned several books by Ukrainians: Stavrovećkyj, Metropolitan Petr Mogila (1596–1647), Gizel', Galjatovśkyj, Baranovyč, and even Simeon Polockij. This policy led finally to the new Patriarch Adrian forbidding the Kiev Cave Monastery in 1699 to print (with a few exceptions) books which did not conform to the Moscow language and orthography. It was Adrian who introduced ecclesiastical censorship.

In reality, the interdictions had little effect. Oddly enough, the Ukrainian writings were especially sought by the Old Believers, but the orthodox readers too – even the high clergy – used the Kievan printings, the more so since a comparable Muscovite equivalent was lacking.

7. The influence of Ukrainian anonymous verses (*virši*) and folk-songs is a chapter in itself. It is difficult to date the beginning of this influence. By the period of the interregnum the songs and verses were already known (see § 1). They are found in transcriptions for the first time in the second half of the century; and very frequently at the turn of the century and in the 18th century. Their influence is apparent in three directions. Firstly,

the "pre-syllabic verse" of the beginnings of the century was being gradually forced out by the syllabic verse, with its equal number of syllables in every line and its genuine rhymes. Secondly, there appear numerous "spiritual verses" (*duchovnye stichi*) which enter popular lore with the *stariny* (*byliny*) and the historical songs, and betray their origin by their syllabic form. Thirdly, school poetry originates, propagating even further types of poetry in Russia; the models are not only Polockij's poems, which had remained mostly in manuscript form, but numerous verses which are in part poetic *nugae*, in part love poems, a genre not practised by Polockij. A few examples may illustrate the variety of the types of the *nugae*; here is a poem which is written thus

and is read as if it consisted of two lines:

Адам преступник небо заключает,
Иисус праведник небо отверзает.

("Adam, the sinner, closes heaven; Jesus, the righteous one, opens heaven.")

In other poems, the words were to be read in a different direction, as here:

Трезвенных возненавидь, люби пьяниц дело,
почти гордых, смиренных убегай всецело.

However, if the words are read from top to bottom, the opposite meaning is obtained:

Трезвенных почти, возненавидь гордых, люби смиренных,
пьяниц дело убегай всецело.

("Honour the sober, hate the proud, love the humble, flee from dealing with drunkards.")

The palindromic poems demanded the highest skill; in these the words or even individual letters could be read backwards (either the same or contrary sense is thus obtained; *versus cancrini*, in Ukrainian *raky* – crayfish). The Russian examples certainly are far behind the Ukrainian and especially the Polish ones. Here is a Russian example:

MURAL DECORATION IN BAROQUE STYLE IN THE METROPOLITAN PALACE IN ROSTOV (OF THE NORTH). 1693

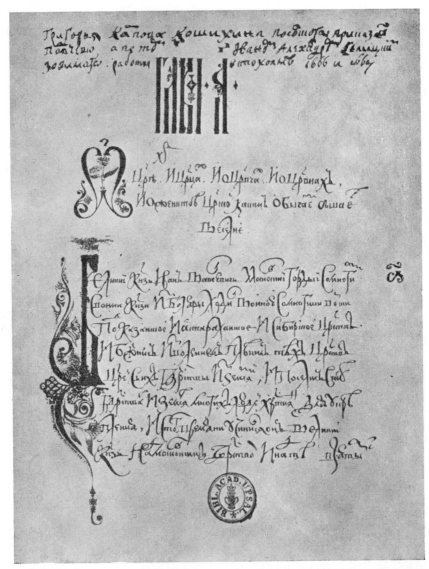

FIRST PAGE OF KOTOŠICHIN'S MANUSCRIPT: CIRCUMSTANCES IN
MOSCOW (WRITTEN IN 1606)

Written by Kotošichin, a Muscovite official fled to Sweden, for the Swedish government.
The manuscript of Uppsala.

Аки Лот и та мати толика,
аки лев и та мати велика.

(Every line can be read, letter after letter, backwards. The meaning is not
very profound: "The mother is as big as Lot, this mother is as big as a
lion." Another variety is, for instance, the *Carmen gryphicum* in which
some letters are read as their names in the Church Slavonic alphabet:

С Богом ЗДЕ пребывати в свѣтѣ,
НОП, нас хранит всѣх от сѣти.

Instead of the letters зде, ноп we read their Slavonic names, and we
obtain the following couplet:

С Богом зѣло добро есть пребывати в свѣтѣ,
наш он покой, нас хранит всѣх от сѣти.

("It is very good to be in the world with God. He is our rest, He protects
us all from the [Devil's] net.") Some of these poems are simply close
imitations of the best Ukrainian contributions. Poems in a particular
shape were later written by Deržavin and by the Russian symbolists
(Brjusov) and futurists (Chlebnikov), whose accomplishments certainly
ranked much higher than those of the baroque poets.

The erotic poems created above all the phraseology and vocabulary of
the language of love. Their themes were mainly praise of the beloved, the
parting, "the enemies"; in general – the melancholy mood (tears) and,
more rarely, joy. The favourite imagery consisted of the arrows of love
which Cupid frequently shoots; the wounds which these arrows inflict as
they hit mainly the heart; love as fire; the lovers' thoughts, which fly like
birds; misfortune (*fortuna zlaja*), etc. Occasionally, some modest elements
of nature are added: gardens, rivers, flowers and trees.

8. The influence of Polish literature and language was extremely strong,
but seldom direct, even when those who knew Polish were at hand. The
intermediaries were again mostly Ukrainians or Byelo-Russians, who
often wrote Polish prose themselves. They also made a considerable
number of translations from the Polish (see VII, 1).

7. THE SCHISM (*RASKOL*)

1. After the shock of the interregnum, life seemed to have returned
once more to the old channels. For over a hundred years the people had

been brought up in the conviction that Russia was the only Christian, indeed the only "holy", land; that everything foreign came from the Devil; that everything inherited – no matter how unimportant it may appear – was of the greatest importance and was even to be considered as "sacred". Above all, piety was reduced to the strictest observance of external rules. Thus calamity was predicted whenever changes were suggested. But the storm came from an unexpected quarter. The traditions of the Church were encroached upon by innovations.

Two problems concerning the life of the Church had to be settled in the 17th century. The printing of books demanded correct texts of works for the divine service. There were attempts to "restore" such texts with the help of quite haphazardly selected "experts". The task proved more difficult than had originally been expected. Conflicts arose, the improvers were called "spoliators", as, on many earlier occasions, Maksim Grek had been (VI, 9, cf. VI, 7, 2). The question of proper decorum (*blagočinie*) at the divine service was also contested; Avvakum, later leader of the opposition to "innovations", had serious conflicts with his parishioners because of his attempts to introduce "decorum" at the divine service. Obviously, he was not at all opposed to the idea of "improving" church life, but he presumably expected that old Russian piety would be restored. What happened, however, was something quite different.

The Russian Patriarch (the Patriarchate came into existence in 1589) was at that time Nikon (1605–1681, Patriarch 1652–67). With the approval of Tsar Aleksej, he could consider as "experts" only the Kievan scholars and the Greeks. Except for a warning from some of the Greeks, the question of decorum in the reform of the Church rites was resolved after the Greek model. The problem of "improving" texts was much more difficult, for here neither the Ukrainians nor the Greeks had any firm views on many of the issues. The texts and their interpretation diverged widely. Moreover, Nikon carried the "innovations" through with a strong hand. And what was discarded and antiquated was declared to be "corruption" and "wickedness" (*nečestie* – atheism). This naturally brought to its feet the opposition which, already during the "work of improvement", had made sceptical objections and complained bitterly. Of course, the clergy and the monks joined the opposition; its leadership was assumed by the clergy, Archpriest Avvakum being the most important among them. The State, whose links with the Church were at the time closer than ever, and which approved Nikon's measures, intervened. The Council of 1666 sanctioned the "innovations"; that of 1667 laid the "schismatics" under an interdict. The same Council, however, also removed Nikon, whose claims to power and authority had meanwhile estranged him from the Tsar. Nevertheless, the schism within the Church (*raskol*) remained.

Later, the magnitude of the schism and the passion with which both sides fought each other were difficult to understand, as there were no dogmatic differences between the two factions. There were merely insignificant differences in cult and rite: the doubling or trebling of the Haleluja, passing by the procession to the right (*posolon'*) or to the left, and so on; and, as if symbolizing the whole quarrel, the most important difference between the parties consisted in the different manner of crossing oneself (here the Old Believers could invoke Metropolitan Daniil and Maksim Grek in support of their point of view). There were also various customs which in themselves did not need religious sanction: the Old Believers were against smoking, and later against the cutting of beards too. This, in their opinion, gave them the right to designate the "innovators" as heretics and servants of Antichrist. But occasionally the official Church also called the Old Believers "heretics" and had recourse to the police help of the State. The Old Believers included in their number clergymen (no bishop however), monks, townsmen and peasants, merchants and boyars. They certainly could have had many more partisans on their side, had it not been for the cruel persecutions of the initial period, which included even mutilation (cutting off the tongue), hanging and burning. Now the Old Believers fled from the "anti-Christian" world; they fled to the northern forests, into the "wilderness", and even out of the country. However, they ran away from the world spiritually, from a world in which there were for them no church, no priests (for no one would consecrate them), no sacraments, no baptism, no communion, no marriage. The eschatological mood gained ground. People awaited the coming of Antichrist or believed that he had already come (Nikon, Tsar Aleksej, later Peter I). In order to escape from the world, they frequently committed suicide, mainly by mass-burning, and after the intensification of persecutions the number of self-burnings increased.

The principles which motivated the Old Believers were varied. Least of all is it possible to see in them – as has been attempted – a defence of freedom of thought or a protest against the intervention of the State into Church affairs, for the Church was here indentified with the State. In reality, the strongest motives were those imparted by 16th-century tradition (Volockij's school), the uncritical faith in the "sacredness" of tradition, with all its small details, together with that version of nationalism which saw truth to be in Russia alone, and Antichrist in everything foreign (in this case – Greek). For the Old Believers the Church and the State were certainly one complete entity and, it seems, the Tsar's "betrayal" of Christianity made an even greater impression on them than the "defection" of the Patriarchs.

2. At the beginning of the Church schism, a few writers appeared in the camp of the Old Believers. Among these Avvakum deserves special attention. Born about 1620, Avvakum was a priest in the north of Russia. He came into conflict with his parish on account of his strictness. In 1652 he arrived in Moscow as Archpriest. Because he soon rose in opposition to Nikon's innovations, he was banished in 1653 to Siberia, to Tobol'sk, but retaining his archpriestship; because of conflict with the local clergy he was exiled even further, to the Mongolian frontier, where until 1663 he had to suffer with his family the greatest privations under a self-willed local tyrant. Then he was called back by the Tsar, who knew him personally, and made welcome. In the meantime however Nikon's reforms and the opposition to them had both made great progress. Avvakum associated himself entirely with the opposition and in consequence he was again exiled to the North of Russia. He was summoned back to Moscow for the Councils of 1666 and 1667, but made not the slightest concession. He therefore was deprived of his priesthood, outlawed, and imprisoned in an underground dungeon in the Far North. In 1682 he addressed a petition to the new Tsar, Fedor, in which he referred to the fate of the Tsar's father, Aleksej, who, he said, was now suffering in Hell. Thereupon Avvakum was burned, together with two of his fellow-prisoners.

   Avvakum wrote the greater part of his numerous works (over seventy) during his last imprisonment, whence they found their way to the Old Believers. Among these works, besides the numerous epistles and instructions, which he arranged in entire series (*Kniga Besěd* – The Book of Sermons, and others), it is primarily his autobiography – extant in different redactions – which is worthy of attention. His writings deal mainly with the fundamental beliefs of the "old faith", with the afflictions of the Old Believers who now live without priests and with the question of self-burning of which he approves; his writings also include admonitions and consolations addressed to his followers, etc.

3. The majority of the sermons (*Kniga Besěd*), interpretations (*Kniga Tolkovanij*), and so on, are very poor in theological content, and yet claim somehow to be theological works. Avvakum deals with the important questions of dogma as seriously as with the minutiae of cult and rite, even with questions which obviously have nothing to do with the Church (how a belt should be worn, etc.). His arguments are only sham proofs. How could he want to prove something, of the truth of which he leaves no possibility of doubt? His proofs are either based on texts from the Scriptures (long and often inappropriate) – and sometimes the explanations are insufficient even for his followers, as when in the case of the Old Believers' sign of the cross, he refers to the Psalter, or he uses rare quotations (from memory), or refers to other writings among which the most doubtful apocrypha are also to be found (at times he himself doubts their value for the purpose of argument, since they are not Church books). His interpretation of the Scriptures is symbolic and pedantic. It is sufficient merely to compare his interpretation of the Gospel parable of the labourer in the vineyard with that of Epifanij (V, 4, 8). Epifanij merely relates the parable and in order to help the reader to understand the content inserts the words "the Permian men"; Avvakum explains in detail every single step of the Gospel story (what the first hour means, the third one, and so on) and misses the point completely – equal pay for all the workers – at the most important moment by seeing in it merely the justification of the divine free pleasure.

As with the personally coloured passages in Avvakum's epistles, his autobiography, together with his personal letters, are entirely different. As far as they depict his own tragic fate and the sufferings of his followers, they are thoroughly human and most moving. But much of the effect is due to the different style employed here by Avvakum.

4. Avvakum's language in the epistles actually follows the Church tradition, with strong rhetorical elements. Avvakum comes to life here only when he speaks directly to his readers, and especially when he is attacking someone in particular (Nikon, Nikon's followers, the current icon-painting, etc.). He then departs entirely from the stereotyped pattern of the ecclesiastical language. But his attacks are the outcome of his point of view that all questions are already solved and that he has the right answers. Therefore he is content to make insulting remarks rather then to raise objections, and moreover remarks of the coarsest kind. Here his language is in a robust popular vein, rich in colour and extremely picturesque. He is rarely tender, for the feeling which he can best express is hatred; all those passages in which he speaks of faith and love are much more anaemic. Some images are very memorable, especially those motivated by hatred; for instance, the description of a proud bishop driving around in a carriage, or of an archbishop who joyously enters supported by devils, etc. But here too Avvakum uses many set formulas, as when exposing the "Nikonian" clergy who "seek ... Rhinewine and wine of Rome, spirits and sifted wines, beer with cardamon, mead with rasp-berries, cherries, and various white liquors" (repeated with little variation several times).

His autobiography and a few personal writings must be judged quite differently from the literary point of view. Their style is highly individual and vigorous. Avvakum produces this impression by an ability which few writers possess, to write exactly as he speaks. This is also the character-istic of the memorable passages of his "theoretical" writings mentioned above. He succeeds, too, with the help of orthography. in rendering the peculiarities of his North-Russian dialect by phonetics and grammar. Thus he uses numerous particles "-*de*" to indicate indirect speech, "-*su*" when apostrophising, "-*ka*" or "-*tko*" with imperatives, "*že*" and so forth. He also uses the article typical of his style, "*tot*" or "*toj*", "-*ot*", "*ta*", "*to*" (declinable):

Как дощеник-от в воду-ту не погряз со мною? Стало у меня в те поры кости-те щемить и жилы-те тянуть, и сердце зашлось, да и умирать стал...

("How is it that this raft has not sunk with me in the water? At that time my bones started to ache, and I began to have pains in my veins, and my heart was hurting, and I was dying.") He accumulates diminutives and pejoratives, popular words which often replace the expected eccles-iastical terms. But the vocabulary is not adequate for Avvakum, who frequently uses set turns of phrase and proverbs: thus in prison he is so deprived of everything that all that is left to him is *mešok da goršok da lapti na nogach* (a bag, a saucepan, and bast shoes on the feet), etc. Most of his sayings, however, are original and always have the pithiness which is often based on puns. Sometimes indeed he utilises the pun in argument (the Catholic church – *kostel* – ought to be named so because it is built *na kostjach* – on bones). As far as the personal passages of Avvakum's works are concerned, it is most significant, however, that he successfully welds ecclesiastical questions, his own fate and Church problems into a single whole, but at the same time completely mixes up ecclesiastical issues with questions concerning the legality of the old forms of daily life (*byt*). One could hardly maintain that Avvakum had in mind the ideal of "Christianizing the whole of life". He is much more inclined to dissolve the religious side in the context of everyday life. This adds force to his exposition, but at the same time it is his essential weakness. One cannot read without spiritual repugnance all those passages in which he mingles his religious considerations with the coarsest insults, and his constantly mixing them detracts from both strata of his language, the high and the popular.

The passages which Avvakum describes as his "idle prattle" or "babble" (*vjakan'e*), and the others which he calls "vociferations" (*krik*) are stylistically uniform. Anything written in between these two tonalities is immediately less forceful. Everything that he says in both these "keys" receives a colouring of intimacy and closeness. In this manner Avvakum deals even with religious questions. He speaks thus of his profession as a writer:

Подобен я нищему человеку, ходящему по улицам града и по окошкам милостыню просящу... Сбираю и вам, питомникам церковным, предлагаю... У богатова человека, царя Христа, из евангелия ломоть хлеба выпрошу; у Павла апостола, у богатого гостя, ис полатей его хлеба крому выпрошу; у Златоуста, у торгового человека, кусок словес его получю; у Давыда царя и Исаи пророков, у посацких людей, по четвертыне хлеба выпросил. Набрав кошель, да и вам даю, жителям в дому Бога моего. Ну, епьте на здоровье, питайтеся, не мрите с голоду! Я опять побреду сбирать по окошкам.

("I am like a beggar who wanders about the streets of the city and asks for alms under the windows. ... I collect from you and also offer to you who feed on the Church. ... From the rich man, from Christ the King, I beg a piece of bread from the Gospels; from Apostle Paul, the rich merchant, I get a crust of bread off the floor; from Chrysostomos, the trader, I get a piece from his sermons; from the prophets King David and Isaiah, the townsfolk, I got a large piece of bread. And having filled my bag, I shall give them to you, dwellers in the house of God. Now, eat in peace, feed yourselves, do not die of hunger! And I shall set off wandering again to collect at the windows.")

Sometimes it is different; Avvakum is not satisfied with the peaceful words (*syn* = son) which, in the Gospels Abraham directs at the rich man in Hell. Avvakum goes further:

плюнул бы ему в рожу-ту и в брюхо-то толстое пнул бы ногою

("I would spit in his snout and kick him with my feet in his fat belly.")

Avvakum depicts his religious life, enumerating his prayers and obeisances; he recommends exactly the same to his disciples and demands the same from his wife (in the evening – 200 obeisances and 400 prayers!).

But this, as well as his other counsels and commands, is also based on his blending of Church and *byt*.

At the same time he is an apologist for the Old Russian Church and the old way of life, where his utopian representation of "old, shining Russia" is pure wishful thinking; his ideal union between the Church and the "world" had never existed in reality. And this retrospective utopia of his would not only impair religious life by its submersion into everyday existence, but would also narrow orthodoxy down to belief in the exclusive genuineness of "Russian faith".

The peculiarity of Avvakum's "spoken-written" language allows him also to depict his personal fate. He writes of everything in this language flowing, as it seems, directly from his pen (and, as he sees it, from his heart), and he is in turn illustrative, concrete and moving (he often weeps and mentions the tears of others). He writes thus of the hen who laid two eggs a day and fed him and his family; but he writes thus also of the decisive and shattering moments of his life – when for instance his wife did not prevent him from going to preach a sermon (*krik*) which had become dangerous for him, but on the contrary urged him to go to church; he writes of one symbolic scene in his life, when he was wandering in winter through Siberia:

Протопопица бедная бредет-бредет, да и повалится, – кольско гораздо! В ыную пору, бредучи, повалилась... Я пришел, – на меня, бедная, пеняет, говоря : "долго ли муки сея, протопоп, будет?" И я говорю: "Марковна, до самыя смерти!" – Она же, вздохня, отвещала: "добро, Петрович, ино еще побредем".

("The poor wife of the archpriest tramped along, and then suddenly fell – it was very slippery. Once she fell while walking. ... As I come up, she reproaches me, saying, "How long, archpriest, are these sufferings to last?" And I answer: "Markovna, until death!" She sighs and says, "So be it, Petrovič, let us be getting on." ")

The genre of autobiography is new or newly originated. Avvakum tried to model himself on Abbas Dorotheos (whose life story, written by himself in the 6th century, was also popular in the West in the 17th century; it was published in Moscow in 1652). But he refers also to the Apostles who have themselves described their lives (he presumably means St. Luke). Avvakum in spite of his assertions of his sinfulness and humility, considers himself a worker of miracles (i.e. cure of the possessed and the sick, appearances of the devil; but also Christ appears to him and informs him, for instance, of the fate of Tsar Aleksej after his death); he also considers himself a prophet, even perhaps a saint (he describes miracles which occurred to save him). And he acts accordingly. Equally inconsistent is his attitude to mankind: of some men who earlier had done him good he speaks with love and is ready to forgive them everything, but elsewhere he would like to exterminate those whose opinions differ from his own: 'ja by ich ... vsech pereplastal v odin den' (I would stab them all in one day) – this he writes in his petition for mercy addressed to Tsar Fedor. Far worse are the incidents which he recounts of himself. He refused to pray for a sick child because its mother had previously called a witch-doctor, though he is convinced that his prayers would help. And again, when a detachment of a hundred men sets out against the Mongols, and the "governor", who himself did not go with the men, called a shaman to learn the future, Avvakum prays "vociferously":

"послушай мене, Боже! ... да не возвратится вспять ни един от них, и гроб им там устроиши всем! приложи им зла, Господи, приложи, и погибель им наведи..."

("Harken to me, O God! ... Let not one of them return, and dig a grave for them all yonder! Cause them evil and bring them to perdition. ....") Avvakum joyfully relates that only one man returned from the expedition, for whose safety he prayed subsequently. And he is just as inconsistent even in his declarations on the minutiae of the rites and forms of life, for which he orders his disciples to throw themselves into fire. On one occasion he writes: "Let them [these trivial matters] go to hell! To Christ and to us they are of no use." He writes in one instance in almost the same vein as the old way of singing in church.

Thus it is with mixed feelings that one considers this man and his tragic and cruel fate, which he could depict so expressively. Even if one admires his courage and energy, and appreciates his writing ability (though not without reservation and remembering that Ivan the Terrible had written previously in a similar style), nevertheless one must see that the ideals for which he fought and died were completely without hope of fulfilment, and that much in Avvakum's writings was the result of illiteracy and spiritual delusion. As a writer he was unable to create a school, even among his followers.

5. Only two works of the early period of the Schism are closely related stylistically to Avvakum's autobiography.

The first of these simply imitates it. This is the autobiography of Epifanij, who was in exile with Avvakum and was burnt at the same time. It was written by "command" of Avvakum. Epifanij's work is also in part reminiscent of tale of Solomonija (VII, 4, 4). Epifanij's autobiography occasionally contains descriptions of impressive and realistic visions of the devil, similar to those of Solomonija; but it includes description of other miracles and visions – his tongue which had been cut off grows again in an instant, Christ Himself appears to him in order to comfort him. Like Avvakum, Epifanij, by slowing down the tempo of his narrative can lend to his images a greater concreteness and plasticity; like Avvakum he can, with everyday words, bring his experiences and thoughts close to the reader; when recounting his religious experiences, however, he uses the "higher" Church style and fails to avoid the set formulas. As moving as Avvakum's autobiography, Epifanij's work is, however, much less effective.

In 1691 a "Council" of Old Believers was called. The participants took a stand against self-burning, which certainly did not extinguish the fires. One of the participants at the Council, Evfrosin, wrote a polemic treatise on the subject, which was named *Otrazitel'noe pisanie* ("The Challenging Writing"). Evfrosin too uses different styles of language mixed. While entire sections of his work are written in a very high rhetorical style with compounds, complicated syntactic constructions and apostrophes, he, however, depicts his enemies, the advocates of self-burning, very clearly and sketches as in a satire, a whole gallery of different types – fanatics, libertines, and simple swindlers; he also draws concrete pictures of their activity, all this – men and scenes – with small typical traits; the faces, glances, beards, voices and clothing, for which he naturally has to use everyday and popular words mixed together. He is rarely insulting; generally he contents himself with irony and sarcasm.

But however popular their works had been, these writers did not create a school. The schism continued, later under somewhat easier conditions. Peter, who appreciated the economic industry of the Old Believers, relaxed some of the rigour; further alleviations were brought about by corruption. A hermitage (with thousands of inmates) was founded in the North, on the banks of the Vyg. At the beginning of the 18th century Andrej Denisov founded a school there in which even rhetoric and philosophy (modelled in part on Raymond Lull!) were taught. Andrej Denisov and his brother Semen also wrote theological treatises displaying vast scholarscip and logical direction of thought. Oddly enough, the Old Believers accepted the writings of the Kievan school as orthodox sources. The literature which now originated was not a little influenced by this typical product of the Baroque. The numerous polemics which appeared on various questions (mainly, because the Old Believers could not have any consecrated priests or any sacraments) are in a quite different style. A somewhat simplified Church Slavonic predominates. The rhetorical sophistry with which the most insignificant questions of ritual are discussed, the numerous texts from the Scriptures and quotations from literature, the elevated style – all these are reminiscent either of Simeon Polockij or of Makarij's school. The Lives of the Saints, the old ones (Maksim Grek and the others) and the new ones (the martyrs of the Schism) are written entirely in the traditional style. Only the apocryphal legends (based on the themes from old paterikons and some other early Lives, as well as on legends concerning Nikon) are really vivid. An essential part of the Old Believers' literature was the copies of old works reproduced as faithfully as possible. Soon forgeries of original texts also appeared (right up to the 20th century), often quite perfect from the graphic point of view, but they betrayed themselves frequently by minor details, such as miniatures in the 19th century fashion, or paper made in the 18th or 19th century.

About this time appear the first songs of the Old Believers and of the sects formed within their midst. These songs are occasionally mere adaptations from the old song repertoire, but some are entirely new and show traces of the syllabic system which did not become generally known until the 17th century. Some songs are taken from literary sources (from Simeon Polockij and the Ukrainians).

8. KOSMA GREK

1. The Greeks who came to Muscovy as teachers (see VII, 1, 6) also left some traces in Moscow's spiritual life but very little however in literature. Arsenij Grek, a man who had already been a Uniate and even a Mohammedan, worked in Moscow after 1649. Strangely enough, in view of the fact that his repeated changes of faith had caused him temporary banishment to the Solovki Monastery he worked on the "improvement" of books. He translated various texts, including Lives of Catherine and Alexis, which had been repeatedly printed after 1660 in bad translations, and in collaboration with his fellow countryman Dionisij, the chronograph of Metropolitan Dorotheos (17th century), which included many apocryphical elements.

In 1673 Nikolaj Spafarij (Spatharios), a Greek or a Rumanian of Greek upbringing, compiled a book on sibyls from Greek sources (see also VII, 15, 3).

Unknown Greek authors translated, about 1700, Ἁμαρτωλῶν σωτηρία ("The Salvation of Sinners") by Agapios of Crete (1641) – a collection of legends which are reminiscent of the old paterikons; some of the legends appeared there via Western intermediaries.

Probably from the Greek, too, came the tale of the proud king Aggej (the origin of the name is not clear), which corresponds to the story of Evinian in the *Gesta Romanorum*. This legend was later used as the foundation of stories by Garšin and Remizov.

2. The most important work by a Greek, however, was the new redaction of Franciscus Skuphos' Greek rhetoric, which had previously appeared in Venice in 1681 (Σκοῦφος: Τέχνη ῥητορικῆς). It had already been revised in Slavonic in 1698 by Sofronij Lichud; however, Kosma Grek revised this work again about 1705, extensively "Russifying" the numerous examples. This is one of the highest accomplishments of the Baroque in Russia. Skufos, a Uniate, linked the Greek tradition of the amplified style with the tradition of the Baroque. The Russification consisted in the insertion of examples from Russian history and Lives of the Saints, where every example, sometimes a whole page in length, was constructed according to a certain artistic device (trope or figure). Thus St. Vladimir gives Kosma the opportunity of introducing a little etymological enquiry (a favourite device of baroque literature): Vladi-mir "the ruler of the whole world" (the Greek adds carefully: "the *Russian* world"). The etymology is false but enables Kosma to write a panegyric which contains, besides, a series of rhetorical questions: "Who was praised at that time?", etc. Quite a good example of irony is a compliment to the Old Believers. In the same way he goes through the entire gamut of tropes and figures. The examples provide, too, a collection of compounds which are un-matched even by Manasses. Worthy of note is the obviously new creation *ad hoc*, or after Greek models, of words which sometimes do not sound quite Slavonic, but which on the whole are successful. Here are only a few examples from several hundreds: *kamenno-serdečnyj, širokopučinnoe more, ètnoplamennyj, muschouchaše, gorodvižnaja cěvnica, svjatověnceu-krasitel'nyj, rogoženosec, Velzevuloučitel'nye vols'vi, Zosimosavvatijnyj, veselovidnye cvěta*, etc. (with a stony heart; sea with a bottomless pit; fiery like Etna; smelt of musk; the flute which moves mountains; adorned with the crown of saintliness; the wearer of mat [as attire]; the sorcerers who have learned from Beelzebub; resembling the saints Zosima and Savvatij; the gay-looking colours).

Moreover, Kosma finds no difficulty in constructing not only noun-compounds, but also verb- and adverb-compounds. It is interesting that numerous compounds are also used now: *povsednevnyj, blagopolučnyj, dušepoleznyj, blagonadežnyj*, though, to be sure, sometimes in another sense: everyday, receiving the good, edifying, trustworthy), etc. Besides, one can see here the exuberance of rhetorical embellishments in a narrower sense: exclamations, questions, apostrophisings, and even a monologue (with epanaphora) is introduced, or the exposition of false rumours which however had been set about earlier (of St. Andreas of Crete). The "examples" offer ancient mythological and historical adornments, too, otherwise not so richly represented in the Russian Baroque; the Russian saints and princes are either compared with or contrasted with Hercules, Theseus, Atlas, Orpheus and others; moreover, geographical and historic-al names appear in unprecedented profusion. Anecdotes are also used, not all of which are properly suited to the predominantly religious content of the examples. We also find here modern material (e.q., *blagopolučnaja Amerika* – prosperous America). Kosma's rhetoric is even today one of the richest Russian sources for the study of baroque poetics.

9. THE THEATRE

1. Theatrical performances in Moscow were planned by Tsar Aleksej

Michailovič as early as 1660. Moreover, some influence might have been exerted by the reports of the embassy to Italy in 1659 which contained a special chapter on "comedies". When in 1672 the Tsar again took up his plan, he might have heard already on the subject from Simeon Polockij. Nevertheless, the Ukrainian theatre, to which Simeon certainly had referred, played no part in the foundation of the Moscow theatre. The Tsar sent for actors and producers from abroad; they, however, did not come, and the first performance was staged by the German pastor, Gregory, with the help of the members of the German colony. It took place on October 17th, 1672, at the Court Theatre. The feminine roles were played by men. The language of the performances was German, so that at first they were regarded by the audience merely as spectacles (*zrelišče*). Then the plays were translated. In the meantime Russian actors were being trained by Gregory. After the latter's death in 1675, the management was taken over by a Ukrainian, a former teacher at the Kiev Academy, S. Čyžynśkyj. However, after the death of Tsar Aleksej in 1676, his successor Fedor discontinued the performances.

2. At first the plays treated only biblical subjects, Esther, Tobias, Judith, St. George, Adam and Eve, Joseph, David and Goliath. Only later were performed an adaptation of the last acts of Marlow's *Tamburlaine the Great* (1587) and a comedy on Bacchus and Venus (probably by Čyžynśkyj). The four plays, which are partly extant in fragments, were – it seems – written by Gregory utilizing German popular theatrical plays and biblical stories. Most of the plays imitated the type of the so-called "English comedies" of the German theatre. The comedy on Adam and Eve by the German collaborator of Gregory, Georg Gviner, is a mystery-play with allegorical figures: Justice, Truth, Grace, Compassion, Peace. Of the comedy on Bacchus and Venus only the list of the *dramatis personae* is known. The cast comprised, beside Venus and Bacchus, thirteen drunkards, ten maidens, musicians and several other persons, and this gives an idea of this type of performance.

The language of the extant plays which were translated from the German by officials is very poor; next to numerous loan translations (*Lehnübersetzungen = calques*) from the German, like *ščastopadenie* (*Glücksfall* – lucky incident) and *okomgnovenie* (*Augenblick* – an instant) and similar others we come across numerous Ukrainian or Byelo-Russian words: *ne maju, šmat chlěba, otpověd'* (I have not, a piece of bread, answer), etc., which probably remained incomprehensible to the audience. Particularly poor is the rendering of the tragic and lyrical passages; better translated are the monologues, which employ biblical language, and the speeches delivered by the comic characters, which are rendered with the help of popular everyday speech. The jokes are primitive, yet sometimes effective. In the comedy about Judith the comic characters are a Babylonian soldier and Judith's servant, Abra. The soldier is a glutton and a coward; Abra says foolish things at the most inopportune moments – when Judith, after having killed Holophernes, says a prayer of thanks, Abra remarks, "What will this poor man say when he wakes up and Judith will be gone with his head?" The Babylonian soldier also makes a similar joke on a different occasion.

The construction of the plays is perhaps their strongest point; the themes are exciting and rich in variety, the authors alternating the tragic and comic scenes. The religious moral was presumably ever-present.

Whether the two plays by Simeon Polockij (VII, 5, 6) were performed, we do not know.

3. The theatrical performances were recommenced in the 18th century. At first the performances began in schools, at the Moscow Academy in 1701, then in many towns, at Rostov (see VII, 6, 3), Novgorod, Astrachan', Tver' (in the 1740's), even in Siberia – at Irkutsk and Tobol'sk. At the instigation of Tsar Peter plays began to be performed in 1702 in the newly built Court Theatre at Moscow, but they ceased in 1707 when the court moved to St. Petersburg. In 1707 the Tsar's sister, Natal'ja, founded a private theatre which existed until 1717. There was also a theatre at the court of Peter's sister-in-law, the widow of his brother Ivan. Another theatre was founded in Moscow at the Surgeons' College. Later, performances were given at the court of Catherine I, Anna, and Elisabeth. This expansion meant first of all a widening of the circle of spectators, as access to Peter's theatre or to the theatre at the Surgeons' College, as well as in the provincial schools, was open to all. In fact, however, visitors were predominantly members of the nobility.

The companies were in part still German (Peter's theatre, since he also allowed the Germans to open a dramatic school; the Empress Anna's); otherwise the actors were amateurs, for instance, students.

4. The theatrical plays were quite varied. In the ecclesiastical schools the Ukrainian movement ruled with plays on religious themes, mystery-plays and morality-plays; next to them panegyrical plays were acted in which Russian rulers and their deeds were glorified. At other theatres it was mostly the translated or adapted plays of the European baroque stage

which were performed; among others there were adapted von Lohenstein's *Sophonisbe*, Moliére's *Amphitryon*, *Le médecin malgré lui* and *Les précieuses ridicules*, a French Don Juan play and a French adaptation of Calderon, a few Italian plays, etc. The plays are of various types, determined by the monarch's whim. The religious plays are the ones most strongly bound by tradition. The heroic plays are an innovation (the heroes are Alexander the Great, Caesar, Scipio), where strong passions, high rhetoric, and elevated style predominate. But nowhere was there any depth to the psychology of the heroes nor in the development of the characters. Still more difficult for the translator and adapter was the rendering of romantic and erotic themes and motifs. In this instance the translation of the foreign texts was hardly ever successful; lyricism was replaced by arid imitation of alien formulas or by rhetoric. Not much more successful was the rendering of the comic element, which was mostly vulgar and coarse. Some spectators, among them Empress Anna, certainly found pleasure in this grossness. The "Interludes" were better; in conformity with Ukrainian tradition, they were presented between the acts of religious plays, and their popular language and topical themes (for example – the Old Believers) contrived to create successful caricatures. There were also plays which were ostensibly meant only as farces; merely the general outline of the plot was sketched, the text being left to the improvisation of the actors. Peter I tried to use the stage for propaganda purposes. There appeared purely panegyrical plays, the content of which was determined only by the declamation; the topical themes were linked with historical or religious ones, so that the audience should be able to recognise the glorified Russian rulers behind the historical heroes represented.

The task of selecting plays was entrusted – as well as to the Ukrainian clergy known to us – almost exclusively to anonymous persons who, it seems, possessed no great ability. That is why the majority of the secular plays which are so far known, although important for the history of culture, are in no way significant from the literary point of view. The authors had not sufficiently mastered their medium. As far as language is concerned, many plays are quite poor; they show the same mixture of language as the 17th-century plays; and, moreover, the use of linguistic levels is by no means regulated, so that in the "light" scenes there occur heavy Church Slavonic forms and turns of phrase, and we come across vulgarisms in the pathetic monologues. Foreign words are numerous; they belonged, however, at that time to the everyday language and also did not have Church Slavonic or Russian equivalents. The religious plays are better; though often with strong Ukrainisms and Polonisms. The most popular play, "The Comedy of Count Farson" (1730), a play of the school theatre, was far more successful in depicting the polite world than were the works of the court-stage. The Count arrives at the Portuguese court where he wins the love of the queen and draws upon himself the hostility of the courtiers. After he has been removed by them, the queen commits suicide, though earlier she had ordered the execution of the courtiers. The language of love and passion is certainly strongly influenced by the language of lyrical poetry (see VII, 6, 7).

On the whole, the theatrical plays of the first half of the 18th century showed no substantial success in the development of *literature*.

6. Under the influence of these works – no matter how one may wish to appraise them – there came into being a small group of plays for the popular theatre. These include *Car Maksimilian*, a story of a heathen emperor who orders the execution of his son Adolf, who had become a Christian. This play continued to enjoy popularity right up to the 20th century. The origin of the subject-matter is probably connected with the execution of the son of Peter I, Aleksej. The Czech popular theatre (viz.: the play concerning St. Dorothea – *Dorotka*) seems to have exerted an influence on it.

10. TRANSLATED LITERATURE IN THE PETRINE PERIOD

1. With the last chapters we have come to the 18th century. To be sure, the works of the Ukrainians and the Greeks in Moscow, of the Old Believers, and partly also the theatre, were a direct sequel of the 17th century literature. In the field of letters, the Petrine period at first brought little that was new.

Peter I did much for the popularisation of books, which were now systematically printed. And what is more, since the introduction of the "civil" type of letter-press next to the Church Slavonic, they were also printed in this new type (*graždanskaja azbuka*). Looking, however, through the titles of some 600 books published under Peter, we are struck by the "practical" orientation of most publications; books for divine service were printed, but among them only the Kievan Paterikon and the Reading Menaea by St. Dimitrij of Rostov (VII, 6, 3) and some further writings intended for reading.

The books in the civil type were just as practical; they were numerous, mainly technical text-books, laws, decrees; to some of those F. Prokopovyč (VII, 6, 5) had contributed theoretical arguments (see VII, 15). The books which were intended for reading were mostly historical or instructive and almost exclusively translations (exceptions are several congratulatory poems and valedictory sermons; only the Kievan "Synopsis" (see VII, 6, 6) and the history of the

A CHURCH IN THE VILLAGE DUBROVNICY NEAR MOSCOW
Beginning of the 18th century. The Western influence in church architecture.

A VISION OF ST. MATFEJ OF PEČERSK

An illustration in a manuscript of the 18th century. An illustration to the tale of St. Isaakij
(already in the Nestor Chronicle under the year 1074, later in the Kiev Paterikon). The
manuscript probably originated in Old Believer circles.

Ottoman Empire by D. Kantemir (VII, 12) were important original works).

The translations to be printed were now systematically selected, but the literary field was neglected. Historical works were published, or works which were erroneously considered as such. Next to the translation of the Introduction to European History by Samuel Pufendorff, both Flavius Josephus and Guido de Columna were now printed; instead of the old Alexandreis, a translation of Quintus Curtius was published. Next to this, the fantastic history of the Slavs by Mauro Orbini, Aesop's Fables and the Apophthegmata were published because they were instructive. The only newly translated printed work of literary significance were the *Colloquia familiaria* by Erasmus; but it was probably classed with such books as the guide to letter-writing (*Kak pišutsja komplimenty*) compiled on the basis of translations, and a manual of good behaviour (*Junosti čestnoe zercalo*). Erasmus was to contribute to the creation of a "new man" who would be able to behave well, write courteous letters, and lead conversations (according to Erasmus). One great value of Erasmus' *Colloquia* lay is its exemplary Latin; now, however, the text was rendered from the Dutch translation and was, moreover, to serve as a reader of Dutch with the help of the parallel printed Dutch text.

Of purely literary significance were the engravings to Ovid's Metamorphoses (without text!) and a compiled emblem book (*Symbola et emblemata*) with the aphorisms in eight languages.

Among the scientific works which were intended for reading, one can properly include only Huygens' Cosmography.

Naturally, the few publications which were intended and suitable for reading were also of great significance. Unfortunately, though many works – mainly those of Flavius Josephus, Curtius, Guido de Columna, and Aesop – were several times reprinted, one cannot thereby conclude that they enjoyed great popularity. It is worthy of note, however, that the language of the printings varied greatly; next to the Church Slavonic, there were now works which had a quite varied linguistic colouring; and which contained to varying extent the typical vocabulary of Petrine times (§ 7). The religious works remained, however, much more popular than the works of secular literature, almost up to the end of the 18th century.

2. Several translations which were also intended for print remained in manuscript, especially those which had originated on private initiative. Some of these existed in two different translations.

The utilitarian principle ruled over the selection of works as well as for their printing. Purely literary interest, however, was decisive only in the case of the new translation of Ovid's Metamorphoses (see VII, 2, 4), this time from the German, and in that of the satirical *Parnasskie izvestija* by Boccalini ("News from Parnassus", original 1649), perhaps also of the anecdotal "Solomon's Judgments", twice translated from the Italian. Most of the translated works were instructive; thus the *Pričti nravoučitel'nye* (with emblems), the original of which is ascribed to a non-existent Italian writer Mirobolius Tassalinus. It is, however, the work of a Polish poet, St. H. Lubomirski *Adverbiorum moralium...libellus* (1688). Also translated at that time were various favourite poetical writings in the form of "Conversations in the Kingdom of the Dead" (for

instance, between Gustavus Adolphus and Charles I of England, and others);
and the emblematic political book by D. Foxardo Saavedra (from the Latin;
one of the two translations is by F. Prokopovyč).

Neither were translations of religious literature lacking; the "Imitation of
Christ" (cf. VII, 2, 2) was translated for the second time in 1719; also another
writing (otherwise unknown) on the "Four Last Things" (cf. VII, 2, 4), as well
as the emblematic-mystical book by Hermanus Hugo, *Pia Desideria*, – an important work of baroque mysticism which served as a basis for the works of Jan
Luyken, Gottfried Arnold and Mme de Guyon.

Attempts were also made to enrich scientific literature, but with little success.
Among the translated works were Fioraventi's *Zercalo nauk* ("The Mirror of
Sciences"; in Italian *Lo Specchio di scienza universale*, 1564; in Latin in
1625); physiognomics by Johannes Taisnier (original 1562); Hippocrates'
aphorisms; Justus Lipsius' political works (translated twice); Ch. G. van
Bessel's "The Tailor of Political Fortune" (German original 1673; in the translation the "tailor" was replaced by a "smith"). Even foreign works concerning
Russian events were taken up; thus a writing on Steńka Razin was translated
from the Dutch.

The haphazard selection of most of these works is striking. Moreover, almost all are quite obsolete.

3. The school education which Peter strove to organise was secular and almost exclusively practical. Its significance for the development of literature was
slight. In any case, Latin was now taught to a greater extent than hitherto. In
1725 the Academy of Sciences was founded, combining scientific work with
educational activity. It consisted at first only of foreign scholars of various
qualifications and ability. Soon the Academy started to publish scientific works,
exclusively in foreign languages (first in Latin). But soon the work of translation
also became organised. This remained, however, very limited and had no
literary character (except for translations from ancient literature). In any case,
even as late as 1743, the Academy complained that it had not available for
purchase even the writings of Petrine times. One has to single out among the
productions of the Academy the translation of B. Gracian's famous book
which contained advice on the art of living (17th century); the neo-Latin
political novel by J. Barclay, *Argenis* (1747, the original appeared in 1621); the
"Conversation on the Plurality of Worlds" by Fontenelle (translated by
Kantemir in 1740; original edition 1686). Thus all these books belonged to the
preceding century.

Of great importance also was the fact that the Academy produced a journal
after 1728 (a weekly at first, later appearing twice a week), and from 1728 to 1748
the "St. Petersburg News" – *Sankt-Peterburgskie Vedomosti* and during the
same period also the popular scientific periodical "Notes" (*Primečanija*) as a
supplement to this newspaper, in which there also appeared occasional poems.
As early as 1727 the publication printed an attempt at a "tonal" translation of a
poem by the German baroque poet, Hancke, and after 1735 the tonal translations of Trediakovskij; between 1733 and 1739 it also published five literary-
theoretical essays mostly concerned with the theatre.

The activity of the Academy was stimulated in 1747 by its new president,

K. Razumovśkyj. At that time two important Russian scholars, Trediakovskij and Lomonosov (see VII, 13 and 14) belonged to the Academy.

Further publishing activity was limited again to Church books, occasional poems, and individual sermons.

4. The manuscript translations of adventure novels and tales constituted a special group of translations. It is a chequered and sorry picture of literary decline. This is not the best section of baroque literature, but rather its meanest product. Their content consisted in fantastic adventures of knights or cavaliers who wander through various lands in order to reach at the end the happy union with the beloved. The heroes are foreigners: Evdon, the Greek prince Kaleander, the Spanish cavaliers Doltorn and Venecian, the English *Milord George*, the Italian prince Cylodon, among them, too, the Elector Augustus of Saxony. The heroines were also all princesses or queens, with similar foreign names. Only by chance is scattered among these translations an occasional work of literary value, which, however, is completely spoilt by the translation, for the translators are merely interested in adventure and obliterate emotional or instructive elements. One of the tales is, like its original, in verse. One should not expect these works to give a true picture of the countries where the action takes place; the plot changes frequently, the field of action being not only European countries, but also Africa, America and Asia. However, there is no question at all of a description of Europe. Only the infiltration of certain elements of knightly and court culture and of erotic motifs has a significance for the development of the reader's ideas.

The translations, which derived from German, French and Polish originals, were themselves often translations of bad translations.

The language is one of the weakest points of this literature. It is an often grotesque and generally inept mixture of Church Slavonic, the colloquial language of the time (with many "barbarisms" characteristic of the period) and the popular language. Only rarely does one succeed in finding a trace of the influence of Russian folk-lore.

5. Another small but noteworthy group of translations is constituted by the publications of the Pietists. This Protestant movement represented the point of view that Greek Orthodoxy had retained many elements of early Christianity. In order to strengthen these elements among the orthodox Christians and also occasionally to convert them to the Protestant faith, a series of translations were undertaken. Luther's short catechism was published by the Swedes for the population of the regions occupied during the Northern War. Other (non extant) manuscript translations were made by some Swedish prisoners who found themselves in Siberia. Instructive literature was systematically published in Halle by the Pietist circle of August Hermann Francke: first, about 1719, the same catechism of Luther (the copy known only from a part-copy), then – after Peter's reign, and with the aid of F. Prokopovyč – a series of works by Pietists, which were all translated by Simon Todorśkyj, at that time a student in Halle and later Bishop of Pskov. Prominent among these was the translation of the main work of a precursor of Pietism, Johann Arndt (16th century) – the "Four Books on true Christianity" (1735). This book achieved a certain dissemination in Russia, and even in monastic libraries. Characteristically, the translators used without exception Church Slavonic: there was as yet no other language in Russia to express theological ideas, although Todorśkyj, the Ukrainian, introduced some Ukrainisms into it. The latter also translated some Latin and German Church hymns into Church Slavonic.

One of the first attempts to treat theological questions in the vernacular was made by the German Pietist H. W. Ludolf, who visited Moscow at the end of the 17th century, in some discourses included in the first grammar of Russian (not Church Slavonic!). The book itself was printed in Oxford in Latin in 1698. An attempt to translate at least the first sentences of the Bible into spoken Russian was made by the German pastor J. Chr. Stahl from Pomerania in 1745.

6. The complicated process of mixing, especially in the area of vocabulary, which the Russian literary language underwent at this time appears now in the translations. Numerous barbarisms are added to the Ukrainisms and Polonisms of the 17th century – further borrowed words and loan translations (*calques – kal'ki*) from German, Dutch, French and English and occasionally from Italian. The fate of these words can be easily followed in the 18th-century literature. Some have survived to the present day, some disappeared after a few decades and were replaced by Russian words or by new borrowings; the third group was retained only in technical terminology of some fields (mainly naval and military); the fourth group found perhaps from the very beginning only scant popularity (possibly in the language of the Tsar himself) and very soon ceased to exist. Here are some examples of words which have become fully absorbed into the Russian language: *adrẹs, ambicija, gavan', gazeta, dama, deboš, genij, žurnal, zontik* (Dutch), *lazaret, medik, osoba* (Polish), *persona, risunok* (Polish), *fabrika*, etc. (address, ambition, port, newspaper, lady, debacle, genius, periodical, umbrella, hospital, physician, person, person, drawing, factory). Some of them have later contracted, or extended their meaning. For instance, *štraf* means now only a fine. The second group were replaced by words such as various designations from the field of fashion and besides by such as *assambleja, vachmistr, viktoria, abšid*, etc. (party, sergeant major, victory, resignation from office). The third group of words contains numerous expressions from the naval sphere (the incomprehensibleness of which is clearly demonstrated in Čechov's comedy, "The Wedding"), also probably *abris, amunicija, kurs, cejchgaus*, etc. (sketch – now only in the language of painters and technical draughtsmen – military equipment, direction, arsenal). Some words of this group have changed their meaning too; thus, for instance, *cirkul'*, which at that time meant both a circle and a pair of compasses, has retained only its second meaning, the first one being replaced by the Slavic *krug*. – For only a short time there survived such words as *ambasada, ambasador, gumor, eksercicija, kollegium, polites, maestat, ekzempel', elekcija, fortuna* and many others (embassy, ambassador, humour, exercise, collegium, politeness, majesty, example, choice, luck). Many words have been contracted to a narrow (often new) meaning: *direkcija* now means board of directors or governing body, earlier – direction; *ministr* – now only a member of the government, meant also a priest at the beginning of the 18th century; *kompliment* – now only the flattering word (compliment), was earlier much wider – politeness, *familija* – now only surname, previously meant the family (*sem'ja*).

With the exception of religious writings, the language of the translated works is mostly a colourful mixture of the various elements which had existed in the 17th century, with the addition of these new words (mainly groups 1, 3 and 4).

The position was similar in the field of morphology, and to a certain extent in syntax. Here, however, the Church Slavonicisms and barbarisms were mostly removed painlessly, even if not always quickly. Only a strong creative hand could bring order into the province of vocabulary. Such was Lomonosov's role (VII, 14, 2), even if he did not solve all the problems.

11.   THE TALES

1. The 18th-century tales are usually designated as belonging to "the Petrine times". This is incorrect. For only one of them can really be dated in the period before the death of Peter I. Peter's times were "void" from the literary point of view. One could possibly find an explanation to fit one's own preferences, but, in fact, the period in question lived to a certain extent on the old literature. Prokopovyč's works, too, belonged in their "tonality" to the old times, as well as the first work of Kantemir (VII, 12, 1), which appeared after Peter's death (1727) and was of religious character (Psalter-concordance). Partly, however, people read foreign literature in the original, as Kantemir did; or poems were written for private circulation, like the early lost poems by the same Kantemir.

The translated tales (see VII, 10, 4) were able to satisfy the need for entertaining reading. A few works of the same type of adventure-erotic novels appeared. Who wrote them we can hardly conjecture, except in a late instance where the author names himself (1750). By a process of elimination, however, one can at least establish that the authors were probably entirely uneducated persons, that they were not attached to the Old, at least not consciously (unconsciously they did not dare to transgress certain limits, for instance they did not question the right of parents to choose the husband for their daughter), that finally they were not very scrupulous as regards morals. Only one positive thing can be said of these writers: they were certainly "The new men", upstarts who in these new times saw all the doors open "to the higher sphere", open to themselves and their like, just as a 20th century servant-girl, under the influence of films, considers it conceivable that she may marry a millionaire, or at least become a film star. Only the servant-girls write no film scripts, but the Russian upstarts (or those who merely aspired to such a status) wrote novels in the first half of the 18th century. There were not many, how-

ever; one can name only half a dozen original works between 1700 and
1750. A "novel in verse", in the form of an autobiography of a minor
official, apparently belongs to the second half of the 18th century.

The fertile soil from which these tales sprang up was the enthusiasm
for the exciting plots of the translated novellas. In addition to these, the
plot of the original tale is always laid in a foreign country; only the hero
is a Russian, who, however, can only find his fortune in Europe. This
Europe has a rather peculiar geography: from Vienna to Florence one
travels by sea, from England to Egypt by land, from Spain to Ethiopia one
one goes on foot, from Moscow to Paris one rides on horseback in a few
days. The objects of the heroes' inclinations are all foreign maidens.
Honours and riches, glory and friends – everything is found only abroad.
One could regard the authors and their novels as an expression of a
"Westernism" driven to extremes, if one could take them seriously at all.
Yet this one cannot do in any case. Without doubt, from the very outset,
they were creating a lower literary level which made no tradition; their
work became extinct without leaving any heirs behind. The tradition of
the older literature, including that of the tales, remained, however. Later
tales tied on to yet another older tradition the tradition of folklore.

2. It is sufficient to become acquainted with only a few such tales in
order to see clearly their value.

"The Story of the Russian sailor, Vasilij" is probably the oldest and
dates perhaps from the times of Peter I. Its second part is a close imitation
of the translated "Story of the Spanish nobleman Doltorn". Vasilij
Koriotskij (or Koriackij), the son of a poor Russian nobleman, is sent by
the government of "Russian Europes" (*Rossijskie Evropii*, plural!) to
Holland to study. There he lives in the house of a merchant whom he
helps in business, and who takes a liking to him. At the conclusion of his
studies, Vasilij betakes himself to his father, but only for a visit, for he has
already found his first good fortune in Holland. Vasilij's ship, however,
founders and he saves himself by swimming to a large island. Here begins
the second part of the story, which also differs from the first linguistically
by a greater simplicity. On the island, Vasilij meets a band of robbers
which he joins; after some time he is chosen leader of the brigands. As
such, he enters the house of the robbers, and finds there in a locked cell a
beautiful girl who is royally arrayed and is in reality the daughter of the
Florentine (*Florenskij*) king – Iraklija. Vasilij now flees together with the
princess, with the help of fishermen who usually supply the robbers. Then
they travel by mail ship to Austria (*Cesarija*) where – thanks to the jewels

taken from the brigands by Vasilij – they can live luxuriously, and where Vasilij soon becomes known to the Emperor and tells him his story and that of the princess. The Emperor receives Vasilij as a brother. This is Vasilij's second piece of good fortune in foreign parts. However, there arrives at Vienna the Florentine Admiral, with a fleet. After long negotiations, the Admiral succeeds in getting Vasilij and the princess aboard his ship. Then he makes drunk the guard whom Vasilij had cautiously taken with him, sets sail, orders Vasilij to be thrown into the sea, and sails to Florence as the saviour of Iraklija. When the Emperor learns all this, he sends 4,000 men under the "General and Cavalier" Flegont against Florence. Vasilij meanwhile, in a small boat in which the officers had against the Admiral's orders put him to sea, lands again on an island where he finds a fisherman who takes him to Florence before the Admiral arrives. Vasilij lives there as a servant in a workhouse (*bogadel'nja*). After three months the Admiral also arrives with the princess. He declares that he had freed Iraklija, and the king orders her to marry the Admiral. But when she is driving to church, she hears Vasilij singing a song (a clumsy imitation of the syllabic verses) in the workhouse, about their misfortunes. The princess alights from her carriage, finds Vasilij, brings him to the palace and tells her parents everything. After three days General Flegont also comes with the Emperor's army. The Admiral is flayed alive. Vasilij marries the princess, later visits the Emperor and, after the death of the king of Florence, reigns in his stead. This is the third and last piece of good fortune. "The Russian Europes", however, are completely forgotten both by the hero and the author.

One cannot deny that not only is the plot of the novella well developed but also that individual scenes and the dialogues, which appear fairly often, are well constructed. However, the narrative art of the author is far behind that of the 17th-century novelists. There is no trace of psychological characterisation. Neither is there a trace of motivation. Various episodes which often occur in folk-lore, for instance, the appearance of the "right" claimant to the hand of the heroine at the very moment of her wedding, are depicted in an extremely clumsy way. Only isolated motifs, for example, Vasilij's successes with the brigands, are dexterously presented. The language is worthy of note. The narrative starts in a completely archaic language with strong Church Slavonicisms and use of aorist and imperfect tenses, turning later to everyday speech in the episode of the brigands. The vocabulary, of course, remains very mixed: next to Church Slavonicisms (lexical and syntactic, e.g., the *dativus absolutus* and the declensions) we find words from chancery language (*poneže* – because) and barbarisms of Petrine times (*frunt, partija, parol', arija* – front; a detachment of troops, here a group of brigands; watch-word, but here promise; aria). Besides these, there are few popular expressions. In many instances, however, the foreign words are falsely rendered or misunderstood. Properly speaking, there are no expressions of love in the story; the author characterizes the condition of the enamoured hero with a reference to a similar situation in one of the tales of "The Seven Sages" (see VII, 2, 6).

Is the hero a "new man"? Hardly. He is depicted as a good pupil and business man, and as cunning and shrewd (among the brigands). He feels a "slave" (*rab*) in the presence of the Emperor, though he himself is of noble birth. He forgets his father, as did Savva Grudcyn; he even forgets the "Russian Europes" – his native land, but still, during the reign of Boris Godunov, i.e., at the end of the 16th century, some young men had been sent to study in England and not one of them returned to Russia. Vasilij has just as little *spiritual* quality as most heroes of the wonder tales who marry princesses indeed, even less than such heroes.

3. A decade later (probably between 1728 and 1732) there appeared a long story much more accomplished from the literary point of view, namely, the "Story of Alexander, a Russian nobleman". This novella depicts a young man who merely pretends (in a long speech to his parents) to want to study abroad; in reality, however, he desires and indeed has several amorous affairs. The narrative is condensed from several tales. Aleksandr sets forth for Paris, and from there to Lille. There he wins the love of a pastor's daughter, Eleonora. But the daughter of a general, Hedwig-Dorothee (*Gedwig-Doroteja*) falls in love with Aleksandr, and she succeeds in estranging him from Eleonora. The abandoned sweetheart dies of sorrow. Then Alexandr abandons Hedwig-Dorothee and returns to Paris. There he forms an attachment with the daughter of the Chamberlain, Tirra, and after a duel with the "Spanish cavalier" Cycil'ko (sic!) he is forced to flee from Paris; Tirra and a Russian friend, Vladimir, accompany him. Together they visit various countries (fantastic geography!), Aleksandr and Tirra lose each other, but meet again after a few years, and set out for Russia. But Aleksandr, who found his good fortune in France, does not reach his native land; he is drowned, and Tirra commits suicide. Hedwig-Dorothee appears again and mocks at Tirra's corpse but dies too. Vladimir goes alone to Aleksandr's parents and becomes their heir.

This "Story" is written in a more artistic manner. It contains long dialogues, declarations of love which make rich use of traditional symbolism (the lover is the sick man, the lady is the doctor, love is a fire, a wound, an arrow, etc., cf. VII, 4, 5 and 6,7). The novella contains seven verse-insertions ("arias") and more than twenty letters. Moreover, short tales are incorporated too: they contain Vladimir's quite cynical accounts of his rather sordid love affairs. Also there is a conversation between three foreign knights (Baron Stark, Baron von Gerd and Silberstern) concerning women; this may perhaps have been borrowed. Besides Vladimir there appear further secondary characters. The beginnings of psychological characterization are present; at least the three women are very different. Vladimir is sufficiently characterized by his stories, while Aleksandr is almost a pawn who allows himself to be ruled by circumstances and other persons (the three sweethearts).

The language, in spite of the rather complicated phraseology, as in the love letters, is from the lexical point of view even more chequered than in Vasilij's story: there occur Church Slavonicisms, both single words and phrases – *věrna sušča, elika, jako, ašče, viždu, obrjaščet* (faithful, like, when, because, I see, he will find), as well as foreign words (*fortuna, rekomendovat', persona* – fortune, to recommend, person) and turns of phrase from love lyrics (see above).

Perhaps not so much this variegation of language, but the fantastic geography of the novella and the fact that the author seems to have sketched provincial life in Germany rather than France, show that he hardly belongs to the educated circles (even within the meaning of the word at that time). To be sure, he is, like his hero, a "new man"; their common ideal is, however, not that education about which Aleksandr speaks in the opening passages, but a voluptuous life not limited by moral scruples. It is a product not of the constructive but of the disintegrating influence of the Petrine reforms.

4. The third novella which may have been written at the same time as the tale concerning Aleksandr is the "Story of the Russian Merchant Ioann". Its action again takes place in foreign parts. The son of a merchant sets out for France "to learn foreign sciences." He lives with the merchant Anis Mal'tik and falls in love with his foster-daughter, the Spanish girl Eleonore, and seduces her with the aid of letters and serenades. But Mal'tik's daughter, Anna-Maria, steals one of Eleonore's love-letters and hands it to her father. The father administers a hiding to Ioann and sends him home. Eleonore is made to marry a "French sergeant of

the Guards" and Ioann returns home where he indeed "lives in well-being"; his happiness, however, remained in France. "He always had Eleonore in his thoughts"; she "never disappeared from his thoughts".

This novella, which is much shorter than the others, is obviously written according to the same pattern as the Aleksandr story. Only the social standing of the hero is characteristic. He certainly is a "new man" among "new men". There is however, some doubt as to whether the tale was written by a man of the same class as the hero. It rather appears to be the work of a man who looks up to merchants. It is by the same token a work of a lower literary type.

5. One can seek in vain in these novellas for the new spirit and the national feeling. Only the 18th-century dress of a Savva Grudcyn or a Frol Skobeev is new. And one can hardly trace a national consciousness (as Soviet scholars do) in these works in which the only function of Russia seems to be that of a country that one would like to leave in order to seek one's fortune elsewhere.

The small number of these novellas is significant (we do not mention further ones, for they are either extant in one single copy or written only about 1750 – cf. VII, 16). Still more significant is the fact that transcriptions of the 17th-century tales are still numerous in the following century. Even such tales as "Akir the Wise", "The Merchant Basarg" and "Varlaam and Josaphat" find numerous readers. Some of these were shortened and revised in the process of copying. Of some there appear new versions, thus of the novellas "Vasilij the Golden-Haired" and "Bova" (VII, 2, 6; VI, 2, 5).

And they are read, as the entries in the manuscripts show, by literate soldiers, petty chancery officials, merchants and bourgeois, squires (who even at the beginning of the 19th century belong to the semi-educated classes); they occasionally fell into the hands of a junior officer or of an educated person who certainly – if only he knew foreign languages and possessed some taste – read them as one reads detective stories today. One cannot see in these works any great literature of the Petrine times, indeed for this reason alone, that only the novella of Vasilij *perhaps* belongs to these times.

12. KANTEMIR

1. Prince Antioch Kantemir (1708–1744), who is called the first modern Russian poet, was significantly a foreigner – the son of the Moldavian

prince Dimitrij, himself a scholar (he published a history of the Ottoman Empire, in Latin and Russian). In 1711 Kantemir's father fled to Russia, where he took part in Peter I's abortive war against Turkey. In Russia the son received an excellent education. At home the Kantemirs spoke Italian and modern Greek. Antioch learned Russian from a certain Il'inskij who acquainted him with the syllabic system of prosody, and who also entered into Trediakovskij's life (see VIII, 13, 1). For a while he attended the Ecclesiastical Academy in Moscow, then the school attached to the Academy of Sciences, where members of the Academy gave some of the instruction. He also accompanied his father on a journey to Persia. Apparently he had even by this time begun to compose poetry; he later mentions his love songs which are not extant. In 1727 appeared in print the "Symphony" of the Psalter (a concordance) compiled by him. Already as a young man (1729), Kantemir had joined Feofan Propokovyč' circle (VII, 4, 6), and at that time he wrote his first satire "Against the enemies of education" – *Na chuljaščich učenie* – which was aimed at the enemies of Prokopovyč's circle. In the following year Kantemir became entangled in higher politics; together with Prokopovyč and his friends he helped the Empress Anna to reject the claims of the courtiers to participate in the government. However, it was not the supporters of Peter I's cultural aspirations who came to power, but Anna's favourites totally uninterested in Russian culture and in part quite uneducated. Even so, in 1732, at the early age of twenty-four, Kantemir became the Russian Ambassador in London, and in 1738 in Paris, where he performed brilliantly as a diplomat. He moved in the intellectual circles of England and France. Kantemir died as early as 1744.

2. Kantemir was is no way a product of the Petrine times. By upbringing he remained a foreigner always. He corresponded with his relations in Italian. To be sure, he considered himself a Russian and wanted to become a Russian poet. He was not a "poet of Petrine times". For him these times were "the golden age" which he did not live to see. He became known as a poet much later. His activity coïncides with the great "literary vacuum" which the Petrine revolution had created in Russia (cf. VII, 1). Even his satire, which did not become known until four years after Peter's death, was only accessible to a narrow circle in manuscript copies. In 1744, it is true, he published his translations from Horace and a treatise on versification. Only the first five of his nine satires were written in Russia; like the three following ones, which were written abroad where Kantemir revised the old ones, they appeared first in 1762 in an

inaccurate edition, so that as a literary work they took effect only in the time of Catherine II. The ninth satire was published for the first time in 1858. But the satires had appeared in a French prose translation as early as 1749, and had been translated into German verse in 1752 by a not insignificant poet, J. Spilker.

3. We have already referred to the First Satire, which is also the most famous one. It deals with four types of enemies of education: an adherent of ritual piety, Kriton; an uneducated landlord, Sil'van; a man of the world, Luka; and a fop, Medor. The objections of the latter are followed by Kantemir's own criticism of contemporary society. Each of the four enemies of education has his own reasons: Kriton thinks that education undermines religion as he understands it; Sil'van considers learning superfluous, as it does not yield any material gain; Luka prefers gay life to tedious studies; Medor is brief – he considers powder, clothes, wigs as much more important than ancient writers. Kantemir himself remarks that education is essential in his times neither for spiritual nor for secular callings. The "golden age" (he means Peter I's time) is gone; now only rank and riches are valued; learning ekes out a wretched existence, unheeded and even persecuted.

All the other satires are weaker, though most are much longer.

The Second Satire is a dialogue between Filaret and Evgenij and bears the title "Against Envy of Evil Noblemen"; Filaret's long observations treat the age old theme that to be sure had gained a new topicality since Peter's day, namely, the pre-eminence of merit over birth. The Third Satire (dedicated to Feofan Prokopovyč) and the Fifth depict various types of people. The Third, "On the Variety of Human Passions", sketches thirteen various types: a miser, a spendthrift, a chatterbox, etc. The Fifth is a dialogue between a man and a satyr, who imparts in great detail his observations on human vices (*zlonravije*). The Fourth, in imitation of Boileau, speaks of the "Danger of Writing Satires". The Sixth, "On True Felicity", starts with the ancient proverb:

Тот в сей жизни лишь блажен, кто малым доволен . . .

("Only he is happy in this life who contents himself with little.") The Seventh Satire, "On Education", is an epistle to Kantemir's friend, Prince N. Ju. Trubeckoj. Kantemir sees the essence of education in the imitation of good models; these ought to be provided by parents and pedagogues. The Eighth Satire is directed "Against Shameless Impudence". The

Ninth, "To the Sun", was not finally revised; the extant text comprises, beside the depiction of Old Believers' "superstitions" and of a similarly "superstitious" and immoral orthodox priest, an enumeration of conditions of this world "repugnant to God".

All Kantemir's other poems – a recast of the psalms, songs (two of these, "Against the Godless" and "Against Evil Men", are, properly speaking, also satires), epistles, epigrams, the beginning of an epos the hero of which was to be Peter I (*Petrida*) – are weaker. His translations of anacreontic songs and Horace's epistles are just as feeble. In the last years of his life, Kantemir also wrote a philosophical and religious treatise "Letters on Nature and Men" (1742). Among his translations one ought to mention chiefly his rendering of two of Boileau's satires and the translation of Fontenelle's work, "On the Plurality of Worlds" (1686) (composed in 1730, printed in 1740 and banned as "atheistic" in 1756). Various further works are lost, among others a treatise on mathematics and the translation of Montesquieu's "Persian Letters". His treatise on Russian versification appeared in print in 1744 (cf. VII, 13, 3).

4. Kantemir wrote his poems in syllabic verse: some he wrote in the "epodic" measure used by Prokopovyč, with alternation of long and short lines (ten and four syllables); at first he preserved the Ukrainian rhyme (ě rhymes with i). Later one can notice in his work various attempts to perfect the syllabic system: he uses masculine rhymes, writes rhymeless syllabic verse (translation of ancient authors), and introduces the caesura while revising his satires.

His verse, however, has two peculiarities which recur later in Trediakovskij and which made and still make some passages of his poetry difficult to understand. The first is the entirely arbitrary word order which he doubtless introduced in imitation of Latin poetry; the older syllabic system (Russian and Ukrainian) endeavoured to keep the "natural" sequence of words. We find in Kantemir, however, lines such as the following (the "natural" word order is shown by the numbers placed above each word):

$$\overset{1}{\text{к}} \overset{5}{\text{какому}} \overset{4}{\text{всяк}} \overset{3}{\text{у}} \overset{6}{\text{него}} \overset{2}{\text{спеет}} \text{ овощь сроку}$$

$$\overset{1}{\text{в}} \overset{2}{\text{двадцать}} \overset{3}{\text{лет,}} \overset{4}{\text{когда}} \overset{6}{\text{юность}} \overset{7}{\text{и в}} \overset{5}{\text{узде}} \text{ ретива (or 1, 2, 3, 6, 4, 5, 7)}$$

$$\overset{1}{\text{когда}} \overset{5}{\text{облак}} \overset{6}{\text{с}} \overset{2}{\text{наших}} \overset{3}{\text{мы}} \overset{7}{\text{прогоним}} \overset{4}{\text{глаз}} \text{ грубый (or 1, 7, 4, 2, 3, 5, 6)}$$

("At what time will he have every kind of fruit ripe: at the age of twenty, when youth is fiery even when restrained; when we chase away the thick cloud from before our eyes.") In other words, Kantemir admits any inversion, and even goes so far as to place a word in an alien context, thus breaking the continuity of words linked to one another. Kantemir also allows enjambments, in this respect following tradition; he has enjambments in fourteen per cent of the total number of his lines, i.e., as many as Simeon Polockij. Also grammatical rhymes still predominate in his poems; at most only thirty per cent his rhymes are non-grammatical.

Rhyme was an important constituent element of syllabic verse. In Kantemir's non-rhymed poems, the rhythmic character of speech can hardly be discerned. For instance:

> Кони убо на стегнах
> выжженой имеют знак,
> и парфянских всяк мужей
> по шапке может узнать.

or:

> или далее отшедши,
> приятные Благодати,
> танцы вы свои водите:
> любимица моя близко
> спочивает тут под древом,
> взбудить ее берегитесь...

("For the horses have a branded mark on their haunches and all can recognise the Parthians by their headgear. – Or dance, beatiful Graces, stepping further back: my beloved sleeps here under a tree, take care not to wake her up. ....") (Noteworthy are the masculine endings in the first quotation!) The language is rendered rhythmical by the use of caesuras and especially by rhyme. Should two lines rhyme accidentally in an otherwise non-rhymed poem, they immediately sound like verse:

> двигайте ноги легонько;
> велите играть тихонько...

("Move the feet lightly, have them play softly....")

Kantemir was more successful in refurbishing the vocabulary. To be sure, folk words and the vocabulary of everyday speech are freely mingled, but the Church Slavonic elements have largely receded into the background. Popular words are frequent: for instance, *nutko, provor, dokuka, oplošnyj,* or the unusual *kopok, žal'* (masculine), *nurit' vremja* (now, keenness, burdensomeness, faulty, kick, grief, to waste time) and so forth. There are also popular turns of phrase, as: *pjalit' glaza, ot golovy do pjat, razvesit' uši, lepit' goroch v stenu, aza v glaza ne znaet*, etc. (to stare, from head to feet, to hearken, to throw peas against a wall [i.e., effort in vain], he does not know the shape of the letter *A*).

There are also some quite unusual words or forms, presumably neologisms: *nachalit'sja, polizaja, tuča deneg* (to become impertinent, licking, a cloud [!] of money*), etc. The morphology and syntax are often either Church Slavonic or artificial.

Kantemir, however, often succeeds in coining forcible expressions, which later gained some currency, of the very least by virtue of his influence, such as:

> Как тебе вверить корабль? Ты лодкой не правил...
> ...итти станет сын тропою,
> котору протоптану видит пред собою.

or about a prodigal fop:

> деревню взденешь на себя ты целу.

or about a fashionable female:

> Настя румяна, бела своими трудами,
> красота ее в ларце лежит за ключами.

("How can one trust you with a ship? You never steered even a boat.... – the son will follow the path which he sees trodden in front of him. – You are dressing yourself in a whole village [meaning the price of clothing]. – Nastja is rosy-cheeked and white, thanks to her labors; her beauty is locked up in a box.") And about the profession of a satirist:

> Смеюся в стихах, а в сердце о злонравных плачу.

("I laugh in my poems, but in my heart I weep for evil men.")

Not without merit, too, are the sentences which he has the victims of his satires utter, as:

> Расколы и ереси науки суть дети...
> Приходит в безбожие, кто над книгой тает...

("Schisms and heresies are children of science... – He who pores over a book becomes godless.")

* Cf. Rumanian *întuneric*, Serbo-Croatian *tušta i tama* = a vast plenty of....

Живали мы преж сего, не зная латыни,
гораздо обильнее, чем мы живем ныне.

("We used to live before, without knowing any Latin, much more luxuriously than we live now.") Or didactic adages:

[нас] благородными явит одна добродетель...
Малым мудрая прожить природа нас учит...

("Only virtue proves [us] noble. – Wise nature teaches us to live with little [expense].") Or the comparision of a chatterbox with fermenting wine:

недавно то влитое ново вино в судно
кипит, шипит, обруч рвет, доски подувая,
выбьет втулку, свирепо устьми вытекая...

"The wine recently poured into a cask seethes, fizzes, bursts the hoop, blows the staves, thrusts the bung out, and pours furiously from the opening.") To be sure, these three lines are lexically uneven: *sudno* is not only a cask, but also any vessel; *poduvat'* – "blow" – is not quite clear; *ust'mi* is archaic. It is possible that these expressions, like many others, are made up of dialect words. The Church Slavonic syntax and morphology do not detract from the popular character of Kantemir's language.

His satires, however, are the product of learning; he himself was in the habit of writing commentaries on his poems and translations in which he explains what he is translating (thus his learned notes on Horace). He mentions the sources of his own poems, with their imagery and allegories; some passages in his satires appear in the light of his notes as centons (verses which are composed of lines from other people's verses). The successful translation, however, remains to his credit.

The satires contained, too, an immense number of pointed allusions to the contemporary scene, only part of which have been unravelled since by learned commentators. To be sure, there also appear in them allusions which reveal Kantemir's ignorance of Russian life, when, for instance, he makes fun of the literary and scholarly life (which certainly at that time did not exist at all in Russia) by having someone publish another's work under his own name, and another work for twenty years on a history of skates. (It would have been fortunate if such people had existed in Russia, but no one worked as a scholar either on a history of skates or on any other subject.) Kantemir was also successful in some of his brief and broad images: thus the description of the reception in the house of a favourite (there is a similar one in Griboedov), or the description of the day of an idler with a beginning that is reminiscent of later scenes in Deržavin (*Vel'moža*, etc.):

> Пел петух, встала заря, лучи осветили
> солнца верхи гор; тогда войско выводили
> на поле предки твои, а ты под парчею
> углублен мягко в пуху телом и душею,
> грозно соплешь, пока дня пробегут две доли,
> зевнул, растворил глаза, выспался до воли...

("The cock crowed, the dawn broke, the sun's rays illuminated the mountain peaks; at this hour your ancestors led the army in the field, whereas now you are snoring awfully, your body and soul softly plunged in an eiderdown, until two parts of the day are gone; you have yawned, opened your eyes, you have slept enough....")

5. Much more important than the external form of Kantemir's poetry is his *Weltanschauung* expressed in it: Kantemir is an admirer of the Petrine period, in favour of education and opposed to "old Russia". However, he conceives education in a much broader sense than even Peter himself; one can hardly discern in his work a purely practical attitude towards knowledge. He is interested in the upbringing of the complete man and primarily in his moral education. To be sure, while Kantemir emphasizes the didactic significance of his satires themselves, his later satires are rather an appeal for self-improvement. The militant note of the first satires has here almost disappeared: the Sixth Satire speaks of "true happiness"; the Seventh treats education in the restricted sense of the word; the Eighth is wholly insignificant. The first satires, however, provide a series of specifically Russian (sometimes, though, only slightly so) negative types whom Kantemir would like to see replaced by educated men, or men serving the State (or mankind; the two notions are not clearly differentiated). His charges against the cleargy seem to arise precisely from the fact that those very men who are called upon to educate society are of so low a character that they are incapable of carrying out this task. The anti-clerical character of many of Kantemir's statements should not blind us to the fact that he remained a devout Orthodox Christian, here too differing from Peter I.

What in fact Kantemir was striving for was a properly educated upper class of society. Even though he emphasizes the equality of nobility and serfs (*cholopi*), this does not prevent him from painting popular mores in extremely gloomy colours (Fifth Satire). The social problem does not interest him at all. Naturally, his contemporaries and posterity could draw from his satirical images many conclusions that he himself did not intend. This they did, only at a time when it was possible to place Fonvizin and the authors of satirical periodicals beside Kantemir.

6. The question remains where Kantemir should be placed in the history of literature. Kantemir himself never expounded his theoretical views on literature. He is often called, with little justification, "the first Russian classicist". His significance, however, is difficult to define. In his satires he is an imitator; he himself designates the themes and some particular motifs and adages of his work as imitations. His knowledge of satirical literature was very wide. Besides Boileau, he makes use of Horace and Juvenal, he alludes to Persius and Régnier, and in one passage he mentions Polish literature as his inspiration. Here perhaps he means the Polish baroque satire (the suggestion of Soviet scholars that in the passages concerned, *po-pol'ski* should read *po-gall'ski* [instead of Polish – Gallic, i.e., French] raises considerable doubts). Kantemir also knew the Italian satirists of the 17th century. And very much indeed distinguishes him from the master of Classicism – Boileau: from the formal point of view – the numerous enjambments which Boileau rejects; linguistically – the use of popular speech and his interest in folk-lore (e.g. proverbial expressions; he quotes a historical song, too). Kantemir could not have been unaware of the fact that Boileau was an opponent of popular lore and was unwilling to accord full recognition to such writers as La Fontaine, Molière and Perrault. Some passages recall Steele and Addison, to be sure, *via* the French imitations of their periodicals, which he names in his diary as early as 1728. Above all, however, Kantemir's satires differ from those of Boileau by the concreteness of his imagery, which stands in complete contrast to the Frenchman's abstract sketches of types. There seem to exist some links between Kantemir's method and the old and new Character Writings (Theophrastus and La Bruyère). Occasional Polish forms (Joviš, in Polish Jowisz – Jupiter) raise the possibility of Polish influence independently of Kantemir's own testimony (see above). He is vigourously opposed to French culture and equally, in part, to French literature (Voltaire). On the other hand, he is concerned with Italian literature, that is to say, as may be judged from chance evidence, predominantly with that of the Renaissance, but also with that of the Baroque (the satirist T. Boccalini). One of Kantemir's Odes ("Praise of the Sciences") is a translation from the Italian (of an unknown original).

In any case, Kantemir is not "the first classicist" of Russian literature. Genetically, his versification derives from the Ukrainian-Russian Baroque, perhaps also from the Polish (see above). Except for a "chronographic" epigram we find in his work no genres especially typical of the Baroque; his satires are stylistically nearer to the Polish satires of L. Opaliński than to Boileau's. It is also characteristic that militant Russian Classicism, such as that of Sumarokov, does not consider Kantemir an ally. It may well be that Kantemir's language, which by no means measured up to classical requirements, was responsible for the rather cool reception of his works among classicists.

Thus Kantemir is left within the period to which he chronologically belongs. A detailed analysis of his style might well assign him a place among the poets of the Baroque.

13. TREDIAKOVSKIJ AND VERSE-REFORM

1. In a biographical legend, Puškin makes Peter I foresee the fate of Vasilij Kirillovič Trediakovskij. The young son of a priest who fled to Moscow in order to study, Vasilij is said to have been presented to Peter, who remarked concerning him, "an utterly indefatigable toiler" (*večnyj tružennik*). This phrase offers the best description of the career of this talented man. Unfortunately, the appreciation of Trediakovskij's accomplishments by his contemporaries did not do justice to their true value; and neither did this value correspond to the efforts which they cost this "indefatigable toiler".

Trediakovskij was born in 1703, the son of a priest in Astrachan'. There he learned Latin from the Catholic monks who belonged to the foreign colony. By chance he met Kantemir's teacher Il'inskij, who was staying there with Kantemir. Il'inskij's stories concerning the Moscow schools filled the boy with such enthusiasm that he ran away from his father's house and studied for two years at the Ecclesiastical Academy in Moscow. Two years later he fled once more, this time to foreign parts where fortunately he gained the patronage of Russian diplomats. He studied for two years at The Hague, and three years in Paris at the Sorbonne and at the University. In 1730 he returned to Russia, where at first his prospects appeared quite good. He joined the circle of Prokopovyč, and his translation of the *précieux* novel by Paul Tellemant (1642–1712), *Voyage à l'île d'Amour* (1633), a novel in prose with insertions in verse, which he had brought back with him, received a favourable reception in certain circles. Despite the attacks of Church circles, he became court-poet, in 1732 translator at the Academy of Sciences, in 1733 secretary of the Academy, and in 1745 Professor, i.e., member of the Academy. He developed an astonishing industry, but in 1741 Lomonosov returned to Russia and the animosity between them caused great difficulties for Trediakovskij; in 1750 Sumarokov, the first representative of Classicism, turned against him too. This sealed Trediakovskij's fate. Fighting against great difficulties, he managed to stay at the Academy till 1759, in which year he was thrown out into the street, and the rest of his life was merely a struggle against want. He tried to earn his living by translating numerous bulky works. He used these translations as vehicles for the publication of at least some of his new poems which he inserted into the prefaces. Otherwise, he would have been unable to find a publisher for his poetical writings, for his name was too unpopular. As late as 1766 there appeared his rendering of Fénélon's *Télémaque* (1699); in 1769 he died in poverty and obscurity.

Trediakovskij certainly was a serious scholar who showed great industry and learning in many of his works. He also was not afraid to express new and daring thoughts. At times, to be sure, these "daring" thoughts turn out to be ridiculous, as when Trediakovskij finds Russian etymologies for all European languages. He arrived at such gems of etymological fantasy as to deduce *Celts* (*Kelty*) from *želty* (yellow, for they were alleged to be blond), *Germany* from *cholmanija* (*cholm* – hill, the country was supposed at that time to be hilly), *Italy* from *udalija* (*dal'* – distance, for it was situated so far away) or from *vydalija* (*vydat'sja* – project, for it protruded into the sea). *Scythians* he derives from *skitat'sja* (to wander), *Caledonia* from *cholod* (cold), *Igor'*, a Scandinavian name, he links with *igrat'* (to play), and so on. That among these grotesque etymologies there are accidentally a few correct ones should not surprise us, for especially in Greek and Latin there are words similar to and cognate with their Slavonic equivalents, but Trediakovskij uses them as proof that all languages derive from Slavonic! To be sure, quite a few equally fantastic theories were current during the age of the Baroque, but mostly in the 17th century. All this, however, should not hide from us the scholarly merits and the diligence of Trediakovskij. The Empress Anna, however, like her entourage, had no cultural interests and considered a poet a nonentity. The Academy was dominated by foreigners who mistrusted the Russians and to whom above all the problems with which Trediakovskij was concerned were completely alien. After the appearance of the first classicists, after the development of the literary court culture, first under

Elisabeth, then later under Catherine II, the old-fashioned poet was entirely displaced.

2. Trediakovskij's most important achievement in the field of literature was his reform of Russian verse. As early as 1735 he submitted a memorandum to the Academy, in which as a first step he proposed an improvement of syllabic poetry. He had became acquainted with tonal poetry abroad; moreover he seems to have been familiar with the experiments of the foreigners in Russia (those of the Germans Paus and Glück from 1680, and the still more effective ones of the Swede, I. Sparvenfeld, before 1672); and he appears to have known a partly tonal poem which had appeared in 1729 in the St. Petersburg journal. Later he also referred to a "Croatian work" which he said had been written in trochees (perhaps I. Gundulić's). The rhythm of such tonal verses consisted in the regular alternation of accented and unaccented syllables. Trediakovskij, however, was influenced only in part by these models, for at first his proposals were quite moderate. As he correctly noted, the long syllabic lines of the poems hardly produce an impression of rhythmic speech, for there recur in them regularly – but at too rare intervals – only a single accent and the rhyme. He therefore attempted to introduce a further tonal constant. He made use of the fact that in the 13- and 11-syllable syllabic verse the caesura was obligatory after the 7th or 5th syllable. This caesura in itself did not create any strong acoustic effect. In Ukrainian poetry the so-called 'leonine verses' were much favoured, for by the internal rhyme they stressed two caesuras in every line (cf. VII, 5, 5), and owing to the obligatory feminine rhyme, in every line they had three immovable stresses, that is to say, three tonal constants. Thus if we designate every "ambivalent" syllable (i.e. one which can be accented or unaccented by "×" and every obligatorily stressed syllable by "′", and the caesura by "‖", we can write down the following pattern of a leonine line:

$$\times \ \times \ ' \ \times \ \| \ \times \ \times \ ' \ \times \ \| \ \times \ \times \ \times \ \times \ ' \ \times$$

A simple caesura without the inner rhyme (feminine or specifically stressed in some other way) produces no strong acoustic impression, because in every single line there occur also several word-endings which do not differ in effect from the caesura, and because the accents without the inner rhyme can be distributed at random wherever one likes. In Polish and French poetry the caesura served to determine an additional stress, for every Polish word has a stress on the penultimate syllable and every French word on the last syllable. Thus the following scheme for an 11-syllable verse is formed:

French	× × × × ′ ‖ × × × × × ′	
Polish	× × × ′ × ‖ × × × × ′ ×	
Russian	× × × × × ‖ × × × × ′ ×	

Trediakovskij introduced yet another constant: the first half of the line preceding the caesura must have a masculine stress, so that the first half of the 11-syllable line appears like that of the French, the second like that of the Polish 11-syllable verse:

$$× × × × ′ \parallel × × × × ′ ×$$

But even this systematisation of stresses seemed to be insufficient for Trediakovskij. He therefore added a further requirement, suggested perhaps by German, Dutch, or classical poetics: every line is to be sub-divided into feet which consist of two syllables each; these two-syllable feet can have any or no stress at all " ′ × " (this Trediakovskij names a "trochee"), or " × × ", which he designates as a "pyrrhic". In exceptional cases he admits iambs: " × ′ ". Two lines from one of Trediakovskij's own poems may serve as an example:

Невоз | можно | сердцу | ах ‖ не и | меть пе | чали
Очи | також | де е | ще ‖ плакать | не пре | стали.

("It is impossible for the heart not to feel any sorrow. The eyes too have not yet ceased to weep."), that is:

$$× × \mid ′ × \mid ′ × \mid ′ \parallel × × \mid ′ × \mid ′ ×$$
$$′ × \mid ′ × \mid × × \mid ′ \parallel ′ × \mid × × \mid ′ ×$$

For us this would be a simple trochaic verse, though, to be sure, every line divides into two parts; a new trochaic line starts after the stressed 7th syllable. Trediakovskij believed that his system derived from popular poetry. It is not quite clear why he rejected the iamb. The sub-division into feet is entirely unnecessary and does not correspond to reality; as can be seen from the above example, the foot limits break up the words.

Trediakovskij wrote verses in accordance with his theories. Moreover, he found imitators, a professor of the Kharkov College, Vytyńskyj, and the young Sumarokov. Only a few of their poems, however, are known to us.

We must note, too, that Trediakovskij, like the other 18th-century poets, erroneously considered every individual word as accented. This makes their calculations questionable, for the Russian language possesses a considerable number of unaccented words (the one-syllable prepositions and conjunctions, also "*že*", "*by*", enclitica and proclitica).

3. Kantemir opposed Trediakovskij, though he did not publish his observations under the pseudonym "Chariton Makentin" (an anagram of his name) till 1744, together with the translation of Horace's epistles.

Kantemir rightly objected to the sub-division of lines into feet. He accepted Trediakovskij's suggestion of having a word with a masculine stress before the caesura. He did not, however, wish to continue the reform of versification merely to the 13- or 11-syllable verse. He wanted to distribute the stresses regularly in every single line at intervals of two or three syllables. He distinguishes four possible metres:

(1) the trochee:	′ × ′ × ′ × ′	. . . . . .	etc.
(2) the iamb:	× ′ × ′ × ′ × ′	. . . . . .	etc.
(3) the dactyl:	′ × × ′ × × ′ × ×	. . . . . .	etc.
(4) the anapest:	× × ′ × × ′ × × ′	. . . . . .	etc.

According to Kantemir, however, the stress should be regulated separately in every line in a poem; thus a poem may consist of an arbitrary mixture of lines in all rhythmic styles (according to one of the four mentioned metres). Kantemir wants to admit, too, not only masculine endings (like Trediakovskij), but also dactylic endings (′ × ×) before the caesura. Further less important details may be omitted.

One can only rarely notice in Kantemir's work the application of his own theory, though in the last years of his life he constantly revised and repolished even his earlier poems. Not even those poems in which he obviously did use his rules differ – to the ear – from the simple syllabic verse. And when Kantemir writes without any rhyme at all, thus abandoning the last rhythmic device of syllabic poetry, the metric character of the verse can hardly be felt (VII, 12, 4).

Kantemir however, did not find any imitators. For even before 1744 further suggestions had been made and numerous poems had appeared in the spirit of these new ideas, which exerted a much stronger poetic influence than those written by Trediakovskij and Kantemir.

4. The author of the new proposals was Michail Vasil'evič Lomonosov (1711–65, cf. VII, 14). As early as 1738 he sent to the Academy a translation written in trochees from Germany where he was studying; in 1739 an ode in iambs on the capture of the Turkish fortress of Chotin, and a treatise on the reform of versification (which did not appear in print, however, until 1751). In 1741 he returned to Russia.

Lomonosov's proposals are certainly indebted to German prosody. His treatise is exceptionally rich, and one can detect in it, as well as the motifs of German prosody, the echoes of the Kiev Academy's poetics. But perhaps just because Lomonosov treated his subject in a more amateurish way than did Trediakovskij, because his proposals were more radical, and, last but not least, because his poetic examples – his own poems – were better than those of Trediakovskij, his theories entered into the practice of Russian prosody before his treatise had even appeared.

Lomonosov's proposals were as follows (he does not expressly mention it, but takes it for granted that a definite metre should always rule the *entire* poem or its strophic units):

1) There are six possible forms of stress-alternation:
    four "pure" forms – two two-syllable ones:

> iambic " × ′ " and
> trochaic " ′ × ",
>> two three-syllable ones:
>> dactylic " ′ × × " and
>> anapestic " × × ′ ";

   two "mixed" forms: iambic-anapestic, in which iambic or anapestic rhythmic units may equally well occur; and trochaic-dactylic, in which the trochees and dactyls may be used interchangeably. All These metres, with the exception of the iambic-anapestic, have indeed been used in Russian poetry. The choreo-dactylic became the basis of the Russian hexameter which, however, was only used much later by Trediakovskij.

2) No trochee or iamb can be replaced by two unstressed syllables (a pyrrhic). Even Lomonosov himself could not manage this substitution because of the length of Russian words.

3) Lomonosov expressly supports the admission of masculine rhymes, which, as a matter of fact, had been used not only occasionally but throughout entire poems and which even some syllabic poets had employed (e.g. Prokopovyč and Kantemir).

4) Finally, Lomonosov emphasizes the connection which ought to exist between the metre and the genre of the poem. This in itself is a laudable dictum which, in practice, however, is not very convincingly applied.

Lomonosov's first and third theses actually came to be basic for Russian versification up to the 20th century, and are still applied by plenty of, indeed by most, poets. This kind of verse is called tonal, for it depends on the stress; the designation syllabo-tonal is better, however, for the number of syllables still remains an essential element of the verse. Lomonosov himself abandoned the second thesis in his own poetic practice; he certainly formulated it under the influence of German prosody, for in German poetry the omission of stresses is much rarer than in Russian poetry. The fourth rule has found no convincing application to this day.

Lomonosov's treatise contains some fantastic things, for instance, his ideas on the "Sarmatic" or "Bulgarian" language in which Ovid was said to have written in exile, and so on.

5. Trediakovskij tried to enter into controversy with Lomonosov. His answer which was submitted to the Academy has unfortunately been lost, but in 1752 he republished in his collected works his first treatise in an entirely revised form. To be sure, he borrowed a great deal from Lomonosov and dealt with his own and Lomonosov's assertions in a most throughgoing and frequently incisive manner. He also published a work "On the Old, Middle and New Russian Prosody", an rich source of material mainly on the "middle" (syllabic) poetry. He here dismissed Kantemir's proposals with clinching arguments. Both these works of Trediakovskij were later widely used.

6. Though as verse-reformer Trediakovsky was in no way inferior to Lomonosov, his poetic practice, however, cannot be highly valued. To be sure, he deserves much credit for the introduction into Russian poetry of all sorts of poetic genres; he wrote odes, fables, epigrams, rondos, sonnets, songs, lyric poems, elegies and idylls, epistles, tragedies and finally an epic in hexameters (the *Telemachida*, as has been noted, a translation of Fénélon's *Télémaque*). Of course, most of these genres had already been represented by Simeon Polockij, but invariably in the same verse-form as his epigrams, whereas Trediakovskij employed various meters and strophes. Moreover, as translator of a series of voluminous scholarly works he contributed much toward the development of a Russian scholarly terminology, even though not all of his terminological inventions were ultimately accepted. His literary remains (among them also a didactic poem, *Teoptija*, which offered proofs in poetic form of God's existence, the complete translation of the Psalter, two tragedies, and others) have been lost.

The main defect of nearly all of Trediakovskij's poems is the same as that of Kantemir's; it is the entirely arbitrary order of words, the result presumably of following Latin poetic models. He inserts long sentences and parentheses not merely between subject and verb or between a noun and its adjective, but between any two words. The understanding of his poems is made still more difficult by the numerous inversions, which

cause him to place even the prepositions after the words which they
govern, and to find room for conjunctions anywhere in the middle of a
sentence. Let us take as examples a few sentences, designating the normal
order of words by numbers placed above the lines. In a poem about
spring, the song of the nightingale is rendered thus:

$$
\begin{array}{ccc}
1 & 7 & 8
\end{array}
$$
...Возгласностию, коя сродна

$$
\begin{array}{ccccc}
5 & 6 & 3 & 4 & 2
\end{array}
$$
к себе другиню в сих местах склоняет...

Or, in an elegy, the nights of a man who knows no unhappy love are thus
depicted:

$$
\begin{array}{ccccccc}
2 & 1 & 5 & 3 & 6 & 4 & 7
\end{array}
$$
В сладком и проходят сне тихи ему ночи, (or: 6–1–4–7–2–5–3)

$$
\begin{array}{cccccc}
5 & 4 & 1 & 6 & 3 & 2
\end{array}
$$
токи проливать и слез не умеют очи...

("With his voice he attracts to himself his lady friend who is a kindred
spirit. – His nights pass by in sweet sleep; his eyes are unable to pour forth
streams of tears.") Or, of Hercules:

$$
\begin{array}{ccc}
1 & 3 & 4
\end{array}
$$
бремена ему дороги

$$
\begin{array}{cccc}
5 & 2 & 6 & 7
\end{array}
$$
и отверзли дверь небес

("The labours opened before him his paths and the gates to heaven.") Or:

$$
\begin{array}{cccccc}
1\,4 & 3 & 2 & 5 & & 6
\end{array}
$$
То б сам и Орфей Фракийский,

$$
\begin{array}{cccc}
2 & 5\,1 & & 3
\end{array}
$$
Амфион бы и Фивийский

$$
\begin{array}{ccc}
7 & 4 & 6
\end{array}
$$
Восхищен был от нея.

Or even:

$$
\begin{array}{cccc}
1 & 2 & 4 & 3
\end{array}
$$
О! не ярости во время...

("Even the Thracian Orpheus and the Theban Amphion would have been
enchanted by her. – O! not at the times of wrath!")

The other peculiarity of Trediakovskij's verse is a multitude of unnecessary one-syllable words which he obviously introduces into his lines in order to preserve the metre: *ach, o, vot* (here, now), instead of *i* (and) – *da i* (and also), *ves'* (entire), *vse* (everything, always), *už* (already), *kupno* (together) instead of *i, sam* (himself), etc., the conjunctions also are often placed where they have no significance. Trediakovskij often breaks the sentence into several subordinate clauses when this is not necessary at all, so that, for instance, an epithet which belongs to a noun is put into a subordinate clause.

One difficulty which Trediakovskij did not notice and therefore took no steps to overcome consisted in the variegation of the Russian vocabulary of that time, a variegation which was already noticeable in many works of the 16th century. Trediakovskij indiscriminately used in his poetry words of various lexical strata. A student of Church Slavonic, he started, however, with songs and the translation of the "Journey to the Island of Love" in which he mixed the everyday vocabulary with popular and even dialect words. In his later years he wrote even idylls or lyrical poems with very strong Church Slavonic elements. These stand in grotesque juxtaposition with words of everyday language and folk-speech which quite often appear in the Church Slavonic context. Here are a few examples:

> В жаре любовном целовал ю присно,
> а неверная ему все попускала чинить.

> нет того, чтоб не возмогл женск пол учинити,
> дабы всегдашнюю иметь с любовником слуку.

> То крастель, в обоей заре
> супружку кличет велегласно...

> Повсюду жавронок поющий,
> и зрится вкось и впрямь снующий...

> То славий, с пламеня природна
> в хврастиных скутавшись кустах...

("In the passion of love he kissed her continually, and she, the unfaithful one, allowed him to do everything; there is nothing that a female would not do in order to be always with her lover. Here a corn-crake calls his mate loudly in the two (evening and morning) twilights: the lark sings everywhere, and he can be seen flying obliquely and straight; the nightingale, hiding in the wood-bushes (!) because of the fire of his nature. ...")

In all these passages we come across "heavy" Church Slavonicisms: *prisno* (always, continually), *daby* (in order to), *vozmogl* (could), *krastel'* (corn-crake), *slavij* (nightingale), *veleglasno* (loudly), *zritsja* (is seen), *chvrastinyj* (wooden). Next to these there are "light" Church Slavonicisms: *činit, učiniti* (to do), and words from everyday speech: *žar lubovnyj* (fire of love), *celoval* (kissed), *vsegdašnij* (constant), *ljubovnik* (lover), etc. Beside these, there also occur folk-words: *popuskala* (allowed), *oboej* (both), *snujuščij* (actually: glide, but here – fly), *skutavšis'* (hiding oneself, probably a dialect word), and even vulgarisms: *vkos' i vprjam'* (back and forth), and *sluka* (reunion, but after a few decades we find this word in the sense of "planking"!). I shall not quote from the early poems of Trediakovskij in which he recasts the poems of the French *précieux* school with the elegance of a dancing hippopotamus. But even later he can still fill a wedding ode with prosaic passages such as:

Цитереины приятности,
что превыше вероятности...

("The charms of Venus which are beyond any probability.")

In the religious odes and in the recast psalms we find, in a Church Slavonic context, popular words like: *zaraz, povsegda, ozlilis', tolsto rasširel, jagodka*, etc. (simultaneously, always, become angry, become fat, small berry); in depictions of nature or of country life we find Church Slavonicisms like *zel'nyj, daby, zret'*, numerous participles, passives and superlatives next to the expressions of everyday life. To these are still added numerous neologisms or rare Church Slavonic words which might have been considered neologisms: *izrjadstvo, beznadeždie, zlat* (! instead of *zlato*), *bezgoda, osaditel', davcy, lukavcy, chlest'*, etc. (profusion, hopelessness, gold, misfortune, besiegers, donor, cunning men, song of the nightingale) or entire sentences: *žužžašča remžet vspjatno čad'* (only from the context can it be understood that here the reference is to bees: "the buzzing folk fly (?) back"), or *bez likovstvá net noščedénstva* (there is no full day without joy). Besides, he has numerous compounds (especially in later years) which are, however, only in part his creation, a large part of them having been borrowed from 17th-century literature, with which he was well acquainted: *gromoperunnyj, gustolistnyj, dolgoprotjažnyj, legkoplyvnyj, poleljubnyj, trizevnyj*, etc. – (with thunderbolt, with dense foliage, long, lightly swimming, fond of fields, with three gullets). There are also numerous words which Trediakovskij uses in an unusual sense, in addition to the above mentioned *sluka* there occurs in his work *zyk garfy* (the sound of a harp) or *zyk* (a bird's song); the word, however, also stands in Church Slavonic monuments for an excessively loud sound, a roar, a howl *Tuk ljubvi* is evidently here "the fullness of love"; *tuk* also means in

Church Slavonic "fat", in which sense Trediakovskij himself uses the word elsewhere. *Sipet'* (otherwise "to hiss") is for him the synonym for "to speak", etc. It is curious that Trediakovskij makes no attempt to follow some of his own injunctions: for example, the avoidance of the "ugly enjambment" and above all the demand for euphony, for his poems have numerous most clumsy enjambments and teem with cacophonies!

It must be granted that in his works which use predominantly Church Slavonic, occasionally good lines and strophes may be found, as for instance in the five lines from the recast Book of the Kings (not to mention, the first verse of the recast of Deuteronomy, chapter 32, which is always cited):

> Господь мертвит и оживляет,
> низводит и возводит в гроб;
> убожит, богатит особ,
> кротит и высит; восставляет
> ниспадших нищетою в дол,
> да их посадит на престол.

("The Lord kills and gives life again, He abases and leads into the grave, He makes poor and enriches, He humiliates and elevates, reinstates those who have sunk into poverty, in order to place them on the throne.") But there are also numerous lines and strophes in which one can hardly perceive the sense through the thicket of inversions and the weeds of the vocabulary, as in Deuteronomy, chapter 32, verse 7:

> Воспомяни те дни веков,
> и купно разумей все лета
> от рода древнего родов;
> спроси у рождшего следов,
> познаешь старших все от света.

("Remember the days of old, consider the names of many generations; ask thy father and he will show thee, thy elders and they will tell thee.")

No doubt, in a certain sense, the notorious *Telemachida* is Trediakovskij's best work. At least the inversions are not too frequent, and the vocabulary is more uniform: the Church Slavonic element has substantially displaced the other elements of the vocabulary. Moreover, Trediakovskij has now noticed the existence of unstressed words and has even indicated them in the text (linked by a hyphen with the other words). It has been asserted that there is only one beautiful line in the entire bulky epic. In reality, there are quite a few, for instance, the description of the Egyptian coast:

Видим всюду. . .стоящи богатые грады,
сельные домы везде приятно росставлены видим,
нивы, на каждый год желтеющи жатвой обильной,
зрим поля, исполнены стад и людей земледельцев,
всех не могущих убрать плодов из земли изнесенных,
множество пастырей зрим, на свирелях своих и цевницах
сладким гласом играющих песнь и по ликам поющих. . .

("We see standing everywhere rich towns, we see everywhere country-houses in pleasant locations, fields yellowing every year with a rich harvest; we see fields filled with herds and peasants who are unable to collect all the fruits of the earth; we see numerous shepherds who with sweet sounds play tunes on their flutes and shalms and sing in choirs.") Unfortunately such continuous passages are not numerous; often a beautiful line is followed directly by a weak, prosaic, confusing line or by one which somehow destroys the impression of the preceding lines.

7. It is interesting that Trediakovskij seems to be the first poet of the declining Russian Baroque who had definite political views. One may perhaps infer this from his three major translations: *Argenis* by John Barclay (1621, cf. also VII, 10, 1), *Télémaque* by Fénélon (1699), which Trediakovskij transformed into an epic in verse, and the *History of the World* by Charles Rollin in a number of volumes. All these works have a certain, though not identical, political slant. *Argenis* and *Télémaque* both reflect the ideology of enlightened absolutism and are not without sallies against the excesses of absolutism. These critical motifs appear far more explicitly in Rollin's volumes which deal with antiquity, particularly ancient Rome; they contain not only a criticism of tyranny, but also sceptical observations about Roman Emperors in general. We do not know whether contemporary readers (1767 ff.) noticed the contrast in these passages between the glorification of Greece's republican virtues and the account of ancient Rome. By the end of the century they certainly did so.

8. Trediakovskij still belongs entirely to the age of the Baroque. In his "Epistle to Apollo" he mentions a number of poets representative of baroque poetry who served him as models, viz.: Régnier, Scarron, Voiture, Mlle de Scudéry, Milton, Lope de Vega, Opitz, J. Chr. Günther, and Brockes. In addition, however, he also mentions Boileau and various

representatives of early German Classicism, among whom Junker inexplicably occupies the first place. But Trediakovskij, like his contemporaries, often regarded the differences between literary trends with indifference and a lack of understanding. Inferences about his taste therefore are to be drawn not so much from the names and works he praises as from the works he translates. And these are all of the Baroque. "The Journey to the Island of Love" is a typical allegorical work of French *précieux* literature. The characters of the novel are in great part personified allegories. On the Island of Love the enamoured Tirsis visits the cave of severity, the wilderness of memory, the gate of refusal, the city of hope, etc. As a supplement to his translation, Trediakovskij published a collection of love-songs, with some poems in praise of Russia and of Paris. Later he wrote numerous odes in praise of the Empresses Anna and Elisabeth. They are much like the numerous congratulatory poems of baroque poetry. Characteristic of his odes are the "high flight" (*parenie*) and the "poetic disorder" which is to suggest enthusiasm. His eulogy of both Empresses is unpleasantly adulatory and servile. His "Epistle to Apollo" announces the birth of a new poetry, that of Russia. His fables on Aesop's themes start the series of verbose Russian fables in a pseudo-popular style. In 1751 Trediakovskij translated J. Barclay's *Argenis;* his adaptation in epic verse of Fénélon's *Télémaque* appeared in 1766. Both works had no success; but in some verses included in *Argenis* Trediakovskij used the hexameter, and his *Telemachida* gave a firm foundation to the Russian hexameter.

The theoretical works of Trediakovskij are also, on the whole, products of the Baroque. Similarly his daring verse and language reforms belong to the favourite exercises of the Baroque. His emphasis on the euphonic side of poetry, too, is typical of the Baroque. Unfortunately in his own poems reigns cacophony! Trediakovskij's three poetic translations are of baroque works: *Voyage à l'île d'Amour, Argenis*, and *Télémaque*. As a baroque poet, Trediakovskij could not succeed in the atmosphere of Classicism. If Lomonosov's animosity toward him was in part the animosity of a rival, Sumarokov's antagonism rested only on the differences between the literary schools to which each belonged. Sumarokov, the classicist, won, at least as far as public opinion was concerned. And thus Trediakovskij's attainments came to be lost for the following generations.

9. Syllabic poetry died without a struggle, but not immediately. The teaching of poetics at the ecclesiastical schools followed the old path for a few more decades. And the pupils of these schools, teachers, priests and bishops, wrote syllabic verse right up to the beginning of the 19th century (some poems are known which originated around 1815–20). To be sure, these were written for private circulation; besides occasional and valedictory poems there were also, however, syllabic lyrical effusions. Still more obstinately did the syllabic prosody survive in the Ukraine, where some Church Slavonic-Russian (beside the Church Slavonic-Ukrainian) and even purely Russian poems were also written.

At the beginning of the 18th-century numerous books of different kinds contained syllabic dedicatory poems, many of which are quite good. Moreover, there were several occasional poems printed.

It is true that few syllabic poets were of any great significance. Among these few belonged the Moscow deacon Petr Buslaev (about 1700, before 1755) who in 1734 published a poem *Umozritel'stvo duševnoe* ("Spiritual Speculations"). It is a long commemorative poem for Baroness Maria Stroganov. Buslaev's speculations seem to have been influenced by Milton (probably *via* a translation); Buslaev himself quotes Homer, Ovid and Vergil. Incidentally he uses in his poem, which on the whole has a pronounced Church Slavonic coloring, modern barbarisms like *instrumenty, elementy, koncerty*. Baroque poetics determine the whole style of the poem. Trediakosvkij mentioned the poem respectfully, but N. Novikov (in the 1780's) also praised Buslaev's thoughts at least.

Another syllabic poet was a school-fellow of Sumarokov, later an army officer and official, Michail Grigor'evič Sobakin (1720–1772). His syllabic poems are, however, occasional poems. He also wrote syllabo-tonal poems. Noteworthy is the use he makes of the artifices of baroque poetry: he wrote acrostics, "gryphic" poems, etc.

As late as in 1756 there still appeared syllabic verses in the body of a syllabo-tonal translation of Alexander Pope's *An Essay on Man*. The translation was the work of the talented pupil of Lomonosov, N. Popovskij (about 1730–1760). Several passages troubled ecclesiastical censors. In order to make the appearance of the book possible, however, the Bishop Amvrosij (Zertis-Kamenskij) recast several passages, making some alterations – doing this in the majority of cases in syllabic verse (for instance I, 461ff; in all twenty-one passages, about 140 lines). In this form the book appeared in four further editions (1763, 1787, 1791, 1802).

It must be stressed that syllabic metres are by no means fundamentally unsuited to Russian poetry! Yet deliberate attempts to use them again were only rarely made later, sometimes in parodies, sometimes in poetical experiments (thus in *Opyty* by V. Brjusov, 1918).

14. MICHAIL VASIL'EVIČ LOMONOSOV

1. Legends are also current about Michail Vasil'evič Lomonosov, Trediakovskij's more successful rival. The most important of these concerns his origin, that he came from a poor peasant family and ran away from home to study in Moscow. Biographical research, however, has recently established that though his father was indeed of peasant stock, he was a "State-peasant" (*gosudarstvennyj krest'janin*), a prosperous fisherman who, with his boats, ventured even to foreign waters. His mother was a deacon's daughter. Born in 1711 in the neighbourhood of Cholmogory (on the Northern Dvina, near the White Sea), Lomonosov while still at home studied what books were accessible to him. These were Meletij Smotrićkyj's Church Slavonic grammar (VII, 6, 5), L. Magnickij's Arithmetic (VII, 5, 7) which also contains a good deal of information on the mathematical natural sciences, and the translation of the Psalter by Simeon Polockij (VII, 5, 4). Lomonosov's stepmother persecuted him and tried to prevent him from studying. In 1730 he left his parents' home but apparently with his father's consent, for he was issued a proper passport which could not otherwise have been secured. He received financial support from his relatives, and thus he was able to set out for Moscow with a consignment of fish. However, his money was all spent on the way and he arrived in Moscow penniless. After having been widely publicized as important new discoveries of Soviet scholars, these details have recently once again disappeared from Soviet textbooks. At Cholmogory, Lomonosov was unable to attend school because children of peasant origin were not admitted. In Moscow he concealed his origin and succeeded in enrolling at the Ecclesiastical Academy. Having jumped grades, he was admitted to the seventh and final one as early as 1734. He decided to go to the Urals as a priest; this plan, however, was frustrated by the discovery at about this time of his peasant origin. Lomonosov was granted permission to attend the Kiev Academy for a year which, however, seems to have had little to offer him. He returned in 1735 and was dispatched as a student to the St. Petersburg Academy. A few months later, however, together with two fellow students he was sent to Germany to study mining. It was planned that at first they should receive general preparatory training, and so, in 1736, they reached the University of Marburg on the Lahn. Lomonosov in particular studied philosophy and mathematics under the famous philosopher Christian Wolf (1679–1754), but at the same time he engaged in the study of literature and of literary theory. It is known that he was enthusiastic about the work of the late baroque poet, J. Ch. Günther (1695–1723), and also studied the works on literary theory by the classicist Gottsched (1700–66). However, from his later "Rhetoric" (see § 3) we see that he had apparently become acquainted with the actual principles of poetics by studying the works of baroque theoreticians when he was still in Moscow and Kiev. At any rate, at Marburg he did not become a classical poet, although the poems of Günther, with their enthusiams and the freshness of youth, colored his own poetry. It was in Germany that he wrote his treatise on Russian versification (VII, 13, 4) and his first syllabo-tonal poems. From Marburg Lomonosov went in 1739 to the Mining Academy at Freiberg in Saxony but stayed there for only one year and left college as a result of quarrels with the professor who was entrusted with the supervision of the Russian students. He returned to Marburg, was married there, went to Holland, set off once again for Marburg but on the way was induced to join the army by the recruiting officers of the King of Prussia, escaped from a fortress and in 1741 was recalled to Russia.

In St. Petersburg Lomonosov became an *Ad'junkt* (lecturer) in physics at the Academy of Sciences and, like Trediakovskij, a member of the Academy. His scientific activities brought him little recognition in those days. A number of his theories, which were ahead of his time, were noted only at the end of the 19th century (the German chemist, W. Oswald, deserves much of the credit for this). Without disparaging Lomonosov's scientific achievements, it must be stressed that on some fundamental questions he actually lagged behind his own times; for example, he was opposed to the Newtonian theory of gravitation. In addition to his work in the natural sciences, Lomonosov also concerned himself with Russian history, and with philological studies, and also wrote poetry. His activities at the Academy did not always proceed smoothly. A number of German members intrigued against him, and Trediakovskij too was his enemy. Nevertheless, Lomonosov succeeded in acquiring a leading position, though one cannot always be in sympathy with him. He also ruined Trediakovskij financially as well; and he openly denounced the two German academicians, Müller and Schlözer, who had contributed much to the exploration of Russian history, because he discovered *nepristoj- nosti* (improprieties) in their works. These consisted in the presentation of various events of Russian history in an objective manner, thus giving them an insufficiently patriotic character. Fortunately, his denunciation was fruitless. In the end, he even created difficulties for the gifted Swiss mathematician, L. Euler, a member of the Academy, who had befriended him. At the end of his life, Lomonosov fell into disfavour with the new Empress Catherine II (after 1762), because he had been too closely connected with a favourite of Empress Elisabeth. He lost influence in the Academy, and his industrial enterprise – a glass and mosaic factory – was not successful. He died in 1765.

2. Lomonosov solved, if perhaps only provisionally and incompletely, the problem that had been facing the vocabulary of Russian literature for some time: he regulated the use of words that belonged to various lexical levels. The Russian vocabulary, permeated as it is with Russian and Church Slavonic elements, and further enriched in the 17th and 18th centuries by an immense number of Slavonic (Polish and Ukrainian) and West European borrowings, was now in a singular position – it was, in fact, a thoroughly mixed vocabulary. This character of the vocabulary required a normalization since hitherto each writer had independently chosen his words as he went along. Trediakovskij at least in part failed as a poet because of these very problems of vocabulary (see VII, 13, 6).

In 1744 Lomonosov published a book on rhetoric, which appeared in a revised edition in 1748, and in 1757 an important treatise "Of the need of Church books in the Russian (*rossijskij*) language" (here he refers to the Holy Scriptures), and in the same year a grammar. What primarily interests us about these works is whether he states and to what extent he solves the problem of the vocabulary. Noting the presence of various lexical strata in the Russian vocabulary, Lomonosov refers here to a notion which he derived from ancient (Quintilian) and Kievan rhetorical works – the distinction between various literary styles on the basis of their "elevation".

Lexical strata exist, of course, in every language, but in Russian, because of the reasons mentioned above, the number of such strata is perhaps even greater than anywhere else. In some instances not only the "elevation" of the word is changed, but also its meaning. This is what happened with words designating "odour"; they might be listed as follows: *smrad – von' – zapach – aromat – blagouchanie, blagovonie – vonja* (this last word in Biblical texts only). The first two words (both Church Slavonic) exclusively convey the meaning of bad odours, the third is "neutral", and the rest designate only good smells and belong to progressively "higher" lexical strata. Likewise words that mean "writing" (both the process and the result) can be arranged in the following way in accordance with the "elevation" of their lexical strata:

verb: *pisnut', pisanut' – pisyvat' – pisat' – načertat'* [*soizvolil*]

noun: *gramotka – pis'mo – gramota – poslanie*

The two underscored words are "neutral".

Lomonosov thus divides all the words of the Russian vocabulary into five groups: 1) very archaic words (*ves'ma obvetšalye*), that is to say, those encountered in "Church books": *ovogda, rjasny* (then, exuberant); 2) words which are rarely used, especially in the spoken language (*v razgovorach*)

like *otverzaju, gospoden', vzyvaju* (I am opening, of the Lord's, I am calling); 3) words which are common to both the Russian and Church
Slavonic languages: *Bog, slava, ruka, nyně, počitaju* (God, glory or
splendour, hand, now, I am venerating), of which *nyně* would probably
now belong to the second group; 4) words which do not occur in "Church
books", e.g., *govorju, ručej, kotoryj, poka, liš* (I am speaking, brook,
which, meanwhile, only); 5) "despicable" words, as examples of which
Lomonosov occasionally quotes popular or dialectical words from the
works of Trediakovskij, e.g., *choduli* (stilts), *kraso[v]uli* (wineglasses),
the first of which would now belong to the fourth group, and the second of
which (a dialect word*) has disappeared from the literary language.

These words were arranged by Lomonosov according to three different
styles. Most important for the literary language is the relationship
Lomonosov establishes between lexical strata and poetic genres. The
first group, in his view, is completely extra-literary. (Trediakovskij used it
frequently and in all genres!) The second and third groups are to be used
in the "high style", in which are written odes, heroic epics and "prose
speeches on lofty subjects" (later tragedy, too, came into this category).
The "middle style" may use words of the third group with a "cautious"
admixture of those belonging to the second and fourth groups. The
advice to use "caution" is, of course, not very precise. In any case,
Lomonosov advises against the use of words of the second and fourth
groups "in juxtaposition". He thinks that this middle style should be
used in the drama, but he recommends the use of the high style in all
instances where it is desired to depict "heroism and lofty thoughts". The
middle style should also be used in epistles in verse, satires, eclogues
(idylls) and elegies. The high style should be avoided in treating "delicate"
subjects. The low style should only use the vocabulary of the third and
fourth groups and avoid Church Slavonic words. Comedies, epigrams,
songs, letters in prose, "descriptions of commonplace events" should be
kept in the low style (later, fables were added). The words of the fifth
group may also be used at discretion (*po rassmotrenii*).

These rules are, as we see, neither wholly clear nor exact nor are they
altogether new (similar suggestions had been made by Quintilian and the
Kievan teachers of Trediakovskij). Nevertheless they provided at least
general directions which were, on the whole, adhered to by the poets of
the first period of Russian classicism. Lomonosov's point of departure
was the lexical usage of his time; actually, though, even among the words
of the third, fourth and even fifth groups there are many words which

* From Middle-Greek κρασοβόλιον.

according to their *origin* should be classified as Church Slavonic (cf. *bran'*, in the sense of "disgrace", *smrad* – stench, *mraz'* – nauseating stuff, *toščij* – lean, etc.). Lomonosov's picture of the Russian language is not genetic but phenomenological, and he considers its many-layer construction as a special advantage; in particular, the existence of the "high style", which is a matter of the vocabulary, appears to him as a point of superiority of Russian over other languages. He is wrong about this, of course. Even so, it is on this point that he bases his encomium of the Russian language, which in some respects seems convincing, but in others exaggerated, especially when one takes into account the Russian language of Lomonosov's times.

3. Considering Lomonosov's poetics (which he expounds in his "Rhetoric"), we shall find it to be typical baroque poetics, and, in fact, in a rather unadulterated form. His principal sources were two works by theoreticians of baroque poetics, Nicolaus Caussin[us]'s (1580–1651) work *De eloquentia sacra et humana* (about 1620), and a book by François Antoine Pomay (1619–93) *Novus Candidatus Rhetoricus* (1650) – that is to say, works not only old but obsolete, even though they were still being reprinted in the 18th century. Lomonosov also copied some material from Gottsched's book (see § 1), the *Ausführliche Redekunst* (1736). But from Gottsched, the classicist, he took primarily the definitions, while the actual precepts were predominantly derived from baroque poetics. There is no doubt that his mind was dominated by the ideas of Kievan poetics (which, to some extent, used the same sources) and by the enthusiastic poetry of J. Ch. Günther (see § 1).

Lomonosov is the theoretician of the heavily ornate style. In his texts he refers to numerous examples from ancient poets, which, however, as is obvious in a good many cases, are interpreted in the spirit of baroque poetics. It is also significant that he likes to quote Quintilian. As baroque poetics demand, Lomonosov wishes to see in works of poetry not only a wealth of ornamentation, but also a wealth of ideas. He begins with advice on the "invention (!) of ideas". The means are old; they are the *loci communes*, the topoi. They enable a poet to develop a rich system of synonyms and to expand his metaphors. The "ideas" are not to be taken in a rationalist sense. Lomonosov builds his poetics on passions (*strasti*). "Reason should guide a man from its high seat to the senses and unite him with them so that he may be set aflame with passion" ("Rhetoric", 1748, § 100). The task of eloquence is to "arouse or pacify the passions" (§ 99). Therefore he urges such representations as will "greatly arouse the senses". Hence, the passion should be represented (§ 124), and lushness of ornamentation appears to Lomonosov as generally the best means to this end. The ornamentation (tropes and figures) gives to the style its splendour (*velikolepie*, § 164 ff.) and fullness (*izobilie*). Lomonosov explicitly recommends "involved speech" *(vitievatye reči)* and "sentences, in which the subject and the verb are connected in a curious, unusual and unnatural way, thus offering something both interesting and pleasant". The effectiveness of words is enhanced by the "mixture of passions". What is more, Lomonosov advises the representation of the union of opposing passions and gives a number of examples from Seneca's tragedy *Medea*, a weak play, which, however, delighted the baroque lovers of antiquity (§ 127). All that is impressive, moving and pathetic thus seems to Lomonosov to be particularly efficacious. So little is he concerned to have poetry be "enlightening" or instructive that he recommends the use of "strategems" to mislead the understanding of the listener or reader: to enthrall him and to make him "forget his cavils" (§ 150; here he speaks explicitly of "orators and *poets*"!)

All these are traits so unmistakably characteristic of baroque poetics that we should not be at all surprised to encounter them again in Lomonosov's poetic practice.

In Lomonosov's works we also meet a trait which is equally characteristic of baroque poetry and is far removed from the "rationalist" poetics of classicism, namely the high estimate of euphony, and the attempt, as fantastic as all other similar attempts (especially by the symbolists, Bal'mont and Andrej Belyj), to assign to the sounds of the Russian language certain definite psychological characteristics (§ 170 ff). He does not merely enjoin the avoidance of cacophony. It seems to him that the frequently repeated use of *A* in Russian "can help to portray splendour, the distant expanse, the height and depth, and sudden terror"; the frequent use of *E, I, Ě, JU* might serve "the depiction of tenderness, flattery, sorrow or small matter"; by *JA* it is possible to express pleasure, joy, tenderness and inclination; by *O U Y* – "the horrific and fierce things, anger, jealousy, fear and sorrow". According to Lomonosov, the consonants *K P T B G D* work in a similar way, and may be used in the portrayal of "phenomena producing blunt, slow and hollow sounds", while *S, F, Ch, C, Č, Š, R* may serve for the description of "strong, great, loud, horrible and impressive matters and effects". *Ž, Z, V, L, M, N* and the palatalisation (ь) might portray "delicate and soft" matters. Lomonosov also offers other euphonic counsels. For us, the principle alone is important here.

Lomonosov also demands a knowledge of the old literature and the "sciences" – a demand which is not necessarily characteristic of the Baroque. But here too he does not forget to add that "a lofty spirit and a natural (innate) poetic fire" should be united with this knowledge.

4. Lomonosov's poems are not numerous and, were he not an innovator, would scarcely have brought him fame. None other than Puškin believes that "one will look in vain for feeling and imagination" in the poems of Lomonosov. This is most striking when one reads them, not one at a time, but all together. One notices then, moreover, that he repeats himself and his predecessors (Günther, Malherbe).

The greater part of his poetic work consists of the seventeen odes addressed to the five rulers who reigned in Russia between 1739 and 1765. That two of them (Elisabeth and Catherine II) came to the throne as the result of palace revolutions does not prevent Lomonosov from delivering broadsides against the former regents whom, but a year earlier, he had praised to the skies. The content in essence, however, amounts to the repetition of the same themes. The odes are of interest to us in part for the very reason that they correspond fully with Lomonosov's poetic theory. The first ode of 1739 (which incidentally is an imitation of a poem by J. Chr. Günther) opens with the line

Восторг внезапный ум пленил

("The sudden ecstasy took my reason captive.") This ecstasy reappears in four other odes as well. To the Church Slavonic use of the word *vostorg* (Latin: *raptus*, Greek: *ekstasis*) belongs the verb *voschiščat'* (to carry aloft). This word recurs in similar forms in seven odes: "reason", "spirit", "feelings", "thought", "the lyre" – all of them are carried aloft. The poet "flies" or "hovers" over mountains, clouds and lightning in six odes. Another expression (repeated with minor variations in eight odes) is the "fire of the heart" (*žar serdečnyj*) which seizes the poet and his imaginary reader, as whose representative he is speaking. Other variants, maintained in the same mood, include the "pierced heart", the "confused mind", reason seized by "sacred awe". Being in this state of ecstasy, the poet – hovering above – is now able to see sweeping images, in which geography plays a significant role: on one hand, "the extended land" between the "seven seas", but on the other, near and distant countries which he wishes every Russian ruler to possess. Here are Damascus and Cairo and Aleppo which burn, quake and are destroyed. Such a flight of imagination might have been incomprehensible, if this whole subject (the capture of the Orient) had not been an imitation of Günther's and Malherbe's odes! At times it is the Rhine and the whole of Germany which allegedly desire the protection of Russia; at others it is Spain (*Ibery*), the Tigris and Euphrates (see above), Central Asia, and – in the later odes – China, India and Japan:

> Чтоб Хина, Инды и Японы
> подпали под твои законы –

("so that China, the Indians and the Japanese should be placed under your laws"), and also America (four times). Of course, lands already belonging to Russia, and especially the Russian rivers, are also enumerated. That a number of times (in five odes) Lomonosov does not forget his Arctic homeland is but natural, and here, too, he has an impressive image which he repeats with variations:

> ... всегдашними снегами
> покрыта северна страна,
> где мерзлыми Борей крылами
> твои взвевает знамена.

or:

> Там мерзлыми шумит крылами
> отец густых снегов Борей.

("The northern land is covered with eternal snow, where Boreas with frosty wings waves your flags. – There, the father of the thick snow, Boreas, rustles his frosty wings.")

Apart from the immense spaces he sees, however, nothing but "heroic landscapes"; smoke (*dym*) or dust (*prach*) rises in the wide steppes. Volcanic eruptions (Etna) appear repeatedly, as well as earthquakes, storms and fires (even at Damascus, Cairo and Aleppo which were as yet inaccessible to the Russians). In these landscapes there move giant figures who work in Nature as natural forces (his source for this is probably Malherbe!). They are, even in the context itself, not fully defined allegorical figures. Thus, he writes in 1742:

> Бежит в свой путь с весельем многим
> по холмам грозный исполин,
> ступает по вершинам строгим,
> презрев глубоко дно долин,
> вьет воздух вихрем за собою;
> под сильною его пятою

кремнистые бугры трещат,
и следом дерева лежат,
что множество веков стояли
и бурей ярость презирали.

and varies the same image in 1746:

...грозный злится исполин
рассыпать земнородных племя,
и разрушить природы чин!
Он ревом бездну возмущает,
лесисты с мест бугры хватает,
и в твердь сквозь облака разит...

("A terrible giant cheerfully makes his way over the hill; he picks his way upon the stern peaks of the mountains, scorns the depths of the valleys: air rushes after him, under his heavy heel the stony mountains resound, and in his wake lie trees that stood for many centuries and had scorned the fury of the storms. – The terrible giant rages; [he wants] to disperse the tribe of those born on earth and to disrupt the order of nature! With his roar he stirs up the abyss [of the sea]; he snatches the wooded mountains from their places and flings them to Heaven through the clouds.")

Countries, towns, and even abstract concepts are personified. Oddly enough, they almost invariably have hands with which to applaud the heroes. Thus the banks of the Neva "applaud with their hands"; elsewhere "woods and meadows ... rivers and seas", and even the White Sea do the same thing. Petersburg raises its hands to heaven, Moscow sheds its grey hair and falls on its knees, sciences stretch out (entreatingly) their hands to Russia. Impressive is the picture of Russia as a giantess leaning her elbows on the Caucasus or stretching her feet as far as China, etc. These personifications appear time and again, as do the many other images or turns of speech: Orpheus and Pindar; appeals to one or another country "to kiss" either the hand or the feet of the one or another Russian Empress (in this he is imitating Günther). Every new Russian ruler ushers in a Golden Age. Historical reminiscences recur; above all, there are innumerable references to Peter I, whose worthly successors, according to Lomonosov's odes, are Anna, Elisabeth, Peter III, Catherine II, and even the few-days old Ioann IV Antonovič, who spent his life in prison (the two odes dedicated to him could not be republished until the end of the 19th century). Sometimes Lomonosov repeats almost the same or even the identical sentence in different contexts; the following is said of both Elisabeth and Catherine II:

Российские мягчит сердца...
Народу грубость умягчает...

("softens the Russian heart, softens the uncouthness of the people");
or of both:

души и тела красота...

and   души и тела красотой...

("Beauty of soul and body").

The impressive personification of dawn, whose "rosy hand" heralds
the new day (probably taken from Homer), appears twice.

5. To be sure, Lomonosov repeats some ideas which were certainly
close to his heart. This happens in the odes idealizing peace (*mir* or
tišina), written in time of war. He summons peace, he describes its blessings in idyllic pictures (ode to Elisabeth, 1747), and he returns to the
same theme on four occasions, opening twice in much the same terms:

Молчите, пламенные звуки...
умолкни ныне, брань кровава...

("Be silent, ye fiery noises... Be silent now, oh sanguinary war....")
And this once more is borrowed from Malherbe! Lomonosov devotes
even more attention to the sciences. He weaves into his praises of each
reign an expression of the hope that the sciences would now at last be
cultivated. The praise of the sciences in the 1747 ode to Elisabeth is,
however, an imitation of a strophe by Günther and of Cicero's speech
Pro Archia poeta. In addition, Lomonosov expresses the hope that:

...может собственных Платонов
и быстрых разумом Невтонов
Российская земля раждать.

("The Russian land can give birth to its own Platos and Newtons of
quick intellect.")

In the 1750 ode, Lomonosov – speaking in the name of the various
sciences – promises practical results, including even the discovery of a new
planet. Similarly in the 1747 ode:

И се Минерва ударяет
в верхи Рифейски копием,
сребро и злато истекает
во всем наследии твоем.

Плутон в расселинах мятется,
что Россам в руки достается
драгой металл его из гор,
который там натура скрыла...

("And then with a spear Minerva strikes the Ural peaks; silver and gold pour out into your patrimony. Pluto is alarmed in his chasms that Russia is receiving into her hands his precious metals which Nature has hidden there.")

We do not encounter a eulogy of pure science, even though Lomonosov was certainly not one-sidedly inclined toward practical accomplishments. Of course, he is expressing his own thoughts when, almost in every ode, he sings the praise of Peter I. Equally, one cannot doubt his "imperialist" tendencies, which certainly went much farther than the modest political visions of Anna or Elisabeth.

An epic, the *Petriade*, was to be devoted to the praise of Peter I. The two cantos which were written down are both cumbersome and prosaic. Equally lacking in poetic merit is a didactic poem "On the utility of Glass". Best of all of Lomonosov's works seem to be the "spiritual odes": eight poetic versions of individual psalms, a poetic recasting from the Book of Job (39–41), and two meditations on God's sublimity (*Razmyšlenie o Božiem veličestve*), one for the evening and the other for the morning. They are also much briefer than the festive odes and include grandiose pictures of Nature: in the paraphrase from the Book of Job these occur in the speech of God to Job; in the Evening Meditation it is the Aurora Borealis, in the Morning Meditation it is the sun. Though Lomonosov is unable to refrain from presenting at least a short exposition of scientific theories in his two meditations, he nevertheless succeeds in placing impressive images in the foreground, as for instance that of the evening:

Лице свое скрывает день,
поля покрыла влажна ночь,
взошла на горы черна тень,
лучи от нас прогнала прочь.
Открылась бездна звезд полна;
звездам числа нет, бездне дна.

("The day has hid its visage; the damp night has covered the fields, black shadows have climbed the mountains and chased the rays away from us; the abyss full of stars has opened, the stars are countless, the abyss has no limit.")

This whole group of odes reveals an influence of Protestant religious poetry and even of Protestant hymnology on Lomonosov. And yet in them the poet is using the grandiose images and emblems of the Baroque. It is not admissible, however, on the basis of an occasional anticlerical motif, to designate him as a "materialist" and an atheist. In any case, even among the *religious* poets of the Baroque one encounters the notion that Nature is perceived "by number, measure and weight". This has nothing to do with "materialism"! (eg. Book of Wisdom, I).

The translations of the so-called "anacreontic" poems form a separate group (one of these was Lomonosov's first tonal poem). These poems are written in light, short iambs, and in a much simpler language than the odes. And in his own appended poems, Lomonosov takes issue with "Anacreon"; he had much rather glorify heroes than love, and instead of the picture of the beautiful maiden which "Anacreon" wants in his poem, Lomonosov designs a picture of a colossal statue of Russia.

Lomonosov also wrote a number of very coarse epigrams and numerous inscriptions for allegorical tableaux at various court festivals. Their symbolism is, as it were, "forced Baroque".

6. Lomonosov's style is marked by its rich ornamentation which the next classicist generation considered "overloaded" and an encumbrance. This ornamentation employs rhetoric as its principal device, the apostrophising of the reader, which at times runs to the length of a stanza. In addition, he makes God and the spirit of Peter I deliver long speeches, and constantly addresses peoples and countries, Russian and foreign rulers. Rhetorical questions addressed to himself are also numerous. Some stylistic devices appear to be borrowed from the theory of the festive sermon. The anacreontic poems are also placed within the framework of a "Dialogue with Anacreon". Three ornamental devices are particularly favoured by Lomonosov: hyperbole, antithesis and climax. Often he concludes his odes in a climactic manner (e.g., summons, defends and comforts; builds, rules and leads, etc.) Allegorical pictures and mythological embellishments are very abundant everywhere.

Lomonosov's odes are all composed of stanzas, each of which is 4–10 lines long; the festive ones are all ten-liners. The stanza is almost invariably a syntactic and semantic unit; the lines, too, are usually endstopped. The arrangement of the whole text of the ode was intended to convey enthusiasm and ecstasy, and therefore a "lyrical disorder" reigns in the greater part of each ode. The far-ranging poet unfolds before the eyes of the reader various seemingly disconnected images, reminiscences and thoughts. Thus, for instance, he describes the future of the then 15-year old heir to the throne, Peter III, in a birthday-ode (after Günther and Malherbe):

> Холмов Ливанских верх дымится!
> Там Навин иль Самсон стремится!
> Текут струи Евфратски вспять,
> он тигров челюсти терзает,
> волнам и вихрям воспрещает,
> велит луне и солнцу встать.
> Фиссон шумит, Багдад пылает,
> там вопль и звуки воздух бьют,
> ассирски стены огнь терзает,
> и Тавр и Кавказ в Понт бегут.

("The peaks of Lebanon are smoking, Joshua the Son of Nun or Samson walks there! The streams of Euphrates are flowing backward, he [Peter III] breaks apart the jaws of tigers; he commands the waves and the whirlwinds, he orders the sun and moon to stand still. Phison roars, Baghdad is ablaze, screams and cries rend the air, fire destroys the walls of the Assyrians, and the Taurus and the Caucasus mountains flee into the sea.")

Actually the heir to the throne, praised in such a way, was not only incapable "of tearing apart the tiger's jaws", but as was already apparent at the time, was a rather limited and retarded boy.

Sumarokov quite effectively parodies this:

> Гром, молния и вечны льдины,
> моря и озера шумят,
> Везувий мечет из средины
> в подсолнечну горящий ад.
> С востока вечна дым восходит,
> ужасны облака возводит
> и тьмою кроет горизонт.
> Ефес горит, Дамаск пылает,
> тремя Цербер гортаньми лает,
> Средьземный возжигает Понт.

("Thunder, lightning and the eternal ice floes, the seas and lakes roar; Vesuvius throws up into the world under the sun the fiery hell from the centre [of the earth]. From the eternal East smoke is rising, it carries with it terrible clouds and covers the horizon with darkness. Ephesus is aflame,

Damascus burns, Cerberus barks with his three mouths, setting fire to the Mediterranean.")

Sumarokov is aware that Lomonosov's imagery is partly derived from Günther, and so he includes here a quotation from Günther: "Damascus burns...." In another poem, he writes even more openly: Lomonosov ...

...Гюнтера и многих обокрал.

("had stolen from Günther and many others.")

Lomonosov solves brilliantly and effectively the problem of word order. In his works there remains hardly a trace of Kantemir's and Trediakovskij's arbitrariness. At rare intervals only do we encounter lines like (1739 ode):

$$\overset{2}{\text{корабль}} \ \overset{1}{\text{как}} \ \overset{4}{\text{ярых}} \ \overset{5}{\text{волн}} \ \overset{3}{\text{среди}}\ldots$$

("Like a ship in tempestuous seas.") Masculine and feminine rhymes alternate (mostly A.B.A.B.; or a.B.a.B.; or A.b.b.A., or a.B.B.a.; only in the Evening Meditation are all the rhymes masculine. The festive odes are very long (more than 200 lines), and the "spiritual" ones are usually from forty to sixty lines long.

Lomonosov's language tends to be archaic; rare or obsolete words occur rarely, however; one may only note *viss* instead of *visson* (byssus), or occasional dialect words like *lyva* (fen). However, the morphology and syntax are antiquated, even words of the vernacular are frequently handled morphologically as though they were Church Slavonic, and the syntax, too, is often Church Slavonic. Nevertheless, later opponents of Lomonosov and even poets who regarded his poetry as a stage that had long since been passed received many suggestions from some of his images, metaphors and hyperboles. And thus his influence persisted into the first decades of the 19th century.

15.   OTHER LITERARY WORKS

1. There are so many 17th and 18th-century works that not all of them can receive mention in a general history of literature. The religious and ecclesiastico-political works may safely be ignored, and besides, we have already mentioned some of them (VII, 5 and 6).

The literature on the order of divine services for Russian saints was now greatly enriched. In addition to the Ukrainians (Satanovśkyj, Slavineckyj, St. Dimitrij, Prokopovyč and others, see VII, 6) the following also contributed to this kind of writing; Simeon Šachovskoj (VI, 12, 1), Karion Istomin, Fedor

Polikarpov (VI, 5, 8) and others. Numerous earlier writings continued to be copied with minor alterations and supplements based on fresh sources (e.g., on the Chronograph).

2. Among 17th-century writings there must be singled out above all a work the origin of which is quite accidental and which, though its description of Russian life is perhaps rather one-sided in its dark colours, nevertheless possesses a great significance for cultural history. Moreover, it provides an incomparable example of the rather lighter style of Chancery language. This is the account of Russian life by the official Grigorij Kotošichin, who fled to Sweden in 1664 and there wrote his report. Two years later he was executed because he accidentally killed somebody. His report especially sheds light on the customs at court and in the boyar households. The picture he paints is very gloomy, and it was used, though without good reason, for the characterisation of earlier centuries as well. Above all, however, it is an outstanding linguistic monument. Its language may be likened to that of the 1649 Codex. Various other memorials (Confession by Sil'vestr Medvedev, etc.) belong in general, from the point of view of vocabulary, to the same linguistic stratum.

3] Of great interest are the treaties on icon painting which unfortunately have only been partly edited and in part been summarized. These treatises are by one representative of traditional art, Iosif Vladimirov, and the "innovators" Simeon Polockij, Karion Istomin, and the painter Simeon Ušakov. To be considered along with these is the decision of the 1667 Council and an epistle (*Beseda*) of Avvakum. All these works develop the foundations of an aesthetic system that is typical of the Baroque: representation can and should adhere to reality, since it merely points to the prototype (archetype), without being able to render it, particularly when what is being represented is invisible (God, for example). Possibly these ideas offer a justification for the symbolic function of art which can also be applied to the poetry of the period. The partisans of tradition see in this new icon painting nothing but secularisation, and they advance their views with no general justification other than reference to tradition.

4. Of interest also are some of the travel accounts of the 17th century, even though most of them were in no way planned as works of literature and are not to be regarded as such. These are the descriptions of voyages to China (Bajkov and the Greek Spafarij – Spatharios), Persia (Kotov), Palestine (Gagara), and the Western countries (Čemodanov: 1656–7; Lichačev: 1659; and at the end of the century Šeremetev and P. Tolstoj). These works give evidence of the development of the language and the powers of observation of the Russian travellers.

5. The scientific treatises are but attempts at theological meditation, and we shall omit them here. In this connection we may single out a work presumably compiled from various sources, *Pričiny gibeli carstv* ("The Reasons for the Decline of States"), which makes use of philosophical quotations (possibly merely extracted from the *Florilegia*). Here, at any rate, is an attempt to think independently. There are probably also compiled manuals of elementary mathematics. The only independent contribution that Russia can show is in the

field of descriptive geography. "The Great Map" was made after 1627, but there survives only a description of it (*Kniga Bol'šogo čerteža*). In addition there are many accounts of journeys, especially in Siberia. By 1701 a map of Siberia (Remezov) was available. For the history of literature all these have significance chiefly as monuments of language. Worthy of mention also is the work on dictionaries (Greek, Latin, Church Slavonic and Swedish), which in many instances were but translations of foreign works or, as in the case of a Church Slavonic dictionary, a recasting of the Church Slavonic-Ukrainian dictionary by P. Berynda.

The Croatian works by the Catholic priest, Juraj Križanić, who visited Russia, do not belong to Russian literature. These, in addition to the description of conditions in Russia in the second half of the 17th century, develop a number of political and ecclesiastico-political themes, among them rather vague Slavophile theories.

6. We may ignore the original scientific literature of the Petrine and post-Petrine times, except for the works of two men.

The first of them is the peasant Ivan Pososkov (1652–1726), the author of a political and economic tract *Kniga o skudosti i bogatstve* ("The Book of Poverty and Wealth"), 1724, as well as of smaller works. This treatise combines on acceptance of Petrine reforms, which Pososkov, however, interprets partly from his own point of view and in part would like to see carried further, with loyalty to old Muscovite Russia, especially as regards the Church. This work, significant from the point of view of cultural and spiritual history, had a tragic effect on its author's fate. In 1725, after Peter's death, Pososkov – whose treatise had become known in manuscript was imprisoned and died in prison. It did not appear in print until as late as 1842.

The other man of that time who expressed in print his ideas on the reforms was of noble birth. This was Vasilij Nikitič Tatiščev (1686–1750) who left behind several works, one of which is written in the traditional form of instructions to his son. These show him to be a loyal partisan of the monarchy, but also a ruthless supporter of Peter's reforms, especially in so far as, in his view, they would lead to the enlightenment of the people. Tatiščev, a man who had traveled widely abroad, even inclined to the enlightenment in the philosophical sense of the term. He also attempted to write a kind of encyclopaedia. His works did not appear in print until after his death.

7. Some annalistic works also appeared at this time. The most important of these are the various "Siberian Chronicles". At the end of the century, the maker of the map of Siberia, Remezov, also compiled a history of Siberia from the material of the Chronicles. Other compilations were the "History" of Russia by the official F. Griboedov (before 1673), and later (1678) the Archimandrite Tichon's edition of a *Stepennaja Kniga* modeled on the great 16th-century work (VII, 10, 3), with the addition of material from other monuments. Both works retain the dynastic pattern of the old *Stepennaja*.

However, even Tatiščev's most significant work, his Russian History, did not appear in his lifetime. This first Russian history was merely a compilation from the chronicles (in which, it appears, Tatiščev also made use of texts unknown to us). He tried to use his sources critically, and even added geographical and ethnographical commentaries. The tireless Lomonosov also left behind some historical works. His first historial work is simply called "a chronicle" (*Kratkij rossijskij letopisec*, 1760). He was able to make a detailed study only of early Russian history, and this did not appear until after his death (*Drevnjaja rossijskaja istorija*, 1766). These works do not mark any substantial advance in historical studies. In the same period the German fellows of the Petersburg Academy, G. F. Müller* and Schlözer, worked on the identical material but with modern methods.

8. In the 17th and 18th centuries there also came into being various records of popular lore. Often these are nothing but attempts to record interesting subject-matter. Prominent among them is the collection of *stariny* and of other songs by Kirša (Kirill) Danilov which probably originated at the beginning of the 18th century. While these records give us an insight into the language of the people, letters of the time give us a similar insight into the language of "society". This language is frequently very primitive and clumsy, but gradually there comes into being a form of expression which, at the end of the 18th century, emerges victorious in the field of literature.

16. THE END OF THE BAROQUE

1. The fate of the Baroque was already determined by the 1740's. About this time Aleksandr Petrovič Sumarokov (1718–1777), then a pupil at a military school, was already writing tonal poems imitating Trediakovskij and Lomonosov. His poetical ideal, however, was diametrically opposed to that of his masters. He developed his own program, primarily, one assumes, under the influence of French poetry and poetic theory (Boileau), but also as a reaction against the clumsiness of language and the opacity of composition of both Trediakovskij and Lomonosov. Sumarokov's technique is characterized by simplicity and lucidity. He demanded:

> чтоб мнение творца воображалось ясно,
> и речи бы текли свободно и согласно.

("that the thoughts of the poet should be clearly expounded, and that the speech should flow freely and harmoniously.") Quite early he entered into a violent controversy with Trediakovskij and Lomonosov. For a long time this polemic appeared to historians of Russian literature to be founded on purely personal grounds. In reality, practically every sentence of Sumarokov's polemical writings may be explained in terms of his "classicist" theories. Sumarokov, to be sure, upheld Lomonosov's poetical reforms and his theory of "three styles". Sumarokov soon won

* Russian: Fedor Ivanovič Miller.

numerous followers, of whose writings the theoretical essays by A. Rževskij (see § 4) and the first works of M. M. Cheraskov (1733–1807) were of special significance. Thanks to a number of short-lived periodicals which he founded in a period beginning in 1759, to his considerable output as a poet and to his success as a playwright, Sumarokov's victory over the baroque movement was assured.

The cultural revival in his environment, moreover, contributed a great deal to this victory. There already existed an educated class – the nobility in the capitals – who knew something of foreign literature, and whose taste could not be satisfied with the all too erudite and cumbersome poetry of Trediakovskij and Lomonosov, so remote from the European literature of the period. Soon the reading public, though still limited, sided with the new movement. Even the talented pupil of Lomonosov, N. Popovskij (about 1730–1760), inclined towards classicism.

Russian Classicism, however, was not simply a feeble imitation of the West European movement. It was faced with peculiarly Russian problems that could not be settled by reference to Boileau's poetics, especially the problem of poetic language. And since the programme of the Russian classicists was by no means clear on every point and since they themselves were incapable of carrying it out completely (because its principles were far from being obvious not only to most readers but also to the majority of poets), Russian Classicism did not evolve along straight lines. And the Baroque, too, was not to be completely conquered at once. Relapses and "recidivists" into the Baroque continued to appear.

2. The Baroque is one of those literary movements which do not disappear speedily and without trace with the emergence of a new literary epoch, in this case the classicist. There are several reasons why the Baroque could resist the new trends. For one thing, even at a later date, the splendours and pomp of the Baroque continued to appeal to some poets. Hence, certain elements of the Baroque style appear in some poets who are by no means the epigoni of the Baroque but who, in some areas or even in individual works, revive the baroque tradition. Moreover, the Baroque style possessed a carefully worked out system of poetic devices which at the same time provided fixed limits for creative work and demanded an originality in application which must have seemed most appealing to a not very creative poet. So there are some imitators of the Baroque who because of a certain uncreative inertia seek in Baroque poetics guidance toward an artificially attained originality.

Moreover, the literary tradition of the Baroque hung on in certain temperately conservative circles. Baroque poetics, after all, had taken deep root in the schools, especially in conservative schools with a theological orientation. The new period, that of classicism, made lesser demands for instruction in the writing of poetry. And in theological schools baroque poetics were still taught for a long time, whereas the new secular schools only gradually defined the new system of poetics. For this reason amateurish baroque poetry still continued to flourish for a long time (cf. VII, 13, 9). But perhaps of even greater significance was the penetration of baroque poetry into the middle and lower classes of the population, and its gradual descent to the level of popular lore. The picaresque novel, the love lyrics, and the religious lyrics became current among these classes in the age of the Baroque (cf. VII, 4 and 11, and also VII, 6, 8). The novel turns into a fairy-tale in short story form, the love poem into a popular song, the religious lyric into a "spiritual song". And indeed, one finds many traces of baroque fiction in the Russian popular fairy-tales, some of the episodes and motifs being preserved in popular anecdotes. The popular songs preserve, for the most part, merely individual images and symbols of baroque lyrical poetry. The Russian spiritual song, which was never admitted into the Church, reveals its baroque origin by the traces of the syllabic system. Amongst the Catholic and Protestant peoples the religious songs of the Baroque found their way into the ecclesiastical hymn books and were thus preserved until the enlightened 19th century "revised" the Church hymnals. In Russia, however, other religious baroque works could maintain a foothold among the people, namely the Reading Menaea of St. Dimitrij of Rostov (VII, 6, 3), and amongst the Old Believers a religious literature which, to be sure, was Ukrainian for the most part, including the poems of Simeon Polockij (VII, 5, 5). It is true, of course, that the Baroque is combined here with more ancient and thus more venerable works. And also some elements of "gnomic wisdom" originated in the writings of the Baroque.

3. We shall make no attempt to trace here the presence of baroque tradition in the folk-lore. From the literary point of view these are lost cultural values. To literature in the true meaning of the term, however, belong those songs which penetrated into the hymnals. These in many cases have appreciably changed their linguistic form. It is far more interesting that the baroque tale continued to survive right up to the 20th century in chap-books (*lubočnaja literatura*) and on illustrated broadsheets (*lubki*). Sometimes they were revised, thus in the second half of the 18th century such a revision was made by a footman, Matvej Komarov;

in the 19th century, too, there were such new redactions, e.g., the short story about Vasilij Kariotskij (VII, 11, 2) was turned into a novel by by I. Kassirov (1894). Even such a poet as N. Nekrasov, in his poverty-stricken youth, was commissioned to write fairy-tales, making use of popular lore and the baroque tale.

Moreover, in the second half of the 18th century, when Russian literary prose was in the process of emerging, a number of novelists continued the tradition of the baroque novel. They were second-rate writers, to be sure, but they won many readers, the more easily because the novels of the classicists, though serious and instructive, were dull (e.g. Cheraskov's) and merely clumsily imitated the style of Diderot or Voltaire.

4. Much more important is the fact that in the classicist period there were significant poets who brought about a return of the Baroque.

The first of them is Aleksej Andreevič Rževskij (1737–1804), an important and profilic poet of the early Russian classicism. He published more than 250 poems, ninety per cent of which (225) appeared between 1759 and 1762. He follows Sumarokov, but the heavily and playfully ornamented style of many of his works actually runs counter to Sumarokov's ideals and, oddly enough, to the author's own views as recorded in his theoretical essays, which demand, above all, clarity of expression. Rževskij, however, is a master of genuinely baroque poetic trifles; he even writes pictorial poems, including a fable in the form of a rhombus. One of his odes consists of only one-syllable words. In a number of his love poems he uses various artistic devices of the Baroque. He writes a love dialogue with identical rhymes; he writes two sonnets from the half-lines of which there emerge two further sonnets whose meaning is not a declaration of love, like that of the whole sonnet, but on the contrary a denial of love. By way of example, here are the first lines of one of the sonnets:

Во веки не пленюсь	красавицей иной
то ведай, я тобой	всегда прельщаться стану
по смерть не пременюсь	во век жар будет мой
век буду с мыслью той	доколе не увяну
не лестна для меня	иная красота
на свете ты одна	мой дух воспламенила etc.

("Never shall I be enchanted by another beauty. Know that I shall always be enthralled by you. I will not change till death comes; my flame will be eternal. For ever, till I wither, I shall have this thought. No other beauty pleases me. You alone, in all the world, have inflamed my spirit. *The first half*: I shall never be enchanted by you, know that. Till death comes, I shall not change. I shall always have this thought: you alone in all the world do not please me. *The second half*: I shall always be enthralled by another beauty. My flame will be eternal, till I wither. Another beauty has inflamed my spirit....")

All three poems are unexceptionable both from the point of view of vocabulary and grammar. Such poems demand, above all, great skill in expressing ideas concisely. In this respect (in his odes too) Rževskij surpasses all his predecessors and contemporaries, not even excepting the head of the school, Sumarokov. Rževskij is, of course, opposed to Lomonosov's excessively cumbersome language. His lavish ornament is of a different kind. He writes, for instance, poems the clue to which is only given in the last line. Others he bases on antitheses (thus, the description of the man in love); these antitheses often culminate in an oxymoron. Finally, he bases the structure of whole poems on the repetition of the same words, in a way similar to that of the baroque epigram. These final instances are in stark contrast to the practice of Sumarokov who rejected and parodied meanwhile, oxymoron and word-repetition. Rževskij, however, was able to write easily-read and easily-understood poems in complicated baroque forms which, for external elegance, have no parallel in the first years of Russian Classicism.

Incidentally, Rževskij's poems had an interesting parallel in Polish Classicism, namely in the *Erotyki* of the somewhat younger D. Kniaźnin (1750–1807) (W. Borowy).

5. We encounter a different sort of revival of the Baroque in Vasilij Petrov (Pospelov, 1736–1799), a very popular and very learned poet. He was a product of the Moscow Ecclesiastical Academy and even lectured on rhetoric there. This accounts for a great deal. When in 1766 he began to publish his poems with great success, he gained access to the court of the Empress Catherine II, and in 1772–74 made a study tour of Europe. He spent most of his time in England, translated Milton and Pope, and on his return became a librarian to the Empress. He wrote relatively little. In addition to writing odes, in which he imitated the festive solemnity of Lomonosov and used both inversions – even if not as ponderous as those of Trediakovskij's – and numerous compounds, he recorded his literary theories in epistles. We find here as clear an exposition of the basic principles of baroque poetics as in any of his precursors and contemporaries. According to him, poetry should be a kind of hieroglyphic art which sets puzzles for the reader. Poetry is a kind of magic (Trediakov-skij had said much the same thing) which should surprise the reader and produce astonishment. Loftiness, abundance of ideas and impressive character of expression, complexity ("The Labyrinth"), novelty and euphony are the basic characteristics of genuine poetry which must shine equally through the use of all that is "beautiful, lofty and marvellous". This is of course a formulation of the basic elements of *baroque* poetry. He decisively rejects the deliberately simple syle of the classicists and, even more emphatically, the conversational style of their fables. In a certain sense, Petrov also quite intentionally reverts to the mixture of lexical strata. In addition to the grandiose images of his odes, he is also capable of presenting idyllic descriptions of nature or of embarking upon euphonic devices (The song of the nightingale).

The sources of the poetry of Petrov – a poet who, along with Lomonosov and Deržavin, was highly thought of in his day – have not yet been investigated.

6. The return of the Baroque appears in yet another form in the works of the most significant Russian poet of the 18th century, Gavriil Roma-novič Deržavin (1743–1816). Coming from an impoverished noble family he received no first-rate education. He is one of the few 18th-century poets who did not know French. He knew German and was acquainted with German poetry, though it is not quite clear to what extent. After a struggling military career, it was only in 1799 that he appeared with success before the public as a poet.

Deržavin's poems, especially the odes, are a complicated blend of elements of various kind and origin. There is the influence of German (baroque and classicist) and Russian (primarily Lomonosov's) poetry, and at the same time that of the emerging "churchyard school" (Young's *Night Thoughts* appeared in Russian translation in 1778), and last, but not least, the unbridled poetic temperament of the poet himself, who not always heeded the counsels of the small circle of classicists who surround-ed him. All in all, his was a brilliant poetry whose god-fathers were talent and a certain amount of provincial parochialism. Deržavin draws without any qualms upon all the sources available to him, including baroque poetry (Lomonosov and the German poets); above all, however, he takes from it, as from all other sources he draws on, suggestions which he assimilates into his own style. Hence there appear in his poetry hyper-bolic descriptions of heroic landscapes and of titanic heroes which certainly are much influenced by Lomonosov's:

Вихрь полунощный летит богатырь!
Тьма от чела, с посвиста пыль;
Молньи от взоров бегут впереди,
дубы грядою лежат позади.
Ступит на горы – горы трещат;
ляжет на воды – воды кипят;
граду коснется – град упадает;
башни рукою за облак кидает...

("The hero – the Northern Wind – flies! Darkness is caused by his brow, dust by his whistling; ahead of him there fly the lightnings of his looks; in his wake, oaks lie in a row. He steps upon the mountains – the mountains crack; he reposes upon the waves – the waters boil; he touches a fortress with his hand – the fortress falls; he throws the towers over the clouds....")

Some of the stanzas of his odes give the impression that Sumarokov's parody (written, however, twenty-five years earlier) was specifically pointed at them. The addiction to hyperbole and antithesis, the pathetic apostrophes, some particular stanzas and lines, make one think that all Deržavin wanted was to excel even Lomonosov. His partiality to the baroque theme of death and transitoriness and his thoroughly lush use of colour are also reminiscent of baroque poetry; but possibly these traits are pre-Romantic ones. There are also many characteristics of his poetry which are purely classicist, and some which, at any rate, can be reconciled with Classicism. But without reference to the Baroque Deržavin cannot be fully understood.

7. There were also minor poets of the age of Classicism who were indebted to the Baroque in some respects. Russian Romanticism, however, found no kinship with the Baroque. Elsewhere the romantics discovered some of the forgotten baroque poets, thinkers and artists (Calderón, Angelus Silesius, Friedrich von Spee, Jacob Boehme, J. S. Bach, etc.). In Russia, however, the revision of the language, begun in Karamzin's school and continued among the romantics, created an impassable barrier against the Baroque. Only a very few poets found a relationship to the late Baroque (Lomonosov), as did, for instance, Küchelbecker (1798–1842), or with the Ukrainian Baroque, as did Gogol'.

A vindication of the Baroque comes only with Symbolism. The high estimate of the amplified style, which the symbolists themselves used, enabled a master of this style, such as Brjusov, to write at least "experi-

THE BAROQUE

mental poems" which made use of baroque poetics and to make the attempt at least to use the syllabic verse technique in modern poetry (*Opyty*). Of much greater significance were the stylizations of old baroque works, short stories and plays, for which, above all, A. M. Remizov deserves credit. To be sure, he also stylized the writings of the earlier Russian literature (viz.: *Stefanit i Ichnilat*, and the apocryphas). But since he based his style on 17th-century literature, he approaches these older monuments in the light of 17th-century tradition.

The revival of theoretical interest in baroque literature as such is due to the literary-historical "formalism". The formalists themselves, however, have not discussed the problem of the Baroque. In Soviet Russia literary Baroque is taboo. Nevertheless, some statements concerning individual poets (Polockij) as baroque poets have been possible. And some other scholars have attempted to set off, from the point of view of style, such poets as Trediakovskij and Lomonosov from 18th-century Classicism, but without being permitted to designate them as poets of the Baroque.

INDEX OF PROPER NAMES

INDEX OF PLACE-NAMES

INDEX OF WORKS

For technical reasons the bibliography of this book will be published as a separate booklet.

ERRATA

page, line:	printed:	should be:
11, 6	1073	1043
39, 16	certainly	certainty
57, 26	Dobolsk	Dolobsk
64, 30/1	acquintance	acquaintance
73, 12/3	of of	of
74, 36	Stavro	Stavr
75, 1	Solov	Solovej
111, running title	RENMAIS	REMAINS
120, 1	three	tree
138, 30	Lay	Tale
154, 17	making	make
166, 2	E. Fedotov	G. Fedotov
190, 38	Aeropagitica	Areopagitica
212, 5	1331	1330
264, 7	majoity	majority
301, 27	Areaopagitica	Areopagitica
331, 24	VII, 6, 2	VII, 6, 3
342, 20	Mikhail	Michail
343, 37	Šemkaja	Šemjaka
350, 4	Rissicisms	Russicisms
359, 19	Innokentij	Ioannikij
371, 33	then	than
388, 9/10	one one	one
399, 30	cleargy	clergy
407, 17	Trediakovsky	Trediakovskij